THE BROADVIEW ANTHOLOGY OF
Nineteenth-Century
British Performance

edited by Tracy C. Davis

broadview press

Library and Archives Canada Cataloguing in Publication

The Broadview anthology of nineteenth-century British performance / edited by Tracy C. Davis.

Includes bibliographical references.
ISBN 978-1-55111-900-7

1. English drama--19th century. I. Davis, Tracy C., 1960-
II. Title: Nineteenth-century British performance.

PR1271.B76 2011   822'.808   C2011-906660-2

Broadview Press is an independent, international publishing house, incorporated in 1985.

We welcome comments and suggestions regarding any aspect of our publications—please feel free to contact us at the addresses below or at broadview@broadviewpress.com.

North America   PO Box 1243, Peterborough, Ontario, Canada K9J 7H5
                               2215 Kenmore Ave., Buffalo, New York, USA 14207
                               Tel: (705) 743-8990; Fax: (705) 743-8353
                               email: customerservice@broadviewpress.com

UK, Europe, Central Asia,   Eurospan Group, 3 Henrietta St., London WC2E 8LU, United Kingdom
Middle East, Africa, India, Tel: 44 (0) 1767 604972; Fax: 44 (0) 1767 601640
and Southeast Asia   email: eurospan@turpin-distribution.com

Australia and New Zealand   NewSouth Books
                               c/o TL Distribution, 15-23 Helles Ave., Moorebank, NSW, Australia 2170
                               Tel: (02) 8778 9999; Fax: (02) 8778 9944
                               email: orders@tldistribution.com.au

www.broadviewpress.com

Copy-edited by Denis Johnston.

Broadview Press acknowledges the financial support of the Government of Canada through the Canada Book Fund for our publishing activities.

This book is printed on paper containing 50% postconsumer fibre.

PRINTED IN CANADA

MIX
Paper from
responsible sources
FSC® C103567

THE BROADVIEW ANTHOLOGY OF
Nineteenth-Century British Performance

To Jacky Bratton, David Mayer, and Laurence Senelick:
stimulating colleagues to so many,
also backroom mentors and generous friends to me.

Contents

List of Illustrations

Acknowledgements

Research for this volume was partially supported by an Andrew W. Mellon Foundation Fellowship at the Huntington Library; Stanley J. Kahrl Fellowship in Theatre History at Houghton Library (Harvard University); Distinguished Visiting Professorship at Queen Mary, University of London; and a grant from the University Research Grants Committee at Northwestern University.

This project was instigated by a timely question from Julia Gaunce and masterfully steered to completion by Marjorie Mather and Denis Johnston at Broadview Press. I am also grateful to Martin Mueller, who patiently leads the way in digital humanities research, and our colleagues at Academic Technologies (Bob Taylor, Bill Parod, Jonathan Smith, Tom O'Connell, and Harlan Wallach) who facilitated development of the website as well as investigations that led to it. Along with Julia Flanders and Syd Bauman (Brown) and Doug Reside (Maryland Institute for Technology in the Humanities, University of Maryland), they helped me grasp the potential—and some of the complications—of new resources and methods of investigation. Staff at Northwestern Library, most notably Sarah Pritchard (Director), Bill Parod, Charlotte Cubbage, Scott Krafft, Bill McHugh, David Easterbrook, and Dan Zellner have smoothed my path in innumerable ways.

Research has been conducted in many private and public collections, and I would like to single out for thanks Jo Elsworth of the Bristol Theatre Collection; the Henry E. Huntington Library; Betty Falsey, Rachel Howarth, and Andrea Cawelti of the Harvard Theatre Collection and Houghton Library; Marcus Risdell, Curator at the Garrick Club; Kate Dorney, Theatre Curator at the Victoria and Albert Museum; Paul Evans, Librarian at the Royal Artillery Museum (Woolwich); Richard Mangan, former Administrator of the Mander and Mitchenson Theatre Collection; the British Film Institute; and Kathryn Johnson, Curator of Manuscripts at the British Library. And to the many, many staff of the British Library (St. Pancras, Colindale, and Boston Spa) whose names I do not know but who make both discovery and preservation possible, my deepest gratitude.

Several individuals warrant special mention. Jim Davis and his students at Warwick University tested components of this volume in 2008-9, aided by Robert O'Toole and other staff at Warwick University Library. I learned a great deal from their process and am indebted to them all. Annette Fern became intrigued by my search for incidental music, and thanks to her expertise and perseverance, innumerable scores and lyrics were located. Laurence Senelick graciously opened the doors to his collection, which solved other musical mysteries. Stefka Mihaylova assisted with research, textual editing, and manuscript preparation, always with utmost professionalism as the consummate collaborator. Research assistants in the Interdisciplinary PhD in Theatre and Drama at Northwestern (Sara Armstrong, LaDonna Forsgren, and Katie Zien) and the undergraduate work-study student Elle Verhelst also aided aspects of the project. Barnaby King, a doctoral candidate in Performance Studies, workshopped the text of *Trip to America* in 2009, helping to reveal numerous editorial problems and endless interpretive potential. Brant Russell and Adam Goldstein joined the project in 2010, and at the time of publication our onstage investigations are continuing. Max Shapey's enthusiasm for etymology uncovered a multitude of pertinent obscurities that enliven the footnotes; in this and so many other ways, he makes my daily work not only possible but joyous.

Many colleagues have answered queries and either shared their work or created congenial occasions that inspired aspects of this volume, including Jacky Bratton, Gilli Bush-Bailey, Stephen Cockett, Tom Crochunis, Adrian Curtin, Scott Curtis, Catherine Goshen, Helena Grahan, Christopher Herbert, Krystyna Kujawinska, Kim Marra, Kate Mattocks, Judith Milhous, Erin Neuman, Kate Newey, Kerry

Powell, Jeffrey Richards, Freddie Rokem, Laurence Senelick, Linnea Starra, Muhammad S. Umar, Peter Webster, and Will West. Special thanks is extended to colleagues who generously read and instructively commented on work in progress, including Jim Davis, Amanda Dehnert, Heidi Holder, Kate Kelly, Sarah Meer, David Mayer, Danny O'Quinn, Tom Postlewait, Richard Schoch, Phyllis Weliver, and Broadview's anonymous reviewers. Insightful students at Northwestern and Warwick opened my eyes to relevant issues. My gratitude to one and all.

Theatre is an iconographic as well as musical art, so inclusion of visual elements is equally important as textual evidence in stimulating readers' imaginations and deepening understanding of historical performance. Thanks are due to numerous collections for permission to publish images and scores: the British Library Board, David Mayer, Garrick Club, Henry E. Huntington Library, Harvard Theatre Collection at the Houghton Library, Milton S. Eisenhower Library at Johns Hopkins University, Northwestern University's Melville Herskovitz Library and Department of Special Collections, Royal Artillery Library Woolwich, and the Theatre Collection at the Victoria and Albert Museum. The John Rylands Library at Manchester University and the Beinecke Library at Yale also provided images for study that proved crucial in research and manuscript preparation.

A portion of the general introduction has been revised from "Nineteenth-Century Repertoire," *Nineteenth Century Theatre and Film* 36:2 (2009): 6-28. A small portion of the introduction to *Trip to America* is revised from "Acting Black, 1824: Charles Mathews's *Trip to America*," *Theatre Journal* 63.2 (2011): 163-89.

Introduction: Repertoire

There is such a premium on claiming originality, innovation, and marked changes that theatre historians are ill-disposed to acknowledge derivation, consistency, or comparability. Exactly those qualities are often negatively inflected. Consequently, originality is privileged over borrowing, and uniqueness over likeness: all noteworthy events are singular, and yet singularity is capable of being rendered through the proxy of textual reconstruction. Studying repertoire constitutes a distinct alternative. In the connectedness and similarity between performances may be discovered what was too commonplace—because it was so pervasively characteristic—to warrant transcription. What was taken for granted in the culture? What was so familiar as to obviate the need for description despite the otherwise verbose tendency of the Victorian press? And conversely, how could a specific event be important enough to be noted yet *not* unique enough to be described? In its standardization, what did it resemble? The answers lie in repertoire: that which constitutes the day-to-day competencies of performers and audiences to make and understand theatre, drawing upon their familiarity with aesthetic conventions, contemporary politics, and cultural preoccupations.

New media are forged from the practices of older media. For example, the visual tricks of magic lantern slides and the plots of melodramas were among the earliest influences on cinema.[1] Likewise, modernist innovations in staging and playwriting are comprehensible in relation to older practices, traceable in the recombinative use of staging techniques and narrative motifs from popular theatre.[2] Performance never breaks wholly from tradition but exists in reference and reconstitution of it. Thus, performance is recognizable as repertoire—a collective entity constituted from many singular events—not only in how artists assemble it but also in how audiences make sense of it.[3] This anthology represents repertoire through experimental performance as well as oft-repeated entertainment tropes; it is less the innovation that matters (in an evolutionary line of development) than the resemblance, harking back, associative resonance, and similarities that make performance cohere as a set of practices. It is as much what *links* these texts (and hundreds of others resembling them) that gives twenty-first-century readers insight into nineteenth-century practices and taste as what makes each example distinct from the others. Some, but by no means all, of the practices have since fallen out of common usage. Evidence of repertoire may be most striking where twenty-first-century readers fail to recognize the conventions: what now requires a struggle to comprehend, nineteenth-century playgoers shared across classes, neighbourhoods, cities, and regions as their *lingua franca*.

In the early-Victorian period, *répertoire* denoted an actor's accustomed parts or a musician's stock of tunes. By the late-Victorian period, it had come to denote a wider body of work, no longer tied to one person but that which was available as a set from which samplings could be compiled. Thus, it came to denote something beyond an individual's proprietorship, as in the repertoire of a theatre company or even a repertoire company. Along the way, the word was anglicized, dropped the acute accent, and

---

1   Tom Gunning, "The Cinema of Attractions: Early Film, Its Spectator, and the Avant-Garde," in *Early Cinema: Space, Frame, Narrative*, edited by Thomas Elsaesser and Adam Barker (Berkeley: U of California P, 1990), 56-62; Rick Altman, *Silent Film Sound* (New York: Columbia UP, 2004), 16-18; and David Mayer, *Stagestruck Filmmaker: D.W. Griffith and the American Theatre* (Iowa City: U of Iowa P, 2009).

2   Martin Meisel, *Shaw and the Nineteenth-Century Theater* (Princeton: Princeton UP, 1963); Marvin Carlson, *The Haunted Stage: Theatre as Memory Machine* (Ann Arbor: U of Michigan P, 2001), 4; C.B. Davis, "Cultural Evolution and Performance Genres: Memetics in Theatre History and Performance Studies," *Theatre Journal* 59:4 (2007): 595-614; and Matthew S. Buckley, "Refugee Theatre: Melodrama and Modernity's Loss," *Theatre Journal* 61:2 (2009): 175-90.

3   Tracy C. Davis, "Repertoire," *Nineteenth Century Theatre and Film* 36:2 (2009): 6-28.

became more malleable than delimiting in its nominative function. A later twentieth-century usage involves repertoires, multiply, as corpora from which a community knowingly chooses in order to do things with what is selectively extracted.[4] Thus, repertoire delineates genre (as in the comedic repertoire, Shakespearean plays in frequent production, or the repertoire of music-hall balladry),[5] or coteries that correlate content to reception communities (as in the repertoire of popular entertainment or of *fin de siècle* New Drama).[6]

In the collection *New Readings in Theatre History*, Jacky Bratton launches a foundational idea, intertheatricality, which "seeks to articulate the mesh of connections between all kinds of theatre texts, and between texts and their users.... They are uttered in a language, shared by successive generations" as memory and "made up of dances, spectacles, plays and songs."[7] Two aspects of this definition are incontrovertible: performance texts are relational, and performances' interpretability depends on artists and audiences making sense of theatre, separately and together. Repertoire refines the conceptual territory that Bratton scopes by drawing attention to the factors that matter in making intertheatricality intelligible. The connection "between texts and their users" foregrounds the issue of what is appropriate evidence of an historical audience's competence to interpret performance.

Since the "successive generations" that share the expressive language of nineteenth-century performance cannot be presumed to extend to our own time, how can we identify vectors that meaningfully connect the sparsely distributed direct evidence of reception? By what criteria can historians recognize a performative corpus, expressing our rationale for pointing out what was probably implicitly sensed by nineteenth-century artists? How is the intelligibility of repertoire subject to proof based *both* on evidence derived from representation by participating artists *and* on the horizon of expectations among the audience? And how can intertheatricality, which implies nonsequentially learned knowledge, accommodate something "new" and thus not yet in repertoire? What constitutes invention or innovation, and how is this intelligible to audiences?

By thinking of repertoire not merely as generic but associational, polytextual, intertheatrically citational, recombinant patterns that sustain intelligibility, historians may begin to recognize where the critical and observational lacunae lie. Those "blanks" are filled by repertoire—the obvious, beyond the need for comment, mundane or entirely expected aspects of performance that make theatre recognizable, predictable, and thereby comprehensible and enjoyable for most playgoers. Some plays and performances are not of themselves innovative but represent a culmination of experiments that add up to a recognizable format despite the idiosyncrasies that make any example unique. The precursors and subsequent circulation of components, rather than the canonicity of any example, matter most in this schema. Innovation and influence exist but are also relative measures of change.

Performative Issues

Repertoire was transmitted least well on the page. It thrived as vital exchange among artists, who migrated and recombined in many rehearsal halls across their careers, and within the memories of spectators

---

4   *Oxford English Dictionary Online*, s.v. "Repertoire," http://www.oed.com/ (accessed 24 July 2008).

5   For example, George Rowell, *The Victorian Theatre, 1792-1914: A Survey* (Cambridge: Cambridge UP, 1978); Michael Booth, *English Plays of the Nineteenth Century*, 6 vols. (Oxford: Clarendon, 1969-76); Clifford Leech and T.W. Craik, gen. eds., *The Revels History of Drama in English*, 8 vols. (London: Methuen, 1976-83); and Richard Schoch, *Not Shakespeare: Bardolatry and Burlesque in the Nineteenth Century* (Cambridge: Cambridge UP, 2002).

6   Gender, popular entertainment, and the New Drama are categories exclusive of the others in Joseph Donohue, ed., *The Cambridge History of British Theatre*, vol. 2 (Cambridge: Cambridge UP, 2004).

7   Jacky Bratton, *New Readings in Theatre History* (Cambridge: Cambridge UP, 2003), 37-38.

who witnessed their century's most compelling mass medium and recognized the permutations and remembered particularly excellent exponents. Many factors were involved. As the twelve examples in this anthology illustrate, repertoire is forged through common experience of venues, actors, authors, plays, variety acts, parlour entertainments, historical events, diplomatic and political developments, foreign and domestic reportage in newspapers and periodicals, and a host of other performative and discursive kinds of sources.

There are numerous intersections among the artists whose work is addressed in this volume. On 29 July 1808, Charles Mathews played in the farce *Mrs. Wiggins* at the Haymarket Theatre. His frequent acting partner, the melancholic farceur John Liston, took a leading role in the main piece, *The Africans*, on the same bill. Liston epitomized the low comedian, and Mathews the character comedian; the latter subsequently developed a sideline in solo performance and sought his fortunes away from regular comedy. Mathews's definitive precursor in the solo entertainment line was Samuel Foote,[8] whose show *Diversions of the Morning; or, A Dish of Chocolate* launched the format in 1747.[9] Another was Charles Dibdin, a prodigious creator of songs who combined music with anecdotes, in the manner adopted by Mathews, accompanying himself on the piano and sometimes a one-man-band contraption.[10] His piece *Observations of a Tour Through ... Scotland and England* (1801-02) also pioneered the kind of traveller's narrative later adopted by Mathews.[11] Mathews experimented with the solo form as early as 1808, when he and his wife Anne performed "an entire new entertainment consisting of recitations, Songs, Imitations, Ventriloquy, &c. &c. entitled The Mail Coach; or, Rambles into Yorkshire."[12] When he played Dick Buskin in the farce *Killing No Murder* (1809), each time he reappeared on stage his "voice, features, and deportment, were so thoroughly altered, that a new man was brought before the audience." As the manager of a strolling company, he gave imitations of the era's leading actors—Kemble, Cooke, Pope, Munden, and Bannister—as well as "a French hairdresser, a rude English hostler, and a cook" in rapid succession, interspersed with songs.[13] This kind of "picture gallery" of actors and service workers—English and French—was repeated later in his "at home" performances "with a fidelity so perfect in posture, step, voice, and manner, as to determine the individual at the first sentence."[14] In 1811, he toured with Charles Incledon in "an entertainment of Recitations and Songs, called the Travellers."[15] In 1813, he first performed Romeo Rantall in the farce *At Home*; he imitated a notorious amateur (Mr. Romeo Coates, who had debuted in 1811) in a succession of

---

8   Foote's earliest followers include George Alexander Stevens, Charles Lee Lewes, John Collins, Charles Dibdin, George Saville Carey and Moses Kean, Jane Scott, and Jack Bannister. Richard L. Klepac, *Mr. Mathews At Home* (London: Society for Theatre Research, 1979), 9-11. Fanny Kelly provides a later example; see Gilli Bush-Bailey, *Performing HerSelf: Autobiography and Fanny Kelly's 'Dramatic Recollections'* (Manchester: U of Manchester P, 2011).

9   Revised by Foote as *A Cup of Tea* (also 1747), this was lampooned by his rival and imitator, Henry Woodward, as *Coffee* (1748). These are notable for their close observation from life and frequently biting satire. Charles Dibdin coined the term "table entertainments" for his *Oddities* in 1788; his solo performances represent the good-natured spirit of Mathews.

10   T. Dibdin, comp., *Songs of the Late Charles Dibdin; with a Memoir* (London: John Murray, 1841), xxvii-xxviii.

11   See *Love, Law, and Physic* in which Mathews and Liston performed from 1812. Liston's character inherits an estate in Yorkshire and while travelling there encounters Mathews's character on the mail coach. Harvard Theatre Collection, unattributed clipping, Anne Mathews's scrapbooks, vol. 1, fol. 122.

12   Playbill, Theatre Royal Hull, 12 April 1808. *Mail Coach Adventures*, a solo performance, is noted in a playbill for an unspecified location on 16 December 1814. Harvard Theatre Collection.

13   Unattributed clipping, Anne Mathews's scrapbooks, vol. 1, fol. 84. Foote had done the same kind of thing (vol. 2, fols. 27-28).

14   Unattributed clipping, Anne Mathews's scrapbooks, vol. 2, fol. 15.

15   Unattributed clipping, Anne Mathews's scrapbooks, vol. 1, fol. 80-81.

costumes.[16] His run of "at homes"—in which the public was invited to join him for a lecture at the English Opera House in the Strand, as if he were entertaining them "at home"—was launched in 1818.[17]

The sites of performance are equally important in linking the artists to this repertoire. For example, the Polygraphic Hall had been a cigar lounge, then a chapel, and in 1854 was converted into an intimate theatre. In 1859 and 1860, the monologuist W.S. Woodin, who performed multiple characters in the tradition of Charles Mathews, rented it. Christy's Minstrels performed at the Polygraphic Hall in their first London season (1857). The same venue was renamed Toole's Theatre in 1882,[18] and there *Ibsen's Ghost* was performed in 1891. J.L. Toole straddled the styles of both his great precursors, Mathews the agile mimic and Liston the droll comedian.[19]

Mathews used songs (and one notable dance) in *A Trip to America* to set a scene or effect a transition. *Dorothy*, the earliest of George Edwardes's musicals, uses songs, spoken dialogue, and dance as enjoyable diversions both conducive of mood and the furtherance of the plot. Combining song, dialogue, and dance was hardly new: it is the variety of ways in which these three elements coalesced into many distinguishable genres that is remarkable, rather than their presence in any one. The incorporation of dance and song in the drama *Elphi Bey* is every bit as "scene setting" as in the opera *Dorothy*; the difference is, in one case, exotically foreign and, in the other, comfortingly English. In this collection, only *The Game of Speculation*, *Ours*, and *The Finding of Nancy* do not include dance, and only *The Game of Speculation* and *The Finding of Nancy* do not include song.

Christy's Minstrels' burlesques reached across many forms. In New York, they included a turn where the minstrels portrayed "Bedouin Arabs": Eastern acrobats is a loose category inserted into performances as varied as *Elphi Bey* and *The Relief of Lucknow* without much regard to geographic or ethnographic plausibility. Also while in New York, Christy's parodied a lecture on mesmerism. Both as medical science and a performance trick, "animal magnetism" fascinated the Anglo-American public from the late eighteenth century until it reached its stage apotheosis in the melodrama *Trilby* in 1895. Set in 1850s Paris, *Trilby* created enough temporal and cultural distinction from 1890s Britain to excuse some implausibility. Likewise, the musical comedy *Dorothy*, set in the English countryside in the mid-eighteenth century, both harked back to comedic and operatic conventions (parodied by William Brough in two Christy's burlesques) and reflected the vaguely feudal mid-Europeanness of what became the musical comedy genre,[20] a setting also resorted to in acts 2 and 3 of *The Finding of Nancy* though more fashionably cast as the French Riviera. The burlesque *Ibsen's Ghost* inverts the formula by bringing "advanced" ideas from contemporaneous Scandinavia and the art theatres of Berlin and Paris into a modern London drawing room where they exist so uncomfortably as to be ludicrous.

Interpretive Issues

As Christy's Minstrels commenced their London career in the summer of 1857, Dr. Livingstone (returned from his transcontinental travels in Africa) conducted a lecture tour of Great Britain, the evangelical

---

16   Unattributed clipping, Anne Mathews's scrapbooks, vol. 1, fols. 139-40, 268. See also Joe Cowell, *Thirty Years Passed among the Players in England and America: Interspersed with Anecdotes and Reminiscences* (New York: Harper, 1844), 27. A brief rivalry ensued between Covent Garden, which employed Mathews, and Drury Lane, which took on Coates in order to give him a platform to rival Mathews.

17   Edward Ziter, "Charles Mathews, Low Comedian, and the Intersections of Romantic Ideology," *The Performing Century: Nineteenth-Century Theatre's History*, edited by Tracy C. Davis and Peter Holland (Houndmills: Palgrave Macmillan, 2007), 198-214.

18   Diana Howard, *London Theatres and Music Halls, 1850-1950* (London: Library Association, 1970), 243.

19   Toole even revived Liston's greatest signature piece, *Paul Pry*.

20   Len Platt, *Musical Comedy on the West End Stage, 1890-1939* (Houndmills: Palgrave Macmillan, 2004).

Baptist phenomenon Rev. Charles Spurgeon captivated audiences of 12,000 at Surrey Music Hall, Catholic soldiers agitated for equal treatment in the military, and the Sepoy Mutiny (the subject of *The Relief of Lucknow*) raged in India. War, religion, and race were never banished from English newspapers: no wonder then that every male comedian had in his wardrobe, as early as 1827, infantry, cavalry, and naval uniforms.[21] Mathews in *A Trip to America* and two young women in *Ours* play at being soldiers: their audiences recognized the calls to "form hollow square!" as easily as they recognized the convention of the harem in *Elphi Bey*. The pantomime *Alice in Wonderland*, performed at Woolwich Barracks, the army's great training and research centre for ballistics at the southeastern outskirts of London, makes the military as much a feature for its martial community as West End theatres did throughout the century. A moderate Christianity is taken to be the characters' faith except when it is flamboyantly something else: Muslim in *The Africans* and *Elphi Bey*, or Muslim and Hindu in *The Relief of Lucknow*. Where the social fabric unravels, atheism might be implied—as in *Ibsen's Ghost* and *The Finding of Nancy*—as the antithesis of the moral compass that steered most Britons.

Ethnographic texts document foreign customs: *The Africans*, *Elphi Bey*, *Trip to America*, Christy's Minstrels, *Ours*, *The Relief of Lucknow*, and *Trilby* all show nineteenth-century versions of this, whether to a respectful, ribald, sentimental, or subversive purpose. *Dorothy*, *The Game of Speculation*, *Alice in Wonderland*, *Ibsen's Ghost*, and *The Finding of Nancy* portray British customs with nostalgia, irony, wistful exuberance, or anxious watchfulness. The military performances—including *Ours*, *The Relief of Lucknow*, and (less explicitly) *Alice in Wonderland*—complicate this pattern further by contrasting Irish and Scottish figures with home-bred Englishness. The Cockney, who features in *The Africans* and *The Relief of Lucknow*, is as liable to be comic as the Irishman, a distant second in romantic potential to the more dignified Scots of *The Relief of Lucknow* and *Ours*, or the fair-skinned Afro-Muslim Foulahs of *The Africans*.

Ethnographic portrayals were perennial on the stage but what makes Mathews's *Trip to America* so notable are the first African Americans on the British stage:[22] neither the tragic figures of *Othello* or *Oronooko*, nor the sentimentalized West Indians of *The Padlock* or Colman's own *Inkle and Yarico*, Mathews's African Americans represent the end-point of the slave captures conducted by the warring Mandingos in *The Africans*. Performance necessitates imitation (of something) before witness-interpreters, and ethnic and racial characters' portrayals both drew on pre-existing impressions and contributed to modifying what was already imprinted on the collective consciousness. A third of a century after *A Trip to America*, how could audiences interpret Christy's blackface performances: as Southern Negroes displaced to Europe, white Americans faithfully imitating enslaved blacks, or Euro-Americans portraying a variety of characters—abject, ingeniously wily, devoted, beloved, and loving—familiar from other ethnically reflected repertoire, grafted onto Americans but signified by nonrepresentational burnt-cork make-up? As Catherine Hall argues, "the mapping of difference" was "the constant discursive work of creating, bringing into being, or reworking these hieratic categories" always as "a matter of historical contingency. The map constantly shifted, the categories faltered, as different colonial sites came into the metropolitan focus and as conflicts of power produced new configurations in one place or another."[23] Was the African Americans' stereotypical speech more reprehensible, or less verisimilar, than what passed for Hibernian, Scotian, or Cockney dialect? For some purposes, the Scots and Irish were inside the boundaries of nation, for others not, just as the sepoy troops of Hindus and Muslims that kept the peace and secured the interests of the British East India Company were integral to empire but became "mutinous" traitors when they acted on long-festering

---

21   Leman Rede, *The Road to the Stage; or, The Performer's Preceptor* (London: Joseph Smith, 1827), 24.

22   Hazel Waters, *Racism on the Victorian Stage: Representation of Slavery and the Black Character* (Cambridge: Cambridge UP, 2007); and Tracy C. Davis, "Acting Black, 1824," *Theatre Journal* 63:2 (2011), 163-89.

23   Catherine Hall, *Civilizing Subjects* (Oxford: Polity, 2002), 20.

ethnography: descriptive study of the customs of individual peoples and cultures.

grievances.[24] Britons were tormented at having lost their American colonies in the eighteenth century, and the sensibility of being a world power was undermined by having suffered an additional defeat by the Americans in the War of 1812. No wonder that the racial differences associated with the republic fixated British attention: the cruelties of chattel slavery could be reprehensibly American while the slaves' songs of longing for familial and community bonds were utterly harmonious with British sensibilities. As the back-story of *The Relief of Lucknow* demonstrates, however, cruelty and exploitation also tainted Britain's foreign policy, if not British characters as portrayed on stage. The farther that performances were set from the homeland, the more relevant to Britain the patterns of self-reflexivity—and collective denial—could be.

Repertoire emphasizes connections, across time and between performances. It does not, however, negate the significance of chronology or cultural specificity. The Foulah of Senegambia are as unlike the plantation slaves of the United States as the villainous Mandingos of *The Africans* are distinct from the mutinous sepoys of *The Relief of Lucknow*. Even within the logic of melodrama, there is scope for reformation, in the case of the Mandingos, and consideration of grievances, in the case of the Muslim and Hindu sepoys. The play *Elphi Bey* could be regarded as one of a legion of orientalist fantasies of the period; however, its referentiality to an important contemporary figure (the eponymous Mameluke chief) and the absence of any European characters mark the action as occurring after Napoleon's withdrawal from Egypt—a time when England pondered the strategic advantage to be wielded by gaining political influence with a resister to Ottoman rule. The melodrama *The Relief of Lucknow* chronicles another situation ripped from the headlines, and though the characters foregrounded by Dion Boucicault were fictional, their liberation is achieved (offstage) by famous officers. *Dorothy*'s plot is a comedic *esprit*, its main events recurring in countless reworkings of *Much Ado about Nothing* and "ring plots,"[25] but its significance in the history of theatre resides not in its plot or structure but in its heralding of musical theatre as distinct from other lyric and operatic prototypes.

Women and children's vulnerability as the captives of war (*Elphi Bey*, *The Africans*, and *The Relief of Lucknow*) or villainy (*Alice in Wonderland* and *Trilby*) made them the special responsibility of heroic men. It was not that women were necessarily frail or susceptible—as these same plays demonstrate—for performance evinces a multitude of womanly expressions of strength and fidelity. Nevertheless gender, like class, is immutable. Mary's predicament in *Ours*—to be female, genteel, poor, and unwanted—is as insurmountable as that of her sparring partner Hugh, the heir to several fortunes, who proclaims, "Pity the rich; for they are bankrupts in friendship, and beggars in love." The young women of *Dorothy* may swagger like men, but faced with duelling pistols they run away and resume their skirts along with the privileges of deference due to their class. Nancy, in *The Finding of Nancy*, is hemmed in by her poverty but most of all by the moral strictures that keep young women from meeting and attracting life partners. Work is her only recourse until she inherits; with money she also gains a limited amount of independence from the strictures that contain women. In her world, however, like that of her modernist prototype Nora of *A Doll's House* (parodied in *Ibsen's Ghost*), there are no longer any heroic men.

Nineteenth-century theatre was just as engaged with political concerns as were broadsheets and newspapers. Theatre lacked journalism's professed devotion to accuracy, though antiquarianism in stagecraft depended on an *appearance* of authenticity. Plotting and characterization streamlined or expanded upon topical situations, political debates, or social struggles, and luxuriated in their emotional content. This is particularly evident in how *The Africans* posits the next challenge for the abolitionist movement just as Britain took a principled stand to abstain from the slave trade; *Elphi Bey*

---

24   Krishan Kumar, *The Making of English National Identity* (Cambridge: Cambridge UP, 2003), 1-17.
25   *Elphi Bey* also has a subsidiary ring plot.

depicts anxiety over the Islamic harem in the light of opportunities for England during a brief power vacuum in the Near East; and *The Relief of Lucknow* and *Ours* track, in triumphant and comic tones respectively, two wars that shattered Britain's sense of security over its empire and Eastern trade routes. Other examples more directly engage familial relations through a framework of social crisis, as with *The Game of Speculation*'s marriage plot set amid a family's catastrophic financial misfortune; *Dorothy*'s reworking of the pastoral form in an eighteenth-century setting, despite the young women's exuberant late-Victorian agency over their marital destinies; Svengali's mesmeric hold over Trilby, wedding an unwitting Irish woman to an Eastern European whose effete yet unbreachable charismatic power is synonymous with anti-Semitism; and *The Finding of Nancy*'s central problem of self-actualization and self-sacrifice, crucially in this case giving a young woman the opportunity to overturn both her culture's gender mores and centuries of dramatic convention. The crisis of marriage as a social institution is highlighted in *Ibsen's Ghost*, a burlesque of continental modernism brought home to two generations of ordinary English couples. Tackling political challenges abroad and (literally) at home, performances also staged the project of forging national unity and identity within Britain. Charles Mathews's reportage in *Trip to America* shows England's common sense and harmony in contrast to the dysfunctionality of the former colonies; the Christy's Minstrels' version of plantation culture from the American South, presented to at least some spectators disposed toward humanistic fellow-feeling rather than racism, reified British commitments to liberty; and *Alice in Wonderland*'s English soldier—one of a legion of deviations from Lewis Carroll permitted by the pantomimic form—struggles to release his darling from the villainous clutches of a home-bred Baron and his otherworldly accomplices, not as class critique but as a realization of the self-made meritocracy of the working and middle classes. As imaginative acts, performances speculated and reflected upon their times, translating facts according to conventions to produce experiences for playgoers. The salient issue is not just what happened in history and how it is represented in performance, but as Eric Hobsbawn posits, "How do or did people feel about it?"[26]

No performance existed in isolation from performance traditions or from sources of cultural prejudice, anxiety, or pride. Though surviving evidence has varying degrees of reliability, performance creates an archive of itself in each new live iteration on stage. Taken collectively, the components that constitute a repertoire can be more faithfully discerned. Ideological factors are frequently expressed through race, ethnicity, religion, gender, and class. In performance, these elements are aligned with imperialist, orientalist, nationalist, classist, and gender orthodoxies. Tending toward levelling middlebrow politics rather than radicalism, the theatre as a collective institution as well as individual businesses needed first to placate the censor before satisfying the public zeitgeist. Chauvinism—of the patriotic and sexist kinds—was *de rigueur*; however, its inevitability could be questioned by getting out of English milieux, sympathetically considering foreign cultures, and enabling the self-determination (or witty banter) of women. This occurs time and again across the repertoire, not just as a modernist innovation but also as an indispensable engine of spectacle, sensation, and thus fascination.

Genre Issues

Genres emerged not merely as expressive traditions and marketing categories but also as a taxonomy for judicial regulation.[27] The greatest restriction on London's theatrical trade up to 1843 occurred along genre lines: the patent theatres (Covent Garden and Drury Lane) could produce "drama" (tragedy, comedy, and

---

26   Eric Hobsbawn, "C (for Crisis)," *London Review of Books* 31:15 (6 August 2009): 12.

27   Wai Chee Dimock, "Introduction: Genres as Fields of Knowledge," *PMLA* 122:5 (2007): 1377-88; and Jane Moody, *Illegitimate Theatre in London, 1770-1840* (Cambridge: Cambridge UP, 2000).

farce, including Shakespeare—which was a lucrative staple), whereas theatres licensed by magistrates could not. These other "minor" or "illegitimate" theatres (which were legion by the 1830s) fostered a wide array of alternative genres including melodrama, extravaganza, pantomime, and circus which, in turn, were enthusiastically (and legally) poached by the patent theatres. Thus, the patents had free rein to adopt the innovations that the minors had developed to cope with their serious restraint on trade. The system was not only commercially unfair but judicially unenforceable.[28] After the law was reformed in 1843, opening the way for every licensed manager to try any fare—provided it was first inspected by the Examiner of Plays—theatres specialized and stratified by genre and class of audience.

Focusing on one theatre, let alone one actor, does not unlock what is necessary to broach audiences' catholicity of experience. Nor does it allow for how that experience could be called upon, when necessary, to recognize a clearly crafted performative joke, an evocation of patriotic sympathy or romantic melancholia in a tuneful refrain, or something deliberately set out of place in order to intrinsically comment on the unflustered normalcy of convention. In London's outskirts, one actor-manager noted,

> they have an audience of their own, and a jolly one it is—hearty and uproarious. An audience with sound lungs, hard hands, and the digestion of an ostrich; always ready to bolt the raw material provided for it. These theatres are seldom visited by the West-end public, except out of curiosity.[29]

Mid-century, at the Bower or Britannia theatres, almost anyone could afford tuppence to sit in the gallery. It cost eighteen times that much (three shillings) to sit in the gallery at Her Majesty's. In the crowded theatres south of the Thames,

> they play there the old standard English tragedies and plays, sometimes even those of Shakspeare [sic], stirring original melo-dramas, spectacles, and pantomimes.... Astley's is a Circus, where they play Battles of Waterloo, Wars in Affghanistan [sic], Mazeppas' [sic], and equestrian spectacles, together with scenes in the [riding] circle, feats of horsemanship, and tumbling in all its branches.... The Victoria is a model house, the type of a school to which it gives its name. It is the incarnation of the English 'domestic drama,' or rather of the drama of English domestics. There you will always find the truest pictures of virtue in rags, and vice in fine linen. There flourish the choicest specimens of all the crimes that make life hideous, robbery, rape, murder, suicide. It is a country abounding in grand combats of four—a region peopled with angelic maid servants, comic house-breakers, heroic sailors, tyrannical masters, poetical clodhoppers, and diabolic barons. The lower orders rush there in mobs, and in shirt sleeves, applaud frantically, drink ginger beer, munch apples, crack nuts, call the actors by their christian names, and throw them orange peel and apples by way of bouquets.... They live upon roast beef and plum pudding, and abominate French kickshaws.[30]

Massinger, Beaumont and Fletcher, John Marston—all neglected since the mid-seventeenth-century Interregnum—and Shakespeare found a home, retired "as to a watering place, for the benefit of its health" as if "a downright dramatic curiosity shop," in Islington.[31] In none of these places were plays by the most prestigious writers of the early nineteenth century (including Byron, Shelley, and Coleridge) seen unless in altered form. Nor were adaptations of the most fashionable Parisian successes seen there. Minor theatres presented "an Apotheosis of the seven deadly sins" relieved by "foreign voltigeurs, rope-dancers,

---

28   Tracy C. Davis, *The Economic History of British Stage, 1800-1914* (Cambridge: Cambridge UP, 2000).

29   Charles James Mathews, *Letter from Mr. Charles Mathews to the Dramatic Authors of France, Translated from Himself by Himself, as a Specimen of "Fair Imitation or Adaptation," according to the Terms of the International Copyright Convention* (London: J. Mitchell, 1852), 9. Charles James Mathews was the son of the solo performer of *Trip to America*.

30   Ibid., 9-10; kickshaws are fancy dishes in cookery.

31   Ibid., 13.

wonderful dogs, men-monkeys, learned pigs, all that can enchant the eye, improve the mind, and enlarge the understanding." Britain's seafaring traditions were featured in nautical plays in which "the object of the management is to 'hold the mirror up' to sailors."

> I leave you to judge whether the pieces are not likely to be pitched tolerably strong to suit the web-footed connoisseurs who roll in at half price, who help to whistle the act music, and only applaud a dialogue made up of cabins, cables, and cabooses, booms, binnacles, and backy boxes; whose nearest notion of attic salt is saltpetre, and whose sides are only to be tickled with points like pikes, quips like quids, and jokes like junk.[32]

The practice of "half price" was facilitated (until after 1870, in some theatres) by having multiple pieces on each evening's bill, changed with great regularity.[33] At nine o'clock, the working classes were admitted at half the regular price (fair enough, since performances began at 6:00 p.m. and stretched toward midnight). Once late-opening shops closed for the evening, their keepers and apprentices flooded into the theatres for entertainment and the meat pies, sandwiches, and ale that often constituted their dinner.

This rendition of mid-century performance culture implies that theatres and theatre-goers were somehow different in the West End. Though their performances might at times be less brisk in dialogue, more subtle in politics, or more refined in acting style, West End houses were just as devoted to spectacle, dance, and variety turns, and every theatre was suffused with music. Pantomime was universally produced, and the example in this anthology—J. Addison's adaptation of *Alice in Wonderland*—typifies the kinds of liberties taken with source material as well as the exuberant fancifulness of pantomime that helped to sustain its popularity across the nation and throughout the century.[34] Pantomime's resilience as a genre was facilitated by its free borrowing from other forms: extravaganza's stupendous processions and scenic transformations, *opéra bouffe's* risible treatment of rhyming couplets, burlesque's promiscuous attitude toward plot and logic, ballet's devotion to celebrating the female form, and (from the 1850s) music halls' fostering of comic soloists and variety acts. While seasons of French plays were regularly presented mid-century at the Haymarket, Lyceum, Princess's, and Adelphi, and later at the St. James's Theatre, these were a highbrow taste, unpruned to prevailing English sensibilities and unproved before fastidious monolinguists.

Amid the overflowing cornucopia of performance types, theatre historians have tended to focus either on the careers of exemplary practitioners, whether actors or those who innovated the function of stage directing; specific theatres; genres (especially melodrama, which was forged at the outset of the nineteenth century); or entertainment zones such as the East End.[35] But studying repertoire across the

---

32   Ibid., 13-15. The oxymoron "attic salt is saltpetre" refers to refined wit landing like gunpowder.

33   Both practices—half price admission and frequent changes of bill—were waning at the time of the 1866 Select Committee on Theatrical Licenses and Regulations. See Jim Davis and Victor Emeljanow, *Reflecting the Audience: London Theatregoing, 1840-1880* (Iowa City: U of Iowa P, 2001), 124, 211.

34   For analyses of the enormous popularity of Victorian pantomime, see Anselm Heinrich, Katherine Newey, and Jeffrey Richards, eds., *Ruskin, the Theatre and Victorian Visual Culture* (Houndmills: Palgrave Macmillan, 2009); and Sharon Aronofsky Weltman, *Performing the Victorian: John Ruskin and Identity in Theater, Science, and Education* (Columbus: Ohio State UP, 2007).

35   Richard W. Schoch, *Shakespeare's Victorian Stage: Performing History in the Theatre of Charles Kean* (Cambridge: Cambridge UP, 1998); Robert Sawyer, Julia Swindells, David Francis Taylor, and Richard Foulkes, eds., *Lives of Shakespearian Actors*, part 3: *Charles Kean, Samuel Phelps and William Charles Macready by Their Contemporaries* (London: Pickering & Chatto, 2010); Allan Stuart Jackson, *The Standard Theatre of Victorian England* (Rutherford: Fairleigh Dickinson UP, 1993); Davis and Emeljanow, *Reflecting the Audience*; and Heidi Holder, *Plays from the Working-Class Theatres of Victorian London* (Peterborough, ON: Broadview, in preparation).

expressive forms of dance, song, narrative music, and sound complicates the historical task. Charles Mathews utilized all these components in his solo performances, and actors of his day had to sing as well as dance. Leman Rede declared in 1827 that "Music has become a mania in this country." Almost all actors need to participate in the opera, and

> there is no line of the drama in which it may not be requisite to sing. Iago, Falkland, Edgar, 'King Lear,' and Incle, all vocalize, and it cannot be very agreeable to the feelings of any tragedian, after being highly applauded for his exertions in the course of the character, to be laughed at for his attempt to sing. In light comedy it is continually requisite to execute music, and sometimes of no very easy character.... Old Men and Low Comedians must sing.[36]

Audiences heard the national anthem every night, and the whole company had to come on stage to participate or else forfeit a sizeable portion of their salary.[37] Audiences heard other tunes on the streets, in their parlours, or at social gatherings, and recognized them when they cropped up in the theatre. Thus, Jessie Brown's Scottish airs were recognizable to her London audience, and the emotional tone of *Ours* is underscored by operatic, folk, and military tunes. Svengali's hold on Trilby is demonstrated by contrasting her tone-deaf rendition of the persistent ballad "Ben Bolt" with her full-throated performance under hypnotic control. *Trilby*'s audiences were also expected to recognize the French nursery tune "Au Clair de la Lune," the military favourite "Annie Laurie" (also performed in *Ours*), incidental music by Schumann and Schubert, and perhaps the strains from Berlioz and Rubinstein that underscored some of Svengali's scenes. Accounting for sound not only disrupts the logocentric grip of text and the emphasis on visuality lent by photographs and engravings, it also points to the interdependency of theatrical and musical repertoires in the nineteenth century.

Parody, which references and reworks a specific source, and burlesque, which more broadly references a form or style, are perhaps the most prominent evidence of repertoire's re-use and re-formation of familiar elements.[38] When musical tunes are recycled—whether from other plays, operas, or street ballads—the reappearance brings with it resonances of the original use. Any associated emotions, plot motifs, or political implications come along in the re-use, whether to undercut solemnity with humour or irony, foreshadow consequences, or claim greater authority or *gravitas* that deepens "understanding of the implications of the dramatic action."[39] In each reiteration, the music gains new associations that can be carried forward to subsequent re-use. Burlesque feeds on recognizability. The connection between a burlesque and what it lampoons is one of the most obvious correlations of repertoire: an audience recognizes the transposition of high-status art into a lampooned version. Tunes and lyrics are retained or substituted, plots are mangled or faithfully retained to reveal their absurdities, and caricatures suffice for readily signified figures.

Editing Issues

Translating performance into print gives texts an unwarranted aura of definitiveness. At its best, print is an infelicitous rendering of performance, a mere suggestion of the live events that unfold in time and space, sometimes again and again. Different problems arise with respect to this imprecision, depending on the relationship between the textual and production histories and the artifacts that remain after the fact. Twelve

---

36 Rede, *Road to the Stage*, 58-61.
37 Ibid., 18.
38 Robert F. Wilson, "Their Form Confounded": *Studies in the Burlesque Play from Udall to Sheridan* (The Hague: Mouton, 1975), x.
39 Carlson, *Haunted Stage*, 117.

of the thirteen pieces in this anthology[40] went through the process of licensing by the Examiner of Plays at the Lord Chamberlain's Office. Each of these manuscripts, now at the British Library and Huntington Library, represents a version that passed through the dramatist's hands some time during (or close to) the rehearsal period.[41] *Dorothy*'s licensing copy includes only the book, so the libretto must be pieced in from published scores. Differences between licensed versions and later print editions—some from authors' desks, others based on stage managers' prompt books[42]—constitute interesting points of comparison between the pre- and post-premiere states of the acting texts for *The Africans*, *Elphi Bey*, *The Game of Speculation*, and *Ours*. In the case of *The Relief of Lucknow*, the text was published (as *Jessie Brown*) between the New York premiere and the first London production, and both the American and British published editions are strikingly different from the licensing copy. The case of *Ours* is very unusual because there is a draft copy that predates the licensed copy, suggesting two incarnations that existed before opening night: one preceding actors' involvement and the other during the process of preparing the London premiere. By contrast, the texts of *Alice in Wonderland*, *The Finding of Nancy*, and the two opera burlesques performed by Christy's Minstrels (*The Gypsy Maid* and *The Nigger's Opera*) exist solely in the licensed versions and cannot be compared or corrected to any other source from before, during, or after rehearsals, while the text of *Trilby* is most reliably studied through the multiple versions of Herbert Beerbohm Tree's prompt copies; the Bristol Theatre Collection documents a succession of revivals and reworkings not only for Tree's own theatre but also a cut-down version for the music-hall stage and a scenario for a film treatment.[43] The more of such artifacts that survive, the more they resemble a "patchwork of speeches and bits of disparate and heterodox writings."[44] Though Charles Mathews's solo performance *Trip to America* was authored by James Smith and R.B. Peake, it did not qualify for licensing because it was neither a comedy (by genre definitions) nor produced at one of the three theatres then subject to such scrutiny. In the absence of Smith and Peake's script, four illicit editions survive; these were created as souvenirs by textual pirates who, presumably, took copious notes during performances, but it is impossible to determine the chronological order of the souvenirs or Mathews's fidelity to the dramatists over the course of the run. The blackface performances by Christy's Minstrels are the least textually coherent or traceable of all the examples because the company constantly recombined its repertoire of songs and burlesque sketches. Two of its sketches were (fortuitously) licensed, but despite many piano reductions for amateur use, there are no authentic instrumental scores for Christy's music, no music at all for the solo dances, and all interpolated speech is inferable only from what is documented later as conventions for the blackface minstrel form (irrespective of company and without being traceable to any performers or date of origin).[45]

---

40 The exception is *Trip to America*, though most of the Christy's Minstrels selections (except Brough's burlesques) were not licensed; details are given below in the introduction to each performance.

41 It might seem more prudent to have submitted a play for licensing before rehearsals commenced, but most plays were submitted and licensed just a few days before opening night.

42 Early in the century, printed plays were "generally set from copy provided by the author; and in it he had the opportunity to restore what the manager had eliminated, or to revise the piece in the light of its reception." Douglas MacMillan, comp., *Catalogue of the Larpent Plays in the Huntington Library* (San Marino, CA: Henry E. Huntington Library and Art Gallery, 1939), viii. Few manuscripts survive other than licensing copies. Jean-Marie Thomasseau, "Towards a Genetic Understanding of Non-contemporary Theatre: Traces, Objects, Methods," *Theatre Research International* 33:3 (2008): 236-37.

43 This plan varies considerably from the 1913 film in which Herbert Beerbohm Tree reprised his stage performance as Svengali.

44 Thomasseau, "Towards a Genetic Understanding," 245.

45 W.T. Lhamon Jr., *Raising Cain: Blackface Performance from Jim Crow to Hip Hop* (Cambridge, MA: Harvard UP, 1998); Michael Pickering, *Blackface Minstrelsy in Britain* (Aldershot: Ashgate, 2008); and T.D. Rice, *Jim Crow, American*, edited by W.T. Lhamon Jr. (Cambridge, MA: Belknap, 2009).

Thus, in tracing these "remains," it is not always performance that is most closely paralleled: sources were prepared for authorial use, censorship, production management, lay readership, and amateur re-production, and each of these purposes shapes the artifact.[46] While there are no examples included of entirely *un*authorized alteration, the questions of *who* made the alteration—author, stage manager, editor, printer, actors in revival, etc.—and under what circumstances are salient.[47] Drawing upon many kinds of source texts for this volume highlights the scope for revision-through-use during the nineteenth century. It also foregrounds textuality-as-process in the transitions from author to actors, actors to audience, and performance to book. In the cases of previously unpublished works (*Alice in Wonderland*, *The Finding of Nancy*, and the two Christy's Minstrels burlesques) this cycle has taken until the twenty-first century to complete. In other cases (*Trip to America*, *The Relief of Lucknow*, *Dorothy*, and *Trilby*), the differences between previous editions and the one presented in this anthology are considerable.[48] "Authorship" is an originary impulse, but neither singularly achieved nor definitive with respect to performance: this confounds the possibilities of what can constitute an edition. Editing is neither simply a question of updating nor improving a text for completeness or accuracy.[49] The volatility of performance ensures that neither perfect historical comprehension nor definitive inscription can occur. As a *set* of texts, however, representing the *processes* and *recurrences* of repertoire, this anthology posits ways in which the dramatists, composers, musical arrangers, performers, and audiences contributed to what was written as well as what was understood in live action.[50]

Nineteenth-century graphic conventions vary between manuscript and print practices. The *virgula plana*, often used in manuscripts to indicate a final pause, is correctly replaced in print by a period. Some-times, however, printers interpreted the *virgula plana* as an em-dash (—), which can be misinterpreted as an actor's distracted, breathy, hesitant, or urgent speaking.[51] When only print survives, one cannot be certain what punctuation was used in the (lost) manuscript from which type was set and thus whether the typesetter consistently re-marked *virgula plana* as full stops or occasionally in a way reminiscent of an actor's delivery. Likewise, when both manuscript and print survive, one cannot be certain whether a dramatist or another person connected with a production amended a printer's proof to more faithfully

---

46   See T.H. Howard-Hill, "The Dangers of Editing; or, the Death of the Editor," in *The Editorial Gaze: Mediating Texts in Literature and the Arts*, edited by Paul Eggert and Margaret Sankey (New York: Garland, 1998), 57.

47   Whereas authorial intention is usually the gold standard for editing, performance overthrows the comparatively simple relationships of author to printer that exist for other kinds of literature (and associated with W.W. Greg and Fredson Bowers's editorial advocacy). See D.C. Greetham, *Theories of the Text* (Oxford: Oxford UP, 1999); Philip Gaskell, *From Writer to Reader: Studies in Editorial Method* (Oxford: Clarendon Press, 1978), 2-9; and Ronald Gottesman and Scott Bennett, eds., *Art and Error: Modern Textual Editing* (Bloomington: Indiana UP, 1970).

48   Richard Fotheringham calls for "radical editorial intervention in order to even partially recapture either ... [nineteenth-century melodramas'] contemporary significance or their modern reading and production values." Richard Fothering-ham, "Editing Popular Nineteenth-Century Melodramas," in *Editorial Gaze*, edited by Eggert and Sankey, 126.

49   Greetham, *Theories of the Text*, 35.

50   See Josette Féral, "Introduction: Towards a Genetic Study of Performance—Take 2," *Theatre Research International* 33:3 (2008): 223-33. As H.R. Woudhuysen reasons,

if all editions can only ever be approximate, if they can only ever be copies of an unrecoverable original, then all editions, and for that matter all performances, betray the work itself. The editorial task is to lay the materials as faithfully as possible before the reader, so that a text can be constructed according to differing sets of uses and requirements.

H.R. Woudhuysen, "'Work of Permanent Utility': Editors and Texts, Authorities and Originals," in *Textual Performances: The Modern Reproduction of Shakespeare's Drama*, edited by Lukas Erne and Margaret Jane Kidnie (Cambridge: Cambridge UP, 2004), 42.

51   M.B. Parkes, *Pause and Effects: An Introduction to the History of Punctuation in the West* (Berkeley: U of California P, 1993), 307, 94.

represent actors' inflections. This indeterminability between artifacts muddies the relationship between evidence and events (texts and performances).[52]

Didaskalia (stage directions, or literally "teaching") are important sources of information about staging.[53] Prompt copies and editions based on them often supply a discursive code of left and right, upstage and downstage, and groupings of players that map movement around the axes of the stage. Some readers may regard this as superfluous, an interruption to the flow of dialogue. Others may find it indispensable—when it exists—to prompt their visual imaginations in ways more compatible with nineteenth-century staging practices. Post-production texts almost invariably include details of scenery (and sometimes costumes) that help a diligent reader to picture settings and sense milieux in which action occurs. Perhaps "authoritative" with respect to a specific production, this is rarely any more "authorial" than the choreography of entrances, crosses, and exits. Multiple texts of *Ours* provide a fascinating example of how Marie Wilton's cast augmented T.W. Robertson's work during rehearsals, changing very little of the dialogue but giving it dynamic form with gesture and properties, and how C.J. James created sets that were integral to the action. Both kinds of contribution become evident in successive renderings of the text. The absence of evidence for similar processes operating in other performance texts nevertheless invites extrapolation, and thus reading *Ours* may be instructive in reading other texts. Charles Mathews's use of props in his solo performances served his need to differentiate characters, but the addition of full costume and scenery only in the last part (the monopolylogue) marks differences in the necessary acting technique as well as demands upon the audience to understand how his depiction of multiple characters serially and simultaneously is manifest *despite* his need to change costumes and navigate the scenery. But whereas the texts of *Ours* outline in detail how actors manipulated their physical environment, *Trip to America* leaves readers guessing.

Pictorial evidence is not always performance documentation *per se*. Spatial conventions of stage blocking may be sacrificed to the compression or extension dictated by illustrative conventions. Frontispieces tend to show actors as if in a three-dimensional environment whether or not that was the scenographic practice of the day. At the time *The Africans* was published, for example, actors performed in front of two-dimensional flats and drops rather than amid three-dimensional scenery, so its frontispiece (illus. 2, p. 36) is misleading. The company that produced *Ours* innovated in exactly this respect, creating a greater illusion of immersion by making the stage a more tactile and material space. Photographs for *Ours* (illus. 24, p. 393 and 25, p. 412) reflect this, though what was posed in a studio to accommodate necessary light levels and held for long periods to meet exposure requirements (as with the photographs of *Dorothy*, *Ibsen's Ghost*, and *Trilby*, illus. 26, p. 433; 27, p. 442; 31, p. 561; and 33, p. 593) may not faithfully capture

---

52   As Thomas Postlewait observes, "we should note that the event, once identified and constructed, can be approached as an object, a text, a discourse, an act, or a performance. In other words, given our wide range of interpretive approaches, we may construct the event in several different ways. Whatever the approach, all of us are involved in a complex interpretive project as we move from artifacts to facts, then from evidence to event. We need to proceed with care through each step in the process." Thomas Postlewait, "Constructing Events in Theatre History: A Matter of Credibility," in *Theatre Events: Borders, Dynamics, Frames*, edited by Vicky Ann Cremona et al. (Amsterdam: Rodopi, 2004), 34.

53   *Nebentext* is a more inclusive term, including stage directions as well as speech prefixes and descriptions that typically precede an act's or a scene's commencement of speech. Roman Ingarden, *The Literary Work of Art: An Investigation on the Borderlines of Ontology, Logic, and Theory of Literature* (Evanston, IL: Northwestern UP, 1978); and John D. Cox, "Open Stage, Open Page? Editing Stage Directions in Early Dramatic Texts," in *Textual Performances*, edited by Erne and Kidnie, 178. *Epitext* is even more inclusive, incorporating "titles and subtitles, pseudonyms, forewords, dedications, epigraphics, prefaces, intertitles, notes, epilogues, and afterwords" as framing devices. Richard Macksey, foreword to *Paratexts: Thresholds of Interpretation*, by Gerald Genette, translated by Jane E. Lewin (Cambridge: Cambridge UP, 1987), xviii. *Trip to America* poses the greatest range of *epitext*. Most of such material has been retained for this volume.

actors' expressions, relationships to properties, or scenery with thorough accuracy. Photographs of an entire stage setting, *in situ*, became possible only at the end of the century. Even then, lighting levels were augmented for the camera.[54] Other illustrative sources and conventions—caricatures (illus. 6, p. 166; 7, p. 212; 8, p. 230; and 12, p. 279), song sheet covers (illus. 23, p. 357), and portraits (illus. 9, p. 268)—are also subject to selection, exaggeration, and excision depending on their medium and marketing strategy.

While print and pictorial evidence are complementary artifacts, in most cases, neither can be as fulsome as performance itself. None of the examples in this anthology was written (or assembled) to be read: performance is the intended mode of transmission though many kinds of artifacts left behind—photographs, books, periodical illustrations, and sheet music—point in different ways to the complexity of theatrical presentation.[55] Yet when they were printed, some texts were oriented to a reader's perspective (as if, in an audience, the action could be viewed left to right) and others (especially in Dick's, French's, or Lacy's editions) were oriented for actor's needs (correlating the locations of entrances to numbered wings alongside the stage, for example).

Each text in this anthology posits solutions to particular problems. More problems exist than can be solved in one edition, and readers are encouraged to become *users*: to get involved with these editorial challenges, make arguments for other solutions, and consider possible variance. Books function to store text and, as material objects, are constrained by size to hold only selected content. Alternate nineteenth-century versions of the texts, ancillary documents (including reviews), images, and bibliographies are available in the electronic archive intended to be used alongside this anthology, at http://drama. at.northwestern.edu. Readers are encouraged to consult these digital files and create dynamic models of the texts (preferably using widely available software or shareware) to add to the website. Thus, communities of readers and performers can offer perspectives on the repertoire. Different editorial choices, page layouts, incorporation of sound or video files, and comparisons and juxtapositions of performance can represent the plenitude inherent to repertoire and the contingency of performance more fulsomely than print ever can.[56] Anyone interested in these kinds of issues is encouraged to contact the editor.[57]

---

54   Photography onstage was possible from 1893 but rare before 1900. David Mayer, "'Quote the Words to Prompt the Attitudes': The Victorian Performer, the Photographer, and the Photograph," *Theatre Survey* 43:2 (2002): 223-51; and David Mayer, "The Actress and the Profession: Training in England in the Twentieth Century," in *The Cambridge Companion to the Actress*, edited by Maggie B. Gale and John Stokes (Cambridge: Cambridge UP, 2007), 80, 89.

55   W.B. Worthen's contention that by the late nineteenth century (and specifically in print editions of George Bernard Shaw) "print is the condition of drama" does not pertain to the vast majority of Victorian stage practice, even in the 1890s. *Print and the Poetics of Modern Drama* (Cambridge: Cambridge UP, 2005), 9. Comparatively few plays were published though the proportion of premieres to first editions dropped precipitously as new-play production burgeoned after 1830.

56   Elizabeth Bergmann Loizeaux and Neil Fraistat argue that electronic editing shapes texts beyond the confines of a book, "creating new forms of textuality and making possible new ways of reproducing, editing, and archiving texts. With its multimedia and networked capabilities, electronic textuality foregrounds the role played by the visual and aural elements of textuality, as well as the social and material ontologies of texts." "Introduction: Textual Studies in the Late Age of Print," in *Reimagining Textuality: Textual Studies in the Late Age of Print*, edited by Elizabeth Bergmann Loizeaux and Neil Fraistat (Madison: U of Wisconsin P, 2002), 5.

57   tcdavis@northwestern.edu.

The Africans; or, War, Love, and Duty (1808)

Editing Issues

As the law required, George Colman (manager of the Haymarket Theatre) submitted a manuscript of *The Africans* to the Lord Chamberlain's office for licensing a few days before the play's premiere.[1] There are innumerable minor differences between this licensed copy and the edition later published by John Cumberland.[2] Cumberland lacks a few passages blue-lined by the Examiner of Plays and so definitely worked from a later copy. Cumberland also alters a lot of punctuation; this seems less likely to reflect changes made during rehearsal and performance than the idiosyncratic habits of the copyist and typesetter, respectively. Though George Colman was never a great writer of iambic pentameter, his metered lines are more regular in the manuscript than in Cumberland, which is surprising given that Cumberland claimed to base the edition on the "acting copy" (presumably the prompt book). In the text presented here, the lines and stage directions are restored to the manuscript, most spelling is modernized, and punctuation is regularized to enhance line sense rather than always reflecting the irregularities of either source text. Both dramatist and manager of the company, Colman knew his cast thoroughly and had every reason to expect his sense of the play to come through in performance. Consequently, the editorial choices in the present version were made to more closely reflect Colman's polemics and actors' rhythms, favouring the manuscript in most instances. Though Cumberland indicates right and left in stage directions, the loss of these details should not impede a reader's ability to envision the flows of movement.

The play has been reprinted once: a facsimile of Cumberland's edition in the eight-volume set *Slavery, Abolition, and Emancipation: Writings in the British Romantic Period*. Its editor, Jeffrey Cox, acknowledges Colman's debt to Pixérécourt's *Sélico* (a Parisian melodrama), in turn taken from Jean-Pierre Claris de Florian's 1792 novella of the same name.[3] The novella was anonymously set to English rhymed couplets

---

1   Larpent 1553, Huntington Library. The play was performed almost every night for the remainder of the summer season for a total of 31 times (Harvard Theatre Collection, Playbills) and revived in 1819, 1822, 1823, and 1824. For more information about the production history of *The Africans*, see also Hazel Waters, *Racism on the Victorian Stage: Representation of Slavery and the Black Character* (Cambridge: Cambridge UP, 2007), 42. The play was also presented in New York in 1810, a production discussed in Heather S. Nathans, *Slavery and Sentiment on the American Stage, 1787-1861: Lifting the Veil of Black* (Cambridge: Cambridge UP, 2009), 116.

2   The exact date of Cumberland's edition has not been determined; however, the text is identical to the American edition, published by M. Carey in Philadelphia in 1811 (Harvard Theatre Collection prompt book), so it almost certainly constitutes the antecedent for the American edition. See George Colman the Younger, *The Africans; or, War, Love, and Duty* (London: John Cumberland, [c. 1808]).

3   Jeffrey N. Cox, ed., *Slavery, Abolition, and Emancipation: Writings in the British Romantic Period*, vol. 5, *Drama*, Peter J. Kitson and Debbie Lee, gen. eds. (London: Pickering and Chatto, 1999), 221-80; Jean-Pierre Claris De Florian, *Sélico, Nouvelle Africaine*, in *Nouvelles Nouvelles* ([Paris], 1792), 64-90. A Spanish stage adaptation also exists: Gaspar Zavala Zamora, *Sélico y Berisa* (Madrid, 1799). In this version, set in 1727 (the year of a Dahomian conquest of the Hueda kingdom), Selico and his brothers move their father Darino to safety in anticipation of an attack by the Dahomians. The Dahomians' enlightened ruler, Truro Audati, dreams of restoring peace in his lands and of turning Sabi, the capital of the Hueda kingdom, into a center of the arts, sciences, and commerce—the envy of the Europeans (the slave-traders in this version are French and Dutch)—and of proving to Europe that his kingdom has to offer more than slaves. As soon as Truro Audati's closest friend and counsellor, Kariskan, brings the captured Berisa to him, Truro Audati falls in love. He is so impressed by her intelligence and lack of artifice that he promises to establish her in his seraglio (Continued)

in 1794, the proceeds of which went to the abolition of the slave-trade.[4] Colman plausibly knew at least two versions, for another of de Florian's works was adapted for the Haymarket in 1789 (the year Colman took over his late father's lease of the theatre).[5]

De Florian's *Sélico* establishes the story of a West African widow and her three sons. The youngest, Sélico, is about to marry Bérissa when their village is attacked. Believing that his beloved is dead, and in anguish at seeing his mother suffer from famine, Sélico joins his brothers in a plan for one of them to be sold into slavery. The grieving Sélico insists that he become the chattel, but upon arrival at the slave market he hears that the king's seraglio has been invaded, his favourite slave visited, and that a reward is offered for the intruder's head. Thinking imminent death preferable to forty years of slavery, Sélico insists that his brothers turn him in for this crime. Sélico and the king's slave are at the brink of death when they discover each other's identities: Sélico rejoices to discover that Bérissa is not only alive but also chaste and faithful. In the anonymously written English verse adaptation, this gives Berissa (with her newly Anglicized name) the occasion for powerful rhetoric, beseeching the king to share her sense of honour and justice, heedless of her own fate:

> "O king of Dahomai," Berissa cry'd,
> (Now to the fatal stake already tied)
> ...
> Behold me cheerfully resigned to death,
> I know that nothing can prolong my breath,
> Nor do I now protract this awful time,
> But to prevent in you a horrid crime;
> Again, O king, I heaven to witness call,
> His guiltless blood upon thy head will fall;
> Put me to instant death, send him away;
> This is, my lord, the whole I have to say.[6]

Berissa's father staggers in, confesses, and the king, implausibly but thoroughly moved by Sélico's filial piety, gives Berissa a 10,000-crown dowry. The tale ends with the motto "Content and Wealth by Virtue only gained."[7]

The verse adaptation provides scope for exotic scenery and vivid stage pictures, such as the wedding, battle, starving family in the wilderness, and slave market.

> With thronging multitudes the place is fill'd;
> In dread array the army to the field
> Advances in slow march, and halting there,

---

but not to force any intimacy on her until she is ready to accept him as a husband. Truro Audati's extreme jealously is ignited when someone tries to break into the seraglio. When Selico learns that the seraglio has been invaded, he begins to suspect Berisa of infidelity. His suspicion is more emphasized in this play than in other adaptations, and even after their reconciliation Berisa harbours bitterness over Selico's misjudgement. Cox also mentions a lost play on this theme, by Charles Kemble (222), but there is no trace of this text. Felicity Nussbaum incorrectly credits a different novel, John Moore's *Zeluco* (London, 1789), as a source in Felicity Nussbaum, *The Limits of the Human: Fictions of Anomaly, Race, and Gender in the Long Eighteenth Century* (Cambridge: Cambridge UP, 2003), 235.

4   *Sélico, an African Tale* (Exeter: R. Trewman, 1794).

5   Jean-Pierre Claris de Florian's *La Bonne Mère* was adapted for the Haymarket as *Look before You Leap*, translated by Horatio Robson (London: Harrison, 1788).

6   *Sélico, an African Tale*, 26-27.

7   Ibid., 31.

Bristled with pikes and muskets forms a square.
The priests their robes of ceremony wear,
Expecting till the destined pair appear,
Their office, e'er they stop the vital breath,
To lay their hands on, and devote to death.[8]

Colman found promising theatrical material in this.[9] He highlights the anti-slavery message by presenting the European slave-traders (who get barely a mention in the sources) as comic grotesques, greatly emphasizing the brothers' and Berissa's codes of duty, and emphasizing the role of intertribal warfare in slave-trafficking. He also exploits the exotic potential of scenery by setting action inside an African hut and then a woodland, depicting the burning of tents after the battle, and staging the procession of slave-merchants over the mountains, even mounting one of the slave-traders on a camel.[10] Music specially composed by Michael Kelly provides a number of character turns and instrumental numbers celebrating the impending wedding, battle and burning of the town, march of merchants and slaves, and march of warriors and prisoners.[11]

Colman also folds in selected aspects of another well-known text: not fiction but the infamous memoir of a Scottish adventurer, *Travels in the Interior Districts of Africa* (1799). Its author, Mungo Park, embarked under the auspices of the scientific Association for the Promotion of Discovery to explore the interior of Africa, concentrating on the area between the Senegal and Gambia Rivers where Colman sets his play.[12] Park's memoir supplies Colman with the names of Selico's middle brother (Madiboo, a Muslim blacksmith who accompanied Park on part of his journey), Demba Sego Jalla (Mandingo King of Kassan), and Daucari (a trader). Though in Britain Park was respected for his intrepidness, Colman cleverly repurposes this explorer to craft Mister Mug, a thoroughly cockney merchant in search of ivory—like gold, a commodity that attracted Europeans to the region—who is simultaneously buffoonish (relative to the dignified Muslim Foulahs and infidel Mandingos) and wise (compared to the avaricious Christian slave-traders). Park found good hosts among the people he encountered but also suffered horribly at the hands of various captors.[13] Mug distills these mishaps by travelling solo in West Africa and being enslaved by three masters: the first severely abuses him; the second is Berissa's kindly father, an imam;[14] and the third is the warring Mandingo

---

8   Ibid., 23-24.

9   The elaborate pageantry may have been written with Covent Garden's 1807-08 season in mind, but it was instead produced at the much smaller Haymarket the following summer. The dimensions of the Haymarket enabled audiences to see the actors' faces, but though this aided natural acting, it made spectacle ludicrous. As Colman quipped, "only clap a Child on a Bulldog, and he'll look like Gulliver taking an Airing in Lilliput." Jeremy F. Bagster-Collins, *George Colman the Younger, 1762-1836* (New York: King's Crown Press, 1946), 205; and George Colman the Younger, *The Plays of George Colman the Younger*, vol. 1, edited by Peter A. Tasch (New York: Garland, 1981), xxix. *Theatrical Examiner*, 30 July 1808: 491.

10   "Mr. Colman's New Drama," *London Chronicle*, 30 July 1808, 108.

11   Michael Kelly, *The Overture, Songs, Duetts [sic], Choruses, &c. in "The Africans"* (London: Kelly's Opera Saloon, 1808); and *Songs, Choruses, &c. in The Africans; or, War, Love, and Duty; A Play in Three Acts, First Perform'd at the Theatre Royal, Hay-market, on Friday, July 29, 1808, the Musick Composed and Selected by Mr. Kelly* (London: Theatre Royal, Haymarket, 1808), Huntington K-D 628. Barry Sutcliffe notes that "Colman was the first playwright of the period systematically to explore" the use of ballads and songs "in a non-comic context." Barry Sutcliffe, introduction to *Plays by George Colman the Younger and Thomas Morton* (Cambridge: Cambridge UP, 1983), 31.

12   Mungo Park, *Travels in the Interior Districts of Africa: Performed Under ... the African Association, in the Years 1795, 1796, and 1797* (London: W. Bulmer, 1799), xviii-xix. Cox notes but does not explicate the connections.

13   Park is a much closer prototype for Mug's adventures than, for example, the travellers taken by Moors in L.F. Jauffret, *Travels of Rolando*, vol. 1 (1804; reprinted by London: R. Phillips, 1823), 42-66.

14   "Maraboou" is the contemporary word used for Muslim religious leaders in Senegal; the Foulah ethnic group uses the terms "cherno/theirno" or "modibo."

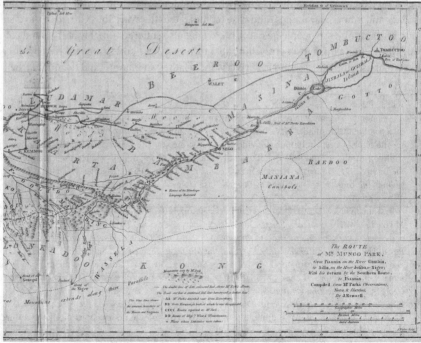

Illustration 1. *The Route of Mungo Park*, from *Travels in the Interior Districts of Africa*, 1799.
Courtesy of the Melville Herskovitz Library, Northwestern University.

king who exploits Mug's literacy to communicate with traders for commercial advantage. A cabinet post goes along with his third situation, yet Mug chafes at his loss of freedom. He selflessly gives food to the afflicted; organizes a petition to free his African friends; and rejoices when reunited with the object of his affections, Sutta, even though she playfully (yet sincerely) proclaims the unredeemable ugliness of his race.

Colman uses details from Park's narrative to give ethnographic specificity to the family-oriented Foulahs (Farulho and Darina's families) and fearsomeness to the bellicose Mandingos and their king (Demba Sego Jalla), who attacks without warning, slaughters the innocents, enslaves the tender, profits from intercontinental commerce in human beings, and resolves to butcher the defiant. These plot elements are in de Florian's story, but Park inspires enhancements of locale and pathos as well as a justification for making the Foulahs fairer-skinned than the ferocious Mandingos. Mug, as the comic *raisonneur* whose speeches constantly remind audiences of London's role in this moral morass, foregrounds the commercial profiteers of human exploitation and serves both to contrast tragic plotlines and to embody the potential for racial turnabout, as Mug is a brutalized captive despite his birthright and irrepressible jolliness.

Colman sets a high moral standard for the African characters; by the mid-point, Selico's jealous brother Torribal meets it by wishing to spare his grieving brother further suffering, and by the end, even the despotic Demba Sego Jalla has evolved to resemble the Mandingo overlord who treated Mungo Park kindly in the midst of his own people's famine. From the outset, the Foulahs embody Eurocentric ideals of love, fidelity, and sacrifice, exhibiting these qualities in supereminent acts of compassion. Demba Sego Jalla rises to their moral level, matching the intercultural compassion shown by Selico's would-be executioner and—by implication—the path of reform modelled for British ex-slavers.[15]

One reviewer referred to these pictures of family life as "truly epic" yet also had difficulty accepting such "intelligent, high-spirited" characters, or the too-logical rhetoric of Selico at the stake, as credibly African.[16] "Vigorous sentiment" was the expression applied by sympathizers to describe this combination of polemics and situation.[17]

> SELICO.
>   Conquest's right
>   Gives a true hero the delightful power
>   Of shewing conquest's generosity.
>   And what's your right? A battle gives it you.
>   What are the ties of those you pluck asunder?
>   Why, time and sympathy have knotted them:
>   And should you die, instead of those you separate,
>   It might be better justice. (3.3)

Such characteristics were more familiar in North American natives than Africans, at least as far as stage convention had assimilated up to 1808. Audiences were more familiar with the ill-guided passion of Othello and the overdetermined fidelity of Oroonoko than an African *raisonneur* who speaks back to British foreign policymakers, but the sticking point was not that eloquence was unfamiliar among stage Africans. The tragedy *Sélico* ends happily, whereas *The Africans* alternated (and ultimately converged) tragic and comic plot lines. Perhaps, therefore, the critic who cavilled at Selico's logic as implausibly African chafed not just at the characterization but also the situation in which his stirring plea resolved.

---

15   Tasch describes the playwright's abiding tendency to create characters that are not individualized: "all the types are heroic, so victor or victim ... vies to be admirable." *Plays of George Colman*, vol. 1, xxvii.

16   *Theatrical Examiner*, 30 July 1808: 491.

17   "Theatre. Haymarket," *Morning Post*, 30 August 1808: 3.

Genre Issues

The Africans begins in the comic mode with an impending marriage. War turns the plot tragic, tragedy entwines with love to inject sentimentality, and the drumbeat of duty ensures that the whole is intensely moralistic. These are the thematic ingredients of melodrama, a genre born with the new century that both satisfied public tastes and enabled the French inventors (and English adopters) of the new conventions to function within censorship and licensing constrictions.[18] Melodrama combines music with drama, underscoring sentiment with melody, linking characters to sonic *leitmotifs*, and cueing audiences to emotive responses through stirring orchestrations. *The Africans*, as an early example that did not need to work around the prohibition on drama (for the Haymarket had an unrestricted licence during the summer months), utilizes aspects of this new pattern along with fragments of other established formats. There are balletic passages taken respectively by the female corps (in the wedding celebrations) and the male *danseurs* (in the processions of soldiers). The comic songs—Sutta and Mug's duet "On the Jet Feathered Raven," Madiboo's "The Priest of Kajaaga," and Mug's hit solo "Mister Mug," a patter song calculated to infect every listener with the line "Crying won't you won't you won't you come Mister Mug"[19] (2.2)—serve as counterpoints to serious action more so than establishing character. Sentimental songs—most notably Sutta's "Slave Come Home" and the trio "All's Well"—establish mood and underscore broad sweeps of narrative, which are features that would not be out of place in opera or sentimental comedy. Solo singing is assigned to just three characters (all with comic proclivities) so it is not opera, nor is it simply a drama with songs. Characters broke into song long before melodrama emerged; this is not what marks the new format, but rather the orchestral underscoring of speech and action (not limited to recitative and choreography).

Melodrama's hallmarks of the spotless heroine, virtuous man of action, vernacular low comedian, suffering parent, and menacing villain are unmistakable within the confines of the plot. This marks *The Africans* as a product of its time. Alongside melodrama's character types is characteristic genre mixing. The comic wooing subplot is worked out alongside serious matters of state, just as the hilarity of Mug is as acceptable as the looming threat of the European slave-traders. Though Demba Sego Jalla's dispensation of poetic justice is unmotivated (by tragic standards), it is necessitated by the demands of comedy. Demba's first appearance, like the entry of the slaves and European merchants, has music that signals to the audience that what will ensue is not an entirely grave event: Demba's theme is majestic, but no irredeemable tyrant could process on the descending staccato scales or ascending trills and grace notes assigned to him, just as no unqualifiedly doomed slaves or slave-traders fated for success could enter to the lively beat assigned to them.

As the low-comic pair, Mug and Sutta provide overt relief from the horrors of Selico and Berissa's fates on the sacrificial pyre. Yet their comic jostling is not certain to result in comedy's conventional unification of lovers by the final curtain. Act 2 ends with Mug having bartered for Sutta in exchange for giving the slave-traders a good deal on another job lot.

> MUG. Now, gentlemen; we finish the market for this day.—Lord, Sutta, I am so happy to see you again.—Can't you like me as a master?
> SUTTA. Very well if you black.

---

18 John McCormick, *Popular Theatres of Nineteenth-Century France* (London: Routledge, 1993); F.W.J. Hemmings, *Theatre and State in France, 1760-1905* (Cambridge: Cambridge UP, 1994); and Jane Moody, *Illegitimate Theatre in London, 1770-1840* (Cambridge: Cambridge UP, 2000).

19 The song was frequently encored and published separately from the rest of the score. Jim Davis, *John Liston, Comedian* (London: Society for Theatre Research, 1985), 19; and *Mr. Mug: A Celebrated Comic Song Sung by Mr. Liston with Unabounded Applause in the Drama of "The Africans"* (London: G. Walker, [1808]).

MUG. Oh come, I see she'll soften down in time. As a famous Squinting Patriot used to say, there is but six weeks difference in point of success, between me and the handsomest man in England. Tomorrow morning, gentlemen, we begin a fresh sale. (2.3)

Now Sutta's master, Mug is confident that six weeks hence he will triumph as her suitor, though his optimism should be tempered in relation to Sutta's racialized world view. By the end of act 3, Sutta acknowledges Mug's kindness but still bemoans his looks. Comedy's romantic threads are pointed toward each other if not fully tied up. Colman's underlying polemic about slavery is renewed in Mug's acknowledgement that even if the pairing of the comic lovers is achieved (the performers playing Mug and Sutta were, after all, John and Sarah Liston, neé Tyrer, married barely a year earlier), commerce in human beings persists: the next day there will be a "fresh sale" of slaves, and one interracial union cannot undo the villainy of slave-trafficking. De Florian's heroic plot is resolved, but in Colman's interleaved story, the slave merchants have not left town. Just as, earlier in the scene, the "Chorus of Mandingo Warriors" includes a counterpoint line between the warriors' song "March brave Mandingos march, in triumph shout" and the prisoners' "Mourn, Captives, mourn! In battle ta'en" (2.3), in the midst of the act 3 finale, Sutta has a melodic solo:

SUTTA.
> Thus after cold and wintry showers,
> The West Wind breathes, and sunshine's ours
> Sweet Spring each heart of care beguiling
> Sweet Spring returns, all is smiling.
> Sweet Peace. (3.3)

Paradoxically, this reminds the audience that peace does *not* reign in Africa as long as slavery persists there. Inserting this solo and giving it to Sutta—not the restored Berissa—keeps her fate to the fore as a traded commodity, emotionally tied to her estranged family and lands, in the midst of the felicitous ballyhoo of the play's conclusion and Selico and Berissa's union. As Julie Carlson states, "*The Africans* enlists sentimental humanism in the service of difference, but a difference that remains plural and relative, rather than one of binary oppositions."[20] While she argues this with reference to Selico and Berissa, whose love is unwaveringly noble, the comic lovers demonstrate pluralism even more strikingly.

Interpretive Issues

The timing of *The Africans*' first performance seems inauspicious for an abolitionist play: just over a year *after* legislation prohibiting England's participation in the transatlantic slave-trade. While public sympathy was with Colman, this phase of the battle had been put to rest after a long and arduous fight. Given the play's two main sources, it is not surprising that it lacks overt topicality, for they were both products of the previous century. Perhaps it seemed that the abolitionist message was still filtering up-river to the outposts of English traders, or perhaps Colman's point was to turn attention to the next abolitionist challenge: the ancient practices of African factions which enslaved each other, without which the intercontinental slave trade among Britain's political enemies and economic rivals could not persist.

Mungo Park reported that in Africa slaves outnumbered freemen three to one.[21] Bondage was neither a recent development nor a European imposition, and though the flow of slaves from the interior to

---

20   Julie A. Carlson, "Race and Profit in English Theatre," in *The Cambridge Companion to British Theatre, 1730-1830*, edited by Jane Moody and Daniel O'Quinn (Cambridge: Cambridge UP, 2007), 183.

21   Park, *Travels in the Interior*, 287.

coastal dungeons found an additional economic incentive in transatlantic export, interethnic capture and indenture was also the basis of African social structure. Abolitionists emphasized European culpability in sustaining this system; Colman reminded audiences of an underlying factor and of the complicated story of victimhood within Africa.

Astute spectators of 1808 might have recalled that Senegambia was technically in French hands. Britain was at war with France. In other words, the British traders who traverse inland at Mug's summons to purchase the prisoners taken in warfare between the Foulahs and Mandingos not only contravene British sentiment (greedy for their last forbidden cargo) but also traffic in their enemy's empire. This enemy terrified Britons. As Madiboo tries to warn Mug, lest he become too comfortable as Demba Sego Jalla's Minister of War,

> MADIBOO. Yes, and he'll poison you, when he has no further occasion for you. He is no rightful ruler; but worked and bullied himself into power. When the troubles, about liberty, broke out among the Mandingoes, he was of low note among their warriors. Enterprise and good luck gave him, at last, complete sway over the fighting men: that's everything when a nation is in a ferment, and the successful upstart is active, cruel, and cunning. But what has it made him?—Why, the usurping king of a people who murdered their true king; and the pillaging protector of some trembling neighbours, whom he forces to say, come and shoot one half of us, that the survivors may thank you for putting their property under your clutches. (2.1)

This double image of a regicidal people (as in France) and usurping black population that wrestled for power among complex interracial groups (as in Haiti) probably resonated with readers' knowledge of both the French (1789-99) and Haitian (1791-1804) revolutions. But it predominantly served to remind them of Napoleon.[22] By Colman's logic, to oppose the Napoleonic system of misrule, despotism, and imperialistic insatiability requires also to recognize British culpability in the slave trade and the work that remained to be done after the Act for the Abolition of the Slave Trade came into effect in 1807. The Foulahs, though portrayed as peaceful (like the British) and god-fearing (like the Church of England), also continued to hold slaves (like the British plantocrats in the West Indies). To know better yet to act in such a way pointed a finger at England; this became a salient point for abolitionists as British interests in the region blossomed following the capture of the island of Gorée from the French in 1800 and as the British realized that France's only remaining hold on the Senegal River was its poorly garrisoned post at St. Louis.[23] Britain saw the chance to undercut France's supply line of slaves to the West Indies and to secure new outlets for British manufactures, but what would be done with that opportunity? Farulho's bridal gift to Berissa is to emancipate his slaves, and thus a man of God becomes righteous. Demba Sego Jalla, a man honed by war and hardened to every story of privation, finally learns to reason on behalf of mercy as well as justice. If only Britons could do as much, jostled by Mug's good nature and inspired by his infatuation with Sutta.

Major plot points turn upon reversals of fortune that result in enslavement, transfer of slaves from one master to another, or emancipation. Slavery's presence as the keynote and abolition's morality as the clarion call are unmistakable. Mug's successive functions as a London craftsman, ivory purchaser,

---

22   Henry Crabb Robinson, an abolitionist, saw *The Africans* on 14 August 1811. He condemned the piece as "a series of commonplace pathetic incidents" parading "refined morality and ostentatious ... sentiment." Nevertheless, he clearly recognized Demba as "a sort of African Buonaparte." Henry Crabb Robinson, *The London Theatre, 1811-1866*, edited by Eluned Brown (London: Society for Theatre Research, 1966), 38.

23   Philip D. Curtin, *The Image of Africa: British Ideas and Action, 1780-1850* (Madison: U of Wisconsin P, 1964), 142, 150-52.

slave, and co-opted Minister of War make him a stand-in for British spectators even though as a cabinet member he experiences social ascendance never available to him in London. Haplessly caught up in Africa's vassalage, he represents not just the stirring story of the white slave but also a white man whose involvement with one commodity is made integral with the traffic in human beings. This points implicitly at the British parliament. Whereas Selico makes a morally conditioned choice to become a slave, sustaining an equilibrium of Africans' making, Mug represents another moral universe—in Europe—that need not be fatalistic about human trafficking.

The play proved popular. Insofar as it was recognizable as an intertext with Mungo Park, the woeful fate of Park's second expedition to the region, begun in 1805 and sealed the next year,[24] would have compelled topical interest even for spectators wearied by abolitionist agitation. Both *Travels in the Interior Districts of Africa* and *Sélico* are Eurocentric sources, yet they seek to portray the complexity of African cultures even as the comparability to Europeans is a not-so-subtle subtext. Identification with subjected others is a key strategy of abolitionist rhetoric. In *The Africans*, identification functions alongside horror to encourage spectators to experience many empathetic affiliations: brothers at odds with one another, a tender-hearted clergyman, children and parents prepared to make any sacrifice for each other, a mourning lover, a woman defiant in the face of a powerful man's sexual threats, a crafty capitalist's adaptation to new circumstances, and a woman who rebuffs a suitor because she finds him physically repugnant. The ultimate permutation of this is the king's prerogative to reverse the fortunes of Selico and Berissa, at the brink of death, not only by restoring them to liberty but also by endowing them with wealth. In the campaign to end slave-trafficking, British abolitionists consolidated emotional appeals into economic strategies which took performative form in product boycotts. Thus, the commodities made by enslaved labourers were experientially linked to consumers' habits and trappings of wealth. Like Berissa, abolitionist sympathizers withstood virtue's trial.

Colman provides significant twists on the idea of the grateful slave: still chafing at her bondage, Sutta is neither an argument for amelioration of the institution of slavery nor a comic character who is "irrationally passionate":[25] "Liberty! Oh, dat make my heart go tump tump," says Sutta (1.2). Only Sutta—enslaved by the Foulahs, and longing for her native village—utters the "black" stage patois. She is too black to be a Foulah and evidently also a foreigner to the Mandingos. While her master, Farulho, is kindly she longs to be restored to her own people: "When I see my home how my eye will trickle joy! Ah! priest Farulho, he dear, good massa;—but some massa, oh! they whippy so!" (1.2). Thus, Sutta underlines ethnic distinctions within Africa and racial difference from Europeans. She also has an uncompromising stance on the desirability of *complete* abolition. She is not deluded that Africa without Europeans will be peaceful, for slavery in itself is not a racialized custom.[26] A comforting division between Christianity, Islam, and barbarity does not pertain.[27] Yet an affective similarity is made apparent in her ballad "Slave Come Home," in which her lyric refrain "Father, Mother, Sister, Brother they will cherish slave come home"

---

24 Park and his remaining bedraggled contingent of fellow explorers reached the head waters of the Niger—just 150 miles inland—and sailed over 1,000 miles downstream, beyond Timbuktu, but were ambushed and drowned far from their destination, the Gulf of Guinea.

25 Compare with George Boulukos, *The Grateful Slave: The Emergence of Race in Eighteenth-Century British and American Culture* (Cambridge: Cambridge UP, 2008), 15.

26 Compare Patrick Brantlinger's characterizations of Romantic and Victorian anti-slavery rhetoric in "Victorians and Africans: The Genealogy of the Myth of the Dark Continent," in "Race," Writing, and Difference, edited by Henry Louis Gates, Jr. (Chicago: U of Chicago P, 1986), 189, 192; and George Taylor, *The French Revolution and the London Stage, 1789-1805* (Cambridge: Cambridge UP, 2001), 216-17.

27 Aphra Behn took a similar stance in *Oroonoko*, where the contrast between "Christian treachery and pagan honour" was marked. Jane Spencer, *Aphra Behn's Afterlife* (Oxford: Oxford UP, 2000), 227.

R. Cruikshank, Del.   G. F. Bonner, Sc.

The Africans.

Mug. Don't kill me! keep me for a show—you'll find it worth
your while.

Act II. Scene 2.

Illustration 2. Frontispiece to *The Africans* by Robert Cruikshank, 1808.
Courtesy of the Henry E. Huntington Library.

makes her family ties as palpable as the enacted sacrifices made by Selico and Berissa for their parents. The musical phrase used for "no more to roam" and "slave come home" (ascending diatonically, ending on the tonic) makes this especially plaintive. The musical flavour is Scots-Irish, by which the composer makes the message hit home for his audiences through religious and racial difference, imparted visually, in contrast to the harmonic familiarity.

Performative Issues

George Colman was the lessee and manager of the Haymarket Theatre: this ensured that *The Africans* was well cast and adequately rehearsed. It did not suffer the usual vicissitudes of new plays under the repertory system, where the bill consisted of several pieces every night and was altered nearly daily.

The frontispiece to Cumberland's edition shows two characters in an attitude of pathos, potentially turned to comedy: Mug (recognizable as the low comedian John Liston) sits on a stump, knees splayed and arms thrust apart in surprise as Madiboo (played by John Fawcett) seizes his neckcloth. Mug's appearance fully conforms to the printed costume plot (striped trousers, shirt with turned-down collar, and broad-brimmed hat), and so does Madiboo's (white shirt and belted trunks, headband, bracelets, and sandals), but it is the additional specification that Madiboo (like his brothers) has "black body, arms, and legs" that accounts for his exotic—as opposed to conventionally comic—ensemble. The brothers' all-over blackness is a significant visual feature even if their colour is superseded by the Mandingos' darker hue. The reigning stage image of Africans was shaped by Oroonoko, the regal hero of Aphra Behn's novel (adapted for the stage by Thomas Southerne), who was pictured in 1776 (portrayed by Mr. Savigny) in the regalia of an eighteenth-century European prince.[28] Though Oroonoko is black and speaks in blank verse, his majesty predominates, no matter how oppressive his circumstances. Madiboo's costume emphasizes his lithe athleticism as integral with his blackness—minus the turban and bangles, this resembles the costume of a contemporaneous acrobat—but his decorum shifts depending upon his company. When speaking with his family, he converses in blank verse, but when talking with Mug or Sutta he descends to prose. This is not a prince dislocated to foreign climes yet indelibly regal, but a middling family man in his own milieu, scrabbling hard for a living. The elder brother's haughtiness and the youngest brother's fine sentiments must be reconciled to Madiboo's ability to code-switch.

The costume plot does not specify black limbs for the female characters; however, it would be an error to assume that their hands and faces were not darkened. Mug describes Sutta as a "dusky Venus," and their by-play depends upon the legibility of her darkness relative to his pallor. Colman also suggests that Madiboo is Sutta's natural pairing, not Mug, though she makes it clear that she has a sweetheart of her own ethnicity and choosing waiting in her native village. Darina and Berissa are also darkened though the Foulahs are "lighter by ten shades" than their neighbours. Portraying a high-caste female such as Berissa in this manner was unusual. (Eighteenth-century stage adaptations of Oroonoko's lover, Imoinda, recast her as white.)[29]

Visual representations of race facilitate both a sense of place and plotting elements. Music and scenery also prime the audience's expectations with respect to character and genre. Percussive wedding music is forecast by Torribal on his first entrance: Berissa and a chorus of dancing girls fulfill the expectation in the next scene, singing of the flutes, bells, and strings that accompany the drums ("Dance and Chorus of Foulah's [*sic*] in Farulho's Tent," 1.2). In Kelly's piano score, an ostinato (repeated melodic phrase)

---

28   See J.R. Oldfield, "The 'Ties of Soft Humanity': Slavery and Race in British Drama, 1770-1800," *Huntington Library Quarterly* 56:1 (1993): 1-14; and Virginia Mason Vaughan, *Performing Blackness on English Stages, 1500-1800* (Cambridge: Cambridge UP, 2005), 149-69.

29   Nussbaum, *Limits of the Human*, 172.

accompaniment marks the drumbeat, a rocking treble line over a repeated staccato chord sounds like bells, and the soprano line resembles the flutes. The orchestration may not have been as segmented as the piano score, but even in this shorthand version, the music onomatopoetically imitates the verses. Later, the instrumental piece "Bridal Dance of Foulahs" (1.3) is definitely not written for a gaggle of mincing European girls: it is fast and, being in D-minor, sonically signals something other than a joyous celebration, which is fitting since the Mandingo attack is imminent. Quiet chromatic phrases alternate with fortissimo chords, at first tonic and then diminished sevenths.

A musicologist studying Foulah music in Banjul, Gambia, describes the sounds he heard at the independence day celebration on a sweltering day in the 1970s. The Foulahs' [Fulas'] emergence in the procession began with

> a shattering crash that rang in my ears for most of the next week.... The Fulas ... were one of the tribes that had won great victories in the religious wars of West Africa in the centuries before the imposed stewardship of the Europeans, and in the steaming heat on the jammed street I could almost believe that they had defeated their enemies by deafening them.... The dark faces, the tall sharpness of the bodies, the swaying robes, the din of the instruments[:] it resembled a scene from the earliest descriptions ... somewhere in the procession there was every kind of Fula instrument. Men were carrying deep, bowled drums with strips of thin metal nailed to the rims to add to their thudding tone. Behind them were a row of men with xylophones strung from their necks. There were also the one-stringed fiddles, the riti that I had heard the Fula jelefo [musician-historian] play.

He also heard flutes, trumpets made from cattle horns, calabash drums, elongated wooden drums, and rattles made of dried calabash.[30] The Haymarket audience had none of this, of course, but only a pit band with the customary assortment of strings, woodwinds, and percussion. Kelly's objective in these instrumental passages was to establish mood and convey action. Music and scenery established locale, correlated to ideas of a religious and ethnic other conditioned by travelogues like Mungo Park's, but did not aim for sonic or visual authenticity.

The wedding celebration is broken up by "*violent shrieks, huzzas, and a discharge of muskets, which appear to proceed from the town*," followed immediately by Madiboo's agitated entrance and call to arms (1.3). The harum-scarum music written for this episode is a classic agitato, with phrasing calculated to enhance tension, mark swordplay or hand-to-hand tussles, the conflagration of the town, and reversals of fortune. The exact cueing for this music is not given in the script. Most likely it begins as Madiboo attempts to pull Selico offstage, continues under the lovers' emotional farewell, and concludes as Mug asks, "Oh, Henry Augustus Mug! what will become of you?" and rushes offstage. The Mandingos then enter, "*yelling and with firebrands*," the wedding tent is torn away, and the burning town is revealed upstage in a new set of scenery. The music for the act 1 finale brings on the conquering corps, torches aloft, no longer with an allegro but a marching beat. The objective is not ethnographic fidelity but a lively sense of action and "wild exultation." The refrain modulates on each repetition, avoiding recapitulation and predictability in favour of organized masculine ferocity. The most striking part of this is the music for the line "Oh! never heed your victim's bleeding": after a sustained tonic chord spanning five octaves, the accompaniment is suddenly minimal and lyrical, grounding the voices' minor and major thirds, followed by ascending cascades of quick thirty-second notes for each "Rush on" and a stately descending dominant arpeggio for "Every foe must fall." The repeated verse ends in unabashed triumph: the chorus of male voices holds

---

30 Samuel Charters, A *Language of Song: Journeys in the Musical World of the African Diaspora* (Durham, NC: Duke UP, 2009), 4-5.

a tonic chord for four bars while the agitated ostinato of the accompaniment finds its way to five unison repetitions of the tonic chord. No victor could sound—and, presumably, also look—more definitive.

As both an entertainment and a polemic, *The Africans* relied upon marking the differences between milieux. Just as costuming an all-white cast equipped the actors with conventions of mimicry rather than imitation—and certainly not illusion—other elements of performance utilized recognizable signals that cued the audience into repertoires of sound, illustration, and narrative. Stage realization was a technique of scavenging, not consistency or authenticity. With reference to illustrations of West Indian culture, Kay Dian Kriz describes a similar practice of presenting "a range of subjects, rhetorical tactics (hyperbole, ridicule, pathos), and time-space relationships."[31] In a comparable way, Colman's play presents "observable knowledge" of Senegambia through a heterogeneous mobilization of elements. To separate out one from all others or to insist upon verisimilitude is to deny the spectating practices of early-nineteenth-century theatre-goers, as well as their competencies to interpret.

The Africans; or War, Love, and Duty[32]

BY GEORGE COLMAN, THE YOUNGER

First performed at the Haymarket Theatre, 29 July 1808.

Original Foreword

'Tis an humiliating truth that the nobler virtues are more practised among barbarian tribes than by civilised society;—that the savage heathen, who wages war to extermination and devours his captives, not unfrequently displays a glorious self-denial, a sublime magnanimity that, with true believers, pass for fable and romance. Mr. Colman lays his scene in an African town; his principal characters are three sable brothers, who exhibit those cardinal virtues, filial duty and affection, in a degree that might startle the polished European. His black Mandingo[33] majesty, who lights up his faggots with Roman Catholic fury,[34] is an honourable exception to the general run of pale-faced potentates; nor would his ebony holiness Farulho suffer in comparison with the full-blown pluralist in canonicals.[35]

Selico is to marry Berissa, the daughter of the priest. His brother Torribal, a wicked wit, rallies the bridegroom on his wedding-day, and accuses him of want of duty to their widowed mother, in quitting

---

31 Kay Dian Kriz, *Slavery, Sugar, and the Culture of Refinement: Picturing the British West Indies, 1700-1840* (New Haven, CT: Yale UP, 2008), 73.

32 Based on Larpent 1553, Huntington Library. Where applicable, song lyrics are corrected to Michael Kelly, *The Overture, Songs, Duetts [sic], Choruses, &c. in "The Africans"* (London: Kelly's Opera Saloon, 1808); and *Songs, Choruses, &c. in The Africans; or, War, Love, and Duty; A Play in Three Acts, First Perform'd at the Theatre Royal, Hay-market, on Friday, July 29, 1808, the Musick Composed and Selected by Mr. Kelly* (London: Theatre Royal, Haymarket, 1808), Huntington K-D 628.

33 Mandingos resided in the area between the upper reaches of the Senegal and Gambia Rivers (now the nation of Mali, with Senegal to the west). More generally, Europeans applied the term to speakers of the Manding (or Mande) language, including Bambara, Malinke, and Djula.

34 i.e., to burn a heretic at the stake.

35 i.e., likening the Muslim priest to an Anglican cleric who holds more than one office at a time.

her roof. But Madiboo, a mahogany harum-scarum[36] and purveyor of eatables to the Day and Martin[37] family, takes the part of Selico, and pays back the sable satirist in his own coin. As the day advances, the jollity becomes more uproarious—the tang-tang[38] thumps; the big tabala[39] beats; bells, flutes, and simbings;[40] shrieks, shouts, and such-like incongruous music swell the nuptial chorus—when, suddenly, an alarm is given that the Mandingo warriors are pouring down in myriads: loud yells are heard; fires are seen raging on all sides; the marriage ceremony is suspended; the town of Fatteconda[41] is surprised, sacked, and burned to the ground!

Pondering on the wide-spread desolation, like Marius amidst the ruins of Carthage,[42] Selico indulges in bitter recollections of the past, and mournful anticipations of the future. His betrothed bride and her father are both slain; his aged mother and brothers, if they yet survive, are either made captives, or fled he knows not whither. He is faint with hunger, and lays down to die. At this moment, a well-known voice salutes him—it's Madiboo's: he receives the joyful intelligence that his parent, borne by her faithful children to the woods, has not perished. Thither he is supported by his affectionate, madcap brother, with famine stamped upon his brow, and despair withering his heart.

The miserable family are pinched by famine, and surrounded on all sides by hordes of revengeful barbarians. News transpires that the Mandingos have invited the English merchants to buy their prisoners. Torribal had charged his brother Selico with want of filial affection—*now* he will prove if the charge be true!

'Tis proposed to draw lots which of them shall sell himself for a slave. To this Selico objects—*his* lot is cast already, more unhappy he cannot be; his early hope is gone—to him the world's sweet garden is a lonely desert.

The biddings of those respectable Christians, Messrs. Grim, Marrowbone, Flayall, and Adamant, are anything but liberal. The market for human bones and sinews is by no means brisk—an able-bodied black is hardly worth the price of a fat bullock; and Captain Abraham Adamant, whom the cruel negroes chucked down the hatchways for stowing *only* fifteen of them in a hammock in hot weather bids a sum for the self-devoted savage, barely sufficient to support his wretched mother through the winter. A reward of four hundred ounces of gold is offered for the apprehension of a man who had escaped through the musketry of his Mandingo majesty's Spanish-liquorice[43] body guards, from the tent of his favourite female prisoner. Selico resolves to give himself up as the criminal and his brother Madiboo is to claim the reward! Nor can Madiboo's pathetic eloquence dissuade him from his purpose. They appear before the king—the accuser weeps on his brother's breast, and is speechless with agony: the self-accused plays

---

36   Rash or heedless person.

37   A London brand of blacking compound.

38   Probably echoic, as with a stringed instrument.

39   A ritual drum native to West Africa. Mungo Park reports Muslim women beating tabalas and singing the entire night before a wedding. Mungo Park, *Travels in the Interior Districts of Africa: Performed under ... the African Association, in the Years 1795, 1796, and 1797* (London: W. Bulmer, 1799), 107-08.

40   A six-stringed Gambian instrument, very likely an ancestor of the American banjo.

41   Fatteconda (Fort St. Joseph) was the capital of Bondou, an area along the Senegal River, a little east of the confluence with the Faleme River. According to Major Rennell's map, Bondou is bounded on the north by Kajaaga (and beyond that, the Sahara), on the east by Bambouk, on the south by Tenda, and on the west by Woolli. See Park, *Travels*, map facing 1; 54. Another map depicting the region may also have been consulted: S. Boulton's *Africa, with all its States, Kingdoms, Republics, Regions, Islands, &C* (London: Robert Sayer, 1787) http://www.davidrumsey.com/luna/servlet/ detail/RUMSEY~8~1~3659~430001:Africa,-with-all-its-states,-kingdo (accessed 6 August 2010).

42   Gaius Marius, a Roman general, went into exile in North Africa in the ninth decade BCE.

43   An intoxicating drink.

his part nobly—acknowledges his guilt—the reward is given to the supposed betrayer of his friend, and Selico is borne off to an immediate and cruel death.

A victim is to suffer with him—the female prisoner, from whose tent the muffled stranger escaped. Two piles of faggots are heaped up; the executioners, with their flaming brands[44] and instruments of torture, are ready to assist at the ceremony; and His Majesty and his court are assembled to see terrible justice done upon the delinquents. The female prisoner is led forth; her veil is thrown aside, and she breathes a prayer of resignation—'tis Berissa! The lovers rush into each other's arms; and Berissa solemnly declares that her fellow-sufferer is *not* the guilty one. But torments shall not wrest from her the real culprit. The drum rolls, and the ghastly ministers of death lift high their blazing torches to fire the funeral piles; when Farulho rushes in, prostrates himself before the king, and pleads the circumstance of a fond father striving to rescue his betrothed daughter from the embraces of a foe. The royal heart feels a touch of pity; and when the mother of the three noble sons enters the imperial presence, and tells *her* melancholy tale, it melts in right earnest. He commands a dowry of two thousand crowns to be given to the affianced bride, and unites her to Selico.

But where is the wood and ivory-turner, "His black Mandingo majesty's white minister of state," Mr. Henry Augustus Mug, of No. 25, Snow Hill? Good luck to the nigger-slave merchant that kidnapped and sold this frolicksome piece of human mutton to a dealer at Fatteconda, where he jested himself into the cabinet as prime minister and buffoon; legislator and ladies man; principal plenipo[45] of the black petticoats, and privy seal;[46] with the run of the imperial kitchen, palace, palanquins,[47] and pretty girls (*à-la-mode d'Angleterre*!) free gratis and for nothing! This comic episode to a tragic drama plays his part with infinite good fun and good feeling, and was originally represented by Liston with all his broad-faced humour and grotesque gravity. His "*Won't you come, Mr. Mug*?" was chanted from one end of Great Britain to the other; and "*Mug*" became a cognomen[48] for any Cockney Adonis whose constitution and countenance were uncommonly concupiscent[49] and charming.

This play was received with very great applause—and deservedly—for Mr. Colman again put his axe to the root of the Upas Tree[50] of Slavery; which, to the honour of British humanity, is now grubbed up and laid prostrate for ever![51]

---

44 Torches.
45 Plenipotentiary: deputized to act on behalf of the sovereign.
46 Royal seal affixed to important documents.
47 Like a sedan chair, carried aloft by human bearers.
48 Nickname.
49 Lustful.
50 Proverbially, the source of the most deadly poison.
51 Literally, dug up and laid face down; figuratively refers to the Act for the Abolition of the Slave Trade, which banned British participation in the Atlantic slave-trade, coming into effect on 25 March 1807.

Farulho, a Foulah[52] Muslim priest	Mr. Thompson[53]
Torribal, a Foulah	Charles Farley
Madiboo, a Foulah	John Fawcett, Jr.
Selico, youngest brother to Torribal and Madiboo	Mr. Young
Demba Sego Jalla, King of Kassan[54]	Mr. Palmer, Jr.[55]
Daucari, Demba's soldier	Mr. Jeffries
Mandingo Chief	Mr. Treby
Mr. Mug, a London ivory-turner	John Liston
Fetterwell, an English trader	Mr. Simmons
Grim, an English trader	Thomas King
Flayall, an English trader	James Powers
Captain Adamant, an English trader	William Wilde
Marrowbone, a London trader	Frederick Menage
Negro (Mandingo) Warriors	
Crier	
Darina, mother to Torribal, Madiboo, and Selico	Mrs. St. Ledger
Berissa, Farulho's daughter, affianced to Selico	Mrs. Gibbs[56]
Sutta, servant to Berissa	Mrs. Liston

COSTUMES[57]

Farulho	Black arms, legs, and face; bracelets; long white shirt; robe; sandals; feather; gold head bands
Torribal	Black body, arms, and legs; white shirt and trunk, all of a piece so as to leave the right arm bare; red head band; sandals; gold bracelets; brass belt
Madiboo and Selico	Black body, arms, and legs; white shirt and trunk; red headband; sandals; gold bracelets; brass belt
Demba Sego Jalla	Black legs and arms; yellow gold-trimmed silk shirt; scarf; beads; tiger skin robes; bird-of-paradise feathers;[58] gold head band; red sandals; bracelets on arms and legs; sword

---

52   Also called Fuli, Fula, Fulani, Fulbe, or Fullatah: an ethnic group of nomadic herders, predominantly Muslim, found throughout West and Central Africa and Sudanese North Africa. They were on the ascendant in the region from the seventeenth through the nineteenth centuries. In 1805, John Cary mapped their territory in two relevant zones: the southern bank of the Gambia River leading to the coast, and the area surrounding the Senegal River, somewhat west of Fatteconda and extending not quite as far as the coast. The intervening land was Jaloof, and the eastern territory was Mandingo. See John Cary's *New Map of Africa* (London, 1805) at www.library.northwestern.edu/govinfo/collections/mapsofafrica/ (accessed 6 August 2010).

53   Thompson originated the role. By December, Mr. Murray had taken over; his name is given in the Cumberland edition.

54   A location on the Gambia River.

55   Mr. Creswell assumed the role later in the run.

56   Martha Norton assumed the role on 7 December 1808.

57   The costume plot is from Cumberland.

58   A genus of birds native to New Guinea, the Moluccas, and eastern Australia, brought to Europe by Magellan in the sixteenth century. The males have spectacular trailing plumes.

Daucari	Black arms and legs; white shirt; buff robes; scarf; beads; feather and gold head band; red sandals; bracelets on arms and legs; sword
Mr. Mug	Large red-striped trousers; white waistcoat and jacket; black kerchief; shirt collar, turned down; large straw hat; white stockings; buff shoes
Fetterwell	Nankeen[59] jacket; striped waistcoat; white trousers; black kerchief; shirt collar, turned down; large straw hat; white stocking, buff shoes
Marrowbone	Blue striped trousers; white waistcoat; red-striped cotton coat
Warriors	White shirts; leopard skin robes; sandals
Darina and Berissa	White muslin decorated with coloured feathers; beads; red bracelets and sandals
Sutta	White bed-gown; buff petticoat; sandals; bracelets; beads

Act I

Scene 1

The Town of Fatteconda, in Bondou,[60] a district of Africa, inhabited by the Foulahs, and situated between the rivers Senegal and Gambia—a large tract of romantic Country beyond the town. The horizon is very faintly tinged with the rays of the sun, which grow stronger as the action proceeds till the sun is completely arisen. Selico discovered (picturesquely placed) watching the progress of morning.

SELICO.
  Rise, orb of light!—those streaks, thy harbingers,
  Are sluggish glow-worms on the mountain's brow;
  Thy bird, the eagle, mourns; and constant dawn,
  Whom thou wert wont to press with hasty fire,
  Weeps dew, in token of thy love's neglect,
  Thou follow'st her so slow. Though oft, ere noon,
  Faint from thy influence, I seek the shade,
  Come, sun, and scorch me now! Dart thy full beam,
  O'er Africk's sands upon me!—Bring me day;
  Bring me to my Berissa!—to my bride!
TORRIBAL (*puts his head through an aperture from a hut*).
  Brother Selico!
SELICO.
  Ha, Torribal! what say you brother?
TORRIBAL.
  I say, that the sun don't get up sooner for your bawling,
  But *I* do!—So I'll come out and speak to you. (*He disappears*).

---

59   Pale yellow cotton. Mungo Park's nankeen trousers were thought both inelegant and indecent by Muslim women. Park, *Travels*, 105.
60   For the location, see Cary's *New Map of Africa*.

SELICO.

Close to a brake,[61] I've seen a playful lion,
Pawing his fellow whelp; 'tis rough diversion.
Much like my brother's wit, a Chimney jester *hurts*,[62]
Often, while he sports: well, he loves me—
And we are brother lions!—I the tamest!

TORRIBAL *(enters from the hut)*.

Now, Selico, my youngest brother!—soon
They'll beat the *tabala*, to tell us all
You're to be married.

SELICO.

Ay, dear Torribal;
With the approval of our much loved mother;
And with the sanction, too, of our good priest
Farulho, father of my bride Berissa.
Prithee, what then?

TORRIBAL.

Why, then, 'tis to be hoped,
You won't (the bride will sour else) hunt for sun-beams,[63]
So soon tomorrow morning, as today.

SELICO.

Still, brother, you will mock.

TORRIBAL.

Mock—Oh, not I!—
Love is a pretty pastime; and last night
Beneath the tabba tree,[64] our marketplace,
Did I harangue the people, on your nuptials.

SELICO.

'Twas kind. What said you?

TORRIBAL.

Africans, said I,
Townsmen of Fatteconda, here, in Bondou
Between the Senegal and Gambia—
We Foulahs are the prettiest of negroes:
For the same sun that dyes our neighbours black,
(Feloops, Mandingoes, Jaloops, and the rest)
Has dipped us Foulahs lighter by ten shades.[65]
Berissa is the prettiest maid among us;
My brothers are the prettiest of your tribe;

---

61   Thicket.
62   This phrase is excised from the published version. Perhaps the line refers to the perils of cavorting in an enclosed space?
63   Arise early.
64   Mungo Park identifies this as a large spreading tree of the species *Sterculia*. Park, *Travels*, 292.
65   Foulahs were thought to descend from the Sudanese and have even been attributed with Caucasian ancestry. As North Africans, they tend to be lighter skinned than their equatorial neighbours.

And brother Selico—except myself—
The handsomest of all our family:
And so this loving couple's love may last,
A little longer than my wedding speech *(crosses to R.)*.
SELICO.
A speech of scoff and ribaldry. My heart
Grieves that it cannot thank you. Side by side,
When, first I followed you into the wars
(A stripling I, you seasoned in the fight),
Remember, Torribal—
TORRIBAL.
That you fought well.
SELICO.
No, no, not that,—but that you saved my life.
You saw the arrow coming; and your arm,
Guarding my breast, received it; in *your* flesh
It quivered; and ne'er scarred the youth you clasped.
You wrenched the barb, then reeking[66] from your sinews,
And smiled, you exclaimed, "they must not wound
My little brother Selico!"
TORRIBAL.
Umph!—Did I?—
SELICO.
Yes, Torribal—you may forget, I cannot;
But, prithee[67] think, good brother, though thy hand *(taking Torribal's hand)*
So fondly screened my bosom, that your tongue
May, very, very deeply, wound my heart.
TORRIBAL.
I hate all honey mouth—all flattery.
Young men may marry; there's no harm in marriage—
What is one wife? Our law allows us plenty;[68]
But—to desert a mother[69]—
SELICO.
What? Desert!
You touch me to the quick! The very wolf
Feels, there, the tie of nature!—why, our mother
Rejoices in my—Prophet Mahomet![70]

---

66 Bleeding.
67 Please, or I beg you.
68 Muslim law allows up to four wives in a polygamous marriage. Foulah wives live in a separate hut from their husbands (and newly pregnant women return to their parents for up to four years), so Colman is applying European expectations of newlyweds' residential and filial patterns.
69 Colman picks up on Mungo Park's observation that Africans revere mothers and tolerate no action against them. Park, *Travels*, 261.
70 Variant of Mohammed.

Whom Africk's converts worship!—who shall say
I leave a mother, if her age required me?
Could I, who—

MADIBOO *(appears in perspective, winding round a pathway on a hill and singing; he continues in sight*
    till he is hid by the intervening bushes as he proceeds on his way).

Kouskous Sinkatoo,[71] for king Ali Beg,[72] o!
But Serawoolli[73] King he eat antelope's leg, o!
Sing shannawang, sing sharrawang,
Sing shongo.[74]

TORRIBAL.

Over the hill comes Madiboo, our brother.
He went before the moon sunk, to fetch home
Provision, by the dawn.

SELICO.

He will not say,
(While you and he remain; and I at hand, too)
I left a mother destitute.

TORRIBAL.

Not he!—
He never thinks; mad-pates[75] have no tomorrow.
His scull holds just enough to oil his limbs,
And make him active; then he runs a-field;
Shoots paroquets,[76] and snares the red-legged partridge,
Hastes back encumbered with more game than brains,
And, so, we go to dinner.

SELICO.

Still, unjust!
His frame, robust and pliant, boasts a nature
Well suited to it, for 'tis bold yet yielding,
Fierce to his foe as panthers; but the dove
Who wings her anxious journey home, with food,
Returns not to her young with more delight
Than he comes laden to his family.
The strong, but generous sovereign of the woods,
And the spring lamb that frolics on the green,
Have mingled both their qualities with him.

TORRIBAL.

Enough.

---

71   A Central African dish made of sour milk and ground meal.
72   Waterfalls in the Punjab; here, probably used generically to indicate an Islamic ruler.
73   Serawoolli (a.k.a. Saracolet) inhabit Kajaaga, in the lowlands between the Senegal and Gambia Rivers. They operated a
     slave market at Galam. James Cowles Prichard, *Researches into the Physical History of Mankind*, vol. 2 (London: Sherwood,
     Gilbert, and Piper, 1837), 80.
74   The refrain consists of nonsense words.
75   Impulsives.
76   Parrots.

SELICO.

    Not quite: They who have heads enough

    To prompt them honestly to use their limbs,

    And work a living for their humble homes,

    Are neither fools nor burdens in a nation.

MADIBOO *(carrys corn and game and sings as he enters).*

    Good wife had Kickawik,[77] she drowny one night, o!

    But Kickawik no fish again, for fear him wife bite, o!

    Sing shannawang, sing sharrawang,

    Sing shongo.

(As he enumerates the articles, he takes them from his shoulders. Speaks)

    There's maize[78]—I'll throw it into the paloon,[79]

    And pound it, for my mother's *kouskous*[80] pudding;

    And here are partridges, ground nuts,[81] and rice;

    And three fat Guinea fowls!—I shot them, Selico,

    For your bride's father.

TORRIBAL *(sneeringly).*

    Aye, priests love good eating.

MADIBOO.

    Bless all their jolly chops!—I love to see

    (When there's a wedding dinner) the good old man

    Who joined the couple, smiling at the feast.

TORRIBAL.

    Well, let him gorge.

SELICO *(warmly).*

    Farulho is no glutton.

MADIBOO.

    A glutton! *(Looking at his brother)*—Oh! I see;—the old work toward![82]

    You have been fretting him about Berissa,

    And on the wedding-day, too, Torribal!—

    Come, come, this is not kind.

TORRIBAL *(very sulky).*

    It all began in a good joke.

MADIBOO *(laughing).*

    Then you did not begin it.

    You are, 'tis certain, as incapable

    Of a good joke, as an owl is of singing.

---

77   Presumably a proper name.

78   Corn (UK Indian corn).

79   Wooden bowl.

80   An African dish consisting of steamed granulated flour (couscous).

81   Peanuts.

82   Presumably "the old work toward," as in the persistent topic.

TORRIBAL.

Why how now, Madiboo!—you bird catcher!

Hunt and be dumb; your wit lies in your heels.

MADIBOO.

And where lies yours? Your muddy gibes[83] are like

The frisking of an elephant. You trample

And fancy you have capered.[84] I have marked you,

A thousand times, tormenting Selico:

Dashing your gall (which you call pleasantry)

Upon his milky[85] spirit, till his heart

Has ached with pain, and mine has boiled with anger.

TORRIBAL.

I tell you, fool, I jested.

MADIBOO.

Jested, did you?

Why, you are grown, of late, as bright as lead;

As comical as malice; and cut

As keen as any rusty hatchet, notched.

Shame on it, Torribal! see how he grieves! *(Pointing to Selico)*

You jeer a brother, as the Moorish Chief

Treated a neighbour, at a merry-making,

He cried, "I'll tickle you!" and chopped his head off.

SELICO *(steps between them and takes them by the hands)*.

Peace, I entreat you!—pray, let us be friends!

We outrage, else, our parent's tenderness—

Who, left in widowed poverty, wept o'er us;

Toiled in her sickness, fasting while we fed,

And clung to life, only to rear her babes.

When brothers are at variance, could they think

On one fond tear a mother shed on them,

That woke their slumbers, while their infant arms

Circled each other's neck, 'twould surely quench

All sparks of strife within their breasts, for ever.

MADIBOO *(affected)*.

My sparks are all gone out: *(to Torribal)* and goodman Gruff,

When you're extinguished, say so, and be friends.

TORRIBAL *(holding out his hand)*.

There then.

MADIBOO.

And there! *(Shaking it)*.

SELICO.

That's as it should be.

---

83   Taunts.

84   Danced.

85   Gentle.

DARINA (*calls without*).

  Selico!

MADIBOO.

  Our mother calls you—run!

SELICO.

  I come, good mother (*exit into hut*).

TORRIBAL.

  He talks it well.

MADIBOO.

  Who—he?

TORRIBAL.

  Aye, Selico.

  But if he bears us all such loads of love,

  Why does he quit us?

MADIBOO.

  Why?—to take a wife.

TORRIBAL.

  Aye, the priest's daughter: she is rich, and grand—

  Else, why not bring her to our little family?

MADIBOO.

  Because, 'tis like, she'll have a little family;

  And then, in time, the cabin couldn't hold us.

TORRIBAL.

  This mother, whom we work for, now she's old—

MADIBOO (*emphatically*).

  Aye—and who worked for us, when she was young—

TORRIBAL.

  Well, her he leaves: and goes—

MADIBOO.

  A stone's throw off—

  How barbarous! There stands the house he'll live in,

  He'll not be able, now, to visit her,

  Above ten times a day.

TORRIBAL.

  Well, well; his labour

  Falls on us now—and added to our own—

MADIBOO.

  We shall be killed!—we're both such puny children!

TORRIBAL.

  Pshaw!—If 'tis right to marry, then how comes it

  He marries first?

MADIBOO.

  Oh, are you thereabouts?

  Now it comes out—you want a wife yourself—

  You would be billing,[86] would you? Oh, you sly one!

---

86 Wooing.

TORRIBAL.

   Not I—but he's the youngest—

MADIBOO.

   That's the reason—

   Girls always like the youngest best, that's certain.

TORRIBAL.

   As things fall out—

MADIBOO.

   Come, come, don't you fall out,

   When things fall out just as we might expect them,

   I shoot; you till a garden—for our mother.

   To gain a daily blessing for her, Selico

   Has paid a daily visit to the priest.

TORRIBAL.

   Well?

MADIBOO.

   When your corn and vegetables sprout,

   Do pretty girls sprout with them?

TORRIBAL.

   No, not one.

MADIBOO.

   And when I've been upon the hunt for birds,

   I never chanced to put a priest's daughter up!

   But Selico went in the way of beauty;

   And she, whom he soon loved, loved him. What said

   Her father—good old soul!—the priest Farulho?

   Just this: "The filial heart of Selico

   Bespeaks him good—and he shall have my girl.

   An honest husband is a wife's best wealth;

   A rich wife helps a poor and kindly son

   To cheer an aged widow, and a mother."

   When every match is made upon this plan

   Family quarrels won't be quite so common.

TORRIBAL.

   Perhaps I've been too bitter.

MADIBOO.

   Worse than wormwood.[87]

   We want no home disturbers of the wedding:

   Others may come, that—

TORRIBAL.

   Others!

MADIBOO.

   Yes—but first

   Swear not to blab.

---

87   *Artemesia absinthium*, a bitter plant used for making vermouth, absinthe, and tonics for expelling intestinal worms.

TORRIBAL.

  I promise.

MADIBOO.

  Well,—your promise

  Is so unlike your joke, that I can take it.

  Hear: the Mandingo king, 'tis looked for, soon,

  Will take us by surprise.

TORRIBAL.

  The usual way

  In war, among our nations.[88]

MADIBOO.

  Coming home, just now, among the thickets, I espied

  A party of Mandingoes, armed in ambush.

TORRIBAL.

  The army's then at hand. I'll raise our people! *(Going).*

MADIBOO *(catches him by the arm).*

  As sure as you attempt to raise the people,

  I take you by surprise, and trip your heels up.

  You'll mar the wedding.

TORRIBAL.

  Yes—*but* are you mad?

MADIBOO.

  Be calm:—these are but straggling spies; we've time,

  Before the main force comes, to give alarm,

  First have the marriage; else it ne'er may happen.

TORRIBAL.

  But if—

MADIBOO.

  Nay, nay, be ruled: the very moment

  Our brother has secured his bride, we'll rouse

  The town.

TORRIBAL.

  Agreed.

MADIBOO.

  'Twill be but a short time.

  And then—hush! Here's our mother! Not a word!

(Enter Darina, from the hut, with a mantle on her arm).

---

88 Mungo Park describes just such an attack which occurred while he stayed at Kamalia. A king's son secretly led 500 mounted men to the village and attacked this and two other towns in the night, carrying off many prisoners. "Several of the inhabitants who had escaped these attacks, were afterwards seized by the Mandingoes, as they wandered about in the woods, or concealed themselves in the glens and strong places of the mountains." Servants, particularly mild-mannered women, taken into slavery, would stay with the conqueror; higher-ranking and discontented persons would be "bartered into a distant kingdom" or killed. "War, therefore, is certainly the most general, and most productive source of slavery; and the desolations of war often (but not always) produce the second cause of slavery, *famine*; in which case a freeman becomes a slave, to avoid a greater calamity." Park, *Travels*, 293-95.

TORRIBAL and MADIBOO.

  Bless our dear mother!

DARINA.

  Blessings on my children!

  On this day double blessings—for it brings

  Joy to my youngest born; and, therefore, joy

  To both his brothers. Oh! the drops that now

  Steal on my cheek are sweet as morning gems;

  For my heart's sunshine sparkles in the eye,

  And grateful is the dew that glitters there.

MADIBOO.

  Come, 'tis full time that we should to the priest;

  The bride will grow impatient.

DARINA.

  I shall follow;—

  And as your custom is, the marriage over,

  We'll join you at the feast.

MADIBOO.

  Good—Brother Torribal,

  Do you go with us?

(While Darina is unfolding the mantle, Madiboo whispers to Torribal).

  Don't! remain at home

  To guard if stragglers come to skirmish,

  Fight like a devil, till I come to back you.

TORRIBAL *(aside)*.

  Enough; *(aloud)* I shall stay behind you, now,

  To stow in the provisions you have brought.

  You and I, mother, can go together *(begins taking up the articles that Madiboo has left near the door, and then exits into hut).*

SELICO *(enters)*.

  Now, mother, once more bless me, and I go.

DARINA.

  Stay, Selico; present this to Farulho.

MADIBOO.

  A curious mantle, that.

DARINA.

  The widow's offering *(gives it to Selico),*

  (On her son's marriage) to the good old priest.

  Say, while she worked it, many and many a prayer

  Of gratitude burst from Darina's lips,

  For him who thus has blessed her and her son.

SELICO.

  Embrace me, mother—and our prophet guard you.

(They embrace).

MADIBOO *(aside)*.

   My mind misgives me—should the foe arrive

   Before we—hum! *(Aloud)* Come, come! Mother, farewell!

   You'll come to dinner.

DARINA.

   Yes—to find all happy.

MADIBOO.

   Aye, to be sure: the priest will have his game,

   And that will make him happy; Selico

   Will have Berissa, that will make *them* happy;

   And Torribal stays here to come with you,

   So you two will be happy.—Oh! there never

   Were such a set of happy, happy people,

   As we shall be today, in Africa.

   Come, Selico and good bye Mother:—come!

(Exeunt Darina into hut, Selico and Madiboo on the opposite side).

Scene 2

The Interior of Farulho's House.

MUG *(enters)*.[89] Oh, Nature! since you formed me amorous, why did Fortune cast me on a soil where to be fair[90] is to be ugly? Oh, Henry Augustus Mug! once a turner, both in wood and ivory, and free of the city of London;[91] you are, now, a slave, among the living ebony ware of the world's creation. The chief folks, indeed, of Fatteconda, the Foulahs as they call themselves, are some patterns[92] lighter than the original natives, and my fellow-slaves. But the town altogether looks like a backgammon board, when the game is over, and all the black and yellow men are jumbled together. Still, that little jade, Sutta, runs in my head, strangely! She's a dingy Venus of the dumpling sort, sprung out of the Black Sea.[93] Eh? Here she comes.

(Enter Sutta crossing the apartment).

   Sutta! Sutta!—

SUTTA. Ah, Massa Mug! me go carry sweet scent to bride, good Missy Berissa.

MUG *(takes her hand)*. But I want to talk to you.—Oh, Sutta! if I had you with me in my own country, I could make you so happy!

SUTTA. Where you live when you at home?

---

89   As the three low-comedy characters, Mug, Sutta, and Madiboo speak to each other in prose. Mug and Sutta always speak in prose; Madiboo switches to verse when he is with other characters.

90   Light-skinned.

91   A member of a craft guild in the City of London; this connotes his deep ties to political and commercial life in the City.

92   Shades, in the published version.

93   An inland sea separating Europe and Asia. Here as elsewhere, Mug puns on Sutta's race and does not make a literal attribution.

MUG. Upon Snow Hill.[94] Mug and Co., goods for exportation. Little did I think, when I exported myself, to buy a cargo of elephant's and hippopotamus's teeth, on the banks of the Gambia,[95] that I should be kidnapped by a Negro slave merchant, and carried up the country to be sold.

SUTTA. How much you sell for?

MUG. Damn the price, it mortifies me! On account of my colour, I didn't fetch more than an English sandman may give for a good donkey.[96]

SUTTA. What dat?—Donkey very poor white man?

MUG. Oh, no—we have many fine gentlemen of the donkey[97] breed, in London, with more money than they know what to do with. But, after pawing me about, in the market, as a butcher handles a sheep, all this handsome human mutton, that now stands before you, was sold for five *minkallis*;[98] value, not quite, two pounds ten shillings, sterling.

SUTTA. But my Massa, Farulho, he, now, you Massa, too.

MUG. Yes; he purchased me from an infernal Serawoolli farmer who knocked me about his green field, every day, like a billiard ball, till he pocketed me in a ditch, at the corner.

SUTTA. Farulho good priest—he kind to poor slave.

MUG. He's a very sympathetic savage. But, ah, Sutta! Should you ever go with me to Snow Hill, what pretty things I would turn for you!

SUTTA. Wish you turn ugly thing for me, now.

MUG. How?

SUTTA. Turn your face t'other way, massa Mug—'cause, when you look me full, it make me jump.

MUG. Jump!—what for?

SUTTA. Skin like tooth—white all over.

MUG *(aside)*. If this girl got over Blackfriars bridge, into the City, she'd refuse the hand of my Lord Mayor, to marry a chimney sweeper. *(To Sutta)* So you object to my complexion.

(Sutta nods).

And, my features, too, perhaps.

SUTTA. No—pity you not black—for your features like negro man, very.

MUG. Damn me, if the best looking Londoner mustn't be smoke-dried, like King Charles at Charing Cross,[99] before he has any chance in this country! Why, I tell you, as I have told you over and over again, white is the handsomest.

---

94   Located at the western extremity of the City of London, near where Holborn and Farringdon Street intersect. This first mention of Snow Hill prompted hearty laughter. *Theatrical Examiner*, 30 July 1808, 491-92.

95   The region is tropical, and hippopotami abound in the rivers. Hippo teeth, which grow up to 70 cm in length, were prized in the ivory trade for their close grain that resisted yellowing over time.

96   A sand-man is a messenger (as in "sendman"); thus a donkey would be a rudimentary form of transport for such a person.

97   Foolish.

98   A measure of gold; in this case, a trifling amount.

99   A statue of King Charles I, by Herbert Le Sueur, still stands at the original location of Charing Cross, on the south side of Trafalgar Square. A nursery rhyme commemorates the sight:

> As I was going by Charing Cross,
> I saw a black man upon a black horse;
> They told me it was King Charles the First—
> Oh dear, my heart was ready to burst!

G.H. Gater and E.P. Wheeler, eds., *Survey of London*, vol. 16 (London: London County Council, 1935), 258-68.

SUTTA. Ah! black for me.

(Duet)

SUTTA.

Oh, the jet feathered raven, how lovely he looks, ah!

When he spreads his black wing to fly over the River Ulacol, Ulacol.[100]

MUG.

Oh, the white swan he swims, in the Thames mighty smugly,

But he hides his black legs 'cause they look so damned ugly.

Fol de rol! Fol de rol!

SUTTA.

Young Negro girls' skin make her eye to shine out, ah!

And sparkle like night star when bats flit about, ah!

Ulalown! ulalown!

MUG.

A white woman's glance, through her eyelashes darting,

Makes black ladies' eyes "all my Eye, Betty Martin."[101]

Derry down! derry down!

SUTTA.

But I be Africk—I be Africk:

Blacky man he be my delight, ah!

MUG.

And, I'm a Cockney—but I'm a Cockney—

I love black when I can't get white, ah!

SUTTA.

Go away, white man!—white man, go—

Then me sing quicka wicka—wit.

(Together)

SUTTA.

Sweet black boy Love me bend before you!

Black boy, Love!

MUG.

White urchin Cupid I adore you!

White boy, Love!

MUG *(speaks)*. Still I maintain that—stay—here's our master, the priest Farulho.

FARULHO *(enters)*.

Come, Sutta; my Berissa stays for you.

Prepare—for Selico will soon be here.

SUTTA. I go, quick, massa! *(Exits)*.

FARULHO.

Our prophet guard you, white man!

MUG. Thank your reverence—but if nobody else guarded me, I should make bold to give you the slip.

---

100 Sutta's refrains are nonsense words.

101 A slang phrase connoting nonsense.

FARULHO.

Be not so sullen, Christian; be not moody,
On my child's wedding day; for I obtained you
From a harsh man, to soften your captivity:
And when I paid your rate—

MUG. Sink the sum, if you please; 'tis devilish disagreeable. I have sold an ivory tooth-pick case, out of my shew-glass, for double the money.

FARULHO.

Nay, I was not the cause of your inthralment.[102]
You were a bondsman when I saw you first;
And, toiling, past your strength, beneath the lash,
I purchased you to smooth your yoke with down
I wanted not the white-man for my slave;
But he could find no friend and wanted one.

MUG. You are the kindest copper clergyman that ever took tithes of the Mussulman[103] negroes; but I shall be as deadly lively at your jollification, as a shut-up shop on a Fast day.

(Wild music and singing is heard without).

FARULHO.

Forget your cares, awhile. My daughter marries:
The house cries holiday; jocund song floats
Down the musky vale, where echo answers.
Each slave, today, shall have his double portion.

MUG. That's as much as to say we are all allowed to get drunk with a sort of African Whitbread's Entire.[104]

FARULHO.

Oh, no! excess befits not me, nor mine,
A priestly festival unbends the brow
As cheerful morning lights the sober hills:
The drunkard's revel is a heated day,
That ends in midnight storm, distorting nature.
Though faiths may differ, all must join in this;
We, seldom, see a wretch that shocks us more
Than a debauched man in a sacred function.

MUG. Pray, did your reverence ever hear of Dolly's Chop-House?[105]

FARULHO.

I know not what you mean.

MUG. You may get a better dinner there for eighteen pence, than all the rich men here could give at a picnic.

FARULHO.

What would you have to make your fare more dainty?

---

102 Slavery (enthralment).
103 Muslim.
104 Whitbread's Entire London Porter, a dark brown malted beer.
105 Frequented by *literati*, this beloved institution near St. Paul's Cathedral served up beefsteak and ale since Queen Anne's day and, though highly economical, became the prototype of men's clubs. Edward Callow, *Old London Taverns* (New York: Brentano's, 1901), 160-65.

MUG. What you have no notion of: a clean table-cloth, and a three-pronged fork, with a neat turned ivory handle; a hot beefsteak, done by a quick fire with mashed potatoes, and red pickled cabbage, the mustard and pepper cruets at one elbow, and a pot of porter with a cauliflower head[106] at the other.

FARULHO.

You talk of things I do not understand.

MUG. And how the devil should you? Lord love your mahogany holiness, how you would stare to see Leadenhall market![107] If I once got home again, damn me if I'd give up the comforts of an English shopkeeper's dinner, in his back parlour, to be archbishop of Africa.

FARULHO.

I would you were at home, since thus you pine.

MUG. Then why do you keep me here?

FARULHO.

To rescue you from death. You would be slain,
In passing through this country to your own,
A strange, lone wanderer: I but detain you,
Poor white man, to preserve you. Should there, ever,
Come Christian merchants, trading through this town,
To them I would consign you, and unransomed,
That you might journey to your native land.

MUG. Why, would you, honour bright!—Do you promise?

FARULHO.

I do, as I love truth, and feel compassion.

MUG (kissing his hand). Heaven bless you!—When we part, we shall never meet again in this world—but though our persuasions are as different as our colours, I think a generous heart on your side, and a grateful one on mine, will bring us together in another.

(Enter Berissa. Slaves preceding her, rejoicing and dancing to Negro music).

CHORUS OF SLAVES.

Now the ting, tong tump,
And the tabala beat,
And the flute and the bells make music sweet.—
And the Negro girl on the simbing play,
For this is Missey's wedding-day.
Then calabash[108] me find for a Massa kind,
And he let slave play as much as he mind.
Hoo ka te boo kow la:
Now the tink tong tump, etc.

FARULHO.

Berissa, my loved child!—my dear Berissa!

BERISSA.

Oh, father! too much happiness, I find,

---

106 Frothy.

107 A grocers' market in the City of London, near the junction of Leadenhall and Gracechurch streets.

108 A gourd used as a vessel.

Yields aching pleasure; for my flurried spirits
Pain me with joy: thus, let me kneel, and soothe them! *(Kneels to her father)*
This day (a solemn day for both!), in which
The anxious father renders up his child;
In which the child doubts whether destiny
Has marked her marriage voyage for calms or storm;
Oh! on this day, with double zeal, bestow
Your priestly benediction!—Raise me, then,
To your fond breast, and add a parent's blessing.

FARULHO *(extending his arms over her)*.

Thy priest, my child, prays Heaven to protect thee!
Thy father's feelings almost choke his utterance—
Come, rise, and let me clasp thee to my bosom *(raises and embraces her)*.

MUG. I gave away Miss Griffin, at St. Andrew's Church, Holborn;[109] but hang me! if the white curate moved me so much, at the marriage, as this African parson, giving his daughter a blessing.

FARULHO.

I trust, my daughter, that you will be happy.

BERISSA.

Yes—Selico is good: but I leave you;
I shall not tend you, quite, as I was wont.

FARULHO.

Well, well—the elder doves, by nature, know
Their callow[110] family, in time, will fly
And pair with youthful mates, in other nests.

BERISSA.

Oh, but they fly for ever: I would not,
For all the kings of Africa could give,
Wing a far distant flight from you, my father.
Your bird will hover near her native tree;
And, though she nestles not where she was born,
Each day she'll plume, to circle round the spot
That gave her birth; rest there to murmur love,
Then flutter off, and soon renew her visit.

MUG. Bless her!—she's a dove indeed!—If I ever carve pigeon pies again, I shall never cut up one without thinking of her.

FARULHO.

All is well—all must be well. A parent's eye
Has marked a bridegroom that, I think, deserves you.
So cheer thee, daughter!—Single out a wish
Wherein I can indulge you—I would make
A wedding present to my child's desires.
Our slaves shall be so happy on this day!

---

109 As Mug was a resident of Snow Hill, this would be his parish church.
110 Inexperienced (literally unfledged, as birds).

BERISSA *(earnestly taking his hand)*.
  Slaves happy!—Oh my father, there's my wish
  To make men happy you must make them free!

(Attendant slaves huzza).[111]

MUG. Miss that's an English sentiment. Go to London, and Parliament will naturalize you, directly.
FARULHO.
  I am a gentle task master; I gall[112] not
  The man I buy. Is this your bridal boon?[113]
BERISSA.
  Yes, yes—your daughter begs it. Do but think
  How the slave's heart must sicken for his home!
  The nightingale's wild carol, to the moon,
  Reminds him of the sweet fellow notes
  Once warbled near his cot of liberty.
  If he's a father, and a prattling child
  Lisps where he labours, "Where are now my babes,"
  He groans, "that I am torn from?" Mothers captived,
  Must still know keener anguish. Man or woman
  In bondage, doubly feel all kindred ties;
  And when they die, 'tis Heaven only numbers
  How many slaves have perished by despondence.
SUTTA *(enters)*. Massa Farulho, Selico be now in you tent, out of door. He wait to take you to mosque,
  Missy, and make you nice wife.
FARULHO.
  Come, Sweet!—though captives chant their bridal song,
  Their burden shall be freedom. *(Addresses the slaves)* They who hear me,
  Spread through my house, and fields, Farulho's promise,
  At dawn, I will assemble all my slaves,
  And give them liberty for ever! *(To Berissa)* Come!

(Berissa kisses her father's hand in token of thanks, while the slaves give a shout of joy: they then dance and sing before Berissa and Farulho as they go out. Exeunt all but Sutta).

SUTTA. Liberty! Oh, dat make my heart go tump tump.—When I see my home how my eye will trickle
  joy! Ah! priest Farulho, he dear, good massa;—but some massa, oh! they whippy so! *(Sings)*
  Sutta home she fly, now;
  To her hut she hie, now;
  Parents' tear she dry, now,
  No more to roam.
  Father, mother, sister, brother,
  They will cherish Slave come home.

---

111 Shout with exultation.
112 Oppress.
113 Prayer or request.

Captive when they make us,
Joy and hope forsake us;
From all dear they take us,
Far, far from home.
Then we languish,
Toil in anguish,
Till slave perish, far from home.

Massa kind and tender;
Sutta he befriend her;
To her hut he send her,
No more to roam.
Though me grieve, now,
Him to leave, now,
Oh! what joy when slave reach home!

MADIBOO (*enters*). Well done, Sutta! The blackbird is a cuckoo to you. I should like to jump down your
throat, steal your voice, and run away with it.

SUTTA. Madiboo! Why you no in tent with Selico—to see dance, and joy, before bride go to mosque?

MADIBOO. Because I've been with Squabba, the cook, plucking guinea fowls, till I am half fledged with
their feathers. We are to have such a wedding dinner as never was known before in Bondou. Besides
kouskous, honeycombs, yams, watermelons and milk, there will be my birds, at one end of the table,
and a quarter of an elephant at the other, a boiled ostrich, garnished with ganders, twenty stewed
magpies, and an antelope's brisket.

SUTTA. Dat nice.

MADIBOO. Very delicate: we shall all gobble like ducks in a frog pond.

SUTTA. And, tomorrow, Massa Farulho, he make all him poor slave free.

MADIBOO. No! does he? Mahomet prosper him!—but 'tis no more than his slaves had a right to expect.
When a priest shows feeling for his fellow creatures, he only performs the duty it is his business to
preach. So, you'll go home, Sutta—and I suppose you have got a sweetheart, there.

SUTTA (*laughing*). Hee! hee!

MADIBOO. Hee! hee!—I understand.—If a woman titters at anything we ask them, they has made up
their minds to say "Yes," when we put the question again. What made you fall in love with him?—
Because he was tall?

SUTTA. He promise, when dey put me in chain, to be good to father and mother, till Sutta come back;—
and if they die, he say—but when he say that, me cry so, me hear no more.

MADIBOO. Marry him the moment you get home. Good daughters, and honest fellows, are something
scarce, and I wish you a large family together, if 'tis only to keep up the breed. Though marriages are
but blind bargains, at best—like the priest's of Kajaaga.[114] (*Sings*)

A priest of Kajaaga, as blind as a stone,
When he took to his bosom a wife,
Cried "Deary, I never shall see you, I own,
But you'll be the delight of my life."
Then his arm o'er her shoulders he lovingly passed,
And says he, "my love, what is this lump?"

---

114 An area adjacent to Bondou, occupied by Serawoolli, considered hostile territory when Mungo Park travelled through.
Park, *Travels*, 53.

She faltered a little but told him at last,
"Please your holiness, only my hump!"

Says the priest, "then we cannot cohabit, d'ye see—
Though I tenderly love you, indeed,
For I've taken an oath that my children shan't be
Of the camel or buffalo breed."
So he married another he fancied would fit,
Coming home in sweet conjugal talk,
She stopped the blind priest, staying, "Sit down a bit,
For my legs are too bandy to walk."

"Bandy legs!" said the priest, "can't be counted for sins,
So sit thou, as still as a mouse;
For Mahomet curse me, if ever your shins
Shall waddle you into my house."
Then he hopped home without her, flumped down on his knees,
And prayed thus to Mahomet, smack:
"Great prophet, afford me a wife if you please
With no humps on her legs or her back."

Then the voice of the prophet, in thunder, was heard,
And rumbled thus over his head:—
"A handsome young woman that can't speak a word,
Shall bless your blind reverence's bed."
The priest he bowed low, crying, "Mahomet's kind;—
Of happiness this is the sum!—
For a handsome young wife likes her old husband blind,
And most men like a wife that is dumb!"

MUG *(enters in a fright)*. Oh, lord! I am scared out of my seven senses!

MADIBOO. What's the matter, whitey?

MUG. Matter enough, whitey-brown. The infernal Mandingoes are making a descent upon us, with a huge army.

SUTTA. Den all poor slave Farulho make free, Mandingo man make slave again!

MADIBOO. Are they in the town?

MUG. Pop your nose out and see. I was just taking a little walk, and ran home again, as if the devil was at my heels—for they are all in an uproar, on the outskirts, where there has been a skirmish already.

MADIBOO *(impetuously)*. And my mother!—Did you pass Darina's?—Did you pass my mother's hut?—Is she safe?

MUG *(wringing his hands, and not attending to Madiboo)*. Oh! if I was but turning teetotums,[115] now, on Snow Hill!

MADIBOO *(springing upon Mug)*. Speak directly or I'll shake you, with your lily cheeks, into sand-grains!

MUG *(trembling)*. Yes, I did; I did pass her hut—but, damn it my dear friend, with the nankeen chops,[116] you frighten me as much as the enemy does.

---

115 An inscribed disk and spindle, like a top, used for fortune-telling.

116 Nankeen chops might refer to yellow whiskers, in which case Mug's allusion to Madiboo is misplaced.

MADIBOO (*still holding him*). Is all quiet, there?

MUG. Still as the Royal Exchange,[117] on a Sunday.

MADIBOO. What's that?—Speak, or (*shaking him*)—

MUG. Why, zounds! all *is* quiet there—and I wish you would be so, too.

MADIBOO. Oh! (*unholds him*). Did you see my brother Torribal?

MUG. Yes, rot him! He gave me a cursed clout[118] of the jaws and called me a coward—then bid me go back, and not say a word, but mind my business at the wedding.

MADIBOO (*apart*). Then they are only skirmishers yet.—Were there any real peril, Torribal would have sent me word.—Let me, once, see the marriage over—then (*ruminating*)—

MUG. Oh, dear! we shall have no quarter.[119] I am afraid the patent blacking generals[120] don't fight half so genteelly as the ivory commanders.

SUTTA. Cheer up, Massa Mug! Mandingo men dey no hurt you.

MUG. No!—Why do you think so?—Why?

SUTTA. When enemy see you, you fright dem so, dey all run.

MUG. Pray, Mr. Madiboo, if I may make so bold, don't you think we are in a confounded deal of danger?

MADIBOO (*assuming ease*). No, to be sure, none at all.

MUG. I am rejoiced to hear it! What, then, these Mandingo gentlemen of the military, are—

MADIBOO. Pshaw!—mere nothings. Don't you be a fool, now, and give an alarm about it, among the merrymakers, in the tent. If you do, you villain, I'll be the death of you!

MUG. I'm dumb.—You have such an amiable way of swearing a man to secrecy, there's no resisting you.

MADIBOO. Pooh! I tell you these little brushes[121] are common in our country.

MUG. And don't your little brushes never sweep a great many off?

MADIBOO. Nothing to fear;—they happen every day. Don't they, Sutta?

SUTTA. Great many fight, since Sutta been here.

MADIBOO. Aye, and here we are still—all safe and sound. (*Aside*) Between my mother's safety, and the wedding, I hardly know which way to turn. (*Aloud*) I'll just go round the town, and you'll see how soon I shall be back, to say all's well.

(*Trio sings*)

MADIBOO.
All's well! all's well;—
Yes, I'm sure that all's well.

MUG.
That's rather more than you can tell.

SUTTA.
Sutta hope that all's well.

MADIBOO.
Fatteconda's a town that is ancient and strong
Its inhabitants staunch, and have lived in it long.
And many a contest have weathered.

---

117 A City of London institution synonymous with banking and the financial market.

118 Blow.

119 Mercy or clemency.

120 Like the reference to Day and Martin's, an association of the Africans with artificial skin darkening.

121 Skirmishes.

MUG.

   Be the gentry assured of this old corporation,

   It would give me most sensible mortification,

   To see the dark freeholders leathered.

SUTTA.

   Madiboo soon come to tell

   Mandingo gone, and all well.

   All well! all well!—

ALL.

   Madiboo soon come and tell, etc.

SUTTA (*solo*).

   There lived an old Chief, in war he grew gray

   Oh to his man in battle he said,

   "See how many ball it whizzed out of the way,

   And how many arrows fly over the head."

MADIBOO.

   Aye, aye, no fear,

MUG.

   Still I wish I was not here.

MADIBOO.

   No, fear, no fear—

SUTTA.

   All well!

ALL.

   Madiboo soon come, etc.

(Exeunt, Madiboo L., Mug and Sutta, R.).

Scene 3

Farulho's tent, adjoining his house. It occupies the whole back of the scene except when Farulho,
Selico, and Berissa are discovered. Its shape and drapery admit a peek at the country, and a
straggling building or two, in the town of Fatteconda, beyond it. The side scenes represent trees.
The stage in the foreground of the tent, the interior of which is fully seen. In and about
the tent, a large company of the priest's domestics and slaves. The Slaves shout.

FARULHO (*to the slaves*).

   Nay, be less clamorous;—for we have yet

   The sacred ceremony to perform,

   That is to make us joyful.—But, I yield

   To custom; and, ere we proceed to mosque,

   The bridal dance shall have its due observance.

SELICO.

   Then strike upon the strings; and as your feet

   Mark the light maze of fancy on the ground,

Be every motion swift as my heart's pulse,
That throbs to make my loved Berissa mine.

(A Negro bridal dance is interrupted by violent shrieks, huzzas, and a discharge of muskets, which appear to proceed from the town).

MADIBOO *(enters in the utmost agitation)*.[122] To arms, directly!—Place the women in safety!—Break off the marriage.

(All is consternation and the following dialogue is rapidly uttered).

SELICO.
   Break off the marriage?
BERISSA.
   What's our danger?
FARULHO.
   Speak!
MADIBOO. I have so much to say, and so little breath to——The enemy is pouring down in torrents.
SELICO. A straggling party, as it often happens.
MADIBOO. I hoped so, at first, myself;—then I had my doubts;—then I smothered my apprehensions;—then—Oh, Selico!—dear, dear brother!—I had so fixed my hopes on this day ending happy, that—but 'tis too late to conceal anything, now. Their whole army is in the midst of the town. Neither age nor sex is spared: at this moment, they are even trampling upon infants, and half our houses are in flames.
BERISSA.
   Oh, Selico!—Oh, father!
SELICO.
   Be firm, sweet! Pray be firm!—
   While I have life, I will not leave you!
MADIBOO.
   Yes, yes—you must, directly.
SELICO.
   What?—leave my love in danger!
MADIBOO. Think, think—*we have a mother*!—a helpless aged woman, that gave us life, and whose life it is our first duty to preserve.
BERISSA.
   True, true; fly to her, Selico—fly quickly!
SELICO.
   Oh! how my separate duties tear me!—
FARULHO.
   They should not, Selico—for Nature points
   Your path of action. I have slaves and servants,
   To guard me, and my child; and I have more:
   The temple of our Prophet—sure they cannot
   Profane religion's mission. Thither will I
   Haste with Berissa.—Nay, we have no time
   For council now.

---

122 Prose indicates his degree of agitation.

(Shouts and musketry).

MADIBOO *(taking Selico by the arm).*
  Come—we shall be too late, else.
SELICO *(with great emotion).*
  It must be so—but oh, my love, this struggle!—
  Farewell! *(Embracing)*—We soon shall meet I trust!
  Oh, guard her, guard her, Farulho!——
MADIBOO *(tearing him from her).*
  Away!—
SELICO and BERISSA.
  Farewell!

(Exeunt Farulho, Berissa, slaves on one side. Selico and Madiboo on the other. Shouts etc.).

MUG *(enters).* Mercy on me! I would give all the goods in my shop to be up to my neck in an English horse-pond![123] I declined being a sharpshooter, because the Tower[124] guns, on a birthday, gave me the colic; and now I have run my unhappy head into an African town, that's invaded by an emperor as black as the kitchen chimney of the London Tavern.[125]

(Musketry discharged close to the tent).

  Here they come, but where shall I go!—Oh, Henry Augustus Mug! what will become of you?—*(Runs off).*

(Enter Mandingoes, yelling and with firebrands[126]—they tear down the tent, and when it is demolished the town of Fatteconda appears in the back scene in flames. A Mandingo Chief and Warriors are discovered: they rush forward with wild exultation).

WARRIORS.[127]
  Rear,[128] rear the torch, to Victory, to Victory proceeding.
  Mandingo men are stout, and conquer all.
  Oh! never heed your victim's bleeding, rush on, rush on,
  Every foe must fall.

Act II

Scene 1

The Town of Fatteconda, in ruins. Selico appears, wandering
distractedly over the ruins with the mantle of Farulho on his arm.

SELICO.
  Monsters of blood! I have borne all—all, all—
  Without a groan, till now. They've murdered her!

---

123 A place for watering horses; also, proverbially, a ducking-pond for obnoxious persons.
124 Tower of London.
125 A tavern and eatery in Bishopsgate Street.
126 Burnt or burning wood.
127 This chorus is included in the published version and with the score but is not in the manuscript.
128 Raise to vertical.

I'll fly to the foe's camp!—I'll do some deed
Shall strike them all with terror. Oh!—my love
Art thou then gone, for ever! By our prophet!
I will have such revenge *(stumbles)*. Fatigue and hunger
Have made me faint. Alas! I'm very wretched[129] *(throws himself on the ground)*.

MADIBOO *(calls from among the ruins)*.

Selico!—Brother!—Brother Selico! *(Sees him and runs forward)*
Now, Mahomet be praised. At last I've found you.
Where have you been these five days, Selico?

SELICO.

Plucking out arrows from the lifeless hearts
That, lately, throbbed in our companions' bosoms,
Turning the faces of dead friends from earth,
Then pondering upon their ghastly lips,
Which, ere the last moon waned, smiled sweetly on us.

MADIBOO.

Fie! this is weakness, Selico:—we want you
To help us for our mother.

SELICO *(wildly)*.

Have I one?

MADIBOO.

Have you? Why, Torribal and you, and I,
Bore her upon our arms, into the woods,
On the same day that they besieged the town,
And, after that, you left us—but she lives.

SELICO.

Well, that's some comfort—she's alive.—Ha, ha!
I have a mother still. Remember, though,
I saw her placed in safety ere I went,
And both my brothers with her.

MADIBOO.

Rise and collect yourself. I have skulked here,
To find, if possible, a little food,
Left in the village; and to find out you.

SELICO.

Well you have one point, if not the other,
You have found *me*.

MADIBOO.

Not quite as I could wish:
We need you to assist us, and you seem
Scarce able to assist yourself.—Our mother—

SELICO *(springs from the ground)*.

I'll fight for her, while I've breath within me!

---

129 Young's utterance of this line, "when he sunk exhausted to the ground, was full of a consummate misery," redolent with
heart-breaking grief. *Theatrical Examiner*, 30 July 1808: 492.

MADIBOO.

Fight for a dinner, then, and win the battle.
Our implements of husbandry—the gun,
Fish-spear, and tackle, bird-snares, hatchet, arrows—
All, all, we foraged with before the war,
Are taken by the enemy:—and still
Their camp remains so near our lurking place,
(A little from the town) we almost fear
To venture out, in search of straggling berries
Our hands may pluck for us—we're famishing!

SELICO.

And nothing to support Darina?

MADIBOO.

Nothing.—
This day, nor yesterday. The night before,
Food was so scanty, that she would not take
The little we could get; till, in her faintness,
We forced it on her.

SELICO.

Would not taste it!—why?

MADIBOO.

Each felt the other's want before their own.
She would not eat, fearing to rob her sons;
Nor they, because they saw their mother starving.

SELICO.

I'll grapple with the lioness, and tear
The fresh-killed wild goat from her sinewy paws,
Ere she who gave me birth shall die by famine.
I know the spot we fixed my mother in;—
I'll fly to succour her.

MADIBOO.

Be cautious then.
Stragglers, from the Mandingo camp, are prowling
All round our pillaged town. Pray, now, take heed,
Or you may lose your life.

SELICO.

My life!—Oh, brother
I wish that it were gone! *(Going).*

MADIBOO *(catches his arm).*

Come hither, Selico
You must not leave me thus. I dread to ask
What have been *your* losses in the town.

SELICO *(distractedly).*

O, something—something!

MADIBOO.

Do not look not so wildly:
You harrow me. You wish your *life* were gone?

SELICO.

    I do; but fear not for me—I shall ne'er
    Commit self-slaughter; the revered Farulho
    Taught me religion, and I know my duties.
    Wretches who killed themselves, when life's a burden,
    Shrink from their fellow men to brave their Maker.
    Too tame to soar above the ills of earth,
    Too rash to bend to the decrees of Heaven,
    They fancy impious weakness resolution,
    Scared into courage, the heroic cowards
    Grow pusillanimously[130] bold—and forfeit
    All ties, divine or human, men acknowledge.

MADIBOO.

    Where are Berissa and her father?

SELICO *(throws his arms on Madiboo's neck)*.

    Dead!—Both dead!

MADIBOO.

    I'll not believe it: Selico—
    Why, Selico! Come, come, dear brother! Rouse!
    Berissa has but fled—fled with her father—
    And to some place of safety. Do not droop man—
    Come, prithee do not.

SELICO.

    Look on this mantle!

MADIBOO *(staggers at the sight)*.

    Well, well—our mother wove it, for the priest.

SELICO.

    I threw it o'er his shoulders, in the tent,
    Just ere I hoped to wed my destined bride.
    He—with a smile of soft benevolence
    Smoothing the furrows in the face of age—
    Vowed to preserve it; every day to wear it,
    In token of the wedding, and in kindness
    Towards our dear mother; yea, that—till he died,
    He ne'er would part with it.

MADIBOO.

    All this is nothing:
    The tumult in the town, might—

SELICO *(interrupting him)*.

    Till today,
    I could not clear the rubbish from the mosque,
    And, there, upon the steps—

---

130 Faint-heartedly.

MADIBOO.

You found the mantle:

Aye, in his flight he dropped it.

SELICO.

No, no, no!—

I plucked it from his headless corpse.

MADIBOO.

Oh, brother!

SELICO.

The porch was strewed with mutilated bodies;

Close to the priest, and headless as himself,

Lay a female's mangled form, whose fingers,

Were twined in his. Some bridal ornaments,

Left (like the mantle in the haste of pillage),

Were scattered round. I have them.

MADIBOO (shudders).

Not Berissa's?

SELICO.

My clay-cold love's!

MADIBOO.

Oh! never tell me so.

SELICO.

Will not nature tell you so, my brother?

Beneath the hatchets of their murderers,

The father and his child, in life's last struggle,

Had pressed each other's hand, and death has clinched them.

She was the good man's only tendril: he

The aged vine she clasped—the storm was cruel;

The grateful shoot embraced the withering trunk,

And clung there, till they perished both together.

MADIBOO.

Selico—I—remember, we are men;

We must bear up, and—pshaw! I cannot speak (weeping).

SELICO.

You are a kind, kind brother!

MADIBOO.

Aye, I trust so:

But there are others, still alive, that still love you.

There's Torribal—a little rough—but kindly.

Then our dear mother. Yours are wringing losses,

But you have still some comfort in your family.

SELICO.

More misery, as you describe it, now.

A family without a home; a mother,

Dying for want—and sons, in manhood's vigour,

Without the means to help her.

MADIBOO.

Well, one evil—the activity
Often required to fight off present ill—softens another:
Serves to efface the memory of the past.
We *must* find methods to support our mother,
Or perish in the search. Go to the wood—
You know the winding.[131]

SELICO.

I can trace it.

MADIBOO.

Go.
Leave me, a little, here—I'll soon be with you.
My strength and spirits are not worn as yours.
Among the ruins of the town, perchance,
I may find something that may save us, yet,
From famishing. Go, brother—and be careful.

SELICO.

Come with me to the outskirts: set me right
Upon my way——

MADIBOO.

You are very faint—

SELICO.

A little: 'tis some time since I have eaten—
And my mind's torment—

MADIBOO.

Cheerly, now! Lean upon my shoulder.
Tut, man! All will, yet, be well.
Come, Selico!—come, come!

(Selico and Madibbo exit over the ruins. Enter Mug, carrying a basket of eatables).

MUG. This has been what I call a complete smash. They have as great a rage for knocking down houses in Africa, as they have for overbuilding about London. What's that? *(Starting)* Only a jackdaw.[132] I'm afraid I'm frightened—for whenever I have caught myself whistling, curse me, if I could tell whether the tune was "Guardian angels now protect me," or "Go to the devil and shake yourself."[133] I wouldn't have ventured into this dismal town again, from the camp of my new master, the Mandingo king, but for the hankering after the fate of my old master, the Foulah priest;—and, if I was quite sure little

---

131 The route, according to natural features.

132 A small crow native to northwest Africa, Europe, and the Middle East.

133 Mug contrasts a secular song's hymn-like lyrics ("Guardian angels, now protect me, / Send me back the youth I love," sung in theatres) with the distinctly impious Irish or Scottish jig "Go to the Devil and Shake Yourself" (also known as "When You Are Sick Is It Tea You Want"). Christopher W. Knauff, *Doctor Tucker, Priest-Musician ... Including a Brief Converse about the Rise and Progress of Church Music in America* (New York: A.D.F. Randolph, 1897), 254; Francis Arthur Jones, *Famous Hymns and their Authors* (London: Hodder and Stoughton, 1905), 55; Francis O'Neil, *Irish Folk Music: A Fascinating Hobby* (Chicago: Regan, 1910), 143; and http://www.ibiblio.org/fiddlers/GNE_GONN.htm (accessed 6 August 2010).

Sutta was deceased, I'd go into short mourning. The poor creatures, here, are all as dead as door-nails! So to keep myself alive (as it is a good English three miles from the conquering king's camp, who has made me his Secretary of State), I'll open my basket and stay my stomach (*sitting down and opening the basket*). We men high in office always make sure of some devilish pretty pickings.

MADIBOO (*enters*). He is safe on his way—now to get some food, if possible, and—(*sees Mug*). Ha! a man! And eating!

MUG. Here's a basket full: but if the English Secretary for Foreign Affairs could see me now, wouldn't he say a Mandingo cabinet minister lunches in style.

MADIBOO (*rushes forward, and seizes him*). You mustn't touch a morsel.

MUG (*terrified*). Don't kill me! Keep me for a show, you'll find it worth your while.[134]

MADIBOO. White man! Is it you?

MUG. Let me look at you—is it—eh?—yes! Lord, Mr. Madiboo! I'm heartily glad to meet you alive, though you almost frightened me to death. You won't hurt your old friend Henry Augustus Mug the ivory turner?

MADIBOO. I can't tell! I'm almost desperate.

MUG. Are you?—(*aside*) then I'm in a funk[135]—pray don't put yourself in a passion, Mr. Madiboo! It will make you angry.

MADIBOO. I must have food.

MUG. I was just going to dinner. You have dropped in a little unexpectedly, but I am vastly happy to see you. Pray take a seat upon the ground; and excuse this bad set out, as I didn't expect the honour of your company.

MADIBOO. Look, Chalk-face! Your fear invites me to eat what I should be very loath to snatch from you, as plunder. The black slave merchants who travel up along the Senegal and Gambia say your nation is famed for humanity and bravery; I won't insult its character for courage by attacking such a paltry specimen of it as yourself. But I apply to you on a score which no Englishman, they say, can withstand: an honest family is perishing—succour the distressed!

MUG. Take all the basket, and much good may it do you. I'm a little nervous—but, hang me, if I do this out of fear. When my heart is full, I'd as lieu[136] my stomach was empty.

MADIBOO. You are a good white man. How can I thank you?

MUG. Don't say a word—munch dumb—Lord love you! I'm made Secretary of State to the Mandingo king, and have got plenty.

MADIBOO. How did that happen?

MUG. Why His Majesty is a monarch of great natural parts—but he can neither read nor write; so, just as he was going to cut my throat, His Majesty humanely considered that I might be of a great deal of use to him, and generously spared my life.[137]

MADIBOO. Yes, and he'll poison you, when he has no further occasion for you. He is no rightful ruler; but worked and bullied himself into power. When the troubles, about liberty, broke out among the Mandingoes, he was of low note among their warriors. Enterprise and good luck gave him, at last, complete sway over the fighting men: that's everything when a nation is in a ferment, and the successful upstart is active, cruel, and cunning. But what has it made him?—Why, the usurping king of a people

---

134 This moment is depicted in the frontispiece (illus. 2, p. 36).
135 Ill-humour.
136 To accept in exchange.
137 An analogous experience happened to Mungo Park. At Kamalia, the Arabic scholar Karfa Taura treated Park kindly after he discovered that he could read *The Book of Common Prayer*. Park, *Travels*, 253.

who murdered their true king;[138] and the pillaging protector of some trembling neighbours, whom he forces to say, come and shoot one half of us, that the survivors may thank you for putting their property under your clutches.

MUG. I happen to be his Secretary of State, for all that—so I must do my duty—and, in my official capacity, see what I have drawn up as my first maiden[139] letter, and sent to the English governor at the factory,[140] at the mouth of the Senegal.

MADIBOO. Well, let me gather all the intelligence I can, before I quit you: but, be quick.

MUG. Don't hurry a cabinet minister—it will spoil your preferment.[141] No merchants have been up the country lately, and His Majesty is out of paper, so I wrote my official letter on a bit of slate, and here is a copy *(pulls out a bit of slate)*. I commanded the State Messenger to be very careful not to spit on the despatches, for fear of rubbing them out.

MADIBOO. Let me hear them.

MUG. A little patience, as I used to say to my creditors. I always took in the *Sunday Monitor*, at Snow Hill, and by conning over extracts from the *Gazette*, I think I'm a tightish dab at this kind of job.[142]

MADIBOO. Begin.

MUG. I'm going *(reads from letter)*. "Sir, I have the honour to inform your Excellency, that my Master, the Mandingo king, whose important cares of state have never afforded him leisure to learn to write, has taken many prisoners now on sale. The capture has been so great that it will be worth the English traders' while to travel up to the camp to inspect them."

MADIBOO. They'll never come so far inland.

MUG. Won't they? The messenger is come back, and they are all expected here, in grand cavalcade, this very day. I knew my style would fetch 'em—for hear what I have added. "I have the honour to inform your Excellency, that if the merchants take the trouble to come, I'll be damned if they don't find a lumping penn'orth.[143] I would send the list of the killed and wounded in this affair, but slate runs short, and no paper. I have the honour to be, with the highest consideration, your Excellency's most devoted servant, Henry Augustus Mug—wood and ivory-turner, No. 25, Snow Hill; where all orders are executed on the lowest terms[144] for ready money only."

MADIBOO. White man, I must hurry from you. The provisions in this basket, which you have given to me, are wanted by those who are now perishing with hunger.

MUG. Why didn't you scamper off towards the desert?—I hear all have run there who were not taken prisoners.—Pray, Mr. Madiboo, if I may make so bold to inquire, what's become of your Mamma—your mother?

MADIBOO. What's that to you?

MUG *(frightened)*. Oh, dear, nothing at all, I didn't mean to be impertinent; but only to make my kind inquiries after the health of the good family.

MADIBOO. I would tell you how we are placed, but unthinking friends often divulge the serious secrets of those they would serve, and bring them into calamity without intending it. Farewell, white man!

---

138 Colman plays on such fears, contradicting Mungo Park's kindly treatment by Mandingos. Ibid., 245-46.

139 Earliest, or first of its kind.

140 A trading station in a foreign country, instrumental to an imperial power's interests in a region.

141 Chances for promotion.

142 The *London Gazette*, printed twice a week, included government appointments and promotions and lists of bankrupts. Mug refers to his ability to imitate official-sounding language.

143 Pennyworth; synonymous with value for money.

144 As inexpensively as possible.

I hope we may meet again—I owe you much, much gratitude.—Oh, Mahomet! can the heart receive more thrilling transport than this basket will afford me, by saving the dear, dear life of her who gave me my own *(exits)*.

MUG. He's off; and what is very uncommon, has taken with him, without fee or reward, all that a Secretary of State had to give, to the utmost satisfaction of the donor. I'll go back to the camp with a clear conscience and an empty stomach. *(Sings)*[145]

By trade I am a turner, and Mug it is my name,
To buy a lot of ivory to Africa I came;
I met a trading blackamoor, a woolly old humbug,[146]
He coaxed me up his land, and made a slave of Mr. Mug.
Crying, won't you, won't you, won't you, won't you come, Mr. Mug?

My skin is lily white, and the colour here is new,
So the first man that they sold me to, he thumped me back and blue.
The priest who bought me from him, in a tender-hearted tone,
Said come from that great blackguard's house, and enter in my own.
Crying, won't you, etc.

Good lack![147] but to behold the vicissitudes of fate!
I'm his black Mandingo Majesty's white Minister of State:
For hours, in my lobby, my petitioners shall stay,
And wish me at the devil, when I hold my Levee[148] day.
Crying, won't you, etc. *(exit)*.

Scene 2

A Wood. A rude shelter is seen among the trees, which Darina's sons have formed as a temporary residence for their mother. Torribal comes from the shelter, supporting Darina.

TORRIBAL.
    Come, mother! This way—more into the air;
    Bear up a little!—Madiboo, I hope,
    Will hasten back to us, with nourishment.
DARINA.
    I'm not in pain; I think the worst is over—
    For they have told me (and I believe it true),
    The famished never struggle at the last:
    Death spreads a gentle languor o'er their limbs,
    And they expire in slumbers.

---

145 The lyrics are not included in the Larpent manuscript; there is just an indication that a song goes here. The *Theatrical Examiner* specifies that this is a parody of Mr. Moore's song "Will you come to the bow'r." *Theatrical Examiner*, 30 July 1808, 492.

146 A blackamoor is a dark-skinned African. Europeans perceived Africans' hair as wool-like (thickly matted like an unshorn sheep). A humbug is a trickster or imposter.

147 An exclamation akin to heavens! or goodness gracious!

148 Assembly in the monarch's presence.

TORRIBAL.

Mother, Mother!

Do not talk so; you cut my very heart!

Here, rest upon this bank *(placing her on it)*. Madiboo loiters—

And as for Selico, let me look out—*(looking out)*

No, not a soul appearing! As for Selico,

Though we are brothers, should we meet again,

I'd cast him from me, as—

DARINA.

Hold, Torribal!

No words of bitterness among my sons.

TORRIBAL.

He has neglected you.

DARINA.

No! No!

TORRIBAL.

He has.

DARINA.

He saw me here in safety.

TORRIBAL.

Saw you distressed!

Then he left you; for five days has left you.

(Passionately) If, e'er again, I cross him—

DARINA.

Peace, I charge you!

I've woe enough; spare me the grief of hearing

One of my children vilify the other.

TORRIBAL *(tenderly, kneeling by her at the dive[149] of the bank).*

Have I offended you?

DARINA *(pressing his hand).*

You are too sudden.

Man, the commanding wonder of creation,

Has, like the insect, his allotted time

To do his task, and perish. Brief, the span,

In which he reckons up these several claims;

Parents, wife, children, sisters, brethren, friend,

And, sometimes more, crowding at once, upon him;

Besides the common social ties, that smooth

Life's road, and gently slope it to the grave.

TORRIBAL.

'Tis very true, my mother!

DARINA.

Sure, then, no blame can fall on Selico,

---

149 Precipitate descent.

Who helps to bear his mother from the war,
Then, leaving both his brothers to protect her
Hastens back to seek his bride, alive, or murdered.

TORRIBAL.

I love him but it frets me to suppose
You can be slighted by him.

DARINA.

Never; never,
By any of my boys; give me not reason
To think they lose that love for one another
That warms their hearts towards me.

TORRIBAL.

Your reprimand
Weighs heavy on me; my anxiety,
In your distress, must plead my pardon *(kisses her hand).*

TORRIBAL.

Hark!—a footstep! *(Looks off)* Ha! 'tis Selico! *(Rises)*
But bearing nothing with him. *(Mournfully, aside)* Still, no food!
If we have no relief, before tonight,
She'll surely perish.

SELICO *(enters).*

I am here again to ask a blessing.
(To his mother) Can you forgive a wanderer?

DARINA.

Forgive!
Oh you had urgent and dear cause of absence.
You seem dejected; tell me 'tis fatigue,
Not disappointment that has made you look thus.
Have you been prosperous?

SELICO.

I left my brother,
Just at the outskirts of our ruined town,
Resolved to bring you food, if food were in it—
But I could find none.

TORRIBAL.

Could not? Chilling news!

DARINA.

'Twas not on that account that I inquired
What has befallen; it was—

SELICO *(distressed).*

I know—I know.

DARINA.

Tell me of—

SELICO.

Our good priest?—and—and—*(pauses).*

DARINA.

    Berissa.

SELICO *(much agitated).*

    Mother, their fate is certain; no more, now—

    Some other time, I'll tell you.

DARINA.

    Selico,

    You torture me! Their fate is certain—speak;

    Have they escaped?

SELICO.

    Not so.

TORRIBAL.

    Concealed within the town, then;

    And, like ourselves, in want of sustenance.

SELICO.

    No, Torribal, not that.

TORRIBAL *(sorrowfully).*

    Then they are—*(hesitates)*

SELICO.

    Aye;—

    Brother, you falter;[150]—what then must I feel,

    When I pronounce—they're butchered by the enemy!

(Darina turns aside, with her hands to her face, and totters to the bank).

TORRIBAL.

    But are you sure of this?

SELICO.

    Too certain! Fearing

    That I might shock my mother with a token

    Which if displayed would break the news at once,

    Within the hollow of a tree, I hid

    (Before I came in view) Farulho's mantle.

    How I obtained it let Madiboo inform you;

    How both the poor souls have perished, prithee, brother,

    Let Madiboo inform you—he knows all—

    And spare me the relation.

TORRIBAL.

    Selico,

    I fear that I have sometimes seemed unkind;

    Forgive me—'tis my nature to be rough—

    But I—in short, we never know how much

    We love a friend, till he is in affliction *(embraces him).*

MADIBOO *(enters).*

    Where is my mother? I've brought provision!

---

150 Spelled "faulter" in both the manuscript and Cumberland. This denotes culprit, but it seems the wrong sense.

TORRIBAL.

Oh, welcome, welcome!

MADIBOO (*pushes by him*).

There's no time for welcome—

For here's the dinner waiting—where is—

Oh! she's there! How fares it, mother?—Courage!—

See, here is something to restore you.

Cheerly[151]—into the shed, and eat! (*Helps her from the bank*).

DARINA.

You'll all partake?

MADIBOO.

Oh, as for me, knowing there was enough,

I snacked as I kept running on the road.

TORRIBAL.

The shed's small, let Selico go with you.

I'll wait—for he, I fear, has fasted longest.

MADIBOO.

Now, Torribal, that's kind! Why Selico!

(*Selico, from the time of Madiboo's entrance, has appeared abstracted and lost in thought*).

MADIBOO.

Never stand musing so, man! Come, and help.

SELICO (*starts and runs to Darina*).

I had forgot—I—now, my dearest mother!

DARINA (*leaning on him*).

My poor unhappy boy!

(*Selico and Darina enter the shelter*).

MADIBOO.

Unhappy boy.

What did she mean by that?

TORRIBAL.

Why, she knows all:

Farulho and his daughter both are dead.

MADIBOO.

Then Selico has told her—that was wrong;

She's weak—such news came too abruptly on her.

TORRIBAL.

Not as he uttered it: he would have strangled

Affliction in his breast; she wrung it thence

By eager questions: first, he reared his head,

Loftily in sorrow, like an aspen struck

By thunderbolts;[152] till, trembling at her breath,

---

151 Cheerfully.

152 Aspens proverbially "quake," so in this case Selico violently trembled.

He whispered out his woe so mournfully,
That, were it not for shame, I could have wept
Worse than the softest wench in Africa.

MADIBOO.
Don't think a tear too weak on strong occasions.
A sniveller's whimpering fills sorrow's puddles;
But when a firm man weeps, each drop's a diamond.

TORRIBAL.
I fear calamity will pinch us harder,
Before we gain another settlement.

MADIBOO.
I'm sure it will, unless we hit on something
Suddenly.

TORRIBAL.
Aye, but what?

MADIBOO.
I know not.
But this I know—there's nothing in the town
That's worth a second venture; and where else
Is there a chance?

TORRIBAL.
Nowhere; and we must starve.

MADIBOO.
No not if we can help it; still we'll struggle.

TORRIBAL.
I see no struggle we can have, but one—
And that is heart-breaking—
We must sit down by our poor mother's side,
And see her die a day or two before us.

MADIBOO.
Here comes Selico.
Let us consult with him how to proceed.

SELICO (enters).
Our mother sleeps: food, after painful fasting,
Has lulled her to repose.

MADIBOO.
Come hither then.
This meal, which the poor white man gave to me,
Has saved her life—but fortune will not send
The white man every day. Have you reflected
About a fresh supply when this is gone?

SELICO.
I dread to think of it.

MADIBOO.
That's worse than folly.

Our inactivity is certain death,
To her, and all of us.
TORRIBAL.
We must do something.
SELICO.
Name it.
MADIBOO.
Aye, there's the point that sorely puzzles us:
For we are girded by the enemy,
And we have neither weapons of attack,
Nor any instruments to gain a livelihood
By hunt or tillage. In a little time, too
The winter rains set in and should that season
O'ertake us here, before a stock's laid up,
There's nothing but a miracle can save us.
TORRIBAL.
Suppose their camp should break up shortly—
Would leave us ranging room.
MADIBOO.
Suppose a dinner,
A day too late, popped under dead men's noses—
That would refresh them vastly.
TORRIBAL.
The camp must soon disperse.
MADIBOO.
Not yet awhile.
There's business that will take at least ten days.
The English merchants are invited up,
To buy the slaves and prisoners.
SELICO (quickly).
Is that certain?
MADIBOO.
They are expected in the camp today.
SELICO.
Aye!—then my mother shall be rich tomorrow.
TORRIBAL.
How, Selico?
SELICO.
I'll be a slave: sell *me*![153]
The traffick we well know, is horrible;
But money will preserve her; she shall have
This body's value, and, for once, the trader

---

153 Park stresses that such things happened: mothers promised their young children in exchange for food through a famine, and individuals volunteered themselves into slavery to avoid starvation. Park, *Travels*, 248-49, 295.

Then be humane, although without his knowledge,
By purchasing a son, to save a mother.
MADIBOO.
That son shall be myself.
SELICO.
No.
TORRIBAL.
Hold a little.
'Tis true the purchase money would procure us
A stock of all we want; and one of us
Must be the sacrifice! Let us decide
By lots, who shall be sold.
SELICO.
No lots, my brother;
For mine is cast already—more unhappy
I cannot be: my early hope is gone.
I breathed, in the soft spring of my desire,
Upon the sweetest violet that ever
Disclosed its fragrant loveliness to Heaven!
Untimely tempest nipped the modest flower,
And the world's garden is, to me, a desert.
MADIBOO.
This must not be.
SELICO.
It must and you shall lead me
Into the camp; 'twill not be difficult
To mingle in the crowd, and find some merchant
Willing to strike the bargain.
MADIBOO.
The bargain!
You make my blood run cold—I cannot do it.
What! sell my brother!
SELICO.
To preserve your parent.
Had we agreed as Torribal proposed
Still one had done this office for the other.
TORRIBAL.
Then let it be by lot.[154]
SELICO.
I'll not consent.
You two are heart-whole; wretched as I am,
I should be useless here.
(To Madiboo) Come with me, brother,

---

154 The published version reads "my lot": quite a different inflection of character.

Or by our prophet! I will seek the camp
Alone, and having found a purchaser,
Trust to some chance to send you back the money.
Hark!—There's our mother stirring—we must part!
Say we go out to forage.

MADIBOO.
   Torribal,
   What can I do?

TORRIBAL *(very mournfully)*.
   It must be as he says.

SELICO.
   Let me embrace her, for the last, last time,
   And leave her, then, for ever!

MADIBOO.
   I shall choke!

DARINA *(appears at the opening of the shed)*.
   Torribal, how you stay—you must be faint—
   Prithee, come in, and eat.

TORRIBAL.
   I come, directly.

SELICO.
   And we, dear mother, now, must leave you.

DARINA *(comes forward)*.
   Leave me!
   So soon, my son?

SELICO.
   Yes to seek more provision.

DARINA.
   Selico, you exert beyond your powers:
   I wish that you would tarry.

MADIBOO.
   So do I.

DARINA.
   Persuade him, Madiboo.

MADIBOO.
   He *will* go, Mother.

SELICO.
   I must farewell!

DARINA.
   Must—say farewell? Farewell!
   There is a something that makes on my heart
   This parting wondrous heavy.

SELICO *(aside to Torribal)*.
   My dear brother,
   May you live happy long! *(Presses his hands—then turns to Darina)*.
   One kiss—still one.

May Heaven shield and bless you, mother!—Now—
I'm ready. Onwards!

(*Exit Selico and Madiboo; Torribal and Darina exit into the shelter*).

Scene 3

The camp of Demba Sego Jalla, Mandingo King of Bambouk.[155] *Enter Mug and several Mandingo Warriors.*

MUG. Pray, black Generals, Brigadiers, Majors, Colonels, and Captains, keep your distance. I am
    Secretary at War, and it isn't pretty to press so strongly upon Cabinet questions.
FIRST WARRIOR. Our prisoners are lying upon our hands: we only want to know when the European
    merchants will come to purchase them.
EVERYONE. Aye, aye, that's all.
MUG. But His Majesty has commanded me not to let you know the time.
FIRST WARRIOR. Why?
MUG. Because you are all so greedy, you would run out of the camp to meet them, and forestall the
    market. Besides, nothing but a verbal message has been given.
SECOND WARRIOR. We don't believe it. Read the letter sent by the factory, that states the day when
    they will arrive.
MUG. Thus far I am free to reply to the gallant General in the black countenance, who spoke last: the
    finances of the country, from our late glorious victory, are in a situation that may make us proud—
    but I assure the gallant General, that on the subject now under discussion, no authenticated papers
    (however loudly they may be called for) have yet reached my office. But set your hearts at ease—I dare
    say you'll all drive your infernal trade to your own advantage, and your unfortunate black and copper
    cattle will go at a good price.

(*A march is played at a distance*).[156]

Hark! (*Looks out*) By the Lord Harry,[157] the merchants are coming already! Run, and draw out your
    prisoners.

(*The black warriors hurry away*).

There they are, in full march! What a capital procession! Some on horseback; some on oxen; and a
    long lanky jockey that looks like their leader, is stuck upon a camel. Lord Mayor's shew, on the ninth
    of November,[158] is nothing to it.

(*The music is heard stronger. The European Merchants come down the stage in procession and range
    themselves on one side. Fetterwell, the chief of the merchants, is seated on a camel*).

---

155 A remote district upriver on the Senegal, inhabited by Mandingos and possessing valuable gold mines. Elsewhere in the
    play, the Mandingo territory is referred to as Kassan (which is on the Gambia). John Ramsay McCulloch, *A Dictionary,
    Geographical, Statistical, and Historical of Various Countries* ..., vol. 1 (London: Longman, Brown, Green, and Longman,
    1851), 287.
156 Instrumental music only.
157 A mild oath referring to the devil.
158 The annual installation of an alderman as Lord Mayor of the City of London took place each 9 November. The festivities
    included a procession of dignitaries through the streets.

FETTERWELL *(to Mug)*. I say—who are you?

MUG. Secretary at war to his Mandingo Majesty, Demba Sego Jalla, King of Bambouk.

FETTERWELL. Are you? Then help me off my camel, and I'll give you a shilling.

(Mug helps him off).

Damn me, but he's a bone-setter![159] He'd never do to carry a lady. A still[160] dock-tail wagon horse, running away with you down Piccadilly,[161] when it wants paving, must be luxury to his long trot.[162]

(The Attendants lead off the camel).

Are you the person that sent the letter to the Governor at the factory?

MUG. I was commanded by the king, my master, to write the despatch.

FETTERWELL. Well, some of our Ministers at home mayn't be remarkable for a dignified appearance; but of all the Secretaries of State I ever clapped my eyes on, curse me if I ever saw such a gig. Then you are Henry Augustus Mug—turner in wood and ivory, when you are in London?

MUG. Yes; and Secretary at War, while I am in Africa.

FETTERWELL. Well, master Mug, your two professions agree nicely, as the world goes: you are not the first, by many, who has wriggled himself into power, when he has been in the habit of turning. My name is Fetterwell, long known as a merchant in the slave trade. Here are other gentlemen of my profession. We've set up a club at the mouth of the Gambia, while we sojourn there. A friend of mine—a poet— before I left London, gave me a double motto, to stick up over the President's Canopy. I'll tell it you. "Hic niger est" and, "Homo sum"[163]—how much money for the man?

MUG. Education is a great advantage.

FETTERWELL. Are we to see His Majesty?

MUG. Not today; he has got the belly-ache.

FETTERWELL. A very odd court excuse for not seeing a sovereign! But let me introduce my friends, and brother traders. Here's Mr. Flayall, bound for Barbadoes; Mr. Grim, going to Jamaica; young Mr. Marrowbone, once a carcass butcher, in Clare Market,[164] but an estate dropping to him in the West India Islands, he now barters for blacks, instead of bargaining for bullocks; Captain Abraham Adamant, who lost his left leg when the inhuman negroes chucked him down the hatchways,[165] for only stowing fifteen in a hammock, in hot weather; and sundry others. Pray, gentlemen, be known to the Secretary.

MARROWBONE. Pray, Mr. Quisby,[166] how do you think we shall find the market?

MUG *(aside)*. Mr. Quisby!—Oh, this is the jimmy[167] young butcher. *(Aloud)* What d'ye buy, Sir?

MARROWBONE. Buy? Why slaves, to be sure.

MUG. I don't know what they may be a pound today; markets vary.

---

159 A specialist who treats bone fractures and dislocations.

160 Meek.

161 A thoroughfare in London's West End.

162 A vigorous two-beat gait, not quite as fast as a canter, in which diagonal legs move in unison (left front and right rear, right front and left rear).

163 From two maxims: Horace's "hic niger est, hanc tu, Romane, caveto" (this man is black, beware of him, Roman) and Terence's "Homo sum humani nil a me alienum puto" (As a man, I consider that nothing human is alien to me).

164 A meat and fish market near Lincoln's Inn Fields. Kosher butchering occurred here, so Colman may insinuate that Marrowbone is a Jew.

165 Into the ship's hold.

166 A quisby is an idler. Marrowbone insults Mug and asserts his own superiority.

167 Pronounced "jemmy": an object that pries things open, particularly locks.

MARROWBONE. I can't see why they should here.

MUG. Can't you? Now, supposing you were put up to sale—

MARROWBONE. Me? *(Laughing)* Ha! ha! that's droll—but what then?

MUG. Why, then a calf's head might fetch more or less today than it would tomorrow.

FETTERWELL. Well, but where are the parties?

MUG. The black generals are arranging their prisoners.

FETTERWELL. We must make short work of this, as this will be our last venture: for, when I left London, a bill was passing[168] that will kick our business to the devil.

MUG. I am very glad to hear it. The work begins in the natural quarter, and the stream of freedom flows from the very fountainhead of true natural liberty. Here come the generals with their prisoners; and we shall have the common marketers pouring in, on all sides, directly.

(A wild march and chorus as the Mandingo Warriors enter with their Prisoners).

WARRIORS.
March, brave Mandingoes, march! In triumph shout
And draw your well-won captives out.
When Africk's conquerors tread the field,
Battles yield.
March, Warriors, march!

(Chorus, together)

WARRIORS.
March brave Mandingos march, in triumph shout.
PRISONERS.
Mourn, Captives, mourn! In battle ta'en.
WARRIORS *(when the Slaves are drawn out. Speaks)*. Halt!

MUG. Rabbit me,[169] if there isn't my darling short bit of a love, Sutta, among the prisoners—and among His Majesty's own proper lot, too. If I could but buy her off, for myself.

FETTERWELL. A pretty decent shew.

MARROWBONE. Yes the women are tricked out as gay as a porkshop on Saturday night;[170] and the men seem tolerably strong.

FETTERWELL. Strong?—Talk of the Africans standing fatigue and climate!—Why, Lord love you! A day's work of a slave in a sugar island is a flea bite to the fag of a British Buck, walking for a wager. The rising generation of England seems to be in training to stump a hundred miles a day, and against time, and post-horses in all weathers.[171]

---

168 The bill passed in 1807, the year before the play's debut. Colman depicts a trade from which English merchants were barred, though other European powers (including France, Austria, Spain, Prussia, Portugal, the Netherlands, Sweden, and Belgium) continued in it unabated.

169 An obscure oath.

170 The allusion is to gaudy adornment. As a butcher, Marrowbone might reflect on brisk business conducted on working-class wage-earners' payday, when they could afford meat.

171 This speech is excised from the published version. It is difficult to imagine it being spoken in the theatre without causing offence to some audience members. It connotes something like the following: a plantation slave's exertion is minor compared to a British dandy's outlay to walk quickly and far on a bet; there is a fad for hiking great distances and hiring horses even when it is inclement, which speaks to our superiority. (This underscores Fetterwell's indifference to the suffering of Africans and obliviousness to the distinction between enslaved labour and voluntary recreation.)

MUG. Don't tip us the trader, and try to run down the article.[172] I must address you in my official capacity: so listen.—Hem!—Gentlemen auctioneers of the two-legged repositories; I am commanded by the king, my master, to inform you that it is His Majesty's humane decree, that you may purchase your fellow-creatures; but if you steal, or smuggle, a single slave, he will with infinite regret, put you to death in the tenderest manner imaginable.

FETTERWELL. The devil he will! I wish we hadn't come here.

MUG. The market will be open a whole week; at the end of which if any of you prove defaulters, so great will be his lenity[173] to you, as his customers, that he will give you the choice of your execution—of which there are three sorts in this country. You may either be burnt, impaled, or scalded, which ever you think the most agreeable.

FETTERWELL. This is a damned arbitrary government. Let's look over the goods. Come, gentlemen under these circumstances the sooner we complete our bargain the better. Now take care, my honest, respectable friends, not to smuggle nor steal. If they were to burn, impale, or scald Messieurs Fetterwell, Flayall, Grim, Captain Adamant, of the Hyaena Cutter,[174] and young Mr. Marrowbone, formerly butcher of Clare Market, how Christian humanity would shudder at so barbarous a massacre in the annals of Africa.

(*They go up the camp to inspect the slaves. Mug accompanies them*).

MERCHANT. He's of the Foulah tribe, I believe.

MADIBOO. Aye.

MERCHANT. I would not give three minkallis[175] for a slave of his breed.—They are not reckoned hardy as the black negroes. You'll get little or nothing for him, now the market is so well stocked.—Good day to you! (*Walks away*).

SELICO.
They all reject us. What did he offer?

MADIBOO.
I can't tell—I forget.—My heart sickens at the business.

SELICO.
I fear my project now may not succeed.
They do not offer anything that could
Support my mother through the winter.

MADIBOO.
No matter. Mahomet forgive me!—
But I had almost rather we should all perish
Than you should be the price of our living,
And I employed to carry home the dross.[176]

(*A bustle is heard*).

Stand aside, Selico!
Something extraordinary has happened.

---

172 Colloquially, do not spoil the auction by decrying the quality of the goods.

173 Mercy.

174 A ship of this name was commissioned by the Royal Navy during this period.

175 A trifle. As a former freeman, Selico is of less value than a man conditioned to lifelong labour through slavery.

176 Impure matter, especially in metallurgy.

Yonder is the white man; he mustn't see us
Or it may lead to a discovery of who we are.

(Enter Crier. Africans crowd round him).

AFRICANS. Hear him! hear him!

CRIER. "Proclamation and reward!—Last night, a man, with his head muffled in his garments, escaped through the fire of soldiery, from the tents of the king's favourite female prisoner.—Whomever shall bring the offender into His Majesty's presence, so that he may be punished by death, shall receive four hundred ounces of gold" (exit)..

SELICO.

Oh! had we but that sum!

MADIBOO.

Hush! This way! The white man is advancing.

(Fetterwell and Mug come forward).

FETTERWELL. That's a good lot. I'll take the whole.

MUG. You have picked out the prime of the market. Those are the tidbits[177] of the prisoners, reserved for His Majesty's own private pocket.[178]

FETTERWELL. There's a little short girl among 'em, though, that I don't think worth a farthing.

MUG (aside). Bless her! that's my Sutta. (Aloud) Hasn't she a sweet face?

FETTERWELL. Why well enough for a blackamoor; but faces do no work in the West Indies.

MUG. You have a devilish bad taste. I had rather have her than all the rest tied up in a bunch.

FETTERWELL. Why, master Mug, it is my opinion you are fond of that little black honey.

MUG. Oh, love!—You know not, Mr. Fetterwell, its power—I am.

FETTERWELL. Then I may throw in a sop for the Secretary; and he'll let me off cheap in a government. I say. See, Mug—let me off at a hundred pounds (wink you know in the official way) let me off at a hundred, for the whole lot—for the whole lot, and I'll chuck the girl to you as a bonus.

MUG. Will you? I'm naturally honest in office—but the tender passion makes me peculate.[179] Done!

FETTERWELL. Then the lot's mine. (Goes among the Slaves, pushes Sutta out from the ranks).

Trundle out, little one, and get a new master.

SUTTA. Oh, dear! who my Massa now?

MUG. Your own Mug.—Sutta, don't you remember your Henry Augustus?

SUTTA. Ah, massa Mug! You alive?

MUG. Alive! Why, I'm Secretary to his Mandingo Majesty. Come this way, and I'll talk to you.

(They go up the camp, and the rest of the characters disperse toward the back of the scene).

SELICO.

That was a large reward the Crier offered.

MADIBOO.

It was.

SELICO.

'Twould make my mother rich, forever.

---

177 Delicate or interesting.
178 Those are not for sale: they are reserved for the king.
179 Embezzle.

MADIBOO.

Aye, but that's hopeless.

SELICO.

No, not so.

MADIBOO.

Not so?

SELICO.

No, certainly; the merchants, you perceive,
Just offer that which would prolong existence,
A few short days—

MADIBOO.

To leave us as we were.
Come home, dear Selico—come to the woods,
And let us trust to fortune.

SELICO.

Never!

MADIBOO.

No!

SELICO.

I never will return—no, never, brother,
While I have means (and hapless as I am)
To save a parent: and the means are offered.

MADIBOO.

What are the means?

SELICO.

You heard the proclamation.
Four hundred ounces, paid at once, in gold,
Would be a treasure. Take me to the king;
Drag me before him as the criminal;
Do you receive the offered sum; depart,
Preserve my mother's life; leave me to death.

MADIBOO.

Oh, God! you drive me mad! Brother! dear brother—
Upon my knees, let me entreat you to hear me!

SELICO.

I am wild—but fixed![180]

MADIBOO.

Think only on the torture!

SELICO.

That may be calculated. She who bore me
Suffered with joy the throes that gave me being;
The pangs I shall endure, to save her life,
Will be as short and grateful.

---

180 Definitely decided.

MADIBOO.
   Don't proceed.
SELICO.
   I'll raise the camp—proclaim myself the culprit,
   If you refuse——
MADIBOO.
   Where would you hurry me!
SELICO.
   Go on my brother: I am resolute—
   Towards the king's tent.
MADIBOO.
   You will repent, dear brother.
SELICO.
   Never! Set on.
MADIBOO.
   I scarce know what I'm doing!
SELICO.
   Go forward!

(Exit Madiboo and Selico. Mug and slave merchants advance).

MUG. Now, gentlemen; we finish the market for this day.—Lord, Sutta, I am so happy to see you again.— Can't you like me as a master?
SUTTA. Very well if you black.
MUG. Oh come, I see she'll soften down in time. As a famous Squinting Patriot used to say, there is but six weeks difference in point of success, between me and the handsomest man in England.[181] Tomorrow morning, gentlemen, we begin a fresh sale.

(Chorus).

Act III

Scene 1

*The Interior of Demba Sega Jalla's tent. He is reclining in
African pomp, surrounded by numerous Attendants. Music.*

DEMBA.
   Who was the leader of the guard, last night,
   Over the females' tents?
FIRST ATTENDANT.
   'Twas Daucari.

---

181 An allusion to John Wilkes, Radical journalist and member of parliament, who advocated electoral representation and other parliamentary reforms in England in the 1770s. He was notoriously ugly and allegedly used a line like this to indicate the head start he would need over another rival in love.

DEMBA.

Where is he?

DAUCARI (*coming forward*).

Here, my king.

DEMBA.

Do you not tremble?

DAUCARI.

At your displeasure? Aye.

DEMBA.

No, for your life:

You must be certain it is now in danger.

DAUCARI.

That is the case when'er I fight for you;

But no one sees me tremble.

DEMBA.

Daucari,

You have been negligent upon your post.

DAUCARI.

You are my king—I dare not contradict you.

(*To one of the Attendants*) Come hither, you! Know you how many years

I've been in battles?

FIRST ATTENDANT.

Thirty, as I've heard.

DAUCARI.

Tell me, in all that time I once was faulty;

Say so, that I may cry 'tis false, and stab you.

(*The Attendant shakes his head, and retires*).

My king, that fellow, who ne'er flinched in war,

Dreads to accuse me, lest I kill a liar.

DEMBA.

You are too bold.

DAUCARI.

I hope not so, my king;

But innocence, though tyrants reign, is fearless.

DEMBA.

Call you me tyrant?

DAUCARI.

I'm too politic.

DEMBA.

Would you betray me?

DAUCARI.

I am much too loyal.

DEMBA.

Skilled as you are in warfare, think you not

I must be very loth[182] to sentence you
To execution?

DAUCARI.

Yes—I'm useful to you.

DEMBA.

On that account, I'll spare your life.

DAUCARI.

That's wise.

DEMBA.

And for your service past.

DAUCARI.

That's gratitude.

DEMBA.

I placed you, Daucari, to guard a female,
One of my slaves of war, whose melancholy
(Death's havoc done) looked softer than the willow
Which graces the wild margin of a lake,
And droops o'er recent wrecks. She mourned so mildly,
That when her anguish forced a tear to fall,
A patient dimple caught it. I had hope
Time would have soothed her girlish grief, and yielded
A willing treasure to me. Your neglect
Has let some lover steal to her in darkness—
She has profaned my tents—and she shall die!

DAUCARI.

You charged me, king, to head the western Guard,
And not to be a sentinel. I watched not
All night, at one tent's mouth: I did my duty—
In visiting the posts—and when, at dawn,
I saw a stranger skulking from your slave,
A cloak before his face, my order was
To fire, but he escaped. Not I—the Sentry—
Was criminal; he's punished, for I shot him.

DEMBA.

Dull fool—and so prevented all the means
Of trying the delinquent, to discover
Who 'twas that fled. But the reward that's offered,
May bring detection yet. Begone!

(Daucari exits. Enter Mug).

DEMBA.

Now, white man; how's our Prisoners' market?

MUG. Damned dull, my Liege.

---

182 Averse.

DEMBA.

    Tell me, what monies, or what merchandise,

    You have obtained among the Europeans,

    In barter for my slaves?

MUG. Bless your royal soul, not a halfpenny yet in hand. We mustn't deal with wholesale traders as if your Majesty kept a chandler's shop.[183]

DEMBA.

    How then?

MUG. Oh, let me alone: I'm up to business, by living in the City. I have your Majesty's interest at heart. You are my king; only be ruled by me, and you'll do.

DEMBA.

    Christian, your words to me are, like your features,

    So very different from other men

    That I both smile and wonder. But explain,

    What is a purchase when no value's given?

MUG. Why the European merchants are what we call good men; and they have entered your Majesty's market to buy stock, just as if they were walking into a black Royal Exchange. Some come on camels, some upon oxen; that's the way they waddled into the country. 'Tis pretty sure they'll come down with the dust[184] on settling day,[185] for without that they know your Majesty won't let 'em waddle out.

DEMBA.

    I cannot comprehend your methods.

MUG. Leave it all to me. Little more than a week will finish the job; in the meantime, may it please your Majesty, don't turn dun.[186] But as I am now joining the fatigues[187] of Chancellor of the Exchequer[188] to the labours of Secretary of War, I humbly hope you'll double my emoluments.

DEMBA. Fear not—you shall have ample honours.

MUG. I am more partial to profits; and, from all I have heard of your Majesty's unprinted court Calendar,[189] if it's the same to you, I had much rather receive a salary than be knighted.

SECOND ATTENDANT *(enters)*.

    There's one without who brings a prisoner,

    For whom he claims reward, by proclamation.

DEMBA.

    Now, by the Serpent that's my Deity,

    The wretch who glided from my captive's tent.

    Set him before me instantly!

(Exit Second Attendant).

    (To Mug) Go, white man; be faithful to your trust.

MUG. Having nothing to do in your Majesty's Old Bailey department,[190] I retire from the Levee *(exits)*.

---

183 A seller of candles.

184 Cash.

185 Day appointed for paying accounts; occurs fortnightly on the Stock Exchange.

186 Debt collector.

187 Additional duties, especially of a soldier.

188 The cabinet minister responsible for finance and the treasury.

189 List of the monarch's activities.

190 Criminal law, a reference to the famous London courtroom.

(Enter Madiboo with Selico, and Attendants).

DEMBA *(to Madiboo).*
  Now, speak.
MADIBOO *(aside).*
  I scarce am able! *(Aloud)* I have brought
  A man to die: don't let it be by torture!
  A man, who—grant me, pray, a little pause,
  For you may see I tremble.
DEMBA.
  Be not daunted. Who is he? Say.
MADIBOO *(agitated).*
  Who *is* he!—he is my—
SELICO *(interrupting him).*
  Prisoner.
  That's plain enough. Your presence, conqueror,
  Awes my accuser, though it awes not me.
DEMBA *(to Madiboo).*
  Proceed, you in your speech.
MADIBOO.
  There's a reward,
  Four hundred ounces, 'tis in gold, for him
  Who brings the culprit who—pray pardon me,
  I cannot utter.
DEMBA.
  One who fled my tents
  Under the muskets of my soldiery:
  Is that the wretch?
MADIBOO *(looks at Selico, then throws himself into his brother's arms in agony).*
  I am the greatest wretch!
DEMBA.
  How! Weeping on his prisoner's breast!
SELICO *(quickly, speaks over Madiboo's shoulder).*
  Ne'er wonder:
  He is this bosom's friend, and has betrayed me.
  (Puts Madiboo gently aside, and proceeds) Hear me avow, what he wants power to tell.
  I left the tent at dawn, escaped the shot;
  Whispered the fatal secret in his ear;
  He heard the proclamation—he is poor—
  Riches too often sap a poor man's virtue
  His need could not resist. He bound me sleeping
  And dragged me hither. Give him the reward;
  Give me my fate.
DEMBA.
  Sure as the evening sun

Closes its sloping course behind the hills
You suffer ere it sets.
SELICO.
I am prepared.
DEMBA *(to his Attendants, points to Madiboo).*
Bring him the recompense.

(Exit Attendant).

Four hundred ounces paid to you in gold.
'Tis fit that I should keep my faith with you,
Though you have broken a dear faith with him.
'Tis said I'm cruel—I may be so in war—
For warriors must be torrents; peaceful friendship
Should be so calm, that if a thought of gain
Ruffle the bosom of a friend, then gold
Should seem a pebble cast upon a pond,
Whose surface for a moment is disturbed,
The cause soon sinks, and all is still again.
MADIBOO.
Then keep your gold, and let my prisoner go.
DEMBA.
Your prisoner?—Mine. Take your reward or quit it,
Still he is mine; and jealousy's revenge
Makes iron justice harder. Vivid lightning
May strike and melt me; a false friend's compunction
Is far too weak a fire to make me bend.

(Re-enter Attendants, with the treasure).

Give him the gold—

(Madiboo receives it with horror).

Go; buy intoxication
And drown your conscience! Guard the prisoner well!
Give order in the camp for execution.
This day, the female slave and he shall die!

(Exit with his Attendants. Several remain to guard Selico).

MADIBOO.
Brother!
SELICO.
Hush—softly—these men left to guard me will overhear us.
MADIBOO.
I never shall see you, dear Selico, again!
SELICO.
No never;

But you will see my mother—think on that—
Think on the treasure in your hands—
MADIBOO.
  I loathe it.
SELICO.
  No, no; it will preserve a parent's life.
  Conceal my fate from her; tell the good soul—
  'Twill not be falsehood—tell her I have journeyed
  To a far distant country, for her good;
  And, if she ask how soon I shall return,
  Evade the question—say we *all* shall meet;
  But do not, brother, let her see you weep.
SECOND ATTENDANT *(to Madiboo)*.
  You must be gone.
MADIBOO.
  One moment. Selico,
  In infancy we often kissed each other—
  Now you must die—I would not ask it else.
  I'll print a manly farewell on your cheek *(embraces him)*.
  Oh, dear, dear Brother! Mahomet support you!

(Rushes out on one side and Selico goes off, guarded, on the other).

Scene 2

A Wood. Enter Darina and Torribal.

TORRIBAL.
  'Tis madness to persist.—Mother, turn back.
DARINA.
  I would not were a lion in my path!
TORRIBAL.
  There's peril in the camp.
DARINA.
  There's torture out on't,[191]
  While my son's there a slave: the shaft of Heaven
  Alone shall stay me—inconsiderate boys!
  Too kind to me, too cruel to yourselves—
  One of my sons to sell the other!
TORRIBAL.
  Famine
  Wrung you, dear mother; 'twas on your account we did this;
  But I beg you to return.

---

191 Outside of it (on it).

DARINA.

I will not.
If they have made my Selico a slave;
And, if the conqueror—

TORRIBAL.

He will not hear you.

DARINA.

Not hear me! The worst of Africans have hearts;
And all surely, who drained their mother's milk,
Imbibed some pity for a mother's feelings.
Oh! when I cling about the conqueror's knee,
And cry, "Restore to me my child!—a gift,
To you a trifle, but to me the world!"
If he be deaf to that, his infancy
Has spurned human breasts, to suckle with a tiger.

TORRIBAL.

I was to blame when I confided to you one word of this.

DARINA.

Confided!—That you did not—
I drew it from you. Very few conceive
A mother's quickness for her absent child.
If she inquire of one who saw him last
How 'tis he fares, a look—nay, half a look—
Alarms her, and a hesitating speech
Is almost confirmation somewhat's wrong.
Go onward, son—if you refuse to guard me,
Why be it so; I am a poor weak woman—
But still maternal love will give me strength
To crawl in the king's camp to save your brother.

TORRIBAL.

Wherever you go, I go: should you rush
Down cataracts, you'll find me by your side.
Stand back! Here's someone coming. Screen yourself
Behind the trees. Ha! Yes—'tis Madiboo.

MADIBOO (enters, carrying the gold).

Who's there?

TORRIBAL.

Friends.

MADIBOO.

Torribal! can it be you?

TORRIBAL.

Yes.

MADIBOO.

And my mother, too! How happens this?

TORRIBAL.

She will go to the camp.

MADIBOO *(shudders)*.
Oh no, no, no!
DARINA.
I will go thither.
MADIBOO *(aside)*.
What a scene of horror.
DARINA.
No power shall prevent me. What is that
You bear about you?
MADIBOO.
Gold, dear mother—gold—
Enough to give you affluence for ever.
DARINA.
Then to prolong my life a scanty term
Which nature soon must end, you sold your brother.
MADIBOO.
I wish I had!
DARINA.
You wish you had! What's done?
TORRIBAL *(takes Madiboo aside)*.
I do not understand you, Madiboo.
What has been done?
MADIBOO *(wildly)*.
Don't ask me!
TORRIBAL.
What's the sum you carry there?
MADIBOO.
Four hundred ounces in gold.
TORRIBAL.
Not for the purchase of one poor slave? Inform me.
How came you by it?
MADIBOO.
Do not question me.
If any means can keep her from the camp
Let us restrain her.
TORRIBAL.
You are agitated.
MADIBOO.
Distracted, brother! Almost heartbroken.
Another time I'll tell you all: at present
My heart's too full.—Keep her away—pray Torribal,
Keep her away! I am too weak, I cannot.
TORRIBAL.
Dear mother, let's return.
DARRINA.
I never will!

MADIBOO.

You know not what you go to see.

DARINA.

My child!

In sickness—health—in slavery—in death—

MADIBOO *(shudders)*.

Death!

DARINA.

Aye, even in the agonies of death,

A mother clings around her child.

MADIBOO *(aside)*.

Oh, God![192] so she *will* cling round him.

DARINA.

Forward, sons!—I am resolved.

(She runs out and Madiboo and Torribal follow).

Scene 3

The Camp of the Mandingo King in which are seen preparations for an execution.
Selico is discovered, guarded by the Executioners. A crowd is collected to watch the ceremony.

SELICO.

Nay, do not torture me before my time.

Your king is not arrived, who is to witness

My parting agonies: then stand aloof

Ye lowest ministers who execute

The sentences of power! How need must warp

Poor human nature when a man turns jailer.

Nor no one, sure, first made it his election,

To live upon his fellow creature's sorrows.

And oh! how flinty must his office make him,

If, when his petty sway might mitigate

The prisoner's woe, he doubles it with vigour—

Is that the stake where I must suffer?

SECOND EXECUTIONER.

Yes.

Yonder the partner of your crime will die.

SELICO.

Poor soul!—poor wretch!—Death in a conqueror's camp,

Is swift in visitation; gives no time,

As oft he will round pallets of the sick,

For leave-takings, and kindly offices;—

---

192 Probably amended in performance to "Oh, heavens!" as in the published script.

Else would I strive to calm her fluttered spirit,
(Whoe'er she be) support the sinking trembler,
And cheer her with a fellow-sufferer's firmness.
SECOND EXECUTIONER *(comes forward)*.
Prisoner, our faiths are different—few Mandingoes
Profess your creed, and follow Mahomet.
You think me cruel from my trade; but you wrong me.
If, in the camp, there's a Mahometan
You wish to pray by you, I'll find and bring him hither.
SELICO.[193]
Thank you, heartily.
There's no religion, as I think, on earth
In which weak man can not exclaim, "The worship
I was born to, others may reject."
But, while I glow with charity for all,
My heart, I trust, pours a prayer
May, at the last, procure my Maker's mercy.
EXECUTIONER.
Say, can I serve you?
SELICO.
No, good fellow, no!
But I am grateful: step aside, and let me
Pray for myself.

(The Executioner retreats some paces, and Selico kneels).

Dear spirit of my murdered love—if ever
It be allowed mortality to soar
Into the breast of Heaven, and look down
On what is left below, behold me meet
Death's agony in smiles. We soon may wander
In airy blessedness—no battle-axe
Can sunder love in those pure realms of bliss;
No ravagers of war can butcher age,
And pinch with famine. Prophet Mahomet!
Now, waft the words I am about to utter,
To try dread Master's throne!—Bless, bless my mother!
Scorn not my prayer though coming from the mouth
Of a poor African!—Oh! bless her! Bless her! *(Rises)*.

(A flourish)

SECOND EXECUTIONER.
Hark! The king approaches!

(Enter Demba Sega Jalla, and Attendant. He places himself on an elevated seat to witness the execution).

---

193 This speech is excised in pencil from the manuscript.

DEMBA.

Criminal—some have murmured 'tis my nature
To be too lavish in decrees of death;
They say I wanton[194] in the shedding blood:
Therefore, I come, that you, yourself, may own
Your sentence just.

SELICO.

More just than merciful.

DEMBA.

Can justice, then, be called unmerciful?

SELICO.

Justice and Mercy are distinct; when joined,
'Tis sweet to see the mild companion smooth
Its stern associate's brow!—and when the sword
Is lifted, smilingly present the sheath.
Atrocious guilt can hope for no indulgence!
But there are cases, where the judge's eye
May drop a tear on him whom he condemns;
And, therefore, when a king has power to sentence,
He might remember he has power to pardon.

DEMBA.

You stole into my camp; the laws of war
Pronounce it death.

SELICO.

Aye, if I came a spy—
But, you have sentenced me on other grounds.
I skulked not hither, o'er my native plain,
That smokes with fire, and blood, to carry back
A vain intelligence to carcasses.
You dread no spy from towns you have subdued,
For there your plan is to exterminate.
Your mode of warfare murders even infants
At shuddering women's breasts, and silences
All fears of a reprise, by butchery.

DEMBA.

Bold wretch! You were received within the tent
Of her who heard my love, and then disdained it,
My favourite slave of war: my guard beheld you.

SELICO.

He who's above all guards, beheld you tear
All of your slaves of war from every tie
Humanity holds dear, and still has spared you.

DEMBA.

Mine is the right of conquest.

---

194 Frolic.

SELICO.

    Conquest's right

    Gives a true hero the delightful power

    Of shewing conquest's generosity.

    And what's your right? A battle gives it you.

    What are the ties of those you pluck asunder?

    Why, time and sympathy have knotted them:

    And should you die, instead of those you separate,

    It might be better justice.

DEMBA.

    Witness, soldiers,

    Your king's forbearance—witness how I hear

    These taunts with patience.

SELICO.

    Oh, mild murderer!

    Every ally[195] you plunder, owns your meekness.

    Specious destroyer! Amiable despot!

    Domestic creature of the tiger breed,

    Who purr upon your prey before you kill it!

DEMBA *(to the attendants)*.

    Prepare for execution. *(To Selico)* You have violated

    The laws of warrior's camp, and you must suffer.

    Bring in the female criminal.

FIRST ATTENDANT.

    She's here.

(Enter Berissa, a woman on each side supports her. A veil is over her face. She appears trembling. Guards follow her. Selico's face is averted, contemplating the pile whereon he is to suffer).

DEMBA.

    Throw off the captive's veil.—She knows her fate.

BERISSA *(removes the veil)*.

    I do—and though I tremble, am resigned.

SELICO *(starts)*.

    Did I hear right? Her voice! It cannot be! *(Turning suddenly round)*

    Berissa!

(Berissa utters a piercing shriek).

    Still alive!—My love! my love!

(He rushes to her and they fall into each other's arms).

DEMBA *(to his Guards)*.

    Force them apart. Woman! One cutting outrage

    Man's pride endures is when his love is scorned,

    By her he's knelt to, whom he might command—

---

195 Kinsman, friend, or supporter.

And insults him to his face, by lavishing
Her fondness on his rival. 'Tis refinement
Of female insult thus to gall my heart—
I can retaliate by the body's torture.

BERISSA.

Hear me!—And I attest my holy prophet;
While bending o'er the awful brink of death
I swear *(and would in my last lingering pang)*—
Though one was in my tent, that was not he *(pointing to Selico)*.

SELICO *(apart)*.

That's truly sworn—but proves her false as wantons.[196]
Oh mother, mother! 'tis for you alone
I now should wish to die!

DEMBA.

I am not fooled
By female oaths. Did he not, e'en this instant,
Rush to your arms while fervently you clasped him?
Nay, has he not himself made full confession?
Captive, you who disdained your conqueror's love,
You, whom I sued to share dominion with me,
What motive, now, in daring to deny
The guilt of your accomplice? Then think you,
To save him? If he be not culpable
Then name the criminal.

SELICO.

Aye. Name him, name him—

BERISSA.

Mark, King!—this man's impetuosity
To hear the culprit named may speak him guiltless.

DEMBA.

That's doubtful: you can clear the mystery.

BERISSA. .

Had I a thousand lives, and every life
Condemned to twenty thousand agonies,
I would never divulge the secret. Conqueror, remember,
I ought not, and will not: but,
When you approached me with your selfish passion
(Selfish I call it, for you urged a mourner),
I then avowed my heart no longer mine.
I dared not utter falsehood: think you, now,
I dare advance it, dying?—I repeat it,
Innocent blood will lie upon your soul,
If he be sacrificed!

---

196 Unchaste women.

DEMBA.

Truth seems to gush
As purely from those lips as bubbling streams,
Forced from the fairest fountain. No, no, no—
Yon slave himself avowed it. Set each pile
On fire, and lead the culprits to their fate!

(The Executioners carry torches to the piles of wood).

SELICO.

King: if one corner in thy human heart
E'er held a drop of pity for the dying,
Grant me one word with my poor fellow sufferer.

DEMBA.

You scarce deserve it: let them speak together.

(Selico and Berissa come forward).

SELICO.

Berissa! how I loved you know. How you
Have loved, I doubt.

BERISSA.

That doubt, dear Selico,
Is worse than any agonies of death.

SELICO.

Is it indeed?

BERISSA.

Indeed!—Oh! if there be a secret
I dare not tell, e'en you, at such a moment,
From the whole course of our pure simple love,
Why should you think me faithless? But inform me,
How came you hither?

SELICO.

We have not, now, the time.

BERISSA.

Say, then, you think me true—for I can swear—

SELICO.

No; do not, love—your words are holy writ—
They're balm to me! Forgive my suspicions:
Your affirmation's everything. Oh, love!
This scene—

(Drum rolls).

We part. Farewell!

BOTH.

Farewell! Farewell!

(They proceed to the stakes where they are to suffer; at this moment a noise is heard in the camp. Farulho rushes in speaking as he enters).

FARULHO.

I will press forward, ere it be too late. *(Prostrates himself before the king)*
King! King! In me behold the real culprit,
A poor old man, who strove to steal his daughter.

DEMBA.

Your daughter!

FARULHO.

Yes; that wretched girl is mine.
'Twas I that sought her tent; 'twas I escaped
The muskets of her guard; she tried, in vain,
To follow her old father. Take your victim:
Save him, who is not guilty, and let *me*
Perish with *her* (if she must die) for whom
I only I wish to live—my darling child!

DEMBA *(to the guards)*.

Release them for a while.

BERISSA.

But for a while!
Then let me snatch this moment to embrace
My dear, dear father.

FARULHO *(embracing her)*.

Oh, my child! my child!

DEMBA *(to Selico)*.

Say, why did you avow yourself the culprit?

SELICO.

Conqueror, to you, who make men's dwellings ashes,
Domestic tales of woe, that follow triumphs
Will not be pleasing.

DEMBA.

Speak.—I need not say
Speak boldly; you have spoken so already.

SELICO.

The dying, wrung with griefs, will use some licence
Towards those that wrung them.

DEMBA.

You had an accuser,
Who brought you to my camp.

SELICO.

He was my brother.

DEMBA.

Your brother!

SELICO.

    Yes—oh, King! you little think
    On all that war, in its extremity,
    Inflicts on nature. You approached with fire,
    When peaceful joy was throbbing in our breasts—
    When I was leading my loved bride to mosque—
    She's there; the daughter of this good old man,
    Our priest, revered by all. I thought them dead,
    For in my search I found two headless bodies
    Clad in their outward habits.

FARULHO.

    Did you so?
    Alas! then, two poor faithful souls have perished,
    In zeal, for me and mine. My honest servant
    Cried to me, "Fly! dear Master, fly! Give me
    Your garments—I am youngest; and your daughter
    Shall change her dress with mine; if they dare
    Invade this sacred place, I'll pass myself
    Upon them for the priest; then, should they battle
    I am more stout than you; my girl less timid
    Than your dear tender child." And so we fled—
    But still I lost Berissa in the tumult;
    Then traced her to the camp; and my poor servants
    Have fallen victims of their love to us.

DEMBA.

    I know not what there is about my heart
    That stirs me thus. In all my victories
    No tale of sorrow I ever heard
    Touched me so near as this. Say prisoner—
    Tell me, when you conceived these people dead
    Why were you rendered as a criminal
    And by your brother too?

SELICO.

    To save a mother
    From perishing with hunger, whom your war
    Had driven to the woods. The sum you offered
    I knew would snatch her from the pangs of famine
    To affluence, and I enforced my brother
    To drag me hither as the sacrifice.

DEMBA.

    And knew she of it?

SELICO.

    No.

DEMBA.

    Her name?

SELICO.

Darina.

DARINA *(without)*.

Guards, give me way—and let me to your king.

SELICO.

Ha! 'tis my mother's voice! They've told her all.

DARINA *(rushes in, throws herself at the king's feet)*.

Pity a mother, king, and spare my son.

TORRIBAL.

Mother be calm; 'tis not the way to soothe.

MADIBOO.

Let her alone; a mother's cries will penetrate

Into a heart of flint—let her alone.

DEMBA.

Rise, your suspense shall soon be over.

Is there a European merchant in our lines?

ATTENDANT.

Here happens to be one.

DEMBA.

Let him advance.

(Merchant comes forward).

DEMBA.

Merchant, have you attended to this process?

MERCHANT.

I have.

DEMBA.

Then prithee tell me, you

Of wisdom and experience—you, who boast

A country, as they say, more civilized

By far, than mine—at how much would you rate

A man like this? *(Points to Selico)*.

MERCHANT.

For his uncommon virtues,

At full a thousand crowns.

DEMBA.

I'll double that,

And give it to this woman *(pointing to Berissa)*. You shall have them—

And not to purchase but to marry him.

(Selico and Berissa fall at Demba's feet).

Nay rise; my heart was never moved till now.

MADIBOO.

My dear mother!—my dear brother!—my good priest! Oh, Mahomet

I'm so happy—I shall jump out of my skin.

MUG *(enters, with a long written paper under one arm and Sutta under the other).* May it please Your Majesty, I have drawn up a petition, which, as you never learned your A.B.C. according to our English fashion, I make bold to read to you.

SUTTA. Ah, Massa Mug! You read so pretty! Oh me wish you look so! For you kind good man for all you face.

DEMBA.

What is it white man?

MUG. Why, I have just heard of some poor condemned folks who were formerly my friends; and, as they have not murdered, nor forged, nor robbed, on your Majesty's highway, it's very hard if a Secretary of State hasn't interest to bring them off. *(Looks round)* Eh!—oh lord! I see by your countenances 'tis settled already. *(To Farulho)* Oh, my dear old master! Lord, Mr. Madiboo how are you, and all the rest of your family, after your confounded fright?

SELICO.

Come, love! My dear Berissa come! My mother

And my father who is soon to be!

Alas we have been sorely wrung.

BERISSA.

But we can say

Whatever we've endured, 'twas virtue's trial.

SELICO.

And, oh! how sweet when after virtue's struggles

We lay our hands upon our heart, and cry

We suffered Heaven's scourge with resignation,

And resignation is repaid with bliss.

CHORUS *(sings).*

The contest's over; war's alarms

Now leave our native plains—

Then welcome Friendship's charms

For smiling peace remains.

SUTTA *(sings).*

Thus after cold and wintry showers,

The West Wind breathes, and sunshine's ours

Sweet Spring each heart of care beguiling

Sweet Spring returns, all is smiling.

Sweet Peace.

CHORUS *(sings).*

The contest's over; war's alarms

Now leave our native plains—

Then welcome Friendship's charms

For smiling peace remains.

Elphi Bey; or, the Arab's Faith (1817)

Interpretive Issues

Britons were fascinated with the eastern Mediterranean and Middle East in the early part of the nineteenth century. Poets, painters, and playwrights joined travel writers, designers, and exhibitors in the attempt to satisfy appetites for reading and entertainments about the region. Sparked by the English defeat of Napoleon's navy in the Battle of the Nile (1798) and the subsequent removal of antiquities to London, a wave of Egypt mania struck Britain. Kept alive by works as famous as Lord Byron's *Eastern Tales* and as ephemeral as the production of Ralph Hamilton's play *Elphi Bey; or, the Arab's Faith* at Drury Lane Theatre, the romance and exoticism of the East went unabated.[1] Not just an antiquarian or folkloric concern accounts for this. Unfolding struggles between European empires and the Turks ensured the contemporary relevance of the region to British fortunes and kept it in the forefront of public concern.[2]

Egypt was part of the Ottoman Empire from 1520, when Suleiman the Magnificent conquered it for the fearsome Turks. The sultan appointed a governor (*pasha*), but Mamelukes ruled regionally on behalf of the pasha. Originally descended in the ninth century from Kurd and Mongol slave-boys, Mamelukes were brought up as soldiers to defend the empire. From the early seventeenth century, Egypt was divided into twelve semiautonomous provinces, each treated by its Mameluke leader (*bey*) as a personal fiefdom. Beys did not practise hereditary rule and rarely held power for more than a few years before being overthrown by stronger rivals. Constant power struggles among the beys also led to a rapid turnover among pashas though Ottoman sovereignty was not directly challenged and Egypt had no independence movement in the modern sense. During the later eighteenth century, the waning Ottoman supremacy was challenged by Russia, with England and France both jockeying for the spoils. Egypt, a strategic route for Europeans trading with Asia, was looked upon as a prize to be taken from the Ottomans. Egypt south of Aswan was ruled by autonomous tribes, which meant that if only the lower (northern) Nile could be taken from the Turks, a route to the Red Sea could be controlled. Napoleon, thinking that England would not risk defence of the homeland in order to stop a French invasion of Egypt, landed his army in Cairo in 1798 and defeated the Mamelukes in the Battle of the Pyramids. He set up an occupying government in Cairo but was unsuccessful in conciliating the beys. The French appointed Christian Copts and Greeks as tax collectors and officials and trained Christians for the army; Egyptians resented them all as intruders.

Britain, correctly perceiving Napoleon's advance on Egypt as a threat to British interests in India, allied with the Russians and Turks against France. Following the decisive result in the Battle of the Nile—one of the greatest naval triumphs in British history—the French abandoned Egypt. Under the Treaty of Amiens (1802), Egypt was returned to the Ottomans, and the British left shortly afterward. In the coming decades,

---

1   After joining Drury Lane's managerial subcommittee in April 1816, Byron actively recruited poets to submit good scripts. Charles Robert Maturin and Samuel Taylor Coleridge are the two most notable compliers. It is tempting to think that he also approached Hamilton—or, at any rate, inspired him—to write this play. Hamilton and Byron both admired the satiric writer William Gifford, to the extent that Byron's *English Bards and Scotch Reviewers* (1809) singles him out for praise, and Hamilton's *Elphi Bey* (1817) is dedicated to him. Byron certainly knew of Elphi Bey: he owned a valuable gold-inlaid dagger that had belonged to Elphi (a gift from Sir Walter Scott). Byron had been a schoolboy when Elphi visited England, but the event may have made a deep impression. See George Gordon Byron, app. 5 in *The Works of Lord Byron*, vol. 3, *Letters and Journals* (London: John Murray, 1904), 413.

2   Timothy Jenks, *Naval Engagements: Patriotism, Cultural Politics, and the Royal Navy, 1793-1815* (Oxford: Oxford UP, 2006).

Britain signed a succession of treaties with rulers along the Arabian Gulf to try to ensure safe passage of British ships to Asia. Viscount Valentia's expeditions to Ceylon (now Sri Lanka), the Red Sea, Abyssinia, and Egypt in 1802-6 gathered the navigational, geographic, and ethnographic data that shaped this foreign policy.[3] The events of 1798-1802, and Elphi Bey's journey to Britain in 1803-4, awakened Britons to the strategic importance of the region. A specific episode in Valentia's accounts of his journeys inspired Ralph Hamilton to write this play.[4]

Mohamed Bey Elphi Morat (Elphi Bey), a Mameluke chieftain who evacuated with the British, arrived in London in October 1803, hoping to make the British fulfil promises made to the beys during the war against Napoleon.[5] Elphi's retinue made a stirring sight: his attendants' liveries were constructed "of superfine scarlet cloth" trimmed with green velvet, gold epaulets and buttons, complemented with "red waistcoat and breeches, worked with gold, cocked hats, gold loop and button, and tall green feathers."[6] Newspaper accounts whetted British appetites for adventure and fuelled orientalist fantasies of exotic masculinity and militant primitivism. Elphi, it was reported, was born in Georgia (east of Turkey), sold in childhood to a powerful bey, and quickly rose to a position of wealth and despotic influence. His feats were the stuff of melodrama; for example, "he has repeatedly cut off the head of a buffalo, at full gallop, with one stroke of his sabre." Not too shabby, especially for a man as corpulent as he. During the French occupation, Elphi "baffled 5 divisions of Bonaparte's army, who were in constant pursuit of him," and at El Hoche, in November 1802, he commanded an army of 1,100 Mamelukes and Bedouins who killed 3,000 Turks but lost only six of their own men.[7] Entertained in grandeur, Elphi was shown many favours. In turn, he impressed his hosts with demonstrations of his retinue's martial abilities. Before the Prince of Wales, a Mameluke groom saddled an unbroken and unruly stallion, and Elphi's principal officer, Mohamet Aga,

> made a spring, seized him by the reins, and in an instant was mounted. The animal, finding himself thus encumbered, and feeling the peculiar tightness of the Mameluke's saddle, plunged in every

3   S.F. Mahmud, *A Short History of Islam* (Karachi: Oxford UP, 1998), 237, 268-69; and Peter Mansfield, *A History of the Middle East* (London: Penguin, 1991).

4   "OSMAN BEY, greatly alarmed at the arrival from England of Elphi Bey,—who, since the death of Murad Bey, had been his rival,—determined to cut him off, and for that purpose sent down two boats with troops, to intercept him.... The boats, with the troops of Osman Bey, passed without seeing him; but he perceived them, and, having some suspicion, immediately landed, and, quitting his baggage, with five or six followers, escaped into the Desert.... At length, after a tedious march of ten hours on foot, he arrived at the tent of Nasr Chedid ... with whom he was on ill terms, and claimed protection. Nasr was himself absent with Osman Bey, whom he had joined with all his people, at his camp, before Cairo, where he waited the event of the attack on Elphi. Chedid's wife received and concealed him ... bringing him one of her husband's favourite horses, and a dromedary, she desired him to escape to Upper Egypt; but to avoid the road which she had directed the troops of Osman to take. Elphi hesitated, and told her he was unwilling to endanger her husband's safety who was in the power of Osman.—She replied, it was no matter; her husband's honour required that she should assist him in escaping; and that, were he there, he would do the same himself, and that he would make her suffer if anything happened to him. Soon afterwards, on being told the way that Elphi had escaped, Osman sent for Chedid, and accused him of having assisted his enemy. He replied, 'You know, Osman Bey, I have been three days with you; how then is it possible that I could do so?' 'Well then,' said Osman; 'it was your wife that did so.' 'It was,' replied Chedid; 'Elphi demanded protection from her, and she only did her duty. Had she done otherwise, I would have cut her head off with this sabre, though you know Elphi was never a friend of mine.'" George Annesley Mountnorris, Viscount Valentia, *Voyages and Travels to Ceylon, the Red Sea, Abyssinia, and Egypt, in the Years 1802, 1803, 1804, 1805, and 1806*, vol. 3 (London: W. Miller, 1809), 348-49.

5   *Cobbett's Annual Register*, 15 October 1803: 503.

6   *Ipswich Journal*, 22 October 1803.

7   Ibid.

direction, but in vain, as the Mameluke firmly kept his seat, where he continued upwards of twenty minutes, to the astonishment of his Royal Highness and every other beholder.[8]

Astley's circus could not have done it more grandly.

When the French left Egypt, the beys emerged from hiding. They attempted to reclaim power but were resisted by the sultan. During a brief period from 1803 until 1805, in the absence of both French occupiers and British ousters, chaotic civil war broke out: neither beys nor Turks could prevail. The beys split into two factions, and Ottoman troops (composed of Albanians and Bosnians) rebelled against the Turkish governor in Cairo while also battling each other. The beys, in control of the upper Nile, seized and sunk all shipments of grain in order to starve Cairo into obedience. Murad Bey died, and in Elphi's absence Osman claimed succession. This is the background to Hamilton's plot.

The play begins early in 1804 when Elphi Bey returned from his English sojourn, conveyed home by the Royal Navy ship *Argo*.[9] Expecting British support,[10] Elphi set out to seize power from Osman, but upon landing, Osman intercepted the riches brought from England, including a diamond-encrusted portrait of King George III. Elphi eluded capture, and a week later landed at the home of the Arab sheik Sedud (renamed Chedid in the play) where the chief's wife was obliged by customs of hospitality to give him protection and provide a dromedary for his escape.[11] Other historical incidents frame the play's action:

> On the first of April, 1804, the Arab Sheik Sedud was encamped about a mile outside of Cairo, on the desert of Suez, a heavy cannonading was heard about Gizah. Soon after a letter was sent in a most private manner to the Arab Sheik, from Osman and Elphy [*sic*] Bey, advising that they had found it prudent to make peace with each other, and that now they were again united with all their Mamelukes against the Turkish government in possession of Cairo; Elphy Bey invited Sheik Sedud with all his Bedouins to join their camp near Gizah, and which the Arab promised to do after he had fulfilled his engagements in escorting a caravan towards Suez.[12]

Rather than wrapping up the plot with the succession of the conflict's ultimate victor, Muhammad Ali (appointed Governor by the Turks in 1805), Hamilton concludes without a resolution to the fighting: familial units are restored, yet the complexities that prevented the beys from uniting to overthrow their foreign ruler are also emphasized. To the extent that Egypt was unstable and France was the agent of instability, Britain represented the way to a dynamic political equilibrium. Yet the British are absent from the play, except as its actors and audience. In historical terms, the play's final chorus is both wrong and ironic: neither were the Turks expelled nor was Elphi the agent of peace. Following half a dozen more years of conflict with the beys, Muhammad Ali had most of them summarily massacred.[13] Instead of aggrandizing British deeds, therefore, the play dramatizes the need for British imperialism, represented in a romanticized figure who had briefly attained *cachet* with the British public.[14]

---

8   *Jackson's Oxford Journal*, 12 November 1803.

9   Zeinaba stipulates in act 1, scene 4 that she has been separated from Elphi for six years; there is no historical justification for this.

10   Valentia, *Voyages and Travels*, vol. 3, 474.

11   Despatches emphasize the Arab code of hospitality, no matter what the previous enmity between families, as asserted in the play. Lawrence Dundas Campbell, *The Asiatic Annual Register; or, View of the History of Hindustan, and of the Politics, Commerce, and Literature of Asia, for the Year 1804* (London: T. Cadell, 1806), 138.

12   Ibid., 139.

13   Mansfield, *History of the Middle East*; and *Jackson's Oxford Journal*, 26 May, 9 June, and 23 June 1804.

14   The *St. James's Chronicle* remarks, fourteen years after his visit, "Our readers will recollect Elphi Bey's embassy here," 19 April 1817: 4.

Muhammad Ali is absent from Hamilton's play in favour of a more schematic depiction of Turkish despotism (in the character of Osmyn) and Arab tribalism (in Othman and Chedid). In this sense, *Elphi Bey* fulfils Paula Backscheider's criteria for "spectacular politics": "a mechanism for the negotiation of a system of knowing and believing" which could "appeal to emotion through unmediated sensation" by bringing many highly mediated arts together.[15] Ideology is not explicitly uttered so much as it is indirectly portrayed through theatrical conventions. Europeans are absent from the *dramatis personae*, yet there are opportunities for spectators to assess what is foreign (Muslim, Arab, or Turkish) and what is familiar (Christian or Western European). As L. Marshall argues about British Ottoman plays of the previous century, "Briton and Turk are placed in a comfortable opposition: one governed by political and personal freedom, the other constrained by political and social tyranny."[16] *Elphi Bey* depicts a sector of the Ottoman Empire, and though the concept of empire is not criticized, the practice of tyranny is implicitly compared to parliamentary monarchy. The formula was so familiar in orientalist plays that "the imagined identity of Britain as the land of liberty" was implicit in the depiction of exoticism.[17] This is complicated by two broadly contrasted types of Muslims. Turks and their collaborators are shallow, avaricious, and opportunistic, motivated not by family or nation but self-interest, comfort, laziness, or personal gain. Arabs, at least in *Elphi Bey*, operate under a code of honour—convoluted and even extreme by British standards, yet founded on recognizable principles of sanctuary and femininized hospitality rather than masculinized revenge—justifying English allegiance with the Mamelukes who form the moral compass. It matters, therefore, that Valentia describes the Egyptian Mamelukes as "fairer than any Europeans."[18] Turks, by contrast, were Asiatic, darker in skin and shadier in values.

At the outset, Zeinaba awaits Elphi's return, but unlike Penelope in the *Odyssey*, who sits at home and spins, she cross-dresses in order to intercept her husband, deliver a fateful message, and save his life. Cross-dressing is a staple device in comedy, allowing women otherwise impossible freedom, but this is an *historical* drama whose comic scenes do not involve Zeinaba. Cross-dressing enables Zeinaba to act out of duty and self-sacrifice, in contrast to the comic ingénue who is typically motivated by romantic intrigue. (The youth, Ageeb, was also played by a cross-dressed woman, but this arose from a casting convention rather than as a plot device.) Disguised as Abdallah (a young soldier), Zeinaba counsels Elphi to take revenge on the Turks as the greater oppressor rather than fight against the other beys. Middle Eastern female characters were usually sensualized, but both principals avoid this in *Elphi Bey*.[19] Emina, who retains her female mien yet exemplifies the Arab code of honour when her menfolk would have faltered, also exhibits courage in sheltering Elphi. She counters the English preconception that Muslim blood feuds require proportionate retaliation.[20] Emina's compassion is repaid when Elphi supplies the money to ransom her son. These plot twists make ethnographic statements while illuminating the role of gender, further likening the Arabs to British ideals: the dutiful yet competent wives who take initiative and aid in their families' security are an early-nineteenth-century version of appropriate womanhood (not yet domesticated to the Victorian angel in the house). If the goal of ethnography (an aspect of Valentia's study) is to learn something about other

---

15   Paula Backscheider, *Spectacular Politics: Theatrical Power and Mass Culture in Early Modern England* (Baltimore: Johns Hopkins UP, 1993), 229.

16   L. Marshall, *National Myth and Imperial Fantasy: Representations of British Identity on the Early Eighteenth-Century Stage* (Basingstoke: Palgrave, 2008), 158.

17   Ibid., 149.

18   Valentia, *Voyages and Travels*, vol. 3, 382.

19   Arguably, Zeinaba's costume undermined this, yet there is nothing in the dialogue or action conducive to eroticized by-play or objectification.

20   Shahin Kuli Khan Khattak, *Islam and the Victorians: Nineteenth Century Perceptions of Muslim Practices and Beliefs* (London: Tauris, 2008), 117-20.

people, depicting the dialectical forces of Egyptian life under the pashas reveals not just an ideology of the East but also its similarity or differentiation from the West in public and private milieux.[21]

Elphi Bey relies upon spectators' awareness of Britain's global connectedness: the navy at Portsmouth and the merchant ships at the port of London needed access to Asia. Though the Cape route could be sailed, moving goods and people overland at Suez—from the Mediterranean to the Red Sea—shortened journeys significantly. The best-remembered event of the recent war with France is Wellington's victory at Waterloo; however, Nelson's triumphs at Trafalgar and Aboukir (the Battle of the Nile) were equally potent in the early-nineteenth-century imaginary, signalling precisely the significance of the route into the Mediterranean, onward to the Red Sea, and thence to India.[22] There is little question, therefore, that Egypt's role in *several* empires was well understood; hence Hamilton's ability to give the merest sketch of politics, emphasizing Eurasian concerns and the widespread practices of empire rather than an explicit and prescribed version of British interests.

Genre Issues

Little is known of Sir Ralph S. Hamilton's career. A colonel in the army and native of Belfast, he was one of the legion of accomplished, yet not brilliant, playwrights who received productions but not celebrity. All three of his plays are preoccupied with political intrigue. *Elphi Bey* was the first of two produced at Drury Lane; the second was *David Rizzio* (1820), about the Italian courtier who ingratiated himself with Mary Queen of Scots and was murdered by agents of Queen Elizabeth. Hamilton's last play, *Almourah, the Corsair* (1821), set on the Barbary coast,[23] is a gothic melodrama laden with exotic locales, dungeons, pirates, a moody forest, zesty sexual threats, and a pitched battle that harmoniously reconstitutes marital and filial pairings.[24] *Elphi Bey* is also melodramatic in structure and incident, featuring the same devices of opposed indigenous tribes, capture, and despotic rule recognizable from *The Africans*. The Arab custom that requires Emina to harbour Elphi when he seeks sanctuary in her tent—giving rise to the play's subtitle—is also a pretext for an 1802 play, *The Bedouins; or, Arabs of the Desert*, though in that case it is Englishmen who seek protection.[25]

Travel literature about the East first appeared in English in 1632. A wave of dramatizations began shortly thereafter and did not abate in four centuries.[26] In many plays, the Islamic Orient is a pretext for voyeurism. *Elphi Bey* retains a trace of this, indulging in scenes of women's work in act 1, scenes 1 and 3,

---

21   See Mita Choudhury, *Interculturalism and Resistance in the London Theatre, 1660-1800* (Lewisburg, PA: Bucknell UP, 2000), 112-13.

22   Timothy Jenks, *Naval Engagements: Patriotism, Cultural Politics, and the Royal Navy, 1793-1815* (Oxford: Oxford UP, 2006), 148-57.

23   The northwest coast of Africa (modern Morocco, Tunisia, Libya, and Algeria).

24   R.S. Hamilton, *Almourah, the Corsair; or, a Brother's Vengeance: A Drama, in Five Acts* (Belfast: Joseph Smyth, 1821).

25   Wallace Cable Brown, "The Near East in English Drama, 1775-1825," *The Journal of English and Germanic Philology* 46:1 (1947): 67.

26   William Lithgow, *The Totall Discourse of the Rare Adventures and Painefull Peregrinations of Long Nineteene Yeares Travayles from Scotland to the Most Famous Kingdomes in Europe, Asia and Affrica* (1632; reprinted by Glasgow: James Maclehose, 1906). See also Matthew Birchwood, *Staging Islam in England: Drama and Culture, 1640-1683* (Cambridge: D.S. Brewer, 2007); and Brown, "Near East," 63-69. For indicative repertoire immediately antecedent to *Elphi Bey*, see James Miller and John Hoadley (adapted from Voltaire), *Mahomet the Imposter* (1744); Isaac Bickerstaffe, *The Sultan* (1775); George Colman the Younger, *Turk and No Turk* (1785); Hannah Cowley, *A Day in Turkey* (1791); Thomas Dibdin, *Mouth of the Nile* (1798); Elizabeth Inchbald, *The Mogul's Tale* (1784), *Such Things Are* (1787), and *Wise Man of the East* (1799); Andrew Franklin, *Egyptian Festival* (1800); and Isaac Pocock, *Zembuca; or, the Netmaker and his Wife* (1815). For later musical repertoire, see Claire Mabilat, *Orientalism and Representations of Music in the Nineteenth-Century British Popular Arts* (Aldershot: Ashgate, 2008), 25-81; and Khattak, *Islam and the Victorians*, 76-86.

though not as a harem of odalisques facilitating overtones of sexual excess or exploitation.[27] Orientalist plays appear in every genre: farce, comedy, drama, tragedy, opera, and countless permutations of these conventions. Given the abundance of generic options and strong traditions of depicting ideas about the Middle East, what is accomplished by understanding the play in generic terms? The classification matters most when considering how audiences were conditioned to respond to particular elements. *Elphi Bey*, like all of Hamilton's plays, is a musical drama "mixed up, according to the modern fashion, of dialogue and music,"[28] yet like many melodramas it loosely employs recent history or social dilemmas, uses a comic servant to establish exposition, and is built up with successive "sensations" of stirring emotional impact.

British dramatists were never constrained by neoclassical dramatic theory in tragedy, yet British tragedy invariably addressed more distant times and often foreign cultures. Melodrama took even greater liberties with the treatment of time, place, and action—provided that plot extravagances could be accommodated by scene painters and musical arrangers—but did not shirk from the contemporary or the local. *Elphi Bey* gestures towards tragedy's concern with affairs of state while it exemplifies how melodrama—in the tragic cadence of iambic pentameter—utilized emotional extremes rather than universal truths. It demanded much of actors' range without giving them the lines or character development to credibly meet the requirements of depicting sensation after arresting sensation within the onslaught of what Matthew Buckley calls "prolonged trauma's successive series of conflicts, shocks, and surprises."[29] The new genre of melodrama, incubated in Paris and London to avoid constraints on trade in commercial theatres, developed a "contained trajectory of crises" into "a dynamic pattern, infinitely extendable, capable of much greater compression and dilation, adaptable to more diverse narratives and contexts, and organized ... as an oscillating movement between absorptive, introverted moments of sympathetic identification and highly spectacular, extroverted scenes of shocking violence."[30] It coalesced around 1800 though elements are recognizable much earlier.

Elphi Bey has a plethora of incidents. From act 1, scene 4, it is compelled forward by a series of escapes that reveal or forge relationships between characters: Hyder's disguise enables Elphi to evade Abu Buk'r, Elphi then facilitates Ageeb's escape from robbers, and Ageeb pleads with his mother to help Elphi keep away from Osmyn's troops. Scenically, this allows for an array of iconic antiquities as well as desert, tent, and riverside settings that reflect Henry Salt's illustrations for Valentia's volumes.[31] The opening of act 3, scene 2 (included in the licensed manuscript but not the published version) provides a contrast in pace, for Emina converses with a pilgrim who crosses the desert on foot rather than at the breakneck speed of horse or dromedary. He sings of the calming effect of music, whereupon Emina comments:

EMINA.
　　Melodious strain! well suited to the scene.
　　Now sunk behind the hills, the scorching sun
　　Gives a short respite to the wearied world.
　　How still the air! How bright across the waste
　　The evening star shoots its silvery light.

27　Mabilat notes the dichotomy that marks "the 'Oriental' female" either as a "proudly predatory, sexual being or conversely as duty-bound, languishing, object of voyeuristic sexual fantasy." Mabilat, *Orientalism and Representations*, 16.

28　"The Drama. Drury Lane Theatre," *St. James's Chronicle*, 19 April 1817: 4.

29　Matthew S. Buckley, "Refugee Theatre: Melodrama and Modernity's Loss," *Theatre Journal* 61:2 (2009): 181.

30　Ibid., 182.

31　Slightly earlier sources were better known through theatrical adaption: *Voyages dans la Basse et la Haute Egypte* (1802) and *Description de l'Egypte* (1809-18). Edward Ziter, *The Orient on the Victorian Stage* (Cambridge: Cambridge UP, 2003), 31.

Illustration 3. *The Shrine at Timai* by Henry Salt, in G.A. Mountnorris [Viscount Valentia],
Voyages and Travels to India, Ceylon, the Red Sea, Abyssinia, and Egypt, 1809.
Courtesy of the Melville Herskovitz Library, Northwestern University.

Audiences were expected to breathe in the evocative atmosphere, but not for too long. The political tempest is never far away, and her husband Chedid responds:

CHEDID.
All still as death! Sullen as this the calm
Ushering the tempest that o'erwhelms the land
With its fell fury from the burning south.
I like it not. Those scattered horsemen too,
We noted late, mysteriously suspicious.
Base, treacherous, and deceitful Osmyn's heart.

Gunfire breaks the idyll, and fighting occurs offstage. Audiences see its effect upon Chedid, who reappears "in disorder" and is taken prisoner by Osmyn. Instead of battle, the audience is shown the emotional rending of the family, especially when the youthful Ageeb is traded for Chedid, who must raise the ransom price. Instead of escape, there is capture.

Alternating scenes of bravado and pathos are varied when act 3, scene 3 returns to a comic mode. The wily servant Hyder, disguised as a drummer, tricks a Turkish soldier into releasing his prospective father-in-law and thus is reunited with his love-interest, Sewda. It bodes well for an imminent happy conclusion; however, after delivering the ransom to Osmyn, Chedid is taken prisoner and condemned to death. Thus, as in George Colman's play *The Africans*, the final scene begins with a procession towards execution. Fortuitous news arrives of Elphi's march upon Osmyn's camp. Osmyn's tyranny is underscored not only by his wrongful decree on Chedid's head but also by his callous treatment of Emina in her distress. Osmyn's heart does not soften even though the priest and Othman make their disapproval very clear. Elphi is the instrument of reprieve, crashing in on the scene in the nick of time and disarming Osmyn. Seeing this, Osmyn's mercenary troops go over to Elphi's side. In the manner of melodrama, the right cause is upheld; however, there is neither melodrama's punishment nor its renunciation of evil. Chedid is liberated and reunited with his wife, yet his concession—by the Arab code—to earlier assaults upon his family by Elphi is merely to allow Elphi to rule unopposed. There is no marker of a tragic hero's greater insight, gained through adversity, leading to a more just government and harmonious domesticity. What transpires instead is far too ambivalent for melodrama. Instead of being clearly either melodrama or tragedy, *Elphi Bey* is a drama predicated as a window on Eastern values—good and bad, felicitous and destructive—interposed with songs and animated against a background of exotic scenery.

Nineteenth-century performance is characterized by mixed-genre as well as downright unclassifiable pieces. The catch-all of musical drama does not quite capture how *Elphi Bey* operates *relationally* to other repertoire, even the melodrama paired with it on the bills at Drury Lane (*The Innkeeper's Daughter*) during its short run of three nights. Elements of melodrama permeated a great deal of other repertoire throughout the ensuing century. Even modernist plays could not escape its influence, as Martin Meisel demonstrates with Bernard Shaw at the century's close.[32] *Elphi Bey* helps to illustrate how melodrama has been falsely held up in a dichotomy with "legitimate" genres (especially tragedy and comedy), not only in the early nineteenth century but well beyond, into the emergence of modernism. This helps to account for the adjective "melodramatic" to pieces that are not melodramas per se. Modern drama has been defined as that which is not melodrama,[33] but this makes no more sense than to sever *Elphi Bey*'s connection to travel writing, comically fantastical renderings of the Middle East, or imperialist panorama.[34] While

---

32   Martin Meisel, *Shaw and the Nineteenth-Century Theatre* (Princeton, NJ: Princeton UP, 1963).
33   Buckley, "Refugee Theatre," 190.
34   See Ziter, *Orient on the Victorian Stage*; and Angela Pao, *The Orient of the Boulevards: Exoticism, Empire, and Nineteenth-*

genre organizes representational conventions, melodrama was a highly permeable category subject to influence from many narrative, musical, and pictorial forms.

Editing Issues

There are three sources for the play: the licensing manuscript (submitted on 2 April 1817, before most rehearsals would have occurred), the published text (which appeared shortly after the production), and a trio of song sheets.[35]

The licensed text, upon which this edition is based, is titled *Alphi Bey*. Nothing accounts for the change in the title character's name except, perhaps, misreading the author's handwriting.[36] The licensed manuscript has many minor variations from the published version: most are changes in capitalization and punctuation. The copyist was conservative in the inclusion of em-dashes, whereas the typesetter was extremely liberal in their use, usually without contributing to readers' understanding or actors' delivery. For the most part, the punctuation of the licensing manuscript has been retained, though in a few places punctuation has been added or deleted if the sense demanded clarification. Contracted spellings, especially of verbs, are modernized where this does not affect the scansion or historical pronunciation.

While the published text adds some lines and substitutes others, for the most part these changes provide unnecessary descriptive flourishes upon what existed when the play was in rehearsal. This seems to suggest that the manuscript is a more authoritative text than the published version. It is difficult to say whether the major omissions from the published text (the pilgrim in act 3, scene 2 and the whole of Hyder's ruse in act 3, scene 3, an episode derided by the critics)[37] point to the excisions made before or during the run (cuts were made prior to the second performance),[38] or whether they reflect the author's preferences, for Hamilton evidently approved the second night's curtailments.[39] There are also plentiful instances where single lines have been omitted or words incorrectly transcribed in the published version, ruining the sense; this supports the idea that the author lacked oversight of the publishing process.

Three songs written for the production by Thomas Attwood, pupil of Wolfgang Amadeus Mozart,[40] were published separately from the play. In contrast to other evidence, the scores' existence lends credibility to the idea that the published text is more representative of the production than the manuscript. The first, "Say Who'd be Great," a duet sung by Hyder and Sewda in act 1, scene 3, helps to establish the reciprocal bond between the comic pair; the lyrics appear in both the manuscript and print versions of the play. These characters otherwise speak in prose, even when Sewda plays opposite her father Hassan, who speaks in verse. The second of Attwood's songs, "The Arab Youth," sung by Emina's servant Zara to while away the time in act 2, scene 2, is not in the licensing manuscript. It is included in the edition below, however, because its inclusion in the performance is documented and it is typical of songs interpolated

Century French Theater (Philadelphia: U of Pennsylvania P, 1998).

35 The play was published in both London and New York: Sir Ralph Hamilton, *Elphi Bey; or, the Arab's Faith: Musical Drama, in Three Acts; First Performed at the Theatre-Royal, Drury-Lane, Thursday, April 17, 1817* (London: W. Clowes, 1817); and R. Hamilton, *Elphi Bey; or, The Arab's Faith: A Musical Drama, in Three Acts* (New York: David Longworth, 1817). The scores were published in London by Chappell, 1817.

36 Other contemporaneous sources use alternate spellings of Elphy and Elfi but never Alphi. There is no need to cloak the eponymous character's historical identity; to the contrary, this is precisely the play's attraction.

37 *Morning Chronicle*, 18 April 1817.

38 "The Drama: Drury Lane Theatre," *St. James's Chronicle*, 19 April 1817: 4.

39 Hamilton, *Elphi Bey* (London), iii.

40 Daniel Heartz, "Thomas Attwood's Lessons in Composition with Mozart," *Journal of the Royal Musical Association* 100:1 (1973): 175-83.

into dramas of the period.[41] The third song, "Can Language Paint the Lover's Bliss," sung by Osmyn at the top of act 2, scene 3, gives him an opportunity to describe his youth when tender-hearted affections still pulsed within him. This gives the character considerably greater depth than the rest of the dialogue and action. Though the lyrics are not present in the manuscript, the song is included here because the score documents its use in performance and its subsequent popularity. Lyrics do not always match in the published edition and the scores; the lyrics printed with the scores have been given preference here. The scores for other songs (by C. Horn and H. Smart) do not survive. The overture came from Mozart (possibly *The Abduction from the Seraglio* (1782), an opera not performed in London until 1827) as well as from additional incidental music.[42]

Scenic details are more elaborate in the published edition than the manuscript, suggesting they might more fully describe the scenery used in production; however, the opposite is true in act 3, scenes 2 and 6, where additional details in the manuscript are evocative of staging needs. Given the more fulsome scenic descriptions at the top of many scenes in the published text, it is surprising that it does not also include more didaskalia (staging instructions) of actors' movements or delivery. This rules out the possibility that the published text was typeset from the prompt copy. What can be known about the staging, therefore, comes more from the reviews than evidence within the script.

Performative Issues

In the early nineteenth century, actors were required to learn new parts with just a few rehearsals, often performed in more than one play each evening, and could see several changes of bill per week.[43] A leading actor could have dozens of parts ready at short notice and play hundreds during a career. It is not unusual, therefore, for playwrights to feel that even the best ensembles gave their work inadequate preparation or undermined literary potential through imperfect memory or fumbled stage movement. If actors were miscast, or displeased with their roles, a new play could be doomed from the outset. If the dramatist had little or no stage experience, and no sway with the management, having a play produced could be a deeply frustrating, disappointing, or even humiliating experience. Hamilton called his Drury Lane premiere "the ordeal of representation." He praised the cast while regretting they could not rehearse more.[44] The performance received "great applause" throughout, and when announced for repetition, "almost unanimous consent" was shouted.[45] Even so, it disappeared after three nights and was succeeded by Edmund Kean in *Richard III*. Theatre history is rife with such scenarios.

To say that *Elphi Bey* was a critical failure would be an understatement. Critics agreed that the cast did the play justice but that the greater credit was due the scene painter and musical arranger than the author. Being largely factual, the plot was "therefore dull and heavy" even if audiences appeared to appreciate it.[46] Only one critic found any of the language "elegant and characteristic"; others called it "inflated bombastical fustian [clap-trap]" resembling the radical newspaper the *Morning Post*, with no other claim to being blank

---

41   The score credits Mrs. Salmon as the singer, however there was no one by this name in Drury Lane's company that season, and Miss Buggins was the actress given Zara's part. See "London Theatres," *British Stage and Literary Cabinet*, January 1817: 4; and *Theatrical Inquisitor and Monthly Mirror* 10 (April 1817): 305.

42   Playbills specify: "The new Musick composed by Messrs. Attwood, Horn and H. Smart. The overture and concerted pieces (selected by Mr. Attwood) from Mozart" (Harvard Theatre Collection and Garrick Collection). The *Times* remarks: "The overture, and some other passages of the music, said to be taken from Mozart, were very pleasing" (*Times*, 18 April 1817: 25). See C.B. Oldman, "Attwood's Dramatic Works," *Music Times*, January 1966: 23-26; and Stanley Sadie, ed., *The Grove Book of Operas*, 2nd ed. (Oxford: Oxford UP, 1992), 182.

43   Tiffany Stern, *Rehearsal from Shakespeare to Sheridan* (Oxford: Oxford UP, 2007).

44   Hamilton, *Elphi Bey* (London), iii, v-vi.

45   *Morning Chronicle*, 18 April 1817.

46   *Belle Assemblée; or, Court and Fashionable Magazine*, May 1817: 230.

verse other than presenting "the usual quantity of syllables."[47] It is not a work of great literature, but few melodramas are. Its value lies in being generically indicative, politically relevant, historically referential, scenically derivative, and thus linked to various kinds of repertoire, on the stage and beyond.

In his dedication to the play, Hamilton describes *Elphi Bey* as "*a joint Composition*" not with his composer but "*in Mr. Salt's name and in my own*."[48] He was right to acknowledge the visual component through his debt to Salt's illustrations for Valentia (also sold separately in expensive portfolios) as a form of stage authorship. The iconic views, along with indicatively islamist props (calligraphic cipher and Koran) and plausible-sounding Middle Eastern names, put knowledge of an exotic culture within reach, or seemingly so, maximizing geocultural associations.[49] As the *Literary Gazette* put it, "The spectacle is superior to the sentiment" though the frequent changes of scenery were "the style of the Westminster Amphitheatre" (Astley's popular circus).[50] The quip was largely justified. Like orientalist poetry, which emphasizes Middle Eastern topography, and orientalist paintings and prints, which emphasize Middle Eastern social life,[51] *Elphi Bey* gives considerable scope to scenes of desert encampments even though Chedid and Elphi's tents were depicted before the same recycled drop cloth.[52] Other settings along the Nile—at Aboukir, the Pyramids, and Cairo—appealed to spectators' taste for the exotic. The most impressive visual effect occurred in the final moments of the play when the gateway opened to reveal a view of Cairo from the citadel. Elphi's troops advanced as the audience viewed the entire depth of the stage.

Apparently there was "much splendor in the dresses,"[53] afforded equally by male and female costume, but racialization was inconsistent. According to the *Theatrical Inquisitor*, "the gentlemen of the chorus had the arms of negroes and the faces of Europeans," possibly not for lack of make-up but because some men wore moustaches and others bound their necks in western-style neckcloths.[54] These were unfortunate oversights, but not unusual in the period before James Robinson Planché introduced rigorous standards for antiquarian scenography and dress, utilizing published studies of the archaeology and ethnography of foreign, distant, or historic peoples, and Charles Kean drilled his supernumeraries in imitation of the German company in Saxe-Meiningen. According to Edward Ziter, antiquarianism "often sought to induce an empathic relation to the actors and events of the past" or, in this case, the near past.[55] For the most part, this succeeded for *Elphi Bey*'s audiences (though not its critics), despite infelicities.

Attempts to charm through exoticism stopped short of the score. Though the music was much admired, it offered neither harmonic nor instrumental evocations of the Middle East. Like other musical stage pieces of the period, it provided "a string of adorable airs linked in a way that was arbitrary or incomprehensible."[56] Some of the music is diegetic (directly narrative of the staged action)—for example,

---

47   *Theatrical Inquisitor, and Monthly Mirror* 10 (April 1817): 305; "Drury Lane," *British Stage and Literary Cabinet* 1 (May 1817): 106; and "Dramatic Register," *New Monthly Magazine and Universal Register* 7 (May 1817): 355. A review of the published text is even more scathing: *Theatrical Inquisitor, and Monthly Mirror* 10 (June 1817): 444-48.

48   Hamilton, *Elphi Bey* (London), iv.

49   Mabilat describes this as the distinction between orientalist and exoticizing art forms. The one broadens artistic palettes through cultural diversity, the other disparages difference. Mabilat, *Orientalism and Representations*, 7.

50   "Drury Lane," *Literary Gazette* 13 (April 1817): 201.

51   Emily Haddad, *Orientalist Poetics: The Islamic Middle East in Nineteenth-Century English and French Poetry* (Aldershot: Ashgate, 2002), 136; and Nicholas Tromans, ed., *The Lure of the East: British Orientalist Painting* (New Haven, CT: Yale UP, 2008).

52   *Theatrical Inquisitor, and Monthly Mirror* 10 (April 1817): 306.

53   "Drury Lane," *Literary Gazette* 13 (April 1817): 201.

54   *Theatrical Inquisitor, and Monthly Mirror* 10 (April 1817): 306.

55   Ziter, *Orient on the Victorian Stage*, 34.

56   Ronald Pearsall, *Victorian Popular Music* (Newton Abbott: David and Charles, 1973), 160; quoted in Mabilat, *Orientalism and Representations*, 28.

the solemn march at the commencement of act 3, scene 6, leading Chedid to execution—but most is not. Arguably, even this march is dispensable except as a strategic counterbalance to the jubilant refrains at the end of the act. Other marches get characters on and off stage (act 1, scene 2, and act 3, scene 2), coordinating choral movements. Most of the airs interrupt rather than promote the course of action, lending aesthetic polish and affective mood rather than narrative propulsion. As Thomas Noble wrote in his preface to his opera *The Persian Hunters* (1817),

> now, as music is an impassioned mode of uttering sentiments, it follows, that the fable and characters of an Opera ought to be framed so as to give frequent opportunities for such impassioned utterance. Yet, on the other hand, if the situations are in themselves of very deep interest, the abrupt transition from declamation to song may disturb the impression which the scene, *of itself*, might be capable of making upon the audience.[57]

Only the pilgrim's song smoothed the transition from dialogue to air with recitative.

Though it is tempting to criticize Attwood for his disregard of musical authenticity, by keeping the musical register recognizable, familiar, and European, he resisted orientalizing the characters, a practice synonymous with disparagement or belittling by implicit or explicit contrast with a Western ideal.[58] Instead, he focused on each song's emotional impact and was praised for writing "compositions [that] are uncommonly beautiful, scientific and effective ... heard with rapture, and several of them, particularly two delicious songs, encored without a dissenting voice."[59] If he knew anything of Egyptian music, he would likely have regarded it as "musically simple, hence emotionally limited," erupting into "violent passions" but sonically incohesive.[60] Though ethnographies touched on the musical characteristics of the Middle East, integration of such elements was rare before the late-Victorian period.[61] Arthur Sullivan included crashing discordant cymbals in *The Mikado* (1885), resonances synonymous with Eastern grandeur but also pomposity. In 1817, such sonic associations had yet to be forged in ways palatable to mass audiences. Antiquarianism came late—and last—to stage music. As Stephen Cockett describes the music for Charles Kean's 1859 production of *Henry V*,

> had Kean applied the principle of historical 'accuracy' to music as rigorously as he did to costumes, setting and props, heraldry and military equipment he would not have employed an orchestra, which was invented some 300 years after Henry's time, musical composition would have been polyphonic rather than melodic and harmonic and played on instruments tuned to a scale not yet adapted to equal temperament, and all accompaniments would have been played within the narrative world of the scene, with no off-stage underscoring. He might also have noted that King Henry, on his return to London, forbade his minstrels to celebrate his victory in song.[62]

57   Thomas Noble, *The Persian Hunters; or, The Rose of Gurgistan: An Opera, in Three Acts* (London: Sherwood, Neely, and Jones, 1817), viii-ix.

58   Mabilat, *Orientalism and Representations*, 7.

59   *Morning Chronicle*, 18 April 1817.

60   Bennett Zon, "'Violent Passions' and 'Inhuman Excess': Simplicity and the Representation of Non-Western Music in Nineteenth-Century British Travel Literature," in *Music and Orientalism in the British Empire, 1780s-1940s: Portrayal of the East*, edited by Martin Clayton and Bennett Zon (Aldershot: Ashgate, 2007), 203.

61   For example, George Forster's *A Voyage Round the World, in His Britannic Majesty's Sloop, Resolution* (London: B. White, 1777) and William Lane's *The Manners and Customs of Modern Egyptians*, 2 vols. (London: William Lane, 1836). See Zon, "'Violent Passions,'" 213, 222.

62   Stephen Cockett, "Documents of Performance: Music and the Representation of History in Charles Kean's Revival of Shakespeare's *Henry V*," *Nineteenth Century Theatre and Film* 34:1 (2007): 3.

Repertoire makes performance interpretable through custom, and in the case of *Elphi Bey* critics found congenial elements in the familiar (conventional music) and the unfamiliar (exotic scenery and costumes), made customary through infinite recombination.

Elphi Bey; or, The Arab's Faith[63]

BY RALPH HAMILTON

First performed at Theatre Royal Drury Lane, 17 April 1817.

Osmyn,[64] a Turkish Chief, usurping the rule during the absence of Elphi Bey	Mr. Horn
Elphi Bey, a Mameluke[65] Chief, supposed the rightful sovereign of Egypt, who has been absent at the time of his predecessor's decease	Mr. Wallack
Chedid, an Arab sheik commanding a powerful tribe, on the east bank of the Nile	Mr. Rae
Othman, minister and friend of Osmyn	Mr. Coveney
Ageeb, son of Chedid	Miss E. Scott
Hassan, an old Arab, attached to Elphi	Mr. Gattie
Hyder, servant to Zeinaba	Mr. Harley
A Pilgrim	
Caleb, Chief in the interest of Elphi	Mr. Pyne
Omar, Chief in the interest of Elphi	Mr. J. Smith
Amalek, Chief in the interest of Elphi	Mr. Cooke
Abu Buk'r, principal Arab of the Desert	Mr. Miller
Saied, principal Arab of the Desert	Mr. Kent
Achmet, principal Arab of the Desert	Mr. Smith
An elderly Sheik[66] or Arabian High Priest	Mr. Powell
Hadjee, a native Arab	Mr. Minton
Emina, wife of Chedid	Mrs. Bartley
Zeinaba, wife of Elphi	Miss Boyce
Sewda, daughter of Hassan	Mrs. Bland
Zara, companion to Emina	Miss Buggins

---

63 Based on *Alphi Bey*, Larpent MS 1965, Huntington Library.
64 Provincial governor under the Ottoman regime.
65 Historically, these are emancipated white military slaves; they ruled Egypt locally under the sultanate from 1250 to 1517, then as a military caste under Ottoman sovereignty for the pasha from 1517 to 1812.
66 Chief of a family or tribe.

Turkish, Syrian, Albanian, and Mameluke Soldiers, Attendants, &c.	Messrs. Ebsworth, Cooke, Saunders, Jones, Dibble, Clark, Cook, Odwell, Mead, Wilson, Warner, Buggins, Caulfield, Mathews, Hope, Goodman, Cooper, Vials, Brown, Appleby, G. Wells
Dancers	Madame Wells, Mrs. T. Cooke, Misses Cooke, Bates, M. Bates, Fairbrother, M. Buggins, Caulfield, Cause, Lyons, Corri, Horribow, Ivers, Vials, Goodman, and Mrs. Taylor

New Music composed by Messrs. Attwood, C. Horn and H. Smart
Overture and concerted pieces (selected by Mr. Attwood) from Wolfgang Amadeus Mozart
Scenery by Mr. Greenwood
Machinery by Mr. Lethbridge
Costumes by Mr. Banks and Miss Smith

Act I

Scene 1

An Arab encampment near a grove of date trees, on the borders of the Desert. Zeinaba, Zara, and Arab women discovered.

CHORUS *(singing)*.
  Our cheerful notes ascending
  Shall swell the balmy gale,
  Our choral voices blending
  Re-echo through the vale.
  The boundless desert ranging
  We fly the city's strife
  Our tented dwellings changing
  How blest the Arab's life.
ZEINABA.
  How harsh the sounds of pleasure
  Forlorn oppressed with fears;
  Absent my bosom's treasure
  My heavy solace—tears!—
CHORUS *(repeat)*.
  Our cheerful notes ascending, etc.
ZARA *(speaks)*.
  Ever in tears, Zeinaba, wherefore thus?
ZEINABA.
  Tears!—were there tears? Am I so weak become?

I, our Sovereign's wife!—forgive me, Elphi!
Thine absence makes me feel a very woman.
But said you not, the chieftains were assembled?
ZARA.
They are, with Osmyn—But that I regret
To wound thy generous heart, I'd name the cause.
ZEINABA.
Withhold it not—more dire the racking thoughts
Of ills uncertain, than the worst disclosed—
Were Elphi even dead, I'd pray to know it.
You pause—my fears have guessed—Allah,[67] support me.
ZARA.
Look up—he lives; but, as I learn his fall
Is the assembled chiefs' determined aim;—
The ship on which he sailed has neared our coast,
And by tomorrow's dawn he lands.
ZEINABA.
Merciful Heaven! the savage tigers prowl;
No friend to warn their unsuspicious victim.
ZARA.
Restrain this burst of passion. Chedid's here.
CHEDID (enters).
Lead forth our horses, Saied—the camel troop
Already halts upon the river's side,
And ere nightfall we must join Osmyn's force.
ZEINABA.
You march then Sheik, in an unrighteous cause,
Against your sovereign prince, to aid a tyrant.
What then becomes of me?
CHEDID.
All comfort we can give
Be (as our captive) yours. But for your husband,
But for Elphi, I am still his deadliest foe:
Our blood is on him.
ZEINABA.
To the gen'rous mind
What rapture like magnanimous forgiveness!
Revenge—an impious passion—
What are its joys, what bliss can it bestow?
CHEDID.
Is it no solace to the starving man,
To riot ravenous on the food he craves?
Or, when the burning fever rages high,

---

67   God.

Is the cool draught of water no relief?[68]

My life itself—nay all that makes life dear—

Freely I'd barter, for this Elphi's head.

ZARA.

Beseech you, Sheik,—this vehemence o'erpowers her.

ZEINABA *(recovering)*.

The shock is past, Allah will give me strength,

That I, with fortitude, may brave the worst.

CHEDID *(to Zara)*.

Greet my Emina—say, I leave my tents,

Our children and, more precious still my honour,

All to her care—to hers, my best beloved.

Bid her good Zara, guard them safe.

Go speed thee straight—farewell.

(Exit Zara).

————Attend me, friends! *(Marches off)*.

HYDER *(enter)*. Aye there they go—huddled together like a troop of jackals, riding faster than their horses gallop, and frightening the very air with the flourishing of their spears—Good-by t' ye, valourous freebooters[69]—But you'll excuse me *(bowing)*—Well now, if my Lady is but in the mind for it, we have the happiest opportunity to escape from this free and easy society. *(To Zeinaba)* Oh, madam, I'm glad to see you—there, through yonder calishe,[70] to the very banks of the Nile, I have passed unmolested. Not the shadow of an Arab horse, Foot, or Dromedary.[71]—That terrible fellow Chedid has carried off his whole tribe with him, a slight Reserve[72] excepted, over the tents and baggage. Let me conduct you.

ZEINABA.

The moment does indeed appear propitious—

I'll venture all to save a husband's life.

HYDER. And see, Lady, thanks to my skill in flower-painting—I have been able to copy the Sheik's cipher[73] so dexterously, that his very secretary could not detect the counterfeit. *(Shewing the flourishing eastern cipher, or signature)*.

ZEINABA.

Good fellow! faithful friend! Cunningly traced!

Guard it against the last extremity.

Passing the Nile, close on its western banks,

An old man lives to Elphi much attached:

You know him, Hyder, or, at least, his daughter.

HYDER. What! Hassan's daughter!—my dear Sewda, let us be gone Lady—I've hauled a boat up, and we'll sweep o'er the river like an ibis—for I shall pull away manfully from slavery and spare diet, to love, liberty—, and my regular daily bread—three good meals and an afternoon's luncheon.

---

68   This line is absent from the manuscript, but restored here.

69   Pirates.

70   Horse-drawn carriage (calash).

71   Troops (mounted or foot soldiers).

72   A small number of troops.

73   Calligraphic monogram.

ZEINABA.
　　Thou art a marvelous chatterer—But away.
　　And, for a wonder, silence, if thou can'st.
HYDER. Not a word Lady,—not a word. Though the mole be under my foot, she shall no more hear
　　than see.[74] Not a word Lady.

(*Exeunt*).

Scene 2

Alexandria.[75] *A vessel in view. Natives on the beach, shouting.*
Hadjee and his attendant Hamed, discovered.

HADJEE.
　　What do they shout for, Hamed? Can'st thou tell?
HAMED.
　　For that good Hadjee, which should cause their tears—
　　The flag of Elphi shewn by yonder ship.
　　But little dreams the Chief the direful change
　　A few short months have wrought.
　　Had he been here when our late ruler died
　　He had been seated firmly on the throne.
　　Now Fortune favour him beyond our hopes,
　　Or the sharp dagger's points his sole inheritance.
HADJEE.
　　Hush! Osmyn's friends!
　　His Myrmidons[76] swarm thick about us
　　Prowl forth like hungry wolves,
　　Drawn by the bleating of these timid sheep.

(*A March—Troops enter*).

CHORUS.
　　Hail, hail, hail!
　　Hail, Osmyn-Bey—hail mighty ruler hail!
　　A thousand years may Osmyn live and reign.—
　　His foes shall fall, his sovereign right prevail
　　And Allah's arm his powerful throne sustain.

(*Osmyn and Othman advance*).

OSMYN.
　　As we surmised my friend, Elphi returns
　　Proudly triumphant to his anxious troops;

74　i.e., even a mole, so near that it is burrowing beneath my foot, will not hear me say anything. (Perhaps proverbial.)
75　The published text specifies that this is at the Pharos (lighthouse built for Ptolemy II, on an island off Alexandria, now
　　a peninsula).
76　Sycophantic supporters.

One month's protracted absence, had secured
The realm I hold but lightly, for my own.
I dread the changeful people—Fickle fools!
Heard you their shouts, as, from the topmast head
His flag insulting mocked our new-raised power?

OTHMAN.

I did, and know them to his cause attached.
Elphi is much beloved.

OSMYN.

But still there's hope—he has not reached his troops.
Nor shall he ever, can my power prevent—
No fond affection now must stay our hands
No visitings of conscience, no remorse
Or he, or I must fall. Egypt can brook
One chief alone.

OTHMAN.

What would your words suggest?

OSMYN.

His death—Why start you? Death alone makes sure.
The man who hourly views a dread abyss
Beneath him gaping, fathomless and wide,
Must dash his foes in, or must sink himself.

(Enter Chedid, attended).

CHEDID.

Osmyn, behold this firm and zealous band—
Yet fancy not that friendship draws me here,—
I am no friend to men in cities born
Men without hearts, enslaved by luxury.
Revenge—fell—deadly revenge to this Elphi.
Now leagues[77] my tribe to yours in common cause.
Do you accept our aid?

OSMYN.

Most gratefully;
And knowing well your daring independence
Shall not too nicely[78] dive into the motive.—
You're welcome, all, and in good time arrived
We must be vigilant against escape.

CHEDID.

My Arabs so beset the eastern shore,
Escape that way's impossible.—
The Nile alone
Offers a scarcely practicable chance.

---

77   Binds.
78   Fastidiously.

OSMYN.
  Then is he ours—My troops secure the Nile.
CHEDID.
  On then—our parties separate,
  We'll foremost cross the arid plain, to where
  In distance rise yon splendid minarets
  Whose blazing tops reflect the setting sun;
  Fortune is with us—foremost in our ranks.
  Hope every thing when next we meet—Farewell! *(Exits).*

(A March).

OSMYN.
  This death, why start you? Death alone makes sure
  The man who hourly views a dread abyss
  Beneath him gaping, fathomless and wide,
  Must dash his foes in, or must sink himself.

  (Sings) Ambition fires my daring soul
  My burning heart sustains;
  My passions rage without control
  My scepter, Might sustains.—
  Hence; weakness, pity, justice hence,
  Your influence I despise
  Hence Friendship, mere assumed pretence
  To power a sacrifice!

  Fixed as fate, yes—Elphi dies—
  His fall ensures my state—
  My rival at my mercy lies,
  To prove my inmost[79] hate.
  He dies, he dies!—My firm decree—
  My mandate seals his destiny *(exit).*

Scene 3

An orange grove on the banks of the Nile. Girls gathering
fruit with Sewda. The sky appears to portend a storm.

SEWDA *(singing).*
  On the verdant banks of the fertile Nile
  There dwelt an Arab's daughter.
  Full many a suitor claimed her smile
  Beys, Sheiks, and Mamelukes sought her.

---

79 Deepest.

They galloped nigh, they skirmished high
While she cried, "Sirs, Pray excuse me!
Till a lover I find that is more to my mind
All your capering but serves to amuse me.
Ha, ha, ha, ha!
All your capering but serves to amuse me."

A barge there came with a splendid sail;
Its gilded oars struck the water;
Round a Pasha's[80] head waved many a tail,[81]
As he stalked to the Arab's daughter.
Rich cloths of gold his slaves unrolled;
But she cried "Dread Sir, excuse me.
Till a lover I find that is more to my mind
All your fripp'ry[82] but serves to amuse me.
Ha, ha, ha, ha!
All your fripp'ry but serves to amuse me."

With a faithful heart then Hyder came
To that faithful heart he caught her.
Her tell-tale eyes confessed the flame
Which love had slyly taught her.
The Pasha sailed,—the Mameluke failed
While she cried "Great Sirs, excuse me!
Here's the lover I find, that is most to my mind
And your vapouring[83] but serves to amuse me.
Ha, ha, ha, ha!
All your vapouring but serves to amuse me."

HASSAN (enters. Speaks).

Well said my girls. Are they all gathered?

SEWDA. All, father, but those so richly coloured near the top:—were Hyder here, he soon would reach
them.

HASSAN.

Ay, ay—
We know the fruit to which his hopes aspire.
Nay, blush not, rosy cheek, your choice is mine.
Were but his Lady safe, he'd soon be with us.

(Music without)[84]

Hark! whence that music borne upon the breeze?
It seems approaching.

---

80   Governor's.
81   An allusion to the bride-price, most likely as a freehold estate.
82   Showy garments.
83   Pretentious talk.
84   The published version indicates "a flute or flageolet [woodwind] upon the water."

SEWDA *(looking out)*. 'Tis Hyder, father. Look! he waves his turban as a signal.

(Enter Zeinaba and Hyder as having landed).

HASSAN.
Welcome, dear lady! bounteous heaven be praised,
My prayers are heard. What miracle preserved you?
ZEINABA.
Enquire not now—The evening fast draws on.
The air is charged with heavy threatening clouds
The lightning flashes in the western sky
And much ere night comes, rests there to be done.
Tell me at once, old man, what news of Elphi?
HASSAN.
This morning as he anchored near our coast
My zeal forewarned him of approaching danger
At Osmyn's wish 'tis fixed he lands tomorrow.
Meanwhile, this very night, he puts ashore,
Near a lone ruin on the adjacent beach;
Baffling his enemies. These feeble limbs forbid
Or his old servant would assist his flight;
Attend him, share—and mitigate his dangers.
Where to engage one faithful for the task
With energy of mind and strength I know not.
ZEINABA.
No further seek—who undertakes it,
Must rise superior to desponding fears.
Bold from the cause, supported by affection,
None else can hope access; who then but I?
HASSAN.
You, Lady, you—You know not half the perils!
ZEINABA.
My resolution's fixed—I therefore sought ye
Firm in my duty, for a husband's life
I trust in Allah, and can brave the worst.
HASSAN.
My noble Lady—thus t' attempt alone—
HYDER. No Hassan not alone. *(To Zeinaba)* Oh, lady! how doubly dear will safety be to my noble master
when it comes in your shape.
ZEINABA.
So my heart whispers—but *(pauses)*—no: till he's safe
He must not know me—I must seem a stranger
Lest fear for me make him neglect himself
And love that sought to save him, should endanger.
Oh! it will cost me many a tender struggle,
But that affection which imposed the trial
Will, if successful, gloriously reward it.

HASSAN.
Come then—I have a soldier's dress within
Will suit your purpose.
ZEINABA.
Allah, look down, support me in this trial.
And you my friends, be steadfast in your duty.
Let no one breathe my name, or hint my purpose.
Discovery e'en to Elphi would undo us.
Then cares for me, doubts, tenderness, anxiety,
The thousand fancied hardships I might suffer
Would damp his noble energies of soul
And yield him up a prey to his enemies.

(Exeunt all but Sewda and Hyder).

SEWDA. And so you do not like these Arabs of the Desert?
HYDER. Like them, girl—I'd rather live among the tombs—turn Santon[85]—go to sea—be lackey[86] to a troop of dancing girls than be exposed to the continual harassings of a wandering Arab's life. They eat nothing but a little unbaked flour and water. Their longest meals do not take up a minute and a half, and they sleep no more than their horses, who stand all night long with bridles in their mouths; I was reduced two-thirds in the short time I passed with them. And well nigh lost the faculty of speech, they looked upon me so fiercely, that every time my mouth opened I expected to be treated like an Indian juggler[87] and have a sword crammed down my throat.
SEWDA. Well now, Hyder, I always admired them. So handsome, brave as lions, and riding so gallantly on horseback.
HYDER. And am not I as brave and as handsome as a lion on horseback too?

(She laughs).

But there's no time for chattering now. My Master's safety; my mistress's happiness, Osmyn's power, Chedid's revenge—nay the very well-being of the State depending upon me! Oh! greatness! greatness!—All the delightful cares and torments spring up like mushrooms. My pillow will be stuffed with asps-stings—and rattlesnakes—and as to a good sound night's rest—I may as well think of raising melons on a sand drift.[88]
SEWDA. Raising a fiddle-stick's[89] end, but down from your altitudes, and remember that he who climbs minarets must expect to fall upon tombstones.
HYDER and SEWDA *(singing)*.
Say, who'd be great, when the road to State
Is a quicksand treach'rous to tread—Love—
Where thorns the feet, each moment meet
And a sword points, hung by a thread Love?
Compared to this, what lowly bliss

---

85   A European term for a Muslim hermit or monk.
86   Servant.
87   Sword-swallower.
88   Sand dune.
89   Absurdity; a mere nothing.

Bids the Arab home to his tent, Love!
While the camels graze, his happy days,
Are a round of ease and content, Love.

The dread Bashaw,[90] today gives law,
And tomorrow he loses his head, Love,
His turrets blaze, the news conveys
And another is raised in his stead, Love.
The lofty date, must meet its fate
When the whirlwinds wind engage, Love.
While the shrub secure, will the shock endure
And thrive in the midst of their rage, Love *(exeunt)*.

Scene 4

Near Aboukir.[91] *Zeinaba enters in an Arab soldier's dress.*

ZEINABA.
By yonder ruin on the sandy shore,
It should be here that Hassan bade us wait.
Why tarries Hyder? 'Tis a fearful night.
How swift the clouds rush sweeping through the sky,
Disclosing to the view, at intervals,
The red moon scowling o'er the sullen waves!
And see, amid the relics of this pile,
The surf beats fierce, plunging with headlong roar,
As if 'twould break its ancient barriers down!
Dreadful the sea! Alas! that he I love
Must tempt its rage.—I tremble but to think on't.
HYDER *(without)*. What ho there!—hist,[92]—*(he enters)*.
ZEINABA.
Ah!—is it you? What news, good Hyder?
HYDER. He is safe on shore, 'twas a hard pull, and once or twice, I thought the boat had been stoved:[93]
but see he's here.
ZEINABA.
Haste then, prepare our horses instantly,
And know me, henceforth, only as Abdallah.

(Exit Hyder).

---

90   Older variant for pasha; high-ranking Turkish military commander or provincial governor.
91   A village on the Mediterranean coast, approximately 14.5 miles (23 km) northeast of Alexandria. Recognizable by its
     castle.
92   Psst!
93   Broken and thus sunk.

Six years long absence,[94] joined to this disguise,
Ensures the wished concealment of my person.

(Enter Elphi and Attendants with luggage).

ZEINABA *(aside).*
  It is himself—How noble is his mien![95]
  But, soft my heart, be still, tumultuous feelings.
  Elphi! most valiant chief! thy friends, by me,
  Greet thy arrival; and, in proof of faith
  Behold, I bear this ring.
ELPHI.
  I thank their kindness.
  Ah! *(looking at the ring),* My wife's!
  Oh! my loved Zeinaba thou art, indeed most welcome—
  Could I but see and clasp thee to my heart!—
ZEINABA *(going to rush towards him, but checks herself. Aside).*
  Down, selfish fondness!
ELPHI.
  Ten thousand fond anxieties arise!
  This ring recalls so many tender thoughts
  The halcyon days of youth and early bliss!
  The modest, blushing, half-suppressed consent
  The rapturous feelings of primeval love!
  (Turning to Zeinaba) Oh, I could question thee till time grew old;
  Speak of Zeinaba—then—her thoughts, her looks!
  Anticipate my hopes. Say, all is well!
ZEINABA.
  Of Elphi's constancy and truth assured,
  All with herself is well—
  But when she thinks upon her husband's danger,
  Doubts and alarm distract her.
  Then, for her sake away—this instant—hence!
  Haste from the perils that surround thee here,
  By various arts,
  Corruption, treachery, intrigue, and murder,
  The common ladder which ambition mounts,
  Osmyn has basely seized the helm of State.
ELPHI.
  Osmyn! In early youth my bosom's friend!
  From him, who loves me what have I to fear?
ZEINABA.
  Much, Elphi, much. He you esteem a friend

---

94 The historical Elphi Bey was abroad for approximately six months. Hamilton may be referencing the longer struggle against Napoleon, which commenced in 1798.
95 Bearing.

With rancorous jealousy now seeks your life.
Had you consented to a public entry
Your head had paid the forfeit—even now,
Amid these very sand hills, wretches wait
Bribed largely, and commissioned to despatch you.—
Horses attend to bear you to the Nile
There, boats are ready—
Myself will be your guide, and, till you're safe
'Twere better in some menial garb disguise you.

ELPHI.

Am I then sunk so low?—are all my hopes
Reduced to this? After six tedious years
Thus to return!—Steal as a midnight thief,
Into a land that should confess my sway!

ZEINABA.

Rouse thyself Elphi and let vengeance take
The full possession of thy manly soul,
Vengeance terrific—Egypt claims thine aid.
Long has the ravenous Turk oppressed her meek-eyed peasants—
Such a cause as this might nerve a woman's arm,
And, with a force overwhelming, fill the timid soul of Age.
Shall Elphi, then, careless of Egypt's wrongs
Be overcome by individual woes?

ELPHI.

No, never, youth—Yet who, with firm composure
Can listen to the fury of the winds,
When the fierce tempest drives his fragile bark?[96]
None—nor can I this Osmyn's treachery learn
Without a struggle. But 'tis past and soon.
This arm shall right me.

HYDER (enter, abruptly). Out with the torches instantly, for, as I passed the beach, a gleam of lightning shewed me a band of the most rascally ill-looking Arabs you ever set eyes upon, lurking behind those sand banks, to the left.

ZEINABA.

To horse then, swiftly—speed we to the Nile
While to deceive them, let a light be borne
Over the ridge of hills upon our right.

ELPHI.

First I'll secure some jewels for our aid
The rest will tempt the villains from pursuit.
Away! (taking some jewels from his baggage).

(Exeunt all but Hyder).

---

96   Small sailing ship (also barque).

HYDER. An excellent example, my master sets me and it is my duty as a good servant, to follow it.—I can overtake them in a moment (*takes up some of the jewels*)—Mahomet![97] how beautiful! had I these little sparklers at our cottage now, they'd make my fortune—purchase the dignities and honours of, at the least, three tails.[98]

(*Puts them under his dress and is stealing off, when he is intercepted by Arabs. He drops the jewels and falls upon his knees. Arabs enter*).

SAIED. I thought I heard them. Ah! who art thou, slave?

HYDER. No slave, but only a poor miserable gardener. Take all, good sir, except my head—that's little worth to any but the owner.

SAIED. On one condition thou art safe—tell us which way thy master went. We know thou belongest to Elphi. Here, take this torch and guide us to him.

ABU BUK'R. Stay Saied—first let us collect our plunder, to us more worth than twenty Elphis.

SAIED. Curse on the tempting bait—no time for trifling now—

ABU BUK'R. Trifling, indeed (*holding up a jewel*) such trifles elevate to power, make great bashaws of fools, and purchase paradise on earth.

SAIED. Paradise, dolt!—and for such as thou and I?

ABU BUK'R. Aye, surely, Saied, for Mahomet's dark girls with coal-black hair, and ever-varying charms would be but thrown away on saintly men. Come, lads, the wind blows keen—let's lose no time, but part our spoil.

SAIED. Why as you all agree, I may as well not lose my share.

(*During this dialogue, by means of the jutting fragment of a rock, Hyder, fixing a spear in the stage, hangs his cloak on it, fastens the torch in the sleeve, puts his turban upon the top of the spear, and steals away unobserved*).

ABU BUK'R. That is right—come, foolish caitiff,[99] thou shalt give us light (*turning to what he conceives to be Hyder and, striking it with his spear, discovers the trick*).—By Mahomet, too much for us!

SAIED. Confusion!—after him comrades! we'll not be fooled thus! follow me! (*Going off*).

ABU BUK'R (*detaining him*). And leave these (*pointing to the jewels*) for a Turkish rummage![100] Who'd be fooled then?—a fellow not worth a sequin to ransom him—What say you lads, shall we hunt down this jackal that has cast his skin (*taking up Hyder's cloak*) or console ourselves with his booty?

ARABS. The booty! the booty! we'll not part with our booty.

CHORUS OF ARABS (*singing*).

Who'd slave and till the stubborn fields
When a soldier's life such rapture yields?
Glory, renown!—dear woman's smile!
His heart of every care beguile.
His treasure's rich, his honour's bright
His days a round of choice delight.

Glory's a mighty sounding name
But dead, pray where's the soldier's fame.

---

97   Variant of Mohammed.
98   Freehold estates.
99   Captive.
100 Casket or ship's hold; i.e., to be taken away to enrich Constantinople (Istanbul).

Bootless[101] his honours;—plunder, spoil
The only fruits to crown his toil.
Then comrades haste and share the prize
Plunder, the Arab gains or dies.

(*They gather round Elphi's baggage*).

Act II

Scene 1

An Egyptian temple. Enter Elphi, Zeinaba, and Hyder.

ELPHI.
    Fatigued and harassed, weary nature sinks
    Here let me rest awhile, and gather strength.
ZEINABA.
    We've traversed far indeed, without repose.
HYDER. Aye, and what's worse, without a regular meal. But we're safe now.—I climbed that palm tree
    and explored the Desert. Far as the hills, not a soul to be seen, friend or foe.
ZEINABA.
    We must extend our search—a spot like this
    May tempt the Arab to enjoy its shade—
    Awhile we part—you, Hyder, to the left.

(*Exeunt Zeinaba and Hyder*).

ELPHI (*alone*).
    Lend me your friendly aid still awful ruin!
    Emblem exact of my dejected state!
    Not far remote it seems in fancy's eye,
    Which with a rapid glance surveys the past,
    Compressing Time's events, when this proud pile
    Reared its bold front, the wonder of the world!
    Now all decayed, defaced, in fragments laid
    By age, by storms; but more by savage man,
    Foremost to lead Destruction's savage bands!
    So on the summit of high fortune, late
    I stood triumphant 'midst surrounding friends
    By distant nations courted.—Idle dream!
    Past is the pageant; while the present hour
    Brings treachery, neglect, and dire dismay—
    But rouse my soul, the brave are ne'er subdued,—
    They, like a spring, with force elastic, bound
    To meet approaching danger.

---

101 Unprofitable.

(Sings) Though Death approach, and dangers rise
The noble mind will bravely—
Will conquer Fate, will fear despise
And rise superior to despair.
The Warrior's dauntless soul succeeds,
And triumphs still where Glory leads.

(A noise—he starts. Speaks).

Ha!—beset already!—
But they shall find my life no easy purchase.
AGEEB *(enter).*

Assist me stranger—wounded, overpowered,
Shame that I speak it, I've been driven to flight.—
Lured by the chase, some distance from our tents
Three desperate robbers fell on, to despoil me.
One I despatched; his fellows pressed upon me,
Till your commanding form appalled their souls.
Still hovering near, they watch the path
Which I must traverse homewards.
ELPHI.

Whence, and what art thou, youth?
AGEEB.

Ageeb my name,—Sheik Chedid is my father.
He forth last evening to join Osmyn's powers,
Led our brave tribe.
ELPHI *(aside).*

Sheik Chedid leagues with Osmyn then—
At hazard of my life, brave youth, I'll guard thee.
Point out the road, and give them to my sabre *(exit).*
ZEINABA *(enter).*

Scarce had I turned yon wall
When a rude voice struck piercing on my ear—
I crept with caution round, still closely hid
By massy fragments that lay heaped together
When lo!—a group of figures met my sight.
On which I crept away. But where is Elphi?
(Missing him, and calling out wildly) Gone!—Taken!—Dreadful!—Elphi!—
HYDER *(enter).* For Heaven's sake, Lady! But I fear those devils of Arabs have already heard you. My master cannot have fallen into the hands of an enemy for all's safe on that side—haste westwards then. I will remain, and try to put them on the wrong scent. Give me that letter; it will assist my plans.

(Zeinaba gives it).

Nay, nay, though I have a little more feeling than a date tree, I'm no coward, so secure yourself, Lady, and I'll soon follow you.
ZEINABA.

Good, faithful, generous friend! my prayers be with you *(exit).*

(Hyder lies down. Enter Hadjee and Arabs).

HADJEE. Here's one of them, at least.

HYDER. Where am I? Is it a dream, or are you living men?

HADJEE. Feel this, and try *(spears him).*—What think you now? Are you awake or sleeping?

HYDER. Too truly I'm awake!—But what may be your will with me?

HADJEE. To provide for you—*(half unsheathing his sabre).*

HYDER. Very much obliged to you indeed gentlemen but I'm already provided for and am your humble servant—*(going).*

HADJEE. Tired of our company already! But we can't part with you yet—who are you?

HYDER. Is that the way to speak to a man of my consequence truly!—The son of Omar—son of Othman—son of Ali!—upon a confidential message from Osmyn to Sheik Chedid!

HADJEE. Chedid!—we are of his tribe!

HYDER. This is a lucky chance! Can any of you read? *(Shows the letter).*

HADJEE. All of us your designs—away with him to Chedid, let the Sheik see his pretended despatch— Son of Omar, son of Othman ha, ha, ha!—

HYDER. Ha, ha, ha! *(Aside)* What shall I think of next? I have it. Ahem! Aloof, miscreants! *(Showing the cipher)* Did you ever see anything like this before?

HADJEE. 'Tis the Sheik's cipher!

HYDER. Now stop me at your peril!—I know whose heads will fall, in that case, while mine's safe!

HADJEE. We are convinced! How can we serve you?

HYDER. Thus—my private instructions hasten me west, and all depending upon despatch, we shall gain time, if you bear on this letter to your Sheik.—That way, at once—and mind no following or observing me.—By the Great Toe of Mahomet,[102] if you do! but you know better. The cipher—remember the cipher!

(Watches at wings until they are gone).

They're fairly off, and I can breathe again!—what an escape!—By Mahomet, I thought myself as dead as Ali Pasha's twenty wives![103]

(Sings) There was Ali Pasha—he'd twice ten wives
And once, in a terrible passion,
From the score complete he requested their lives
In a very odd sort of a fashion.
In a muddy pond, he the ladies crammed,
Where a legion of frogs they were croaking,
The water ran deep, it was tightly dammed
Oh! what a Turkish method of joking![104]

---

102 A comical oath akin to "by the beard of the Prophet."

103 Ali Pasha (1744-1822) allied with the Turks and took despotic control over much of Albania, western Greece, and the Peloponnese. His ruthlessness was legendary. It was, in fact, his son's mistress (not his own wife) and her companions whom he vindictively had thrown into Lake Pamvotis. (Byron's Eastern poem *The Giaour* features a similar incident of drowning.)

104 A middle stanza is excised from the printed score but appears in the published play:
Mild Mustapha-Bey had a gentler mode,
He began by a sample of banging,

(Continued)

Had I twenty wives, would I treat them so?
Though twenty times more plague more than pleasure
I'd give 'em their wings, let nineteen of 'em go
One sweet little pet my heart's treasure.
Bone-o-bone of my bone! not a hair of her head
Should be hurt were she ne'er so provoking
Dear dimpled-faced rogue, better living than dead
We'd have no Turkish method of joking *(exit)*.

Scene 2

A tent. Enter Emina, Ageeb, and Zara.

EMINA.
  Blest be the hand that saved thee boy!—A stranger!
  And of commanding mien! Hadst thou before e'er noted him?
AGEEB.
  Never! and instant, when we gained our lines[105]
  Rejecting thanks, on conference,[106] he departed.
EMINA.
  Mysterious chieftain! would that Chedid knew,
  And met to greet him.
AGEEB.
  Oh let me hasten and apprize my father—
  Perchance he'll place me in his warriors' ranks—
  To climb the hills and brave the glorious sun,
  Is nobler far than to live idling here,
  Like a tame antelope
  As if created but to play and sleep.
EMINA.
  Such is thy father's gallant spirit, boy,
  In strength a lion,—but thy youthful limbs
  Are yet unequal to the toils of war.
AGEEB.
  In truth I long for trial of my strength—
  You are impatient.—I'll ascend the hill

  And then, if his charmers they restive rode,
  Why,—he finished the matter by hanging!
  A nice silken cord to each lovely bride,—
  And thus, on the system of choking,
  By tying one knot, he another untied,—
  O! what a Turkish method of joking!
105 Arrived at our territory.
106 After discussion.

And on his first approach,
Bring the glad tidings that my father comes *(exit)*.
EMINA.
  Child of my heart!—How do I love thee boy!
  Thy rising spirit charms thy mother's pride!
  While it alarms, I own, thy mother's weakness!
  Too soon thy early sports must end and war
  With all its train of dangers, veiled in glory
  Will fire thy soul and from our tents allure thee.
  Good Zara, to beguile the tedious hours,
  Sing me the favourite ballad of our tribe.
ZARA *(sings)*.
  The Arab youth, at early dawn,
  Eager seeks the wildfowl's nest;
  Or pursues the bounding fawn,
  While rising ardour fires his breast.
  Soon a nobler foe he dares,
  Marks the gaunt hyena's way;
  Seeks the treach'rous panther's lairs,
  Starts the lion from his prey.
  Thus matured to glorious deeds,
  Proud he treads the tended field;
  His tribe's defender freely bleeds,
  Their rights to guard, their faith to shield.
EMINA.
  I'm tired of waiting—would that he were come
  My spirit still forebodes approaching ill.

(Enter Elphi, faint and exhausted).

EMINA.
  Ah!—What art thou?
ELPHI.
  A wretched fugitive—one close pursued
  By your tribe's faith![107]—protection!—safety!
  My life is in your hands.
EMINA.
  Man, thou art safe—
  This floor was never stained with stranger's blood.
  But say what brings thee here? Though fallen, thine air
  Bespeaks a chieftain of no common rank.
ELPHI.
  Above the vulgar, true; though sunk beneath
  The meanest of mankind in misery—

---

107 Trust.

Thus far I've reached but by a miracle—
E'en now the circling dust that, rising, forms
Yon distant cloud marks my pursuers near.
Give then the means of flying instantly,
Or I am surely lost! You hesitate
Fixed as a Basilisk's[108] intent, your eye
Would seem to penetrate my inmost soul.

EMINA.

'Tis he the man of blood, who proudly dared,
With desolating hand and impious rage,
Pour direful vengeance o'er a smiling land.

ELPHI.

I know you not. You do mistake me, woman.

EMINA.

No *Elphi*, no—I never can forget
The lightning's flash from that determined eye
My father fell beneath thy sabre!
Still on mine ear ring his last dreadful cries—
Still his last call for vengeance thrills my bosom.
Vengeance on thee, his murderer!—Know you not
The Sheik Abdalla's daughter?—Aye, 'tis so.

ELPHI.

Too well—and know your tenet—"Blood for blood."
But your sire fell in the fierce battle's rage—
Fell fairly fighting—

EMINA.

By thy ruthless hand—
What ho—within—But hold, perturbed soul
Where are thy passions leading me astray!
Thou spok'st of danger, of pursuit—Oh, true,
It is my husband, Elphi, that pursues thee
Achmet, I say—What, ho! *(Exit).*

ZEINABA *(enter).*

Ruined! undone!——This is Chedid's tent!

ELPHI.

I know it well—but even have hope
Relying on the faith by Arabs shewn,
To all who claim protection in their tents.

ZEINABA.

Away, away!—trust not fallacious hope.

ELPHI.

Hemmed in on every side, no means of flight—
My horse sunk lifeless as I gained the tent.

---

108 Mythical serpent with a fatal stare.

ZEINABA.

    Mine yet remains—fatigued indeed, and harassed;
    Yet while he breathes he'll bear you, to the last
    True to his gen'rous[109] blood.—You yet may reach
    Your friends in safety!—

ELPHI.

    And leave thee behind!
    No, good Abdallah, be our fates alike—

(Enter Emina and Attendants).

EMINA.

    What stranger's this?

ELPHI.

    A faithful friend attendant on my fortune.

EMINA.

    Excuse that keen resentment of the past
    Led me to speak in terms so harsh and grating,
    So unbecoming to a wearied guest—
    Now let me make by gentler acts, amends—
    I've brought refreshments to recruit your strength.
    Horses, and camels wait to bear you hence
    Safe to your friends.—To Achmet I commend you
    He with a guard of horsemen waits your orders.

ELPHI.

    Can you most noble woman then forget—

EMINA.

    Touch not the jarring string[110]—it vibrates still—
    Not Pity, Elphi, now inclines my heart—
    A binding, sacred, and imperious duty
    Never by Arab broke, compels to this
    For both by Heaven and man accursed is he
    Who turns aside from mortal in distress,
    Pleading, pursued, defenceless, at his threshold.

ZEINABA.

    Exalted!—generous woman! Allah for this
    With choicest blessings prosperous mark thy life,
    Thy husband's love, thy duteous children's smiles,
    Gladden thy days, and lead to endless bliss.

AGEEB *(enter).*

    Mother he comes, I saw from yonder height
    Wide in the extended plain, a noble throng
    Of horsemen proudly urging their fierce steeds,
    Behind them far remote as eye could reach

---

109 Noble.
110 Painful memory.

A train of dromedaries half obscured
By clouds of rising dust, bring up the rear.
By the gay shew of glittering arms and banners,
I judge that Osmyn's troops attend our friends—*(perceiving Elphi)*
Ha! 'tis himself—Mother the very same
The valiant chief to whom I owe my life.

EMINA.

To him!—
Merciful Heaven! to him!—thy life to Elphi!
Inscrutable the ways of Providence!
Contending passions harrow up my soul
This noble action *binds*, but not *resolves* me.
Duty alone directed, and our faith—
Elphi—a moment's pause undoes thee now.
Reply not—come—to none else dare I trust thee.
Away, away! To horse—fly for thy life!

(Exeunt).

Scene 3

Outside of the tent.

OSMYN *(enter).*[111]

Futile my purpose—vain our close pursuit!
Fool!—to forsake my former tranquil life,
And yield the reins to uncontrolled ambition.
Days of my youth! regretted 'midst my splendor,
Sweet your remembrance still!—attuned, in peace,
To all the fond endearments of affection.

(Sings) Can language paint the lover's bliss,
When first through sighs, through smiles and tears,
The soul enchanting thrilling yes.
Half breathing softly sweet he hears?
That heavenly yes elates, inspires,
His heart expands, his bosom fires.

Does fate ordain him cloudless hours
A life of ease and joy to prove?
Remembrance gilds, with magic powers,
The crown of Hope propitious love!
That heavenly yes elates, inspires,
His heart expands, his bosom fires.

---

111 The licensing manuscript does not include this speech or song; instead, the scene commences with Othman's speech. Because the score was published as "Sung by Mr. Horn," it is restored here.

(Enter Othman, Chedid, and Chiefs).

OTHMAN *(speaks).*
　We've travelled fast—our jaded horses shew
　The toilsome march we've made—and after all
　Vain our pursuit.

(Enter attendant).

ATTENDANT.
　Achmet has marched upon Emina's orders
　With our reserve of Horse—attendant on
　A chief unknown—this moment marched.
OSMYN.
　What! is it thus your Arab wives beguile
　The tedious hours? thus stifle the fond sigh
　For a loved husband's absence?
EMINA *(enter).*
　Welcome my husband, welcome once again—
　Oh! I have much to greet thy private ear.
CHEDID.
　In private nothing—publicly declare
　The chief who fled from our polluted tents—
　Your life and honour are with mine at stake!
　Who was the chief?
EMINA.
　My father's murderer—our invet'rate foe
　Elphi, the man I *cherished* in your absence.
　Closely pursued by you, of hope bereft
　He gained our tents exhausted by fatigue,
　And claimed protection on our Arab's faith—
　I did my duty—gave him instant aid
　Though the determination wrung my heart—
OSMYN.
　Reveal the track he took—Instant to horse!
　We may pursue and still arrest his flight.
EMINA.
　Nor threats, nor dangers, tortures, lingering death,
　Shall force me to such complicated baseness.
CHEDID.
　Nay—say they did—what would the knowledge serve?
　Could Chedid tamely stand to witness that
　Which must with ignominy brand his name?
　Chief know us better,—all the neighbouring tribes
　In such a cause would rise in arms t' oppose ye!
　Retire my love!

(Emina exits).

OSMYN.
Othman, what troops are here?
OTHMAN.
But fifty horse.
The Syrians[112] turned aside, lured by the smoke
Of scattered villages, that flanked our march.
OSMYN.
Dogs!—It is ever thus! foremost in plunder
But the last to fight—recall them instantly!

(Exit Othman).

CHEDID.
Osmyn displeased?
OSMYN.
Oh, no, in sooth, not I!
While useless toils still overpower my frame
And disappointed vengeance mocks my view;
I cannot fail but smile, and look content
To hear detailed a woman's prejudice.
Last night indeed you held a diff'rent tone
Futile as false—the morning sees you give
Protection to my foe and means of flight.
CHEDID.
But that the truth
In part is mingled with the foul reproach
I should disdain reply.—Such were my words—
Such were my acts—I'm proud to call them mine.
How different my intent, this swelling breast
That rankles still with deadliest hate can prove;
How then suspect he'd fly to me for life?
To me!—I'd stretch my neck to th' uplifted sword
And have my head borne round your hated walls
A spectacle for curious fools to gaze at,
Sooner to beg, with supplicating meanness,
The respite of an hour from him.
OSMYN.
You gloss it well.
Say rather 'twas a scheme too deeply planned,
Thus drawing our attention from the Nile
Whose turbid waves now from our vengeance bear
To give him safe to his expecting troops—
But such is Arabs' faith!
CHEDID.
Osmyn forbear.
Or know the faith you scoff will scarcely save you.

---

112 Part of the Ottoman Empire.

Allah dealt different portions to us all—
To thine, the world would call a favoured race.
He in his goodness, gave, unthanked the while,
Gold, gems, palaces; rich garments, slaves,
And to confirm them yours, he gave you power—
Our lot the desert and the mountains' heights.
Rude are our habits—loose and uncontrolled
But smiling independence glads[113] our tribes.
By vigorous toil and manly courage fostered
Temperance[114] we boast, and proud fidelity,
Inviolably firm.—Witness this proof—
Scoff as thou wilt—the man whom most we hate
Gaining our tents, defenceless and oppressed
Our faith preserves.—But Osmyn's narrow mind
Admits no ray of genuine greatness—
Then tempt my rage no further—at a call
My tribe is armed, and eager for the conflict.

OSMYN.
I must dissemble yet *(aside)*. We know full well
Thy bravery Chedid.—As a friend, excuse
What disappointment wrested from a heart
Too warm its inmost feelings to disguise.

CHEDID.
Enough!—Thus ever may dissenting friends,
When passion's heat subsides, be reconciled.—
Now to our tent, while fierce the sun still rages,
There rest awhile, enjoy the cooling shade;
Then rise refreshed, and share an Arab's meal,
The pledge of Peace.

(Strikes his spear upon his shield; a party of his tribe enter).

CHORUS *(sings).*
An honest welcome meets the guest
The Arab bids partake his board;
Secure the sheltered trav'llers rest
And Peace the pledge his meals afford.
Treachery he scorns—Deceit he flies
Direct his words, his meaning clear
On faith and truth his soul relies
His dealings just, his acts sincere.
Then while the sunbeams fierce descend
A welcome cheers the Arab's friend!
Welcome friends, securely rest

---

113 Makes glad.
114 Self-restraint, e.g., toward alcohol.

Faith pervades the Arab's breast.
Then, while the sunbeams fierce descend
A welcome cheers the Arab's friend *(exeunt)*.

Illustration 4. *The Pyramids from Old Cairo* by Henry Salt, in G.A. Mountnorris [Viscount Valentia], *Voyages and Travels to India, Ceylon, the Red Sea, Abyssinia, and Egypt*, 1809. Courtesy of the Melville Herskovitz Library, Northwestern University.

Act III

Scene 1

*A Camp between Giza and the Pyramids, which are seen in the distance—
Chiefs attached to Elphi (Amalek, Caleb, Omar, and others) meeting.*

AMALEK, CALEB, OMAR, and CHORUS *(sing)*.
Solemn silence reigns around!
Hark!—the lowly whispering rill[115]

---

115 Stream.

Lends a distant murmuring sound,
Trickling down the date-clothed hill.

Vain we wander far and near
No clue to guide, no hope to cheer!
Elphi—Chieftain, Sovereign, Bey—
Dear shall thy foes their treachery pay.

AMALEK *(speaks)*.

Busy report proclaims our Sovereign's fall
Our force, disjointed, needs a present chief.
The general voice demands an instant choice.
I would propose his successor.

CALEB.

Trust not these vague reports, nor name again
Thy rash design; lest from our faithful ranks
We chase thee, doubting thy allegiance.

(A distant shout heard).

But hark!—to dash these rumours to the ground
Those shouts of joy proclaim the Bey's approach.

(The shout increases, ending with "Our Chief! Our Chief! Elphi our Chief!" Enter Elphi, Zeinaba, Achmet, and suite).

ELPHI.

Blest be the hour that brings me back once more
To friends like these. Dangers and hardships past
Give to the present moment tenfold joy.
To all our thanks—my faithful honest friends.
Achmet, to thee our warmest tributes due
This, as the token of our favour, wear. *(Taking off and giving him his own sabre)*
And to your Sheik, bearing acknowledgments,
Present this ring, with it my earnest suit
All enmity between us hence may cease.
Needs he assistance ever from our arms,
Though all the force of Turkey should oppose
We fly to aid him. Peace to your tents, farewell.

(Exeunt Achmet and suite, attended. Elphi turns towards Zeinaba, who appears greatly fatigued, and takes her hand, presenting her to his principal Mamelukes).

Behold this youth—your chief's deliverer
Ah! he sinks! Nay nay—
Now that we've gained the haven of our hopes
Be not o'ercome at last.

ZEINABA.

Oh Elphi, each reverse, save this, I've borne

And stoutly too—But the full flood of joy
To see thee thus o'erpowers—and still not know me! *(Reveals herself)*.
ELPHI.
Good Heavens! Zeinaba! *(Embracing her)* Is it possible?
Wert thou so near me, and I knew thee not?
Best loved of women! Saved too by thy care!
But why, unkind one, from thy husband's eyes
So long conceal thyself?
ZEINABA *(faintly)*.
Inquire not now,
But read in that disguise a proof of love!
ELPHI.
Of matchless love!—yet how could such a form—
So soft—so delicate, endure such trials?
ZEINABA.
Think you the mind, by fond affection prompted,
Could ever shrink from danger? But I faint—
Lend me your arm—I must awhile retire.
ELPHI *(supports her)*.
In the dread hour of trial woman stands
Pre-eminently bold—but danger past,
Delight, with its full tide of rapture, flows,
And overpowers at once her tender spirit.
Look up love.
Cheerly—so—so—rest will recover thee.

(Exeunt Elphi supporting Zeinaba).

CHORUS OF MAMELUKES *(sing)*.
Elphi returns—our choral strain
Triumphant rising, rend the skies.
The boundless joy let none restrain
Nile from thy verdant banks arise.

Nature with smiles shall deck her vales,
Her mountains welcome thunder round
Till borne on undulating gales
Remotest climes the notes resound.

Elphi returns
Our hopes to crown
To freedom, Victory,
Fame, Renown *(exeunt)*.

Scene 2

The Desert. Outside of a tent. Camels, horses, etc., described as resting
after a march. Chedid, Emina, and Zara. Other camels seen coming in with
travellers—amongst whom a Pilgrim passes by. Time about sunset.

EMINA.

How light yon Pilgrim seems to tread the ground,
I heard him singing all the way we came,
With jocund voice enlivening the dull march,
So sweetly innocence of heart can smooth,
When duty prompts, the rugged path of life.
Where bound good Pilgrim?

PILGRIM.

To Mecca, Lady.

EMINA.

Well, speed the Youth—thou hast a merry heart.

PILGRIM.

Have I good Lady? Joy befits our age
When nature bounds elastic, when the mind
Unclouded by misfortune, warmly feels
The thrilling powers of soul enchanting music!

(Recitative)

Who has not felt, whose soul can feel
The magic power to music given,
That power which fires the warrior's zeal
And lifts the saint's pure thought to heaven.

(Air)

If on the way-worn pilgrim's ear
The sultry breeze soft music bear
The sound though he through wilds must roam
Suspends the thoughts of toil and home.

But if that breeze should waft along
His earliest lays,[116] his country's song,
Then, though through deserts downed[117] to roam,
Before him glow the joys of home.

Thirst, heat and toil, no more he feels,
Like Mecca's balm, that music heals,
And though his feet through deserts roam
That well-known strain transports him home.

---

116 Lyric or narrative poems, usually meant to be sung.
117 Lined with birds' down.

EMINA *(speaks)*.

    Melodious strain! well suited to the scene.
    Now sunk behind the hills, the scorching sun
    Gives a short respite to the wearied world.
    How still the air! How bright across the waste
    The evening star shoots its silvery light.

CHEDID.

    All still as death! Sullen as this the calm
    Ushering the tempest that o'erwhelms the land
    With its fell[118] fury from the burning south.
    1 like it not. Those scattered horsemen too,
    We noted late, mysteriously suspicious.
    Base, treacherous, and deceitful Osmyn's heart.

EMINA.

    Too true indeed, I tremble for our safety,
    If unawares attacked. Our followers few—
    Our camp exposed—ill-suited for defence.

CHEDID.

    Fear not Emina; in our hearts we're strong,
    A match for thousands such as Osmyn leads—
    Slaves to his power alone, but unattached,
    By any ties of feeling or affection;
    Ruled by a force oppressive, dragged from home,
    Torn from their relatives, and driven to fill
    The hated ranks of an ambitious tyrant.
    Our tribes adore us—for their tents they fight,
    Their wives, their children, all their social joys.
    Such, if a torrent's force o'erwhelm them not,
    We may esteem invincible.

EMINA, ZARA, and PILGRIM *(sing)*.

    Could faith and justice aid us,
    Behind their triple shield,
    Should countless hosts invade us
    We'd dauntless brave the field.

    But power and fraud assailing
    Sweep with the torrent's force
    Our efforts unavailing
    To stem their furious course.
    No, no, no, no!
    Destruction marks their course.

(A gun is fired).

---

118 Savage.

CHEDID *(has been looking out anxiously at the wing; endeavouring to conceal his surprise exclaims).*
  The evening gun.
EMINA.
  It is not yet the hour.

(Another gun fired. The alarm given. Arabs behind, and entering).

CHORUS.
  To arms! To arms!
EMINA.
  Whence these alarms?
ARABS.
  Our tents the Turks insidious gain
  They sweep the hills, they scour the plain
  To arms! To arms!

(Exeunt Chedid heading the Arabs. Emina and Zara remaining).

ZARA *(singing).*
  Preserve him Heaven! Our champion save!
  Where death and danger mark the field,
  His manly daring bosom shield
  And crown, with victory crown the brave.

(They retire into the tent. An attack and skirmish behind the scenes. A retreat. Enter Chedid, his sword drawn, and in disorder, as from fighting).

CHEDID *(speaks).*
  All skill is vain—their numbers bear us down.

(Enter immediately, Osmyn with his guards, etc., who arrange themselves so as to hold Chedid prisoner, one of them disarming him. Osmyn receives his sabre).

OSMYN.
  Where are your deserts now, your mountain heights,
  That yield such certain refuge to your tribes?
CHEDID.
  I do not yet conceive your full intent;
  True that my life is in your hands; what then?
  Think you an Arab Sheik will basely crouch
  Like a low peasant in his master's presence?
OSMYN.
  Still, haughty chieftain, towers thy spirit thus?
  So soon forgot the injuries thou didst me?
  Such injuries Osmyn never can forgive,
  Though to console, thou hast thine Arab faith.
CHEDID *(tauntingly).*
  Deeper the hatred of thy baseness Osmyn.
  Deeper my scorn—but not a thought of fear.
  At once disclose my fate I'll boldly meet it.

OSMYN.

    Thou art far in our arrears.[119]

    Five hundred purses[120] by tomorrow's dawn

    Or forfeit be thy life.

CHEDID.

    Poor are our villages, and much depressed

    With late exactions, raised in wanton mood

    By thy dependents: vampires on the land

    Draining its sweetest blood!

    And thus a prisoner, how command the sum?

OSMYN.

    Leave thy son hostage.

CHEDID.

    My son! My noble boy!—But down, fond heart,

    Affections are denied the Arab Sheik,

    His public duties must at once decide,

    They claim the sacrifice—then be it so.

    Ageeb!

(Calling—Ageeb enters).

    In Osmyn's conquering hands remain

    Our hostage, till with gold, I ransom thee.

OSMYN.

    Tomorrow's dawn, we shall expect thee Chedid.

    And mark me well, thy son's head answers it.

    Back to our palace, friends!

(Chedid looks earnestly on Ageeb, rushing to and taking him in his arms—they embrace. Ageeb is placed amongst the Turks. A March. Exeunt Osmyn and his suite, Chedid remaining for a moment lost in thought—looking after Ageeb, rouses, and, turning towards the opposite wing, calls).

CHEDID.

    Come forth, Emina!

EMINA *(entering).*

    My husband! praised be Allah!

    Did then the savages at last relent?

    But where's my boy? was he not with thee Chedid?

CHEDID.

    Collect thy fortitude—he rests our hostage.

EMINA.

    Ageeb in Osmyn's hands! You could not sure—

CHEDID.

    Compose thee love. This instant I proceed

    To raise his ransom. Osmyn's faith is pledged.

---

119 Your debt to us is great.

120 An Ottoman monetary unit. The ransom equates to approximately £2,500 (over £200,000 in 2010 currency).

EMINA.

    His faith!—a Turk's!—Sooner the rugged lion

    His trembling prey beneath his bloody fangs,

    I'd trust, than any of this monster's race.

    Our boy is lost. Cruel, unnatural father!

    Thou'st placed him bound within the assassin's gripe![121]

CHEDID.

    My duty to our tribe, not our own safety

    While my heart bled, determined me.

    But I repent it now.

    Reflection tells me not a hope exists

    To raise one half the sum. Five hundred purses!

EMINA.

    Ha!—surely Heaven suggests the blessed thought

    And I shall save my boy!

    Chedid, nor seek to question or prevent me.

    Thy swiftest courser instant bears me hence.

    Tomorrow's dawn restores me with the gold,

    Or thou ne'er seest thy loved Emina more. *(She embraces him, and hurries off).*

CHEDID *(alone).*

    I dare not, though I would arrest her course;

    Nature will rise still paramount to duty.

    The means she seeks I know and disapprove,

    But others there are none.

    Yet be exertion to the utmost strained.

    Allah forbid the weight of obligation

    Where every feeling of an Arab's soul

    Calls for revenge! *(Exit).*

Scene 3

The Suburbs of Cairo. Enter Hyder, in a loose cloak and turban, disguised as a Turkish drummer, and wearing one of the little round Drums of the country called Tom-toms.[122]

HYDER *(alone).* I've had as many hair-breadth escapes in twelve short hours looking for Sewda, as would satisfy the most ravenous Turk's appetite in perpetuity. But all's well now—thanks to this dress, which I pilfered from a sleepy-headed drummer at the serai;[123] so let me but discover my little evergreen[124]—my budding nosegay of heartsease,[125] and if I ever wander from home again, rambling

---

121 Clasp.

122 An East Indian drum, or more generally any hand-beaten drum from Asia or Africa.

123 Travellers' rest stop, as in caravanserai.

124 Never failing.

125 Bouquet of pansies.

from Cecca to Mecca,[126] may crocodiles once more ingest the river,[127] and seahorses bed themselves 'midst my pineapples.[128]

(*Sings*)Who wanders about is a fool for his pains,
He brings home his trouble alone for his gains,
And sure his allowance of brains must be small.
Who always is running his head to the wall.

Quiet, quiet. Oh give me quiet!
We battle for peace, and for rest we riot.

But a wife brings—what? A legion of brats,
And a house must run over with mice or cats;
A wife will scold and a brat will squall,
Rats, kittens and cats—are the devil and all.

Quiet, quiet. Oh give me quiet!
We battle for peace, and for rest we riot.

A peaceable man then should sit down alone,
Should twist his own griskin,[129] and broil his own bone.
Yet ere I'm in quest of a rib with a tongue,[130]
Which though she may be short, I may find to be long.

Quiet, quiet. Oh give me quiet!
We battle for peace, and for rest we riot.

(*Looking out at the wings. Speaks*) Eh!—Who have we here? Good old Hassan in the clutches of those rascally Turks! And Sewda too!—That's right my fine fellows! Every dog his day—and we bite next. To cheat such scoundrels as these, does me more good than to feast on a young kid[131] with cloves and raisins, after that terrible month fasting in Rhamazan.[132] (*Considering*) I have it—I'll bribe my little sleepy-headed drummer at the serai. He'll act with me—and then—call me Turk too—if I'm not even with you (*exit*).

(*Enter Turkish soldiers dragging in Hassan prisoner. Sewda following*).

TURK. Bring him along—a hoary-headed[133] traitor.
HASSAN. Traitor! But what avails complaint, when in a ruffian's power?
SEWDA. Look soldiers—look on those reverend locks—look and respect—

---

126 "Cecca to Mecca" is from Cervantes' *Don Quixote*, an alliterative phrase usually translated as "from pillar to post." Mecca is the site where Mohammed proclaimed Islam; subsequently the destination for Muslims on the hajj (holy pilgrimage).
127 Possibly an allusion to Job 23:40: "Behold, he drinketh up a river, and hasteth not: he trusteth that he can draw up Jordan into his mouth."
128 Fanciful nonsense suggesting that will never happen.
129 A lean cut of pork loin; here, it refers to preparing his own meal.
130 An allusion to the biblical Eve, created from Adam's rib.
131 Goat.
132 Variant of Ramadan, the month-long Islamic rite of fasting and prayer.
133 Grey-haired.

TURK. "Respect" quotha![134] What he must turn state gardener, I warrant him, planting new rulers, and rooting out old ones—But he'll find it a dangerous trade, and the lopping part of it, begins with his own head. Away with him!

HASSAN. Soldiers release me, and take all I'm worth—This purse of gold—*(producing one from his girdle)*—the savings of a long industrious life—

TURK *(snatching it)*. Is ours, you see—what else to offer?

SEWDA. I will go round amongst my friends, and by tomorrow bring you three times the sum.

(The roll of a distant drum is heard behind, followed by two taps, and answered immediately by a similar roll, and two taps close to the wing).

TURK *(starting)*. Eh! What the devil's this comrade? A roll-call![135]

(Enter Hyder—he advances beating his drum).

HYDER *(in a disguised voice)*. Any soldier absent at roll-call, shall be bastinadoed for a twelvemonth,[136] at the rate of twenty sound blows on the soles of his feet daily, in the first place—in the next—

TURK *(interrupting him)*. Hold, hold good master thumper of the tom-tom—one twentieth part of the first punishment would stiffen the best of us—so you may spare your breath—the rest is superfluous—we must be off—But what shall we do with our prisoner, and his promised ransom? Our captain would save us the trouble of receiving that, if we lodged him in the guard room, and give us the bastinado instead of it.

HYDER *(first beating his drum)*. Why look ye comrades, if you share handsomely *(Hassan beating his drum again, the Turks appear alarmed)*. I don't care, now that my rounds are done, if I take charge of him myself. But you must pay beforehand *(again beating drum)*.

TURK. Share and share, comrade—this included—*(giving him Hassan's purse)* But keep a sharp eye to him.

HYDER. Aye, aye—I'll lodge him safely—the snug little choky,[137] by Yuseph's[138] Terrace, west of the Citadel. Why you know me?

TURK. Can't say we do, exactly.

HYDER. What!—Not know Mustapha? That comical droll fellow, born to make a noise in the world! *(Beating his drum)* Everybody knows me, I am everybody's messenger, everybody's companion, and everybody's friend. But I must do my duty. *(Repeating the roll on his drum)* Any soldiers absent at roll-call, shall be—

(Another Drum beats behind, and towards the back of the stage, upon which the Turks start, look at each other, and run off. Hyder watches them till they are fairly gone, at the wing, giving a final smart roll, and the two taps).

SEWDA *(advancing to—without knowing Hyder)*. Oh dear, good Sir.

HYDER *(discovering himself)*. Why Sewda!

(She runs into his arms).

HASSAN. Hyder!

---

134 An interjection calling attention to the sarcastic quotation of another's words.

135 A military procedure: every soldier answers when his name is given.

136 Beaten, especially on the soles of the feet, for a year.

137 Prison.

138 Yusef, variant of Joseph.

HYDER. There, take this cloak, drum, and your purse, again *(giving them to Hassan)*. Thump your way to the advanced post—get into Elphi's lines with a flag,[139] and we'll soon follow you. We must not venture in a body through these hyenas. Away! No time to lose!

(Pushing him off. Exit Hassan).

And now we're met again my dear Sewda, we'll never separate, but take your father back to Rosetta,[140] get married at once, and be as happy as the day is long my girl.

SEWDA. Prettily said, Hyder—But make a husband of you, and you'll be as bad as the rest of them I warrant me.

SEWDA and HYDER *(singing)*.
You teasing men are all alike
But once the wedding over,
Come doubt and gloom, distrust, dislike,
Good bye the timid Lover.

"Zounds[141] Madam! This will never do
This Rice so hard, what teeth can chew?
And who the devil ever saw
A mess[142] like this, such cursed pillaw!"[143]

Then nothing for it left the wife
Must scold it out for very life.
Or pout and sigh, and beg and pray
And rue to death her wedding day.

HYDER.
You saucy minx, no more of this
The Moullah[144] once writing,[145]
We'll laugh and coax the toy and kiss
No wrangling, jangling, fighting.
For better and for worse, you know
Then smoothly down the stream we go—
In amber ships on seas of milk
The rudder gold—the sails of silk.
A cottage snug—a parsley bed—
Our olive branches round us spread,
A quiver full to frisk and play[146]
And make us bless our wedding day.

---

139 A signal that one side requests parley with the other.
140 A port city 40 miles (65 km) east of Alexandria, also called Rashid.
141 An interjection derived from "God's wounds!"
142 A meal.
143 A dish of rice typically with meat and spices (pilau).
144 Cleric (mullah).
145 This presumably refers to the recording of a marriage.
146 Foreshadows their resulting children: "a quiver full of children" proverbially refers to a large family.

SEWDA and HYDER.
  A Cottage snug, a Parsley Bed
  Our olive branches round us spread,
  A quiver full to frisk and play
  And make us bless our wedding day *(exeunt)*.

Scene 4

The interior of Elphi's Tent, his own Apartment, Mameluke Arms[147] *hung round. Elphi enters with a letter, which he delivers to, and despatches one of his Mameluke Chiefs with. His Guards and Attendants fill the back of the Scene, the most conspicuous bearing his buckler,*[148] *helmet, firearms, etc.*

ELPHI.
  Now all's in readiness, my heart beats high,
  My cause is just—we shall return triumphant!

(Receiving his Commander's staff of iron, or his battle-axe, from an attendant officer. Enter suddenly Emina, preceded by a Mameluke Officer who passes over the stage).

EMINA.
  Elphi! behold me now a suppliant here;
  I in my turn imploring bend to thee. *(Kneeling)*
  Late to our tent thou earnest, I now seek thine,
  With all the mother's feelings roused to madness!
ELPHI *(raising her)*.
  Rise noble, excellent, revered Emina.
  But that it pains me aught[149] disturbs thy peace
  Rapturous I'd hail the moment given to serve thee,
  Most blest, most fortunate in Elphi's life.
  At once disclose the means—oblige—command me.
EMINA.
  The daughter and the mother war within me,
  One bids me hate thee, and the other bless.
  His very life's blood
  Thy sabre's point drank from my father's heart—
  But thou didst save my son.
ELPHI.
  Trust me Emina, much it grieves my heart,
  That war erst[150] led me to thy father's tents,
  And much I mourn the hapless chance befell him.
  But let the past be buried in oblivion.

---

147 Either heraldic symbols or weapons.
148 Strap of the helmet.
149 Anything.
150 Formerly.

One common interest now demands our care—
To drive the Turk beyond our country's bounds,
End our unhappy feuds, and seal our freedom.
EMINA.
  Oh! let it animate our souls, and rouse
Each latent spark of patriotism. My hand
I tender,[151] Elphi, in a cause so glorious,
And Chedid's noble nature will commend me.
Chedid!—Alas! this moment of enthusiasm
Led me from present woe to future hopes,
Vain as they're fleeting!
Osmyn surprised, subdued, dispersed, our tribe.
My son's head answers it—should Chedid fail
This very day to raise the extorted ransom.
ELPHI (quickly).
  Gold! Generous woman! Till his sordid mind
Is glutted with the despicable dross,
Osmyn shall find our treasury supplies him.
The swiftest steeds our trusty Mamelukes boast
Shall bear to Chedid, under escort sure,
Purses beyond his need.
More would I tell thee, but by deeds we speak.
Commend me to your Sheik, or name me not
To wound his feelings or alarm his pride.
Best as befits your son's immediate safety.
Join we Zeinaba till your escort mounts
And prayers and blessings to thy tents attend thee.

(Exeunt).

Scene 5

Interior of the Palace at Cairo—a State Apartment.

OSMYN (alone).
  Is this then power? Ambitious fools! are these
The charms that lure ye to such desperate heights?
Say what is life, that we still doting seek
To eke it out with such insatiate fondness?
Is it a fair assemblage of delights,
A social intercourse of kindred minds
In early bonds of amity allied,
Who onward move along a roseate path?

---

151 Offer.

(Sings) Retired beneath the splendid dome,
The monarch sinks, his heart oppressed
For them will troubled fancy roam,
Nor balmy sleep his eyelids rest.

But, hark! the voice of Fame resounds—
He springs!—his soul with ardour bounds—
He rears his crest on high.
He vaults—his neighing charger flies—
He spurns the ground, his spirits rise
To conquer or to die.

In vain the death-charged shell may soar,
The cannon's thunder vainly roar,
Drums beat, and clarions[152] sound
Amongst the dying and the dead
His blood-stained horse shall furious tread,
His toils with victory crowned.

His bright reward, the laurel wreath
His soul's desire, his hopes achieved.

(Speaks) Such is the dream of youth—but the reverse
Experience paints in truer tints—a scene
Of warring passions, fierce dissension, wrongs,
Desires ungratified, and hopes destroyed!
OTHMAN *(enters)*.
The Arab sheik demands an audience.
OSMYN.
Othman, you know our will. Let him approach.

(Enter Sheik Chedid, followed by Osmyn's guards, and after him, an elderly Sheik, or High-Priest, in the Arabian pontifical vestments[153] (in this instance representing also the Governor of Cairo). He is attended suitably, and bowing in a stately manner to Osmyn, retires towards the back of the stage, conversing apart so as to be observable by the audience, with Othman).

CHEDID.
Osmyn, you see I'm punctual to my time.
Behold the money—let them count it forth
And now my tribe is free. Release my son.
OSMYN.
Such our intention—Go, release the boy!

---

152 A shrill trumpet used in war.

153 In practice, there is no ensemble designating a Muslim cleric. "Pontifical" is Roman Catholic; Hamilton indicates the
      loftiness (and perhaps the pomposity) of the office rather than a corresponding priestly hierarchy in Islam. On stage, the
      office of cleric needed to be signified; a civic dignitary's robes would have been adapted (or invented) for the purpose.

(Exit an Officer, to whom he had addressed himself. Chedid, going out, is opposed by Osmyn's Guards).

OSMYN.

Hold Chedid, hold. Thyself our prisoner now.
Thought'st thou so meanly,[154] Sheik, of our revenge?
Thy gold we wanted first, that gained, thy life!
A public execution crowns our triumph.

CHEDID.

Dishonoured wretch. The earth no more shall groan
Beneath such turpitude.

(Chedid draws a dagger, and advances upon Osmyn—his arm caught by one of the guards).

OSMYN.

Disarm him instantly. Idiot! to think
I'd leave thee means t' escape from my revenge.
The gates of death shall open from the scaffold.

CHEDID.

The coward only flies to self-destruction!
Coward, thou knowest, thy Turks know, I am none.
Thou canst not shake my soul, detested monster!
E'en from the scaffold Chedid shall defy thee!

OSMYN.

We'll put thy boasted courage to the proof,
By pain and ignominy. Bear him hence!

CHEDID.

Pain! Puny tyrant! Rack thy troubled mind,
Exhaust invention, till unheard-of pangs
Seize every nerve. Unmoved, I still deride thee.
On thine own head be ignominy.
Glorious his death, however vile the means,
Steadfast in principle, resolved in truth,
And spurning treachery—he the block ennobles,
While meanness, groveling, base, degrades the throne.

(Chedid exits under guard).

OSMYN.

Sealed is his fate! Elphi is surely mine.
Our cares were ended, and my reign secure.

(Enter a Turk hastily).

What means this interruption?

TURK.

Elphi breaks up his camp, and suddenly
Hither directs his march.

---

154 Slightly.

OSMYN.

    Let him approach. We may defy his efforts.

    Strong are our towers, our frowning ramparts high,

    And troops of prong[155] undaunted man the walls.

    Quick, to your stations friends; but ere we fight

    Hasten to gratify our deep revenge.

    Bring forth your prisoner to the citadel.

(Exeunt).

Scene 6

*A platform in the citadel, with a gateway partly overlooking the walls. In the distance
the ancient aqueduct, and a reach of the Nile. A procession of solemnly marching troops
leads Chedid to execution. Amongst those attending is Emina, leaning on Ageeb.
The full effect of this scene is not entirely shewn till the gateway opens. Enter Osmyn,
attended suitably, the High Priest and his suite, with Othman following.*

OSMYN.

    Chedid, thine hour is come.

CHEDID *(steps intrepidly forwards)*.

    And chose most aptly Osmyn to inspire

    Thy troops with courage. *(Sneeringly)* Yet reflect awhile

    My friends are numerous, their connections strong

    E'en in your city. Tremble then to give

    The order that o'erturns thy tottering throne.

OSMYN.

    Lead him to execution.

EMINA *(rushing forwards)*.

    Osmyn stay!

    Mine was the crime, if crime it may be called,

    Be mine the punishment. He unconscious fought

    Beneath thy banner, steadfast in thy cause,

    While by my aid, your common foe escaped.

    On me pour out thy vengeance then, but spare

    Hear me, in mercy spare my husband's life *(kneeling)*.

CHEDID.

    Forbear Emina. Rouse thy nobler spirit,

    Thy sire and husband, both were Arab Sheiks.

    Disgrace us not, disgrace not thus thyself,

    Thine high descent, thy known, acknowledged virtues,

    By servile pleadings at a monster's feet.

---

155 Spears.

At best, but for a few short fleeting years,
For which I'd barter not an hour of honour.

(Emina rising while Chedid speaks, goes and rests upon him, greatly agitated).

OSMYN.
Obey me, guards!
CHEDID *(leaving Emina to Ageeb).*
Tyrant thy cup is full, and though my blood
May seal the horrid catalogue of guilt,
Our Arab tribes shall gloriously avenge it.
Allah! for ends inscrutable to man,
Permits a scourge on earth—some dire offence,
Some crime unheard, Egypt must expiate.
But purified from sin, justice divine
Shall thunder death.
Blast thee devoted wretch—and leave thy name
For generations yet unborn to execrate.
OSMYN.
And thine posterity shall bless, no doubt,
Cherish that blessing—for, of this be sure,
Thy name alone survives the passing hour.
Had thou ten thousand lives, the whole I deem
Too poor a sacrifice to my revenge.
CHEDID.
Short-sighted being!—Vain, presumptuous man!
His name but breathed, when Chedid murdered falls
Destruction overtakes thy guilty course.
Living, remorse shall haunt, contempt pursue thee.
Fame will report us truly at the last.
Unstained my life—unstigmatized my death
Thy days dishonoured, and thy fall descried.[156]
Strike when thou wilt, the blow recoils on thee.
What yet remains is precious to my heart
These few short moments love, be Heaven's and thine.

(Turning towards and encouraging Emina, who leans upon him overcome by feeling and scarce able to support herself. The elderly Sheik (High Priest) bearing the Koran,[157] steps forward).

HIGH PRIEST.
I warn you Osmyn, pass not on, for here
The limits of your earthly power determines.
I speak our Prophet's will—he must not die.

(A commotion amongst the bystanders).

---

156 In the published version, this is "desired"; in the manuscript it is "descred," presumably intended as "descried" (made known).
157 Holy book of Islam.

A CHIEF.

We're deep enough in blood!

OSMYN.

Ha! Am I thwarted? Vengeance be then mine own.

(He draws his sabre—the High Priest interposes, placing himself between Chedid and Osmyn. Chedid gives Emina over to Ageeb—turning boldly towards and confronting Osmyn).

HIGH PRIEST [(to Osmyn)].

Impious profaner of our holy laws!

Against the high behests of Mahomet

By me promulgated, darest thou rebel?

Advance a single step, and we depose thee (holding open the Koran before Chedid).

OSMYN.

Dotard,[158] beware! Thy superstitious dreams,

Thy prophet's vengeance, and thy priestly craft,

I laugh to scorn, and tread beneath my feet.

Learn, that whate'er opposes Osmyn's way

This hand removes.

An instant longer dare dispute my will

And through thy rebel heart I strike the blow.

(Othman here interposes, and appears as entreating Osmyn, who shakes him off angrily, and is furiously advancing upon Chedid, when (at the very moment), a crash is heard behind the gateway. He starts and pauses).

HIGH PRIEST.

Hark! Roused by thy blasphemies, Heaven intervenes.

(Osmyn turns round—a second crash, and Elphi's advanced guard burst open the gateway. Elphi rushes forward, crosses Osmyn's raised sabre with his own, and parries it, disarming him. His Mamelukes, following up, halt in the gateway, and Osmyn's party goes over to them).

ELPHI.

His life be spared.

Memory recurs to former happy days,

They call for mercy. I admit the appeal

Though prudence doom thee to perpetual chains.

Secure him Mamelukes, our prisoner.

(Advancing, and at the same time, his troops drawing up on each side of the gateway. The whole extent of scenery opens upon the audience. Osmyn taken off guarded—Othman following).

ELPHI (to Chedid).

Brave Sheik. Shame on these ignominious bonds!

(Loosening his chains) Be free—all that thou late possessed restored.

Forget the past; we live as friends in future.

---

158 Imbecile, especially due to advanced age.

CHEDID.

Elphi—no—our father's fate forbids it.
These hands in amity can ne'er be joined
With thine—polluted by our nearest blood.
Thus much I promise—free us from the Turk,
Rule justly, anxious for thy country's good,
Our tribes shall not oppose thee. So farewell!

(Emina takes Elphi's hand, presses it to her heart, then throws herself into Chedid's arms, who supports and leads her off with much dignity, followed by Ageeb and Attendants. The High Priest and suite range themselves near Elphi).

ELPHI.

Give them safe conduct, guard them to their camp,
With presents ample. Allah! Just thy ways!
He, in his humble tent, shall happier rest
Than careworn sovereigns on their splendid thrones.
Brave friends and comrades! share the general joy.
Throw wide our palace gates, prepare the feast,
And peace shall bless our late distracted land.
Strike and lead on, let pleasure rule the hour
When loyalty supplants illegal power.

(Finale)

ELPHI'S TROOPS *(singing).*

Gloom and sorrow hence away
Egypt rejoice
With heart and voice.
Hail our Sovereign Bey.

The ravenous Turk no more oppressing.
Freed from his heavy galling chain,
Our songs re-echoing glad the plain,
In peace against our valleys smile,
Again abundance crowns the Nile,
Elphi's return brings every blessing.

Gloom and sorrow hence away
Egypt rejoice
With heart and voice.
Hail our Sovereign Bey.

Trip to America (1824)

Editing Issues

Beginning in 1794, Charles Mathews was a leading low comedian of the provincial and London stages. From 1811, he experimented with two-person shows that enabled him to exhibit a variety of eccentric characters. This established relationships with playwrights who became accustomed to writing for Mathews's talents. In 1818, he gave up his life as a contracted actor in a dramatic company and relaunched his career as a solo performer, presenting the first in a series of fifteen shows in which he invited audiences to join him as if "at home" for an excursion into storytelling, lecturing, and comic vignettes. They were authored, at least to some degree, by playwrights but based upon Mathews's suggestions of characters he had observed from life, wished to reprise from earlier performances, or had invented.[1] None of the playwrights' texts survives, nor do we have the equivalent of an actor's version (reflecting Mathews's further interpolations) or prompt script. Instead, for each of the "at homes," there are one or two souvenir texts cribbed by hacks: all are illegitimate, and in the early years, Mathews sued the publishers of these six-penny pamphlets.[2] *Trip to America*, the "at home" he presented after returning from a US tour in 1824, is unique in having four such texts (some in multiple editions), illustrated with frontispieces;[3] these afford the opportunity, through comparison and contrast, to confirm details observed in performance while also compounding the degree of variation among presentations that might be considered valid. Apart from reviews, which confirm some details, these illegitimate texts are the main sources for understanding Mathews's "at homes."

Though arguably rendered from spectators' perspectives, the texts are far from perfect as sources. Comic acting, particularly from someone as versatile as Mathews, is devilishly challenging to notate. How does one concentrate on the words, gestures, dialect transcription, intonation, as well as physical

---

1   Nowadays, Mathews's methods might be called performance ethnography: personal observation among other people, leading to a rendition of the visited group's identificatory characteristic of belonging, using acting techniques but not abnegating the researcher's own persona or obscuring the practice of observation. There are some problems with this paradigm when applied to Mathews. First, Mathews consistently disparaged lower-class white Americans in private correspondence. Second, Mathews bemoaned his difficulty in coming into contact with "real" Americans, failing to recognize European immigrants or the descendents of Africans as authentic. Third, his claims of authenticity are untraceable; for example, the "authentic" native tune for "Possum Up a Gum Tree" has not been identified. And finally, his material resembles earlier travelogues and newspaper accounts such as William Faux, *Memorable Days in America: Being a Journal of a Tour to the United States, Principally Undertaken to Ascertain the Condition and Probable Prospects of British Emigrants; Including Accounts of Mr. Birkbeck's Settlement in the Illinois* (London, 1823); and Henry Bradshaw Fearon, *Sketches of America; a Narrative of a Journey of Five Thousand Miles through the Eastern and Western States of America* (London: Longman et al., 1818).

2   Unattributed clipping, Anne Mathews's scrapbooks, vol. 2, fol. 82, Harvard Theatre Collection. Thr 483.3.35.

3   These exist in multiple printings, but the base texts are *Account of Mr. Mathews' at Home; as Delivered in an Annual Lecture on Peculiarities, Characters, and Manners, Founded on His Own Observations and Adventures during His Late Trip to America ... Also a Monopolylogue, Called All Well at Natchitoches; Embellished with a Representation of the Scene, &c. &c.* (London: Duncombe, [1824]); *The London Mathews; Containing an Account of This Celebrated Comedian's Trip to America ...* (London: Hodgson and Co., [1824]), reprinted in Philadelphia by Morgan and Yeager, and in Baltimore by J. Robinson; *Sketches of Mr. Mathews's Celebrated Trip to America Comprising a Full Account of His Admirable Lecture on Peculiarites, Characters, and Manners; with the Most Laughable of the Stories and Adventures, and Eight Original Comic Songs ...* (London: J. Limbird, [1824]); and *Supplement to the Numbers Already Published of* The Vocal Gleaner and Universal Melodist; *a Sketch of Mr. Mathews's Entertainment, Entitled A Trip to America ...* (London: J.D. Bird, 1824).

gags—all potential justifications for why a bit is humorous—with equal felicity and completeness? And how should such a performance be rendered: as dialogue (though there is only one actor); as running commentary upon action, effects, and text (as if it were not orally delivered, alternating between first and third person); or as verbatim text (which would account for what Mathews said but not how he said it or what he did)? No wonder Mathews disapproved of all attempts to transcribe his work, for comic acting's many valences are not subject to capture. It is crucial to remember that these source texts are mementos rushed into print by profiteers, not in any way equivalent to a dramatic score rendered by an author and given the imprimatur of the artist who brought it to the stage.

The solo piece *Trip to America* took Mathews three-and-a-half hours to perform. That implies a great deal of ad-libbing and action beyond what was transcribed. It is not known when the shorthand clerks who made the transcriptions attended, how often they attended, or the order in which the versions were published. It is likely, however, that some of the variations can be explained by Mathews's expansion or truncation of some parts, substitution of material, or hitting the comic tone differently over the many months that he performed the piece. The four versions credit different tunes for the songs, and these are not always reconcilable to each other or the meter of the verse; they may be misattributions or genuine changes that Mathews implemented.

The souvenir texts alternate between puns, jokes and jests, songs, characters' banter, comic recitations, *bon mots*, catch-phrases, linking narrative, and appeals to the audience, rendered variously in third-person narration, dialogue, first-person narration, summary description, and direct address. These are transcription conventions for what was essentially an autobiographical lecture, larded with incidents and anecdotes intended to convey the authenticity of Mathews's reenactment. All the pirated texts stipulate that Mathews drew upon well-known tunes for many of the songs and reflect how the performance—loosely organized as a travel narrative in which he likens himself to Columbus "discovering" America—resembled Mathews's well-established repertoire of characters and comic business. The "at homes" hook a narrative onto the people encountered in various kinds of conveyance (here, the transatlantic sailing ship, American steamship, stagecoach, and sleigh) and while taking in the local sights (here, including inns, a boarding house, theatre, battle site, post office, and courthouse). Across the versions of *Trip to America*, many of the jokes, some of the wording, and almost all the episodes recur, tracking Mathews's theatrical tour back and forth along the eastern seaboard; thus, evidence of consistency in the performance is cumulative rather than definitive.

Only one version exists in a modern edition.[4] It is a transcription, and the editor made no attempt to refer across the other three sources. The edition printed here is derived through comparison of all four sources and aims to present as integrated a version as feasible. This compound edition is a "critical archive" rather than a definitive edition of the first—or any other—night's performance.[5] Where alternative passages exist, compatible portions are knit together; some alternatives are left out, especially in the songs, but the sense is retained. The order of episodes is based on the preponderance of evidence, and all but the Duncombe edition usually agree in this regard. Performative information is prioritized and rendered with modern lexigraphic methods. Only one passage, the encounter between the ship *William Thompson* and another vessel, was originally rendered as dramatic dialogue; elsewhere in the pirated editions, long dashes usually separate different characters' speeches. For readers' ease, whenever the intended speakers are decipherable (or inferable) these passages are rendered with name tags, and stage directions are

---

4   This is the Duncombe edition, reprinted in Richard Klepac, *Mr. Mathews at Home* (London: Society for Theatre Research, 1979).

5   Comparability among the source texts can be seen in a side-by-side presentation on the website; this more closely resembles a variorum of the four sources. See http://drama.at.northwestern.edu/.

italicized and ascribed to particular characters. Since the performance was metadramatically narrated by Mathews, all but the opening "exordium" and the afterword are rendered as either first-person narration or in the form of dramatic dialogue.

Illustration 5. Playbill for *Trip to America*, 25 March 1824, in *Charles Mathews at Home.* Courtesy of the Garrick Club.

Illustration 6. Frontispiece to *Account of Mr. Mathews at Home*, depicting characters from the monopolylogue, Duncombe ed., c. 1825. Courtesy of the Henry E. Huntington Library.

Genre Issues

Starting with his second "at home," *A Trip to Paris* (1819), Mathews settled upon a three-part structure. The first two parts consisted of anecdotes and songs delivered sitting or standing at a cloth-covered table, accompanied by his pianist, on the pretext of a lecture. During these parts, Mathews employed no props or costume pieces, working as a raconteur who recounted conversations (with the appropriate use of voices) rather than fully enacting them. The second part is even less driven by narrative than the first and reads like a series of vignettes, or performative "turns," such as the Frenchman who praises General Jackson (a candidate for President in 1824 who came to national prominence as leader of the American forces in the Seminole Wars), the German magistrate, the Yorkshireman whose Illinois farm has failed, and Mathews's search for a servant. Only in the third part—for which Mathews coined the term "mono-polylogue," designating multiple interlocutions from a single performer—did he gave full embodiments of the characters, usually sequentially, utilizing scenery and costume quick-changes. *Trip to America*'s monopolylogue is called "All Well at Natchitoches" and includes five or six characters (and a live pony) appearing in front of a streetscape of shop fronts with a water-well at centre stage.[6] The monopolylogue is the least well-documented aspect of *Trip to America*[7] even though several prints depict its characters, and two give a detailed rendering of the set. Mathews may have extensively extemporized both the comic business and words, making it more challenging to notate, or its pace and execution may have been so much more complicated than the earlier parts that it defied anything but a skeletal rendition.

Performative Issues

Mathews's facility for transformation was legendary. This was achieved through physiognomic flexibility, mimetic precision, and exacting use of make-up and prostheses.[8] A contemporary remarked that

> Mathews, the mimic, could effect so extraordinary a change in the appearance and expression of his face, by simply [t]ying up the tip of his nose with a piece of catgut, that he has frequently taken leave, as if for the evening, of a company, amongst whom were some of his most intimate friends, and returned to them sometime afterwards so transformed that not one of them recognized him.[9]

But it is one thing to meticulously apply make-up for a comedy, farce, or social prank and quite another to make the multiple on-stage transformations necessitated in the "at homes." He could just as deftly make his nose grow longer in view of his audience as shorten it. When imitating the singing actor Charles Incledon, "his nose seemed actually to become aquiline,"[10] which is a greater feat than making it appear shorter by attenuating it with catgut. Gender, physique, and age were all elements of his transformations. As a young man learning his trade on the York circuit, he asked a group of gentlemen who had seem him act many times "to settle a wager about his age." Each one recorded a figure on a piece of paper and slipped

---

6   Three versions give a cast list for the monopolylogue, but only one (*The London Mathews*) specifies Miss Mangel Wurzel as a character. Illustrators agree on how she looked, but no speeches are attributed to her in any version. Perhaps she was a painted silhouette (as in the escape on the pony?) or another puppet proxy.

7   One of the sources, *The Vocal Gleaner*, omits it entirely.

8   Johnny Winter, the tailor and wardrobe keeper for Tate Wilkinson's company, where Mathews spent his apprenticeship, complained especially of Mathews that he "would soil a napkin from one end to the other in cleaning, and painting, and marking his face, again and again, to obtain some particular expression." Joe Cowell, *Thirty Years Passed among the Players in England and America: Interspersed with Anecdotes and Reminiscences* (New York: Harper, 1844), 32.

9   Unattributed clipping, Charles Mathews folder, Harvard Theatre Collection.

10 Leigh Hunt, *Lord Byron and Some of His Contemporaries; with Recollections of the Author's Life, and of His Visit to Italy*, vol. 2 (London: Henry Colburn, 1828), 14.

it under a candlestick. The estimates ranged from nineteen to eighty.[11] After his debut at Covent Garden, in a new farce called *Schniederkins*, a critic noted, "nothing but the felicity with which he transformed himself into a *tall Irishman*, a *short Scotchwoman*, and an *old Man*, could have induced the audience to enure [tolerate] it all."[12]

Despite being lame[13] and forty-eight years old when he performed *Trip to America*, Mathews effected the monopolylogue's costume changes at breakneck speed, rarely remaining offstage more than thirty seconds while keeping up a running commentary, sometimes using his facility with ventriloquism to throw his voice elsewhere and create the impression of deflected or concurrent action. Some of the action is described in the source texts, but the time it took to present this had to be significantly greater than the time it takes to read it. The sources give a sketchy account of Mathews's ability to depict multiple and concurrent action.[14] For example, two suitors for Miss Mangel Wurzel's hand are successively presented—the tippling Kentucky cobbler and French tailor—and as Mathews changes costume off stage, the two annoy each other, bashing the implements of their respective trades in counter-rhythms, singing and calling out insults. Someone—perhaps Mathews's pianist—battered out the rhythms and counter-rhythms while Mathews alternated their voices from the wings and his dresser assisted his costume change. In the midst of this organized cacophony, an Irish lyric is heard from offstage, and then a third suitor, Mr. O'Sullivan, is turfed out of his hotel. Mathews developed techniques to visually as well as aurally represent multiple characters; for example, once the Irishman entered, he somehow eloped *with* Miss Wurzel on the pony. Even for an actor capable of taking many forms, taking two at once—as the cobbler and tailor, then as Sullivan and Miss Wurzel—or doubling two into four—as the disappointed suitors look toward the eloping couple—or adding a fifth for good measure—as the slave Agamemnon assists the couple to escape—is challenging. *Trip to America* was a *tour de force* in performance.

Another passage from the monopolylogue suggests a performance problem that complicated the quick-changes. The Yankee Jonathan W. Doubikin, introduced in the first part of the evening, returns in the monopolylogue in pursuit of Agamemnon, whom he has purchased from his wily Uncle Ben, a character who is described at length but never brought on stage. Reportage of this passage specifies:

> Agamemnon, a runaway Negro, is a fat unwieldy fellow who has been sold by Uncle Ben to his nephew Jonathan W. Doubikin. He enters, pursued by his master; after singing a Negro song called "Oyanwaw," but finding his master is gaining ground upon him, he determines to get down the well and conceals himself until he [Jonathan] has passed. Jonathan W. Doubikin, the real Yankee, enters with a gun, in pursuit of his runaway Negro.

Corpulent characters recur throughout Mathews's work.[15] They could be nimble despite their bulk, as with Mr. Wiggins, a character in a farce whose "agility in bolting his cumbrous body out at window was an edifying exhibition ... to say nothing of his particular enquiries whether the street door was open

---

11   *Mirror*, 291-93, Charles Mathews clippings folder, Harvard Theatre Collection.

12   Unattributed clipping, Anne Mathews's scrapbooks, vol. 1, fol. 116.

13   Mathews's leg was badly injured, and permanently shortened, when he was thrown from a carriage.

14   The same problem exists with harlequinades, the manic free-for-alls that ensue after each pantomime's final transformation. In these zany wordless slapsticks, the basic plot lines are sketched in, but how effects are achieved is a matter of repertoire: too expected to require transcription or not conducive to more fulsome linguistic treatment.

15   In *A Trip to Paris* (1819), Hezekiah Hulk, an enormous attorney from Size Lane, squeezes his bulk into the *diligence* to return to Calais; in *Youthful Days* (1822), Ab Llewelyn ab Llwyd, esq., who is "not thin enough," eccentrically travels from spa to spa with his own shower-bath; in *Mathews in America; or, the Theatrical Wanderer* (1822), the publicans Mr. and Mrs. Drainemdry were both in fat suits; the *Memorandum Book* (1825) included the lugubrious Friaswaffen; and the *Comic Annual for 1833* featured Josephu (Joseph?) Jollyfat, the Gastonomer Astronomer.

'quite wide' when he proposes to take 'bolt the second!'"[16] Agamemnon is the chosen colossus in *Trip to America*, which affords comic business as he huffs his way on stage, plays the violin, and probably dances through his song, then compresses his bulk into the well. That would be ordinary enough except that Mathews then needed to remove the neck-to-knee fat suit, don the lanky Doubikin's costume, and dash to the wings to re-enter as the pursuing master. And that would be straightforward enough (for Mathews) except that Agamemnon is an African American slave, and his master is Caucasian. Did he remove the blackface make-up in this rapid turnaround (only to reapply it later when Agamemnon returns to assist O'Sullivan and Miss Wurzel with their elopement)? How much could Mathews do and still keep up the momentum? Whereas the contrast between the Kentucky cobbler and the French tailor could be signalled through minor costume changes, physical stance, accent, rhythmic signature, and perhaps ventriloquism, how did he depict the contrast between the African and the Yankee?

Perhaps, with a superb dresser and much practice, Mathews could have removed the blackface before returning as Jonathan W. Doubikin.[17] All the illustrations of Agamemnon show him with a black—not just dark—countenance, so illustrators (and presumably audiences) had no doubt of his race. He is one of several African Americans in *Trip to America*, but the others appear in the earlier parts when characters were expressed yet not fully embodied or reclothed, and Mathews was at his table rather than in front of the scenery. Then he was the raconteur and mimic, not the animate low comedian of the monopolylogue.

One of these black characters is Maximilian, a waiter who participates in two rapid-fire discussions at the boarding house's dinner table. Mathews describes throwing his voice into a snuffbox whenever Maximilian carried in a new course, bringing the waiter into paroxysms of laughter and causing him to drop a succession of serving dishes and their scorching contents. Here, physical comedy prevails through Mathews's demonstrations of ventriloquism, the waiter's immoderate laughter, and other diners' mimed reactions to having hot food poured into their pockets or down their backs. To achieve this, it would have been necessary not only to narrate but also to demonstrate the ventriloquized voice, the diners' reactions, Maximilian's growing mirth, and Mathews's development of the prank in response to Maximilian. Everything had to be indicated physically and verbally: there was no time to change costume pieces, let alone make-up. The evidence points to how Mathews indicated the co-presence of multiple characters—sometimes a whole stagecoach, streetscape, or dinner party of them—interacting with each other, emphasizing the contrasts between voices and attitudes. He shifted between narrative and performative modes, giving what a contemporaneous critic called "successive portraitures" interspersed with "intervening links of introduction and connexion [that] evidenced the intrinsic man."[18]

Interpretive Issues

The episode for which *Trip to America* has received the most scholarly attention involves the black actor whom Mathews claims to have observed at the African American theatre.[19] It was most likely an impersonation of James Hewlett, who was affiliated with the African Grove Theatre, which operated

---

16   George Danile, remarks on *Mrs. Wiggins: A Comic Piece in Two Acts, etc.*, by John Till Allingham, vol. 29 of *Cumberland's British Theatre* (London, 1829), 7, quoted in Jim Davis, "Representing the Comic Actor at Work: The Harlow Portrait of Charles Mathews," *Nineteenth Century Theatre and Film* 31:2 (2004): 6.

17   Mathews travelled with his servant George. Anne Mathews, *Memoirs of Charles Mathews, Comedian*, vol. 3 (London: Richard Bentley, 1838), 305.

18   "My Acquaintance with the Late Charles Mathews," *Fraser's Magazine* 8 (March 1836): 344.

19   Here, as elsewhere, he stipulates what has become an offensive epithet which is glossed for British readers as "Negro."

in New York for a few years beginning in 1821.[20] Despite a change in setting, many lines and gags are recycled from Mathews's 1822 "at home" in which performers audition for a strolling company, and a hopeful young British actor, Mister Flourish Jr., raised to the stage by the wife of an old prompter, declaims in a parlour demonstration to his mother's circle of friends.[21] These episodes and the Kentucky Roscius of *Trip to America* draw upon one of Mathews's standard *lazzi*: imitation of fellow actors (sometimes historic and revered colleagues, and sometimes buffoonish aspirants).[22] Mathews has been accused of racism, specifically over his mimicry of the New York actor.[23] The dialect and botched Shakespearean verse particularly suggest that interpretation; however, Mathews drew upon his own repertoire, combined elements of speeches, foibles associated with amateurism, and some of the same gag lines to fashion the anecdote he tells about the New York theatre. Blackface minstrelsy had not yet emerged: the first exponent, George Washington Dixon,[24] would not appear in New York City until four years later, and though Ira Aldridge sang "Possum Up a Gum Tree" in London in 1825, T.D. Rice did not perform "Jump Jim Crow" in New York until 1830 and in London until 1836.[25] Mathews may indeed have witnessed the African Grove Theatre company, but he cast the anecdote in terms of material with which he was already familiar and which Richard Peake, the playwright of the 1822 "at home," had already lampooned in the personages of an English boy raised to the stage, a misguided French marquis, and a Blackamoor. When it came to their unfitness to be actors (Mathews, Peake, and *Trip to America*'s author James Smith seemed to argue), the Briton, Gaul, and African were on a par.

In Mathews's England, there were no taboos against racial or ethnic insensitivity. He "took off" Yorkshiremen without aggravating the English; Welsh, Scottish, and Irish characters without antagonizing fellow Britons; and countless continental Europeans without inciting international incidents. Yet he was aware of the potential to offend Americans and peppered *Trip to America* with reflections on both the accuracy of his presentations and his tact, hopeful of his own ability to heal the rift between the United States and Great Britain caused by two wars (and very nearly a third over the Seminole Wars *c.* 1818)

---

20 See Shane White, *Stories of Freedom in Black New York* (Cambridge, MA: Harvard UP, 2002); and Marvin McAllister, *White People Do Not Know How to Behave at Entertainments Designed for Ladies and Gentlemen of Colour: William Brown's African and American Theater* (Chapel Hill: U of North Carolina P, 2003). This has been mistakenly taken as Ira Aldridge, who appeared at the African Grove somewhat after Hewlett began there, toured Europe beginning in 1825, and became renowned as an interpreter of African roles. See, for example, Walter Blair, "Charles Mathews and His 'A Trip to America,'" *Prospects: An Annual of American Cultural Studies* 2 (1976): 1-23; Hazel Waters, *Racism on the Victorian Stage: Representation of Slavery and the Black Character* (Cambridge: Cambridge UP, 2007), 61; and Eric Lott, *Love and Theft: Blackface Minstrelsy and the American Working Class* (Oxford: Oxford UP, 1993), 45-46.

21 *Mathews in America! A New Dramatic at Home; Written for and Intended to be Delivered by Mr. Mathews Abroad ...* (London: Duncombe, [1822]), 12, 15-17.

22 This featured in the "at homes" in 1818, 1825, 1827, and 1833.

23 Mahar's study of early-nineteenth-century orthography of black English vernacular and frontiersmen's rhetoric concludes that comic conventions of speech contrasted one group with another; in minstrelsy, blacks got the worst of it, yet it is naïve to say that this is a clear-cut case of white prejudice. McAllister regards Mathews's performance as comparable to contemporaneous newspaper, almanac, and pamphlet transcriptions of black speech, all "counterfeit" on a par with the (mis)appropriations of blackface minstrelsy. William J. Mahar, "Black English in Early Blackface Minstrelsy: A New Interpretation of the Sources of Minstrel Show Dialect," *American Quarterly* 37:2 (1985): 260-85; McAllister, *White People Do Not Know*, 151, 157-58. Jane Moody states that "the Kentucky Roscius is a composite satire which denigrates an ethnic group utterly disenfranchised from American Society and its theatrical institutions." Jane Moody, "Dictating to the Empire," in *The Cambridge Companion to British Theatre, 1730-1830*, edited by Jane Moody and Daniel O'Quinn (Cambridge: Cambridge UP, 2007), 38.

24 Charles Hamm, *Yesterdays: Popular Song in America* (New York: W.W. Norton, 1979), 117.

25 E.W. Mackney, A.J. Park, and C.D. Stuart, eds., *The Life and Reminiscences of E.W. Mackney, the Original Ethiopian Entertainer* (London: Greyfriars' Publishing; 1897), 12-17.

while cognizant of the ideological differences that created a growing rift in social practices.[26] When he tries to hire a servant, a class of whites that Mathews complained of in his correspondence as particularly recalcitrant,[27] Daniel Doolittle turns him down flat.

> DANIEL. No; I must beg leave to decline off. America is the first country in the world, and England may be the second: now for a genu-*ine* native of the first to serve one of the second is putting the cart before the horse.
> MATHEWS. Well, I hope I have not offended you.
> DANIEL. No; I hope I have not mortified you.
> MATHEWS. Not much.

Mathews implies that the American credo of liberty has gone too far, yet he also allows himself to be taken down a peg. Elsewhere, he has the foppish English youth Topham express his nation's stereotype of Americans, as well as his discovery that they are not so bad after all:

> TOPHAM. Why, I am agreeably surprised to find you all so different from what I expected—knives and forks, spoons, and all that sort of thing, like the hotels in Bond-street.
> PENNINGTON. Why, Sir, what did you suppose?
> TOPHAM. Don't know; thought they were only used by the tip-tops: had heard of squatters; thought you all squatted, and chewed tobacco, and spit in each other's faces.

Pennington realizes that Topham conflates the American Indians that visited the English Opera a few years before (bedecked in full native regalia) with all Americans, and laments,

> PENNINGTON. That young man is in a very fit state to write his tour! I deplore that tourists should so often misrepresent this country. *(Mildly)* I know little of the natives. I deplore that prejudice should give birth to such misrepresentations, and hope modern tourists will in future forbear giving wounds with the pen which go deeper, and reach further than the sword. May one nation endeavour to do justice to the other, and prosper under those blessings which heaven is daily pouring upon them.

Pennington despairs of Topham, but Topham is a foil—the mouthpiece for English prejudice—against which Mathews displays his own good-natured caricatures. He makes equal fun of his English touring companions—one droll, the other witless but good-humoured—and the Americans whom they encounter. Mathews needed Americans to like him so he could have a prosperous tour. His American manager, Stephen Price, hand-picked Mathews's travelling companions in order to reduce the number of his blatant insults that leaked to the public and the press,[28] yet Mathews seemed utterly unaware of how he grated on his hosts. In performance, back in London, Mathews sought to tailor his opinions into an impression of amity. He has Pennington, a prosaic Yankee "of the better order," admonish: "I hope you will speak of us as you find us."

> I assured him, there was not a person who had a heart more inclined to speak them fair than the humble individual he then addressed; and however I might have my jokes, and laugh at their

---

26 He was not entirely successful in this regard. After he opened *Trip to America* in London, Americans reacted angrily to press reports describing the performance. And when he returned to America in 1834, the enmity resurfaced despite his presentation of the material he had performed in London. Mathews had worried about Americans taking offence long before *Trip to America*'s premiere: Smith conceded all, allowed the conciliatory encomium at the end of part 2, but discouraged other effusive compliments. Mathews, *Memoirs of Charles Mathews*, vol. 3, 428.

27 Ibid., 308.

28 Cowell, *Thirty Years Passed*, 62.

peculiarities, yet I sincerely hoped, that nothing for the future, might divide England and America but the billows of the Atlantic.

As Mathews narrates his departure for England, he breaks into song, reprising the keynotes of some of his chief characters, and musing:

> And when in England seated,
> I think how I've been treated,
> Depend on't, to your prejudice;
> That nought shall be repeated,
> I please my English friends best,
> By giving still an harmless jest,
> For England the most tolerant
> Of nations, always is confest.

In so doing, he beseeches his English audience to find his performance apt: they, not the Americans, paid the piper for his tune. While in the United States, he was a cultural ambassador; after he returned home, he was a living souvenir.

Was *Trip to America* a negative portrayal of Americans? Mathews's characters in all the "at homes" ranged across the absurd, jesting, droll, freakish, flakey, capricious, facetious, hilarious, touching, and touched. Portraying the Militia Muster as a rag-tag force of local shopkeepers and farmers who drill with "umbrellas, fishing-rods, and pitchforks" instead of muskets implies that though they seem inept, these are the resourceful people who won their independence from Britain and then routed the Redcoats again in the War of 1812. The episode at the Boston post office juxtaposes the sensible Yankee with the overwrought Frenchman as well as an Irishman whose news from home details that all is "very peaceable and quiet, with the exception of a good deal of bloodshed that takes place occasionally." The unspoken question is whether the Americans' creed of political representation is a trust any more or less misplaced than in the British system. The Yankee individualist whom Mathews quests to know is cunning in the extreme, yet Jonathan W. Doubikin is as likely to be cheated by his own uncle as to be thwarted by his slave. As a Belfast review noted,

> Next comes Jonathan W. Doubikin, a fine picture of American independence in the midst of slavery—asserting the freedom of the human mind at the moment he is basely *bargaining for the liberty of his black brother*—this is a cruel hit against the Americans, but it is as just as it is severe, and should be the topic of the Senate, the Pulpit, and the Bar, as it is now the subject of ridicule in such hands as those of Mr. Mathews.[29]

The British were justifiably proud of ending their part in the transatlantic slave trade, but Mathews depicts the enduring problem with, not an opinion about, Agamemnon's plight. British audiences caught that "American liberty and negro slavery jostle each other in the same parenthesis" when Uncle Ben again gets the better of Jonathan.[30] In Louisiana, where the monopolylogue is set, Agamemnon faced severe consequences for his misdeed, but runaways from slave states could also be taken in New York.[31] British liberals would know this, and so the potential for the garrulous Agamemnon's flight to become a struggle against all that the plantocracy held dear and that the Northern Yankee failed to protest could have registered in London as a critique. In America, however, it was a blast across the bow.

---

29   Review of 31 December 1824, Anne Mathews's scrapbooks, vol. 3.
30   *Theatrical Observer; and Daily Bills of the Play*, April 1824: 3.
31   Under New York law, all slaves had to be freed by 4 July 1827. White, *Stories of Freedom*, 16.

Mr. Mathews's At Home, Trip to America,[32]

COMPRISING A FULL ACCOUNT OF HIS ANNUAL LECTURE ON PECULIARITIES, CUSTOMS, AND MANNERS, FOUNDED ON HIS OWN OBSERVATIONS AND ADVENTURES IN THREE PARTS PARTS I AND II BY JAMES SMITH PART III (MONOPOLYLOGUE) BY R.B. PEAKE[33]

First performed at the English Opera House [Strand Theatre, London], 25 March 1824.

Exordium

The daily increasing interest and importance which the American States have created in every quarter of the inhabited world, have not been of the least vital consequence to the commercial progress of this country. Our great English Lecturer, Mr. Mathews, impressed with the advantages which might result from a more perfect knowledge of the growing manners and cultivation of the *New World*, determined by a Trip to America to afford the British public an entertainment, which should comprise information on this most interesting subject, with an ample portion of that good humour and enjoyment for which he has become so celebrated among his countrymen.

Never was public attention and curiosity more upon the stretch than when Mr. Mathews ceased to be 'At Home' in England and, Don Quixote like,[34] determined to try his fortune in the United States of America. What could he do with the Americans, when caricatures, burlesques,[35] and every description of ridicule had, it was supposed, been carried to the utmost excess at their expense? Yet he did not go at hazard; to him every new situation presented a new character—every new character a new caricature—ev-

---

32   Based on several illicitly transcribed and published texts: *Account of Mr. Mathews' at Home; as Delivered in an Annual Lecture on Peculiarities, Characters, and Manners, Founded on His Own Observations and Adventures during His Late Trip to America ... Also a Monopolylogue, Called All Well at Natchitoches; Embellished with a Representation of the Scene, &c. &c.* (London: Duncombe, [1824]); *The London Mathews; Containing an Account of This Celebrated Comedian's Trip to America ...* (London: Hodgson and Co., [1824]), reprinted in Philadelphia by Morgan and Yeager, and in Baltimore by J. Robinson; *Sketches of Mr. Mathews's Celebrated Trip to America Comprising a Full Account of His Admirable Lecture on Peculiarites, Characters, and Manners; with the Most Laughable of the Stories and Adventures, and Eight Original Comic Songs ...* (London: J. Limbird, [1824]); and *Supplement to the Numbers Already Published of* The Vocal Gleaner and Universal Melodist; *a Sketch of Mr. Mathews's Entertainment, Entitled A Trip to America ...* (London: J.D. Bird, 1824).

33   Either Smith or Peake had written each of Mathews's "at homes" up to this point (Charles Mathews's clippings folder, Harvard Theatre Collection; and Anne Mathews's scrapbooks, vol. 2, folios 189 and 197, Harvard Theatre Collection). Correspondence from Mathews to Smith in early 1824 establishes Smith as the author of the main piece (Huntington MssHM 63356). A manuscript, possibly in Peake's hand, stipulates him as the author of the monopolylogue ("List of dramatic pieces, written by R.B. Peake, 1843," Harvard Theatre Collection MS Thr 270). Peake expanded elements of the monopolylogue in a separate play, *Americans Abroad; or, Notes and Notions*, later in 1824 (London: John Dicks, [1884]).

34   The hero of Cervantes's early-seventeenth-century romance: Don Quixote has a romantic vision and naïve idealism.

35   A droll caricature, especially in dramatic form.

ery new caricature something beyond our imagination, something burlesque, and something laughable.[36] John Bull[37] began to laugh in anticipation at the Jonathans,[38] and to fancy the French valet would out-do them, both in conveyancing and coin.[39] Nor is he disappointed; Mr. Mathews is now 'At Home' with an inexhaustible collection of fun, whim, frivolity, pun, song, activity, Joe Miller,[40] and the like, calculated to drive away melancholy, and most agreeably exceed the expectations of the most sanguine after the above qualifications.

Strange stories have been told about the Americans by many persons, who have called themselves tourists; and strange it is to find, that thousands are ready to give ear to them, and by leaning to the wrong side of the question, not only become the victims of prejudice, but sow discord between the very people whose forefathers were our own, and whose blood comes from the same stock, although it flows through other veins, and upholds the interests of a land which our fathers cultivated, and our brothers now exist upon, and deal out the blessings of their industry to the various nations of the earth.

Mr. Mathews has met with a unanimous and most cordial welcome from all ranks of society, and his present lecture, which has been attended with crowds of fashionable visitors, who have testified their satisfaction and delight with enthusiastic tokens, at the very humorous and excellent detail of his reception and adventures. He carries us through America, and describes its particular places. Although he does not describe it as a land flowing with milk and honey, he makes it the land of promise; and finding himself very much 'At Home,' delineates it, according to promise, to the pleasure of all denominations. He has given a true picture of the Americans, though forced into wit and burlesque; he allows no quarter to the idle, the proud, the fanatic, and the sharper, and upon these lays the chief weight of his performance. To the industrious his talents for ridicule have no sting, for they are placed by him in most respectable conditions. The Americans originally descended from our own countrymen, who, disappointed here, endeavoured to gain wealth and renown in the rising country of America. Industry seconded their efforts, and valour procured for them independence. Independence is, in some respects, carried too far by them; and Mr. Mathews shews in what this consists, and makes us, at the same time, acquainted with their style, demeanour, and eccentricities.

---

36   This is far from the impression Mathews gave in a letter to James Smith, the author of the "at home," where he complained of the Americans'

> universal sameness of manner and character, so uniform a style of walking and looking, of dressing and thinking, that I really think I knew as much of them in October as I know of them now in February.... If I excelled in Narrative, and were a lecturer, allowed to be occasionally grave, I could find infinite variety of materials to dwell upon, and rather amusing too; but as I feel perfect conviction that I am never amusing without I assume the manner of another, I know not how to suggest matter for comic effects, out of mere observations. (Anne Mathews, *Memoirs of Charles Mathews, Comedian*, vol. 3 [London: Richard Bentley, 1839], 354, 333)

37   Colloquially, the English people.

38   Often "brother Jonathan," a generic Britishism for Americans.

39   Mathews draws upon cant meanings; roughly, to cheat, skew, and fabricate.

40   Joe Miller (1709-38) was a British actor whose name became synonymous with a hackneyed joke through the posthumous publication of a jest book in his name. This was constantly updated and by 1824 had run through many editions. [Anonymous], *Joe Miller's Jest; or, the Wit's Vade-Mecum* (London: T. Read, 1739). Here is a typical example:

> There being a great disturbance one night at Drury Lane play-house, the late Mr. Wilks, coming upon the stage to say something to pacify the audience, and an orange being thrown full at him, which, when he had taken up, making a low bow, with the orange in his hand, This is no *civil* [Seville] orange, I think, said he. (John Mottley, ed., *The New Joe Miller's Jest; or, the Wit's Vade-Mecum* [London: D. Tissier, 1824], 3)

Mathews complained that Americans "are apparently dead to the fascinations of punning" (Mathews, *Memoirs of Charles Mathews*, vol. 3, 354), whereas for him it was a significant aspect of recreational conversation. See Charles James Mathews's letters home from Italy, 1823-24, Harvard Theatre Collection TS 1197 289.

The Trip to America varies not in its style from those which have been already before the Public; but there is more originality, more work for the mind, and more judgment required than in any entertainment which he has yet delivered; and when it is considered that one man is for the whole evening before an audience, and has mind sufficient to remember, and capability to give effect to every word and action, it must create surprise, nay, astonishment, in those who have not the possible means of witnessing his wonderful powers. It is astonishing that one man should be possessed of the power of pleasing all who hear him in all his undertakings; he merits all, and even more than he gets; the applause was universal; for he truly suits the action to the word, and the word to the action.

Part I

Commences as Mr. E. Knight plays the Medley Overture, which includes
several of Mr. Mathews's popular songs. Mr. Mathews then speaks.

Ladies and Gentlemen, it is with the utmost deference, I beg leave to inform you, that since I was last 'At Home,' I have been abroad—to America, to which Columbus had been before me. And now having come from *abroad*, I am very happy to find myself *at home* again. Like a traveller who begins his tale at a proper place, I shall tell you my motives for going to America.

It is said, some tourists travel to explore foreign regions, to find men black, or women brown, the precise height of a mountain, or depth of a cave. No such motives influenced me: mine was a search after Peculiarities, Character, and Manners. My object in crossing the Atlantic was to find out and secure the *yellow boys*,[41] being like the great prototype Columbus, lured to the new world by the yellow fever, the *auri sacra fames*.[42] I thought I had every reason to anticipate success; but friends viewed the thing on the other side, particularly my old friend Mr. Verbiage,[43] who requested me not to venture my dear figure upon the water, and assured me, if I once got to that savage land, America, I'd be eat up by the Scalps, the Mammoths, and Tomahawks.[44] This reasoning had not the desired effect. *(Pathetically)* All must travel, and to prove it *(he sings)*:

TRAVELLERS ALL
To the tune of "Fishermen All"[45]

Some men, you'll confess, must travel by stealth,
The world too they see as they travel about,
While others they travel, improving their health,
But mostly improving their pockets, no doubt.
Travellers all, tol de rol.

The soldier, he travels to conquer the brave,
The sailor, for prize-money, buffets the storm,

---

41   Gold coins worth, in 1824, one pound (twenty shillings).

42   The holy (or cursed) lust for gold. Yellow fever is also a dangerous viral infection, spread by mosquitoes, that broke out frequently in tropical areas or in hot and humid conditions; one such outbreak occurred in Barcelona in 1821.

43   Mathews speaks figuratively, presumably of the loquacious aspect of his conscience.

44   Perhaps indicating fictitious names of indigenous tribes. Scalps and tomahawks were popularly associated with indigenous Americans' ferocity. The mammoth excavated in the Hudson Valley in 1801 became an icon of Charles Willson Peale's museum in Philadelphia; see his painting *The Artist in His Museum* (1822).

45   Source unknown.

The old man is travelling into the grave,
And the stoic is seeking a climate that's warm.
Travellers all, tol de rol.

The lawyer, he travels to gather his fees,
The preacher, he travels to find out new grace,
A vixen will travel her husband to tease,
And a statesman will travel to better his place.
Travellers all, tol de rol.

The husband, he travels for comfort and peace,
The lady, she travels new fashions to find,
The rake goes a travelling, his joys to increase,
And the wisest of men travel out of their mind.
Travellers all, tol de rol.

The author, he travels for subjects so rare,
Your composer will travel to pick up new notes,
Your lover, he travels, although in despair,
And your singers will travel to strengthen their throats.
Travellers all, tol de rol.

Your miser, he travels in poverty's ways,
Your spendthrift, he travels to make himself poor,
Our dandies, they travel, well laced up in stays,
While the aged are travelling fast to death's door.
Travellers all, tol de rol.

Your parson, he travels with mitre[46] in view,
Your farmer, he travels, new tithes to procure,
Your creditors travel for debts that are due,
And your patriots travel, their rights to ensure.
Travellers all, tol de rol.

Your gambler, he travels, his money to lose,
A sinner, he travels without much belief,
Some tourists will travel, all lands to abuse,
And a judge often travels to halter a thief.
Travellers all, tol de rol.

The merchant oft travels, his fortune to mend,
The Frenchman, he travels with capers[47] and shrugs,
The pawnbroker travels, his money to lend,
And the chemist, he travels by nothing but drugs.
Travellers all, tol de rol.

---

46   Bishop's headdress, shaped like a pointed arch (from the front view).
47   Leaping dance steps.

A king, if he travels, is very much prized,
Some travelers, at sea, they are oft taken ill,
A wife, if she travels, is soon advertized,[48]
And some folks now travel into the tread mill.[49]
Travellers all, tol de rol.

The player, he travels for frolic and fun,
Ambassadors travel to set nations right,
The poor man oft travels to get from a dun,[50]
And watchmen, they usually travel by night.
Travellers all, tol de rol.

Now, I have been travelling far from my friends,
Still I trust they oft travel to me for good cheer,
And if, by my adventures, I make them amends,
I shall hope long to see them all travelling here.
Travellers all, tol de rol.

I embarked on board a fine vessel, romantically called *The William Thompson*, laden with molasses, melancholy, mustard, soda-water, etc.; and by a strange coincidence, the vessel is commanded by Captain Thompson, the master's name is Thompson, and the owner's name is Thompson, although not related.[51] The description of a sea voyage being generally of an uninteresting description, I shall pass that over, except relating a conversation held by means of a speaking trumpet, with a Dutch vessel bound for Havre de Grace,[52] who hails us as follows:—

FRENCH CAPTAIN. Vat is de nomme of your vaisseau?
MATE OF THE WILLIAM THOMPSON. The William Thompson.
FRENCH CAPTAIN. Vat is de nomme of de Capitaine of your vaisseau?
MATE. William Thompson.
FRENCH CAPTAIN. Eh! bien! Vat is de nomme of de owner of your vaisseau?
MATE. William Thompson.
FRENCH CAPTAIN. *Sacrableu!*[53] Vot is de nomme of de Mate of your vaisseau?
MATE. William Thompson.
FRENCH CAPTAIN. *Peste!*[54] Have you any of de Mademoiselles, de ladies on board?
MATE. One.
FRENCH CAPTAIN. Vot is her nomme?
MATE. Mrs. Thompson.

---

48 Warned. Mathews also plays on the sense that to advertise is to give public notice, for example, that a husband would no longer take responsibility for a wayward wife's debts.
49 This is a topical reference: the treadmill was invented *c.* 1817 as a punishment for prisoners.
50 Creditor.
51 Mathews relates this anecdote almost verbatim in a letter to Mrs. Rolls, 4 January 1823, so presumably he copied it into a (lost) letter to James Smith. Mathews, *Memoirs of Charles Mathews*, vol. 3, 351.
52 A port on Chesapeake Bay in the state of Maryland.
53 *Sacrebleu*: a French oath (sacred blue) referring to the Virgin Mary.
54 Pestilence.

FRENCH CAPTAIN. *Diable!* by gar[55] you be Thompson all over.

I thought this a curious coincidence, and was laughing heartily when New York became the topic, and our conversation turned upon the yellow fever, which I certainly had to a small extent, but anticipated a speedy cure, provided I had the good fortune to fall in with the *yellow-boys* I before mentioned. No sooner was New York in view, than I got my first lesson on American peculiarities. The captain of the vessel asked:

CAPTAIN THOMPSON. Is the fever at New York?
ANOTHER CAPTAIN. Yes, *I guess.*[56]
CAPTAIN THOMPSON. Is it fatal?
ANOTHER CAPTAIN. Very fatal, *I reckon!*
CAPTAIN THOMPSON. Are there many dead?
ANOTHER CAPTAIN. A great many, *I calculate.*

Mr. Price,[57] the manager of the New York Theatre, who accompanied me from London, finding it impossible to induce me to land on the New York side of the water, now took his leave. I expected the next time I met him, to find him *only half Price.*[58]

In a steam-boat, I then set off for New Brunswick,[59] in company with two Englishmen just imported, and who were the companions of my tour. The first is Jack Topham, a young blood from Saville-row,[60] a dandified young spendthrift, full of life and gig,[61] particularly fond of murdering Joe Miller, with a strong prepossession in his own favour. Having arrived at "years of indiscretion," and having contracted rather more debts than himself or his friends are able to answer, he is transported by the latter to America, to be out of "harm's way." Bray, his charming cousin, a kind of guardian to Jack, is a fat delightful lover of old jokes, with short breath and short legs, and almost splitting his sides with laughter, exclaims:

BRAY. Oh! That boy, his wit is astonishing; he'll be the death of me some day; there's a joke! Well, I never heard that afore. What do you think he says, Mr. Mathews?—that you have come to take the inhabitants off,[62] but he says, they have been beforehand with you, for they have taken themselves off.[63]

---

55   By God.

56   Mathews repeats this trope over and over again. George Colman, the Younger records the same affectation from an American in the early 1780s. The joke Mathews makes is on the Yankee usage of "I guess," not as a conjecture but misapplied as a synonym for "I believe" or "I think." "Calculate" and "reckon" are used similarly. He complained to James Smith, however, that he had difficulty discovering distinctive American expressions: "the language, *generally*, is better spoken than in London, or any part of England." "They are chiefly remarkable for accenting the wrong syllable, in (en*gine*, gen*uine*, en*quiry*).... 'Guess' is always used in cases where no doubt exists:—'I *guess* I have a headach[e].'" Mathews, *Memoirs of Chares Mathews*, vol. 3, 384-86; and George Colman, the Younger, *Random Records*, vol. 2 (London: Henry Colburn and Richard Bentley, 1830), 211-12.

57   Stephen Price managed the Park Theatre, New York, 1808-40. He had previously handled the American tours of the English actors George Frederick Cooke and Edmund Kean.

58   A pun on the practice of half-price admission to theatres: at nine o'clock tradesmen and apprentices finished work and were sold lower-price tickets.

59   A town in New Jersey.

60   In the 1820s, Saville-row was a fashionable residential street.

61   Jokes and merriment.

62   Portray them.

63   Disappeared.

On our arrival at Elizabeth Town,[64] we put up at an hotel, kept by Jack Rivers. In the Waterloo Hotel, Liverpool, it is all life and bustle, ready attention, obliging behaviour, and moderate charges: 'Coming, sir, coming—a boot-jack[65] for this gentleman, John. Betty, clean sheets and a warming-pan in No. 1; attend on you directly, sir,' and all that. In the American hotel, all was quietness, deliberation, determined independence, and due charges.[66] 'You can't be accommodated here, I guess; your bill is five dollars, *I reckon*, and the *helps* will take three more, *I calculate*.'

TOPHAM (*lustily*). Hollo, I say, what are you all dead? Here's a go, eh! this is what I call a pretty go.
BRAY (*laughing*). Don't John, don't, you'll kill me, you will; where are the waiters?
TOPHAM. Waiters, phoh! Plenty; *we* are the waiters now.
BRAY. Don't John, don't; what humour the boy has; he'll be the death of me some day.

After waiting a considerable time, we saw a respectable old gentleman sitting in a passage, smoking a segar,[67] see-sawing in a chair.

TOPHAM. Any body alive in this inn?
INNKEEPER. I am alive, I *guess*.
TOPHAM. Aye; but any body belonging to the hotel—who keeps it?
INNKEEPER. This is my hotel, I guess.

But as he was a curiosity, I will indulge with a magnifying glass, and shew him as he sat. (*Imitation*)

TOPHAM. Can we have a private room?[68]
INNKEEPER. Yes; if there's no one in it, I guess.
TOPHAM. Can we have any dinner?[69]

The host is a genu-*ine* cha-*rac*-ter, and very ac-*tive*, and is *con*-siderably kind in letting them have any thing at all, under such circumstances, as it is not right.[70]

INNKEEPER. Can't tell, I reckon; very awkward time to come for dinner, the *helps* won't like it: you should never come so late to dinner: there was forty dined here at two o'clock; but I'll see what I can do for you.

---

64   Elizabeth, New Jersey, is in Newark Bay. Mathews has put to shore, *en route* to the town of New Brunswick.
65   An implement that assists in removing boots.
66   Mathews advised James Smith,

The strongest *character* is the *Landlord* of an inn. He is the most independent person in America. You *must* be impressed with the idea that he confers a favour upon *you*, or it is in vain to expect any accommodation. He can't be caricatured; I won't spare him an inch. He is, too, the most insolent rascal I ever encountered.... It will be my main stay, my sheet-anchor. I have already three or four distinct specimens of the same species. The effect will depend more on manner than matter. *Par exemple*. If you arrive at the inn, the regular system of inattention and freezing indifference is instantly apparent. No one appears. You enter the house, and search about for a landlord or waiter. Probably you pass the former, but fearing he may be the Judge or the Governor of the state, you are afraid to address him. (Mathews, *Memoirs of Charles Mathews*, vol. 3, 387-88)

67   Cigar.
68   Mathews reported this dialogue to James Smith. Mathews, *Memoirs of Charles Mathews*, vol. 3, 388.
69   Dinner was the chief repast, usually taken midday, whereas supper was the last meal of the day.
70   These syllabifications indicate how Mathews heard American speech.

BRAY. Hope we shall get some dinner. I am very hungry, and I generally eat a great *deal*[71] for dinner.

TOPHAM. Eat a great *deal*, do you? Then I suppose you generally dine in a timber-yard.

(A black help, Othello, now brought in a leg of lamb).[72]

TOPHAM. Is it mutton senior, or mutton junior?[73]

BRAY. Mutton junior! Don't John, don't; you'll be the death of me.

We get a bottle of what Jack Topham calls mulled Day and Martin,[74] but what the host says is Port wine that has been kept in his warm bar for the last three months.[75] During dinner, the landlord sat down very *coolly*, smoking his segar, and questioning the travellers:

INNKEEPER. Where did you come from?

TOPHAM. England.

INNKEEPER. Where's your plunder?

TOPHAM. Plunder! what the devil, do you take us for highwaymen?

MATHEWS. No, he means baggage.

INNKEEPER. Mean to stay long?—What are you?—Are you married?—Where are you going to?

TOPHAM. This is Captain Poodle, that is Mr. Macfoozle, and I am Colonel Foozle.

INNKEEPER. Where from?

TOPHAM. Foozle Hall.

INNKEEPER. Where's that?

TOPHAM. Foozle Town.

INNKEEPER. Where?

TOPHAM. Foozle County.

I regretted I had not followed the plan of the celebrated Benjamin Franklin, who, being aware of the customary inquiries, to supersede that trouble, on entering an inn, always had the landlord, his wife, children, and helps summoned together, and put a stop to all questions, by saying: "I am Benjamin Franklin, by trade a printer, formerly of Boston, now of New England, and at present travelling to Phila-delphia[76]—now bring me a boot-jack."

Having retired to rest, judge my surprise, at about twelve o'clock at night, to find the landlord walk into my room, with a lamp in one hand and a letter in the other, which by the description given, he *guessed* was for me.

MATHEWS. Hollo! What do you want?

LANDLORD. A letter for you, I guess.

---

71   A plank of pine or fir, not more than seven inches wide and three inches thick.

72   Mathews describes this encounter to James Smith: "A Hottentot Adonis appeared, with his sleeves tucked up to his shoulders (thermometer 90°), an affluvia arising from his ebony skin, that he ingeniously overpowered by one of greater power from a leg of lamb." Despite "the *musk*," Mathews was glad to find anyone prepared to serve him in the English manner. Mathews, *Memoirs of Charles Mathews*, vol. 3, 388-89, 315.

73   In other words, he inquires whether mutton or lamb is being served.

74   A blackening compound.

75   A mulled drink is wine, ale, or spirits heated with sugar, spices, fruit, and sometimes egg yolk. In England, wine is kept in the cellar and served cool. Mathews, *Memoirs of Charles* Mathews, vol. 3, 389.

76   Franklin was born in Boston. At age fifteen, he began working on his brother's newspaper, the *New-England Courant*, and at age seventeen, ran away to Philadelphia. Mathews's usage implies that Boston is different from New England, which is erroneous except, perhaps, to imply that Franklin's orbit became larger than his native city.

MATHEWS. For me; this is a most unusual time to deliver a letter; you wasn't told to deliver it in the middle of the night.

LANDLORD. I have done the right thing, I judge; it was all my contrivance; I have done the right thing, I reckon; I do every thing with propriety, and don't mind remarks.

This letter called me to Bristol,[77] in America; of course we wanted some one to conduct us thither, we therefore sent for a person to drive us, and while we were waiting, a person came up with[78]

DRIVER. How d'ye do friend? Believe you're going to Bristol?

I answered in the affirmative, when he said

DRIVER. That's all correct *I guess*; as, if you are going to Bristol, I am the gentleman sent to drive you, *I reckon so.*

With this independent driver, we passed along where MacAdams[79] is unknown, but where they certainly stand very much in need of that colossus of *Rhodes*.[80]

I next went to Baltimore, my first appearance before a crowded audience; there, I imagined myself in the midst of my friends at the English Opera House in the Strand.[81] The same rows of beauty and fashion in the boxes; the same smiling, joyous faces in the pit; the same laughing and friendly disposition in the galleries; the same stage; the same lamps; and almost the same Mr. Knight at the piano-forte,[82] that I almost fancied I had, like a second Gulliver, packed up the theatre, and brought it out with me. Mr. Price, the manager, tells us his voyage did not half agree with him; here my success like a soothing medicine took effect, and I found myself better of yellow fever when Mr. Price gave me some of his yellow boys.[83]

I next transported myself to Washington, from Washington to Philadelphia, and from Philadelphia en route to New York in one of those floating palaces, the American Steam Boat, the most stupendous things imaginable.[84] Some idea may be conceived of their magnitude: they can accommodate 200 persons by night as well as day. While on the voyage, Bray made the only attempt at a joke I ever heard, which I did not rightly understand, as follows:

BRAY. Mr. Mathews, do you know this steam-boat puts me in mind of the British Museum?
MATHEWS. The British Museum; why?
BRAY. I don't know why; but it does.

---

77   Bristol, Pennsylvania, the home of Thomas Abthorpe Cooper, an actor friend to Mathews and Stephen Price.

78   Colloquialism for a person approached, saying thus and thus.

79   i.e., via bad unimproved roads. In the 1810s, John McAdam, a Scottish engineer, invented a system of road-making that involved layering crushed stone or gravel on a raised and slightly cambered surface. This "macadamization" method significantly improved travel conditions; the first such road was created in America around 1830.

80   A pun on "roads." The Colossus of Rhodes, one of the seven wonders of the ancient world, was an enormous statue of Helios (who drove the chariot of the sun across the sky) erected in the third century BCE.

81   This is where Mathews performed his "at homes" in London, including *Trip to America*. He flatters his current audience and heaps compliments upon Baltimore.

82   Mathews travelled with his dresser but almost certainly used local pianists when performing his solo pieces in America.

83   While performing in Baltimore, Mathews had contracted with Stephen Price for £50 per night, but having made £230 on his benefit night, subsequently held out for £100 per night. Mathews, *Memoirs of Charles Mathews*, vol. 3, 318, 329.

84   Probably a sternwheeler. These boats' flat hulls and high position in the water made them spacious and light-filled. They were used on American rivers and lakes, as well as for limited ocean-going routes.

At one end of the vessel were a quantity of live turtle on the deck, which seemed much to attract the attention of an Irish sailor, who was talking to himself, and gazing with the greatest astonishment.

IRISH SAILOR. What the devil is it? I never saw such a thing before. Arrah! sure now, but that's a very curious odd sort of bird.

MATHEWS. A bird: It is not a bird.

IRISH SAILOR. Not a bird—faith, then, what may it be, if I may be so bold, sir?

MATHEWS. It is a turtle.

IRISH SAILOR. A turtle! and is it a turtle—sure, and I never saw a turtle before—arrah! It's mighty curious, but pray, sir, axing your pardon—is it a real turtle or a *mock* turtle.[85]

Being landed, we take places in one of the stage-coaches, which are always ready on the arrival of a steam-packet, and which are a kind of covered caravan, with curtains on both sides, carrying sixteen or eighteen *inside* passengers, but no *outside*.[86] *(Introduces the stage-coach characters in great style)* Mr. Raventop, a lachrymose soft-speaking gentleman, who is compiling an American Jest Book, of which he has written the title page, and found the motto, but is at a loss whether to call it *Raventop's Merry Jester* or *Every Man His Own Wag*. Also Major Grimstone, a fine tall personage, with his coat buttoned up close to his throat, blushing with military ardour, and a tight black stock,[87] whose whole vocabulary of conversation appears to consist of the words—'Oh I very well, very well, very well,' which he applies to almost every thing that is said or done. But one of the most amusing persons appears to be the driver, a consequential pragmatical formal fellow, who is a gentleman to his passengers; and holds his head up so high, that we should be led to suppose he never looked so low as the moon. And wherefore, thus? Why, because he was once a Major, in the American army:[88] as independent as Moses in the bulrushes,[89] he answers every interrogatory with "Oh yes," and occasionally enquires:

DRIVER. Does any gemman choose Backey?[90]

JUDGE *(borrowing some pigtail of a Counsellor that sits beside him)*. Yes, I *chews*.

PASSENGER. Do you stop anywhere?

DRIVER. Oh, yes; at Brine's;[91] but we are not there by a pretty considerable damned long way off there yet.

---

85 Soup made from a calf's head.

86 English stage-coaches were less commodious, and fee-paying male passengers often rode hanging onto the exterior of the vehicle.

87 Collar.

88 Mathews stressed to James Smith the preponderance of ex-officers in menial jobs:

    They tenaciously exact their titles. On every road, even at the meanest pothouse, it is common to call out, 'Major, bring me a glass of toddy!' 'Captain Obis, three segars, and change for a dollar!' 'Why are we so long changing horses, colonel?' This was addressed to our coachman—A fact! 'Why, Achilles is gone to get one of the horses shod, but the major is a good hand, he'll soon clap four shoes on.'—'Othello, run to Captain Smith's for a pound of cheese.' (Mathews, *Memoirs of Charles Mathews*, vol. 3, 385)

    Achilles and Othello would, undoubtedly, be African Americans, for Mathews encountered no whites susceptible to being ordered about it this way. The same point about Americans' excessive use of titles is expressed by an anonymous writer in "Speculations of a Traveller, Concerning the People of North America and Great Britain," *Blackwood's Magazine* (Edinburgh), June 1824: 692-93.

89 Exodus 1:15-2:10.

90 "Does any gentleman choose tobacco?", leading to the pun in the next line. A pigtail, as the name suggests, is a thin roll of chewing tobacco.

91 Probably McBrine's: the typeface is illegible in the source text.

PASSENGER. I should admire[92] to stop there to have a drop of sangaree.[93]

TOPHAM. Sangaree! What the devil's sangaree?

PASSENGER. Negus.[94]

TOPHAM. I say, Major Whipcord, Jarvey,[95] hollo!

BRAY. Don't John, don't; call him Major; you see every body else does.

Jack Topham fires off a Joe Miller or two in the course of the journey, at this consequential Jersey,[96] which draws forth from Bray his usual exclamation of

BRAY. That boy'll be the death of me.

Pursuing the conversation, and not knowing the company, one of the passengers remarked *(various voices)*:

PASSENGER. They say Mathews the player is come among us; have you seen him?

PASSENGER. Oh, no.

PASSENGER. Is he a favourite with you?

PASSENGER. Oh, no; not by any manner of means.

PASSENGER. They say, he is a smart[97] chap.

PASSENGER. They say, he is a double-faced fellow, not two minutes alike.

PASSENGER. Ah! Give me a steady actor, one who will give you time to find out his beauties.

PASSENGER. Yes, I suppose he's coming here to take us off[98] when he returns to his own country.

PASSENGER. We wouldn't suffer it; I wonder Congress doesn't put a tax upon these foreign players.

PASSENGER. The sooner he takes himself off the better, I reckon.

PASSENGER. He is such a double-faced fellow, never two moments alike; I don't like such players, beside, I think, we have raw material enough of our own.

We next arrive at New York. I wish to make it appear that the Americans are more sinned against than sinning: men must indeed be curious characters, who pay a visit to that part of the world, and calumniate[99] its inhabitants, because they are not at all times ready to bend before them in servility, or bow like slaves, in a land of independence. No: let's hope that tourists in future may try rather to heal the wound than to agonize it; and may that good understanding always exist between the two countries, which will make them happy; and, to the end of time, may nothing but the Atlantic exist to divide them.

Having crossed the Hudson River, I declare the streets look just like a back-gammon board, with such a mixture of black and white men in them. I am immediately surrounded by black porters, offering to carry my luggage: one of whom I call, and inquiring his name he replies:

PORTER. Agamemnon Julius Caesar Hannibal, massa!

MATHEWS. Do you know Mrs. Bradish's boarding-house?

PORTER. Yes, massa; she live in de Broadway.

---

92   To be inclined to do this.

93   A punch made with Madeira wine or port (cf. *sangria*).

94   Like sangaree, this is a punch (made with red wine, port, or sherry mixed with hot water, sugar, and flavourings such as orange or lime).

95   A hackney coachman.

96   Man from New Jersey.

97   Clever, quick-witted, and good at repartee.

98   Mimic us.

99   Slander.

MATHEWS. Good house?

PORTER. Yes, massa; first grade.

MATHEWS. Well, Major, if agreeable, we'll go to Mrs. Bradish's.

GRIMSTONE. Oh very well, very well, very well.

TOPHAM. I say, cousin Barnaby, let us push on, for I am confoundedly sharp-set,[100] and then for fun and laughter.

BRAY. Why?

TOPHAM. Why, because we're in *a merry key*—never be sad here.

BRAY. *A merry key*, America he means, ha! Ha! Ha! Well, I never heard that before, how good, that boy'll be the death of me!

PORTER. Massa, you come wi' me, I take you to the best Hot-hell in New York.

A very curious place this: all houses, shops, hills, hackney-coaches,[101] carts, wagons, Day and Martin's blacking, genuine tea, and every thing just as natural as if we were in London. *(Sings)*

MRS. BRADISH'S BOARDING-HOUSE
Air—"Murphy Delaney," "Who's for Calais," "Lary O'Lashem," or "The Parson in his Boots"
Now at New York we're all landed so merrily,
Strangers begin to make use of their eyes;
Niggers and Yankees are crowding so cheerily,
Every thing causes us monstrous surprise:
Up steps a blackee, and takes your portmanteau,
"Massa, you want Boarding house, or Hotel?
Me take you to both"—away then you canter,
To where Mrs. Bradish from all bears the bell.

Now all upon deck, soon the luggage is landed,
We step in the boats, and we make no delay;
But gladly we smile as we safely are stranded,
And off to some boarding-house toddle away.
There are Yankees and Niggers all gazing and pressing so,
While we so merrily through the crowd dash,
And the Nigger a portmanteau there is caressing so,
To find out the virtue of English cash.

Oh all in a boarding house free is and easy,
Acquaintances, strangers, alike are good friends;
Your company ne'er for a moment need tease you,
You leave when you please and the matter soon ends.
And then at the table d'hôte[102] all is so hearty,
You appetite gather by seeing folks eat;
And can't for your life but do just like your party
Oh sure Mrs. Bradish's isn't a treat?

---

100 Hungry.
101 A hired coach seating four people and drawn by two horses.
102 A table at a hotel, restaurant, or tavern where diners share a set meal at a stipulated time.

Success to the mortal who first found out eating,
For surely there's not such a joy on the earth,
For hunger, blue devils, and misery cheating,
And giving the password to frolic and mirth.
And those who would wish to have a good dinner,
May speedily gain every bliss of the treat,
By just dropping in, whether saint or a sinner,
At old Mrs. Bradish's, in thingumbob[103] street.

Now being all seated, and dinner quite ready,
I wondered that tourists should make such a fuss;
For this land of Columbus has wild folks and steady,
And do you know that they eat, and they drink, just like us.
And really, 'tis true what I say, without joking,
They can eat beef and mutton whenever they dine;
There are some fond of snuff too, and some fond of smoking,
And after their dinner they drink grog[104] or wine.

(Rapidly alternating impersonations)

AMERICAN. Fine eating these, certainly; how do you like it, Sir?
ENGLISHMAN. Aye; I don't know; the veal is red, the beef is white, the wine is thick, and everything
    sour except the *vinegar.*
AMERICAN. Ah! that's just like you English; you find fault with every thing.

All sorts meet at a boarding-house, and sure there never was a stranger collection of hungry mortals than
flanked the table of kind-hearted Mrs. Bradish.

MATHEWS. I say, Topham, what do you think of the inhabitants?
TOPHAM. Oh, they're all fair enough.
MATHEWS. What, you mean the Black people?
TOPHAM. No, not exactly; but I'll just ask this long stick of black sealing-wax[105] a question—*(to waiter)*
    I say, *Teapot,* how many black fellows have you got in the house?
MAXIMILIAN. Twenty, massa.
TOPHAM. Twenty! Damme, yours must be a house of mourning.
BRAY. Ha! ha! ha! that boy will be the death of me!

Maximilian, a Nigger, or Negro, waiter at Mrs. Bradish's boarding-house, is attending at dinner.[106]

*(Mr. Mathews uses ventriloquism to cause some excellent sport, completely astonishing the poor black
waiter. On one occasion he brings in a dish, and when Mr. Mathews has his snuff-box on the table,*

---

103 Like "what do you call it."
104 Alcoholic spirit diluted with water.
105 Referring to the tall and thin Maximilian. Drops from sticks of sealing wax were melted onto the folded edge of letters
    (or, when an envelope was used, the overhanging flap) to hold it closed, and imprinted with the author's signet. Mourners
    used black wax.
106 This episode appears in three sources (all except *The Vocal Gleaner*), always just after the "Illinois Inventory." While it
    serves to reintroduce Maximilian prior to Mathews's leave-taking, it does not accord with the narrative flow of part 2.

he imitates a child calling from within; Maximilian drops the dish and begins laughing. When the joke is again repeated, the Negro is bringing in a tureen of soup, and just as Mr. Mathews begins the conversation from the snuff-box, Maximilian pours all the soup down a gentleman's back, and begins to laugh most immoderately. Various voices).

DINER *(enraged)*. What do you mean by laughing?

MAXIMILIAN. Him only laughing to hear Mr. Mathews's child cry in de box.

DINER. Have the kindness to help me to some of that cod.

DINER. Yes; and give some *sound*[107] to that *deaf* lady.

DINER. Dear me, this meat is done to a stick.

DINER. Then you may make a *stake* of the joint.

DINER. This beef is exceeding *rare*.

DINER. I don't wonder at it, considering how much you have eaten of it.

TOPHAM. Now, gentlemen, I wish to put a conundrum. Why is this stuffed goose like the tub of Diogenes?[108]

DINERS. Can't tell.

TOPHAM. Nobody tell—why, because it has *sage* in its inside.

BRAY. Well, I declare that boy will be the death of me, some day.

DINER. There's a *time* for all things, but you should *rue* making such a bad pun.

TOPHAM. Shall I help you to a merry thought?

RAVENTOP. No, no, give it to me, I am compiling a jest-book, and the favour will much oblige the public.

TOPHAM. I think your wit will be on the *wing*, or in the *bill* of your landlady.

DINER. Talking about our landlady ...

ANOTHER. Help me to a piece of that maid.[109]

DINER. Our landlady is charming—with a little sauce—and when she smiles—some mustard.[110]

DINER. Can you help me to a piece of that beef?

WAITER. How shall I cut it? Are you outside or in?

DINER. Oh, either; but I've booked my appetite for *four*.

(Sings)

> So thus runs the frolic, no wight[111] melancholic
> Can keep up the mask at this excellent treat;
> And those who shall cross, may ne'er be at a loss
> For a pun and a dinner, at thingumbob street.

> All hunger thus conquered by fresh fish and pastry,
> With wine and with walnuts, we crack shells and jokes;
> Whilst *living* Joe Millers, those jolly care-killers,
> Get time in a hobble,[112] and give him a hoax

---

107 The swimming bladder of a cod.

108 Diogenes was a fourth-century-BCE Cynic philosopher famous for his extreme asceticism and doctrine of self-sufficiency and uninhibited behaviour. He eschewed other Greeks' luxuries and opted to live in a large storage vessel (his tub).

109 A type of fish, such as skate, ray, or shad.

110 A pun on "pass the mustard" and the false smile of a churlish hostess.

111 Person.

112 Perplexing situation.

A pun and a brimmer,[113] whilst brains gently simmer
Above the warm vapours of brandy and grog,
Jeux d'esprit[114] hatching, and newcomers catching,
Whilst gambling fancies this mortal top flog.[115]
After dinner every one gets his desert.[116] *(Various voices)*

DINER. I'll thank you for a couple of those apples.

ANOTHER. A couple, why that will be a *pear*.

Cloth cleared, enter candles, slippers, and segars and all sit round for serious drinking.

DINER. What wine do you take, Sherry?

ANOTHER. No, *Inveni Portum*.[117] I have found a *Port*.

ANOTHER. Very good wine. A gentleman might carry six bottles of that, comfortably.

ANOTHER. Carry six bottles, why then he'd be a *porter*.

TOPHAM. I've heard that before: you're only a *reporter*, sir, a man deserves to be stretched on his *bier*[118] that would make such a joke.

BRAY. Ha! ha! ha! how good; well, I never heard that before, that boy'll be the death of me.

DINER. Now the ladies have left the room, give the fair sex,[119] gentlemen.

ALL. Oh, very well, very well, very well! *(Toasting)* "The fair sex."

(Sings)

Thus joking and laughing, and chaffing,[120] and quaffing.
We hail Mrs. Bradish's snug boarding house.

YANKEE. Charge[121] your glasses, gentlemen—here's Success to Liberty—you infernal black neger,[122] what are you about—don't you see you are emptying that tumbler[123] into my waistcoat pocket?

MAXIMILIAN. Massa, me only giving you small change for dat dollar me owe you.

TOPHAM. That's as much as to say that he is liquidating the debt.

DINER. So it should seem, and the payment passes current. Well, we'll wave that subject, and see something new.

Raventop, the American jester, almost in his dotage, who complains that Irish, French, German, and English, are all alike in refusing to acknowledge the Americans have any *fun*,[124] asks looking all the time like Patience on a monument smiling at Grief.

---

113 A full glass of wine.

114 Witticism (literally, games of spirit).

115 Obscure.

116 Mathews later puns on dessert, but "just deserts" (from Old French *deserte*) means getting one's reward.

117 From the Roman epitaph: In Fortunam Inveni portum spes et fortuna valete Nil mihi vobiscum ludite nunc alios. (I have found harbour. Farewell hope of fortune: you have deceived me enough, now mock others.)

118 Stretcher for a corpse.

119 Toast to the ladies.

120 Good-humoured banter.

121 Fill up.

122 Negro.

123 Drinking vessel.

124 The meaning of this—amuseenth and joking—is unchanged since the mid-eighteenth century, but in Mathews's day, it still carried its original cant connotation. By contrasting "fun" to "wit" (the ability to draw distinctions between unlike things), he both shows himself old-fashioned and claims an affiliation with intellectual humour rather than silly pranks. Mathews found the upper orders melancholic, even more grave than the English. Mathews, *Memoirs of Charles Mathews*, vol. 3, 354.

RAVENTOP (*querulously*). Pray sir, what do you think of our fun, as you seem to have paid peculiar attention to us Americans?

MATHEWS. Fun, sir! Fun, sir! Really I don't know what you mean.

RAVENTOP. Our fun, sir, our American fun.

MATHEWS. Upon my word, sir, I am at a loss, I don't understand you.

RAVENTOP. You don't, you don't understand what fun is; ah, it's just like you all: all you English. Why you have fun in England. I mean wit, wit is what I mean.

MATHEWS. Oh! I understand now, sir; why, I think you are a very good-natured sort of well-meaning people; but ...

RAVENTOP. Ah! you English won't allow us our merit; you will not allow us to be witty. Now, sir, you must know, I am preparing a jest-book, having the title-page and preface already finished, only wanting the body of the work. Now I'll tell you one of the best jokes I intend putting in:—"There were two farmers, who had made up their minds to go the distance of ten miles; so one of them said to the other, 'As we have this journey to walk, you must walk five miles, and I'll walk the other five, and then we two shall have walked ten.'" There: I was present, and heard that myself.

TOPHAM. Ha! ha! Why, I heard my father tell that before I was born!

BRAY. Ha! ha! ha! That boy will be the death of me!

Just then in came the American calculating boy, and Jack Topham began to ask him several questions.

TOPHAM. Oh, Oh, damme I'll puzzle him.—I say, old one, if one pound of cheese cost two pound of soap, what will a cart-load of paving stones come to?

CALCULATING BOY. Three-and-sixpence.

TOPHAM. If a pair of breeches cost sixpence, what will ten miles of rubbish come to?

CALCULATING BOY. Just as much as you're worth.

(*Sings*)

> Thus, while we're joking, and laughter provoking,
> We at Mrs. Bradish's drive away care.
>
> Mrs. Bradish's boarding-house now is in motion,
> Some coming, some going, by night and by day;
> And many a vessel now rides on the ocean,
> With passengers anxiously looking this way.
> "*I guess*," and "*I calculate*," here they're exclaiming,
> But still we can't blame them for that I will show;
> And "*I reckon*" the Yankees we mustn't be blaming,
> For we have expressions in England, "*you know*."[125]

MATHEWS. Raventop, my boy, can't you give us a song?

RAVENTOP. No, Sir; I never sung but once.

MATHEWS. And what was that?

RAVENTOP. Why not *All's Well*,[126] you may be sure.

---

125 Yankee expressions are described by Constance Rourke "not so much a dialect as a lingo" with "consciously assumed" oddities. Mathews highlights a few. *American Humor: A Study of the National Character* (1831; reprinted New York: Doubleday, 1953), 28.

126 A sea shanty by Thomas Dibdin, with music by John Braham (1805), in which a sentry keeps watch on deck.

MATHEWS. Well, play us a tune upon your flute.

TOPHAM. No, damn his flute, I'd rather he'd give his flute the *sack*, and make a *bagpipe* of it.[127]

KENTUCKY GENTLEMAN. Do you carry snuff, Sir?

RAVENTOP. No, Sir, I reckon I don't.

KENTUCKY GENTLEMAN. Don't you? Then you are worse than a tallow-candle, I calculate.

RAVENTOP. We can't see your wit without *torch* light, Sir.

KENTUCKY GENTLEMAN. Then you'd better look with that gentleman's carotty[128] head.

RAVENTOP. That gentleman's head is fire-proof, Sir.

KENTUCKY GENTLEMAN. Yes, and so is your hat, I should think.

RAVENTOP. Why, Sir?

KENTUCKY GENTLEMAN. Because it has been so long above your nose.

(Sings)

And this is the prattle, the pun and joke battle
That's fought every day, where the cormorants[129] meet,
With wit in a posse,[130] so harmless and glossy,
At kind Mrs. Bradish's in thingumbob street.

There's a time too for smoking, and also for joking,
For telling of stories, and cracking of nuts;
There's a time too for laughing, or (*Anglice*)[131] for chaffing,
And making from soft ones, some two or three *butts*;[132]
But in all the gay scenes amid this gay world,
There's none that can yield more frolicksome din
Than the circle at Boston,[133] where good humour is twirled
Like a teetotum, every one giving a spin.

Jack then attacks Mr. Pennington, a highly worthy, but somewhat prosaic American of the better order, whom, as well as the other Americans present, he is continually calling "Yankee."[134]

TOPHAM. Why, I am agreeably surprised to find you all so different from what I expected—knives and forks, spoons, and all that sort of thing, like the hotels in Bond-street.[135]

PENNINGTON. Why, Sir, what did you suppose?

TOPHAM. Don't know; thought they were only used by the tip-tops. Had heard of squatters; thought you all squatted, and chewed tobacco, and spit in each other's faces.

PENNINGTON. My dear Sir, why did you think so?

---

127 "Sack" affords a double pun: to add a loose pocket to the flute (and thus make a bagpipe) as well as to give the flute the sack (dismissing it).

128 Red-haired.

129 Large, dark, sea-going birds; also rapacious people.

130 Among a group of peers.

131 In plain English.

132 To try the good nature of the person who is chaffed.

133 Sic: New York.

134 One review specifies that Pennington is a member of Congress and a recognizable imitation of a senator. *Theatrical Observer; and Daily Bills of the Play*, April 1824: 2.

135 A luxury shopping street in London's fashionable Mayfair district.

TOPHAM. Don't know; but I fancied it. What do you do with your prisoners of war, eh! Do you eat them? You know you do; there's a great picture of it done by West,[136] one of your own people; so it must be true. Besides, I saw a great many of you come out two years ago at the English Opera.

PENNINGTON. Do you recollect their names, Sir?

TOPHAM. Yes; there was *Silver-top, Blue-mountain, Grey-squirrel*, and I don't know what all; all dressed in fur, feathers, and tomahawks.

PENNINGTON. Why, my dear Sir, they were the native Indians.

TOPHAM. Oh! What you confess it, do you? I thought I should find you out; but, however, you are not half so bad as I thought you were.

PENNINGTON *(lamenting)*. That young man is in a very fit state to write his tour! I deplore that tourists should so often misrepresent this country. *(Mildly)* I know little of the natives. I deplore that prejudice should give birth to such misrepresentations, and hope modern tourists will in future forbear giving wounds with the pen which go deeper, and reach further than the sword. May one nation endeavour to do justice to the other, and prosper under those blessings which heaven is daily pouring upon them.

While residing at Mrs. Bradish's, I take an opportunity of visiting the Niggers (*Anglice*, negroes) Theatre.[137] The black population being, in the national theatres, under certain restrictions,[138] have, to be quite at their ease, a theatre of their own. Here I see a black tragedian (the Kentucky Roscius)[139] perform the character of Hamlet[140] *(Imitating dialect)*

To-*by*, or not to-*by*, dat is de question,
Wedder it be noble in de *head*, to suffer
De *tumps* and *bumps* of de outrageous fortune,
Or to take up de arms against a sea of *hubble bubble*,
And by *opossum*, end 'em.

No sooner had he said the word 'opossum,' which he meant for 'oppose them,' than a universal cry of 'Opossum! Opossum! Song! Song!' ran through the sable auditory. This, I learnt from a Kentucky planter, was a great favourite with the negroes, and a genu-*ine* melody. I was informed that "Opossum up a Gum Tree" was the national air, a sort of "God save the King" of the negroes, and that being reminded of it by Hamlet's pronunciation of "oppose 'em," there was no doubt but that they would have it sung. The opossum is addicted to climbing up the gum tree,[141] thinking no one can follow him; but the raccoon hides himself in the hollow of the tree, and as poor opossum goes up, pulls him down by the tail, and that's the plot. The following is a translation from the original Indian *(Sings)*:

---

136 Benjamin West's famous painting *The Treaty of Penn with the Indians* (1772) depicts a shoreline in Pennsylvania. This American painter was well known for his history paintings. West died in London in 1820.

137 Mathews modelled his anecdote on the African Grove, a New York theatre founded by William Brown in 1821, whose audiences included African Americans as well as a sizeable number of whites.

138 African Americans were prohibited from sitting anywhere but the "third tier" (the highest gallery) in many theatres.

139 Any outstanding actor or, as in this case, someone with pretensions to that stature; after Quintus Roscius Gallus, a famous Roman actor of the first century BCE. Adding a qualifier (such as the Infant Roscius, or the Kentucky Roscius) designated what distinguished one aspirant from another. Mathews is unlikely to mean that this actor was necessarily from Kentucky: the term was widely used in minstrelsy to reference the plantation South.

140 Mathews most likely observed James Hewlett play Hamlet. At Mathews's premiere, this character was called Caesar Alcibiades Hannibal Hewlett. In Dublin, he evidently designated this character Maximilian Alcibiades Caesar. *British Press*, 26 March 1824; and undated Dublin clipping, Anne Mathews's scrapbooks, vol. 3, Harvard Theatre Collection.

141 A Southern hardwood, also known as sweetgum (*Liquidambar styraciflua*).

OPOSSUM UP A GUM TREE
Air—"Negro Melody" or "Native Melody"[142]
Verse

Possum up a Gum-Tree,
Up he go, up he go
Raccoon in the hollow
Down below, down below
Him pull him up hims long tail
Pully-hawl,[143] pully-hawl
Then how him whoop and hallow
Scream and bawl, scream and bawl.
Possum up a Gum Tree
Raccoon in the hollow
Him pull him by hims long tail
Then how him whoop and hallow.

Massa send we Negro Boy
Board a ship, board a ship
There we work and cry "ye hoy"
Cowskin whip, cowskin whip
Negro he work all de day
Night get groggy, night get groggy
But if Negro he go play
Massa floggy, Massa floggy.
Possum etc.

Caesar steal him Massa's boots
Last Whitsunday—Whitsunday
'Cause him marry Polly Cootes
Look fine and gay fine and gay
Caesar all day walk in pain
Boot so tight, boot so tight

---

142 Three distinct versions are printed in the souvenir editions. The lyric reproduced here is from a fourth variation, published as sheet music explicitly to commemorate Mathews's performance ("Possum up a Gum Tree," arranged by T. Philipps, London, n.d.). It matches the tune published in *Chappell's 100 Christy Minstrel American and Negro Melodies for the Violin, Flute, Cornet, Clarionet, or Concertina*, arranged by Franz Nava (London: Chappell, [1858]), 30. Described as "remarkable not only for its whim and character, but for the exceeding pretty native air" (*Theatrical Observer; and Daily Bills of the Play*, April 1824: 2). The Duncombe edition includes an explicit reference to slavery:
    Black boy, him love Til Jenkins,
    Tink he'll wed—tink he'll wed.
    His massa chide him tinking,
    Beat him head—beat him head.
    Black boy him love rum too,
    Make him groggy—make him groggy;
    But massa make him come to,
    When him floggy—when him floggy. (12)
143 Pull with all one's might.

He no get them off again
All de night, all de night.
Possum etc.

Miss Polly say "you nasty brute
Get out of bed, get out of bed
If you come near me wid de boot
I break your head, I break your head."
Caesar he no more entreats him
He quite dummy, he quite dummy
Massa see his boots and beat him
All to mummy,[144] all to mummy.
Possum etc.

(Speaks) Hamlet proceeded:—

——————————'Tis a *coronation*
Devoutly to be wished—to die—to sleep—
To go to sleep—den to dream—ah! dere's de *rub-a-dub dub.*

This rub-a-dub[145] was mistaken by a little black drummer, placed behind the scenes to announce the king's drinking to Hamlet. This appeared to discompose Hamlet extremely, for on his recommencing the part *(strutting down with one arm a-kimbo,*[146] *and the other spouting out in front, just for all the world like a black teapot, and bellowing out):*

Now are de winter of our dis-a-contents
Made glorious summer, by de *son of New York.*[147]
PLANTER *(from the side-boxes).*[148] Young man, what's the name of the play?
TRAGEDIAN. *Hamlet,* massa.
PLANTER. Because that speech is from *Richard III.* I guess.
TRAGEDIAN. Ees; I thought every fool know dat; but I just thought of New York then, and I couldn't help talking about it.

---

144 Pulp.
145 "Rub-a-dub" indicates the sound of a beaten drum: the drummer-boy evidently thought his cue was being called out.
146 "Akimbo": hand on hip and elbow splayed outward. The "teapot" position described here was synonymous, by the early nineteenth century, with bombastic or amateurish acting.
147 The *National Advocate* review transcribes the actor saying, "Now is de vinter of our discontent made glorus [glorious] summer by de son of New-York." Review of *Trip to America,* by Charles Mathews, *National Advocate* (New York), 21 September 1821, 2. "*New*-York" is interpolated by the actor. All four of the *Trip to America* texts record this detail, so presumably this interpolation was retained over the course of twelve to eighteen months, heard by Mathews, and inspired a reliable laugh line in his performance. The actor's idiosyncratic pronunciation is lampooned in the review, and also by Mathews, but only the Duncombe edition has the ludicrous version printed here. It is the least faithful to Shakespeare though it also offers the most interesting take on the lines' scansion. Two of the sources (*Sketches of Mr. Mathews* and *The Vocal Gleaner*) include the more conventional "Now is de winter of our discontent made de glorious summer by de sun of New York."
148 Locating the Kentucky planter in the side-boxes designates him as higher-status than if he sat on the lower floor or mezzanine.

The Americans are not, constitutionally, fond of fighting; and not being often at war, the army of course was not in the finest state of regulation, as all above twenty and under forty-five years of age are liable to be called upon. They have five musters[149] in the year; fine for non-attendance is five dollars, however they are allowed to send a substitute. The accoutrements, too, are bad: umbrellas, fishing-rods, and pitch-forks, are allowed to take the place of guns at a short notice, and hope for the usual indulgence. Having been present at one of these muster-folk, it struck me that I could glean the same amusement from an imitation of one, as I had before done from one of our "Volunteer Field Day and Sham Fights."[150] *(Sings)*

MILITIA MUSTER FOLK
Air—"Hey for the life of a Soldier," "Roll drums merrily March away,"
or "Voulez-vous dansez"
Chorus

Come militia men so gay—
Bring your drums, your guns, and sabres,
While the fife, shall briskly play;
Assemble all your neighbours.

Verse

See the officer is near,
See the troops in crowds appear;
Every soldier now is near
To prosecute his labours.

CAPTAIN BLUEAPRON *(speaks)*. Aye, aye, friends and neighbours, we must make no distinction of personages now. The tradesman must be lost in the officer, the gentleman sunk in the soldier. Captain *Blueapron* on the ground—Silence, gentlemen—considerably well silenced—those gentlemen who have only umbrellas must go to the rear; those for ploughshares may file off in a separate body; while the veterans with muskets, may keep the front rank—considerably well done—handsome—considerably handsome. Come, fall in, or we shall fall out—form a line, there, form a line, if you please. Why, bless me, do you call that a line? Why you're zig-zag at both ends and crooked in the middle. Why neighbour Swigger, don't you see your inside is hollow?[151] It wants filling up.

SWIGGER. Yes, and so would yours too; if you had come from home without your breakfast as I have.

CAPTAIN BLUEAPRON. You should put a biscuit in your pocket, when you come to drill; but come, we must get on. Stand at ease. Neighbour Cripplegait, why don't you stand at ease?

---

149 Military drill practices.

150 Mathews refers to the military exercise described in his 1822 "at home," *Master Charles Mathews's Youthful Days*, in which a song of this name is included. A rag-tag group of "tailors, and barbers, and butchers, and bakers" practised manoeuvres.

But lord! When they all began to fire,
It sounded like children sneezing.

The London Mathews; Containing an Account of Master Charles Mathews's Youthful Days (London: Hodgson, [1822]), 31-33. The structure of the tale and many of the jokes are borrowed from Oliver H. Prince's "Militia Muster," first printed in a Georgia paper, the *Monitor*, in 1813, reprinted in the Louisville *Public Advertiser* 21 June 1823, and eventually collected in A.B. Longstreet, *Georgia Scenes, Characters, Incidents, &c., in the First Half Century of the Republic. By a Native Georgian* (Augusta: H.R. Sentinel Office, 1835), 157-64. See also Walter Blair, *Native American Humor (1800-1900)* (New York: American Book Company, 1937), 26.

151 Pun on the infantry formation of the hollow square: two or more ranks of musketeers or riflemen poised to volley fire at charging cavalry.

CRIPPLEGAIT. I can't, Major; for these here last breeches you've made me are so tight they screw me like a vice.

CAPTAIN BLUEAPRON. Well, send 'em back after exercise, and they shall be let out. Now then, eyes right, you there with the spectacles.

GAZE-ALL. That's a thing I should like to do, and perhaps Mr. Officer, you'll tell me how to manage it, for look, I squint.

RATTLEPOT. That's true, and that's the reason you always looks *so cross* at the Captain when he commands you.

CAPTAIN BLUEAPRON. What dog is that running after the troops?

GUARD. She's mine, Captain, I have got her two puppies in my great coat-pockets.

CAPTAIN BLUEAPRON. Puppies must never come to parade in future.

GUARD. I am very sorry we are going to lose you, Captain.[152]

CAPTAIN BLUEAPRON. Don't you be impudent; I do not approbate impudence to the commander. None of your remarks; I am but little,[153] but I'll throw up you in the air so high, that you shall be starved to death before you come down again. Silence, gentlemen! Silence for the word. Now gentlemen, you with the guns, come forward. You with the umbrellas, wheel to the right. You with the bean-stalks and fishing-rods, turn to the left; and you with the pitch-forks and spits go behind, and mind you don't stick 'em in any body. Now shoulder—there, now, I say arms.

PRY. Well, but you might have said it, you know.

CAPTAIN BLUEAPRON. Fall back, fall back, there. What the devil do you leave the ranks for, Pry?[154]

PRY. Only came out, Captain to ask if there had been any reduction in broadcloths,[155] and what the news was.

CAPTAIN BLUEAPRON. Pooh, nonsense; we shall never finish, if we begin in this manner—fall in, fall back.

(Sings)

Verse

The maneuv'ring now begins,
Dressing, forming,
Charming, charming;
Now they exercise their pins,
Marching, counter-marching.
Now the corps is at a fault,
Now they wheel, and now they halt
Hours employing,
In deploying,
Till their throats are parching.

CAPTAIN BLUEAPRON *(speaks)*. Now, gentlemen, I must ask you the favour, as we are all met for the benefit of our country, not to quarrel one among the other, but let the evolutions of war go off in the

---

152 A puppy is a foolish young man.

153 Short, like Napoleon; or young, like a puppy.

154 It is tempting to attribute this as an allusion to Paul Pry, a character from John Poole's eponymous play, made infamous by Mathews's friend John Liston, but this did not premiere until 13 September 1825. Poole may have developed a social type (his catch-phrase was "I hope I don't intrude," spoken with his umbrella tucked beneath his arm and his rear end prominently protruding) or picked up on Mathews's fleeting characterization.

155 Plain woven cloth, usually black, used for men's clothing; evidently Captain Blueapron is a tailor.

most peaceable manner. I trust I need not explain to you, gentlemen, what *war* is; you are all, I believe, married men, and know too well its properties. Every married man is in fact a soldier, inasmuch as he may sleep with *loaded arms*; but, gentlemen, I will now proceed to the business of the day.

YANKEE *(tremulously)*. Captain, Captain! You must excuse me, but there's a customer at my shop, and my wife can't give him what he wants; I must go.

CAPTAIN BLUEAPRON. Stop, stop, that is against the regulations, for a soldier to run away.

YANKEE. Not at all, Captain, for I am going to *charge* and so I am off in a shot.

CAPTAIN BLUEAPRON. Now, gentlemen, shoulder arms!—Handsomely shouldered, gentlemen—considerably handsome; only don't some of you shoulder on one side, and some on the other; it don't matter which, only be all alike—handsomely altered, gentlemen. Halt! halt! halt!—why, gentlemen, you've left the rear guard behind.

GUARD. Yes, so we have, we're beforehand with them.

CAPTAIN BLUEAPRON. Now, gentlemen, we're going to exercise, and in order that all may be correct, I'll give the word from my book of the New System, *Rules and Regulations for Regulating the Rules that Rule the Regulars*—Stand at ease! Attention! Shoulder arms! Fix bayonets!

GUARD. Why, Captain, how are we to fix bayonets when our guns are on our shoulders?

CAPTAIN BLUEAPRON. Oh, I beg pardon, I've turned over two leaves[156] at once—order arms—unfix bayonets.

GUARD. Why, we haven't fixed them yet, Captain.

CAPTAIN BLUEAPRON. That's true, but never mind—ground arms—why, bless me brother Falter, you've tumbled down—I hope you haven't hurt yourself?

FALTER. Yes, I've cut my nose and bled a bushel, *I guess*.

GUARD. Yes, he's wounded in the service, and has shed blood in the cause, *I calculate*.

FALTER. Yes, and there's one gentleman has run his bayonet into a very tender part of my frame, and I've only to inform this here corps that I am not bomb proof.

CAPTAIN BLUEAPRON. What have you put up your umbrella for, Sandy?

SANDY. Because *I guess* we shall have a very particular damned heavy shower of rain soon, and though you may expect us to be able to stand fire, I believe there is no rule to oblige us to stand water.

CAPTAIN BLUEAPRON. Why, egad that's true, and it is beginning to rain, sure enough—forward umbrellas! Shoulder umbrellas! Fall in three deep! Take close order! Prepare umbrellas! Now, then, fire umbrellas! That's right—they're all up. I say, Little, how long are you in this regiment?

LITTLE. Five feet nine without my shoes, how long are you?

CAPTAIN BLUEAPRON. Six feet three.

GUARD. A pretty size for a coffin.

LITTLE. Pretty well, *I guess*.

CAPTAIN BLUEAPRON. Quick, march!

(Sings)

Verse

Thus they exercise away,
   And you'll say it is a joke, sirs,
For I've been on many a day,
   With militia muster folk, sirs.

---

156 Pages.

Now all formed to work they go,
And no regiment e'er looked prouder;
I'm sure their looks would scare a foe,
When they're supplied with powder.

Chorus

All are ready for the fray.
All exclaim come don't delay,
All prepare to fire away,
And where's the corp's fired louder.

Verse

Yes militia muster folk,
Friends and neighbours,
Glory's labours,
Call upon us 'tis no joke,
Then hey for guns and sabres!
Every heart with ardour burns,
Paws[157] for glory,
Live in story,
Each all thoughts of yielding spurns,
Like a true-born Yankee.

Chorus

Now Columbia's valiant sons,
Prove that they are sons of guns,
Fire and thunder,
Spreading wonder,
But no harm done, I thank ye.

CAPTAIN BLUEAPRON. I shall not intrude very long upon your valuable time, because I am aware that patriotism is an expensive virtue, at least, when encouraged by such as ourselves; therefore, gentlemen, I guess I shall read over the regularly made regular rules for regulating the irregularity of the regular irregulars. Now, gentlemen, kneel down.—Very good; this is what we call Platonic[158] firing.—Fire!

(They fire irregularly).

Why, gentlemen, that is the most irregular firing for a regular regiment I ever heard. Now, gentlemen, I must trouble you not to stand at ease; it is quite opposite to the design of war for any man to stand at ease. All attention.—Handsome—considerably handsome—Advance!

GUARD. How can we advance, when we are down here upon our knees?

CAPTAIN BLUEAPRON. Gentlemen, to avoid accidents, and perform our evolutions with military precision, you in the front row must kneel, and you in the second row must stand up; this is what we call Platonic firing; but mind, the gentlemen in the second row are not allowed to shoot the gentlemen's heads off in the front row; and if any of the gentlemen in the front should fall down, the persons behind shall pick them up again—now return ramrods[159]—Eh! bless me, Master Clayskull what are you doing?

---

157 Impatient (literally, striking the ground as a horse with its hoof).

158 Theoretical rather than practical.

159 Muzzle-loaded rifles required a rod to pack the projectile against the propellant. Soldiers were drilled to return the ramrod to its groove under the gun barrel to ensure they always kept it with their weapon.

CLAYSKULL. Why, I'm returning my ramrod to neighbour Longstaff, I borrowed it of him the first time we went out shooting together, and now I'm giving it him back again; if that ain't returning ramrods, you may do the exercise yourself another time.

CAPTAIN BLUEAPRON. Gentlemen, if any of you should bite your cartridge at the wrong end, just be good enough to spit the ball out again. Make ready—

(One of them discharges his musket).

Who's that firing before the time; for shame, friend. Quick, present.

(Another fires).

Really gentlemen this is a waste of powder, I never heard anything so bad as

(Another fires).

There, again—now gentlemen—fire—

(They fire one after the other).

Really I never heard such irregular firing in a regular regiment. Fishing-rods, I never heard you report. Eh! why gentlemen, what are you all dancing about in that manner for—stand at ease—

(They knock the mosquitoes off with their hands).

Attention! Damn the mosquitoes—

(They still keep knocking them off).

Shoulder arms! (Knocks mosquitoes off his shoulders, arms, legs, etc.).

(Sings)

Chorus

Bravo militia muster folk,
Friends and neighbours,
Glory's labours,
Call upon us 'tis no joke,
Then hey for guns and sabres.

Part II

Hiring a servant in London is one thing, and hiring a servant in America is another. In the former place, they are generally civil and well-behaved; at all events, they put on their livery.[160] In the other, they always consider they are conferring a favour on you. I am in want of what we in England call a servant, and am very soon accosted by a person, introduced as Daniel Doolittle. I ask him if he wishes to become

---

160 Servant's costume. Mathews wrote to James Smith:

  I should feel ... disposed to scourge, to flagellate, to score to the back-bone, ALL the middling and lower orders.... Not merely sullen and cold, but studiously rude.... The stage-driver says, 'Yes, sir,' and 'no, sir,' to the ostler [stable-man], but to a question from a person who has a clean neckcloth, he instantly draws up, and, in the most repulsive manner, answers, 'No,' 'ay,' or 'very well.' The upper orders are literally slaves to the lower.

  Mathews could not find servants who were not African, Irish, or Scottish—whom he did not regard as American—and everyone dressed alike so he struggled to find individuals worthy of imitation. Mathews, Memoirs of Charles Mathews, vol. 3, 382-83.

my servant, but the man don't seem to understand. At length he asks me if I 'wants a help?' which is as unintelligible to me as I was to the other, but when I reply that I certainly do want a help, the servant says:

DANIEL. Being in a pretty considerable damned hurry, I should like to ask you a few questions; for I should like to know all about you, if you have no objection.

MATHEWS. None in the world.

DANIEL. Aye, that's right; you are quite free and affable; not a bit of pride; not a bit of a gentleman about you.

MATHEWS. You are pleased to compliment.

DANIEL. No, I don't; it is just what I think. What are you? Where do you come from? How did you get your living when you came of age? And what have you done since?

MATHEWS. Not to trouble you with any more inquiries respecting me.

DANIEL (correcting his pronunciation). In-quiries, you mean.

MATHEWS. Well then, in the first place, I am an Englishman.

DANIEL. Oh! you are an Englishman, are you? Well, I should not have thought it; you speak English almost as well as I do myself: if you are an Englishman, you won't do for me.

MATHEWS. What then, you won't *help* an Englishman?

DANIEL. No; I must beg leave to decline off. America is the first country in the world, and England may be the second: now for a genu-*ine* native of the first to serve one of the second is putting the cart before the horse.

MATHEWS. Well, I hope I have not offended you.

DANIEL. No; I hope I have not mortified you.

MATHEWS. Not much.

Jack Topham, and his admiring double Barnaby Bray, now entering and hearing the circumstances, Jack attempts to have another go at the natives, calling the worthy Mr. Pennington, who then joins them, and every American indiscriminately, 'Yankees, Jonathans,' and the like. The calm reflecting American is not quite satisfied with Jack's facetiousness, and asks him if he really knows what the meaning of the term "Yankee" is.

TOPHAM. Oh, yes; a Yankee is what you may call an American, and of course, an American is what you must call a Yankee.[161]

PENNINGTON (unsatisfied by this very classical description). My dear sir you are wrong; you might, with equal propriety, apply the word *cockney* to an Irishman or a Scotsman; *Yankee* is only applied to those of the back settlements. When the English first came to America, the Negroes called them L'Anglais, which soon became corrupted into Inglée; and at length, as a matter of course, every Englishman in the end was called a Yankee.[162] I once knew a Farmer whose partiality for the English was so great

---

161   Topham follows the contemporaneous English practice of referring to all Americans as Yankees, whereas Pennington reflects the American practice of limiting the term to New Englanders. Originally used pejoratively by residents of the Southern states about their northern brethren, by the 1820s it had a neutral connotation and self-identified Yankees hailed from the area north and east of Boston. The Yankee "was a mixture of amiable rustic simplicity and hardy independence, with which he threw his adversaries off guard, and a shrewd and cunning intelligence, with which he unfailingly won his bargains." Francis Hodge, *Yankee Theatre: The Image of America on the Stage, 1825-1850* (Austin: U of Texas P, 1964), 44.

162   Pennington's etymology cannot be verified.

that he applied the word Yankee to every thing that was good; thus good beef, was Yankee beef; a good fowl, was a Yankee fowl, and since he imagined all Englishmen good, he of course called every Englishman a Yankee.

Thus we got a definition of the word, which completely overthrew the stale wit of poor Jack Topham; and cousin Bray stood gazing for a joke, to aggravate his risible muscles, but only yawned, and seemed to say,

BRAY (through his yawn). That boy'll not kill me yet.

My reception at Boston, whither I next repaired, surpassed my most sanguine expectations: I found as many friends there as I had ever done in any place where I was better known. Although it is uncommon to drink toasts there, I felt not only delighted, but highly honoured, and gratified, by hearing the health of his most gracious Sovereign George the Fourth given upon almost every occasion, by way of compliment, to me as an Englishman and a stranger.

Bunker's Hill,[163] where the celebrated battle was fought, between the English and the Americans, on the 17th of June 1775, was visited. There is nothing very remarkable here, except a sort of column, raised in commemoration of that event, and on which certain wags scribbled over with anonymous wit, like some of our inn windows

This monument was built of brick,
Because we did the English lick.

And another, of equal merit, but far more elegant, which runs thus:

This monument was built of stone,
Because Lord North[164] wouldn't let the Americans alone.

While looking at the inscriptions I was accosted by a real *Yankee*, one Jonathan W. Doubikin, who is very fond of relating long stories, which turn to no account.[165]

JONATHAN. Uncle Ben; my Uncle Ben's desperate cute;[166] if you like I'll tell you all about my Uncle Ben—it was he as that wrote that letters to the ship's owners, I guess, when all the crew died but Uncle Ben and the mate; it was a ge-nu-ine letter, I'll tell you what it was—"I am well—the mate's well—As for the rest they are gone to—you know where." One day he was riding up town on his mare, Uncle Ben had a mare, he had, a great many little children followed him, crying out "Uncle Ben the devil's dead—Uncle Ben the devil's dead"—for you see they knowed him—at which he was a little damned

---

163 Bunker Hill is the site commemorating the first major battle of the American Revolutionary War. During the siege of Boston, the colonials attempted to fortify a position at Breed's Hill (adjacent to Bunker Hill) to prevent the British from taking Dorchester and Charlestown and thus surrounding the city. The poorly trained colonials withstood two major assaults before retreating to Cambridge. Both sides suffered heavy casualties. Mathews must have seen the first monument, an eighteen-foot wooden pillar erected in 1794. During Mathews's visit, the citizens were organizing to erect what stands there now; the cornerstone was laid in 1825.

164 Frederick North, 2nd Earl of Guilford (1732-92) was Prime Minister of Great Britain during the American Revolutionary War.

165 Mathews may have seen one of several Yankee poetic monologues published in American newspapers in the 1820s and borrowed elements (see Rourke, *American Humor*, 29). "The Yankee portrayed in travel books was a lanky and awkward bumpkin who talked through his nose. Tight-lipped and shrewd, he most often appeared as a peddler who played sharp tricks and revealed his tarnal cuteness in every section of the country." Blair, *American Humor* 28-29; see also 26-27.

166 Sharp-witted.

mad to be sure; but Uncle Ben took no manner of notice, but continued on. Well, they kept following him, crying "Uncle Ben the devil's dead—Uncle Ben the devil's dead," at which he turned round, being in a pretty dam'd considerable passion, and lifting up his arms in this manner, said, "Poor *fatherless* children." One day Uncle Ben said to me "Jonathan," said he, for he always called me Jonathan, though I was christed[167] Jonathan W., but I was a pretty considerable favourite with him I was; so he said "Jonathan," said he, "don't you want to go out a gunning tomorrow." "O yes!" said I, "I do," and with that Uncle Ben and me went out a gunning; and we walked and walked and never shot nothing; but, as we were coming home, Uncle Ben stopt short. "Jonathan," said he, looking up a tree, "there's a squirrel I guess?" So I looked. "Yes," said I, "it is a squirrel I calculate." A small little thing it was, jumping from tree to tree, a little grey one, not a brown one, for it was a grey one—so Uncle Ben took his gun and aimed at it; there was no salvation for it then, for he walked into[168] his body and killed it outright. But the little thing lodged in the tree, so Uncle Ben said: "Jonathan jump up the tree for that damned squirrel," for he knowed I was very *sprive* [sic] and ac-*tive*. "No," said I, "I shan't, unless I likes." So he says, "I reckon if I give you a shilling you will"—so up I got in a minute, for I was very ac-*tive*, and when I came down, and gave it to Uncle Ben, he never offered to pay me the shilling; so I said, said I, "Uncle Ben," said I, "I'll trouble you for that trifle," but he took no notice and quitted. I did not see Uncle Ben again for a fortnight, at last I saw him walking up the street; so I goes up to him and says, says I, "Uncle Ben," says I, "I'll thank you for that trifle you owes me?" "What trifle?" said he; so I up and told him all about the gunning and the squirrel, he had got money for I heard it rattle in his pocket. "Oh, I remember," said he, but he quitted again. Well, a good bit after I saw Uncle Ben in the street again; so I goes up to him and says, says I, "Uncle Ben," says I, "I'll thank you for that little trifle you owe me." So he looks at me and says, says he, "Oh! ah? you are a little too damned particular, you are." "Why Uncle Ben," said I, "it's not for the matter of the money, but it is for the *principle altogether*." And do you know I have not seen my Uncle Ben from that day to this.[169]

About this time the winter set in and, in company with Bray and Topham, I had an opportunity of witnessing a custom, on the first fall of snow, of the maidens in a *sleigh*, drawn by horses with bells on their heads, visiting the villages at a short distance, for the purpose of regaling themselves: they always start at midnight.[170] On the first night the noise of the bells awoke Bray and Topham, who rushed to the window in alarm.

TOPHAM. Hollo! what the devil's the matter, oh! a fire, oh! why don't you fetch the engines?[171]
YANKEE. The in-gines you mean.
TOPHAM. Oh! very well, in-gines if you like.
YANKEE. We don't want no ingines, we don't; it's only the maidens in the sleigh, I guess.

---

167 Christened.
168 Vigorously attacked.
169 The rustic Doubikin's anecdote shows the shrewd and tricking nature of the Yankee personified by Uncle Ben. Curiously, when W.T. Moncrieff develops Uncle Ben's character in *Monsieur Mallet; or, My Daughter's Letter* (London: Hailes Lacy, 1851), first acted by T.P. Cooke at the Adelphi on 22 January 1829, Uncle Ben is "Mr. Commissary Benjamin Brom Von Gunnery" from the Knickenbocken Settlement near Albany, New York, and speaks with a heavy German accent.
170 Mathews was fascinated by this mode of transport, silent except for the horses' bells. He wrote home,
     They whisk along at about the rate of twelve miles an hour, and in *open* carriages like the half of a boat. So fond are they of the sport, that it is common for parties to go out at night ten or fifteen miles to adjacent villages, dance there, and then return in these open sleighs. (Mathews, *Memoirs of Charles Mathews*, vol. 3, 356)
171 Fire engines.

TOPHAM. You shouldn't say I guess—you ought to know whether it is a sleigh or not.

YANKEE. Well, if I say I guess, you always say you know.

TOPHAM. Why a good many do, you know; but you know, I never say you know.

YANKEE. There, you said you know then, I guess.

TOPHAM. And you said I guess, you know.

YANKEE. Well, I have a right to say I guess, if I like, I reckon.

Generally going every morning to the Boston Post Office to look after my letters, I discover all fighting for the grand material, the first beautiful morsel of our existence—News! There they are like wasps round a sugar cask. At this moment opens the little door, and out pops the post-master's hand ringing a kind of muffin[172] tintinnabulum.[173] *(Various voices.)*

POSTMASTER. Now, now, the dollars and cents.

AMERICAN. Have you ever a letter for me?

POSTMASTER. I don't know, I guess.

AMERICAN. I calculate you have.

POSTMASTER. I guess you must wait till I see, I reckon.

ANOTHER. Have you ever a letter for me, I ask?

POSTMASTER. I don't know, I guess.

ANOTHER. Well, I'll ask you once more—have you got ever a letter for me?

POSTMASTER. I can't tell, I reckon.

ANOTHER. Can't tell, you are a pretty fellow for a post-master, I shall report you to Congress.

POSTMASTER. You!—psah!—you're only an individual.

ANOTHER. What am I!

POSTMASTER. An *individual*.

ANOTHER. You're another!

POSTMASTER. Here's a letter for you, Jonathan Tomkins.

TOMKINS. How much?

POSTMASTER. One dollar twenty-five cents.

TOMKINS. That's a pretty considerable damned shame, that is.

SAILOR. Have you 'ere a letter for me?

POSTMASTER. Yes, ah! this is it; it came from your friend, Captain Grampus, of the Greenland whale fishery.

SAILOR. How do you know?

POSTMASTER. Why by the *seal* at the back of it.

MALLET.[174] Pray Sare, I beg your pardonne, avez vous von lettre pour Monsieur Mallet *(pronouncing his name Mallay)*.

POSTMASTER *(looking over letters)*. Mallay, no, no letter of that name.

The next day he attends again:

MALLET. Um tres sorry to give you de grande trouble, sare, but have you von lettre for Monsieur Mallet?

---

172 Cup-shaped.

173 Small tinkling bell.

174 This character became the inspiration of H.W. Montagu's verses *Monsieur Mallet; or, My Daughter's Letter, a Random Record*, illustrated by Robert Cruikshank (London: Thomas Griffiths, 1830).

POSTMASTER *(looking as before)*. No: no letter for Mallay.

MALLET. Thank you, sare, I would not come so oft, but it is from my daughter, sare, she is at Bourdeaux,[175] she is my only child. I shall come again tomorrow, sare. Good day, good day.

Week after week passed away, and the poor Frenchman never received the wished-for consolation. One day, however, he went to the office and while the man was sorting the letters he named several persons, and among the rest.

POSTMASTER. Mr. Mallet; to be left till called for.

MALLET *(shrugging his shoulders, exclaims)*. It was very strange; might I look over the list myself?

Reflect, and conceive his astonishment, when he casts his eye upon the identical letter he had been so long searching after. His joy at having received the letter for a moment subdues his rage.

MALLET *(kisses the treasure, presses it to his bosom, then recalling the agent of the delay exclaims)*. Sare, don't you see this letter is for me!

POSTMASTER *(coolly)*. Why, had you said Mal-*let*, I should have given it to you before. That letter's been lying here these three mouths. Why don't you learn to pronounce your name properly, that one might understand you?

MALLET. Vot yon mean by dat? *(Seizing the letter, which he rapturously kisses, and affectionately presses to his bosom forgetting for a moment the neglect of the post-office-keeper, then returning to his former indignation)* Vot do you mean by dat, I say? To keep my lettre all dis time, ven I came so oft, and tell you it was from my dear daughter at Bourdeaux—my child I love so much. You are very neglect, insolent, ignorant man. I shall complain of you to Congress. If I had learn vot de Aungliesh call de box,[176] I would blow your nose for you!

(The postman retorting in turn, his apathy and conduct so provoked the poor Frenchman, that in his rage he tears up the letter he had sought so long; and is only aroused to a sense of what he has done by the laughter of the republican; his despair at the circumstance, and the manner in which he departs, are, as Mr. Mathews delineates them, beyond description, and must be seen to be properly appreciated. Sings.)

BOSTON POST-OFFICE
Air—"Tom Thumb"[177] or "Oh! what a day"

Oh! what a town the Bostonians have to talk about,
There's the Bank, the Theatre, the Church and the Exchange;
Then so many fine streets for the pretty girls to walk about,
On high day with their sweethearts when to show themselves they range.
And then there's the Post-office, where all the men of letters go
That place of fun and bustle, when election time begins,
And that he's independent, every man can let his betters know,
And settle o'er his pipe and pot who shall be outs and ins.

---

175 Bourdeaux is in the Gironde department of southeastern France. Mathews noted in his letters home that because the French were so numerous in America, any imitation of their broken English is "a sure hit" with American audiences. Mathews, *Memoirs of Charles Mathews*, vol. 3, 310.

176 Boxing.

177 In 1780, Kane O'Hara's adaptation of Henry Fielding's play *Tom Thumb* debuted at Covent Garden. The burlesque had music by J. Markordt (including this duet) and Thomas Arne.

A new governor is to be elected, and every body is six inches higher, trying to sniff the intelligence over his fellows' head.

AMERICAN. I'll bet you my hat to a blanket that the election is not settled.

ANOTHER. No, I won't do that; but I'll bet you my wife's gown to your wife's petticoat that we have all the news this day.

An American election now takes place, and the Post-office becomes a scene of bustle. (Sings)

> All the folks of Boston crowd about the gay post-office now,
> A governor they must elect to manage matters well;
> How they gaze and talk aloud—Oh, there is a mighty row,
> For not a man his conscience, nor a single vote, will sell.
> Come boys, be ready now, and let us have a man that's good;
> Yes, honour is the best, my lad, and never could be yet withstood;
> We'll have a proper man to rule—oh, yes, we will, and nothing less;
> Some one that's good, *I calculate*, and one that's honest too, *I guess*.

(Various voices) 'Pray, Sir, does the election take place today?'—'Yes, Sir.'—'Who's to come in, pray?'—'Why, that gentleman that's just gone out.'—'And who's to go out, Sir?'—'Why, that gentleman just coming in.'—'Here's a letter for that gentleman with the threadbare coat: I mean A. B.'—'That's not me, Sir, for I'm C. D.[178]—'Sir, you're standing in the way—you're standing in the way, Sir.'—'Did you speak, Sir?'—'Yes I did, Sir; you're standing in the way, and you know it; that's as clear as A. B. C.'—'So it may be, Sir, but I am D. E. F.'[179]

MALLET. *Sair,* I beg your pardon, but when it is quite convenient I shall tank you to stand off my toes.

YANKEE. Oh! I beg your pardon, Sir—I hope I haven't hurt you in *toto.*

MALLET. Yes, *Sare,* you have, and you have hurt me in foot foot, and have trod upon my wheat wheat.

YANKEE. Trod upon your wheat! what the devil does the man mean?

MALLET. I mean my corn, Sir.

YANKEE. Oh! is that the case, then I'll cut you and your corn too, Sir.

(Sings)

> Thus with laughter and prattle
> They gaily, gaily rattle,
> At Boston Post-office, for wit, joke, and whim.
> Verse
> Come, stand aside, I say, and let us to the office go,
> Letters in abundance there are waiting now for me;
> To see you all assembled here, I think a very mighty show,
> And strangers cry to see the sight—what can the matter be?
> Pushing, squeezing, roaring, teazing, every two in warm debate,
> Stand aside, you stupid elf, I must get in at any rate;
> I've a letter waiting there, and must receive it now, I say,
> Here are letters waiting—take them quick, and quickly too the postage pay.

---

178 Seedy.
179 Deaf.

POSTMASTER. Here are a great many returned letters; James Franks, that's unpaid; Jonathan W. Doubikin, Patrick O'Flaherty.

O'FLAHERTY. That's me, Sir; my name is Pat O'Flaherty.

POSTMASTER. Then it's not for you: I said, Patrick O'Flaherty.

O'FLAHERTY. Well, and isn't Patrick Pat all the world over?

POSTMASTER. Here, take your letter, it comes to half-a-crown.

O'FLAHERTY. But then, Sir, I can't read, and where's the use of my taking the letter; perhaps you'll be kind enough to open it and read for me?

POSTMASTER. Certainly, with great pleasure. *(Reads)*

"Dear Pat,

In sitting down to write this letter I have to inform you, that I'm standing on the same spot where you left me, but I have lost the use of both my hands. The people in this country are very peaceable and quiet, with the exception of a good deal of bloodshed that takes place occasionally; and we haven't had one execution in this part of the country, with the exception of fifteen that were hanged last week. Your uncle Tim died last week, and remembered you in his will, for he has acknowledged owing you twenty-five thirteens,[180] but expressed great vexation after his death that he couldn't pay you, because he had no money. Your sister still remains single, but was safely delivered of twins the day before yesterday. All your absent friends desire to be remembered to you. I wouldn't conclude, only I have nothing more to say. I am, my dear Pat, your honoured father, Peter O'Flaherty."

There, Sir, now you must pay me half-a-crown.

O'FLAHERTY. What for, Sir?

POSTMASTER. Why, for the letter.

O'FLAHERTY. Pooh! bother! you read the letter—I did not. What use is the letter to me now? I'm sure you're welcome to it; sell it to somebody else, and get as much as you can for it.

Refrain (Sings)

Thus with laughter and prattle,
They gaily, gaily rattle,
At Boston Post-office for wit, joke, and whim.

Chorus

The governor's elected, the people are departing now
The conquerors are merry, and the losers sad;
With joy the one's elated, with grief the other's smarting now,
To lose the day one candidate is nearly mad.
Never mind, the time will come, and then our friend shall take his turn,
And then the winner of today from out his office we will spurn.
We'll let him know we can elect a man of true gentility,
And one who far outshines that knave in manners and ability.

(Various voices) 'So, Surety has got in.'—'Yes, and we're all out, I reckon; he's got in by a pretty considerable d—d large majority.'—'Here's a paper for you, Sir.'—'What! a newspaper.'—'Yes, Sir, it's the *Quizzical Gazette*.'—'Oh! then I'll read a little: "Last week, as a man was running down Fish-street-hill, he came in contact with the Monument, and upset it by the velocity with which he ran

---

180   An Irish silver shilling, worth thirteen pence of Irish copper currency.

against it.[181] After he had committed the act, he was daring enough to pick it up, and went and concealed it in St. Paul's Cathedral."'—'Well, I don't believe that; do you, Mr. Jonathan Doubikin?'

JONATHAN. My name's not Jonathan Doubikin: it's Jonathan W.; but, talking of stories, when my Uncle Ben was at sea, he met a sea-serpent; it put its head under the ship, and lifted it up; and after they sailed sixty miles they found themselves opposite its belly, and had one hundred and twenty to go before they got to the end of the tail.

(Sings)

Refrain

Thus with laughter and prattle,
They gaily, gaily rattle,
At Boston Post-office for wit, joke, and whim.

From Boston I proceed to Providence, at which place was a theatre; the manager of which appeared to depend entirely upon *providence* for support, was extremely anxious that I should perform. Among a variety of other inducements held out by him, to effect so desirable a consummation, is one of the very last we should have thought of holding forth:

MANAGER. Mine is a considerable respectable theatre, Mr. Mathews, many first-rate actors, I guess, have played in it, Mr. Cooper[182] has honored it with his performance, it was the last house he ever appeared in, for he died two days afterwards; and many other eminent actors who have played here lie in our church-yard; indeed I may say, it's half full of your English stars.

Moved by the oddity of this recommendation, I am induced to brave superstition, and comply with the manager's request. I performed to crowded and delighted audiences, thus proving that under any circumstances, if a man only has faith, he is not unlikely to benefit by Providence.

My companions and I next take the coach, and depart for Worcester;[183] on the road we meet with a fiddling Negro, who causes much amusement *(business: this fat stage-coach driver fastens the reins around his neck and urges his horses by different tunes on a fiddle),*[184] till we reach our destination. We meet with another particularly cool landlord, who enters into long arguments with his visitors, and gives us red port, which Jack Topham compares with mulled "Day and Martin."

A grand dinner is given in commemoration of the American war; and General Jackson[185] is invited, and attends solely on condition that he shall be allowed to pass unnoticed, and that no speech shall be

---

181 Fish-street is the main street running from London Bridge to the Monument (commemorating the Great Fire of 1666). The anecdote is apocryphal: the Monument is far too solid to suffer such treatment.

182 Thomas Abthorpe Cooper (1776-1849), an English tragedian, first appeared in America in 1796.

183 In central Massachusetts.

184 The nature of this character is specified in Mathews's letter to James Smith but not in any of the souvenir editions:
    A very fat negro, with whom I met, driving a stage-coach ... and urging his horses by different tunes on a fiddle, while he ingeniously fastened the reins round his neck. This would give an opportunity for the only costume which differs from that of our own country, the summer dress. (Mathews, *Memoirs of Charles Mathews*, vol. 3, 384)

185 Andrew Jackson (1767-1845) was the new state of Tennessee's first representative to Washington. He served as Major General in the War of 1812 and commanded defences in the Battle of New Orleans in 1815. He was again in (Continued) the limelight as the ruthless commander in the Seminole War (1817) in which the Americans successfully took Florida

made to, or desired from him, he labouring under a peculiar degree of *mauvaise honte*,[186] this is agreed to.[187] Dinner is served up, and all passes off very well till a little grinning Frenchman rises, and pays the General a most ridiculous compliment, by comparing him to:

FRENCHMAN.[188] The great Hannibal: because he shoot all the English, and can shoot anybody, and kill them all to death with his own grand sabre. I was once intended for Poet Laureat having such great talent for a muse *(gives a few ludicrous specimens of his talent)*; bat that when I mounts my pegasus, it runs away so fast, I never know when to stop. I am unfit to express all I could say; because I is so very eloquent, that by once beginning, I thinks it will be impossible for me ever to leave off again.

These observations are merely prefatory to delivering an ode of thirty verses, in praise of the General, which he has written.[189] *(Sings)*

ODE TO GENERAL JACKSON
Air—"Marlbrook"[190]

I will sing of General Jackson
Who the foe he has ne'er turned his back on.
But his soldiers, with all their knapsacks on,
Did make all *de* English stray.
He fought them one and all,
And his courage was not very small,
For he cut them with his sabre,
And their backs he did belabour;
Then we'll sound the pipe and the tabor,
Hurrah! hurrah! hurrah!

Refrain

Hurrah for General Jackson! the noble General Jackson!
Hurrah for General Jackson!—Hurrah! hurrah! hurrah!

When this place they would put one great tax on,
Ha! ha! says brave General Jackson,

---

from Spain. He ran for President in 1824 and though receiving a plurality of votes from the Electoral College, the House of Representatives declared John Quincy Adams the victor. Jackson ran again for President and served in 1829-37.

186 Bashfulness.

187 Jackson was known for this reticence: "If private humble citizens invited the General to dinner, he invariably went there in preference to a public dinner." William Faux, *Memorable Days in America: Being a Journal of a Tour to the United States, Principally Undertaken to Ascertain, by Positive Evidence, the Condition and Probable Prospects of British Emigrants* (London: W. Simpkin and R. Marshall, 1823), 199.

188 Colonel Peglar reprises this in the monopolylogue to annoy his French rival.

189 As they crafted the script, James Smith advised Mathews on how to phrase the introduction to this song: "Where you end by saying, 'A hundred verses, of which I unfortunately only retain ten,' say, 'unfortunately (or perhaps I should say *fortunately*).' This self-humility will cause you to be exalted." Mathews, *Memoirs of Charles Mathews*, vol. 3, 428.

190 Also known as "Malbrook" and "Malbrouk," this tune (a corruption of "Marlborough") is still in the repertory as "For He's a Jolly Good Fellow." As a result of the tune's popularity, Malbrook was commercially linked to all sorts of fashionable goods prior to the French Revolution. *Musical World*, 25 October 1856: 685, reprinted from the *Dublin Review*.

Begar[191] here's no time to relax on,
So their blood I will instantly draw.
Then he pulled out his sabre so,
And he gave them one, two, three, great blow!
He kicked up the very devil to pay, Sirs,
He knocked off all their legs, people say, Sirs,
And *den dey* all try to run away, Sirs.
(Refrain)
Now it's peace, and the war is over,
So let us all live in clover,
For he is his country's lover,
And still will protect her law.
He'll always shed his blood,
And fight for a cause that's good;
And if he's shot through the head, Sirs,
Or his blood it should flow so red, Sirs,
We'll sing in his praise when dead, Sirs.
(Refrain)
And when *dis* brave man *dey* send off, in
A very nice[192] gay looking coffin,
No one shall his burying be scoffing,
Nor on his brave skin set his paw;
For, *begar*, if e'er he does,
He vill shake him out of his shoes;
But at this I must say, oh, fie! Sirs,
For that day I am sure is not nigh, Sirs,
And brave Jackson he never shall die, Sirs.
(Refrain)

At the Boston sessions,[193] a supreme judge presides, and the rest of the bench are magistrates, chosen from the wealthy inhabitants and farmers of the neighbourhood. From some cause or other, the supreme judge could not attend. The day I was present, his place was filled by one of the magistrates, whose ancestors were of German origin, and who retained part of the dialect of his forefathers; in his charge to the grand jury he endeavours to expound the law: in a very ludicrous manner, he says,

MAGISTRATE. Perjury is when von man swears von thing, and anoder man swears anoder. False-swearing is ven von man takes his oath, and never kisses de pook, which is a very common practice. Bigamy is ven a man marries two wives; and polygamy is when von voman marries two husbands. Rapes and seductions are too vell known by every gentleman of education, when he comes to years of discretion, that it is useless for me to enlarge upon that subject. But the greatest crime of all, is selling vood made to imitate nutmegs. I hope I have made it clear to all parties; if not, dey must consult their

---

191 By God.
192 Tidy or smartly made.
193 Sittings of the court of justice.

attorneys out of court; but for myself, no man shall offer greater *obstructions* to the course of law, than I vill.

Mr. Raventop, the jester, now sings in a most melancholy whining manner, grinning all the time a ghastly smile, what he calls a very funny song. *(Sings)*

AMERICAN JESTER'S SONG
Medley air[194]

Merry are the bells, and merry do they ring,
Merry is myself, and merry do I sing,
For a lass is good,
And a glass is good,
And a pipe to smoke in cold weather;
The world is good,
And people are good,
And we're all good fellows together.

Merry is New York, and merry are its folks,
Merry are the Niggers, and merry are their jokes,
For the country is good,
And the victuals is good,
And the climate in all sorts of weather,
The Yankees are good.
And the natives are good,
And we're all good fellows together.

In England, farmers are too pat[195] to be discontented with their own country, and are very fond of trying their fortune in others—America for instance—imagining everything there to be of superior growth.[196] Walking through the streets of New York, I am very much surprised at meeting with a Yorkshire farmer I had formerly known extremely well, one John Houghton, who had emigrated from comfort and honest labour, in the vain hope of finding affluence and independence. He appeared overjoyed to see me, and inquired whether I intended to become a settler. I replied I did not think it would answer my purpose; as I doubted whether I could *draw* a *house*[197] so well as in England.

HOUGHTON. Oh, no need of that, Sur; we can build one, you know; I built one.
MATHEWS. Indeed! What with?

---

194 Source(s) unknown. In the Hodgson edition of *Mathews in America*, purportedly written for his performances abroad, the medley in part 3 switches airs after every verse: "Adieu, My Native Land," "Roast Beef," "Malbrook," "The Castilan Maid," "Ting a Ring," and finally "Paddy's Wedding." *Mathews in America; or, the Theatrical Wanderer* (London: Hodgson, 1823), 31.

195 Exactly suited to their circumstances.

196 "The wretched English who have been lured here, and have not the means of getting back, are pictures of misery and despair. The second and third year is sure to make inroads on their constitution. They all bear the first summer and winter well." Mathews, *Memoirs of Charles Mathews*, vol. 3, 366. Illinois became the twenty-first state in 1818; there were few settlers at this time, concentrated along the Ohio and Mississippi Rivers. In 1825, the Erie Canal (connecting Albany to Buffalo) eased access for settlers travelling from the east rather than the south. When hostilities with Native Americans were concluded by the Black Hawk War (1832), Illinois's population grew steadily.

197 Attract so large an audience.

HOUGHTON. LOGS.
MATHEWS. What's your cattle?
HOUGHTON. HOGS.
MATHEWS. What do you protect them with?
HOUGHTON. DOGS.
MATHEWS. And what's your land?
HOUGHTON. BOGS.

Honest John said the place would not do for him, and that for his part, he should go back to Yorkshire immediately; that he had just been making out a description of all his 'goods and chapels,' for the auctioneer, to sell them forthwith. Upon looking over this catalogue of farmer John, I found it to be a very curious collection, as he had not only enumerated all his 'goods and chapels,' but all his *wants* at the same time. *(Sings)*

ILLINOIS INVENTORY[198]

Recitative

I'll give you an inventory of what belongs to me,
And then you will be enabled to judge of my property;
So, to commence, pray notice what I mention,
For I think they'll prove quite worthy your attention.

Air

I've a house that's built with logs,
A sty that's built for hogs;
A kennel built for dogs,
And near me lots of bogs;
My pig's without a sow,
My calf's without a cow;
A boat without a paddle,
No horse, but I've saddle;
A gun without a trigger,
A whip without a Nigger;
A knife without a steel,
A chest without the meal;
A clock without a hand,
A basin without a stand;
A spade without a handle,
A stick without a candle;
A steel without a flint,
A purse with nothing in't;
And this my friends, do ye see,
Is a part of my inventory.

---

198 Described as "rapid and pleasing." *Theatrical Observer; and Daily Bills of the Play*, April 1824: 2. Illinois was the frontier in 1824. William Faux paid a visit in November 1819 and reported back to British readers that Illinois was not a profitable settlement. Faux, *Memorable Days in America*, 268-69, 198.

Recitative

But wait, I have a few things more to mention still,
And you can listen to me silently if you will,
For I'm determined you shall hear the whole,
And I am not deceiving you upon my soul.

Air

I've mice without a cat,
A trap without a rat;
Panniers[199] without an ass,
A bottle without a glass;
A box without the treasure,
A yard, but nothing to measure;
Some bills that ne'er will be paid,
A kitchen without a maid;
A guinea not worth a ducat,
A well without a bucket;
A nose without any snuff,
Some powder without a puff;
Some very good water just handy,
But the devil a drop of brandy;
Some excellent land, you must know,
Without any seed to sow;
I've an appetite quite complete,
But then I've got nothing to eat;
And this my friends, do you see,
Is the whole of my inventory.

(*Speaks*) Having now collected as much of American manners and American gold as tantamount to my purpose, I began to yearn for old England again. Feeling not only satisfied with my reception, but pleased with my adventures, I trusted they might not prove tedious or unseasonable in my own country. The day before I came away, Mr. Raventop, Major Grimstone, Jack Topham, Mr. Pennington, and all my friends and acquaintances dined with me to take their farewell. Even Bray and Maximilian had a tear.

MAXIMILIAN (*affectionately*). Good bye; God bless you, massa!
TOPHAM. Good bye, Mr. Mathews. I wish you very well, and a safe voyage. If you should go near Saville-row, call on dad: tell him, here I am; haven't met with any savages yet.
BRAY. That boy will be the death of me some day. You may tell his father, he may let him come home now; for he's so changed, not even his oldest creditor would know him.
PENNINGTON. I hope you will speak of us as you find us.

I assured him, there was not a person who had a heart more inclined to speak them fair than the humble individual he then addressed; and however I might have my jokes, and laugh at their peculiarities, yet I sincerely hoped, that nothing for the future, might divide England and America but the billows of the Atlantic. (*Sings*)

---

199 A pair of baskets carried on either side of a beast of burden.

FAREWELL FINALE

Air—"Molly Pops," "London out of Town," or "Each Pious Priest, Since Moses"[200]

Now ere for England starting,
I'll soothe the hour of parting,
By wishing those I leave behind,
May find one more diverting;
Indeed I will, to be sure I will.
A more sincere or true one,
I'm sure they never knew one,
He'll ne'er forget the kindness,
And the care he has from you won.

Do not condemn, I pray, sirs,
Jack Topham, Cousin Bray, sir,
Nor Doubikin, nor Uncle Ben;
Nor Raventop the gay, sirs;
Indeed I don't, to be sure I don't.
Grimstone, who is so brave, sirs,
And Pennington the grave, sirs,
The Nigger Maximilian too,
That very laughing slave, sirs.

And when in England seated,
I think how I've been treated,
Depend on't, to your prejudice;
That nought shall be repeated,
Indeed it won't, to be sure it won't.
I please my English friends best,
By giving still an harmless jest,
For England the most tolerant
Of nations, always is confest.

So now my travels ended,
And if by you befriended,
I may once more quit England's shore,
To get my budget[201] mended;
Indeed I may, to be sure I may.
But, if you say 'tis right, Sirs,
As it is given tonight, Sirs,
With grateful heart, I now depart,
For you'll crown me with delight, Sirs.

---

200 The music for the verse of "The Amours of Geoffry Muffincape and Molly Popps" is from *Amateurs and Actors*, by Mathews's friend and collaborator R.B. Peake. It is evidently based on an older tune, "Pease upon a Trencher," sung in John O'Keeffe's *The Poor Soldier* (1783) which fits the meter, as do the verse and chorus of "Each Pious Priest Since Moses." I am grateful to Judith Milhous for helping to track some of these relationships.

201 Revenue, or the sack in which money is kept.

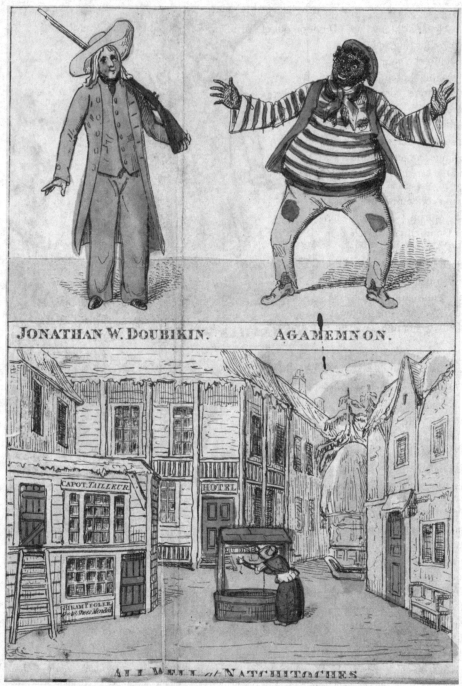

Illustration 7. Frontispiece to *The London Mathews*, Morgan & Yeager ed., 1824. Upper image depicts Jonathan W. Doubikin and Agamemnon of the monopolylogue; lower image depicts the setting for the monopolylogue. Courtesy of the Department of Special Collections, Northwestern University.

Part III

*The Second Part ends with the Finale by several of the Characters; and we very soon
are introduced to the following Characters, in a Monopolylogue, called*

"*All Well at Natchitoches*"[202]

COLONEL HIRAM PEGLAR, a Kentucky Shoemaker
AGAMEMNON, a poor runaway Negro
JONATHAN W. DOUBIKIN, a real Yankee, his Master
MONSIEUR CAPÔT, a French Emigrant Tailor
MISS MANGEL WURZEL,[203] a Dutch Heiress
MR. O'SULLIVAN, an Irish improver of his fortune

*The scene is laid at an American village in the winter season; the stage, scenery, etc. appear as if covered
with snow; at the back of the stage is an American hotel; on the right, is the house of Miss Mangel Wurzel,
the Dutch heiress; on the left, is Hiram Peglar's stall; over which is the shop of Monsieur Capôt. In the
middle of the stage is a draw-well,*[204] *down which Agamemnon, the negro, will descend to escape his
master, Jonathan W. Doubikin.*

*Enter the cobbler, Hiram Peglar, a thirsty soul who not only thirsts after liquor but also for the money
of Miss Mangel Wurzel;*[205] *he indulges at the same moment in the pleasures of the bottle, and the
anticipation of marrying the Dutch heiress. He is a major in the army, and talks of mending boots, and
soling shoes, and circumventing the French tailor, who is likewise a suitor for the hand and fortune of the
fair Dutch lady. Colonel Hiram Pegler resolves to teaze the Frenchman to death, or come off triumphant.*

*Monsieur Capôt, the French emigrant tailor, enters with a dress he intends as a present for the Dutch
lady, tied up in a bundle, and a salad he has been gathering for his breakfast. He detests his military rival,
and swears to subdue him and endeavours by every means he can devise, to tease and perplex; still he
endeavours to tantalize the cobbler.*

CAPÔT *(crying out).* Monsieur Peglare how you do?—how you do, Monsieur Peglare? *(in the same breath
he calls him)* a d—d vagabone. *(Roaring)* Monsieur Peglare, you are von rascal! I have found out your
histoire, your grand grand *père* was *von transporte.*[206]

*(Miss Mangel Wurzel, the Dutch heiress, seems to view their discord without regret, and is only waiting
for the right man to take possession of herself and fortune. Agamemnon, a runaway Negro, is a fat
unwieldy fellow who has been sold by Uncle Ben to his nephew Jonathan W. Doubikin. He enters, pursued
by his master;*[207] *after singing a Negro song called "Oyanwaw,"*[208] *but finding his master is gaining ground*

---

202 Pronounced "nak-a-dish."
203 This character is only included in the *London Mathews*'s *dramatis personae*. Mangel-wurzel is a yellow or red-fleshed
  beet, known in the early nineteenth century as "the Root of Scarcity." The roots weigh up to thirteen pounds and along
  with the leaves were used as cattle feed. *The Farmer's Cabinet*, vol. 2 (Philadelphia: John Libby, 1838), 154.
204 A deep well from which water is drawn in a bucket suspended from a rope.
205 "*Colonel Hiram Peggler*, who thinks that every thing 'does him a deal of good,' whose voice is thick with rum, and whose
  head is filled with deadly hatred for the lodger on the first floor of his stall, Monsieur *Capot.*" *Theatrical Observer; and
  Daily Bills of the Play*, April 1824, 2.
206 Transported, i.e., forcibly removed to America as a prisoner.
207 Agamemnon indicates pursuit, but the characters are not simultaneously seen.
208 No other trace of this song has been discovered. Also called "Oyangwaw."

upon him, he determines to get down the well and conceals himself until he has passed. Jonathan W. Doubikin, the real Yankee, enters with a gun, in pursuit of his runaway Negro. Jonathan tells a long story about his Uncle Ben, who sells Agamemnon. The bargain with his uncle was concluded nearly as follows).

JONATHAN. "Jonathan W., do you want a *nigger?*"—"Well, Uncle Ben, I calculate you have a Nigger to sell?"—"Yes, I have a Nigger, I guess. Will you buy the Nigger."—"Oh, yes! If he is a good Nigger, I will, I reckon; but this is a land of liberty and freedom, and as every man has a right to buy a Nigger, what do you want for your Nigger?"—"Why, as you say, Jonathan," says Uncle Ben, "this is a land of freedom and independence, and as every man has a right to sell his Niggers, I want sixty dollars and twenty-five cents. Will you give it?"—"Oh, yes!" *(Pause)* But the Nigger has proved a bad one: he is good for nothing, except eating, drinking, and fiddling. Now I've lost the Nigger, Uncle Ben's got the money; but I'll not forget to tell him of that, and the small trifle he owes me too, the next time I see him.

(During the absence of a character from the stage, the interest of the piece is kept up by the annoyance and tantalizing spirit evinced by the tailor and cobbler towards each other. The cobbler hammers away with his lapstone,[209] strap, etc., and sings in praise of General Jackson.[210] The Frenchman, in return, abuses the cobbler, and raps his implement of trade, the sleeve-board,[211] against the cobbler's stall and tells him).

CAPÔT. Monsieur Peglare, you are beneath me.[212]

(Mr. O'Sullivan, an Irish improver of his fortune is seen at the instant of being turned out of the hotel, being unable to pay for his entertainment.[213] He is heard, prior to his appearance, singing the following strain).

SAINT PATRICK WAS A GENTLEMAN[214]

Saint Patrick was a gentleman, and he came from dacent[215] people,
In Dublin town he built a church, and on it put a steeple.
His father was a Wallaghan, his mother an O'Grady,
His aunt, she was a Kinaghan, and his wife a widow Brady.
Sing tooralloo, what a glorious man our saint was. etc., etc.

---

209 A stone held in the shoemaker's lap; beating on it softens leather.

210 Reprised from part 2.

211 Part of the tailor's stock in trade: a shaped implement over which sleeves are ironed.

212 Indeed he was: Peglar's shop was below Capôt's.

213 "The unfortunate Hibernian speculator, *Mr. Cornelius O'Sullivan*, a funny mixture of mirth and rags, *want* and *wit*, who finishes the entertainment with perfect satisfaction to himself and to the audience." *Theatrical Observer; and Daily Bills of the Play*, April 1824: 2.

214 Based on a song of the same name that begins:
       OH! St. Patrick was a gentleman, and came from decent people,
       He built a church in Dublin town, and on it put a steeple;
       His father was a Gallagher, his mother was a Brady,
       His aunt was an O'Shaughessy, first cousin to O'Grady.
       Oh, success attend St. Patrick's fist, for he's the handsome Saint, O.
       Oh, he gave the snakes and toads a twist, he's a beauty without paint, O.
     From the broadsheet, Henry Bennett and W. Toleken, "Primrose Hill" and "St. Patrick was a Gentleman" (Boston: L. Deming, n.d.). A similar version was published as Bailie Nicol Jarvie, "Bailie Nicol Jarvie's Journey to Aberfoil, to Which Are Added, St. Patrick Was a Gentleman, and The Auld Sark Sleeve" (Glasgow: J. Neil, n.d.).

215 Decent (imitating Irish pronunciation).

(O'Sullivan enters. His wardrobe has the appearance of hard service).

O'SULLIVAN. My elbows, are looking *out* for fresh situations, and I've not been able to get my hair cut since I left old Ireland. I wish for a few yards of *Irish* linen, to make myself some *Holland*[216] shirts with.

(He laments leaving his own country in many laughable Irishisms. He observes Agamemnon down the well, and releases him, making him serviceable in his intended elopement with Miss Mangel Wurzel, which takes place before the audience, in a sledge drawn by a chestnut pony. On driving off, he says)[217]

O'SULLIVAN. I am now a happy man, and fully satisfied; and if my friends do but approve, I shall have no cause to regret my Trip to America.

Afterword

Thus ends a performance, which lasts for at least three hours and a half;—a performance requiring great exertion of body and mind, with most wonderful powers of imitation and amusement; all of which are certainly embodied in Mr. Mathews, in a more eminent degree than in any other actor at present before the public. The interest gradually increases from its commencement; and the liberal sentiments with which it abounds tend greatly to increase its value, and advance it in public estimation, who nightly cram the house in every part. So great has been the demand for places, that thousands nightly leave the doors of the theatre, while some of the first people in the country are contented to take their seats in the gallery. The songs cause reiterated laughter; and Mr. Mathews will no doubt, reap a plentiful harvest from his Trip to America.

---

216 Linen.

217 Mathews could not impersonate all three characters at once, but this moment was evidently a *coup de théâtre*. A live pony was incorporated, so one solution would be for Agamemnon to lead the pony in a straight cross upstage while the pony draws a sledge containing cutaways of O'Sullivan and Miss Mangel Wurzel. The cutaways could be made to wave to the audience while Mathews (attired as Agamemnon) threw his voice in imitation of O'Sullivan.

The Game of Speculation (1851)

At the midpoint of Victoria's reign, John Ruskin penned the ultimate statement on the sanctity of the home:

> It is the place of Peace; the shelter, not only from all injury, but from all terror, doubt, and division. In so far as it is not this, it is not home: so far as the anxieties of the outer life penetrate into it, and the inconsistently-minded, unknown, unloved, or hostile society of the outer world is allowed by either husband or wife to cross the threshold, it ceases to be home; it is then only a part of that outer world which you have roofed over, and lighted fire in.[1]

This represents a caution and aspiration, not necessarily a statement of achieved fact. Victorian fiction and drama are founded upon various kinds of intruders and imposers crossing the domestic threshold and compromising the sanctity, safety, and stability of family life. Almost all marriage plots, according to Rebecca Stern, reference "the potential for fraud" in the highly speculative venture of wedlock. Fraud, as it pertained to marriage and home life, "was a fundamental component of the Victorian imagination," not in the abstract but as a daily reality.[2] The more that a marriageable daughter had to offer, the more negotiable her assets and the higher the risk became in settling her fate. She extended faith in civil bonds, yet allied to this was the system of assets, credit, debt, and capital exchange. Speculators and brides discovered what was a gain or a loss only after they pledged themselves.

Marriage plots cannot stick to matters of the heart; they also become, to greater or lesser degrees, financial plots that bring the masculine world of commerce ruthlessly into the feminine realm of feelings. For the wealthier classes, marriage contracts were business ventures whereby the groom benefited from the use of his wife's dowry; since most business was conducted within family circles, the bride and groom's respective wealth functionally became part of the circulating capital of the conjoined families rather than of just the couple.[3] Misrepresentation on either side resulted in disappointment (at best) or misery and ruin (at worst). In *The Game of Speculation*, the intimacy of the Hawks' household is made contiguous with world-wide circulation of capital, all bearing down on the question of Julia's dowry: government bonds and the London Stock Exchange are a short hop to speculations in Siberian mines and Indian emeralds, and the prosperity of these enterprises determines how much Affable Hawk can commit to his daughter's marriage settlement. The young bride's fate thereby hinges on global wealth. The "affectionate economy of the nuclear family"[4] is manipulated, manoeuvred, and finagled in common with venture capital for enterprises conducted thousands of miles away from London. The games of love and speculation are equated in what Ruskin called "The Goddess of 'Getting-On.'"[5]

Editing Issues

The Game of Speculation is the second of a dozen plays by "Slingsby Lawrence" (playwriting pseudonym of George Henry Lewes) and by far the most successful. He made adaptations from the French, mainly

---

1   John Ruskin, "Of Queen's Gardens," lecture 2 in *Sesame and Lilies: Two Lectures Delivered at Manchester in 1864* (New York, 1870).

2   Rebecca Stern, *Home Economics: Domestic Fraud in Victorian England* (Columbus: Ohio State UP, 2008), 116, 6.

3   Leonore Davidoff and Catherine Hall, *Family Fortunes: Men and Women of the English Middle Class, 1780-1850* (Chicago: U of Chicago P, 1991), 198-208.

4   Stern, *Home Economics*, 35.

5   John Ruskin, *The Works of John Ruskin*, vol. 18, *The Crown of Wild Olive* (London: George Allen, 1905), 488.

for Charles James Mathews (son of the solo comedian) at the Lyceum.[6] Lewes probably learned about stagecraft in 1847 when he toured with Charles Dickens's company of amateur actors. Meanwhile, he made his living and considerable reputation writing a prodigious range of books on philosophy, science, Calderon, Lope de Vega, and Goethe, and contributing to most of the liberal periodicals of the day. Lewes claimed that he completed his work for *A Game of Speculation* in just thirteen hours, transforming Honoré de Balzac's play *Mercadet* as a vehicle for Mathews's benefit night.[7] As Jane Moody notes, "Mathews went on to make this ingenious swindler one of his most famous roles, taking the character of Affable Hawk abroad on tours to Australia and America and choosing it for his farewell performance at Paris in 1877."[8]

French dramatists were unprotected against piratical translations. In an open letter to French playwrights, Mathews admitted to being "one of the dramatic weasels of the 'Perfide Albion,' who have so long sucked the eggs of your Gallic nightingales.... I have robbed you, maimed you, assassinated you; I admit it all; and the love of virtue only enters my head at the very foot of the gallows."[9] The situation could have been a lot worse for the profits of French dramatists and the prospects for writers of original English plays. According to Mathews, adaptations from French plays were presented in only four of London's 23 theatres (in another, the St. James's Theatre, visiting Parisian companies performed in French).[10] He estimated that in 1851, when the theatrical season was three months longer than usual due to the Great Exhibition, there were 263 new pieces in Paris, but only eight (about 3 per cent), including *The Game of Speculation*, were translated for London.[11] They would steal more, but English audiences could not stomach French fare that was "too full of indecency, anachronism, immorality, and dirt."[12] In a typical piece at Paris's Théâtre du Gymnase-Dramatique, where *Mercadet* originated,

> the curtain rises. In walks a pretty woman—a woman of rank and fashion—into an elegant boudoir. 'Ah, ah!' you say, 'now we are all right!' Are you, my good friend? Wait a moment. It soon comes out that the lady is the affianced bride of one worthy man, the wife of another, in love with a third, and with a child by a fourth; notwithstanding all [of] which, she is just as much beloved by indulgent audiences, who invariably contrive to find some mitigating circumstance to justify her interesting little irregularities.

At other Parisian theatres, there are performances with

---

6   Lewes's play *A Strange History* is witless and convoluted, a domestic melodrama with an excess of plot and insufficiency of motivation. British Library Add MS 52938(AA), licensed on 24 March 1853. *The Lawyers* is more in the mode of *A Game of Speculation*'s keen dialogue, well-crafted plot, and clearly drawn characters. British Library Add MS 52940(B), licensed on 18 May 1853.

7   Balzac's *Mercadet* premiered in Paris on 23 August 1851 and opened in London on 2 October; so even if Lewes's claim is exaggerated, he must have worked very quickly.

8   Jane Moody, "The Drama of Capital: Risk, Belief, and Liability on the Victorian Stage," in *Victorian Literature and Finance*, edited by Francis O'Gorman (Oxford: Oxford UP, 2007), 94.

9   Charles [James] Mathews, *Letter from Mr. Charles Mathews to the Dramatic Authors of France: Translated from Himself by Himself, as a Specimen of "Fair Imitation or Adaptation," according to the Terms of the International Copyright Convention* (London: J. Mitchell, 1852), 2.

10 Ibid., 8.

11 The full list includes *Mlle. de la Seiglière* (as *Man of Law*, Haymarket); *Paysan d'aujourd'hui* (as *Only a Clod*) and *Mercadet* (*Game of Speculation*) both at the Lyceum; *Bataille de dames* (as *Ladies Battle* at the Olympic); *Second mari de ma femme* (as *My Wife's Second Husband)* and *Doctor Chiendent* (as *Poor Relations*) both at the Strand; *Paillasse* (as *Belphegor*) and *Un vilain monsieur* (as *An Unwarrantable Intrusion*) both at the Adelphi. See Mathews, *Letter from Mr. Charles Mathews*, 17.

12 Ibid., 18.

milliners' girls and lawyers' clerks, living together in the most unceremonious manner; Actresses talking openly and unblushingly of their numerous lovers; Ballet-girls, with accidental children by unknown fathers; Interesting young ladies, who fall asleep, they don't know why, at the end of the first act, to awake with a baby, they don't know how, at the beginning of the second. In short, nothing but mistresses, accoucheurs,[13] midwives, wet nurses, infants, cradles and feeding-bottles, in every direction.[14]

The English stage did not welcome literal translations, so the 2-3 per cent of selected French plays chosen for this form of thievery were adapted. Mathews claimed that "the taste of the two countries is so essentially different, that it requires a very skilful hand to adapt, expand, retrench, and arrange even the most available foreign dramas—especially as it is a well known circumstance that the details which produce the most effect in Paris are frequently those which produce the least in London."[15] It is curious, therefore, that *The Game of Speculation* passed Lewes's test for "harmless amusement," as "a sprightly petite comedy." True, it avoids "adultery, seduction, and all the worst passions of our nature," but it makes a comedic *tour de force* out of greed, unscrupulous business practices, and the bartering of a daughter in marriage to avoid financial ruin.[16]

Hawk cajoles and bullies, as circumstances dictate, identifying each mark's weakness and manipulating him to willingly give up whatever Hawk requires. In the midst of deflecting Hardcore from fleeing the room, Hawk references their mutual self-interest while setting him up to relinquish shares in the Indian Emerald Company. He appeals to Hardcore's vanity by asking how "an adroit, intelligent man, thoroughly up to all the knowledge of the humbug of speculation" can "dabble in such schemes." As Hawk reels Prospectus into his plan to adorn Julia, Prospectus wonders, in an aside, "Is he humbugging me?" Later, Prospectus reports,

> PROSPECTUS. There is a fixed determination to rid 'Change of all the speculative humbugs who now infest it.
> HAWK. The fools! Do they want to convert 'Change into a desert! And yet to be driven from the scene of my operations, the field of my glory!—ruin, shame, want!

Hawk, proclaimed a humbug, is also called by Hardcore "a giant in business" and by Grossmark "the prince of speculators, a man capable of gaining a million, the moment he has a thousand!" The successful man of business was synonymous with a humbug, but this was not pejorative. When P.T. Barnum declared to his audience at the St. James's Theatre in 1859, "you have the honour of beholding before you the most notorious humbug on the face of the habitable globe," the audience "uttered a wild shout of applause, conscious that at last the right man was in the right place."[17] Scoundrels-turned-saints confessing their deeds at revival meetings were not cheered louder. The English public embraced Barnum's bunk, and no wonder: he was one of a long line of hustlers very like Affable Hawk. England, claimed Barnum, was a haven for humbugs. "Here Tom Thumb was kissed by 500,000 ladies," the speculators Leopold Redpath and Sir John Dean Paul defrauded investors on a spectacular scale, "lacqueys are K.C.B.s,[18] and Princes, who never saw a shot fired in anger, have the batons, and better still, the pay of Field Marshals." By this

---

13   Male midwives.
14   Ibid., 20-21.
15   Ibid., 31.
16   Ibid., 19-20.
17   *Weekly Freeman's Journal* (Dublin), 8 January 1859: 5.
18   Knights.

standard, a thoroughly French play—noted by reviewers as uncharacteristic for the English stage—became a solid favourite.

Despite Lewes's haste in preparing the English version, he knew precisely what would play well, for the text presented for licensing is remarkably like what was later published in an acting version by Lacy's.[19] The adaptor's job was not only to rewrite any character or situation to better conform to British sensibility but also to alter francophone literary allusions and turns of phrase to better suit English ears and tighten up the dialogue where it ambled.[20] A scene between Hawk and Prospectus was added at the end of act 1, testing their friendship and showing Prospectus willing to dig deeper into his pockets for the sake of his goddaughter's prospects. The other major change is in Hawk's final winding-down. The licensed version declares Hawk's intention to resettle in the country and study agriculture:[21] he renounces his former friends, gives Sir Harry Lester £1,000 on a whim, extols the pleasure of being a creditor, and exits to greet the long-lost Sparrow. He implicitly allies himself with Adam Smith's view of sensibility: he shall take pleasure in seeing his child's happiness. In the published version—developed during the run—rather than reference his family, he identifies emphatically with his fellow men of business, now as a creditor. He reminds his friends of their role in equipping him with the weapons of their undoing and urges them henceforth to exercise patience and perseverance while waiting for fortune to smile on them. Though wild speculations are a thing of his past, his adherence to Smith's moral sentiment is based on his self-command coupled with instructions to others. In the end, Hawk becomes a creditor. Be courageous, play your cards right, reap your reward, then eschew the game of speculation. How sincere is this? Is satire, which had drawn the moral on his earlier activity, forgone in this version of Hawk's final proclamation?

The following text follows the published edition, including notations for entrances, exits, and movement around the stage. In a play so dependent upon servants' guiding visitors in and out of rooms at propitious moments, it is useful to picture everyone's whereabouts. Just as importantly, the servants sometimes remain onstage, as do Julia and her mother, as silent witnesses to Hawk's shenanigans. "L.D.," for example, designates left door, and "1 E.L." means first entrance left, correlating to a box set framed as interior space with walls—introduced in Mathews's joint management with his wife Eliza Vestris at the Olympic Theatre in the 1830s—as a realistically furnished interior rather than the more traditional flats and drops. As in farce, the doors "served as concrete representations of suspense through which a character might burst at any moment," propelling the plot in a new direction.[22]

Interpretive Issues

Ever since the Renaissance, English drama has been rife with "stories about prodigals, debtors, and long-distance merchants whose ventures failed." Jean Howard describes how in Ben Jonson's *Every Man out of*

---

19   Slingsby Lawrence, *Game of Speculation* (London: Lacy, [1851]).

20   There are several source texts in French. The earliest, unproduced version, containing five acts, was printed in Paris in September 1848 in only four copies. Of these, Balzac kept one for himself, sent one to his assistant Laurent-Jan, another to the actor Joseph-Philippe Simone (known as Lockroy), and the last one to the printer Étienne Poitevin. One of these copies remains at the Bibliothèque Lovenjoul, another at the Bibliothèque de l'Institut. Between 28 August (five days after the premiere at the Théâtre de Gymnase) and 13 September 1851, the play was published as *Mercadet*, in several parts, in *Le Pays*. Two years later it was published as *Le Faiseur* (Paris: Cadot, 1853). The play was adapted in three acts by M. Dennery before presentation on stage; Lewes clearly worked from this version. For the textual and production history, see *Œvres complètes de M. de Balzac*, vol. 23, *Théâtre* (Paris: Les Bibliophiles de l'Originale, 1970). An English translation of the three-act version is included in *The Plays of Honoré de Balzac*, 2 vols. in 1 (New York: Howard Fertig, 1976).

21   A first-night review mentions the agricultural resolve. *Morning Chronicle*, 3 October 1851: 5.

22   Jeffrey H. Huberman, *Late Victorian Farce* (Ann Arbor, MI: UMI Research Press, 1986), 15.

His Humour (1598) "Carlo outlines a certain logic of credit. The more you owe, the more the world will take you for a great man of immense wealth and importance; consequently, the less likely are honest and modest tradesmen to want to offend you by demanding payment in an unmannerly way. Only bankrupts ... are so desperate that they will cause a commotion in seeking repayment of loans."[23] Charles James Mathews played debtors in *Used Up* (1844) and *Bachelor of Arts* (1853); *The Game of Speculation* (1851) is in this mould.[24] Mathews was one to know how the system worked, for he became insolvent three times. When managing the Olympic Theatre, he was committed to Fleet Prison for debt. He and Vestris went into management at Covent Garden in 1839, but a string of productions failed to yield profits. In 1841, they scored a great success with Bellini's opera *Norma*, which brought the landlord down on them for arrears of rent. By that time, Mathews had established a chain of debt, borrowing from one creditor to pay the next, discounting his bills of exchange until the interest rate reached 60 per cent. He was committed to Queen's Bench Prison. Carrying forward his personal liabilities, Mathews took up lesseeship of the Lyceum, continuing to struggle with debt until the daunting sum of £28,000 had accumulated in 1855.[25] He was made bankrupt by a single impatient creditor, and later imprisoned at Lancaster Castle.[26]

Hawk is the London-based partner of Sparrow, but when Sparrow absconds and remains abroad unexpectedly long, Hawk's cash flow reaches a crisis point. Household as well as business creditors pester him incessantly. He, like Sir Harry Lester, has issued bills of exchange which obligate him to pay, upon expiration, a fixed sum. The problem with such negotiable instruments is that they can be transferred as collateral from one payee to another so the drawer is never quite sure who will present the bill or when. With tradespeople credit is simple: households buy goods, the traders present themselves at the door demanding payment, and commerce is face-to-face. In Hawk's world of high finance, however, third and fourth parties become involved, eliminating the personal nature of lending and borrowing. The play shows the two systems in tandem. Hawk has acquired Mr. Bradshaw's bills of exchange, not realizing that this is the same person as Sir Harry whose assets he intends to work in a new speculation in exchange for Julia's hand. But instead of acquiring a wealthy son-in-law with land, Hawk holds the bills for Lester's worthless mortgages. The marriage scheme now a bust, Hawk turns to the stock exchange, generating an artificial panic over the value of the Indian Emerald Company so he can buy up stock cheaply (with borrowed money) on options, let the panic dissipate, then sell shares for their true value. He just needs enough time so that he can stall his creditors until hoaxing them again by pretending Sparrow has returned.

The British financial system was not exactly broken, yet Hawk demonstrates how it could be manipulated to the detriment of investors and trade in general. He skirts the boundaries of ethics, taking everything to extremes, yet operates within common practices. Therein lay the dilemmas: what is moral within capitalism, should the government regulate the market, and what practices warrant suppression? Mrs. Hawk's insistence that people be properly paid is a primitive belief in exchange value; she is moral, of course, but also financially naïve compared to her husband. He is of his time, believing that men (and it is always men) who owe nothing receive no regard, and that regard, fanned by rumour, is what propels

---

23   Jean E. Howard, *Theater of a City: The Places of London Comedy, 1598-1642* (Philadelphia: U of Pennsylvania P, 2007), 82, 84.

24   Dion Boucicault and Charles James Mathews, *Used Up*, produced at the Haymarket 6 February 1844; and P. Hardwick, *Bachelor of Arts*, produced at the Lyceum Theatre 23 November 1853.

25   This is approximately equivalent to £1,890,000 in 2009 sterling, calculated relative to the retail-price index. This converts to around US $2,790,000 in 2009 dollars (the range of values is from $1,850,000 to $3,800,000). See www.measuringworth.com/index.html (accessed 9 July 2010).

26   Tracy C. Davis, *The Economics of the British Stage, 1800-1914* (Cambridge: Cambridge UP, 2001), 187-88; and V. Markham Lester, *Victorian Insolvency: Bankruptcy, Imprisonment for Debt, and Company Winding-Up in Nineteenth-Century England* (Oxford: Clarendon, 1995).

the commercial world. For one person to make money, another must lose it; and as Hawk's schemes spiral, the basis of wealth becomes more and more abstract. When Parliament created new ways to enable investment by passing the Companies Acts in the 1860s, legions of small holders invested in the stock exchange for the first time; they had the advantage of limited liability (putting in exactly what they agreed to invest, and being liable for no more calls regardless of the company's success or failure). This would not curb the Hawks of the world, but it would give their financiers alternatives.

One of Lewes's earliest jobs was writing for John Stuart Mill's quarterly, the *Westminster Review*. Mill argued that the family and the marketplace were subject to the same market forces. Lewes shows how domesticity might "civilize" capitalism—through alliance with Hawk's clerk, the "man of sense" Frederick Noble—but never serve as a refuge from it. In the ethical union represented by Julia and Noble, loyalty and compassion hold sway over competition.[27] Noble, allied with the female characters' more naïve belief in payment for services rendered, is the standard-bearer for ethical practice. Yet, without the unexpected windfalls of Noble's inheritance and Sparrow's return from India, Hawk would face ruin or (as he says) "the wet sheets of the Thames."

Genre Issues

Balzac had a penchant for showing a prosperous and likeable character then "peeling off his moral skin, layer by layer, till he has been successfully exhibited as liar, coward, cheat, and humbug, and finally kicking him down stairs for a fool," revelling in this exposure of "respectability" with *gusto*.[28] While this was not customary in Britain, there were French precedents for this "most remarkable figure of modern comedy. In shiftiness, inexhaustible fertility of resource, and other similar qualities, Mercadet approaches Scapin and Figaro, of Moliere's *Les Fourberies de Scapin* (1671) and Beaumarchais's *Le Mariage de Figaro* (1784).[29] The satire is bitter in *The Game of Speculation*, and at first "the stunning blows ... seemed to astonish the audience," but they soon caught up with its vigour and wit.[30] The *Era* found *The Game of Speculation* particularly well suited to the Lyceum's clientele:

> It is light, amusing without being farcical, abounds with lively dialogue, and interesting but natural
> situations, is descriptive of modern and social life, and represents the prominent edges, as it were, of
> that portion of polished society which is more remarkable for tact than principle, more worldly than
> moral, looking, indeed, more to an end than the means of attaining it, so that they be not outrageously
> or vulgarly scandalous.

This is not the modern and social life that most English drama (or English behaviour) is modelled upon: it is essentially French, yet onstage delights an English audience.[31] Lewes's satire presents an instructive contrast to Netta Syrett's play *The Finding of Nancy*, produced half a century later (see below, p. 650-84). Whereas *The Game of Speculation* is a thoroughly moral drama *vis-à-vis* sexual relations (the money be damned), *The Finding of Nancy* has an immoral plot *vis-à-vis* sexual relations (though money is handled appropriately). By the end of the century, the depiction of morality versus wealth does not come down to national taste or custom but to gender politics and business ethics.

Lewes achieves his effect without injecting anyone or anything evil into the play. Even Sparrow, who "decamped with all our funds," is not condemned. It is just as likely that he has been prevented in

---

27   Compare Edward Bulwer Lytton's play *Money* (1840).

28   *Morning Chronicle*, 3 October 1851: 5.

29   This description references the role performed first by Geoffroy in 1851 and taken over by Edmond Got at the Comédie-Française in 1868. *Athenaeum*, 6 June 1874: 774.

30   *Observer*, 5 October 1851: 3.

31   *Era*, 5 October 1851.

returning from the Indies by storm or shipwreck as having been delayed because he encountered an additional speculative opportunity. The former scenario—typical in eighteenth- but not in nineteenth-century plots—could still ruin any speculator whose trade depended upon sea travel. The latter scenario put foreign venturers at physical risk but left London investors on tenterhooks, wondering whether they profited or failed. There is no villain, such as George Hudson the "Railway King" who made and then lost his fortune and that of countless investors in a matter of years.[32] Nor are there equivalents of the Cheeryble brothers to set off Ralph Nickleby in one of Charles Dickens's novels, or Daniel Doyce and Arthur Clennam to counter the tactics of Merdle the banker in another.[33] Affable is Hawk's first name (it was Auguste Mercadet in the original, so Lewes's point is sharpened), and his relentless yet genial juggling of fortunes—always letting others' greed drive their actions—is not a morality tale about the sin of avarice or the practice of gambling set opposite the virtues of thrift and self-denial.[34] Insofar as compulsive speculation was associated with mental illness in the Victorian period, "the desperate speculator would stop at nothing to feed his habit: all moral considerations, all rational calculation, were suspended."[35] But Lewes's speculator is *affable*, and his colluder in getting up the shares panic is Prospectus, Julia's godfather, an extension of the family. Not even the unpaid servants breach his façade. This is a comedy not because it is humorous (though it is) or frivolous (which it is not) but because the gambits result in marriage. Noble has some agency in this quest, Mrs. Hawk has a little, but Julia has none. In the time-honoured custom of comedy, the fate of a daughter lies in the hands of men. Notably, however, this maiden does not resort to the intrigues of cross-dressing, sending servants with messages, hiding lovers in cabinets, or other subterfuges of young women who oppose their fathers' choice. She has her preference, but the decision is Hawk's. Marriage has both sacramental and contractual aspects; comedy emphasizes the latter. Whereas drama is driven by the consequences of marriage, comedy depicts the business of arriving at a marital bargain within an economy of exchange. The plot twists suggest that wedlock is the stage equivalent of the survival of the fittest, with Hawk as the nominal arbiter after nature has buffeted the competitors, leaving only Noble in view to claim his prize.

Performative Issues

According to reviews of the premiere, the creditors gave superbly contrasted character studies—Earthworm "was particularly effective as the sycophantic lucre lover"—and the whole cast was the elite of the Lyceum's stock company, but it was Mathews who carried the play. His speech rang with perfect and rapid diction (more in the French than English style),[36] "his composure was the essence of self-confident audacity, and his energy would have inspired a statue. His make-up was admirable, the regulation baldness of middle-aged respectability being most artistically managed."[37] Percy Fitzgerald recalled how invariably Mathews's "face reigned *finesse*.... there was an airy nervousness at the corners of the lip, where you saw the satire fluttering before it took wing." In other words, an attentive spectator could spot each scheme as it was conceived and take predictable delight as it fledged. Yet it was not just Mathews's face that carried the story. He exuded "refined enjoyment and good-humour" even from the rear, for at calculated

---

32   Robert Beaumont, *The Railway King: A Biography of George Hudson, Railway Pioneer and Fraudster* (London: Review, 2002).

33   See *Nicholas Nickleby* (serialized 1838-39) and *Little Dorrit* (1855-57).

34   James Taylor, *Creating Capitalism: Joint-Stock Enterprise in British Politics and Culture, 1800-1870* (Woodbridge: Royal Historical Society, 2006), 56.

35   Ibid., 71.

36   *Era*, 5 October 1851.

37   "Lyceum Theatre," *Morning Chronicle*, 3 October 1851: 5.

moments he turned away from the audience and expressively communicated with the back of his head, neck, and torso.[38]

Lewes consistently uses metaphors from the theatre to demonstrate how speculation is a matter of manipulation. Hawk borrows in order to stage a pretence of prosperity when entertaining Sir Harry Lester. Anyone in the audience might be implicated in the same metatheatrical conceit, subject to Hawk's garrulous influence. Indeed, the ironic image of the play depicts Hawk not just describing but demonstrating to his wife how he achieves this:

> HAWK. The speculators who enriched themselves quietly under the shadow of my former successes, are now the toys and puppets with which I divert my leisure and dispel my melancholy. When I am dull I pull their strings *(imitates the action of pulling the strings of a puppet)*, and they dance till I am merry again. The game of speculation, which I formerly played for love, I now play for money, that's all.

This business of jerking his dupes' strings was "a conspicuous feature" of Mathews's performance and he only ceases to be the puppetmaster when he ceases to speculate.[39]

At every plot twist, the creditors willingly *allow* themselves to be duped: or, rather, they dupe themselves into believing Hawk's schemes will profit them. Yet if business is (like theatre) an elegant deceit, what genre does it deploy? Sir Harry Lester deflects Hawk from going too far in delineating the part he is to play as the false Sparrow: he will neither commit robbery at gunpoint nor pretend to raise someone from the dead. "My dear Hawk," Lester says, "melodramatic situations in real life are no longer taken in good part." Mrs. Hawk wants to squelch any plotting and persuades Lester to quit his role. Hawk, thoroughly immersed in the plot-within-the-play, believes that Sparrow's arrival—which could be undermined by his wife's devotion to veracity—is instead excellently played by her. "How well she does it," he admits in an aside even though she pretends nothing. But the ultimate act of reversal—the complete paying off of all his creditors—is so fantastical that it throws Hawk out of the more explicable realms of comedy and into extravaganza or pantomime:

> PROSPECTUS *(re-enter down C.)*. There they are all, and all paid! It was quite true!
> HAWK. All paid?—yes, paid—all paid! Damn it, they're all paid! I see fire!—the room spins round!— this is fairyland—enchantment—devilry!

It is as if Fairy Moneybags waved her wand and converted everything topsy-turvy in a transformation scene. Yet in fact the scenery stays as is, and the play continues to operate within the stage logic of comedy. Hawk's change in fortune is prosaic, not supernatural: so prosaic that though Sparrow's arrival is announced, he is never seen by either the audience or Hawk, and instead the setting remains the drawing-room, the locus of middle-class life (and comedies). Here, the *lack* of a scenic transformation is what makes the moment funny, not just coincidentally convenient. Hawk is no longer a puppet master. Cash has arrived—though the audience does not see its bearer—and thus wealth is the *deus ex machina* rather than Sparrow himself. The unravelling is complete, and comedy's conventional pairing-up can commence: first, the creditors and their wealth, then Julia and Noble.

---

38   Percy Fitzgerald, *The World behind the Scenes* (1881; reprinted by New York: Benjamin Blom, 1972), 117-18.
39   John Coleman, *Players and Playwrights I Have Known* (London: Chatto and Windus, 1881), 228.

The Game of Speculation[40]

ADAPTED BY GEORGE HENRY LEWES[41]

First performed at the Lyceum Theatre, London, 2 October 1851.

Affable Hawk	Charles James Mathews
Sir Harry Lester	Robert Roxby
Earthworm	Frank Matthews
Prospectus, Julia's godfather	Basil Baker
Grossmark	Mr. Suter
Hardcore	H. Horncastle
Frederick Noble, Hawk's clerk	H. Butler
Thomas, a servant	Mr. Oxberry
Mr. Graves	Mr. Clifford
Mrs. Caroline Hawk	Mrs. Horn
Miss Julia Hawk, her daughter	Miss M. Oliver
Mrs. Dimity, chambermaid	Miss Grove
Mrs. Mason, cook	Miss Ellis
Other Creditors	

Costume Plot

Affable Hawk (First Act—blue body coat, waistcoat, dark grey trousers. Second Act—blue body coat, white waistcoat, black trousers. Third Act—blue surtout,[42] light waistcoat, grey trousers)

Sir Harry Lester (fashionable morning dress)[43]

Earthworm (black old-fashioned coat, black waistcoat, black knee-breeches, grey stockings, black short gaiters,[44] low-crowned hat)

Prospectus (blue body coat, buff waistcoat, black trousers, gaiters)

Grossmark (dark surtout, light waistcoat, grey trousers and umbrella)

Hardcore (blue surtout, red velvet waistcoat, blue trousers, white bat[45])

Frederick Noble (suit of black)

Thomas (First Act—footman's jean[46] coat, white waistcoat, black trousers. Second Act—blue body coat, white waistcoat, black trousers)

Mr. Graves (fashionable morning dress)

Mrs. Caroline Hawk (First and Third Acts—fashionable chocolate silk dress. Second Act—handsome flounced muslin)

---

40   Adapted from Honoré de Balzac's three-act comedy *Mercadet, ou le faiseur*, produced posthumously at the Théâtre du Gymnase-Dramatique, Paris, 23 August 1851. British Library Add MS 43037 fols. 324-61. Published as Slingsby Lawrence, *Game of Speculation* (London: Lacy, [1851]).

41   Under the pseudonym Slingsby Lawrence.

42   Overcoat.

43   Formal suit with striped trousers and cut-away coat.

44   Coverings for the ankles.

45   Stick.

46   Twill.

Miss Julia Hawk (First and Third Acts—fashionable lavender silk dress. Second Act—white lace dress)
Mrs. Dimity (muslin[47] dress, apron)
Mrs. Mason (Cotton dress, Holland linen[48] apron, cap)

Act I

*Drawing Room in Mr. Affable Hawk's House, handsomely furnished;[49] table and
two chairs, R.; table and two chairs, L.; doors, R. and L.; window, L.; sofa, R..,
at back.—Mrs. Dimity, Thomas, and Mrs. Mason discovered.*

THOMAS (*R.C., seated*). Yes, my dears, our respectable and respected master, Mr. Affable Hawk, may swim well, but he'll be drowned this time.

MRS. MASON. Lor! Do you really think so?

THOMAS. Burnt his fingers, I can tell you; and although there is always pretty pickings in a house where the master is in debt, still, you know he owes us all a year's wages, and it is time now to be turned out of doors.

MRS. MASON. It ain't so easy with some Missuses! I have already been impertinent two or three times to our'n, but she always pretends not to hear.

DIMITY. As for me, I have been lady's maid in a great many families, but never in such as this. One has to become quite an actress! A creditor arrives—you have to throw astonishment into your eyebrows, and exclaim—"What! you don't know, sir?" "Know what?" "Mr. Affable Hawk is gone to Manchester, about some new speculation." "Oh! gone to Manchester, is he?" "Yes, sir, a splendid affair, I hear—discovery of a copper mine." "So much the better! When does he come back?" "Really, sir, we don't know."

ALL. Ha, ha, ha!

DIMITY. He's settled! But what a countenance it requires to lie with that superiority! And my wages are none the higher for it.

THOMAS. Besides, these are all such coarse-minded creatures; they bully as if they owed the money.

DIMITY. It must end. I shall formally demand my wages, because the tradesmen absolutely refuse to serve us any longer.

BOTH. Yes, let's have our wages and go.

DIMITY. A pretty family to pretend to gentility, indeed!

MRS. MASON. Genteel people are those who spend liberally in eating and drinking!

THOMAS. And become attached to their servants.

DIMITY. To whom they give little annuities—that's what a gentleman ought to do.

MRS. MASON. Well, for my part, I most pity Miss Julia, and her lover, Mr. Noble.

THOMAS. Her lover! Do you suppose a man like Mr. Affable would give his daughter to his clerk, with one hundred and fifty pounds a-year salary? No! He has better than that in his eye.

MRS. MASON. Oh, do tell us!

THOMAS. You remember the two gentlemen who came yesterday in their cab? The groom tells me that they are going to marry Miss Julia.

---

47   Light cotton, plainly woven.
48   Plain-woven.
49   In the licensing copy, all the action is set in "*Hawk's Sanctum; papers tied with red tape; tin boxes etc. All the appearance of the room of a Man of business.*" This emphasizes Hawk's realm rather than the domestic and feminized portion of the house. The published version moves to Hawk's "salon" in act 2 and back to the drawing-room in act 3.

MRS. MASON. Lor! What, are those gentlemen in white kid gloves and flowered waistcoats going to marry Miss Julia?

THOMAS. Not both, you simple creature!—we don't allow bigamy in England. It's only in France that women have two husbands.

DIMITY. And do you believe that a rich man will be brought to marry Mr. Hawk's daughter, now his ruin must be suspected?

THOMAS. If you knew Mr. Affable Hawk half as well as I do, you would believe anything of him. I have seen him with creditors around him like hornets, till I have said to myself—"Well, at last he's done for!" Not a bit of it! He has received reams of writs, tons of protested[50] bills—Basinghall Street[51] has gasped for him—when, hey presto! he bounds up again, triumphant, rich! Then his invention—was there ever such invention! every day a new speculation; every day a new committee formed! Wood pavement—quilted pavement—salt-marshes—railways—waterworks—and yet always in debt!

MRS. MASON. But he don't seem to care for creditors.

THOMAS. He! To see him cajole and caress them—how he wheedles them, and diddles them, and sends them away delighted with his affable manner and magnificent promises. I have often seen them come with arrest written in every line of their faces; but they have gone away smiling, shaking him by the hand, the best friends in the world. We hear of men who tame lions and tigers! but he does more; he pacifies a creditor! I call him the Van Amburgh[52] of the City.

MRS. MASON. There is one I especially hate—Mr. Grossmark.

THOMAS. A shark that feeds on post obits.[53] Then there is old Earthworm.

MRS. MASON. Ha, ha! a begging creditor—I always feel that I ought to offer him some broken victuals.[54]

DIMITY. Then there's Hardcore—

MRS. MASON. And no end of 'em! But here's missus!

MRS. HAWK (enter L.D.). Thomas, have you bought the things I ordered? (Sits, R.).

THOMAS. Bought them, ma'am, but not got them. The tradespeople refuse to send things home.

MRS. MASON. And the butcher, ma'am—and the baker, ma'am—and them all, refuse to send the things.

MRS. HAWK. I understand. It is useless to conceal from you my anxiety about my husband's affairs. We shall need your discretion; and we may count upon you, may we not?

ALL. To the last, ma'am!

DIMITY. We were saying, but now, that we had a most excellent master and mistress.

THOMAS. And that we would go through fire and water to serve them.

(Hawk appears at back, C.).

MRS. HAWK. Thanks!—you are good creatures!

(Hawk shrugs his shoulders contemptuously).

Mr. Hawk only wants to gain time; he has so many plans—a rich husband is in view for our daughter—

---

50   Unpaid.

51   A street near the Guildhall, the seat of civic power for The City of London.

52   Isaac A. Van Amburgh was an American animal trainer who toured Britain and Europe c. 1838-45. He emphasized his dominion over large cats, putting his head in a tiger's mouth and his blood-smeared arm in a lion's mouth. He was painted twice by Sir Edwin Henry Landseer: Isaac Van Amburgh with His Animals (Royal Collection, Windsor, 1839) and Portrait of Mr. Van Amburgh as He Appeared with His Animals at the London Theatre (Yale Center for British Art, 1847).

53   A bond secured by money the borrower expects to inherit.

54   Meat scraps.

HAWK (*advancing and interrupting*). My dear Caroline!

(*The servants draw aside*).

HAWK (*speaking to her aside*). That is the way you speak to your servants!—tomorrow they will be impertinent. (*Aloud*) Thomas, go at once to Mr. Prospectus, and tell him to come here immediately, about an affair which admits of no delay. Be mysterious, for he must come—I want him. You, Mrs. Mason, go back to the tradespeople, and tell them, indignantly, to send the things ordered by your mistress. They shall be paid—yes, cash down—go! And stop!—if those—gentlemen call again, admit them.

THOMAS. Those—gentlemen? What! the creditors?

HAWK. Precisely.

MRS. HAWK. Are you serious?

HAWK (*throwing himself into a chair*). I'm sick of solitude, and I want to see them. (*To Thomas and Dimity*) Go!

(*Exeunt Thomas and Dimity, C.D.*).

—Mrs. Mason, has your mistress ordered dinner?

MRS. MASON. No, sir; besides, the tradespeople—

HAWK. Today you must surpass yourself—you must make Soyer[55] pale with envy. We have four persons to dinner, besides ourselves—Prospectus and his wife, Sir Harry Lester, and Mr. Graves. Let me see—there must be all the delicacies of the season.

MRS. MASON. But the tradespeople won't—

HAWK. Don't talk to me of my tradespeople, the day my daughter is to see her future husband!

MRS. MASON. But I must, for they won't send in the orders.

HAWK. Nonsense! What are tradesmen for, but to serve their customers?

MRS. MASON. But they are creditors.

HAWK. Well, what are creditors, but to give credit to their customers? We're their customers! If they are obstinate, go to others—their rivals—promise them my custom, and they will give you Christmas-boxes.[56]

MRS. MASON. And how am I to pay those whom I leave?

HAWK. That's their business and mine—leave that to me!

MRS. MASON. They mustn't look to me for money, that's all!

HAWK (*aside*). Holloa! Mrs. Mason has saved money! (*Aloud*) Mrs. Mason, in these days credit is everything—credit is the wealth of commerce, the foundation of the State! If my tradesmen refuse credit, it is a proof they have no respect for the British Constitution, our safeguard and our pride! They are radicals and Chartists of the worst description![57] The man who would refuse credit would erect a

---

55   Alexis Benoît Soyer, at the time a fashionable cook.

56   Collections of coins made by apprentices at Christmas time; when full of gratuities, the clay boxes were smashed open and the proceeds shared.

57   Radicalism arose in the 1770s, bringing artisans into alliance with middle-class reformers (especially Unitarians). In the aftermath of the French Revolution, radicals called for parliamentary reform, relief from economic distress, and lower taxation. They sought extension of the 1832 Reform Act and free trade through the repeal of the Corn Laws in 1846. Chartists constituted the first mass working-class movement in the 1830s and 1840s. They agitated for political reform to eliminate social and economic injustices in a six-point charter that called for annual parliaments, universal male suffrage, abolition of property qualification for the position of Member of Parliament, secret ballot, equal electoral districts, and salaries for Members of Parliament.

barricade! Don't distract me any more about people who are in open revolt against the vital principles of Government! Mrs. Mason, you look after the dinner—I depend upon you for it; *(rising)* and if Mrs. Hawk, in settling with you on the day of Julia's marriage, finds herself a trifle in debt to you, I'll take care you are no loser.

MRS. MASON. Oh, sir! *(Aside)* I'll buy the things myself, if the tradesmen refuse.

HAWK. And I will put you in the way of getting your ten shillings interest for every five pounds, twice a-year—that's a little better than the Savings' Bank, eh?[58]

MRS. MASON. I should think so—the interest there is next to nothing!

HAWK *(aside to his wife)*. I told you that she had money. *(Aloud)* Then I may rely upon you, Mrs. Mason?

MRS. MASON. That you may, sir!—come what will, the dinner shall do you credit *(exit C.L.)*.

HAWK. That woman has fifty pounds or more in the Savings' Bank—all pilfered from us: it is but right she should pay for dinner on the occasion.

MRS. HAWK. How can you descend so low!

HAWK. My dear Caroline, do not attempt to judge my means of action. In this world, nothing is trifling—nothing too insignificant. Just now, you were trying to win over the servants by gentleness. Error, my dear—complete error! You should be firm as the Iron Duke, and as brief.[59]

MRS. HAWK. And why issue commands, when you cannot pay?

HAWK. My love, the principle of social existence is extremely simple. Pay with gold, when you can—when you can't, pay with brass.

MRS. HAWK. But we often obtain, through affection, services which are refused to—

HAWK. Through affection! How little you know the present age. Now, nothing but selfishness exists. Everyone places his future in the three-per-cents.[60] There lies our paradise. The wife knows her husband is insured; the son insures his father's life. All our morals lie in dividends! As to servants, we change them every day. Attachment, indeed! pay them their wages regularly, and they leave you without regret; but owe them money, and you keep them devoted to the last.

MRS. HAWK. Oh! You, so honourable, to utter such things?

HAWK. I utter what we all feel, but what few have the boldness to avow. Here lies modern honour *(holding up half a crown)*.[61] Chivalry has shriveled into that!—Shall I tell you why plays succeed which have scoundrels for their heroes? It is because the spectator is flattered, and says to himself as he goes away, "Come, come, hang it, after all I'm not such a scamp as he is."

MRS. HAWK. No, no!

HAWK. My dear Caroline, I see my levity wounds you, but consider our positions. Are we not suffering for the crime of our partner, Sparrow, who decamped with all our funds? You know the honour and integrity with which I raised our house to wealth—a house untainted in reputation till that fatal act reduced us all to beggary. The fault was not mine, but what was to be done! A coward would have destroyed himself. Not I. Die! Never. I had not lived so long in the world, my dear, without discovering its weakness. I had not mixed so much with moneyed men, without reading their inmost souls—and so, like a man of that world in which I had studied, I gaily accepted the new position forced upon me. Necessity, mark me, not choice, compelled me to it—and I thenceforth determined to give the world the benefit of the lessons it had taught me, and turn my very ruin into an amusement.

---

58   Savings banks enabled even the lowliest to set aside pennies for a rainy day.

59   The first Duke of Wellington, who prevailed over Napoleon in the Battle of Waterloo. Prime Minister from 1828 to 1830, he held the Tory line, resolutely opposed to expansion of the franchise and parliamentary reform. He was, as a result, extremely unpopular, and the people rioted. In 1830, the Whigs were returned to power for the first time since the 1770s.

60   Government securities.

61   A coin worth two shillings and sixpence.

MRS. HAWK. Your elasticity of mind was commendable, no doubt, but is the line you have taken justifiable?

HAWK. Perfectly. The speculators who enriched themselves quietly under the shadow of my former successes, are now the toys and puppets with which I divert my leisure and dispel my melancholy. When I am dull I pull their strings *(imitates the action of pulling the strings of a puppet)*, and they dance till I am merry again. The game of speculation, which I formerly played for love, I now play for money, that's all.

MRS. HAWK. Aye, but your former worshippers are now turned into ravenous creditors.

"MR. AFFABLE HAWK," MR. CHARLES MATHEWS.   "MRS. HAWK," MRS. HORN.

SCENE I., ACT I., FROM "THE GAME OF SPECULATION," AT THE LYCEUM THEATRE.

Illustration 8. Charles James Mathews as Affable Hawk, pulling his creditors' strings, and Mrs. Caroline Hawk, in *A Game of Speculation*, 1851. Courtesy of the Harvard Theatre Collection, Houghton Library.

HAWK. Creditors? Not at all. They are my bankers. If I did not use their money they would be miserable. Besides, after all, where is the dishonour of debt? Is it not national? Every man dies in debt to his father, to whom he owes life, which he can't repay. What is life, Caroline, but one enormous loan? A perpetual borrow, borrow, borrow. Moreover, there is some skill required to get handsomely in debt—it is not every one that can get trusted. Am I not greatly superior to my creditors? I have their money—they must wait for mine. I ask nothing from them—they pester my life out with importunities. Think, my dear—a man who owes nothing, what a solitary, miserably incomplete being! Nobody cares for him; nobody asks about him; nobody knocks at his door. Whilst I am an object of intense and incessant interest to all my creditors. They think of me in going to bed; they think of me in rising every day— their lips grow familiar with my name; their hands love my knocker.

MRS. HAWK. Yes; but remember that we owe their money to their confidence in your probity.[62]

HAWK. Well, isn't that an agreeable reflection? But the truth is, that we owe it more to their avidity[63] than to their confidence. The speculator is no worse than the shareholders. They are both moved by the desire of becoming rich, without trouble, and without much care for the means. All my creditors have been enriched by me, and they still hope to gain something more. Were it not for my knowledge of their interests, I should be lost; as it is, you will see how I make each of them show their cards, and play their little game before me. I have given orders to have them admitted.

MRS. HAWK. For what?—to pay them?

HAWK. Pay them, my love! No; to make them lend me more money. Don't be astonished. The marriage of our daughter is our last hope, our last resource. I must have money for the jewels, for the trousseau, the wedding breakfast, and the many exigencies of the hour. Sir Harry Lester, who is to marry Julia, must have no suspicion of our being in difficulties; so that ready money is indispensable just now. By the by, what amount of jewels will she require, with a fortune of twenty thousand pounds?

MRS. HAWK. But you can't give her twenty thousand pounds.

HAWK. The greater reason for giving her the jewels. How much? Eh? Eight hundred—nine hundred?

MRS. HAWK. And you count upon your creditors?

HAWK. Of course! who should I count upon?—are they not, so to speak, all of my family? Find me a relation who desires to see me rich, as much as they do. Were I to die tomorrow, I should have more creditors than relations inconsolable. Relations feel grief in their hearts, and put crape on their hats; creditors feel the loss in their pockets. The heart forgets, the crape wears out, but the unpaid debt is ineffaceable—the blank is never filled up.

THOMAS (enter C.). Mr. Hardcore wishes to know if it really be true that you desire to see him, sir.

HAWK. That amazes him. Beg him to walk in.

(Exit Thomas, C.)

Hardcore, the most inexorable of all—a walking writ;[64] but withal, a greedy speculator, and timid as a fawn, venturing on the wildest schemes, and trembling the moment he has set them going.

(Thomas announces Mr. Hardcore, who enters, C.)

HARDCORE (angry). So, sir, you are to be found when it pleases you.

MRS. HAWK (R.). Mr. Hardcore, this tone—

HAWK (C., calming her). My dear, Mr. Hardcore is a creditor.

HARDCORE (L.). And one that will not stir from here until he is paid.

---

62   Good, honest character.
63   Greed.
64   i.e., he is forever presenting legal demands for payment.

HAWK (*motions Hardcore to take off his hat. Aside*). One that will not stir from here till he has given me some money. (*Aloud*) Ah! you have not behaved handsomely to me, Hardcore, to have a writ out against the man with whom you had so many transactions.

HARDCORE. Transactions which have not been all profit.

HAWK. Otherwise, where would be the merit? If all affairs brought profit, all the world would be speculators.

HARDCORE. You have not sent for me, sir, I presume, to give me proof of your wit—I know you are cleverer than me, for you have got my money.

HAWK. Money, my dear Hardcore, must be *somewhere*. Yes, Caroline, strange as it may appear to you, Mr. Hardcore has hunted me like a hare. In my place some people would avenge themselves—for I have him in my power, and can make him lose an enormous sum.

HARDCORE. If you don't pay me I shall; but you will pay me—the writ is in the hands of the Sheriff's officer.[65]

MRS. HAWK. Heavens!

HAWK. Sheriff's officer! Are you entirely losing your sagacity? Poor devil! you don't know what you are doing—you ruin me and yourself at one blow!

HARDCORE. Eh! *You* I understand, but me—how me?

HAWK. Both, I tell you—both, you stupid fellow! There, sit down and write at once—delay is frightful! (*Hardcore crosses to L.*) Moments are precious!

HARDCORE (*taking the pen, alarmed—sits L.C.*). Write! What?

HAWK (*C.*). To your head clerk, to stop proceedings—and to send me two hundred pounds I want.

HARDCORE (*throwing down the pen*). I dare say indeed!

HAWK. You hesitate?—you, when I am about to marry my daughter to a man immensely rich? You have me arrested? You lock up your debt, not me. You ruin your debtor. Your brain is softening!

HARDCORE. Oh! you are about to marry Julia to—

HAWK. Sir Harry Lester—as many thousands as years!

HARDCORE. As many thousands as years? How old is he, though?—all depends upon that. If he is a middle-aged man, that is no reason for suspending proceedings. But two hundred pounds—two hundred pounds? No, no—I can't stand it!—I'm off!

(*Crosses up C., with hat on. Every time Hardcore puts on his hat, Hawk motions him to take it off*).

HAWK (*with vehemence*). Go, then—go, you dolt—your blood be upon your own head!

HARDCORE (*stops*). Eh?—my blood?

HAWK. In your ruin, remember that I offered to save you!

HARDCORE. Save me?—from what?

HAWK. From what? Simply from utter ruin!

HARDCORE. From ruin! Impossible!

HAWK (*motions for Hardcore to take off his hat. Sitting himself, L.*). What, you! An adroit, intelligent man, thoroughly up to all the knowledge of the humbug of speculation—for he is, Caroline, perfectly wide-awake in general—you dabble in such schemes? (*Mysteriously*).

HARDCORE (*C., getting more fidgety*). To which do you refer?

HAWK. I was quite angry when I heard you had been duped so—not out of love to you, observe. No, out of pure selfishness; for, in some sort, I look upon your fortune as my own: I said to myself: "I owe him

---

65   Sheriffs could execute writs and order imprisonment.

too much, not to be certain that he will aid me on great occasions"—such as the present, for instance: and you are about to risk all, to lose all, in one scheme.

HARDCORE *(in agony)*. Hawk, my dear friend, is it then true? Is that Indian Emerald Company really a flam?

HAWK *(aside)*. Oh, you have shares there have you. I knew I should make him betray himself. *(Aloud)* A flam! You, the knowing Hardcore, ask me if it is a flam?

HARDCORE. But it is considered such a splendid scheme. Shares are at three per cent above par already.

HAWK. Oh, yes, a splendid scheme for those who sold yesterday.

HARDCORE. They sold yesterday?

HAWK. Yes, in secret—hush!

HARDCORE. Adieu. Mrs. Hawk, good morning.

HAWK. Hardcore?

HARDCORE. Well?

HAWK. And your note to the chief clerk—

HARDCORE. I'll speak to him.

HAWK. No; write. When a man says he'll speak, he means to forget. Write! Meanwhile, I may tell you of some who will buy your Emerald shares.

HARDCORE. All my shares? *(Reseats himself, L., and takes pen)* And who, pray?

HAWK *(aside)*. There's an honest fellow, now; eager to rob someone else, as a cat to pounce upon a mouse. A promise of three months delay?[66]

HARDCORE. There—it's done! *(Comes down, L.)*.

HAWK. My friend, who is buying in secret, believing the scheme as splendid as you believed it, wants three hundred shares. Have you as many?

HARDCORE. Three hundred and fifty!

HAWK. Fifty more—well, I have no doubt he'll take them. *(Looking upon what Hardcore has written)* Have you mentioned the two hundred pounds.

HARDCORE. And what's your friend's name?

HAWK. His name is—but you have not written two hundred pounds.

HARDCORE. His name?

HAWK. The money!

HARDCORE *(crosses to L. and sits at table)*. What a man you are. *(Writes)* There it us.

HAWK. His name is Grossmark.

HARDCORE *(rising)*. Grossmark?

HAWK. At least, Grossmark is the man commissioned to buy. Go home, and I'll send them to you.

HARDCORE. I'll go myself *(crosses to C.)*.

HAWK. If you run after the buyer, he'll lower his terms.

HARDCORE. True! You are my preserver. Adieu, my dear friend—you are my friend, my very dear friend. *(Hardcore retires, and returns to bow very obsequiously to Mrs. Hawk, shakes hands with Hawk, turns, and exit C.)*.

HAWK. Yes, dearer to you than you imagine *(imitates the action of pulling the strings of a puppet)*.

MRS. HAWK *(R.)*. But is that true, what you told about the Emerald Company?

HAWK *(L.)*. There is truth in it. My friend Prospectus is anxious to get up a panic in these shares, which will eventually turn out a magnificent property. Ah, if I had but a thousand pounds to purchase with, my fortune would be—but, no, I must first marry Julia.

---

66   Hawk manipulates Hardcore to write a 90-day note of credit.

MRS. HAWK. Do you know this Sir Harry Lester well?

HAWK. Intimately! I have dined with him.

MRS. HAWK. Oh!

HAWK. Charming house, splendid plate, everything the first in style. Our child will make a famous match. And as to him—bah! in marriage, it is devilish lucky if one of the happy pair is satisfied.

(Enter Julia, L.D.).

MRS. HAWK. Here comes Julia. *(Crosses to C.)* My dear, your papa and I have just been talking of you; and apropos to a subject young ladies always like to hear of—marriage.

JULIA *(L.).* Has Frederick Noble, then, been talking to papa?

HAWK *(R.).* Noble! *(Crosses to C.)* Mrs. Hawk, were you prepared to find that gentleman comfortably established in your daughter's affections? What! my clerk?

JULIA *(R.).* Yes, papa.

HAWK. You love him?

JULIA. Yes, papa.

MRS. HAWK *(L.).* Does he love you?

JULIA. Oh, dearly!

HAWK *(C.).* What proofs have you?

JULIA. His wish to marry me.

HAWK. How sharp these chits[67] are with their answers. Miss Julia Hawk, permit me to inform you that a clerk, with one hundred and fifty pounds a-year, does not know how to love. He has not the time—'tis too luxurious—he can't afford it.

JULIA. But Frederick loves me, and I love him.

HAWK. In that case, you shall marry him.

(Julia is overjoyed).

Wait a bit. I said in that case: the case isn't yet proved. You know that you will not have a penny. How are you to live after you're married? Have you thought of that?

JULIA *(overjoyed).* Yes, papa!

MRS. HAWK. She's out of her senses.

HAWK. Well, my child, tell me your plans. Confide in me, as your best friend. How will you live?

JULIA. Live upon love, papa!

HAWK. Pleasant and cheap. But will love from his quiver, wing[68] his arrows with bank-notes?

JULIA. Yes, for it will give us both courage. Oh! I will work for him. Frederick has ambition—he will get on.

HAWK. An ambitious bachelor may get on: but, married, he has no chance. The great Bacon said—"The man who has a wife and children, has given hostages to fortune."[69] In other words, has pawned his whole existence. But a thought occurs to me—your Frederick believes me rich?

JULIA. He has never spoken of money.

HAWK. Exactly. I see it all. Julia, you may write to him at once to come and speak to me.

---

67   Impudent young women.

68   Feather.

69   The whole passage reads, "He that hath wife and children hath given hostages to fortune, for they are impediments to great enterprises, either of virtue or mischief. Certainly the best works and of greatest merit for the public have proceeded from the unmarried or childless men, which both in affection and means have married and endowed the public." Francis Bacon, 1st Viscount St. Alban (1561-1626), "Of Marriage and Single Life," (1625) in *The Essays or Counsels Civil and Moral of Francis Bacon*, edited by A. Spiers (London: Whittaker, 1854), 57.

JULIA (*throwing her arms around his neck*). Oh, you darling papa!

HAWK. But you will marry Sir Harry Lester. Instead of being the wife of a poor clerk, you will be Lady Lester—rich, flattered, and courted. I'm sorry that I've nothing better to offer you.

JULIA. But Frederick—

HAWK. Oh! he will give you up of his own accord.

JULIA. Never, never!

MRS. HAWK. Suppose Frederick really loves her?

HAWK. Suppose he loves her fortune?

(*A knock is heard. L.U.E.*).

MRS. HAWK. A knock! and no one to open the door.

HAWK (*sits, R.*). Let them knock again.

MRS. HAWK. It's very strange, but I can't help fancying that every knock must be Sparrow returned.

HAWK. Sparrow? I think you said Sparrow—did you not? Ha, ha! Well, that is good! What! after running away with our funds—after eight years' absence, and no hint of his existence—you believe in Sparrow's return? Why, you are like the old French soldiers, who still live in hope of Napoleon's returning to them.[70]

(*A knock*)

MRS. HAWK. Another knock!

HAWK. Go, Julia, and say we are out. None but a creditor can have the indecency to disbelieve a young girl—and, in that case, let him enter.

(*Exit Julia, C.*)

MRS. HAWK (*L.*). That child's love—sincere, at any rate, on her part—has quite moved me!

HAWK (*R.*). You women are all so romantic! We shall see what Mr. Noble says.

JULIA (*enter C., comes down L.*). It is Mr. Grossmark, papa.

HAWK (*R.*). Grossmark—the laughing hyena—coarse in speech as in mind. His bantering is like the badinage of a young elephant; but he is civil to me, because he thinks I still have resources. I tame him as we tame wild beasts—by audacity, and an unflinching eye. If he thought I feared him, he would swallow me up whole! (*Going to door*) Come in—you can come in, Grossmark.

(*Ladies cross to L.*).

GROSSMARK (*enter C., cross L.C.*). Ha, ha! I've come to compliment you. I know that Miss Julia is going to be married to a *millionaire*; the rumour has already got abroad.

HAWK. *Millionaire!*—no. Some hundred thousands—that's all.

GROSSMARK. That magnificent dodge[71] will make many of your creditors patient—ha, ha! And even I—

HAWK. Thought of arresting me.

JULIA. Arresting you, papa?

MRS. HAWK. Oh, Mr. Grossmark!

GROSSMARK. Hear me. The money has been owing two years; but this marriage is a superb invention, and—

---

70 After his defeat at Waterloo, Napoleon was exiled by the British to the island of St. Helena, where he lived from 1815 until his death in 1821.

71 Deflection.

MRS. HAWK. An invention, Mr. Grossmark!

HAWK. My son-in-law is Sir Harry Lester, a young man of—

GROSSMARK. What! really a young man? Ha, ha! How much do you pay him? Oh, come now—

MRS. HAWK. Oh!

HAWK. Enough of this impertinence; or else, my dear Grossmark, I shall insist upon settling accounts; and at the price you sell me money, I rather imagine you would be something the loser by that.

GROSSMARK. But, my dear—

HAWK (*haughtily*). Mr. Grossmark, I am about to become rich enough to permit no longer the vulgar jests of anyone—not even a creditor.

GROSSMARK. But—

HAWK. Not another word, or—I pay you. Enter my private room, and we will settle the affair about which I sent for you.

GROSSMARK (*humbly, and crossing to R.*). At your service, Mr. Hawk. (*Aside*) What an imposing chap he is (*exit D.R. 2 E.*).

HAWK (*following him, and speaking to them*). The wild beast is tamed—I will have his skin ere long (*exit D.R. 2 E.*).

JULIA. Oh, mamma, I shall never be able to marry this baronet.

MRS. HAWK (*R.*). But he is rich.

JULIA (*L.*). Yet, I prefer poverty and happiness.

MRS. HAWK. My child, there is no happiness possible in poverty. Let our experience be a lesson to you. We are at this moment going through a terrible crisis. Marry well, my child, while you can.

(*Enter Thomas, followed by Dimity, C.*)

THOMAS (*C.*). All your orders are executed, ma'am.

DIMITY. The tradesmen are civil again, and Mrs. Mason says the dinner will be superb.

THOMAS. As to Mr. Prospectus—

(*Enter Hawk with papers in his hand, D.R. 2 E.—Exit Dimity, C.*)

HAWK. What of Mr. Prospectus?

THOMAS. He is coming at once; he had to take some money to Mr. Johnson, who lives next door.

HAWK. You keep at the door, and manage that he speaks to me before he sees Johnson. Tell him 'tis a case of immense importance, admitting of no delay.

(*Exit Thomas, C.*)

MRS. HAWK (*C.*). And Grossmark?

HAWK (*L.*). That is all I could extract from him—delay, and these bills of exchange for some shares.[72] Bills on a certain Bradshaw, a man of fashion, very insolvent, but who has a rich old aunt in the environs of Dublin. Sir Harry comes from Dublin—he will tell me, perhaps, whether the bills are worth anything.

MRS. HAWK. But the tradespeople will be here immediately.

HAWK. And I shall be here to pay them. Never fear, Caroline, the money will be ready. But leave me to myself.

(*Mrs. Hawk and Julia cross, and exeunt, 1 E. L.*)

---

72   Post-dated orders (rather like modern cheques) specifying an amount payable. In this case, the bills are probably exchangeable for shares (or their face value) signed by Bradshaw.

—They are coming! Everything now rests upon the doubtful friendship of Prospectus—a man whose fortune I made. But the world is so ungrateful; where the benevolent people are, I know not. Prospectus and I like each other very well. He owes me gratitude, and I owe him money—neither of us pay.

THOMAS (*without, C.D.*). Yes, sir, master is at home.

HAWK. 'Tis he—my friend!

(*Rushes to the door—Earthworm appears*).

—Oh, it's Mr. Earthworm!

EARTHWORM (*L.*). I have been here eleven times during the last week, my dear Mr. Affable Hawk; and want obliged me to wait for you three hours in the street yesterday; and I saw that they told me the truth, in saying you were in the country, so I came today.

HAWK (*R.*). My dear Earthworm, we are equally miserable.

EARTHWORM. Um, um! I am in a wretched plight—everything I have pawned!

HAWK. Pretty nearly my case.

EARTHWORM. I never reproached you with my ruin, for I believed it was your intention to make us rich; but, after all, fine words pay no baker, and I am come to beg the smallest installment of interest, to keep my family from starvation. Starvation!—imagine what a fearful thing starvation must be!

HAWK. Earthworm, you unman me! Be reasonable—I will share with you what I have. (*In a low voice*) There is but five pounds in the house, and that is my daughter's money.

EARTHWORM. Is it possible?—you, whom I have seen so rich!

HAWK. I have nothing to hide from you.

EARTHWORM. Between those who are wretched, truth is a sacred debt!

HAWK. Ah! if that was all we owed, how promptly it might be paid! But mind you keep my secret. I am on the point of securing a husband for my daughter.

EARTHWORM. I have two daughters, and they must work, work, work, without hope of marriage! In the circumstances in which you are placed, I would not importune you, but my wife and children await my return in anguish and anxiety.

HAWK. You move me deeply. Come, I'll give you three pounds (*Exit R.D.*).

EARTHWORM. My wife and children will forever bless you!—you have saved them from starvation— starvation! (*Aside, during Hawk's brief absence in another room*) The others who pester him get nothing but by my doleful and modest complaints, I gradually get from him all the interest due to me. Ah, ah! starvation is a fine ferret! (*Taps his pocket*).

HAWK (*re-enters in time to observe the latter part of Earthworm's pantomime*). Eh? Oh, the old miser! Ten installments on account, each of three pounds—that makes thirty pounds. I have sown abundantly— now I must reap. (*Aloud*) Here is the money.

EARTHWORM (*L.*). Three sovereigns—three golden sovereigns? Eh, eh! what a time it is since these fingers have touched gold! Adieu!—my whole family will pray for the happiness of Miss Julia.

HAWK (*R.*). Good bye! (*Holding him back*) Poor fellow! when I look at you, I fancy myself rich. Your misery so affects me, that I can't express it. And to think of my being only yesterday on the point of repaying you all—capital and interest!

EARTHWORM (*eagerly*). To repay me?

HAWK. It hung upon a thread.

EARTHWORM. Tell, tell me all about it!

HAWK. Imagine the most brilliant invention—a speculation so grand—which appealed to all interests— which was certain to realize gigantic profits—and a stupid banker refused me the paltry sum of two hundred and fifty pounds, when perhaps there was a million to be gained.

EARTHWORM. A million?

HAWK. A million to begin with—for no one can tell the limits to which commercial vogue might not push the "Conservative Pavement."

EARTHWORM. Pavement?

HAWK. Conservative—a pavement upon which and with which barricades are impossible![73]

EARTHWORM. Really!

HAWK. You see, all the Governments interested in the maintenance of order, become at once our shareholders. Kings, princes, ministers, form our committee, supported by the banker lords, the cotton lords, and all the commercial world. Even the very Republicans themselves, finding their chance ruined, will be forced to take my shares, in order to live!

EARTHWORM (eagerly). Ah, yes!—that is grandiose—colossal!

HAWK. And so philanthropic! And to think of my being refused three hundred pounds to advertise and start this magnificent scheme.

EARTHWORM. Three hundred. I thought it was only—

HAWK. Three hundred; Not a sixpence more; and I would have taken the lender into partnership, he should have had half the profits, that is to say ten fortunes!

EARTHWORM. Wait a bit—I will see—I will speak to someone who, perhaps, will be glad.

HAWK. Hush! not a word; Above all things, don't speak of it—they might steal the idea; or, perhaps, they might not see at once the enormous fortune certain to be realized, as your sagacity has seen it. Capitalists are so stupid; besides, I am expecting Prospectus.

EARTHWORM. Prospectus—but it is quite possible that I may know someone.

HAWK. Lucky dog, that Prospectus! He's speculative too. If he only has the wit to see how easily he may make his fortune—five hundred pounds is all that are required.

EARTHWORM. Five hundred? Just now, you said three hundred.

HAWK. Three, yes, exactly. It was three hundred I was refused; but it is five hundred I must have. And Prospectus, whom I have so often enriched, will become a *millionaire* through me now. After all, he's a good fellow, Prospectus.

EARTHWORM. Hawk, if I were to find the sum.

HAWK. You? No, no my friend, think nothing of what I told you; besides, Prospectus is coming, and he is certain to give me the money; and then I shall soon pay you the two thousand pounds I owe you.

EARTHWORM. But you won't listen to me.

MRS. HAWK (enter L.). Mr. Prospectus has arrived, dear.

HAWK (aside). Bravo! (Aloud) Detain him one instant.

(Exit Mrs. Hawk, L.).

—Now, my dear Earthworm, I must say good bye to you. Prospectus is here, and my money is secure. I needn't appeal to your gallantry. (Forcing him)
All things, you know, my friend, give place,
When there's a little money in the case.[74]

EARTHWORM. Stay, stay, I have the sum by me, and I will give it you (takes out his pocket book).

HAWK. You! Earthworm! Five hundred pounds.

EARTHWORM. It—it—some one—a friend commissioned me to invest it for him; and I don't think I could do better than invest it in your hands.

---

73   This is a preposterous concept: a road surface on which civil disturbance cannot be mounted.

74   This couplet appears to be a quotation or aphorism, but of obscure origin.

HAWK. Oh! For an investment, I defy you to find a better (*taking the notes*). So much the worse for Prospectus—he ought to have come before.

EARTHWORM. Then you will prepare the agreement (*crosses to R.*).

HAWK. At once! Good bye! Go out through my private room (*shows him out, 2 E.R.*).

EARTHWORM. You have got the money safe?

HAWK. Safe (*putting it in his pocket*).

EARTHWORM. Oh, Mr. Hawk. Oh! Oh! (*Exit R.*).

MRS. HAWK (*enter 1 E.L.*). My dear, Prospectus says, if you're engaged, he'll look in again, as he must call on Johnson, next door.

HAWK. I'm with him directly. Oh, my dear Caroline, I ought to blow my brains out.

MRS. HAWK (*L.*). Heavens! What has occurred?

HAWK (*R.*). Not five minutes ago, I asked Earthworm, the old miser, to lend me five hundred pounds.

MRS. HAWK. And he refused you?

HAWK. On the contrary, he gave them!

MRS. HAWK. Well?

HAWK. I'm miserable to think that he gave me the money so readily—it might have been a thousand, had I been adroit!

MRS. HAWK. What a man you are!

THOMAS (*enter C.D.*). Please, sir, the tradesmen are waiting in the hall.

HAWK. Have they their little bills with them?

THOMAS. Yes, sir.

HAWK. Then show them into my study.

THOMAS. What! all of them, sir? And what in the world am I to do with them there?—they would eat me up!

HAWK. Do with them?—why pay them, of course!—what should you do with them?

THOMAS. Pay them?—what! with money?

HAWK. With gold!

THOMAS. Oh! (*Exit C.D.*).

MRS. HAWK. Come and see Mr. Prospectus—don't keep him—he's in a dreadful hurry!

HAWK. True!—send him to me, while I'm in the vein. I've sufficient already for the jewels; and a few hundreds now, for the tradesmen and sundries, will carry me through.

MRS. HAWK. You must succeed with Mr. Prospectus—he is such an old friend! (*Exit L.*).

HAWK. An old friend! How comfortable that sounds!—what a crutch to lean upon!—and what a delusive reed it really is! Prospectus is an old friend; but I'm afraid that he's more the friend of money than of myself.

PROSPECTUS (*enter L. 2 E.*). Good morning, Hawk! What is it you have to say to me? Quick! Thomas stopped me on my way to Johnson's.

HAWK. What! Do you visit such a fellow as Johnson?

PROSPECTUS. My dear Hawk, if we only visited those whom we esteem, we should never pay visits at all, for bang me if I know a door I could knock at!

HAWK (*R., laughing, and taking his hand*). No, not even your own—not even your own.

PROSPECTUS. Well, what is it you want of me?

HAWK. You leave me no time to gild the pill.[75] I see you have guessed.

---

75   Soften the tone of unpleasant news.

PROSPECTUS. Money? My dear fellow, I have none; and, frankly, if I had, I couldn't lend it you. I have already lent you all that my means permitted. I have not dunned[76] you for it—between friends, you know. But if my heart was not filled with gratitude; if I were as other men are, the creditor would long since have absorbed the friend. If I had money enough to save you altogether, I'd do it: but you are done up. All your recent speculations, though ingenious, have failed. When ruin comes, you will always find a home, and a knife and fork, in my house; but for the present, depend upon it, your game is up. It is the duty of friendship not to conceal unpleasant truths.

HAWK. A duty friendship very steadfastly avails itself of. You may always trust to your friends for that. What would friendship be, without the luxury of complimenting oneself while saying disagreeables to one's friend? So, I am a lost man in public opinion, am I?

PROSPECTUS. Well, I don't say that. There is no man for whom the public has a greater admiration than yourself, but it is thought that necessity, the mother of all evil, has forced you to have recourse to expedients.

HAWK. Which are not justified, because they are not successful! Success, success! what an idol it is!—and of how many infamies is it not frequently composed? I'll give you a proof of it, I have this very morning brought about that fall in Indian Emeralds so necessary for your operations, that you may buy largely before the news is published of its—

PROSPECTUS. Hush? *(Taking him, by the waist)* My dear Hawk, is that true? Ah, how like you that is now! There's no one has your genius after all.

HAWK. That will show you that I don't want advice, but money. Nor do I ask that for myself; I ask it for my daughter, whose marriage depends on it. We are at the last pinch. Poverty reigns in this house, though under the form of plenty—and, unless I have a little ready money, Julia's chance is lost. In a word, I want a week's opulence here, as you want four-and-twenty hours' untruth on 'Change.[77] To be frank with you, my wife and daughter have not the wherewithal to provide the wedding dresses.

PROSPECTUS *(aside)*. Is he humbugging me?

HAWK. This very day my future son-in-law is to dine here, and all my plate is—having my crest engraved on it! All I ask is, to lend me three hundred pounds—and your service of plate—for a day.

PROSPECTUS. Three hundred pounds! no one has three hundred pounds to lend. Lucky him who has the sum for himself; *(crosses to R., and sits upon sofa, R.)* and if he lent it continually, he would never have it *(goes to the fire-place)*.

HAWK *(following, sits by him)*. Look here, my dear fellow. I love my wife and child; their love is the only consolation amidst my present troubles; and they have been so patient, so resigned! My greatest anxiety is, to see them safe from misfortune. *(Coming down the stage arm-in-arm with him)* I have suffered much of late. I have seen my best hopes frustrated—my best schemes fail—but all these are nothing compared with the pain of being refused by you.

PROSPECTUS. Well, I'll step home and see if I have as much at my banker's, and I will drop you a line. I will write to you.

HAWK. No. When a man says he will write, he means to refuse. I have promised to pay dressmakers and other tradesmen on the certainty of your aiding me. You will not suffer Julia, your god-daughter, to miss a splendid marriage.

PROSPECTUS. My dear Hawk, I haven't the money. I will lend you the plate with pleasure. *(goes R., and sits at table)*.

---

76 Pestered.
77 The Exchange.

HAWK (*sinking into chair, L. of table*). Enough! All is over. My child must suffer for her father.

(*Enter Mrs. Hawk and Julia, L.*).

MRS. HAWK. What is the matter?

HAWK (*drawing them both to him*). Look here, Prospectus—here are my anxieties! Oh, the sight of them unmans me! I could implore you on my knees.

JULIA. Papa, I will implore for you. Oh, sir, whatever his request, grant it! (*Crosses to R.*).

PROSPECTUS. Do you know what that request is?

JULIA. No.

PROSPECTUS. Three hundred pounds for your marriage.

JULIA (*R.C.*). Oh! sir; then forget what I have said. My marriage must not be bought with the humiliation of my father.

(*Hawk kisses her*).

PROSPECTUS (*moved*). Julia, you are a good girl—and my god-daughter—and—and—I'll go and fetch the money.

(*Prospectus goes quickly up stage, towards C.D.—Hawk towards door, R.—Julia and Mrs. Hawk towards L.*).

Act II

Hawk's office. Doors R. and L. 1 E.; window, L.; a large desk, with drawers and compartments for letters, deeds, papers, etc., R.; two chairs and table, L.; writing materials at back, bookcases, tin cases, etc. ; doors 1 and 3 E. R.; 1 and 3 E. L.; window, 2 E. L.; fireplace, 2 E. R. Enter Thomas, followed by Frederick Noble, 1 E. L.

NOBLE. You say Mr. Hawk wishes to speak to me?

THOMAS. Yes, sir, but Miss Julia begs you to wait here for her, before you see her father.

NOBLE (*aside*). Her father wishes to see me—she wishes to speak with me before the interview: something has happened!

THOMAS. Here is Miss Julia.

NOBLE. Julia!

JULIA (*enter R. 1 E.*). Thomas, inform papa that Mr. Noble has arrived.

(*Exit Thomas, U.E.R.*).

—Frederick, if you wish our love to shine as brilliantly in the eyes of others as it does in our hearts, you must summon all your courage.

NOBLE (*L.*). What has happened?

JULIA (*R.*). I am threatened with a husband—young, rich, titled. My father is evidently eager for the match.

NOBLE. A rival! And you ask me if I want courage? Tell me his name, and you shall soon—

JULIA. Frederick! You terrify me; is it thus you hope to persuade my papa!

NOBLE. He is here.

HAWK (*enter U.E.R., goes C.*). So you love my daughter?

NOBLE (*L.*). I do, sir.

HAWK. At any rate, she believes as much. You have had the cleverness to persuade her of that.

NOBLE. Sir, these insinuations, from another, would be unpardonable insults; from Julia's father I will let them pass. Not love her? How could I help loving her? The friendless orphan has no one in the world to love; none but her, and she has been a world to me. She has smiled upon me in my darkness; she has comforted me; she has made ambition a duty and a delight; and yet you ask me if I love her.

JULIA *(R.)*. Ought I not to leave the room, papa?

HAWK. Oh! Your modesty suffers from these praises? Mr. Noble, I happen to entertain those ideas on love, which usually accompany age and experience. My doubts are all the more rational in this case; as I am not one of those parents who believe their goslings are cygnets, I see Julia as she is—without being plain—she wants that beauty which arrests the eye.

NOBLE *(L.)*. You are mistaken. I venture to assure you that you do not know your daughter.

HAWK. I don't?

NOBLE. You do not know her.

HAWK. On the contrary, I know her perfectly. I know her as well as if—in fact, I know her.

NOBLE. No, no! You know the Julia seen by all the world; but love has transformed her! Tenderness, devotion, gentleness, invest her with a beauty which love alone creates.

JULIA. Oh! Let me leave the room; I'm in all confusion!

HAWK *(C.)*. You are all gratitude and delight, hussy! *(To him)* And if you say such things to her—

NOBLE. I can say nothing else?

HAWK *(aside)*. Who can wonder that lovers are such bores to other people, if that is the staple of their talk? *(To him)* I fancied I was Julia's father, but you are the parent of a Julia so charming, that I should be glad to make her acquaintance.

NOBLE. Have you ever loved then?

HAWK. Considerably—and often. Like most men, I have been a fool and a dupe.

NOBLE. Is it to be a dupe, to feel that exalted passion, which attaches us to the ideal? Which charms every hour of life?

HAWK. Yes, every hour, except the dinner hour.

JULIA. Ah! Now you are laughing at us; we love each other truly—our love is pure and holy, founded on our knowledge of each other; and on the conviction that, together, we could battle through life bravely and cheerily.

NOBLE. What an angel she is!

HAWK *(aside)*. Yes, yes—we shall see what you say to the angel without wings! *(Aloud)* So, you love each other desperately? What a charming romance! You will marry her?

NOBLE. It is my highest ambition.

HAWK. In spite of every obstacle?

NOBLE. In spite of everything!

HAWK. Julia, my dear, you may leave us. I have to mention a few details not quite so romantic, but quite as necessary, as those we have just had.

JULIA *(going)*. Remember, I shall never love anyone but Frederick *(exit R. 1 E.)*.

NOBLE *(aside, L.)*. I feel certain of his consent.

HAWK *(R.)*. Young man, I am ruined!

NOBLE. Mr. Hawk!

HAWK. Totally, irretrievably ruined! Now, if you still claim my daughter's hand, it is yours. I feel bound in honour to be explicit with you. She will be at least saved from want, as your wife; whereas she must, at home, share worse than poverty.

NOBLE. Worse?

HAWK. I have enormous debts—ruin stares me in the face!

NOBLE. Impossible!

HAWK. You don't believe me? *(Aside)* He's obstinate. *(Taking out book from desk)* Look here—our property is here reckoned. Here are the protested bills—the mortgages—the lawyers' threats. You see how imminent the ruin is. Look at them—they are all in order—all classed. For, my young friend, bear this in mind—it is above all things, in disorder that order is necessary. In a well ordered disorder you are at your ease—you are master of the field. What can a creditor say, when he sees his debt methodically inscribed in due order? It gives bankruptcy a business-like air—makes it quite respectable; and nothing goes down so well with men of business, as business-like appearances. Order, my dear young friend, methodical order, is the hypocrisy of commerce! They ought to make me librarian to the British Museum—I'd make them a catalogue *(replaces book in desk)*.

NOBLE. And you have paid nothing?

HAWK. Little more. I pay alphabetically, and have not come to "A" yet. My debts amount to seventeen thousand pounds and odd shillings.

NOBLE *(absorbed in thought)*. Ruined! ruined! No help!

HAWK *(observing him—aside)*. I was sure of it—I knew how a *douche*[78] of reality would cool the ardour of the ideal. *(Aloud)* Well, my young friend?

NOBLE. I have to thank you sincerely for the frankness of this confession.

HAWN. And the Ideal? and your love for my daughter?

NOBLE. You have opened my eyes.

HAWK. I knew I should.

NOBLE. I fancied that I loved her to extremity—

HAWK. And now?

NOBLE. Now I feel that I love her ten times more.

HAWK. What?

NOBLE. You have opened my eyes to the sacred responsibility of my love—to the need of all my courage, of all my devotion; and with that increased demand has come increased love to meet it! I give my life to labour for her, and she will love me the dearer for my toil!

HAWK. What! you still think of marriage?

NOBLE. Still!—more than ever. I believed you rich—it was a drawback. With trembling and shame, and fear lest my motive should be misinterpreted, I asked for your daughter. Now I can hold my head erect; and ask you, without shame, to give me her hand.

HAWK *(aside)*. Um! I did not think there was so much goodness in the world. *(Aloud)* Forgive me the opinion I had formed—I had wronged you: and, above all, forgive me the pain I must cause you—Julia cannot be your wife.

NOBLE. No! What, in spite of our affection, and your ruin?

HAWK. Precisely on account of my ruin. I have told you all; and thereby discovered what a generous spirit lives in your breast. To that generosity I must now appeal. I have a brilliant marriage in view. That marriage will give me money; and, that which is more than money—*time*. By its aid, I can re-conquer my position—pay off my debts, and save my family from ruin. Thus, the marriage of my daughter is my last hope—my last resource—the plank that floats past the shipwrecked family: without it, I lose all, even my honour—with it, I save all. Now, since you so truly and disinterestedly love my daughter, I appeal to the very generosity of your love; do not condemn her to poverty.

---

78   Water jet.

NOBLE *(with emotion)*. But what—what is it you ask? What would you have me do?

HAWK *(taking his hand)*. I would have you seek in your affection a courage, which I should not have—

NOBLE. What is it? There is nothing I would not do for her.

HAWK. Brave and generous fellow! Listen to me. If I refused you her hand, she would refuse the man I intend her to marry: so that it is necessary that I should give my consent, and the refusal come from you.

NOBLE. From me? She wouldn't credit it.

HAWK. She will believe it, if you tell her that you fear poverty for her.

NOBLE. She will think my love is mercenary.

HAWK. But she will owe to you her happiness.

NOBLE *(with pathos)*. But she will despise me.

HAWK. She will.

NOBLE. And can I bear that?

HAWK. If I have read your heart aright, you would bear that, or worse than that, to secure her happiness. What is love but self-sacrifice? I ask you to do what I could not do myself—I confess it: what thousands could not do, because the thousands are selfish: but you will do it, because your heart is high-placed, and your love unselfish. Am I not right? May I not count on you?

NOBLE *(after a struggle)*. Yes, you may.

HAWK. I knew it *(shakes his hand warmly)*.

(Enter Mrs. Hawk and Julia, R. 1 E.).

MRS. HAWK. Julia is so impatient to hear the result of your conversation that she has found me to come with her.

HAWK. I have laid before Mr. Noble a frank statement of our position, and it remains with him to decide.

NOBLE *(aside)*. How shall I tell her? My heart will break.

JULIA. Well! Well?

HAWK *(C.)*. I have told him that we are ruined.

JULIA. But that has not altered his intentions—that has not affected your love, Frederick.

NOBLE. My love!

(Crosses to C.—Hawk, unobserved seizes him by the hand).

I—I—I should deceive you, Julia, if I were to say my intentions—remained the same.

JULIA. I cannot believe it! It is not you who say this?

NOBLE *(with animation)*. There are men to whom poverty gives fresh energy—men whose happiness would be intensified by the devotion of each day, by the toil of each day; and would hold themselves as a thousandfold repaid by the smile of a loved wife. *(Restraining himself)* I—I—am not one of those. The thought of poverty subdues me. I could not sustain the idea of your being in want.

JULIA *(throws herself, sobbing, into her mother's arms)*. Oh! Mother—mother—mother!

MRS. HAWK *(R.)*. My child!—my darling Julia!

NOBLE *(aside to Hawk)*. Have I said enough!

JULIA. I should have had courage for both. I would have slaved for him!—Poverty would have been light to bear with his love! But oh! he never—never—never loved me!

NOBLE. In pity, sir, let me go away at once!

HAWK. Come!

NOBLE. Julia, farewell! You know not what is beating in my heart at this moment! You despise me! The love which would drag you into want is madness! My love is that which sacrifices itself for you and your happiness!

JULIA. Go—I no longer believe in you! *(To her mother)* He was my happiness!

THOMAS *(enter L. 1 E., and announces)*. Sir Harry Lester and Mr. Graves.

HAWK. Caroline, my dear, take Julia to her room. *(To Noble)* Follow me. *(To Thomas)* Ask the gentlemen to wait here a minute.

(Exeunt Hawk and Noble, U.E.R.; Mrs. Hawk and Julia, R. 1 E. Enter Sir Harry Lester and Graves, L. 1 E.).

THOMAS. Master will be here in a minute, gentlemen *(exits)*.

GRAVES *(L.)*. Well, my boy, you have entered the citadel at last. Have a care, though, Hawk is deuced keen!

LESTER *(R.)*. Yes, I'm rather afraid he won't be gulled.

GRAVES. Tut! never fear, if you play boldly. There is no man more easily duped than he who is always duping. He relies too much on his own sagacity. Hawk is a speculator—rich today, tomorrow he may be a beggar. To guard against this, my belief is that he wants to place a fortune of his money in the shape of a dowry for his daughter, so as to be secure against a rainy day. He wants a son-in-law who will aid him in his plans.

LESTER *(R.)*. I've no objection, provided he does not look too closely into my affairs.

GRAVES *(L.)*. I have primed him.

LESTER. Well, fortune assist, for I'm in a sad plight! If I had not, luckily, two names[79]—one for the usurers and bailiffs, the other for the fashionable world—I should be on my last legs. The only chance I have lived upon for some time, has been that of meeting with an heiress or a rich widow; but the race seems almost extinct—like the pug-dogs.[80]

GRAVES. It's very sad.

LESTER. Then the money-lenders are such scoundrels;—Grossmark sends me to old Earthworm, after having emptied my pockets himself. My tailor refuses to understand my prospects—the brute! The horse lives on tick.[81] As to my tiger,[82] I don't know a d—n how he breathes, nor where he feeds; that is a mystery I dare not fathom. So, you see, I must do something. Besides, I'm sick of idleness. I see that the shortest way to get wealthy is, after all, to work for it: but the devil of it is, that we gentlemen feel ourselves fitted for everything, and so, in reality, are fitted for nothing. A man, with such whiskers as mine, what is he to do? Society has created no employment for us.

GRAVES. Join Hawk, and become a speculator.

LESTER. And you are positive he won't give less than twenty thousand pounds with his daughter?

GRAVES. That was the sum he named to me. And from the magnitude of his affairs, the elegance in which he lives—

LESTER. Oh, as to elegance, damn it, look at me!

GRAVES. Ah! but look around, and observe that the opulence here is that of a merchant.

LESTER. That's true.

GRAVES. Besides, Hawk is a great city name.

LESTER. Yes, but it suggests uncomfortable ideas to the pigeons! However, he can't hurt me, so I'm all safe.

GRAVES. Not counting me, how much do you owe?

---

79   His family name (Bradshaw) and his inherited title (Lester).

80   Pugs flourished in Victorian England, in part due to Queen Victoria's fondness of the breed. Lester's remark is ironic, as if to say that pugs are everywhere but each already claimed by a master.

81   Credit (also a small bean).

82   Smartly liveried boy-groom or footman who stands on a platform behind the carriage.

LESTER. Oh, a mere nothing! Some five thousand pounds, which my father-in-law will pay. I always said I should never become rich till I was penniless; that critical moment is arrived.

GRAVES. Have you prepared yourself to answer Hawk's questions?

LESTER. Yes; I have the Lester estates. Three thousand acres of the finest land in Ireland—several houses in Dublin—two marshes—and powerful political connections, the more useful, as I am resolved upon playing a political part.

GRAVES. A good idea!

LESTER. I shall commence with journalism; do as they do in France—make the newspapers carry me into the Cabinet.[83]

GRAVES. But you never wrote a line in your life.

LESTER. Innocent gentleman! Why do you suppose that it is necessary for the editor of a newspaper to know how to write? He leaves that to some poor devil who is paid for it, and whom nobody hears of. I shall shave my whiskers, and assume a dignified demeanour. *(Speaks with emphasis)* "The question before us has still to be understood; it lies deep, sir, deep; I shall expose it altogether, very shortly." To another—"Russia, sir, is a bugbear nobody understands." Or I may do something in the grandiose and prophetic style—"We are rolling down the abyss; we have not yet evolved all the evolutions of the revolutionary phases." A man establishes a high character upon such pedestals as these: especially if he publish a bulky volume of statistics, which no one opens, and everyone pretends to have read—that settles him as a serious thinker, a solid politician.

GRAVES. Ha, ha! I believe you are right.

LESTER. The moment I am married I put on the air of a man of principles! I can take my choice of principles, for we have them of all colours. Stay! I shall be a Protectionist.[84] The word tickles me. In every age, there is some word which is the latch-key to the Cabinet—and Protection sounds so kind, so generous, so fatherly! Decidedly, I shall go in for the farmers' friend![85] *(Crosses to L.).*

GRAVES. Here comes your father-in-law.

HAWK *(enter R.—cross to C.).* How do you do?—delighted to see you. Sorry to have kept you waiting, but I was occupied with—I may as well tell you, as you are to be one of the family. Poor fellow!—an admirer of Julia's. I'm afraid I was rather stern with him—but what could I say to an offer of marriage from a man with only a miserable five hundred a-year, and no great prospects?

LESTER. Five hundred a-year—poor devil!

HAWK *(C.).* People may vegetate upon that sum.

LESTER *(L.).* Not live on it, assuredly.

HAWK. The ladies will be here immediately. Meanwhile, shall we talk business?

LESTER *(aside).* The crisis is come.

(They sit down).

HAWK *(L.).* You love my daughter?

LESTER *(C.).* Passionately!

HAWK. Passionately?

---

83   In other words, by editing a newspaper, he will garner public favour and go into politics. This makes light of the fate of Ernest Charles Jones, the Chartist editor and poet, who was imprisoned for sedition and kept under brutal conditions from 1849 to 1850. (In France, the allusion may have been recognizable as Pierre-Jean de Béranger, the songwriter elected to the Constituent Assembly in 1848.)

84   Conservative (against free trade).

85   Favouring British agriculture even if foreign imports could be cheaper.

GRAVES (*R., aside to Sir Harry*). You are going too far.

LESTER. I am ambitious—very: and, in Miss Julia Hawk, I see a lady so *distinguée* in manner and appearance, that, as my wife, she would not only adorn any position I might attain, but assist me onwards by her influence.

HAWK. I understand. A wife is easily found; but to find a wife for a Minister, or an Ambassador, is not quite so easy. I see, Sir Harry, you are a man of capacity.

LESTER (*with emphasis*). Sir, I am a Protectionist!

HAWK. Um! I don't know what to say to that speculation. I doubt whether it will pay a dividend. However—to our affairs.

GRAVES. Should they not be left to the lawyers?

LESTER. No, no! let us settle amicably. Don't let the lawyers have anything to do with the affair.

HAWK. No—damn the lawyers—they confuse everything.

LESTER. Frankly then, my fortune is limited to the Lester estates, which have been in our family for a century, and will, I trust never quit it.

HAWK. Perhaps, now-a-days, hard cash would be better; it is always at hand. However, a slice of the good fat earth is not to be despised: what's its extent?

LESTER. Three thousand acres—Lester Hall—some houses in Dublin—a salt-marsh of considerable extent, which might be worked by a company, and give enormous dividends.

HAWK (*rising, and shaking his hand*). A salt-marsh? My dear sir, why were we not sooner acquainted? We can form a company for the working of the Lester salt. I see a million of money there.

LESTER. I am sure of it—the only difficulty is to get it.

HAWK. But you have debts, of course? Is it mortgaged?

GRAVES. You would have a poor opinion of Sir Harry, if he had not a few debts.

LESTER. Frankness is the order of the day. I will confess that there is a mortgage of about two thousand pounds on it.

HAWK (*aside*). Innocent youth! Only two thousand pounds, when he might have got—(*Aloud*) Sir Harry, you shall be my son-in-law. I feel proud of such a man's belonging to me. You don't know the fortune that awaits you.

LESTER (*to Graves*). I say—he's too easy. That looks suspicious.

GRAVES. Pooh! He is dazzled with the salt-marsh. You can always lure him with a speculation.

HAWK (*aside*). The Lester salt company. The shares will go like wildfire—I'm a made man! (*Aloud*) We shall get on together I foresee.

LESTER. And now, Mr. Hawk, perhaps, you will allow me to ask—

HAWK. What is the dowry I give my daughter? I am not so rich as it is generally imagined, and I cannot put down now more than twenty thousand pounds; but Julia is our only child, and will inherit all.

LESTER. Twenty thousand pounds!

HAWK. You expected more? But that is the last farthing I can afford. On my honour! You shall receive the interest until we can find a safe and profitable investment—for I can promise you we shall not live idle. You wish to distinguish yourself?

LESTER. I do.

HAWK. I sympathize with you. Together, we shall be able to make superb speculations.

LESTER. We shall—I feel we shall succeed.

HAWK (*aside*). I begin to feel uncomfortable—he is too easy.

LESTER (*aside*). He has plunged into my salt-marsh, head foremost.

HAWK (*aside*). He accepts the interest.

GRAVES *(aside to Lester)*. Are you satisfied?

LESTER. Well, I don't see the money to pay my debts with, just yet.

GRAVES. Wait a bit. *(Aloud)* My friend, Sir Harry, is too frank a man to hide from you that he has a few debts.

HAWK. Debts! who has not? How much?—a couple of thousand?

GRAVES. About that.

LESTER. More or less.

HAWK. Mere nothings!

LESTER. A bagatelle![86]

HAWK. It will be the subject of a little comedy between you and your wife—but I will pay them—*(aside)* with shares in the salt-marsh! *(Aloud)* As you say, a mere bagatelle. So all's settled, I think.

LESTER. All's settled—all's settled—and without the lawyers.

HAWK *(aside)*. I'm saved *(rising)*.

LESTER *(aside)*. My debts are paid—I'm a rich man.

THOMAS *(enter L. 1 E.—aside to Hawk)*. Mr. Grossmark wishes to speak to you, sir—he says it is a very important affair.

HAWK *(aside)*. What the devil can he want? *(Aloud)* My dear Sir Harry, you'll stay and dine with us, I hope—and you too, Graves?

(They bow).

That's right! Well, then, I'll ask you to step upstairs and see my pictures, while I see a gentleman who has just called upon me.

(Graves goes to R.D.).

LESTER. Stand on no ceremony, I beg. Come, Graves—I adore pictures! *(Aside)* All right, eh?

GRAVES *(aside)*. I told you it would be.

(Exeunt Graves and Lester, U.E.R.).

HAWK. Show up Mr. Grossmark.

(Exit Thomas, L.).

Well, at last I think that fortune is in my hand. Julia's happiness—our happiness—everybody's happiness—lies in that salt-marsh. What a prospectus I will issue!

GROSSMARK *(enter L.)*. Good morning, Mr. Hawk! I am come about those bills which I gave you this morning, drawn on Bradshaw of Dublin.[87] They are waste-paper almost, as I told you at the time.

HAWK *(R.)*. I know you did.

GROSSMARK. I'll give you one hundred and fifty pounds for them.

HAWK. That's too much to be enough. If you offer one hundred and fifty pounds for them, they must be worth infinitely more—good day! *(Goes up to desk)*.

GROSSMARK. Two hundred pounds.

HAWK. Thank you!

GROSSMARK. Three hundred pounds.

HAWK. Much obliged!

GROSSMARK. Four hundred pounds.

---

86   Trifle.

87   Bills of exchange drawn against Bradshaw (Lester).

HAWK. Deal openly with me. What do you want them for?

GROSSMARK. Bradshaw has insulted me, and I will have vengeance—I can put him in prison.

HAWK. Four hundred pounds' worth of vengeance? No, my boy—you can't stand such expensive luxuries. Bradshaw has dropped into a fortune, and the two thousand five hundred pounds of acceptances are worth two thousand five hundred pounds. Tell me the truth, and let's share.

GROSSMARK. Well, we will share. Bradshaw is about to marry the daughter of some bamboozled nabob,[88] who gives her an immense fortune.

HAWK. Where does Bradshaw live?

GROSSMARK. Um! that's not easy to say. He has no fixed residence. In London, all his furniture is in the name a friend of his—a baronet; but his family lives near Dublin. When I say "family," I mean he has an aunt living there, who is struggling to exist on fifty pounds a-year, and whom he christens—Lady Balbriggan,[89] in delicate health, with three thousand a-year.

HAWK. I'll find him out. Well, that's settled—we share and share alike.

GROSSMARK. Agreed—good day! (Aside) Well, I've only got half! I tried to do him—I threw him a bit of meat, but the hawk wouldn't pounce (exit L.).

HAWK. That's twelve hundred pounds nicely fallen in! We shall be able to do things in style at Julia's wedding!

(Enter Thomas, L.)

—Beg Sir Harry Lester to step this way.

(Exit Thomas, R.U.E.)

—I certainly am in luck today! How the aspect of affairs changes.

(Enter Sir Harry and Thomas, R.U.E.)

LESTER (R.). Will you allow me to send your servant with a letter?

HAWK. By all means. Thomas, take the letter.

LESTER (giving him a letter and half-a-crown). There's something for your trouble.

THOMAS (aside). Money begins to circulate again. Welcome, little stranger! (Exit L.).

LESTER. You wished to speak with me?

HAWK. Yes. I assume the family privilege at once with you. Sit down a moment. I want to ask you something about a gentleman whose property lies near Dublin. You know most of the people there, I suppose?

LESTER. All. At any rate, my aunt does.

HAWK. You have an aunt there?

LESTER. Yes, dear old lady—I'm her only nephew; and her health is very delicate.

HAWK. Eh! Health delicate?

LESTER. She has a nice property there of three thousand a-year.

HAWK (aside). The very sum.

LESTER. So you see, I have every reason to keep well with the Lady—

HAWK (vehemently and rising). Balbriggan.

LESTER. You know her name?

HAWK. And yours.

LESTER. The devil!

---

88 Either a wealthy foreigner or a Briton who made a fortune in India.

89 A coastal town north of Dublin.

HAWK. You are over head and ears in debt; your furniture is made over to a friend—your aunt has fifty pounds a-year. Grossmark has acceptances[90] of yours, amounting to two thousand five hundred pounds;—you are Mr. Bradshaw, and I am a bamboozled Nabob!

LESTER (stretching himself in the chair). Egad! You know as much as I do.

HAWK. Sir Harry, your conduct is more than equivocal.

LESTER. In what?—did I not tell you I had debts?

HAWK. Everyone has debts, but where is your property?

LESTER. In Ireland.

HAWK. Of what does it consist?

LESTER. Principally of bogs.

HAWK. And is worth—

LESTER. About three thousand pounds.

HAWK. And is mortgaged for—

LESTER. Five.

HAWK. You had talent to do that?

LESTER. Yes.

HAWK. And your salt-marsh?

LESTER. Is on the coast.

HAWK. What, the sea, I presume?

LESTER. Well, people were malicious enough to say so, when I wanted to borrow money on it.

HAWK. Borrow money on the sea?—No—that surpasses even my faculty! Sir Harry, your morals seem to me—(sits).

LESTER. Well, sir.

HAWK. Somewhat lax.

LESTER. Mr. Hawk? (Rising, calming himself) We will not quarrel (sits).

HAWK. Are you aware, sir, that I have in my possession, acceptances of yours amounting to two thousand five hundred pounds.

LESTER (starts up). What! to Grossmark's order.

HAWK. Exactly.

LESTER. And they came into your possession this morning?

HAWK. This morning.

LESTER. In exchange for shares of no value.

HAWK (starts up). Sir Harry!

LESTER. And Grossmark accorded you a delay of three months for it.

HAWK. Who told you so?

LESTER. Who? Grossmark himself, a little while ago, when I wanted to arrange with him.

HAWK. The devil!

LESTER. Oho, Mr. Hawk! You give ten thousand pounds to your daughter on the verge of ruin. Between you and me, it looks very much as if you wished to entrap a son-in-law.

HAWK. Sir Harry!

LESTER. You take advantage of my inexperience.

HAWK. The inexperience of a man who raises money on Irish bogs, and borrows money on the sea! But let me be calm. At least, do not divulge the fact of the marriage being broken off.

---

90   Bills of exchange.

LESTER. I'll swear—except, however, to Grossmark; to whom I have already written.

HAWK. Written to Grossmark!

LESTER. This moment. You saw the letter. To set his mind at rest.

HAWK. And you told him the name of your father-in-law?

LESTER. Yes. I believed you were Croesus.[91]

HAWK. All's lost! In half an hour, the whole Stock Exchange will know it. I'm undone! I must write to him at once.

(Enter Julia and Prospectus, R.).

JULIA *(R.).* Here's papa.

HAWK *(C.).* Ah, Prospectus? It's you, is it? Come to dinner?

PROSPECTUS *(R.C.).* Dinner be damned!

HAWK *(aside).* He knows all—he's in a fury.

PROSPECTUS. This, then, is your son-in-law? *(Bowing)* A superb marriage indeed!

HAWK. My dear Prospectus, the marriage is broken off.

(Sir Harry bows in confusion).

JULIA. Oh, how delightful *(exit R.D.).*

PROSPECTUS. And so it was only another scene of comedy you played this morning to extort money from me; but the affair is blown upon. The whole Stock Exchange echoes it.

HAWK. Echoes what?

PROSPECTUS. That you have your son-in-law's bills in your pocket-book; and Grossmark tells me that all your creditors are assembling at Hardcore's house, to come down upon you, tomorrow, as a single man.[92]

HAWK. Tomorrow! Have I till tomorrow to turn round? Why, I've hours before me, then: and the world itself only wants twenty-four to turn round in.

PROSPECTUS. There is a fixed determination to rid 'Change of all the speculative humbugs who now infest it.

HAWK. The fools! Do they want to convert 'Change into a desert! And yet to be driven from the scene of my operations, the field of my glory!—ruin, shame, want!

LESTER *(L.).* Believe me, my dear Hawk, that I am sincerely sorry for having been instrumental—

HAWK *(C. looking him in the face).* You! *(Aside to him)* You have hastened my fall—will you assist me to rise?

LESTER. On what conditions?

HAWK. Oh! the easiest. I see consent in your eyes. *(Walks across the stage)* The idea is bold, novel, and triumphant! They force me to it—be it on their own heads. My plan is here *(striking his forehead)* and tomorrow Hawk shall once more flutter over 'Change! *(Takes stage R. and L.).*

PROSPECTUS. What does he say?

HAWK. Tomorrow all my debts shall be paid; and the house of Hawk and Co. shall deal with thousands—I shall be the Napoleon of Finance![93]

PROSPECTUS *(R.).* But your troops?

---

91   Proverbial personification of wealth, after the excessively wealthy King of Lydia in the sixth century BCE.

92   They will confront him *en masse* and force him into debtors' prison.

93   Supreme through ruthless ambition.

HAWK *(L.)*. Did I not tell you I should pay? What can be said to a man of business who hands you a cheque? My dear Prospectus, a moment ago the battle was lost, and now the battle is gained. Dinner is on the table—come! Tomorrow, I shall have the control of thousands.

PROSPECTUS. The control of thousands! Oh! in that case, I will dine with pleasure. *(Aside)* What a man it is!

HAWK *(aside, as they approach the door)*. Tomorrow, I have the control of thousands, or I sleep in the wet sheets of the Thames![94]

(Exeunt, R.).

Act III

Same as Act I. Enter Thomas, C.D., making signs to Dimity and Mrs. Mason, Thomas steps forward, and looks through keyhole, R.D.; Thomas, R.—Mrs. Dimity and Mrs. Mason, L.

MRS. MASON. They are not going to hide their situation from us, are they?

DIMITY. Oh, I know that master is to be arrested today. He must settle my wages first.

THOMAS *(at keyhole)*. I hear nothing; they speak so low—yes, I think I hear.

(The door opens, and Hawk appears; Thomas goes to table, R., pretending to put the things to rights).

HAWK *(crosses to L.C.)*. Do not disturb yourself.

THOMAS *(R.)*. I—I—I was arranging—

HAWK. Were you?

(Dimity is going off, C.).

Pray stay where you are, Mrs. Dimity; and you too, Thomas. Why did you not come in? We could have talked over my affairs.

THOMAS. Master is pleased to be funny.

HAWK. Away with you all; and remember that henceforth I am visible to all the world. Be neither insolent nor humble to whoever calls. You will only receive paid creditors for the future.

THOMAS. Oh!

HAWK. Now go.

(Exeunt Thomas, Dimity, and Mrs. Mason, C.D. and R.).

Here come my wife and daughter. In such circumstances women spoil all; they've what they call nerves.

(Enter Mrs. Hawk, Julia, and Noble, L.D.).

MRS. HAWK. My dear, you thought that the marriage of Julia was to consolidate your credit, and calm your creditors; whereas the events of yesterday have only placed you at their mercy.

HAWK. You think so? Well, you are altogether deceived. My dear Noble, may I ask what brings you here? *(Aside)* And yet, if with that I could get a delay of a month—if by some splendid turn I could bring up the value of the shares—No! The money of these children would weigh upon my heart—my

---

94   Commit suicide by drowning. Suicide is the frequent fate of failed financiers, whether real (John Sadleir) or fictional (Melmotte in Trollope's novel *The Way We Live Now* and Murdle in Dickens's *Little Dorrit*). Nevertheless, all these examples post-date *The Game of Speculation*.

calculations would be confused—the figures would be blurred through the tears in my eyes. 'Tis easy enough to play ducks and drakes with the money of shareholders—but one's children's!—(*Aloud*) Frederick, you shall have my daughter.

NOBLE. Julia mine?

(*Julia crosses to L.C.*).

HAWK. As soon as she has got ten thousand pounds.

JULIA. Oh, papa!

NOBLE. Oh, sir, when will that be?

HAWK. Why, in a month—perhaps sooner.

ALL. What?

HAWK. Yes, with good brains and a little money.

(*Noble offers notes*).

Pooh, pooh! put it into your pocket. Give my daughter your arm, and take her away—I must be alone.

(*Julia and Noble cross to L.*).

MRS. HAWK (*going L.—aside*). What plan has he now? But I shall know. (*Aloud*) Come, Julia.

(*Exeunt Mrs. Hawk, Julia, and Noble, at door, L.*).

HAWK. I resisted. It was a good impulse: and yet, perhaps I was wrong to follow it. Those *good impulses* lead one into such monstrous follies! However, if I do fall, I'll manage that little capital for the youngsters. I'll speculate with it! Oh! they shall be rich—rich! What an excellent couple they will make! (*Going towards door, R.*) Now to commence their fortune! Sir Harry is there, waiting for me. I do believe he is sleeping! Sir Harry!—Bradshaw!

LESTER (*enter, R.D. as if just awakened*). Eh, who calls?

HAWK (*L.*). Oh, don't be alarmed! I thought Bradshaw was the best cold pig[95] for you—it has completely awakened you. The wine hasn't done you any harm?

LESTER. Wine? Lord! I refresh my intellects with wine as a gardener does his flowers with water.

HAWK. Yesterday we were interrupted in our conversation.

LESTER. I remember perfectly well. We had come to a distinct understanding that our respective houses could no longer keep their engagements. You've the misfortune to be my creditor. I have the happiness to be your debtor for two thousand five hundred pounds, seven shillings, and threepence.

HAWK. I see your brain is not heavy.

LESTER. There is nothing heavy about me—neither purse nor conscience. Yet, who can reproach me? In devouring my own fortune, I have encouraged commerce. It is a mistake to call us gentlemen useless. We idlers? Not a bit of it! We animate the circulation of money!

HAWK. By the money of the circulation. Ah! I see you have all your intelligence.

LESTER. I have nothing, else.

HAWK. Never mind—intellect is our mint. But to the point. Do you feel within you a capacity of sustaining yourself in patent leather boots and canary-coloured gloves? Or do you begin to perceive the Bench[96] in perspective?

LESTER. Why, you are breaking into my conscience like a burglar! What do you want?

HAWK. I want to save you, by launching you upon the sea of speculation.

---

95   Wake-up call, as in receiving a dash of cold water.

96   Judge's seat; in other words a trial.

LESTER. I'm ready.

HAWK. You must begin by personating the man who is to compromise himself for me.

LESTER. I understand—a man of straw. Unfortunately, straw burns.

HAWK. You must be incombustible!

LESTER. Oh! If you insure me, I'm prepared.

HAWK. Assist me in the desperate situation in which I am now placed, and I will return you the two thousand five hundred pounds, seven shillings, and threepence, that you owe me. To accomplish it, you only require a little address.[97]

LESTER. What! with the pistol?

HAWK. There's nobody to be killed—on the contrary, somebody to be resuscitated.

LESTER. That will never do! My dear Hawk, melodramatic situations in real life are no longer taken in good part. There is a very ugly interference of the Police, ever since the abolition of feudal privileges; and, you see, one cannot thrash the Police now—they are gross and muscular.

HAWK. But the Bench?

LESTER. Um! Well, certainly, I don't like the Bench. However, let's hear your plan: all depends on that— because, as yet, my honour is intact; and—and—

HAWK. I understand. You consider it to be too good an investment to be lightly placed. So do I. I have as much need of it as you. It's only a Stock Exchange hoax I propose.

LESTER. Well, but what is it?

HAWK (giving paper). Here are your written instructions. You will be my partner, returned from the Indies.[98]

LESTER. Very well.

HAWK. Go to Long Acre[99]—buy a travelling carriage—get the horses put to it—and drive here, in a fur pelisse[100] and a long pigtail,[101] with your teeth chattering like a man who looks upon our summer as a winter. I shall be ready to receive you—to introduce you. You will have interviews with my creditors, not one of whom knows Sparrow; and you will make them suspend operations.

LESTER. Long?

HAWK. I only want two days—two days, to make the purchases Grossmark and I have arranged—two days, to send the shares up.

LESTER. And I shall cease to play the part, as soon as you have realised the two thousand five hundred pounds, seven shillings, and threepence, that I owe you?

HAWK. Precisely! But someone comes—it's my wife.

MRS. HAWK (enter L.). Here are some letters, dear, to be answered.

HAWK. At once. Good bye, my dear Sir Harry! (Aside) Not a word to my wife—she won't understand the subject, and might compromise us. (Aloud) Good bye! all luck attend you!—and forget nothing.

LESTER. Never fear!

(Exit Hawk, R. Sir Harry is going. Mrs. Hawk detains him).

MRS. HAWK (L.). I beg your pardon, Sir Harry.

---

97 Preparation and/or adornment.

98 This is tantalizingly vague: the East Indies (India) is specified later, though the West Indies (Caribbean) is also warm. Proverbially, the Indies connotes any region where huge fortunes can be made.

99 A street near Covent Garden, a centre for cabinet-makers and custom carriage-builders.

100 Fur-lined cloak or cape.

101 Either to make him seem old-fashioned or Chinese.

LESTER *(R.)*. Pray excuse me, madam, but I'm in a hurry.

MRS. HAWK. You will not stir a step!

LESTER. But you do not know—

MRS. HAWK. I know all.

LESTER. Eh!

MRS. HAWK. You and my husband have been plotting schemes that will do very well in a comedy. I have employed one that is still older, and, as I think, better. I tell you I know all.

LESTER. She was listening!

MRS. HAWK. The part my husband wishes you to play is a disgraceful one—give it up.

LESTER. But, my dear madam—

MRS. HAWK. Oh! I know to whom I am speaking. It is only a few hours I have had the pleasure of knowing you; and yet I do know you.

LESTER *(R.)*. Indeed, I do not know what opinion you may have of me.

MRS. HAWK. One day was sufficient for me to judge you; and while my husband was seeking, perhaps, for the amount of folly in your breast, which he might turn to his purpose, I discerned that your heart was in the right place, and concealed honourable feelings which might save you.

LESTER. Save me? Oh! My dear madam!

MRS. HAWK *(L.)*. Yes, sir, save you—you and my husband—you are going to ruin each other. Do not you understand that debts dishonour no one, when they are avowed? We can but work to pay them. You have before you your whole life; and you have too much intelligence, if not too much heart, to wish to disgrace that life forever, by a scheme which justice would repudiate, if not punish.

LESTER. Why, the truth is, madam, I never should have thought of playing such a dangerous game, if your husband had not my bills.

MRS. HAWK. He shall return them to you, sir; I will undertake to see it done.

LESTER. But, my dear madam, I cannot pay them.

MRS. HAWK. We will be satisfied with your word, and you will pay them when you have honourably made your fortune.

LESTER. Honourably! I'm afraid that will be rather long.

MRS. HAWK. We will have patience. Now, Sir Harry, go—seek my husband, and persuade him to renounce this scheme, which you can do more easily, now that he will no longer have your assistance.

LESTER. I am rather afraid of seeing him. I should prefer writing.

MRS. HAWK *(pointing to the room from which she entered)*. There—in that room you will find writing materials. Remain there until I come to take your letter—I will give it to him myself.

LESTER. I obey you, madam. *(Crosses to L.)* After all, it appears that I am better than I thought I was. It is to you, madam, that I am indebted for the knowledge *(kissing her hand with respect)*—I shall never forget it *(exit L.)*.

MRS. HAWK. I have succeeded. Oh, that I may now succeed with my husband!

THOMAS *(enter C.)*. Oh, ma'am, here they are all!

MRS. HAWK. Who?

THOMAS. The creditors!

MRS. HAWK. Already!

THOMAS. There are such a number, ma'am!

MRS. HAWK. Ask them to walk in. I'll go and tell my husband.

(Thomas opens the centre door. Enter Grossmark, Hardcore, and Earthworm, C. from L., talking offstage, as if with other creditors).

HARDCORE. Well, gentlemen, we are quite decided—are we not?

ALL. Yes, yes.

GROSSMARK *(C.)*. We will have no more dust thrown in our eyes.

HARDCORE. Believe in no more promises; be moved by no more prayers and supplications!

GROSSMARK. Believe no more lies.

HARDCORE. Take no more shares!

GROSSMARK. Read no more prospectuses!

EARTHWORM *(R.)*. No more of those installments *on account*,[102] by means of which he always, somehow, dipped his hand deeper in our pockets!

HARDCORE. We will be paid.

ALL. We will.

HAWK *(enter R.)*. So, gentlemen, you are determined?

HARDCORE *(L.)*. Unless you pay everything today—

HAWK. Today?

GROSSMARK *(C.L.)*. This very day!

HAWK *(sitting in chair, R.)*. My dear fellows, do you think that I am the Bank of England? Or do you think I have discovered a mine in California?

EARTHWORM *(coaxingly)*. Is it possible you have nothing to offer us—not an installment?

HAWK. Absolutely nothing.—If you like, incarcerate me at once, but take care who pays the cab, for my assets will not reimburse him.

HARDCORE. Don't be uneasy. I'll pay for it, and add it to the rest of my bad debts.

HAWK. Thank you; you're a real friend. And you are all quite decided, are you?

ALL. We are.

HAWK. You are only three—but the others?

EARTHWORM. We represent all the rest.

HAWK. You are all agreed?

ALL. Yes, all—all.

HAWK. Touching unanimity! *(Taking out his watch)* Two o'clock. *(Aside)* Sir Harry has had time enough—he must be en route. *(Aloud)* Upon my life, gentlemen, I must confess that you are devilish clever fellows, and have chosen well your time.

GROSSMARK. What does that mean?

HAWK. For several months—I may say, years—you have allowed yourselves to be played with, in a foolish, idiotic manner! Yes, played with—gulled by stories that would not take in a child—gulled, in fact, by your own cupidity. And this is the day you select to show how implacable you can be. Ha, ha! Egad, it is very amusing! Now, then, let's be off. Send for the cab—I'm ready!

HARDCORE. But, my dear sir—

GROSSMARK. He laughs—I begin to suspect something.

EARTHWORM. There is something in it, gentlemen—I am sure there is something! That manner of his conceals something!

GROSSMARK. Will you explain yourself?

HARDCORE. All we desire to know is—

EARTHWORM. Mr. Affable Hawk, there is something hid—tell us what it is?

HAWK. No, there is nothing—at least, nothing that I shall tell you. I choose to be incarcerated—I shall rather like the change. Besides, I shall be a gainer by it.

---

102 On credit.

GROSSMARK. What do you mean?

HAWK. I shall rather like to see your physiognomies tomorrow—or this evening—when you hear of his return.

HARDCORE. His return?

GROSSMARK. Whose return ?

EARTHWORM. Oh, I knew there was something in it! Do tell us, whose return?

HAWK. The return of—of nobody! Let's go—send for a cab!

HARDCORE (with a change of tone). But my dear Mr. Hawk! if you are awaiting some assistance—

GROSSMARK. If you have any hope—

EARTHWORM. If you have inherited anything—

HARDCORE. If somebody is dead—

GROSSMARK. Oh, explain!

EARTHWORM. Tell us—do!

HAWK. Take care, take care, gentlemen!—you are yielding, you are yielding—you know you are!—and if I chose to give myself the trouble, I could gull you again—easily, pleasantly, affably, as is my manner. No!—play your parts as creditors!—forget the past—forget all the brilliant speculations I have helped you to—forget all the sums I helped you to gain, before the sudden departure of my worthy, excellent Sparrow!

HARDCORE. His worthy and excellent Sparrow!

EARTHWORM. I have it! Oh! If—yes! Sparrow has returned!

HAWK. Yes! forget all the brilliant past, and call a cab!

EARTHWORM. Hawk, look me in the face—you are expecting Sparrow!

HAWK (hesitating). No—no!

EARTHWORM (as if inspired). Gentlemen, I know it!—he's expecting Sparrow!—Sparrow has returned!

HARDCORE. Can it be possible?

GROSSMARK. Speak!

ALL. Speak—speak!

HAWK (pretending confusion). No, no! I cannot say that I—certainly, it's quite possible that some day or other—in fact, it's very probable that he will return from the Indies, with an enormous fortune. (With assurance) But I give you my word of honour, that I do not expect Sparrow today.

EARTHWORM. Then it's tomorrow! Gentlemen, he expects Sparrow tomorrow! I am sure of it—I can read it in the wrinkles about his mouth!

HARDCORE (in a low tone to the others). Unless it is another dodge of his, to gain time.

GROSSMARK. Do you think so?

HARDCORE. It is not impossible!

EARTHWORM (aloud). Gentlemen, it must be so!—he is laughing at us! I'll fetch a cab myself!

HAWK (aside). The devil! (Aloud) Well, gentlemen, shall we go?

HARDCORE. Yes, at once!

(Noise of a carriage is heard—then a loud knock at the street door).

HAWK (aside). At last! (Aloud) Heavens! (Places his hand upon his heart, and sinks into chair).

HARDCORE (rushing to window, L.). A carriage!

GROSSMARK (after him, L.). A post chaise![103]

---

103 A closed carriage drawn by four horses.

EARTHWORM (*after him, R.*). Gentlemen, it is a post chaise, with the luggage of a traveller behind it!

HAWK (*aside*). Sir Harry is just in time!

HARDCORE. Look—it is covered with dust!

EARTHWORM. And is splashed to the roof! It must have come from the Indies, to be splashed like that! He's come overland!

HAWK (*blandly*). My dear Earthworm, you do not know what you say—people do not come from India by land.

HARDCORE. Come and see, Hawk—do look at that man descending from the post chaise!

GROSSMARK. Enveloped in a fur pelisse—come!

HAWK. No—excuse me!—the joy—the emotion—I—

EARTHWORM. He carries a box under his arm—oh, such a large box! Gentlemen, it's Sparrow! I know him by that box, and the pigtail! Gentlemen, it's Sparrow! I know him by his tail!

HAWK (*rising, R.*). Concealment is useless—I expected Sparrow!

HARDCORE. Who comes back from Calcutta?

HAWK. With an incalculable fortune.

EARTHWORM. Did I not say so?

(*They all go and shake hands with Hawk*).

HAWK. Oh! gentlemen, friends, brothers!

MRS. HAWK (*enters from R.C.*). My dear, such news!

HAWK (*aside*). My wife! The devil! I thought she was gone out. She'll ruin everything.

MRS. HAWK. Oh! You do not know the news!

HAWK. No. Yes—that is, I—

MRS. HAWK. Sparrow has returned!

HAWK. What do you say? (*Aside*) Hollo!—does she?—

MRS. HAWK. I have seen him—I have spoken to him; it was I who received him at the door.

HAWK (*aside*). Sir Harry has converted her. What a man! (*Aside to her*) Bravo!—my dear! You do it capitally!

MRS. HAWK. I tell you it is Sparrow—he is there!

HAWK (*aside*). Silence! (*Aloud*) I must go and welcome him!

MRS. HAWK. No—wait a bit!—wait a bit! Poor Sparrow had counted too much upon his strength. Scarcely had he entered the parlour, when the fatigue and the exertion produced a nervous crisis.

HAWK. Indeed! (*Aside*) How well she does it.

EARTHWORM (*L.C.*). Poor Mr. Sparrow! Poor Mr. Sparrow!

MRS. HAWK. He begged me to see you, and to carry back to him your forgiveness. He says he cannot meet you face to face until he has wiped out the past.

HARDCORE (*L.*). How sublime!

GROSSMARK (*L.C*). What an excellent man!

EARTHWORM. It brings tears into my eyes! Gentlemen, you see the tears!

HAWK (*aside*). Upon my life, I had no conception of what a wife I had! (*Putting his arm round her waist*) My dear Caroline! Excuse me, gentlemen. (*Kisses her*) Bravo!—all goes on capitally. You could not do it better.

MRS. HAWK. How lucky; and how much better, than what you contemplated.

HAWK. It is indeed! It is ten times as plausible. (*Aloud*) Return to Sparrow, my dear;—and you, gentlemen, be kind enough to pass into my study, where we will settle our little accounts.

(Exit Mrs. Hawk, C.).

HARDCORE. At your service, my excellent friend *(crosses to R.)*.

GROSSMARK. At your service, our best of friends *(crosses to R.)*.

EARTHWORM. If there is one man that I admire and respect above all others, it is you, Mr. Hawk *(crosses to R.)*.

HAWK. And yet they said I was a humbug!

HARDCORE *(at door)*. You!—a giant in business.

GROSSMARK *(at door, R.)*. You!—the prince of speculators, a man capable of gaining a million, the moment he has a thousand!

EARTHWORM *(R.)*. Dear friend!—excellent, Mr. Hawk!—we will wait as long as ever you please.

ALL. Certainly! Any time that Mr. Hawk likes.

HAWK. Gentlemen, I thank you as much as if you had said that this morning—meanwhile, step into my study.

(Exit Earthworm).

(Beckoning Hardcore) In one hour I'll sell all your shares.

HARDCORE. Good! *(Exit R.D.)*.

HAWK *(beckons Grossmark)*. Stop! Now we are close. There is not a moment to be lost. There was a fall yesterday, and another this morning, in the shares of the Great Indian Emeralds. Rush to the Stock Exchange—buy up as many as you can—two hundred—three hundred—four hundred! Hardcore, alone, will sell you more than half.

GROSSMARK *(R.)*. But on what terms?—and how will you cover it?

HAWK *(L.)*. Cover it! Pshaw! Bring me the shares today, and I pay you tomorrow.

GROSSMARK. Tomorrow!

HAWK *(aside)*. Tomorrow the rise will have taken place.

GROSSMARK. It is quite clear that in the situation in which you are, you are buying for Sparrow.

HAWK. You think so?

GROSSMARK. He must have given you the orders in the letter which announced his return.

HAWK. Well, it is possible. Ah, Grossmark, you're a knowing dog!—there is nothing escapes you. We shall yet have some excellent business together. Before the year's out, I shall have put ten thousand pounds of commission into your pocket.

GROSSMARK *(overwhelmed)*. Ten thousand pounds!

HAWK. Bull the market[104] with the Tobolsk Mines,[105] and get this letter inserted in the *Times*, and tomorrow we shall clear our twenty per cent. Swift!—away.

GROSSMARK. I fly! Good bye. *(Aside)* To think that I was about to send such a man to the Bench! *(Exit, C.L.)*.

HAWK. Ha, ha, ha! All the steam is on, and away we go! The moment Mahomet had three followers who believed in him, he had won his empire. I have moved the mountain. Thanks to the pretended arrival of Sparrow, I gain at least a week's delay—and a week always means a fortnight in a matter of payment. I buy shares to the tune of ten thousand pounds, in the Emeralds, before Prospectus can get at them—and, when Prospectus wants them, up they go! From today's affair, I see a clear profit of twenty thousand pounds; with seventeen thousand pounds I pay my creditors, and am master of the place *(walks up and down stage)*.

---

104 Force the prices up.

105 Tobolsk, capital of Siberia. The region is rich with metal deposits.

THOMAS (enter C., cross to L.). Oh, sir!

HAWK (R.). What is it, Thomas?

THOMAS. Oh, sir, oh!

HAWK. Well, what is it, I say? Speak.

THOMAS. Old Earthworm offers me five pounds, if I will let him see Mr. Sparrow.

HAWK. Thomas, allow yourself to be bought.

THOMAS. No objection at all, sir—but there's Mr. Hardcore. He wants to buy me—and all the others, they want to buy me. It's very pleasant, but a little puzzling.

HAWK. Oh, sell yourself to all of them! You have my permission. It is the only way I can pay you your wages.

THOMAS. Thank you, sir, I'll certainly do it (going).

HAWK. Let them all see Sparrow. (Aside) Sir Harry will be sure to play his part well. (Aloud) When I say all—all except Grossmark. (Aside) He will recognise Mr. Bradshaw.

THOMAS. I understand, sir. Ah! here's Mr. Noble (exit).

NOBLE (enter L.D.). My dear sir!

HAWK (R.). Well, Noble, what brings you here?

NOBLE. Despair!

HAWK. Despair?

NOBLE. Mr. Sparrow has returned, and I hear that you have become a rich man again.

HAWK. And is that what alarms you?

NOBLE. It is.

HAWK. Upon my word, you are a strange fellow! I reveal to you my ruin, and you are enchanted!—you learn my good fortune, and you are in despair! And yet you wish to be one of my family: why, you are more like an enemy!

NOBLE. It is my love which makes your fortune terrible to me. I fear lest now you should be no longer willing to give me your daughter's hand.

HAWK. Frederick, we men of business do not all place our hearts in our banker's book—our sentiments are not always reckoned up by double entry.[106] You offered me the two thousand pounds which you had: it is not for me to reject you on account of a few thousands—(aside) which I have not.

NOBLE. I breathe again!

HAWK. So much the better, for I have a real affection for you. You are brave, generous, honest—you have touched me here, sir (touching his heart).

(Enter Grossmark and Prospectus, C.D.).

HAWK (to Grossmark, without seeing Prospectus). Well?

GROSSMARK (R., with confusion). The business is terminated.

HAWK (R.C., gaily). Bravo!

PROSPECTUS (C., to Hawk). Good day, old fellow!

HAWK (aside). Prospectus!

PROSPECTUS. So, you have been buying before me, have you? I shall be forced to pay dearer! Never mind! You have played your game well. Let me pay my compliments to the Napoleon of Finance! Ha, ha, ha!

HAWK (troubled). What does this mean?

GROSSMARK. It seems Mr. Prospectus does not quite believe in the return of Mr. Sparrow.

---

106 A bookkeeping system with balanced entries for credits and debits.

NOBLE *(L.)*. Oh, Mr. Prospectus!

HAWK. What! he doubts?

PROSPECTUS *(ironically)*. Not at all—no longer! I fancied, indeed, first, that this return of Sparrow was the bold stroke that you told me of yesterday.

HAWK *(aside)*. Fool that I was!

PROSPECTUS. And that, by means of the pretended return of this Sparrow, you intended to buy for a rise tomorrow, though you had not penny today.

HAWK. And you fancied that?

PROSPECTUS. Yes! but when I saw that post chaise at the door—such a perfect model of Indian carriages—I saw at once it was impossible to find its fellow in Long Acre, and all my doubts disappeared. But, Grossmark, why do you not hand Mr. Hawk the scrip![107]

GROSSMARK. The scrip?—but—

HAWK *(aside)*. Audacity alone can save me! *(Aloud)* Yes, the scrip!—come!

GROSSMARK. Stay a moment. If Prospectus should be right—

HAWK *(haughtily)*. Mr. Grossmark!

NOBLE *(L.)*. But, gentlemen, Mr. Sparrow is here! I have seen him—spoken to him.

HAWK *(R.C., to Grossmark)*. Noble has seen him.

GROSSMARK *(R., to Prospectus)*. I have seen him myself.

HAWK. You?

GROSSMARK. Yes, at the window.

PROSPECTUS. Oh, I have not the slightest doubt of it! By the way, in what vessel did Mr. Sparrow come over?

HAWK. What vessel?—why, the—why, the—Oh! it was the *Triton*.

PROSPECTUS. How inaccurate the newspapers are!—they announced it as the *Minnow*.

GROSSMARK. Is it so?

HAWK. No more of this, Mr. Grossmark—the scrip!

GROSSMARK. Allow me one moment. Unless this scrip be covered,[108] I should prefer seeing Mr. Sparrow.

HAWK. You shall not see him, sir! If I were to suffer you to see him now, it would show that I allowed you to doubt my word.

PROSPECTUS. Magnificent!

HAWK. My dear Noble—*(crosses to L.)*—go and see Sparrow—tell him that I have bought the scrip he ordered, and beg him to send me—(with marked emphasis)—two thousand pounds to cover it. *(Aside)* At all events, you bring your own money!

NOBLE. Certainly! *(Exit L.D.)*.

HAWK *(with coldness)*. Does that satisfy you, Mr. Grossmark?

GROSSMARK. Oh! Doubtless!—doubtless! *(To Prospectus)* I say, he must have come back.

PROSPECTUS. Yes, when you have got your two thousand pounds.

HAWK. Prospectus, I should be justified in calling you to account for so insulting a doubt; but I am still your debtor.

PROSPECTUS. Oh!—don't mention it—for you must certainly have in your spacious cash-box the means of paying it; and then your scrip in the Indian Emeralds, will bring you a fortune.

---

107 Certificate issued in lieu of money.
108 Secured by real property or cash.

HAWK. I understand your anger. *(To Grossmark)* You see where the shoe pinches *(crosses to R.C.)*.

PROSPECTUS *(L.C.)*. The shoe will no longer pinch me, when I see Sparrow's money.

(Enter Earthworm and Hardcore C.).

HARDCORE *(L.C.)*. Oh, my dear friend!

EARTHWORM *(C.)*. Excellent Mr. Hawk!

HARDCORE. What an excellent man that Mr. Sparrow is!

HAWK *(R.C. aside)*. Good!

EARTHWORM. What probity—what generosity.

HAWK *(aside)*. Better and better!

HARDCORE. What greatness of soul!

HAWK *(aside)*. Go on!

PROSPECTUS. Have you seen him?

EARTHWORM. And spoken to him.

HARDCORE. And been paid by him.

ALL. Paid!

(Grossmark crosses to L.C.).

HAWK. Eh! What do you say?—paid?

HARDCORE. Entirely, five hundred pounds in two bills.

HAWK *(R., aside)*. Oh! I understand.

HARDCORE. And eight hundred pounds in notes.

HAWK. Notes?

HARDCORE. Bank of England notes!

HAWK. Now, I do not understand. If they had been Bank of Elegance, it would have been clearer. Oh!—I see. Noble must have given it out of his money. Well!—he'll bring so much less to Grossmark, that's all.

EARTHWORM *(C.)*. And me too—me, who would willingly have consented to a discount, a slight discount—I have received every farthing!

HAWK. In bills also?

EARTHWORM. In excellent bills of fifteen hundred pounds!

HAWK *(aside)*. What a magnificent fellow that Sir Harry is!

EARTHWORM. And the other five hundred pounds—

PROSPECTUS. Well, the other five hundred pounds?

EARTHWORM. In ready money—here it is *(shows notes)*.

HAWK. The devil! Noble will only bring back seven hundred pounds?

HARDCORE. And, at the present moment, he is paying all the creditors.

HAWK. In the same way?

EARTHWORM. Yes, by bills and ready money.

HAWK *(aside)*. Ah! it's quite clear, Noble won't bring a penny to Grossmark.

NOBLE *(enter L.D.)*. I have executed your commission.

HAWK *(nervous)*. Oh! you have—seen him—you have brought back some money—

NOBLE. Some money, indeed! Mr. Sparrow would not hear of the two thousand pounds covering.

HAWK *(aside)*. I understand!

NOBLE. He wrote a cheque[109] for the whole amount.

---

109 A negotiable instrument drawn against a bank account.

HAWK (*rushing across to L.*). Hey! what the devil's that!

(*Earthworm, Grossmark, and Hardcore cross to Noble*).

NOBLE. A cheque for ten thousand pounds.

GROSSMARK (*R.*). Ten thousand pounds!

PROSPECTUS. It is true then (*runs off, C.D. and L.*).

HAWK (*overcome*). A cheque for ten thousand pounds! I have it!—I see it!—I touch it! Ten thousand pounds!—and where did you get that?

NOBLE. Why, he gave it me.

HAWK. He! Who?

NOBLE. Why, Sparrow.

HAWK. Sparrow! What Sparrow? Cock Sparrow![110]

HARDCORE (*R.*). The Sparrow that's come back from India!

HAWK. What India?

EARTHWORM (*R.*). And who's paying all your debts.

HAWK. Oh! I am going mad—I'm going mad! Am I, Hawk, to be the victim of such Sparrows as that?

PROSPECTUS (*re-enter down C.*). There they are all, and all paid! It was quite true!

HAWK. All paid?—yes, paid—all paid! Damn it, they're all paid! I see fire!—the room spins round!—this is fairyland—enchantment—devilry!

(*Enter Mrs. Hawk and Julia, C.; Sir Harry Lester, L.D.*).

MRS. HAWK (*L.C.*). My dear, Mr. Sparrow feels himself equal to seeing you now.

HAWK (*R.C.*). Come here, my dear!—you, Caroline—you, Julia—you, Frederick.

(*Noble crosses to L.C.*).

All friends—you are not making an ass of me, are you?

JULIA (*L.C.*). Why, what's the matter with you, papa?

HAWK. Tell me frankly—(*sees Sir Harry, L.*) Sir Harry, what is this?

LESTER (*L.*). Lucky for me that I followed the counsels of your wife—you would have had two Sparrows at a time, since good luck brings you back the real one.

---

110 As in the nursery rhyme,
      A Little Cock Sparrow
      Sat on a tree,
      Looking as happy
      As happy could be,
      Till a boy came by
      With his bow and arrow:
      Says he, "I will shoot
      The little cock sparrow."

      "His body will make me
      A nice little stew,
      And his giblets will make me
      A little pie too."
      Says the little cock sparrow,
      "I'll be shot if I stay,"
      So he clapped his wings
      And then flew away.

HAWK. Has he, then, *actually* arrived? What! Sparrow—my dear Sparrow?

PROSPECTUS *(L.C.)*. What! you did not know it, then?

HAWK *(drawing himself up)*. I? How the devil should I know it?—Come back? Now I am a *man*! Oh! I always said of him—"Sparrow has a heart—Sparrow has the heart of an eagle! What integrity!—what probity!" *(Embracing his wife and daughter)* Didn't we always bless his name? *(To his wife)* And you, Caroline—you, who bore all adversity so bravely!

MRS. HAWK *(R.C.)*. The delight overpowers me! To think of you rescued, rich!

HAWK *(C.)*. And honest. For my dear Caroline, and you, my children, I will confess to you I was nearly succumbing. I was nearly beaten. A Giant of honesty might have fallen. But all that is over now. *(To Lester)* Sir Harry Lester, I give you up your bills.

LESTER. Oh, sir.

HAWK. And I lend you one thousand pounds.

LESTER. One thousand pounds! But I really do not know when—

HAWK. No ceremony. Accept it.—It's a fancy I have.

LESTER. Then I do accept it.

HAWK. Ah, what a sensation!—how soothing, how noble! I am a creditor! Look at me—I am one of you. *(To creditors)* I, too, am a creditor! Magnificent development of human faculty!

MRS. HAWK. My dear, remember he is waiting for you.

HAWK. That's true! Come, let us go! I have so often held up Sparrow before the eyes of others, that it is high time I should behold him myself. *(To creditors)* Gentlemen, we shall have no more business together, but we remain good friends. If I have dealt too hardly with you, forgive me. Remember, you yourselves first taught me to handle the dangerous weapons with which I have kept you at bay; and at parting, accept one word of advice from a man of the world:—when adversity comes, wait. Don't follow old Weller's advice, and run for a halter at once;[111] but bear up manfully and cheerfully—go round with the world, and bide your time. I dare not, I confess, attempt to justify the unwarrantable means I have adopted to keep my head above water—though we all know that a drowning man will catch at a straw. Still, this I do say—while avoiding my errors, imitate the energy, perseverance, and good humour with which I formed a raft to float on till succour arrived; and if you are honest fellows at heart, and really wish to pay, you will get into smooth water at last, depend on it. Only play your game boldly and steadily, till some good card turns up—then reap the reward of your courage and your toil—burn the cards, and eschew for ever—as I shall do—THE GAME OF SPECULATION!

(Characters form semicircle, R. to L.: Earthworm, Grossmark, Hardcore, Mrs. Hawk, Mr. Hawk, Julia, Noble, Prospectus, and Sir Harry).

---

111 If this is Samuel Weller's father, in Charles Dickens's *Pickwick Papers*, chapter 33, he gives the opposite advice:

"Wot'll be a trial?" inquired Sam.

"To see you married, Sammy—to see you a dilluded wictim, and thinkin' in your innocence that it's all wery capital," replied Mr. Weller. "It's a dreadful trial to a father's feelin's, that 'ere, Sammy—"

Christy's Minstrels (1857–61)

In the early nineteenth century, the terms "minstrel" and "minstrelsy" connoted traditional music, whether from Bardic Ireland or the barrel-organists and ballad singers that busked in the streets. Sacred or secular, the minstrel's fare was pleasing yet "primitive": the resemblance between Hebridean laments, Bavarian carols, and Sandwich Islanders' sagas was not so much a musicological as an ethnological idea of "the folk."[1] Minstrels came from somewhere other than industrialized, imperial Britain; they had stories to tell of distant lands and sensibilities, and told them with distinctive harmonization, idiosyncratic gestures, steps, costumes, and affects. Minstrelsy was localized as "national" music but never contemporary. Minstrelsy could be performed in concerts and entertain modern Britons yet never supplant what they esteemed as "concert music," based upon the composers performed in a circuit of cosmopolitan European capitals.

Blackface minstrelsy, consisting of white performers supposedly imitating African American slaves and freedmen, is an "invented tradition" with a precise point of origin. Singing and dancing soloists with blackened faces were popular on London stages from 1836, when T.D. Rice arrived from America and "jumped Jim Crow."[2] After 1846, troupes such as the Ethiopian Serenaders formed which cemented the dance, song, and narrative repertoire into a group performance, but no combination was ever so popular as Christy's Minstrels. As minstrels, Christy's were fully recognizable in the old mould: they delivered, with superb musicianship, songs about life in the plantations of the American South as well as British melodies of ancient lineage.

> While their 'negro ditties' are essentially characteristic of the negro, and consequently exceedingly droll and catching, they are utterly devoid of coarseness or vulgarity, and would not be out of place even in the drawing-room of the most fastidious. Then, again, their serious melodies are rendered with a truthfulness, sweetness, and simplicity, that not only strike a deep sympathy into the heart of the listener, but at once carry him to the distant habitations of the 'bondaged.' Indeed, it would puzzle singers of much higher pretentions to render those beautiful melodies with that plaintive, thrilling accent so peculiar to the Christy's Minstrels. Not alone are their talents confined to vocalization; as instrumentalists they ably acquitted themselves, adding to the vocal rendering of their brother artists additional pathos and delicacy.[3]

Christy's objective was not to pass as Southern slaves, or even as persons of African descent, but to utilize established tropes to deliver a repertoire that aurally, visually, and narratively referenced African American slavery. This meant incorporating a wide range of folk material.

Some of their repertoire was directly borrowed from Austrian troupes that toured in the 1820s and 1830s. Some of the jokes and jests were similar to pantomime and harlequinade. Some of the "plantation"

---

1   Edmondstoune Duncan, *The Story of Minstrelsy* (London: Walter Scott, 1907); "Minstrelsy in the Sandwich Islands," *Penny Magazine of the Society for the Diffusion of Useful Knowledge* 4 (14 February 1835): 59; "Fairy Minstrelsy," *Glasgow Herald*, 12 August 1857; W.Q., "London Minstrelsy," *New Monthly Magazine and Literary Journal* 13 (January 1825): 542; "The Tyrolese Minstrels and Mr. Hyman," *North Wales Chronicle*, 24 January 1828; and James Hardiman, *Irish Minstrelsy; or, Bardic Remains of Ireland*, 2 vols. (Joseph Robins, London: 1831).

2   Rice had performed in the United States since 1830. He, in turn, had progenitors: "in 1799 a Mr. Grawpner blacked up and appeared at the Old Federal Street Theatre, Boston, and sang a song of a negro, in character." Colonel T. Allston Brown, "The Origin of Negro Minstrelsy," in *Fun in Black; or, Sketches of Minstrel Life*, edited by Charles H. Day (New York: R.M. DeWitt, c. 1874), 7. See also Hazel Waters, *Racism on the Victorian Stage: Representation of Slavery and the Black Character* (Cambridge: Cambridge UP, 2007), 98-116.

3   *Morning Chronicle*, "Christy's Minstrels," 13 February 1862.

specialties were adapted from Irish or Scottish jigs, reels, or other tunes. Other turns were purportedly discovered in the fields, on the riverboats, and in the cabins of the plantation slave. Thus, for stage purposes, "American" idioms aggregated from both European and African influences manifested through artists' talent to mimic (but not mock).[4] The American South was not depicted as a dynamic, evolving society—contemporaneously the subject of intense debate among those disputing slavery's economic rationality and ethical defensibility—but was instead a zone of agrarian elementalism. Lamentations and exultations alike reflected the same anxieties as medieval song: courting, mourning, longing across distance, the relations of master and serf, the rigours of travel, and the soothing familiarity of nature.[5] As song repertoire, Christy's brand of minstrelsy drew upon old patterns, but their progenitors were also in the newly emergent realms of music hall, where from 1850 novelty tunes, dances, and popular ballads were exhibited nightly all over Britain. Music hall, in turn, had evolved from local entertainments in public houses and glee clubs—industrialized England's counterpart to the folk—into a multi-million-pound industry, featured in large halls in the West End, suburbs, and provincial capitals.

Blackface minstrelsy first emerged in newly urbanized America. George Christy formed a troupe in Buffalo in 1842 and settled into a long Broadway run in 1847. He retired in 1854, and in 1857 the remaining company split into two; those who crossed the Atlantic—taking what Frederick Douglass called "a bridge to connect" Britain and America—never went home again.[6] In America, there were high social stakes involved in "collecting" authentic dances, songs, and snatches of dialogue from slaves and ex-slaves, distilling these into a variety act performed by white men and entertaining Northeastern audiences.[7] These American blackface artistes did not necessarily draw on different repertoire than exponents in England, but the repertoire's immediate referentiality altered when transplanted to Europe. In England, blackface impersonators alluded to a distant culture, separated from English rule for several generations, preserving practices rejected by British law in 1833 and detested long before. Blacks constituted up to 3 per cent of Londoners,[8] yet for Britons neither the sentimental songs nor the comic sketches delivered by minstrels depicted people resident among or near them: slave culture was a fading memory, something foreign, abhorred where it still existed but seemingly not impinging on Britons' daily interactions. Exactly what it did mean to see white men with blackened faces represent Southern culture (and sometimes citified dandies of the Carolina or New York boardwalks) eludes history, but in Britain Christy's specific brand of it was scrupulously decorous family fare. Praised for "their gentlemanly conduct and the extremely fastidious character of their entertainment," Christy's Minstrels attracted many of the same music lovers who patronized concerts of Beethoven, Mozart, and Mendelssohn.[9] The music was widely published and

---

4   W.T. Lhamon Jr., *Raising Cain: Blackface Performance from Jim Crow to Hip Hop* (Cambridge, MA: Harvard UP, 1998), 170; and Kay Dian Kriz, *Slavery, Sugar, and the Culture of Refinement: Picturing the British West Indies, 1700-1840* (New Haven, CT: Yale UP, 2008), 120.

5   For a discussion of antebellum American themes, see Robert C. Toll, *Blacking Up: The Minstrel Show in Nineteenth-Century America* (London: Oxford UP, 1974), 72-88.

6   Frederick Douglass, *Northern Daily Express*, 24 February 1860, reprinted in Frederick Douglass, *The Frederick Douglass Papers: Series One; Speeches, Debates, and Interviews*, vol. 3, *1855-63*, edited by John W. Blassinghame (New Haven, CT: Yale UP, 1985), 335.

7   See Lhamon, *Raising Cain*; Toll, *Blacking Up*, 50; and Howard L. Sacks and Judith Rose Sacks, *Way Up North in Dixie: A Black Family's Claim to the Confederate Anthem* (Washington: Smithsonian Institution Press, 1993).

8   For estimates of the number of blacks, see Douglas A. Lorimer, *Colour, Class and the Victorians: English Attitudes to the Negro in the Mid-Nineteenth Century* (Leicester: Leicester UP, 1978), 212-13.

9   *Era*, 14 November 1858; and *Examiner*, 21 May 1859. The designation "gentlemanly" is significant: it suggests that Christy's was regarded as distinct from the crass minstrels who populated the stages by this time, and had more in common with the deportment and perceived social desirability of antislavery lecturers such as William Brown and Frederick Douglass. Lorimer, *Colour*, 52.

"many pairs of fashionable little lips ... sing songs learned from artificially dusky gentlemen, with large collars and woolly heads."[10] The sheet music sometimes reproduced images of Christy's artistes: *not* in blackface but undisguised, as if audiences saw through the burnt cork make-up to the white Americans underneath or, in any case, were fascinated to see the artists as Caucasians like themselves (whatever that might mean). For Rev. H.R. Haweis, seeing the performers represented with and without blackface sparked the following reflection:

> It is not without emotion that we gaze at the portraits of the most successful "Bones" of the age outside St. James's Hall, representing above the mighty W.P. Collins, black as to his face, and otherwise equipped for action, while underneath, the same face, only washed, looks appealingly at us, and seems to say, "You see the black all comes off. I am not so bad-looking either. You can hardly see me at night. But remember *P*. Collins is white, and, although his initial is *P*., he was not christened Pompey."[11]

In Collins, an exceptionally sweet-voiced alto, the duality (and perhaps the contradiction) of appearance and self prompted identification. And thus Christy's tunes emanated from all manner of instruments in middle-class parlours—piano, concertina, and guitar[12]—and were sung by fine ladies, hummed by labourers, and bellowed by gutter urchins.[13] Banjos were plucked by the Prince of Wales, Prime Minister Gladstone, and the Tsar of Russia.[14] In Michael Pickering's view, audiences could be entertained without being either morally improved or morally tainted and "escaped from the seriousness of being white without contaminating whiteness."[15] Contrary to Eric Lott's view of American minstrelsy,[16] Christy's could signal an abject class but not represent them, attired (as was their custom) in the same evening clothes as the gentlemen in the stalls (except during burlesques). Christy's were not counterfeit blacks but whites performing a sometimes noisy shivaree in the spirit of what W.T. Lhamon calls "a thoroughly nested cultural struggle,"[17] its causes and effects intertwined. As Melanie Dawson discovered in contemporaneous American home entertainment, impersonating the "barbarities" of foreign others more firmly established the hierarchy of an idealized whiteness.[18]

---

10   "Christy's Minstrels," *Lloyd's Weekly*, 24 March 1861.

11   Rev. H.R. Haweis, *Music and Morals* (New York: Harper, [1871]), 473.

12   See, for example, *Christy's Minstrels: The Original Christy's Minstrels; Complete Repertoire of Plantation Melodies, from Which the Programme of Each Evening Is Selected* (London: B. Ford, [1857]); *Boosey's 200 Christy's Minstrels' Melodies for the German Concertina* (London: Boosey & Sons, [1862]); and *Popular Songs Sung by Christy's Minstrels and Other Celebrated Vocalists Arranged with an Accompaniment for the Guitar ... by Henry Lea* (London: H. Lea, [1859]).

13   *Musical World*, 6 April 1861: 215.

14   Programme for "The Famous Royal Bohee Bros. Banjoists and Entertainers ...," n.d., Mander and Mitchenson Theatre Collection.

15   Michael Pickering, *Blackface Minstrelsy in Britain* (Aldershot: Ashgate, 2008), 106.

16   Eric Lott, *Love and Theft: Blackface Minstrelsy and the American Working Class* (New York: Oxford UP 1995), 68.

17   Lhamon, *Raising Cain*, 54.

18   Melanie Dawson, *Laboring to Play: Home Entertainment and the Spectacle of Middle-Class Life, 1850-1920* (Tuscaloosa: U of Alabama P, 2005), 91. The *Uncle Tom* melodramas featured on British stages in 1852-55 incorporated blackface minstrelsy acts; this may have sullied Americans' reputation, or as Sarah Meer also postulates, they would "equivocate about slavery." As with Stephen Foster's tunes, delivery was everything. Sarah Meer, *Uncle Tom Mania: Slavery, Minstrelsy and Transatlantic Culture in the 1850s* (Athens: U of Georgia P, 2005), 50-53, 56. Variance and ambiguity may not have had an effect on Unitarians, who regarded themselves as "theological Negroes" outside the British power structure and subject to persecution. David Turley, "British Unitarian Abolitionists, Frederick Douglass, and Racial Equality," in *Liberating Sojourn: Frederick Douglass and Transatlantic Reform*, edited by Alan J. Rice and Martin Crawford (Athens: U of Georgia P, 1999), 57.

MR. J. W. RAYNOR, MANAGER OF THE TROUPE CALLED
CHRISTY'S MINSTRELS.

Illustration 9. J.W. Raynor in evening dress.
Courtesy of the Theatre Collection, Victoria and Albert Museum.

Genre Issues

The eight men[19] comprising the original Christy's troupe in London imported some of their acts from the United States: Stephen Foster's tunes and other blackface troupes' standards; lively dance solos and duets (in turn derived from European clog dancing as much as African tap rhythms); popular operatic arias and concert songs; Tyrolean solos "exhibiting great compass and volume of voice"[20] and suggesting "a plum in the mouth [yodelling] ... usually considered the attribute of Swiss maidens;"[21] and burlesques of

---

19   J.W. Raynor, W.P. Collins, D.S. Wambold, E.H. Pierce, W. Burton, T. Christian, A. Nish, and Joe Brown. They accompanied themselves on bones, banjo, two fiddles, and a cello (*Musical Gazette*, 8 August 1857: 377). Harry Reynolds augments the number of the St. James's troupe to eleven, adding E. Thompson, J.T. Donnelly, and the instrumentalist G.W. Meeker (Harry Reynolds, *Minstrel Memories: The Story of Burnt Cork Minstrelsy in Great Britain from 1836 to 1927* [London: Alston Rivers, 1928]). By January 1859, when the troupe was in the midst of their first tour, it had ten members (*Freeman's Journal and Daily Commercial Advertiser* [Dublin], 1 January 1859). Earl Horton Pierce died in June 1859, and his comic repertoire was initially taken on by W.P. Collins, then G.W. "Pony" Moore (*Era* 12 June 1859; 26 June 1859; and 4 March 1860). See also "Mr. J.W. Raynor, Manager of the Troupe Called Christy's Minstrels," [*c.* 1857], Christy's clippings file, Harvard Theatre Collection. When Raynor retired, Wilson, Nish, and Collins took over. Moore left to form the Christy's Coloured Comedians, managed by Mr. Burgess; eventually this troupe reformed as the Moore and Burgess Minstrels which assumed the mantle of the original British Christy's Minstrels. E.W. Mackney and A.J. Park, *The Life and Reminiscences of E.W. Mackney, Ethiopian Entertainer* (London: Greyfriar's, 1897), 18-19.

20   Christy's playbill, Metropolitan Opera House, New York, n.d., Harvard Theatre Collection.

21   "Christy's Minstrels," *Lloyd's Weekly*, 21 February 1858.

Illustration 10. Playbill for the Christy's Minstrels, Bush Street Theatre, San Francisco, 16 November 1854. Courtesy of the Harvard Theatre Collection, Houghton Library.

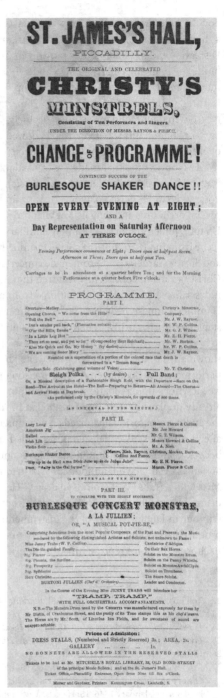

Illustration 11. Playbill for the Christy's Minstrels, St. James's Theatre, c. 1858–59. Courtesy of the Harvard Theatre Collection, Houghton Library.

popular entertainments.[22] Circus was a favourite target of burlesques: in New York, Christy's performed a "burlesque combat with 'Equestrian Manouevres,' à la Hippodrome, concluding with a grand Acrobatic Display,"[23] and in London, they took off an Astley's Amphitheatre act, "Star Riders" (featuring horses and mules) by prancing childishly on wooden hobby-horses,[24] then proceeding to "balance each other, throw mock sommersaults [sic] ... [and] wind up with 'a walk on the ceiling.'"[25] Whereas in America Christy's featured "Life Among the Happy," "Pourtraying [sic] the peculiarities of the Southern or Plantation Negroes in their Holiday Pastimes," featuring banjo tunes, a corn shucking, Arkansas reel, and Louisiana jig,[26] in London this was soon overshadowed by burlesques of Italian opera (evidently the local equivalent of exaggeration, exotica, and unfathomable mannerisms).

Two burlesques that made the transatlantic journey are both send-ups of popular concert acts. One was the "Terpsichorean Divertisement [sic]," titled the "Grand Burlesque Concert à la Jullien" on New York and San Francisco playbills of 1853 and 1854, which parodied "monster concerts" that combined several orchestras and long lists of virtuoso soloists conducted by Louis Antoine Jullien during a 1853-54 US tour. Jullien's tactics were amply familiar to London audiences too, for he was a regular on the concert scene from the 1840s until 1858, performing bal masqués as well as monster concerts at the Crystal Palace and Surrey Gardens, and promenade concerts at the Royal Italian Opera House (Covent Garden Theatre). Christy's version consistently featured the "American Quadrille" and comprised "a general 'POT PIE' of indescribable Musical Combination—from a Penny Whistle to a considerable sized Tin Horn, Sledge Hammer, Chinese Bells, &c. &c." How this was danced, and thus made terpsichorean, is unspecified. A staple of Christy's British repertoire, it certainly would have required engaging the spectators' imaginations to bridge between Jullien's touring orchestra of 125 and Christy's troupe of eight or ten. Jullien's flamboyant showmanship, such as receiving a jewelled baton and white gloves on a silver tray before commencing a performance of Beethoven—whom he sought to make the British public appreciate—were reflected in Mr. Raynor's impersonation, which culminated with him fainting exhausted on the drum. Jullien was already implausibly self-important: clad in "the largest white waistcoat ever seen," he conducted facing the audience, occasionally seized an instrument from a performer to emphasize a climactic moment, and, after a concert, sank exhausted into a gilded chair.[27] Christy's likely showed up these glittering diamond-bedecked antics and, through racial inversion and musical buffoonery, demoted them to absurdities. A St. James's Hall playbill announces W. Burton as Chef d'Orchestre presiding over the cantatrice d'Afrique Miss Jenny Trabs (W.P. Collins in drag), "Herr Christine" the snare soloist, other soloists on the monster drum, penny whistle, AwfulClyde, and trombone, and the Dis-tin-guished Family on their sax horns. On tour in Dublin, "some of the instruments used in the burlesque caused shouts of laughter on being produced. They consisted of pyramids of tin, with monster keys, through which some pieces were played in chorus, the voice representing the tone of the horn or 'AwfulClyde.'"[28] Christy's musical selections are

---

22   Toll mistakenly calls these farces. Toll, Blacking Up, 56-57.

23   Ibid.

24   Lloyd's Weekly Newspaper, 4 July 1858; and Theatrical Journal, March 1858: 98.

25   Freeman's Journal and Daily Commercial Advertiser (Dublin), 1 September 1858.

26   Christy's playbills, Harvard Theatre Collection.

27   "The End of Jullien," Times (London), 16 May 1867: 7; Michael Broyes, "Art Music from 1860 to 1920," in The Cambridge History of American Music, edited by David Nicholls (Cambridge: Cambridge UP, 1998), 232; "Jullien's Concerts," Theatrical Journal, January 1846: 18; Haweis, Music and Morals, 417; Louis and Susan Foreman, London: A Musical Gazetteer (New Haven, CT: Yale UP, 2005), 255; and Dave Russell, Popular Music in England, 1840-1914: A Social History, 2nd ed. (Manchester: Manchester UP, 1997), 78.

28   "Christy's Minstrels," Dublin Evening Post, 4 January 1859: 3.

not specified apart from Miss Jenny Trabs's "Tramp, Tramp"[29]—a send-up of mezzo-soprano Henrietta "Jetty" Treffz's performance of "Trab, Trab, Trab, or The Ride," sung at Jullien's concerts in 1850[30]—but may have included selections from Jullien's albums of scores, such as his original quadrilles, polkas, or waltzes; popular music by Auber, Mozart, and Mendelssohn; and "Yankee Doodle," arranged by Jullien to appeal to American audiences[31] and including "wonderfully imitative effects of the battle, as well as the deep boom of the 'monster drum.'"[32] It would have been difficult to resist putting at least one of his gimmick-laden pieces on Christy's programme, such as "The Fireman's Quadrille," which sonically depicts the kindling and growing roar of a fire, alarm, approach of fire engines, battle with the infernal enemy, and eventual triumph of the firefighters.[33] John Tasker Howard describes the premiere of the Quadrille: "Suddenly the clang of firebells was heard outside. Flames burst from the ceiling. Three companies of firemen rushed in, dragging their hoses behind them. Real water poured from the nozzles, glass was broken ... and all the while the orchestra was playing at a tremendous fortissimo."[34] The potential for comic foolery in Christy's scaled-down version is evident, comically imitating both the massed musicians and the firemen.

Christy's other popular musical burlesque, which parodied the New Hampshire-identified Hutchinson Family singers, also became a staple "quaint drollery" of British programmes.[35] The Baptist Hutchinsons' folksiness combined with their fervent belief in the abolition of slavery, abstention from alcohol, and Christian salvation. The ardent and pious quintet (sometimes a quartet) were well known in the American Northeast, including New York where they often performed, but are little more than a footnote in the history of British concert music: they toured Britain in 1845-46, competing against the Ethiopian Serenaders for patrons; and though they received respectable reviews in London, it is doubtful that they made a sufficient impression to stick in the British public's imagination.[36] Their signature tune was "We're a Band of Brothers." Christy's replaced the lyric

We have come from the mountains of the Old Granite State
We're a band of brothers ...
... a band of music we are passing 'round the world.

with

---

29   St. James's Hall, London, playbill [1857-58], Harvard Theatre Collection. This is not the same as the popular Civil War tune "Tramp! Tramp! Tramp!" written in 1863. Paul D. Sanders, comp., *Lyrics and Borrowed Tunes of the American Temperance Movement* (Columbia: U of Missouri P, 2006), 192-93.

30   Composed by Friedrich Wilhelm Kuecken. See the Levy Sheet Music Collection's "Trab, Trab, Trab" at https://jscholarship. library.jhu.edu/handle/1774.2/27950 (accessed 10 August 2010).

31   "Yankee Doodle" was written *c.* 1755 to make fun of Americans who helped the British battle the French. The British played it on the way from Boston to Concord and marching to Bunker Hill, after which the Americans adopted it as their own triumphal theme. Lewis Winstock, *Songs and Music of the Redcoats: A History of the War Music of the British Army, 1642-1902* (London: Leo Cooper, 1970).

32   John Graziano, "Jullien and His *Music for the Million*," in *A Celebration of American Music*, edited by Richard Crawford, R. Allen Lott, and Carol J. Oja (Ann Arbor: U of Michigan P, 1990), 198.

33   This appears on a Christy's bill from St. James's Hall, Liverpool, 15 August 1864; "The Sleigh Polka" is on a Polygraphic Hall bill *c.* July 1858, Harvard Theatre Collection. "The Fire-Bell Galop" appears on Christy's bill for St. James's Hall, Liverpool, from 15 August 1864, Harvard Theatre Collection. Most likely, this is the version composed by Charles Blamphin and performed by Templeton's African Opera Troupe. Copies of Blamphin's and Jullien's piano reductions are available in the Lester S. Levy Collection of Sheet Music, Johns Hopkins University (http:// levysheetmusic.mse.jhu. edu/index.html).

34   From *Our American Music* (New York: Thomas Y. Crowell, 1931), 230, quoted in Graziano, "Jullien and his *Music*," 208.

35   Era, Christy's Minstrels," 15 July 1860.

36   Dale Cockrell, ed., *Excelsior: Journals of the Hutchinson Family Singers, 1842-1846* (Stuyvesant, NY: Pendragon Press, 1989), 336-44.

We have come from the mountains, from Carolina State
... We are the sons of Dinah,
And we go just where we're a mind to.[37]

It is understandable that when Christy's first came to London they would perform what they already knew. But how is it that the Hutchinson brothers registered as objects of hilarious parody in London sufficiently so to remain on Christy's programmes into the early 1860s?

While this burlesque was Christy's repertoire, on a deeper level its elements must also have had commerce with British repertoire: the close vocal harmonization of a family's identical inflections was the Hutchinsons' trademark, but their songs were based on hymns as well as blackface songs (both given new lyrics). They expounded an American identity, and any topical reference could have been adapted to update this idea, much as any allusion to zealous reform politicking—or the temperance songs of Henry Russell[38]—would recall this type of troupe. As the most recent biographer of the Hutchinsons, Scott Gac, explains,

> The key to the Hutchinson Family Singers' triumph was their moral fortitude combined with an uncanny ability to transform the meaning of their often borrowed melodies with catchy lyrics. The Hutchinsons' antislavery anthem 'Get Off the Track!' changed the minstrel tune 'Old Dan Tucker' from a dim characterization of black society into an abolitionist vehicle; 'King Alcohol' transformed the traditional British melody of 'King Andrew' into a comical temperance caution; 'The Old Granite State,' remade a revival hymn into a sacred song about antislavery, temperance, religion, and family. Add to these selections the Hutchinson Family Singers' many sentimental songs (the musical equivalent of sentimental literature) which borrowed lyrics from famous poets, and the group's catalogue implored listeners to identify with the downtrodden, with the powerless—with children, family, and, ultimately, all humankind.[39]

Merely the claim to give a "chaste and fashionable" performance could have been enough to invoke the Hutchinsons, their style, or their pious counterparts in Britain.[40] As a Washington newspaper reported in 1844,

> The Hutchinsons do not torture us with this most romantic and affected Italian jargon—nor with this nerve-rasping, krout-digesting [sic], Hessian minstrelsy, nor with French squalling, nor Spanish squealing; but they give us the eloquence of music in the natural harmony of their natural voices. There are no shrieks like the yell of a Pottawatomie squaw in the hug of a grizzly bear—no swoonings, no crocodile tears, no supercilious rolling up of the eyes, no affected palpitations of the heart; but all is as simple and graceful as an alderman dissecting a canvass-back duck.[41]

Christy's version might have reset solemn sounding diatonic part-songs with contrapuntal portions, *à la* Christy's other choruses. In any case, their send-up of the Hutchinsons' piety and no-nonsense Yankee earnestness was kept within the bounds of good taste, for this was calculated to amuse rather

---

37   "We're a Band of Brothers," song no. 1976 of *Christy's Minstrels Popular Songs for the Piano-Forte, with Choruses* (London: Musical Bouquet, [1863-64]).

38   The composer of "Cheer Boys, Cheer," "The Maniac," and other standards, Henry Russell (*c*. 1812-1900) came to prominence in New York in 1836 then resettled in London in 1842. He was the most important US composer prior to Stephen Foster.

39   Scott Gac, *Singing for Freedom* (New Haven, CT: Yale UP, 2007), 16.

40   Ibid., 227-28. See also Vicki L. Eaklor, *American Antislavery Songs: A Collection and Analysis* (New York: Greenwood, 1988).

41   *Whig Standard* (Washington), 4 February 1844, quoted in Cockrell, *Excelsior*, 284.

than offend Protestant Nonconformists[42] who were the mainstay of the Hutchinsons'—and possibly Christy's—audiences.[43]

Burlesque feeds on recognizability. The connection between a burlesque and the genre (not just the individual work) that it squibs is one of the most obvious correlations of repertoire: an audience recognizes the transposition of high-status art into a lampoon.[44] Tunes and lyrics are retained or substituted with deliberate intertextual referentiality, plots are mangled or faithfully retained to reveal their absurdities, and caricatures suffice for readily signified figures. The two Christy's operatic burlesques included here epitomize how this works. Whereas in America Christy's programs featured the stump speeches and stamp oratory full of buffoonish malapropisms, piccaninny grammar, and *idiot savant* folksiness of the most outrageous racism, these were less prominent in Christy's British troupe.[45] The barrage of punning jokes between the end-men finds a place in their twenty-minute burlesques of operas, *The Gypsy Maid* (based on *The Bohemian Girl*) and *The Nigger's Opera; or, The Darkie That Walked in Her Sleep* (based on *La sonnambula*).[46] In *The Gypsy Maid* a good deal of the comedy depends on everyone being in blackface, even though the characters are central European nobility. "Blackness" has a metaphorical resonance in the portrayal of Gypsies, though again the discrepancy between their appearance and that of real Gypsies called attention to blackface as a performance convention. In *The Nigger's Opera*,[47] the source opera's whiteness is inverted amid a community of "darkies" though separated by class (Dolphus is the out-of-town swell) and degrees of superstition and sophistication. The tale of a young woman who sleepwalks to a compromising locale, struts obliviously across a narrow plank suspended over a raging torrent, and awakens to find her fiancé aghast at her behaviour—taken as normal in the opera house—is lampooned as unfit for even the näifs of this blackened-up topsy-turvy retelling.

Studies of blackface minstrelsy invariably relay a structural formula for the genre: dances and songs, followed by olio acts and speeches, then a one-act skit. The bill presented here is a compound version of typical elements—all taken from playbills, but not adhering to any one—which the troupe took as its standards. Not all aspects of the programme can be properly represented in a print anthology: the virtuosic

---

42 Members of congregations other than the Church of England (Anglicans or Episcopalians) such as Methodists, Unitarians, and Baptists.

43 J.S. Bratton, "English Ethiopians: British Audiences and Black-Face Acts, 1835-1865," *Yearbook of English Studies* 11 (1981): 127-42.

44 Robert F. Wilson, *'Their Form Confounded': Studies in the Burlesque Play from Udall to Sheridan* (The Hague: Mouton, 1975), x.

45 Meer notes that the British preferred puns over malapropisms. (Meer, *Uncle Tom Mania*, 151). It is unclear whether Christy's invariably, or even often, included stump speeches (they are not indicated in programmes) during their first years in Britain. Reviewers did note their incorporation of "Tambo and Bones," end-men who delivered successions of punning verbal jokes.

46 These scripts have survived by happy accident: for a few months in the spring of 1861, Christy's performed at the Bijou Theatre, a concert-hall annex of the Haymarket Theatre. In a venue licensed by the Lord Chamberlain, they were obliged to submit their scripts for examination, which thus became part of the British Library's collection. These are the earliest known British blackface minstrel burlesques. The opera *La sonnambula* featured in several other burlesques: *La sonnambula; or, The Ghost Vot Haunts the Mill* (licensed for the Britannia in November 1859, British Library Add MS 52987A); Elias Howe, *The Ethiopian Glee Book* (Boston: n.p., 1848), 112-16; J. Caulfield (words) and J. Harroway (musical arrangement), *La sonnambula*, sung by Sam Cowell; and Gilbert A. A'Beckett, *The Roof Scrambler: A Grand Burlesque Ballet Opera*, performed at the Victoria, 1835 (London: John Cumberland, n.d.).

47 It is impossible to document blackface minstrelsy without repeating what has subsequently become an offensive epithet. For mid-nineteenth-century Britons, "nigger," "negro," "sable," "Ethiopian," and "African" all connoted the same people and characteristics with very little nominal differentiation, pejorative or otherwise. Following Charles Mathews's Kentucky Roscius (see pp. 190-92 above), they are all portrayed as partial to the antics of the "coon" and "possum," but are also distinct from white Americans as a result of both history and self-identification.

banjo solos and vigorous dances must be imagined, but so too must the cut-and-swap between arias and minstrel tunes during the burlesques.

The programme's overture and opening chorus gave the troupe the opportunity to introduce their instruments and their other performing specialties. By the 1840s, walk-arounds were indispensable aspects of any minstrels' programme. Typically, troupes would circle while singing verses of well-known minstrel repertoire such as "Dixie's Land" (1861). Vocal solos of sixteen measures would be followed by the chorus and then by eight measures of a "'grotesque' dance."[48] The lyrics could be nonsense, non sequiturs, or culturally specific references, as in "Dixie's Land":

> Den hoe it down an scratch yer grabble,
> To Dixie's land I'm bound to trabble.[49]

This serves as a variant on what Washington Irving described in an African American dance at the turn of the nineteenth century:[50] "hoe corn and dig potatoes" is a literal description of two contrasting movements performed by field hands. In the 1840s, the hoe-down was described as vigorous movements, including knocking the shins with heavy boots. In "Dixie's Land," to "hoe it down an scratch yer grabble" juxtaposes these well-known steps with something imitative of angling, for "fishing on the grabble is when the line is sunk with a running plummet fast to the bottom, so that the hook-link plays in the water":[51] one part of the apparatus scratches the river bottom while the other—metaphorically the narrator—trabbles (travels) downstream to Dixie.[52] This lyric does make sense, but it in no way coheres overall with the story of the jilted Old Missus that occupies three of the six verses.[53] The song's failure to cohere as a narrative adds to the sense of absurdity and fun but also upsets expectations that a consistent identity will be taken by the performers. This is because "Dixie's Land" adopts the walk-around's convention of letting each performer introduce himself in a solo interleaved with dance and choral song, made dizzying by the

---

48   Gilbert Chase, *America's Music from the Pilgrims to the Present*, 3rd ed. (Urbana: U of Illinois P, 1987), 242. See also Hans Nathan, *Dan Emmett and the Rise of Early Negro Minstrelsy* (Norman: U of Oklahoma P, 1962), 233-37.

49   Chase, *America's Music*, 176. The two 1861 versions published in London elide some of the Americanisms and include only four verses: "I wish I was in the land of cotton," "His face was like a butcher's cleaver," "While missis lived, she lived in clover," and "Buckwheat cakes are good strong batter." They preserve the dance music. [Dan Emmett], "Dixey's Land, Sung by Buckley's Serenaders" (London: H. and E. Swatton: [1861]); and Frederick Buckley, arr., "Dixey's Land, Plantation Song and Dance" (London: Joseph Williams, [1861]).

50   From Washington Irving, *Salmagundi* 7 March 1798. See *Oxford English Dictionary Online*, s.v. "hoedown," http://oxforddictionaries.com/definition/hoedown (accessed 2 October 2011). This also appears in the lyrics of the minstrelsy standard "Sich a Gittin Up Stairs":
     Trike he toe an heel—cut de pigeon wing
     Scratch gravel, slap de foot, dat's just
     [refrain] Sich a gittin up stairs, &c.
   Jim Crow Vagaries; or, Black Flights of Fancy: Containing a Choice of Nigger Melodies; To which is added, the Erratic Life of Jim Crow (London: Orlando Hodgson, [1889]), n.p.

51   *Oxford English Dictionary Online*, s.v. "grabble," http://oxforddictionaries.com/definition/grabble (accessed 2 October 2011).

52   Howard and Judith Sacks attribute "hoe down" as a reference to tobacco farming ritualized into "dance figures in which the dancer moves down and around a line of stationary dancers." That is possible too. They do not offer a meaning for "grabble" but note that "bound" may refer to a group of slaves chained together for transport. Sacks and Sacks, *Way Up North*, 180.

53   Incongruity and even conundrums feature in early minstrel songs. One version of "Clare de Kitchen" includes this verse:
     I have a sweet-heart in dis town,
     She wears a cloak and a new silk gown,
     And as she walks the streets around;
     The hollow of her foot makes a hole in the ground.
   Philip D. Jordan, *Singin' Yankees* (Minneapolis: U of Minnesota P, 1946), 134.

narrative incongruities, jaunty arpeggios, and quick runs of notes. Walk-arounds could mix vocal and instrumental sections or be entirely instrumental, accompanied by dance which added to the percussive instrumentation. In purely instrumental walk-arounds, the sudden juxtaposition of tunes works in a fashion similar to "Dixie's Land," syncopating abruptly in jolts to which audiences had to successively adapt. They often utilize a medley of popular tunes and—as in traditional Gaelic performance—include multiple instantaneous transitions: not just variations on a melodic theme, but incongruous vignettes allied to jig, reel, and polka tunes.[54]

Interpretive Issues

Christy's evenings commenced with a concert. The programme posited here consists of a succession of the major song types utilized by Christy's. "Kiss Me Quick and Go," by F. Buckley, is an up-tempo comic courting song, invariably demanded by audiences in Christy's first years in London.[55] Impetuous rather than naughty or titillating, its story of a constantly interrupted couple ends, like all comedies, with an imminent marriage. The ballad "In a Little Log Hut" is set in "old Virginny" and narrated by a "darkey" who came from "Guinea." Since new infusions of African-born slaves to the United States dried up with British Abolition in 1807, this implies both a far-away and long-ago sensibility. The "darkey's" fellows are subservient to a benevolent master who works them only until sundown, when they express quaint allegiance to General Washington and entertain their fellows on the plantation.[56] The rhythmic chorus, explicitly set in the South, and temperate evocation of slave-holding culture are precisely the characteristics about which later critics of blackface minstrelsy complain:[57] who ever saw hard-working yet irrepressibly fun-loving, nonsense-jabbering, and naïve slaves voluntarily singing a paean to their master? What could be more preposterous? In the context of Christy's performance, however, this may have pulled the audience back into the referential world of the walk-around (where skill and composure were presented in equal measure) not exactly *as* slaves but in ethnological reference to them. Reviewers noted that Christy's were the first troupe to "introduce sentimental songs without any attempt at extravagance or burlesque":[58] sincerity in their approach may have amounted to pathos towards their performed personae. After all, the converse of the contented slave is the insurrectionist.

Lyrical abstractions are open to interpretation: racists may have found confirmation for their views while antislavery advocates may have heard echoes of hymns sung at abolitionist meetings. The American repertoire of the period includes songs explicitly describing the wrenching separation of enslavement

> Forced from home and all its pleasures,
> Afric's coast I left forlorn;
> To increase a stranger's treasures,
> O'er the raging billows borne;

---

54 For example, the medley "Old Johnny Boker," "Jim Along Josey," "Back Side of Albany," and "Old Zip Coon," track 7 of the CD *The Early Minstrel Show*, compact disc 80338, New World Records, 1998. The Ethiopian Serenaders' "Walk Along John" (London: John Reid, [1855]), sung in London *c.* 1855, resembles the lyrical *non sequiturs* and absurdity of "Dixie's Land," a walk-around distinguished by its very simple melody with a limited range and highly syncopated rhythm over a plain walking bass.

55 They also performed "The Gal in Blue," but most of the published courting repertoire is sentimental (for example, "Lulu Is Our Darling Pride," "Silver Shining Moon," "Twinkling Stars," "We Meet by Chance," and "Oh Gently Breathe"). "Katy Dean" is a comic courting song, a rare example in dialect.

56 Other repertoire in the "happy darkies" mould includes the songs "Ginger Bluff," "Ring Ring de Banjo," and "Yo Yah Yo." "Some Folks" is similar, but the narrator is not definitively black.

57 Jan Nederveen Pieterse, *White on Black: Images of Africa and Blacks in Western Popular Culture* (New Haven, CT: Yale UP, 1992).

58 *Musical World*, 6 April 1861: 215.

the socio-economic basis of slavery

> O slavery, where are the charms
> That "patriarchs" have seen in thy face;
> I dwell in the midst of alarms,
> And serve in a horrible place;

the sexual exploitation of human property

> The Slaver led her from the door,
> He led her by the hand,
> To be his slave and paramour
> In a far and distant land;

and the obligations of Christians

> Hark! I hear a sound of anguish
> In my own, my native land;
> Brethren, doomed in chains to languish,
> Lift to heaven the suppliant hand,
> And despairing, And despairing,
> Death the end of woe demand.[59]

In all these cases, anti-slavery songs make explicit the figures whose thoughts are being expressed—captured or captor, brutalized or brutalizer, witness or perpetrator—and rightful action is never in doubt. In contrast, Christy's songs often trade on ambiguity in first-person address, the timelessness of the slave's predicaments, and imprecision in the call to action. One reviewer noted that when performing the pathetic ballads "Hard Times Come Again No More" and "We Are Coming Sister Mary," "the imitation of negro manners and pronunciation is very judiciously suppressed."[60] The Reverend Haweis admitted that "if we could divest ourselves of prejudice, the songs that float down the Ohio River are one in feeling and character with the songs of the Hebrew captives by the waters of Babylon." Sorrow and tenderness at bereaved separation establish the cognitive link; decorum makes the songs palatable to all listeners.[61]

"The Mocking Bird"[62] is a mourning song, one of a raft of similar tunes that use a nature image to evoke the melancholia of lingering grief.[63] The loss and the pain that it instills are universals, and as such mourning songs are not racially marked. Christy's made rapid transitions between sentimental and comic

---

59   These are excerpts from the songs "The Negro's Appeal," "I Am Monarch of Nought I Survey," "The Quadroon Maiden," and "Hark! I Hear a Sound of Anguish," in George W. Clark, ed., *The Liberty Minstrel* (New York: Leavitt and Alden, 1845), 14-15, 18-19, 29-31, 24-25. Clark's book *The Free Soil Minstrel* (New York: Martyn and Ely, 1848) is of the same ilk. Even the dialect songs, in which blacks are the apparent narrators, sing of the imperative of emancipation. See "The Negro Emancipation Song" and "The Slave's Consolation," in *The Patriotic Glee Book*, arranged by John Molten (Chicago: H.M. Higgins, *c.* 1861-65), 45-47, 168-71. See also Eaklor, *American Antislavery Songs*.

60   "Christy's Minstrels," *Morning Chronicle*, 11 November 1857.

61   Haweis, *Music and Morals*, 430.

62   By A. Hawthorne [pseud.], also accredited to Septimus Winner.

63   For example, "Toll the Bell." Mourning songs are the most prevalent category in the published repertoire, the most famous being "I Dream of Jenny [or Jeannie] with the Light Brown Hair." A few more examples include "Ellen Bayne," "We Are Coming Sister Mary," "Eulalie," "Gentle Annie," "Happy Haidee," "Evangeline," and "Hard Times Come Again No More." "Good Old Jeff" is a rare example that references not only a lost wife (or female sweetheart) but also the woman's father. "Nancy Bell" is the only example in dialect.

set pieces, and the amusement of one gave added piquancy to the other.[64] "Dat's Another Pull Back," by contrast, is a comic plantation tune, a "sure enough corn song" claiming cultural authenticity.[65]

> At a regular home-spun Virginia or Kentucky Corn shucking, a Negro having the finest voice and the best descriptive powers, and who is termed the Rhymer, is selected. Mounting a stump or some other elevation he sings a couplet. At the end of the couplet another singer especially appointed, answers, "And dat's another pull back."[66]

What ensues is probably a dance step: the "pullback" latterly describes a move where the body is propelled backwards while the foot strikes the ground with an audible slide. An exchange of stock verbal responses follows, and then the Rhymer's improvisation recommences. It "ends with the Chorus 'Ha-ah,' which the Negros sing in Unisons [sic] with a nasal twang peculiar to themselves, and which is difficult to imitate." The verses are non sequiturs, and in the American edition are topical. The threat of beating, which looms in verse six, is not acted upon yet it reminds listeners of the stakes. The song's imitation of dialect is more common in Christy's repertoire than that of other British blackface troupes[67] (though it is also used in "In a Little Log Hut"), yet when it occurs, it points directly to African Americans.

"Good News from Home" matches a lilting melody with a minor key: the narrator, parted from his family by an ocean, never expects to go home. The heartache was recognizable to many Victorians, as was the happy receipt of word that the loved ones were well.[68] Introduced in 1858, this song does not allude to race or location, and whereas "Kiss Me Quick" presents a universal and tame courting scenario, "Good News from Home" allows listeners to imagine voluntary emigration from Britain, the singer's parting *en route* to London, the forced separation of slaves, or even the Middle Passage that slaves travelled, in shackles, from Africa to the Americas. In other words, it *could* evoke a racial identity but just as likely did not if audiences listened to rather than looked at the blackened singer. In 1859, Christy's introduced a new hit song, "Nelly Gray." It tells the first-person story of an avaricious man of business who, despite his waking demeanour as an "iron man," wistfully dreams of his youthful love, Nelly Gray.

> Then years flow back I'm young again,
> New hopes my bosom cheer,
> I carol forth a joyous strain,
> In gentle Nelly's ear.

The warmth and joy he recalls in sleep cannot be conjured by the light of day, and his ruefulness passes, unspoken, in instrumental passages. Calculated to appeal in much the same way as Dickens's Scrooge—without the opportunity to repent and make good—this song was almost certainly perceived to have a white, well-to-do narrator. In "Seeing Nelly Home," another Christy's tune, the heart-warming pastoral tale

---

64 *Somerset County Gazette*, 22 March 1862, reprinted in *Era*, 30 March 1862; and *Freeman's Journal and Daily Commercial Advertiser* (Dublin), 4 January 1859.

65 Authenticity implies "replication of the creator's intentions," "dependency on the performer's imaginative act," and dependency on the "historical and social context in which the work was created." Anything short of this might be accurate but not authentic. Rodreguez King-Dorset, *Black Dance in London, 1730-1850* (Jefferson, NC: McFarland, 2008), 13.

66 Frank Williams, "And Dat's Another Pull Back," (Cincinnati, OH: W.C. Peters, 1854).

67 Song collections published in 1859-60 reveal that 38 per cent of Christy's repertoire was in dialect, compared to 30 per cent and 14 per cent for two of their competitors. *50 Songs Sung by the Christy Minstrels* (London: Davidson's, [1859]); *50 Songs, Music and Words, Sung by the Ethiopians at Canterbury Hall* (London: Davidson's, [1860]); and *50 Songs Sung by the Coloured Opera Troupe* (London: Davidson's, [1859]).

68 Other examples in Christy's repertoire include "I Dream of My Home" and "I Long for My Home in Kentucky." Some lyrics are interpretable as emigration stories ("Maggie by My Side" and "Do They Miss Me at Home?"), and only "Good Bye Sally Dear" is unambiguously about the separation of slaves.

of a young couple racing to old age and still blessing the moment they fell in love is Victorian sentimentality at its height. Yet, during this song, the narrator details the couple in a specifically racialized manner:

> Jetty ring-lets softly flutter'd
> O'er a brow as white as snow,
> And her cheek, the crimson sunset
> Scarcely had a warmer glow.

The white hair and furrowed brows of the subsequent verse level all races, but Nelly is definitely marked as white. When Christy's lyrics do not specify the race of the narrative voice, or of the loved one, either through dialect, context, or description, what was assumed? Did the "white" voices of the performers determine the matter, or did their darkened faces?

All the preceding songs set choruses in four-part harmony, which was Christy's musical trademark. The Stephen Foster classic "Come, Where My Love Lies Dreaming" was delivered as a quartet in "a display of exquisite vocalization which ... is utterly impossible to describe."[69] The lyrics are repetitive: the listener is invoked by the title line to imagine "visions bright redeeming" in the "happy hours" of dreamland. This vision is personified as a woman, carefree as a "gushing melody," light of heart, "bright and free." Here, too, there is no hint of anything but the (white) Victorian domestic scenario.

Performative Issues

The first part of the programme ends with two specialty turns. T. Christian's Tyrolean solo capitalized on the craze for alpine music (initiated in the 1820s), part of the *volksleid* movement to collect authentic songs from south-central Europe and fuelled by Eliza Vestris, who as Pandora in the burlesque *The Olympic Revels* "sang songs based on Swiss yodelling melodies in order to best display her coloratura."[70] The Rainer Family troupe made a sensation with this musical style when they visited London in 1826 and America in 1841.[71] The men performed in *lederhosen* and plumed hats, and Margaret Rainer wore a traditional costume with apron and played the guitar. Madame Vestris drew on this music's immense popularity with her solo "Dear Happy Tyrol!" in which the refrain was yodelled; this is the particular feature most likely featured in Christy's version. "The Sleigh Polka" was one of Jullien's instrumental standards. The English comedian Charles Mathews noted the American craze for winter sleighs during his stay in Boston in 1823:

> They whisk along at about the rate of twelve miles an hour, and in *open* carriages like the half of a boat. So fond are they of the sport, that it is common for parties to go out at night ten or fifteen miles to adjacent villages, dance there, and then return in these open sleighs. Funny people! They declare it is right *arnest* fun. I believe it is all they enjoy; so rest them merry![72]

"The Sleigh Polka" echoically narrates the departure of a happy group, cracking whips as they race on the snow, arrive at a ball, and make the return journey. The jingling sound of sleigh bells was pleasing but also distinctly foreign to British ears. Another composition in this mould is retained in modern Christmas fare: "Jingle Bells," anthologized as a blackface minstrel tune in the 1870s.[73]

---

69   *Era*, 25 September 1859.

70   Edith Hall and Fiona Macintosh, *Greek Tragedy and the British Theatre, 1660-1914* (Oxford: Oxford UP, 2005), 357.

71   Gac, *Singing for Freedom*, 133.

72   Charles Mathews, letter to Anne Mathews 12 January 1823, quoted in Anne Mathews, *Memoirs of Charles Mathews, Comedian*, vol. 3 (London: Richard Bentley, 1839), 356. See p. 200 above.

73   Listed as "Sleighing Song" (sung by W. Matthews) in *Matthews Brothers' C! C! C! Christy's Minstrels: Book of Words from Which the Programme of Each Evening Is Selected* (London: J. Miles; [*c.* 1870s]).

Illustration 12. E.H. Pierce in costume, from *Christy's Panorama Songster*, New York, early 1850s.
Courtesy of Department of Special Collections, Northwestern University.

The programme ends with virtuoso acts. The very popular banjo solo "Hoop de Dooden Doo" was comically performed with "unction and sly humour," drawing laughter and applause.[74] The dancing was considered "almost obsolete" though excellent of its kind.[75] In 1861, when Mr. Howard introduced a Highland Fling, "decked out in kilt and philobeg [bagpipe], and gyrating with the speed of a youthful *gasteropod* [mollusc]," the *Era* declared that the discordance with blackface was too extreme.[76] "The Silver Belt Jig," which Mr. Howard performed with such agility that he appeared to have boneless legs, was more in keeping with the Jim Crow tradition.[77] Interspersed, "the fearfully stale jokes of Messrs. Bones and

---

74 "The Last Appearance of the Christy Minstrels," *Morning Chronicle*, 3 August 1858. The piece was borrowed by numerous Christmas burlesques in 1857-58. "Christy's Minstrels," *Era*, 24 January 1858: 11.

75 "Christy's Minstrels," *Morning Chronicle*, 11 November 1857.

76 *Era*, 8 December 1861.

77 "Christy's Minstrels," *Era*, 2 June 1861; and "The Last Appearance of the Christy's Minstrels," *Morning Chronicle*, 3 August 1858.

Banjo" (W.P. Collins and E.H. Pierce) livened the proceedings.[78] British and Irish reviews suggest (by omission) that Christy's was not particularly well known for stump speeches or the kind of low verbal humour associated with other minstrel troupes, but they did utilize jokes of the calibre of "Why is a husband like a Mississippi steam-boat?"[79] For example, a garrulous individual tells how

> the government has been paying him great attention—providing him with excellent board and lodging, and a new suit of clothes, and they have set a guard to see that no harm comes to him. And all just because he was poor and had to borrow some money—only it was difficult to borrow, and he was obliged to knock a man down four times before he would lend it.[80]

In a duo, Pierce sometimes played an elocution professor whose "oblique-minded pupil" demonstrated "a peculiar faculty for misapprehending everything that he is taught."[81]

By 1860, London easily supported five or six blackface combination troupes like Christy's Minstrels. The appetite for this entertainment was nearly unquenchable. As the *Saturday Review* commented, this demonstrated "the close connexion that exists between Puritanism and extreme frivolity," yet it also illustrated the permeable border between stage performance and audiences' home entertainments.[82] Musicianship, comedic exuberance, and acrobatic dancing sustained Christy's in esteem, and they remained before the public longer than any other blackface troupe before them, becoming "as a part of London itself—like the Monument,"[83] even as the personnel were replaced and name of the troupe altered after 1864. They were not authentic representations of Southern slavery—as Frederick Douglass remarks in his book *My Bondage and My Freedom*, he only ever heard the "wailing notes" of Southern slaves' rapturous, sorrowful, and plaintive spirituals in one other place: Ireland during the Great Famine of 1845-46[84]—but drew upon a multitude of repertoires, rather like the synthetic borrowing of any immigrant culture.

Christy's Minstrels Programme[85]

Cast

J.W. Raynor (bass-baritone and conductor)[86]
William P. Collins (alto and bones, stump orator, female impersonator)
Earl H. Pierce[87] (banjo and vocals, comedian)
William Burton (baritone)
Tom Christian (yodeling songs)
Dave S. Wambold (tenor and banjo)
G.J. Wilsom (tenor)[88]
Anthony Nish (violin and musical director)

78   *Daily News*, 6 April 1858.
79   "Christy's Minstrels," *Morning Chronicle*, 19 March 1861.
80   "Christy's Minstrels," *Lloyd's Weekly*, 21 February 1858.
81   "Christy's Minstrels," *Era*, 2 June 1861.
82   "Nigger Minstrelsy," *Saturday Review*, 11 May 1861: 477-78.
83   "Christy's Minstrels," *Lloyd's Weekly*, 2 June 1861.
84   Frederick Douglass, *My Bondage and My Freedom* (1855; reprinted by Hardmondsworth: Penguin, 2003), 74.
85   Based on London and Liverpool programmes at the Harvard Theatre Collection and British Library, *c.* 1857-61.
86   Replaced by Mr. Rainford in 1861.
87   Died 5 June 1859; replaced by George W. "Pony" Moore.
88   Joined in 1859.

Joe Brown (jig dancer)
G.W. Meeker (instrumentalist)
E. Thompson (instrumentalist)
J.T. Donnelly (instrumentalist)

[Items with an asterisk are reproduced below]

Part I

Overture—Instrumental Medley, introducing the whole Troupe
Opening Chorus, arranged by the Company
Songs
"Kiss Me Quick and Go," by F. Buckley (W.P. Collins)*
"In a Little Log Hut," by E.H. Pierce (E.H. Pierce)*
"The Mocking Bird," arranged by A. Mullen (J.W. Raynor)*
"Dat's Another Pull Back," by Frank Williams (W.P. Collins)*
"Good News from Home," by P.S. Gilmore (W. Burton)*
"Nelly Gray," music by M.W. Balfe and words by John Oxenford[89] (J.W. Raynor)*
"Come Where My Love Lies Dreaming," by Stephen Foster (quartet)*
Tyrolean solo, exhibiting great volume and flexibility of voice (T. Christian)
"The Sleigh Polka," a musical description of a Fashionable Sleigh Ride, with the Departure; Race
    on the Road; the Arrival at the Hotel; the Ball; Preparing to Return; All Aboard; the Chorus and
    Arrival Home at Daybreak, by L. Jullien (Full Band)*

An interval of ten minutes

Part II

Musical and Miscellaneous Olio "We're a Band of Brothers," burlesque on the Hutchinson Family,
    John, Judson, Jesse and Asa (Messrs. Raynor, Burton, Meeker, Christian)
Polka Burlesque (Pierce and Collins)
Ballad (D.S. Wambold)
Violin Solo (A. Nish)
American Jig (Joe Brown)
Burlesque Italian Opera by William Brough
    *The Nigger's Opera; or, The Darkie That Walked in Her Sleep**
    OR
    *The Gypsy Maid**

An interval of five minutes

Part III

Hoop de Dooden Doo (E.H. Pierce)*
Duet (E.H. Pierce and Collins)
Banjo Solo (E.H. Pierce)

---

89   Balfe (1808-70) was the composer of the opera *The Bohemian Girl* on which the burlesque *The Gypsy Maid* was based.
    Oxenford (1812-77) was a playwright. The lyrics for "Nelly Gray" are also attributed to Benjamin Russel Hanby.

Illustration 13. "Kiss Me Quick and Go!" by J.F. Buckley, song sheet. Courtesy of the British Library Board H 1401 (1).

Illustration 14. "In a Little Log Hut," song sheet. Courtesy of the British Library Board H 1401 (1).

Illustration 15. "The Mocking Bird,"
song sheet. Courtesy of the British
Library Board H 1401 (12).

Illustration 16. "And Dat's Another Pull Back" by Frank Williams, song sheet. Courtesy of Lester S. Levy Collection of Sheet Music, Special Collections, Milton S. Eisenhower Library, Johns Hopkins University.

Illustration 17. "Good News from Home" by P.S. Gilmore, song sheet. Courtesy of the British Library Board H 1401 (1).

Illustration 18. "Nelly Gray" by John Oxenford (lyrics) and J.W. Balfe (music), song sheet.
Courtesy of the British Library Board H 1401 (14).

Illustration 19. "Come, Where My Love Lies Dreaming" by Stephen Foster, song sheet. Courtesy of the British Library Board H 1401(1).

Illustration 20. "Sleigh Polka" by
Louis Antoine Jullien, song sheet.
Courtesy of the Lester S. Levy
Collection of Sheet Music, Special
Collections, Milton S. Eisenhower
Library, Johns Hopkins University.

The Nigger's Opera; or, The Darkie That Walked in Her Sleep[90]

BY WILLIAM BROUGH

First performed at the Bijou Theatre (Haymarket), London, 12 March 1861, by the Christy's Minstrels.

Dinah, known in operatic circles as Amina the Darkie that Walked in her Sleep	Mr. Collins
Aunt Sally, sometimes called Aunt Sally Dinah's Mother	Madam Anne Boddi[91]
Dandy Jim from Caroline, who would probably have been called Elvino had he been a native of Switzerland	Mr. Wilsom
Dolphus, a heavy swell of color according to his own account a count being empowered by Royal Italian Opera license to change his name to Rodolpho	Mr. Rainford
Caesar and Pompey, two coloured celebrities who have kindly consented to combine the duties of the old Greek and the modern operatic chorus—their first appearance in the musical world	Messrs. Nish and Moore
Peasants, Villagers etc.	

(Enter Pompey meeting Caesar).

POMPEY. That you Caesar?

CAESAR. Well yes I s'pose so, I don't like to be too positive about it. I lost a wager yesterday to that conceited Nigger Brutus, through being positive.

POMPEY. How was that?

CAESAR. Why yesterday when the clock struck twelve, he pulled out his chronometer—you know that large copper one as big as a warming pan[92]—and it was half past twelve. "Halloa Brutus," says I, "your watch is fast." "It ain't," says he. "'Tis," says I, and we got 'sputing[93] about it, and at last we laid a wager—and what d'you think I found out?

POMPEY. What?

CAESAR. Why that his watch had stopped and instead of being half an hour too fast, it was eleven hours and a half too slow.

POMPEY. So you lost.

CAESAR. Why of course I did. It was half past twelve the night before by his watch, don't you see?

POMPEY. Well come, Massa's given us all a holiday today. So we're going to have some rare fun. We're "going to try our hand at an uproar."

CAESAR. What an uproar—a Row?

POMPEY. A "Row"? no you stupid nigger. An uproar's a sort of foreign country where every body's lost the way of speaking and they're forced to put up with singing instead. Here, lend a hand to put the place in order and we'll show you. It's what we saw one night all of us to the play. It's about a nigger gal as was going to be married, but took to walking in her sleep instead.

---

90   British Library Add MS 53003 A. Burlesque of *La sonnambula*, composed by Vincenzo Bellini with libretto by Felice Romani after Eugène Scribe (1831).

91   As in "Any Body."

92   A long-handled pan filled will live coals, covered, and passed between the sheets to warm a bed.

93   Disputing.

CAESAR. But they don't have niggers in the play do they?

POMPEY. No they paint them white for fear the ladies should be jealous of their complexions. Come on, these chains will do for the orchestra.

CAESAR. What's that?

POMPEY. Why a musical box as they shut the fiddlers up in. Here, this is Dinah's cottage. *(Sticks placard with "the Kottidge" on down Left)* Now then "we must have a mill."[94]

CAESAR. Must we? Come on then *(shows fight).*[95]

POMPEY *(running away).* No, no not that sort of a mill. A mill with a wheel where they grind things, you know.

CAESAR. All right. I'll fetch him *(exits).*

POMPEY. Of all the stupid niggers I ever met. Oh here's the mill door *(writes with chalk on door Right: "The Mill").* And this table for the Bridge *(arranges chairs and table to form a walk from the door).*

CAESAR *(return with Grind Stone).* Here you are Massa Pompey. Here's a mill for you. That's the chap to grind.

POMPEY. Yes he'll do, put him under the bridge now, then come with the fiddles.

(Enter Band).

POMPEY *(to double bass player).* Here, you first you're biggest bow.

(They take their places).

You and I'll be pheasants.

CAESAR. Pheasants? What, birds?

POMPEY. No not that sort of pheasants. Men pheasants as sing in the chorus.

CAESAR. Sing? Pheasants don't sing. You should call us blackbirds, not pheasants.

POMPEY. Well, well. Stand at the wings.

CAESAR. I tell you I ain't got no wings. I ain't a bit like a pheasant.

POMPEY. Come let us begin. The tale we have to unfold is—

CAESAR. Well but I ain't got no tail either—how can I be a pheasant without wings or tail?

POMPEY. Be quiet, will you. Play up Music.

CHORUS *(enter).*
   La-la-la-etc.

(Air "Happy Are We")[96]

   Happy are we niggers so gay
   We'll laugh and we'll sing and banjo we'll play
   Pretty Miss Dinah's married today
   So it's la-la-la-la and hip hip Haragh.

---

94   A fist-fight (slang).
95   Prepares to box.
96   From the minstrel tune by E.P. Christy:
      Happy are we, darkies so gay!
      Come, let us sing and laugh while we play.
      We darkey minstrels' favorite lay,
      With a ha, ha, ha, ha, and laugh while we play.
      Music delicious!
      O, den how sweet!
      Your kind applauses,
      We hope to greet.

1st VOICE.

Cakes so delicious

2nd VOICE.

Oceans of Wine

1st VOICE.

Dinner they'll dish us

3rd VOICE.

Won't that be fine

CHORUS.

Happy are we, etc. etc.

CAESAR. But where's Dinah? We can't have a wedding without the bride.

POMPEY. Why you stupid darkie, you wouldn't have the prima donna come on with the chorus would you? Of course she must have an entrance to herself. Hark, she's coming.

DINAH *(enter from Cottage. Recitative from La sonnambula).*[97]

Dearest companions, good friends and you too darkies all. I'm glad to see you most sincerely hoping you're pretty middling.

CHORUS.

We're pretty middling.

DINAH *(Aria).*[98]

In my heart such joy now pushes

In my cheek the bright hue gushes

Spare oh spare my maiden blushes

I've not cheek enough for this.

CHORUS.

For a bride that's not a miss.

POMPEY. But where's the Bridegroom? 'Tain't what you call polite to keep the lady waiting.

CAESAR. Look out. Here he comes.

(Music. "Dandy Jim of Caroline").[99]

JIM *(enter, extravagantly dressed. Embracing Dinah).* Oh Dinah you lovely creature.

DINAH. Go away black man. Don't know as I shall speak to you keep me waiting all this time. What you been doin' all the morning?

JIM. Ay what? Can't you guess?

---

97 The libretto used for comparison is *Boosey and Sons' Complete Edition of Bellini's Opera, Sonnambula for Voice and Pianoforte, with English and Italian Words* (London: Boosey and Sons, [1860]); English translations (mangled though they are sometimes) are drawn from this contemporaneous source. This passage is from act 1, scene 3.

AMINA.

Dearest companions, ye also my earliest friendships

Making joy too joyous thus partaking its bounties;

How sweetly grateful unto Amina's bosom

The welcome with whose flowrets, you carols blossom!

98 This continues in act 1, scene 3 and is the moderato passage of the song.

AMINA.

While this heart its joy revealing,

Beats, O, beats with grateful, grateful feeling,

Still my lips in vain appealing

Cannot speak my soul's delight.

99 A comic courting song in the minstrel tradition of dandies. Here it would connote Jim's vanity.

DINAH. Why you've been dressing of course.

JIM. Haven't I rather *(turning around)*. What you think of this? But what else besides dressing?

DINAH. Washing.

JIM. What else?

DINAH. Having your hair curled.

JIM. Yes! What else?

DINAH. Getting your boots cleaned.

JIM. What else? Buying something—guess what.

DINAH. I know—a clean collar.

JIM. No.

DINAH. Give it up then.

JIM. The ring!

DINAH. Oh don't, I shall faint.

(Duet from La sonnambula)[100]

JIM *(producing a very large ring. Sings)*.
   Take now this ring from me dear
   I think 'twill fit you to a T dear
   Like this our love shall be dear
   It has no end as you see!

DINAH *(taking it)*.[101]
   Oh I cannot give expression
   In this time to my confession
   So suppose we try a fresh'un
   Since this time for me won't do
   oh-no-no—

JIM.
   Yes oh yes that air will do love
   In this Ear when breathed by you love
   But now I'm off my time love
   For the parson I must see.

DINAH *(to the tune of "Kiss me Quick")*.[102]
   Oh kiss me quick and go my honey
   Kiss me quick and go
   Your time don't waste so pray make haste
   To kiss me quick and go.

CHORUS.
   Come kiss her quick and go my honey, etc.

(Cracking of whip heard without).

CAESAR *(looking off. Speaks)*. Hallo'a. Hold on niggers somebody's coming.

POMPEY *(looking off)*. Oh golly what a swell.

DINAH *(looking off)*. Getting out of his own post say[103] at the door.

---

100 This seems to refer to Elvino's song "Prendi. L'anel ti dono" (Take now this ring, 'tis thine, love) in act 1, scene 4.

101 This is most likely a second verse for "Prendi. L'anel ti dono" though Amina does not sing this melody in *La sonnambula*.

102 A standard Christy's tune; see part 1 of the programme, p. 282 above.

103 Post-chaise: a four-wheeled closed carriage.

(Enter Dolphus. They all bow and curtsey to him).

DOLPHUS. How do you common fellows, eh?

(They crowd round).

There, keep your distance niggers. I'm very fond of the lower orders in their proper places, when we men of fashion honor the country with a visit we don't like to be scrouged[104] by common rustics so. I tell you *(looking round with eye glass)*. Hah—very pretty—nice place. I like the country for a change when it don't rain, and when the sun's not too hot for the complexion.

(Recitation)[105]

JIM.
  Who is he?
CHORUS.
  Yes who can he be.
DOLPHUS *(using eye glass)*.[106]
  Scenes, so, so rural pretty
  Nothing like it in the city

(Symphony plays "As I View" from La sonnambula *then Air "Robbing Joase").*[107]

  Truly rural scenes, and truly rural people
  A truly rural church with a truly rural steeple.
JIM.
  Tooral-ooral lay
DINAH.
  Toral ooral—
DOLPHUS.
  Tooral ooral lay
CHORUS.
  Torral-ooral do—
DOLPHUS *(speaks)*. There, hold on, that'll do. But tell me what's up darkies? A wedding?
JIM. Yes Sir. That is, we sign the contract today. The wedding tomorrow.
DOLPHUS. And this lovely creature is the bride then.
DINAH. Yes Sir, I's the lovely bride.
DOLPHUS. And the bridegroom.
JIM. This interesting coloured gentleman Sir, I.
DOLPHUS. Very good, niggers. I'll be at the wedding tomorrow, but I must now go to my inn, yonder, where I sleep tonight.
POMPEY. You sleep there? Oh don't please don't!

---

104 Encroached upon.
105 Unidentified.
106 This is probably Rodolpho's cavatina, act 1, scene 6.
    RODOLPHO.
       As I view now,
       These scenes so charming,
       All my pulses, and heart are warming
       With remembrance of days long vanished;
       But my bosom but my bosom fills with pain.
107 Unidentified.

DOLPHUS. Why not?

POMPEY. Oh, low, the Ghost—the Ghost.

(All look round terrified).

DOLPHUS. What ghost? Tell me about it niggers.

POMPEY. We'd rather not Sir, indeed.

DOLPHUS. Go ahead I tell you.

(Phantom Chorus from La sonnambula. *At each forte note all express the most abject terror).*[108]

POMPEY.

Oh dear oh dear Sir to speak my fear sir
All shivering, shaking, all quivering quaking
To lay before you this dreadful story
Oh! I thought I saw, I thought I saw the Phantom there.

All dressed in white Sir, twelve feet in height sir
This bogy[109] stalking, each night comes walking
With eyes all firey and hair all wirey
Oh. I thought I saw. I thought I saw the ghost again.

Whene'er she comes sir, the critters dumb sir
Their fears bespeaking, let up a shrieking.
The coon he holla's—the possum follows[110]
The bull-frog roars and screams "Oh murder" and "Oh dear."

CHORUS.

The bear he whistles butts up[111] his bristles
The oyster shrieks out the lobster squeaks out
And alligators as is their waters
Their heads beneath their wings poor things concealed for fear.

(All exit except Pompey and Caesar. The latter in a fearful state of alarm).

POMPEY *(looking at Caesar. Speaks).* Halloa what's the matter with you?

CAESAR. Say, is it true?

POMPEY. What?

CAESAR. About the ghost?

POMPEY. True? No. It's in the uproar.

CAESAR. Well, then don't let's have any more uproar, I don't like it frightnin' a nigger out of his wits like this all for nothing.

---

108 This is most likely the choral passage in act 1, scene 6 that begins

And wheresoever its pathway falleth,
A hideous silence
All things appalleth,
No leaflet trembles,
No zephyr rambled,
As 'twere a frost
The brook congeals.

109 Goblin.

110 As in "Possum Up a Gum Tree," first introduced to Britain by Charles Mathews (see *Trip to America*, pp. 191-92).

111 Sticks out.

POMPEY. But you haven't heard half of it yet.

CAESAR. Well then I don't care about the other half, tell it to somebody else.

POMPEY. But what you think this ghost was?

CAESAR. Don't want to know nothing about it.

POMPEY. Why 'twas Dinah herself. She as is going to be married. I told you she'd a way of walking in her sleep.

CAESAR. More shame for her—and folks thought she was a ghost?

POMPEY. Yes, till they found her asleep one night in the wrong bed.

CAESAR. What bed?

POMPEY. Guess.

CAESAR. A hotbed?[112]

POMPEY. No.

CAESAR. A watercress bed?

POMPEY. No, guess again.

CAESAR. An oyster bed?

POMPEY. Certainly not. The bed in the haunted inn where that swell nigger was going to sleep.

CAESAR. No?

POMPEY. Fact.

CAESAR. And what did the young man say to that?

POMPEY. You'll hear. He's coming. He's just found her there.

(Enter Jim, indignant. Dinah following with Peasants, etc. Recitation).[113]

DINAH.

Here what's up say what's the row

JIM.

Hence ungrateful deceitful maid

DINAH.

Mother 'Oh' Mother.

(Duet)[114]

DINAH.

Hear me swear then, upon my say so,

---

112 A frame filled with soil, for nurturing or forcing plants (as in a greenhouse).

113 Act 1, scene 10:

    AMINA. Here! for why? of what suspected ?

    ELVINO. Search that black heart it *well* doth know,

    AMINA. Mother! dear mother!

114 This could be the duet between Amina and Elvino, act 1, scene 11.

    AMINA.

      Not in Thoughts remotest dreaming

      Was a crime now, was a crime by me intended;

      Is the little faith, the faith now granted,

      Is the little faith now granted

      Fit return for so much love?

    ELVINO.

      Heav'n forgive ye, this guilt redeeming;

      May *thy* breast, may *thy* breast be ne'er thus rended;

      With what love now my soul was granted,

      Fit return for so much love?

It's all right. Oh don't give way so.
I've done nothing—why this disgrace oh.
Sure 'twill break this darkie's heart?

JIM.

Oh false darkie. How can you say so.
When my love you could betray so
To deny it have you the face oh,
I could act Othello's part!

(Recitation)

JIM.

Go false darkie

DINAH.

I ain't done nothing

JIM.

Away I hate you.

DINAH and JIM *(Duet)*.

Oh my goodness Oh my gracious
Once my hopes were so splendatious,
Now to nothing do they dwindle
What a sell and what a swindle
Just when all appeared so jolly
To turn out so melancholy
Oh my goodness Oh my golly,
What will this poor darkie do.

(Recitation)[115]

DINAH.

But hear me!

JIM.

Go!

DINAH.

But hear me.

JIM.

Go!

(Air "Get Away Black Man")[116]

---

115 This is a continuation of the same song, likely the passage scored as a quintet.

AMINA.

Deign to hear me, deign to hear me I am not guilty, no!

116 "Get Away Black Man! Don't you Cum a Nigh Me," also known as "My Yaller Busha Belle," was a minstrelsy ballad sung in London by J.W. Sharp. It chronicles the courting, marriage, and death of a "yellow" (light-skinned black) woman by a darker man. The chorus is:

[*(Spoken)*] Says she "Yow, Yaw"
[*(Sung)*] Get along black man, don't you cum a nigh me
Scorch you wid a chunk if I don't, blue di me!
To de radi inka day! Oh! ra di inka day!
Grimin nigger see her feed on possum all de way.

JIM.

Go away black maid don't come a nigh[117] me

You'll only get my dander up if more you try me.

DINAH.

Oh dear lack a day,[118] dear lack a day

Never was poor nigger gal ill treated in this way.

CHORUS.

Oh dear lack a day etc.

Never knew a nigger so ill treated I must say.

(Exit all except Jim).

JIM (speaks).

All is lost now. This poor darkie's goose is cooked completely

He's done brown and sewn up neatly,

And with him it's all U.P.[119]

(Aria)[120]

Still with gentlemanly feeling,

I my cause of grief concealing,

Will declare 'twas onions peeling

This poor darkie's tears had cause like this to flow.

Tho' some other darkie charm you

And t'would serve you right to warm[121] you

Yet don't fear I will not harm you

No. I couldn't, no I couldn't wop you, no

Still with gentlemanly feeling

I my cause of grief concealing

Would declare 'twas onions peeling

Still I love you. Still I love you so—

DOLPHUS (entering. Speaks). Come here black man, I want to talk to you.

JIM. Go away Sir. Don't like your company.

DOLPHUS. Come here, you've quarreled with Miss Dinah—what you done that for?

JIM. What for!

---

117 Near.

118 An expression of woe.

119 Obscure.

120 Elvino's solo in act 2, scene 2:

ELVINO.

Still so gently o'er me stealing,

Mem'ry will bring back the feeling,

Spite of all my grief, revealing

That I love thee, that I dearly love thee still.

Though some other swain may charm thee,

Ah, no other e'er can warm me,

Yet, ne'er fear I will not harm thee,

No, that false one, no, no,

I fondly love thee still.

121 Beat.

DOLPHUS. Yes. What for? She's done nothing wrong.

JIM. "Nothing" wrong?

DOLPHUS. No. It's true you found her in my room. But what then? She was fast asleep when she came there.

JIM. Asleep. Hold on Massa. I'm too wide awake for that.

DOLPHUS. I tell you she's a sonnambulist.

JIM. Come don't you call her names, 'cause even if we have quarreled I won't stand it *(showing fight)*.

DOLPHUS. Hold on nigger it's not names. Sonnambulists are people as walk about when they're asleep. It's a sort of doctor's shop word. "Sonnamus"—that's sleep you know—and "ambuls" that's—

JIM. Oh, walker.

DOLPHUS. Just so. How well you know your French, nigger!

JIM. Walk in her sleep. Don't believe a word of it.

DOLPHUS. Listen.

(Symphony. Air "Someone in the House with Dinah")[122]

She came there in her sleep I distinctly state
I saw how matters stood and so I did not wait
But I bolted through the window and I left her there alone
And she went to bed supposing she was in her own.
There was no one in the House with Dinah
No one in the house I'll swear
No one in the house with Dinah
Till you came and found her there.

JIM.
What? no one in the house with Dinah

DOLPHUS.
No one in the house I'll swear

BOTH.
Till (I/you) came and found her there

(Enter Villagers).

POMPEY *(speaks)*. Hush. Be quiet niggers. Poor Miss Dinah. She's worn out with her troubles. And now she's just taking a nap in the mill yonder.

JIM. Taking a nap? Ah! She always was of an-appy[123] disposition.

DOLPHUS. But I guess she won't be so much longer, unless you make it up with her. Do! Now!

JIM. Well, if I could believe she was fast asleep all the time.

DOLPHUS. Do you doubt my word?

JIM. No. Only I don't believe it!

DOLPHUS. You don't. What an obstinate nigger you are. *(Stares)* Look'ee there! Golly if she ain't at it again.

JIM. At what?

---

122 A popular minstrelsy tune:
> There's someone in the house with Dinah
> Someone in the house, I know—
> Someone in the house with Dinah
> Strummin' on the old banjo.

123 Punning on nap, (h)appy, and "nappy" hair.

DOLPHUS. Here. She's coming from the mill sound asleep as any top.[124]

(*Music.*[125] *Dinah comes from mill with candlesticks in hand. Mounts chair to get on table*).

JIM. Asleep and going across that dreadful narrow plank. Stop her.
DOLPHUS. No, no you mustn't wake her.
POMPEY. Caesar—go and turn the mill directly.

(*Caesar works grindstone*).

CHORUS. Yes she is sleeping. Mind, Miss, how you go. Look out. It's breaking!

(*Dinah falls through table dropping candle*).

CHORUS. She's down!

(*Dinah gets up*).

DOLPHUS. Don't touch her, don't wake her.
CHORUS. She's safe. She's sound.

(*Dinah comes down stage to symphony.*[126] *Recitation*).[127]

DINAH.
    Oh why are I not dressed then
    Where oh where's my new lace bonnet,
    With orange blossom
    In thick clusters upon it?
DOLPHUS.
    Hear her she is dreaming thinking of dress.
DINAH.
    Sad is my fate then
    As I walked out by the light of moon
    Merrily singing this same tune.
    There I spied my Dandy Jim
    Sitting on a Rail.

    (*Change to Air "Sittin' on a Rail"*)[128]

JIM (*Sings*).
    Sitting on a Rail.
DOLPHUS.
    Sitting on a Rail.

---

124 Idiomatic: sleeping like a top (sound asleep).
125 Act 2, scene 5.
126 In *La sonnambula*, it is during the quartet that Amina crosses on the plank: the lamp drops from her hand and falls into the torrent, yet she safely reaches the stone steps. Brough probably puts the dialogue over this music in a truncated version of similar action.
127 Following the quartet in act 2, scene 10, Amina arrives downstage with the flowers given her by Elvino in act 1 still attached to her breast. She sings:
    AMINA.
        O were I but permitted only once more to see him,
        Ere that another he doth lead to the altar.
128 "Sittin' on a Rail, or Raccoon Hunt" was a popular early minstrelsy song about a man who encounters a raccoon "sittin on a rail," attacks it, but (in the wily way of raccoons) it escapes with its life.

DINAH.
There I spied my dandy Jim
CHORUS.
Sitting on a Rail!
JIM (speaks).[129]
Let me go to her,
But if we're yet in time dear,
Let us be going.
DOLPHUS.
Now go and take her hand.
DINAH.
The ring you gave me.
Where is it?
Oh give it me once more dear.
DOLPHUS.
Oh yes return it.
DINAH (taking ring).[130]
Once more 'tis mine then.
Oh ain't that fine then
Embrace me, tenderest of parents
With happiness I'm busting.

(Falls into her mother's arms and wakes).

(Spoken). Hallo! Whats all this? Fancy I've been dreaming.
JIM (holding out his arms). Dinah!
DINAH. What, all right?
JIM. Most particularly serene.

(They embrace. Finale Symphony "Do not mingle" from La sonnambula).[131]

DINAH.
Let's be gay and banish sorrow,
All our work is done today,
Laugh and sing until tomorrow,
For it is our holiday!
CHORUS.
Let's be gay, etc. (Repeat Chorus).

---

129 Presumably this is part of the trio in which Elvino sings "No, più non reggo" (No more restrain me).
130 In the same ensemble, Amina (still asleep) sings.
    AMINA.
        I'm thine again, love; thou, mine for ever—
        Embrace me, tenderest mother, Now I at last am happy!
131 AMINA (sings).
        Do not mingle one human feeling
        With the rapture o'er each sense stealing;
        See these tributes, to me revealing
        My Elvino, true to love.

The Gypsy Maid [132]

BY WILLIAM BROUGH

First performed at the Bijou Theatre (Haymarket), May 1861, by the Christy's Minstrels.

Count Arnheim, Governor of Presburg	Mr. Rainford
Thaddeus of Warsaw, a proscribed[133] Pole disguised as a Gypsy	G.J. Wilsom
Florestein, Nephew to the Count	
Sam and Pete, two niggers, expressly engaged for "general utility"[134]	
Arline, the Count's daughter, stolen when a child by Devilshoof, a gypsy who is so ashamed of his wicked deed that he has not the face to appear in the present version	William P. Collins
Queen of the Gypsies	
The Count's Retainers, Gypsies, Citizens	

Scene. Hall of Justice, in the Palace of Count Arnheim. A large chair, centre, elevated on a dais, and having the Austrian Eagle emblazoned upon its back. Over the chair in the wall, a kind of signboard with the inscription "The Hall of Justice—by Count Arnheim." Smaller placards in frames about the wall, having on them "Chancery Suits made to measure," "the Noted House for Nisi Prius,"[135] "Prosecutions conducted by the day, job, or hour," "Judgements delivered free to all parts of the town," etc. Sam is discovered standing on the chair with a hammer in his hand fixing the board with "Hall of Justice" on it. Enter Pete.

PETE. Holloa! There! What are you doing nigger?

SAM. Who do you call nigger. That the way to speak to your superiors? I'se not a nigger—I'se a hama-teur.

PETE. A what?

SAM. A hamerteur.

PETE. And what's a hamel-ture?

SAM. Not "hamel"—stupid "hammer."

PETE. Well I see the hammer plain enough in your hand there.

SAM. Who's a-talking about a hammer?

PETE. You was.

SAM. No I wasn't. I said a hammer*ture*.

PETE. What's that?

SAM. What's that! Well of all the stupid darkies I ever see. Why a hamerteur is a sort of a—well—a hammerteur.

PETE. Oh!

SAM. Yes, of course, a hammerteur, a man as does something as he's no business to do and as he don't get paid for doing.

PETE. Oh! Hold on then nigger. I'se as good a hammerteur as you then.

---

132 British Library Add MS 53004 N. A burlesque of the opera *The Bohemian Girl*, music by Michael William Balfe, and lyrics by Alfred Bunn (1843).

133 A banished outlaw.

134 Someone who plays small parts, as needed.

135 Literally "unless before." Nisi prius is an assize court trial of actions in a civil case. Cases were heard at Westminster "unless before" they had already been heard in the periodic assizes in the counties.

SAM. How do you make that out?

PETE. How? Why t'other day I made a pair of boots for that swell nigger Dolphus, and I ain't got paid for making of them yet.

SAM. Oh nonsense! That ain't amateuring that's cheatin'. What we'se a goin' to do is a hamateur performance of a opera. It's called the "Bohemian Girl."

PETE. What sort of gal's that?

SAM. Oh, a young woman as was stolen from her father by the gypsies when she was a little baby.

PETE. No! What did they steal her for then?

SAM. Why to serve out the old gentleman, her father. He's a kind of magistrate—this is the shop where he sells justice you see. Well, he'd sent some of the gypsies to prison—so they stole his baby to spite him.

(A loud blubbering outside).

PETE. What's that?

SAM. Hold on. That's the old gentleman himself. He's been crying for his stolen child ever since they took her off—twelve years ago.

PETE. What? Been a crying for her all the while?

SAM. Never leaves off, 'cept when he takes his victuals.[136] He keeps fifteen women constantly at work drying his pocket handkerchiefs. Look here comes.

(They retire. Music "The Heart Bow'd down," from The Bohemian Girl).

COUNT *(enters, very miserable. Wiping his eyes etc. He expresses his grief in dumb show to the music, and then sings in a very doleful style, and in a very slow time, to the tune of "There's nae luck about the house").*[137]

The heart bow'd down by weight of woe
    I've never ceased to sing
Though twelve years is full long I know
    To harp on that same string.
My life, since by that gypsy scamp
    Arline was borne away
Has been all gloomy sloppy damp
    Like any washing day.

---

136 Food (pronounced "vittels").

137 This pairs two complaint songs: "The Heart Bow'd Down" (a lilting melody in which the Count expresses his grief) and "There's Nae Luck about the House" (a rollicking Scots tune in which a wife eagerly anticipates the return of her husband from the sea).

"The Heart Bow'd Down," from *The Bohemian Girl*	"There's Nae Luck about the House"
The heart bow'd down by weight of woe,	And are ye sure the news is true,
To weakest hopes will cling,	And are ye sure he's weel?
To thought and impulse while they flow,	Is this a time to think o' wark?
That can no comfort bring ...	Ye gauds fling by your wheel!
To those exciting scenes will blend,	Is this a time to think o' wark when Colin's at the door?
O'er pleasure's pathway thrown	Reach me my cloak
But mem'ry is the only friend	I'll to the quay and see him come ashore.
That grief can call its own.	*(Chorus)* For there's nae luck about the house, there's
	nae luck at a'
	There's little pleasure in the house
	When my gude-man's a-wa'.

It's dumps, glumps, snivel, drivel
 Cry, sigh away
As sloppy and as comfortless
 As any washing day.

(*Music changes to "Old Bob Ridley"*).[138]

Oh! white folks give ear to my ditty[139]
This poor old object please to pity
Twelve years spent in crying is a shame
But old Count Arnheim is my name
 I'm old Count Arnheim oh—
 I'm old Count Arnheim oh—
 I'm old Count Arnheim oh—oh—oh—
(*Spoken*) White folks. Is you a looking at this washed out relic of humanity.
I'm old Count Arnheim oh! (*Sits down*) Another handkerchief!

SAM (*gives one*). Yes sir—but don't you think it's almost time you left off crying.

COUNT. Certainly not, nigger. The man that wrote the opera ought to know best, and he said I was to keep on crying for twelve years, so here goes. (*Count blubbers again*).

SAM. Hold on a minute Massa. Somebody coming.

COUNT. Somebody! Who! (*Looking off*) Oh! my distracted sight—my nephew.

FLORESTEIN (*enter*). Oh my prophetic soul, my uncle!

PETE (*to Sam*). Who's that?

SAM. Be quiet, can't you. Dont interrupt the hamerteurs. That's Massa Florestein. You'll hear.

COUNT. What do you want?

FLORESTEIN. Oh uncle I've been robbed, assaulted, positively frightened out of my wits.

COUNT. Out of your what?

FLORESTEIN. My wits.

COUNT. I hope not lad, you've none to spare.

FLORESTEIN. A lot of fellows last night stole my watch, my ring, and all the valuables I had about me.

COUNT. Hold on there, I 'spects you've been a drinking. Why you've got your watch and rings on now.

FLORESTEIN. Yes, that's the queer part of it. A woman came, as soon as I had been robbed and sung out to the thieves, in a voice that sounded as hollow as if it came out of an empty rum-puncheon.[140]

(*Sings from* Bohemian Girl)[141]

To him from whom you stole
Surrender back the whole.

---

138 This is a comic minstrel tune (by Charles White) in which a plantation slave makes his way to New York City. It begins,
 Now white folks, I'll sing you a ditty,
 I'se from home, but dat's no pity,
 Oh, to praise myself, it am a shame,
 But Robert Ridley is my name.
 (*Chorus*) Oh, Bob Ridley ho ...

139 Song.

140 Rum cask.

141 After the chorus of Gypsies in Balfe's opera surrounds Florestein and takes all his valuables, the Gypsy Queen enters and sings the lines "O-là! tutto rendete, / Al nobile messere"; Florestein requests his diamond medallion; the Queen commands its return, but Devilshoof has already absconded with it.

COUNT. And did they?

FLORESTEIN. To be sure they did. The thieves were gypsies, and this woman was their queen.

COUNT. Gypsies! Hold on! Another handkerchief.

(Sam gives one).

FLORESTEIN. Why what's the matter?

COUNT. You mentioned gypsies. Hah! hah! *(laughs wildly)*. Gypsies—who stole the—?

FLORESTEIN. What?

COUNT. Arline, my long lost child *(going)*.

FLORESTEIN. Where are you going?

COUNT. Going! To have another good cry about the gypsies that ran off with my child twelve years ago *(exit blubbering)*.

FLORESTEIN *(calling after him)*. But uncle stop! You haven't heard the worst. I didn't get all back. There was one jewel I prized more than all the rest. It was an order—

QUEEN *(entering)*. Of the thistle![142] No wonder that an ass should prize it.

FLORESTEIN. Holloa! What brings you here.

QUEEN *(sings)*.

"'Tis I am the Gypsy Queen, ha! ha!"

FLORESTEIN *(speaks)*. Yes, I know. You told me so—in the same style last night. But what about my order?

QUEEN. Come with me to the fair which is now being held outside the palace gates, and you will find a gypsy girl wearing it round her neck.

FLORESTEIN. You don't say so. Come then—

QUEEN. One moment. Suffer me first to inform you that—

FLORESTEIN. That what?

QUEEN *(sings)*.

"'Tis I am the gypsy Queen, ha! ha!"

FLORESTEIN *(speaks)*. Yes, yes. I know you mentioned it before. Come on.

QUEEN. Hah—hah—Revenge—revenge! *(leads him out)*.

PETE *(to Sam)*. Say, who's this gypsy girl that's got the jewel?

SAM. Who indeed? Why the Bohemian Girl herself—the old gentleman's daughter.

PETE. No! Did she steal it then?

SAM. Steal it! Not she. It's that old she alligator of a gypsy queen, made her a present of it just to get her into trouble.

PETE. What for?

SAM. Because she's jealous of her.

PETE. Oh. Then look here. When that old female rattle-snake comes here again, if I don't pound her into mince meat I'm—

SAM. Be quiet you stupid darkies. It's all in the play. You mustn't interrupt the Amateurs. See here's the Count come back.

(Enter Count).

Feel better sir?

---

142 A Scottish chivalric order of knights. Membership is conferred by the sovereign, though foreign monarchs are also admitted. The insignia is a gold, green, and purple depiction of St. Andrew surrounded by the motto *Nemo me impune lacessit* (No one provokes me with impunity).

COUNT. A little, nigger. Give me another handkerchief, and see if here are any prisoners want trying.

SAM (*looking off*). Prisoners! All right massa, here's a beauty.

(*Music. "Marble Halls" to which Arline enters guarded, followed by Thaddeus, Florestein, retainers, gypsies etc.*).

COUNT. What now?

FLORESTEIN. I have been robbed. That girl's the thief.

ARLINE. I ain't. I tell you.

THADDEUS. Certainly not.

COUNT. Order!

FLORESTEIN. Order—yes, here it is—a jeweled one stolen from me (*pointing to medallion round Arline's neck*).

COUNT. Where did you get it, young party.

ARLINE. It was given me by our queen.

COUNT. Walker.[143]

FLORESTEIN. I say she stole it.

THADDEUS. Well and I say she didn't, and so I'll fight you for it—there—come on (*showing fight*).

COUNT. Order there! Prisoner you're found guilty. So attend to what the law states.

RETAINER. Si-lence!

COUNT (*reads from big book*).

　"Him as steals what isn't his'n

　When he's catched he goes to pris'n."

ARLINE. A prison! Never! Thus I free myself (*draws a dagger and attempts to stab herself*).

(*The Count seizes her arm and stops her*).

COUNT (*sings from the opera*).[144]

　Hold! hold!

　With justice this should play the deuce

　A prisoner cooking her own goose

　Sad thing—

　(*changes to "Lucy Long"*)[145]

143　An interjection indicating incredulity, as in "Nonsense!"

144　This is from the act 2 finale.

　　　COUNT [(*sings*)].

　　　　Hold! hold!

　　　　We cannot give the life we take,

　　　　Nor re-unite the heart we break!

　　　[(*Speaks*)] Sad thing—(*taking the hand of Arline, and suddenly seeing the wound on her arm*).

　　The libretto is taken from the version licensed for Her Majesty's Theatre in 1858, [Alfred Bunn, librettist], *The Bohemian Girl* (London: W.S. Johnson, 1858).

145　"Lucy Long"—a comic dialect song in which a woman declines to marry—is a blackface minstrelsy standard. Brough seems to draw on a version that includes Lucy's answers to her suitor. It begins,

　　　　I've come again to see you, I'll sing another song,

　　　　Jist listen to my story, It isn't very long.

　　　　(*Chorus*) Oh take you time Miss Lucy ...

　　Lucy's answer:

　　　　I'd like to know de gemman,

　　　　Dat wrote dat little song,

　　　　Who dare to make so public

　　　　De name ob Lucy Long.

Oh! take your time Miss, you see
    This is really very wrong.
It grieves me much miss to see
    You come out so very strong.
ARLINE.
    To live while thus degraded seems
        To me extremely wrong
    So let me please just stab myself
        It will not take me long.
COUNT, THADDEUS, and FLORESTEIN (in chorus).
    Oh take your time miss, you see
        This is really very wrong
    It grieves us all miss to see
        You come out so very strong.
COUNT (starts as he looks at her arm. Speaks). Hah!—Can I trust my eyes? You have a scratch upon your
    arm. How came it there? Speak—
ARLINE. How should I know? Spose it was the cat.
THADDEUS. Don't you believe her, sir. Everything's laid to[146] the cat. Listen to me and I'll let the real
    cat out of the bag.
COUNT. Go ahead.
THADDEUS (sings from the opera).[147]
    That wound on her right arm
    Whose mark is left you see
    In saving her from greater harm
    Was somehow caused by me.
ARLINE (sings).
    By he?

(Accompaniment from opera continued for some bars, then change to the Air "Nothing More").[148]

    Oh get away, you darkey, oh take away your song,
        You'll nebber be de husband ob dis Miss Lucy Long.
    "Miss Lucy Long" (Boston: C.H. Keith, c. 1843).
146 Blamed on.
147 Thaddeus sings this earlier in act 2. This is the duet "Oh qual contrasto rio!" ("The Secret of her Birth"):
        THADDEUS.
            That wound upon thine arm,
            Whose mark through life will be,
            In saving thee from greater harm
            Was there transfixed by me.
        ARLINE.
            By thee?
148 This courting ballad dates from 1856, music by William Winn, words by J.B. Rogerson:
            In a valley fair I wandered
            O'er its meadow pathways green,
            Where a singing brook was flowing
            Like the spirit of the scene.
            And I saw a lovely maiden
            With a basket brimming o'er
            With sweet buds and so I asked her for a flower and nothing more.

THADDEUS.
> In a valley where I wandered once
>> Some years since there were seen
> A lot of chaps with hunting speaks, all
>> dressed in Lincoln Green.
> I made enquiries who they were, this
>> fancy garb who wore
> The Count and his retainers, going hunting
>> Nothing more!

ARLINE *(sings from the opera).*[149]
> Strange feelings move my breast
> I never knew before
> And bid me here implore
> That you'll reveal the rest.

COUNT *(sings).*
> Go on.

(Accompaniment as before).[150]

THADDEUS.
> The deer they hunted turned to bay, the
>> hunters cut and run.
> The daughter of the Count the deer attacked
>> I found a gun.
> I brought him down, the baby to her
>> father did restore
> Her arm was wounded by his horns—a
>> scratch—and nothing more.

ARLINE. And was that me?

(Thaddeus makes a sign in the affirmative).

COUNT *(exclaims).* Ha! ha! He! He! It is my long lost daughter *(embraces her).*
FLORESTEIN. He! he! Ha! ha! It is my long lost cousin.

(About to embrace her. She throws him off).

ARLINE. Get along with you, do. Fathers is very well, but cousins is an article as I objects to—so I tell you.
COUNT. Pattern of female modesty and gentleness. Come to my arms again *(embraces her).*
THADDEUS. I say, old gentleman, when you've quite done with her.

---

149 This verse is also in "Oh qual contrasto rio!"
> ARLINE.
>> Strange feelings move this breast
>> It never knew before,
>> And bid me here implore
>> That you reveal the rest.

150 That is, resume the tune from "Nothing More."

COUNT. And you—brave young man, how shall I repay you? For twelve long years you have watched over her, and now restore her to my loving arms. Let this bespeak a father's gratitude. Here's fourpenny bit[151] for you—take it—and be happy.

THADDEUS. Away! I scorn the wealth you proffer.

COUNT. You do. Very good *(puts it in his pocket)* only don't say as I didn't offer it mind, now then be off.

THADDEUS. What! Leave Arline? Never.

COUNT. Now just look here you darkie. I ain't going to stand any nonsense. I'm a magistrate, I am. So if you don't absquatulate[152] about as quick as you know how I shall commit you as a rogue and vagabond.[153]

THADDEUS. Tyrant!

COUNT. Halloa! Here's nice contempt of court.

ARLINE. Spare him! *(She kneels to Count and sings from the opera.)*[154]

See at your feet a suppliant—one
Whose place should be your heart.
Do let that darkie there go free.
Think what he's done for me:
He saved my life he brought me up
Provided me with bite and sup.
Twelve years all this he's done
Let him then free depart.

(To Thaddeus. Air "Haste to the Wedding")[155]

Go! haste! for I'm dreading my father's displeasure
We'll meet again soon though compelled thus to part

THADDEUS.

I go at your bidding, though leaving my treasure
Behind me like this is near breaking my heart

(To Count)

---

151 A coin of little value.

152 Vamoose.

153 Persons with no fixed address, wandering outside their home parish, could be punished with imprisonment.

154 From the aria "Padre, sereno guardami":

    ARLINE.
      See at your feet a suppliant one,
      Whose place should be your heart;
      Behold the only loving thing
      To which she had to cling,
      Who sav'd her life and watch'd o'er her years
      With all the fondness faith endears.

155 A traditional Irish tune. It begins,

    Come haste to the wedding ye friends and ye neighbors,
    The lovers their bliss can no longer delay.
    Forget all your sorrows your cares and your labors,
    And let every heart beat with rapture today.
    Come, come one and all, attend to my call,
    And revel in pleasures that never can cloy.
    (Chorus) Come see rural felicity,
    Which love and innocence ever enjoy.

Old man though I leave you, I would not deceive you
I'll come back again when your temper's got cool.

COUNT.
Well go, go, or I soon shall believe you
Not only a rogue but a bit of a fool.

ARLINE, COUNT, FLORESTEIN, and CHORUS (*2nd part of tune repeated*).
You'd better be going, there's really no knowing
The scrapes you'll get in if here longer you stay
So go, go. The gratitude owing
For all you have done we in time will repay.

(*Exeunt Count, Arline, & Florestein L. Thaddeus R.*).

PETE (*speaks*). Well. I consider they've treated that young gentleman uncommon bad after all he's done for the girl. It's a shame—that it is.

SAM. But she's a fine lady now. You wouldn't have her keep company with a common gypsy nigger would you? There's her fine cousin is a sticking up to her now.

PETE. But you don't mean to say as she'll have him?

SAM. Don't ask impertinent questions, nigger, just you wait and see. Look out. She's coming back.

ARLINE (*enter*). Well I can't say as I think much of high life by the little I've seen of it. It's kinder slow after all. But to think I should be a fine lady. Jehoshaphat![156] If I didn't dream it too! And what's funny is it's all coming true—just as I dreamt it.

(*Song, "Marble Halls" from The Bohemian Girl*)

I dreamt that I dwelt in marble halls
    And in marble halls now I reside
And with all that I dreamt what today me befalls
    Seems every way to coincide.
I've riches too great to count—can boast
    Of a high ancestral name
But I also dreamt 'twixt ourselves and the post
    I should find it uncommonly tame.

I dreamt that suitors besought my hand
    Now my cousin comes courtin' of me
I dreamt we had dances and parties so grand
    And a ball there's tomorrow to be.
I dreamt as my partner to dance the post
    Horn gallop young Thaddeus came
And since all that I dreamt thus takes place I almost
    May hope that will come true all the same.

(*Speaks*) Oh! don't I wish it would come true though—that's all. I don't want to be a fine lady—that I don't. I want my Thaddeus.

THADDEUS (*enter*). Does you? Then here you've got him.

ARLINE (*running to him*). Oh golly! Ain't that nice?

---

156 A biblical name (2 Sam. 8:16, etc.), used interjectionally as a mild expletive (as in "jumping Jehoshaphat!").

THADDEUS. Then you ain't a-going to cut a poor darkie—now you're a grand lady.

ARLINE. Cut you? Go away with your nonsense black man.

THADDEUS. What then you won't forget me when, when, you know what I mean.

ARLINE. Of course I knows—when—why don't you sing it?

THADDEUS. Eh? Hold on then. Here goes.

(Song. "You'll remember me" from The Bohemian Girl)[157]

> When other lips and other hearts
>> Their tales of love shall tell
> When wealthy snobs and proud upstarts
>> And every kind of swell
> Shall offer love d'ye think intact
>> Your heart as now will be?
> In other words, in point of fact
>> That you'll remember me.

ARLINE (speaks). Remember you? O' course I will. But hark, there's someone coming. Get in here and hide (opening door R.).

THADDEUS. What should I hide for? I don't want no hiding.

ARLINE. Don't want no hiding don't you? You'll get one whether you want it or not if you're found here,[158] so I tell you. Get in.

THADDEUS. Well but—

ARLINE. Get in I tell you, do (pushes him in violently). So just in time. What a flustration[159] it has put me in!

(Enter Count and Florestein).

ARLINE. Ah! Pa!

COUNT. My child! But how's this? You are pale.

ARLINE. Am I Pa? I was always noted for a delicate complexion.

COUNT. Well, well. I've come to intercede for my nephew here, whom it is my intention you shall marry.

FLORESTEIN (kneeling). Fair cousin, I—

ARLINE. Can't do it Pa, at any price. (To Florestein) There get up do. You'll only soil your Sunday what's-his-names.

COUNT. What? You reject him?

ARLINE. Well, that's just about it, old 'un.

COUNT. And why?

QUEEN (enter). Shall I tell you why?

---

157 Thaddeus's aria begins,
> When other lips and other hearts
> Their tales of love shall tell,
> In language whose excess imparts
> The power they feel so well:
> There may, perhaps, in such a scene,
> Some recollection be
> Of days that have as happy been,
> And you'll remember me,
> And you'll remember, you'll remember me!

158 Arline puns on "hiding" in the sense of "beating."

159 Agitation; probably a conflation of "fluster" and "frustration."

COUNT. And who are you when you're at home?

QUEEN. As I observed before (*Sings*)

"I am the gypsy queen ha! ha!"

COUNT (*speaks*). And what on earth might you happen to know about it?

QUEEN. Tell me first. Do you allow followers in this place?

COUNT. What do you mean?

QUEEN. That there's a man concealed here.

COUNT. A man here! Fudge![160]

QUEEN (*sings from the opera*).[161]

Open that door—and thyself be judge.

(*Count goes towards door R., where Thaddeus is concealed. Arline stops him. Sing together*).

COUNT.	ARLINE.
Stand not across my path.	Pa, you may go to Bath[162]
Brave not a father's wrath	You and your father's wrath.

(*Music. Count pushes her away. The door opens and Thaddeus appears*).

THADDEUS (*speaks*). Good morning Squire.

COUNT. Oh! Somebody hold me. I shall faint.

THADDEUS. No, don't.

COUNT. Slave, leave my house this instant.

THADDEUS. Well, I don't seem to care about staying. Arline dear go and put your things on.

COUNT. What do I hear? My child—

ARLINE. Yes Pa!

COUNT. You'll not disgrace your family by going off with a fellow like that?

ARLINE. Well I reckon my family will have to look out for itself—I'm going with him—that's a fact.

COUNT. With him? A low-bred, good-for-nothing, ugly—

THADDEUS. Here—hold on I say. I can't stand this. Tell you what it is, old gentleman. I'm just as well-bred as yourself, and as for beauty, you'd best just try a looking glass—so there—

---

160 Drat!

161 In the opera, the Gypsy Queen tells Arnheim that his daughter is in love with a gypsy youth:

QUEEN.
List to the words I say—
He is now conceal'd beneath thy roof;
COUNT.
Base wretch, thou liest—
QUEEN.
Thy faith I begrudge,
Open that door, and thyself be the judge.

(*Count, rushing to the door of the cabinet, which Arline in vain opposes*).

COUNT.
Stand not across my path,
Brave not a father's wrath.
ARLINE.
Thrown thus across thy path,
Let me abide thy wrath.

162 i.e., go where I shall not see you again.

COUNT. You! A base-born gypsy slave![163]

THADDEUS. Nothing of the kind, old chap. A swell in disguise.

COUNT. Hah!

THADDEUS (sings).

  Start not, but hear me!

(Song, "The Fair Land of Poland," from The Bohemian Girl)[164]

  When "The Fair Land of Poland" is played by the band
  You're of course well aware what's to come
  So to cut matters short sir, at once understand
  I'm a noble, I swear it, by gum![165]
  In the Rifles enlisted, 'gainst Austria I fought[166]
  A Pole here proscribed do you see
  Condemned to the scaffold—and had I been caught
  I then should a scaffold Pole be.
  My birth is noble, and for the rest
  My quality let this attest (gives paper).

COUNT (looking at it. Speaks). What do I see? An officer?

THADDEUS. In the Rifle Volunteers.

COUNT. Noble too! Ha! ha! (laughs hysterically) My child.

ARLINE. Yes, Pa.

COUNT. Embrace your future husband.

ARLINE. Oh golly, ain't it nice.

QUEEN. Defeated! Foiled! No matter—I'll be revenged.

(Takes from her pocket a pop-gun pistol, points it at Thaddeus. Pete gets behind her, and turns it towards herself. It goes off. She falls. All start).[167]

---

163 Until 1856, Gypsies were enslaved in what is now Romania.

164 This is the line "Start not, but listen!"—just before Thaddeus begins his aria "Allor che l'Ardente Brioso."

  THADDEUS.

  When the fair land of Poland was ploughed
  By the hoof of the ruthless invader,
  When might, with steel to the bosom and flame to the roof,
  Completed her triumph o'er right.
  In that moment of danger, when freedom invoked
  All the fetterless sons of her pride,
  In a phalanx as dauntless as freedom e'er yoked,
  I fought and I fell by her side;
  My birth is noble, unstained my crest
  As thine own—let this attest.
  (Takes his commission, seen in Act 1, from his bosom, and gives it to the Count, who stands fixed and bewildered).

165 By gosh.

166 Part of Poland was occupied by Austria; a nationalist uprising in 1846 failed miserably.

167 In Balfe's version, the sight of Thaddeus about to embrace Arline enrages the Queen.

  (In a transport of rage, points him out to a Gypsy by her side, who is in the act of firing at him, when Devilshoof, who has tracked their steps, averts the Gypsy's aim, and by a rapid movement turns the musket towards the Queen—it goes off, and she falls).

  The finale then ensues.

SAM (to Pete). Halloa! What you interfering for?

PETE. Told you I'd serve out that old crocodile. I've done it.

COUNT. The verdict of the Count is "Serve her right." My child.

ARLINE. Yes, Pa.

(Count leads her down to footlights, and points to Audience. Finale, Bohemian Girl).[168]

ARLINE.
> Oh! what full delight
> > Through our hearts will thrill
> If you say "all right"
> > As I trust you will.
> On our nonsense smile
> > and before you go
> In your good old style
> > Your applause bestow.

---

168 In the final moment of the opera,
> (The distant sound of joyous instruments heard in the saloons, which the intelligence of the catastrophe is supposed to have reached, ceases, and crowds of nobles, ladies, guests, etc., pour in at each door. Arline rushes into the arms of Thaddeus, and then passes over to the Count).
> ARLINE and CHORUS.
> > Oh! what full delight,
> > Through my bosom thrills,
> > And a wilder glow
> > In my heart instills!
> > Bliss! unfelt before,
> > Hope! without alloy,
> > Speak, with raptured tone
> > Of that heart the joy!

Illustration 21. "Hoop de Dooden Doo" by A. Nish, song sheet. Courtesy of the British Library Board H 1401(1).

presentation → Nov. 10
& essay → Nov 17

The Relief of Lucknow (1862)

Interpretive Issues

The indefatigable Irish dramatist, actor, and manager Dion Boucicault was on tour in the United States when the uprising of native soldiers against the British occupiers commenced in India. The first overt acts of insurrection occurred in February 1857, and for two years newspapers were full of the events known as the Mutiny. Mutinous outbreaks were concentrated in northern India and were most numerous from May through July 1857. The British Army fought a formidable enemy: one drilled by British officers, equipped from British stores, and munitioned with British artillery. The British were, in some cases, duly routed.

Two episodes moved Westerners most profoundly: the slaughter at Cawnpore and the long siege at Lucknow. The atrocities committed upon, and by, the colonizers shook British culture to its roots, causing what Christopher Herbert calls "nothing less than an alarming disorganization of national personality."[1] The large garrison at Cawnpore had forewarning of the trouble that erupted on 5 June. Faced with overwhelming odds and no chance of relief, the Europeans struggled under increasingly desperate circumstances. Twenty-two days into the stand-off, after negotiating for the safe passage of besieged women and children down the Ganges, Major-General Wheeler led a column of expectant civilians toward the river. As the overladen boats began to get underway, thousands of mutineers opened fire in an ambush. Survivors were taken prisoner. Weeks later, during the punishing temperatures of July, Brigadier Havelock marched a relief column of 1,800 Britons 126 miles from Allahabad in eight days, winning four battles and taking 24 guns *en route* to recapture Cawnpore. Anticipating their arrival, Nana Sahib[2] ordered the slaughter of all his captives. Havelock's forces found nearly 200 bodies of European women and children hacked to pieces, stripped of clothing, and dumped in a dry well. Those not killed outright by the sword had suffocated from the weight of corpses pressing down upon them. When news filtered back to Britain, readers were horrified by eyewitness reports: "all that remained of these women above ground was 'long tresses of hair, dresses covered with blood, here and there a workbox or a bonnet.'"[3] As the bodies were tossed down the well, Nana Sahib had allegedly ordered musicians to strike up the favourite air from the long siege at Sebastopol: "Cheer, Boys, Cheer."[4] Cawnpore successfully conveyed the message that the mutineers—or freedom fighters—would stop at nothing.

Lucknow, capital of the province of Oudh, preoccupied newspaper reports through summer and autumn of 1857. Brigadier Inglis, commander of the extraordinarily gallant garrison, was dubbed "the Homer of our Modern Troy."[5] Many memoirs were produced of this episode. Captain Thomas Wilson's was among the earliest. Deputy Adjutant-General to Sir Lawrence (who died in the earliest days of the siege), Wilson was in a position to move within the entire post and ascertain its condition round the clock. He describes how, following an uprising on 30 May, officers oversaw the stockpiling of ammunition,

---

1 Christopher Herbert, *War of No Pity: The Indian Mutiny and Victorian Trauma* (Princeton, NJ: Princeton UP, 2008), 24.

2 Nana Govind Dhondu Pant (1827-?), adopted son of Baji Rao II, heir to the last Peshwa of the Maratha Confederacy.

3 "The Sepoy Rebellion," *London Quarterly Review* 9 (October 1857): 252-53.

4 Charles Mackay, *Through the Long Day; or, Memorials of a Literary Life During Half a Century* (London: W.H. Allen, 1887), 137. This song functioned like "a second national anthem" during the Crimean War, the Indian Mutiny, and the American Civil War. "It was played by the 61st when they first marched on to Delhi Ridge, and it was sung at a party in Lucknow when the defenders learned from a spy that help was on the way." Lewis Winstock, *Songs and Music of the Redcoats: A History of the War Music of the British Army, 1642-1902* (London: Leo Cooper, 1970), 168, 177.

5 George Thompson, letter to Amelia Thompson, 9 January 1858 from Calcutta, Raymond English Collection REAS/2/267, John Rylands Library.

guns, and supplies, and reinforced their stronghold within the city. British women and children from surrounding territories crowded into the fortified area, which fell under attack from 10,000 men on 30 June. When the enemy moved at the perimeter, the shuffle of thousands of human feet and the noise of elephants drawing cannons augmented the nocturnal soundscape.

Lucknow was under near constant bombardment, and the sepoys lobbed not only ammunition but also corpses, wooden mortars, and stink-pots composed of iron shell embedded in flax and resin sewn up in canvas. There were funerals daily, yet the garrison could not keep up with the removal of the dead. The climate contributed to the occupants' misery. Temperatures rose to 106°F (41°C) by 8:00 a.m., with regular downpours during the rainy season. Between the putrefying dead, open drains, and saturating dampness, the resulting stench was suffocating. Fatigue, painful boils, smallpox, and other fevers ailed many within the cordon; those stricken with cholera could go from duty post to the grave within a few hours. Lucknow was also under attack from below: Royal Engineers endeavoured to track sappers' tunnels under the city, as these conduits for explosives were potentially more destructive to buildings than airborne projectiles, and early countermining was vital.

Wilson was concerned about provisions in early July; by mid-August many children had died, "all greatly emaciated." The enemy was closing in by late August, but a rare incoming communiqué informed the garrison that no relief could be expected for at least 25 more days. Native servants and camp followers were fast deserting. Survivors crowded into fewer and fewer buildings, while soldiers slept in damp trenches. Half the officers were on the sick list. On 22 September, word came that General Outram had crossed the Ganges and should reach Lucknow in a few days. The next morning distant cannonade could be heard from the direction of Cawnpore. On the twenty-fifth, the relief troops pushed through to Lucknow, having suffered dreadful losses along the way, to face an enemy 50,000 strong.[6] The men who greeted them at the Redan,[7] guarding the place of last stand in the besieged city, had a nearly empty arsenal and a highly irregular appearance: as clothing wore out or was given over for bandages, officers adopted "the most extraordinary costumes; few, if any, had any semblance of a military uniform, and very many were in shirts, trowsers, and slippers only; one gallant civilian having found an old billiard-table cloth, had contrived to make himself a kind of loose coat out of it, while an officer wore a shirt made out of a floor cloth."[8]

Privation, shock, and mourning imprinted upon Lucknow's survivors, as well as the British psyche. The experience did not always do the nation credit. Martial law sanctioned acts of vengeance that, to some cooler heads, seemed to negate the difference between the two sides. The British "came to regard the lives of the natives with perfect indifference," for without due process of law natives were tied to cannons and shot without trial, or qualm, in "cannibal ferocity."[9] To many British, savage retaliation for Cawnpore was justified by the loss of vulnerable women and children. Members of imperfectly understood religions (Sikhs, but especially Muslims and Hindus formed into native regiments) were targeted. At home and abroad, civilians and military of Britain's three ancient kingdoms—English, Irish, and Scottish—were brought together under an indivisible flame. "Remember Cawnpore" became the refrain of countless memoirs, novels, and dramas.[10]

---

6   "The Relief of Lucknow," *Bombay Times*, reprinted in *Era*, 6 December 1857: 6.

7   Redans were forward thrusting V-shaped fortifications, common features in British forts of the period.

8   T.F. Wilson, *The Defence of Lucknow* (1857; reprinted by London: Greenhill, 2007), 88, 119, and *passim*.

9   George Thompson, letter to Amelia Thompson, 22 January 1858 from Calcutta, Raymond English Collection, REAS/2/2/68, John Rylands Library.

10   Herbert, *War of No Pity*; Gautam Chakravarty, *The Indian Rebellion in the British Imagination* (Cambridge: Cambridge UP, 2004); and Patrick Brantlinger, *Rule of Darkness* (Ithaca, NY: Cornell UP, 1988).

One especially persistent, though fabricated,[11] account of Lucknow tells of a Scottish woman who, suffering from starvation and fever, thrilled to the distant sounds of the relieving regiment's bagpipes when no others could hear it and all her compatriots had lost hope of rescue.

Death stared us in the face. We were fully persuaded that in twenty-four hours all would be over. The Engineers had said so, and all knew the worst. We women strove to encourage each other, and to perform the lightest duties which had been assigned to us, such as conveying orders to the batteries, and supplying the men with provisions, especially cups of coffee, which we prepared day and night. I had gone out to try and make myself useful, in company with Jessie Brown. Poor Jessie had been in a state of restless excitement all through the siege, and had fallen away visibly within the last few days. A constant fever consumed her and her mind wandered occasionally, especially on that day, when the recollections of home seemed powerfully present to her. At last overcome with fatigue, she lay down on the ground, wrapped up in her plaid. I sat beside her, promising to awaken her when, as she said, 'her father would return from the ploughing.' She at length fell into a profound slumber, motionless and apparently breathless, her head resting in my lap. I myself could no longer resist the inclination to sleep, in spite of the continual roar of cannon. Suddenly I was aroused by a wild unearthly scream close to my ear; my companion stood upright beside me, listening. A look of intense delight broke over her countenance; she grasped my hand, drew me towards her, and exclaimed, 'Dinna ye hear it? dinna ye hear it? Aye, I'm no dreamin'; it's the slogan o' the Highlanders! we're saved! we're saved.' Then flinging herself on her knees, she thanked God with passionate fervour. I felt utterly bewildered; my English ears heard only the roar of artillery, and I thought my poor Jessie was still raving, but she darted to the batteries, and I heard her cry incessantly to the 'men.' 'Courage, hark to the slogan of the Macgregor, the grandest of them a'. Here's help at last.' To describe the effect of these words upon the soldiers would be impossible. For a moment they ceased firing, and every soul listened in intense anxiety. Gradually however there arose a murmur of bitter disappointment, and the wailing of the women who had flocked out began anew as the Colonel shook his head. Our dull lowland ears heard nothing but the rattle of the musketry. A few minutes more of this deathlike suspense; of this agonizing hope, and Jessie who had again sunk on the ground, sprang to her feet, and cried in a voice so clear and piercing that it was heard along the whole line—'Will ye no believe it noo? The slogan has ceased indeed, but the Campbells are cumin'. D'ye hear, d'ye hear?' At that moment we seemed indeed to hear the voice of God in the distance, when the bagpipes of the Highlands brought us tidings of deliverance, for now there was no longer doubt of the fact. That shrill, penetrating, ceaseless sound; which rose above all other sounds, would come neither from the advance of the enemy nor from the work of the Sappers. No, it was indeed the blast of the Scottish bagpipes, now shrill and harsh, as threatening vengeance on the foe, then in softer tones, seeming to promise succor to their friends in need. Never surely was there such a scene as that which by one simultaneous impulse, fell upon their knees, and nothing was heard but bursting sobs and the murmured voice of prayer. Then all arose, and there rang out from a thousand lips a great shout of joy which resounded far and wide, and lent new vigour to that blessed bagpipe. To our cheers of 'God SAVE THE QUEEN!' they replied in the well-known strain that moves

---

11   There was no one at Lucknow named Jessie Brown, so the account, or whom it names, is a fabrication—though that was not known at the time. Pipers denied that they played on the day in question though they did on 17 November when Sir Colin Campbell's force relieved Lucknow. The 93rd Highlanders took the Shah Njaf, a domed mosque, and signalled their success to Campbell with the slogan. In case this was insufficient, they also hoisted their colours and sent a twelve-year-old bugler aloft to sound the company's calls. After the youngster played "The Cock o' the North," he broke out into verses of "Yankee Doodle Dandy." Winstock, *Songs and Music*, 180-83.

every Scot to tears, 'SHOULD AULD ACQUAINTANCE BE FORGOT', &c. After that nothing else made any impression on me. I scarcely remember what followed.[12]

This story was musically adapted in several versions in 1858, 1860, and as late as 1901. The basic narrative units—the siege, dream, and rescue by the Highlanders—culminate with the triumphal rendition of "The Campbells Are Comin'," the rejoiceful "Auld Lang Syne,"[13] then the stately "God Save the Queen."[14] The exhaustion of the regiment, vulnerability of the women, and fervid zeal of Scottish national symbols and song are all embodied in Jessie Brown.

themes of the play

Genre Issues

Boucicault seized upon the same story for the melodrama he first presented as *Jessie Brown* in New York (February 1858).[15] Melodramas require villainy to be personified, and Boucicault used Nana Sahib to embody unmotivated treachery, performing the role himself. The historical figure Nana Sahib inherited a personal fortune in 1851 but neither a kingdom nor a pension from the British. Disappointed, he sent an emissary, Azimullah Khan, to London to plead his case.[16] Handsome and erudite, Azimullah charmed the British but was unsuccessful in his suit. He returned via the Crimea, where he concluded that the British were so entrenched in their war with Russia that they could not possibly send reinforcements to India. Azimullah and the Nana studied the British military encampments stretched across northern India, sounded out Indian princes, and laid the seeds of the rebellion as early as 1855. They focused not upon the tens of millions of Indian civilians but upon a few hundred thousand Hindu and Muslim troops formed into native regiments to enforce the rule of the East India Company (and, by extension, the British Crown) alongside the regular army of Europeans, whom they outnumbered ten to one. Grievances were many, and their causes entrenched, ranging from unfair pay to the recent British annexations of land, but another factor looms larger in the lore of the Mutiny: the inflammatory rumour that the new, lighter Enfield rifles used ammunition greased with pig fat (anathema to Muslims) or beef lard (abominable to Hindus).[17] Loading procedures required soldiers to bite off the cartridges' paper wrappings with their teeth, but doing so brought fear of contamination, and with it perdition. No precautions taken by the British—including appointing men trusted by the native troops to supervise local production of cartridges—could squelch the rumour. To be ruled by Europeans was one thing; to have one's soul condemned by physical contact with corruption was another. The Enfield cartridges were "the puff of wind which fanned the smouldering mass of embers—accumulated for ages—into a flame."[18]

---

12   "Dateline Calcutta," 8 October 1857, printed in *Le Pays* (Paris), reprinted in *Jersey Times*, 10 December 1857, and in *Times* (London), 14 December 1857; and Winstock, *Songs and Music*, 180; reprinted in Dion Boucicault, *Jessie Brown; or, The Relief of Lucknow: A Drama, in Three Acts* (London: Lacy, 1858), 2-3.

13   The tune was frequently used as an anti-slavery song in this period, as was "The Campbells Are Coming." Vicki Eaklor, *American Antislavery Songs: A Collection and Analysis* (New York: Greenwood, 1988), *passim*.

14   The version written by Edward Wiebe, "The Pipes at Lucknow" (New York, S.T. Gordon, [1858]), dedicated to Agnes Robertson, omits "God Save the Queen." See also John Blockley (music) and J.E. Carpenter (lyrics), *The Highland Rescue, an Incident of Lucknow* (London: Cramer, Beale, [1858]); John Blockley (music) and Grace Campbell (lyrics), *Jessie's Dream (a Story of the Relief of Lucknow)* (London: Chappell, [1858]); John Blockley, *Jessie's Dream; or, the Relief of Lucknow, a Descriptive Fantasia* (London: John Blockley, [1860]); Felix Godard, *Jessie's Dream (Descriptive Fantasia)* (London: Mathias & Strickland, [1901]); and John Blockley, *Jessie's Dream (Song)*, arranged by J.E. Newell (London: Leonard & Co., [1906]).

15   Richard Fawkes, *Dion Boucicault: A Biography* (London: Quartet Books, 1979), 98-99.

16   "Stories of the Indian Revolt," *Tait's Edinburgh Magazine*, November 1857: 675.

17   Saul David, *The Indian Mutiny* (New York: Penguin, 2002); and "The Indian Mutiny," *Eclectic Review*, October 1858: 334.

18   Hope Grant and Henry Knollys, quoted in Herbert, *War of No Pity*, 10.

Nana Sahib named himself Peshwa (Mahratta priest-king, his father's title) on 1 July 1857, but he disappeared shortly after, probably into the forests of Nepal, and played no further role in the Mutiny. Boucicault settled blame on the Nana for not only Cawnpore but also Lucknow, making him the engine that sparks the troops' mutiny as well as an emblematic inversion of British manliness in his callous treatment of women and children.[19] Five years after calls for sadistic retribution for the Cawnpore massacre had eased, in the revised version for the London premiere Boucicault renamed his villain the Rajah Gholam Bahadoor (generalizing his perfidy to the princes who sided against the British), billed the play *The Relief of Lucknow*, a "Scotch Drama and Military Spectacle," and took for himself the role of the Irish corporal Cassidy. It was the custom, at the conclusion of theatrical performances, for pit orchestras to strike up "God Save the Queen," whereupon audiences rose to their feet in patriotic observance. In this case, however, rather than undertaking the patriotic ritual after the curtain rang down, the orchestra played the song while the actors held the final tableau.[20] It was an opportunity to heal trauma and redirect national memory into a feminine figure—played in New York and London by Agnes Robertson, the dramatist's wife—put into service of Britain's historical destiny.

Opportunities to display military valour in historically reminiscent plots with children (for pathos) and women (for romance) attracted numerous dramatists to the Indian situation. The Victoria Theatre and Astley's Amphitheatre produced melodramas about the siege of Delhi in 1857, in which exhausted soldiers bear children down precipitous inclines, and women find strength that makes them fearsome. Indeed, when it came to melodramatic patriotism, there was no such thing as the gentle sex. In *The Storming and Capture of Delhi*, Matilda, a General's daughter, becomes like a tigress defending young ones, revolver in hand:

MATILDA. British thunder now clears the way and British Lions rush to tear these Bengal Tigers limb from limb.[21]

Scottish clansmen rather than English heroes are in evidence, kilts lending colour and variety to the equestrian spectacle, as well as humour when the men are pestered by mosquitoes. William Seaman's melodrama *Jessie Brown or the Relief of Lucknow* (1858)[22] interposes a back story of Jessie's choice to marry a noncommissioned officer in the Highlanders' troops against her father's wishes. Three subsequent scenes trace the increasing desperation of Lucknow's residents and Jessie's pluckiness; the final scene closely follows the memoir that gave Jessie's name to the world. Another version, *Highland Jessie Brown or Lucknow Reserved* (1858),[23] makes Nana Sahib as bloodthirsty as Jessie is brave. She is repeatedly in the

---

19 Boucicault also shadows the abductions at Cawnpore of Margaret Wheeler and Amy Horne in his villain's lust for Mrs. Campbell.

20 "Drury-Lane Theatre," *Times* (London), 16 September 1862: 10.

21 *The Storming and Capture of Delhi: A Grand Military Spectacle*, licensed for Astley's Royal Amphitheatre, produced on 23 November 1857, British Library, Add MS 52969K, fol. 26. Similarly, in act 2 of Boucicault's play, Rev. O'Grady, who gave up a military commission to become a chaplain, takes up arms again out of necessity, becoming martial when manliness is needed just as (in other melodramas about the Mutiny) brave women had done. Audiences may have remembered the fate of General Wheeler's youngest daughter, Margaret, who was abducted by a *sowar* at the boats. She may have been sexually abused, but in any case she rose in the night and slew the *sowar*, his wife, son, and mother-in-law, then threw herself in a well. *Lloyd's Weekly Newspaper*, "Foreign Intelligence," 22 November 1857: 1.

22 William Seaman, *Jessie Brown or the Relief of Lucknow: A Drama in One Act and Prelude*, licensed in 1858, British Library, Add MS 52971 (J).

23 *Highland Jessie Brown; or, Lucknow Reserved*, Queen's Theatre, produced on 6 March 1858, British Library Add MS 52,972 (L).

Nana's clutches but cheers herself with a rendition of "The British Grenadiers."[24] Comic characters sing "Jim Crow" thinking it will befuddle the sepoys—they may be rather befuddled themselves, occasionally referring to their opponents as Afghans—though this episode is crossed out in the licensing manuscript. The melodrama *The Fugitives* (1858) is set during the first days of the rebellion. It interweaves the stories of two Sisters of Mercy whose charitable values are at odds with Hinduism; an affianced bride whose wedding is postponed by the outbreak of the mutiny; the return of this would-be bride's true love, presumed dead in the Crimea; and various escapes as the Europeans flee the spreading rebellion. In effect, India and its historic events provide local colour and particularity, but the formulae could be reconstituted anywhere.

Performative Issues

Boucicault returned from the United States in June 1862 and opened at Drury Lane with *The Colleen Bawn*, an Irish play of star-crossed lovers that he had already performed over 300 times. In August, he added an *entr'acte*, "The Arab Troop, Thirty Moors of the Beni-Zoug-Zoug," to the bill.[25] These gymnasts moulded themselves into pyramids, an Arab arcade, the Atlas Mountains, and scenes with lions, antelopes, tigers, and serpents. In mid-September, *The Relief of Lucknow* had its London debut, including several new "sensation scenes."[26] Similar "showy pieces" had characterized Drury Lane since the 1820s, and this combination of "dialogue, fighting, and smoke" still reigned at Astley's. Even so, the subject's topicality had faded for the fickle public.[27] It succeeded principally through a succession of stirring tableaux.

In act 2, the Rajah sets out to make a blood sacrifice to Shiva: this is to be Mrs. Campbell's child, shot from a cannon. A scene of rapid exposition shifts to a grand ballet in which Jessie (the child's nanny) is disguised as a Hindu girl. The Zoug-Zoug Arabs (and, likely, the Apsara Girls mentioned in the playbills) form the Hindu revellers:[28] a spectacular distraction which enables Jessie to secure the child, mount a horse, and gallop away.[29] In the next scene, Jessie's progress is anxiously monitored by Captain Randal

---

24   This is the best-known British march and war song. It was probably composed in the late seventeenth century, and words were added for the burletta pantomime *Harlequin Everywhere* (Covent Garden, produced in January 1780). Winstock, *Songs and Music*, 32.

25   The *entr'acte* was performed at 7:00 and 10:00 p.m., with *The Colleen Bawn* intervening at 8:00 p.m.

26   Earlier in 1862, Drury Lane featured H.J. Byron's *Miss Eily O'Connor*, a burlesque of Boucicault's highly successful Irish melodrama, with Miss L. Keeley cross-dressing as Myles na Coppaleen. This played with the pantomime and then continued in repertory with Charles and Ellen Kean's season of *Louis XI*, *Hamlet*, *The Wife's Secret*, *The Merchant of Venice*, *Much Ado about Nothing*, and *Othello* (Drury Lane Playbills, Theatre Collection, Victoria and Albert Museum). *The Relief of Lucknow* opened on 15 September and continued until 7 November. Boucicault then took the lease of the Theatre Royal Westminster (formerly Astley's Amphitheatre), and the run resumed there. See Templeman Library, University of Kent, Playbill UKC/CALB/JES/POS/LDN AST: F190671.

27   "Public Amusements of the Metropolis," *New Sporting Magazine*, October 1862: 323.

28   This recalls the Bayadere-esque ballet *divertissement* in George Conquest's *The Fugitives [or, a Tale of India]*, produced at the Royal Lyceum on 1 November 1858, British Library, Add MS 52976 (O) fol. 15. See also *Le Dieu et la bayadère*, choreographed by F. Taglioni, music by Auber, Paris Opèra, 1830. The *Journal des débats* described the Paris debut of a troupe of Bayaderes as follows: "They dance with their whole frame. Their heads dance, their arms dance—their eyes, above all, obey the movement and fury of the dance.... [It is] something strange, impetuous, passionate, and burlesque. It is a mixture of modesty and abandonment—of gentleness and fury." This troupe was employed for an Adelphi melodrama in 1838, *The Law of Brahma*, about a widow saved from suttee (ritual self-immolation) by British troops. Joep Bor, "Mamia, Ammani and other *Bayadères*: Europe's Portrayal of India's Temple Dancers," in *Music and Orientalism in the British Empire, 1780s-1940s: Portrayal of the East*, edited by Martin Clayton and Bennett Zon (Aldershot: Ashgate, 2007), 58, 62-63.

29   Acrobats were typically billed as non-English, and especially East Asian, during this period. When the *Illustrated London News* attested that "an air of reality is superinduced on the entire action by the employment of the Arab troop of the Beni-Zoug-Zoug in the train of the Rajah" (20 September 1862: 307), it meant that the spectacle came across as orientalist and fantastical, rather than in any sense accurate to a religious tradition or authentic to those who enacted it.

McGregor, the child's mother, and other British protectors who watch from a forest as a waterfall roars offstage. This olio scene[30] shifts to reveal the Ghoorka Falls. In a scene with just five short speeches, the Rajah and his henchmen dismount to form a trap for Jessie; the British snipers position themselves on

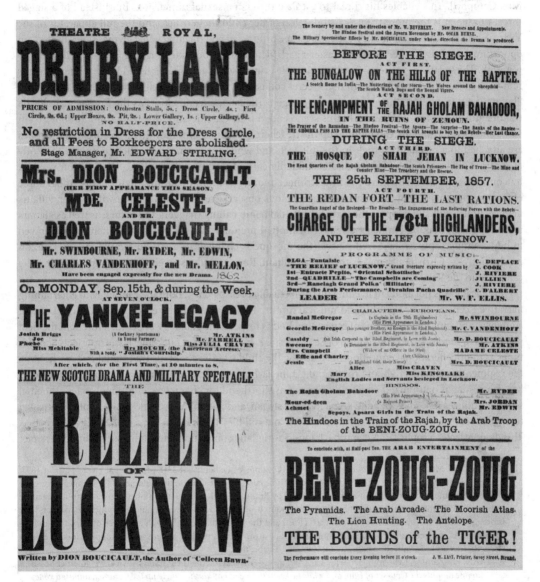

Illustration 22. Playbill for *The Relief of Lucknow*, Drury Lane, 15 September 1862.
Courtesy of the Theatre Collection, Victoria and Albert Museum.

30 Olios required no practical scenery and could be played in front of a painted drop, far downstage, while a major set change occurred concurrently behind the drop.

a precipice; and as Jessie approaches, she unwittingly protects the villains from the snipers. She gallops onward, the child in her arms, and geeing her horse, ascends the cataract in a shower of water.[31]

Boucicault underscores the Rajah's villainy, rather than his humanity, by having him besotted with Mrs. Campbell. This enables his threat to escalate through a sexual dimension. But instead of a staged threat of rape, it is the more theatrical abduction of her child that ensues, and the full apparatus of the Victorian stage is utilized to make the child's escape protracted and thrilling while giving Agnes Robertson opportunities to display her figure in Eastern garb, demonstrate her skill at riding, and be soaked in the waterfall. The sedateness of act 3, in which Geordie is imprisoned by the Rajah and Jessie tenderly nurses him back to health, culminates with their secret collusion with the tunnelling Sweeny and Cassidy who liberate them just before they are due to be hanged. The act 3 curtain closes as the Engineers hold the traitors at firing point. In New York, this scene ended with Cassidy and Sweeny taking the ropes from Jessie and Geordie and instead binding up the treacherous Achmet. But they do not realize that the ropes are attached to a mechanism high in the minaret, and when the faithful are called to prayer, the body of Achmet forms a counterweight and is suddenly carried up through the flies. The London version, by contrast, puts the British troops in a stronger moral position, detaining their enemy under force of arms rather than using an instrument of religious observance to cause (even unwittingly) a villain's demise. Boucicault still peppers the text with mutual name-calling (naggers and kaffirs, as well as giaours and feringhee), making language a matter of mutual prejudice. As vicious as the enemy is portrayed to be—holding captives in sacred places (the mosque is changed to a Hindu temple for the London production)[32]—Christianity makes the British valiant. Rev. O'Grady is given clemency specifically so he can attest to the Rajah's vengeance.

Boucicault was not alone in livening up the factuality of dispatches about the Mutiny with entertaining narrative, scenery, choreography, and musical motifs. This aligns with the ethnic prejudices of London audiences and multiple traditions of repertoire. In this respect, the gallantry of Scottish forces in the field played into a romanticized convention of Scots on stage. In *The Relief of Lucknow*, Jessie interjects Scottish tunes as multigenerational conditioning, teaching the child Charlie about his traditional culture, holding the regiment true to its Highland roots, and (Ophelia-like) demonstrating how privation has unhinged her. Thus, song is naturalized while it also serves as shorthand for characters' emotional states. The final sequence utilizes folk song, popular song, military slogan, and nationalistic anthem into a fully-motivated (diegetic) *coup de théâtre* wholly justified by civil and military tradition to stir a metropolitan audience. This demonstrates a sophisticated approach to melodramatic convention and canny use of sound to depict

---

31   Based on W.T. Moncrieff, *The Cataract of the Ganges* (London: W. Oxberry, [1823]), produced at Drury Lane in 1823. In the final, eponymous, scene, "The Sacred Wood of Himmalaga [*sic*], leading to the Cataract of the Ganges" where the trees are in flame, Mokarra leads in Zamine, followed by Brahmins with torches alit. Mokarra gives Zamine one more chance to accept him, but she will not live thus dishonoured. The men are ordered to put her on the fiery pile, and she is dragged off by the Brahmins. Her sweetheart (Iran) and the Jahrejahs break through and force off Mokarra and his Brahmins. As the trees fall all around, Zamine is in Iran's arms, surrounded by the emperor's troops, who come on in strength. Iran seeks in vain for a pathway for Zamine's escape, then:

IRAN. Fly, Zamine, fly!—my steed will bear you safely!—The Cataract!—the Cataract!—we have no other hope! (*Zamine mounts the Courser of Iran, and while he keeps the foe at bay, dashes safely up the Cataract, amidst a volley of musketry from the Enemy on the heights—the Rajah, Mordaunt, and Robinson enter at the head of the combined Mahratta and Jahrejah Army—the contest becomes general—horse and foot are engaged in all parts—Mokarra vainly endeavours to rally his Forces, who are overpowered by the Rajah—Mokarra is killed by a pistol shot from Robinson—Iran brings forward Zamine in safety—the Rajah joins their hands—and the Curtain falls on the shouts of the Conquerors*). (fol. 50)

32   This is specified in the licensing copy, but a review specifies that this act is set in "the mosque of Shah Jehan in Lucknow." *Morning Herald*, 19 September 1862: 3.

an historical event while reinforcing xenophobic sentiment, but it also requires Jessie to be an elemental figure, almost tribal in her musicality.

Jessie has a pair of lovers who vie for her attention with acts of heroism. These comic men are Irish[33] and Cockney; in aspiring to win Jessie's love, the Union of Scotland with Ireland and England is symbolically strengthened. Geordie the Highland lieutenant, companion of Jessie's childhood, newly branded with brave deeds, is in some ways her natural match (even the pacifist minister follows the regiment to India for this man's sake), but he is interested in Alice, sister to the widowed Mrs. Campbell beloved by Geordie's brother Randal. Nevertheless, instead of ending with comedy's traditional coupling of loving pairs, Jessie's apotheosis comes in a grand tableau with the besieged soldiers and a relieving column of Highland warriors in hand-to-hand combat with the mutineers.

The same regimental piper played "in triumph and disaster, at births and deaths.... in battle it was his duty to animate his clansmen and to be with them where the blows fell thickest, so that he assumed something of the importance of a standard bearer."[34] On marches through the Indian subcontinent, pipers would play not only to cheer on the troops but also to intimidate the locals.[35] The march "The Campbells Are Coming" was used in the Jacobite Rebellion of 1715 and the Napoleonic Wars; playing it in *The Relief of Lucknow* recalled a tradition of military valour and signalled the imminence of dramatic transformation. Pantomime and extravaganza utilized scenic transformation to contrast regimes of sensibility (the fairies' bower and the demons' lair, or a sylvan glade and the gritty urbanscape of the underclasses), but Boucicault did something comparable in the final onrush of redcoats and tartan through the smoke of the cannonade. A scene of desperation and destitution turned, visually and sonically, into the onrush of foot soldiers. The relief of Lucknow—promised on the playbills and as inevitable as destiny—was achieved.

Editing Issues

The two published editions (Lacy's in London and French's in New York) differ only in some changes of nomenclature (e.g., lamp for candle) and rewording of oaths. (In Britain, the Examiner of Plays exercised a strict prohibition against bringing the church into disrepute, but that assumed that only the Christian religion warranted protection.)[36] Boucicault liberally sprinkles place names and Indian words to establish authenticity and an authoritative sense of locale. By the same token, details of Hinduism and Islam exoticize as well as menace. Beyond the putative memoir recounting Jessie's exploits, his precise sources are unknown but likely came from newspaper reporting and ethnographic accounts in periodicals and travelogues.[37] Nineteenth-century place names have been retained in the following edition though the spelling of some terms has been modernized.

---

33 Richard Allen Cave, "Staging the Irishman," in *Acts of Supremacy: The British Empire and the Stage, 1790-1930*, edited by J.S. Bratton et al. (Manchester: Manchester UP, 1991), 62-127; and Elizabeth Cullingford, "National Identities in Performance: The Stage Irishman of Boucicault's Irish Drama," *Theatre Journal* 49:3 (October 1997): 287-300.

34 Winstock, *Songs and Music*, 136.

35 Ibid., 45, 137-38, 178.

36 The principle was clarified in 1909, but until then, judgements were *ad hoc*. In 1853, McKean Buchanan's historicist arrangement of a play based on the life of Mohammed was licensed (British Library, Add MS BL Add MS 52939 E), but when de Bronier's *Mahomet* was proposed in 1890, the Examiner was made to see the offence that would be incurred by allowing the play. Helen Freshwater, *Theatre Censorship in Britain: Silencing, Censure and Suppression* (Basingstoke: Palgrave Macmillan, 2009), 12-13; and Tracy C. Davis, *The Economics of the British Stage, 1800-1914* (Cambridge: Cambridge UP, 2000), 148-50.

37 For discussion of English views of India at this time, see Angelia Poon, *Enacting Englishness in the Victorian Period: Colonialism and the Politics of Performance* (Aldershot: Ashgate, 2008), 75-98. Rev. Alexander Duff's *India, and India Missions: Including Sketches of the Gigantic System of Hinduism, Both in Theory and Practice* (Edinburgh: John Johnstone, 1839) is typical of accounts of the "Gigantic System of Hinduism" rendered into festivals.

This edition is based on the 1862 licensing manuscript, which was prepared subsequent to both published editions; thus, this edition documents the London performance and not the play produced in New York as *Jessie Brown*.[38] Rather than accruing stage directions based on the American run, the 1862 manuscript elaborates dialogue in comic exchanges, tightens up plot-moving dialogue, and gives Jessie subtle opportunities for character delineation in acts 1 and 2. The scenes following Charlie's abduction, including Jessie's escape, are added, and the mosque/temple scene is significantly rewritten and shortened. The final act, where the British make their last stand at the Redan, shows Boucicault's impulse towards concision: Boucicault restricts comic by-play, making broad strokes towards the inevitable sequence of relief, and gives notably less description of staging, music, and sound effects than he did in 1858. This indicates ways in which Boucicault reshaped the historical story for later consumption, retaining and augmenting melodramatic elements, without definitively establishing how the New York and London productions compared in setting the final moments. These are not textual instabilities, for Boucicault was both the dramatist and stage arranger in both cases, and it is reasonable to assume that he submitted a text for licensing that he endorsed. They are the kinds of indetermin-abilities characteristic of nineteenth-century scripts created for different purposes (reading versus producing); even so, neither is definitive documentation of a particular production nor a blueprint for subsequent productions. The additional scenes interjected in the licensing manuscript reflect the resources at Drury Lane (such as the Beni-Zoug-Zoug Arabs and stock scenery) as much as the mar-ketability of the story in 1858 versus 1862, and London reviews stress the abundance of scenic effect and spectacular success with the audience.

---

38   The use of the revised version in London is confirmed by reviews which detail incidents not found in the earlier published editions.

The Relief of Lucknow[39]

BY DION BOUCICAULT

First performed at Wallack's Theatre, New York, beginning 22 February 1858 and running upwards of eighty nights. The same text was performed at Theatre Royal Plymouth, November 1858, with a company other than Boucicault's that toured Bristol and the West Country. Boucicault's company performed a revised version (the licensed text, printed here) at London's Theatre Royal Drury Lane, 15 September 1862.

	New York	*London*
Rajah[40] Gholam Bahadoor[41]	Dion Boucicault	Mr. Ryder
Achmet, his Vakeel[42]	Mr. Grosvenor	Mr. Edwin
Mour-ed-deen,[43] a Rajpoot[44] Prince		Mrs. Jordan
Capt. Randal McGregor, 78th Highlanders	Mr. Lester	Mr. Swinbourne
Lt. Geordie McGregor	A.H. Davenport	C. Vandenhoff
Rev. David O'Grady,[45] Chaplain to the 32nd Regiment	Mr. Blake	H. Mellon
Private Sweeny, 32nd Regiment	T.B. Johnston	Mr. Atkins
Corporal Cassidy, 32nd Regiment's drummer	Mr. Sloan	Mr. Dion Boucicault
General Havelock[46]		
Jessie Brown, a Scottish girl	Agnes Robertson	Agnes Robertson[47]
Amy Campbell, Widow of an officer in the 93rd	Mrs. Hoey	Madame Celeste
Charlie and Effie, her children	Master and Miss Reeves	Master White and Miss L. Raymond
Alice, her sister	Mary Gannon	Miss Craven
Mary	Miss Orton	Miss Kingslake
Hindu Revelers		Beni-Zoug-Zoug Arabs

Soldiers, Highlanders, Sepoys, Hindu Servants, English Ladies and Servants Besieged in Lucknow, and Apsara[48] Girls in the Train of the Rajah

---

39   Based on the licensing copy, British Library Add MS 53016(G), licensed on 11 September 1862. Where songs are specified, lyrics have been added.

40   King.

41   In New York, this character was named Nana Sahib, Rajah of Bithoor, after the notorious rebel, and played by Dion Boucicault. The published edition reflects this. Bithoor, part of Cawnpore (now Kanpur City), is considered by Hindus to be the centre of the universe. It was Nana Sahib's headquarters. Playbills and reviews indicate a further name change, to Rajah Gholam Bahadoor. Gholam Bahadoor recalls Ghulam Muhammad Khan Bahadur (1763-1828), the tyrannical viceroy of Rampur.

42   (Anglo-Indian) agent, envoy, or representative.

43   Named Mahoon in the published edition.

44   A Hindu military caste.

45   Named Rev. David Blount in the published edition.

46   A non-speaking part.

47   Mrs. Dion Boucicault.

48   Hindu dancers.

Drury Lane: Scenic Design William Beverley
Choreographer Oscar Byrne
Musical Director W.F. Ellis

COSTUMES[49]

Rajah Gholam Bahadoor	White turban with jewels, white tunic and trousers, red Morocco[50] shoes, yataghan.[51] Second Act: Morocco boots, sword and pistols
Achmet	Red turban, shirt and trousers of a bold stripe—the same pattern not worn by any other character
Capt. Randal McGregor	Red coat, plaid trousers and scarf, broad sword, white cotton topi,[52] with lappet[53] round the neck
General Havelock	Blue frock coat, cocked hat, dark trousers and gauntlets
Rev. O'Grady	Black cut-off coat, trousers, broad brimmed hat, white cravat, and grey hair
Corp. Cassidy and Pvt. Sweeny	Red coat, white trousers, and white cotton toupee
Mrs. Campbell	White muslin dress
Charlie and Effie	Neat white dresses
Alice and Mary	White muslin dresses, white hats, and parasols
Jessie	Grey stuff[54] dress, light paid scarf, and hood
Rebel Sepoys	Red coats, white trousers and shakoes[55]
Servants	White turbans, shirts, trousers, and leather slippers
Natives	All have dusky complexions
Soldiers	Uniforms of different regiments
Highlanders	Full Highland uniforms

Scene 1

The summer residence of Mrs. Campbell in the province of Oudh, India. Table laid for tea etc. Enter Mrs. Campbell, Alice, Mary, and Achmet from the house.

MRS. CAMPBELL. It is nearly sunset, and Jessie has not returned with the children. Alice do you see my little ones coming home?

ALICE. No—I am watching Geordie McGregor who is crawling up the hill.

MRS. CAMPBELL. He is just in time for tea.

---

49   From the printed (London) edition.
50   Fine flexible goatskin leather.
51   A slightly curved double-bladed sword without a guard.
52   Pith helmet (corrected from "toupee" in London edition).
53   Loose flap.
54   Smooth woven wool.
55   Cone-shaped caps, topped with plumes or pompoms.

GEORDIE *(enter R.H.)*. Here I am—dead beat—I have walked over from the fort to bring you the news. *(Gives paper)* Here is the latest from Calcutta.

MARY. Is the overland mail in?

GEORDIE. No, but there's the deuce to pay. It seems down below there, the native regiments at Patna[56] have mutinied.

(Achmet stops to listen).

MRS. CAMPBELL. I thought that foolish man was at an end.

GEORDIE. It seems not. My brother Randal arrived at the fort last night—

MRS. CAMPBELL. Randal returned?

GEORDIE. We are ordered to vacate the fort and march to Lucknow.

MRS. CAMPBELL. How provoking. We only arrived here last week to spend the hot months in these cool mountains, and now you are going to leave us.

O'GRADY[57] *(enter L.)*. Going to leave us?

GEORDIE. Yes, Sir, we are under orders to march. All our plans for enjoyment for the summer are destroyed. I reckoned on making love to Alice there, while Mrs. Campbell relied on billing and cooing with my brother Randal.

MRS. CAMPBELL. Geordie!

GEORDIE. Our charming dovecote here is demolished.

O'GRADY. I hope this sudden order does not mean that this rebellion is approaching this part of the country.

GEORDIE. Oh! no fear of that. The fact is we have spoiled our Sepoy troops—those black rascals are mere scum. *(To Achmet)* Well what are you grinning at?

ACHMET. Because the Sahib[58] speaks truth. In Hindoostan there are one hundred millions such as I am, and there are one hundred thousand such as you, yet for a century you have had your foot on our necks. We are to you a thousand to one—a thousand black necks to one white foot. God is just; and Mohammed is his prophet. We are scum!

GEORDIE. I can't answer for the truth of your calculation, but I agree in the sentiment—you are scum.

(Exit Achmet).

MRS. CAMPBELL. Beware of that man, Geordie, I did not like the expression of his face as you spoke.

GEORDIE. Bah! there is virtue enough in one redcoat to put a whole army of them to flight.

MRS. CAMPBELL. Have you ever been in action?

GEORDIE. Never, but when I'm on parade and hear the drums and see the uniforms, I feel like the very devil!

ALICE. There is no chance of that war coming here—is there?

GEORDIE. Here—not the slightest. London itself is not more peaceable than these mountains, the natives here are faithful and docile as dogs.

MRS. CAMPBELL. Yes thank Heaven. We are far away from any fears. But when I read of the atrocities already perpetrated by the Sepoys—when I think of my two little children—oh, why do I remain here in the neighbourhood of such scenes of horror?

---

56 In Bihar.
57 Rev. David Blount in both published editions.
58 Respectful term of address to Europeans (equivalent to "Sir").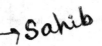

GEORDIE. Because you are in love with my brother Randal.

MRS. CAMPBELL. Yes, and to gratify that selfish love I keep my little ones here in the midst of death, when we might be in safety at home.

GEORDIE. Safety—why yonder is the fort with a detachment of thirty men in it—Queen's troops—twenty of the 32nd and ten of Randal's Highlanders the 78th.

ALICE. Yes—thirty sick men and you a mere boy.

GEORDIE. A what? I'm twenty next May.

MRS. CAMPBELL. You were at school last year.

GEORDIE. Well if I was, a McGregor of nineteen is worth three other men of five and twenty.

ALICE. Geordie's Scotch blood is up.

GEORDIE. Then don't you call me a mere boy. Wait till you see me in a fight.

O'GRADY. My dear boy, I was in the same army once. I felt like you, until I saw the field of battle in which I had a share. That dreadful sight, those sufferings to which I had contributed so shocked my poor weak nature that I sold my commission and entered the church—a vocation more congenial to my humanity.

GEORDIE. Our men say that you are as brave as a lion, although you pretend to be as gentle as a lamb.

ALICE. A cup of tea, Mr. O'Grady?

O'GRADY. Thank you. I prefer a cup of Sangaree.[59] I'll lie down under this mango and read the news.

MRS. CAMPBELL. Jessie keeps the children out too late.

GEORDIE. You need not be anxious. She has our bodyguard with her—her two lovers.

ALICE. Two lovers—that is an extra allowance.

GEORDIE. Bless her bright Scotch face, she might have *seven hundred* if she wished, for that is the effective strength of the 78th Highlanders, and there's not man there that wouldn't die for her.

MRS. CAMPBELL. She is indeed a faithful creature.   *Speaking of Jessie*

ALICE. And she loves the children better than anything in the world.

GEORDIE. Except my brother Randal—or the McGregor as Jessie insists on calling him to his great annoyance.

MRS. CAMPBELL. Ha, here she comes.

JESSIE (enters). Gude day leddies,[60] I am certain it's maister Geordie an in his braw[61] red coat and gold lace. There's mo' McGregor in every inch o' him.

GEORDIE. There she goes on the McGregor again.

JESSIE. The bairns[62] here they come my leddie the devil awa in the laggards.[63] (Calls Cassidy) Hand the parasol over the bairn ye laut.

GEORDIE. Look at the use to which she puts Her Majesty's 32nd regiment—makes under-nurses[64] of my men—you see to what base uses love may bring the bravest of our sex.

(Enter Cassidy with Effie, and Sweeny with Charlie).

MRS. CAMPBELL. There girls, I wish you a pair of lovers as useful and faithful as those of Jessie.   *Speaking of Cassidy & Sweeny*

JESSIE. Haut no leddie, they're na lovers o' mine.

ALICE. Come Cassidy, Sweeny which is the favoured one?

SWEENY. Please, Mum, it's this 'ere Hirishman we Henglish haint no chance mum.

---

59   Cold wine, diluted and spiced.
60   Lads.
61   Splendid.
62   Children.
63   Here come the children, the devil take the slowpokes.
64   Assistant nannies.

CASSIDY. If you please, Miss, it's this thief o' the world Sweeny—bad luck to him. She's dying for the spalpeen.[65]

SWEENY. She isn't.

CASSIDY. She is, and that's why. I saved your dirty life at Berhampore.[66]

SWEENY. She isn't.

CASSIDY. She is.

JESSIE. Are ye daft, ye fools?[67] Fall in! Attention 32nd Dress. Left face. March!

(Exit Sweeny and Cassidy).

GEORDIE. There's discipline.

MRS. CAMPBELL. See, do my eyes deceive me—yonder—a horseman dismounts at the brack[68] below and ties his charger to a tree.

GEORDIE. 'Tis Randal, he has galloped across from the fort.

JESSIE. The McGregor.

ALICE. Come Geordie shall we not be generous and leave Randal to meet Amy alone?

JESSIE. Eh? Master Geordie—that's one word for the McGregor—and twa[69] for herself.

GEORDIE. Come Mary.

(Exit Alice, Geordie, and Mary).

MRS. CAMPBELL. Randal is coming. I cannot hear his footsteps, yet I feel he is there. It is the air he breathes that conveys his presence to me as it flutters through my heart.

RANDAL *(enters).* Amy—

MRS. CAMPBELL. Dear Randal!

CHARLIE. Oh! there's Randal. Kiss me.

RANDAL. Dear ones—ah—Jessie—lassie—

MRS. CAMPBELL. How her eyes sparkle, as she looks upon you. It is with pride—kiss her—Randal, you will make her so happy.

RANDAL. What folly—there—go along, Jessie *(kisses her forehead).*

JESSIE. Oh—ma—leddie, ye dinna ken[70] how a Scottish heart grows warm—to the tartan o' their bluid.[71]

RANDAL. Leave us Jessie, and send here Cassidy and Sweeny.

(Exit Jessie).

RANDAL. Amy—I have had news. The rebels are at Meerut[72]—Delhi has revolted—the disaffection of the Native troops is more extensive than our worst fears prompted us to believe—

---

65   Rascal.

66   A small encampment 120 miles upstream from Calcutta where, in late February 1857, sepoys refused to accept new ammunition because they believed it was improperly greased. A morning parade was ordered when anyone not accepting cartridges would be court-martialled. At midnight prior to the parade, fearful Hindus seized their muskets; officers tried to reason with them and the commander, Lieutenant-Colonel William Mitchell, threatened to fire on them with grapeshot. It took three hours to explain the cause of the rising and subdue the men.

67   In the manuscript, "ye Jules" (obscure).

68   This could mean either a crag or a piece of uncultivated land.

69   Two.

70   Do not know.

71   Blood (figurative for clan).

72   Meerut, forty miles northeast of Delhi, mutinied on 10 May 1857. Early the next morning, the rebellion broke out in Delhi.

MRS. CAMPBELL. Thank Heaven we quitted Benares[73]—we are in safety here.

RANDAL. Fatal security! Yonder country seems to you to be in repose—yet to me it looks like a sleeping tiger. Death is humming in the air.

MRS. CAMPBELL. You exaggerate the danger—the people are kind and gentle—not a look of anger in any face—our servants are devoted to us.

RANDAL. Are they? One of them is watching us now—don't turn—a fellow in a crimson turban—

MRS. CAMPBELL. Achmet.

RANDAL. Look away—I will keep my eye on him. Listen—tonight you must leave this place.

MRS. CAMPBELL. Tonight! Is peril so near?

RANDAL. Your servants are in league with Mour-ed-deen the bay[74] prince of—Shahjahanpore.[75]

MRS. CAMPBELL. My servants—

RANDAL. The lives of your children are paid for—your honor is sold. In a few days this peaceful abode will be a pile of bloodstained blackened ruins—

MRS. CAMPBELL. It is impossible! Oh, Randal—

RANDAL. Hush, they come—dissimulate your fears, or we are lost.

(Enter Achmet and servants, who remove the service. Randal dances Effie on his knee and sings).

MRS. CAMPBELL. They are gone.

RANDAL. Regain your courage—think of your children—

MRS. CAMPBELL. Oh Randal, let us hope that you are mistaken—why do you suspect my household of treachery?

RANDAL. Because one of them is a spy of Mour-ed-deen—This letter was intercepted yesterday. Do you know the Rajah—

MRS. CAMPBELL. The Rajah! Yes, once only I saw him at Benares a year ago at the feast of the Mahurran[76]—

RANDAL. You do not understand Hindi—

MRS. CAMPBELL. No.

RANDAL. Listen then as I translate.

(Achmet glides on at back).

(Reads) "My faithful Achmet—on the night you know of—at one hour after the set of moon, I shall be with 500 men at the Raphee Ghat,[77] when the Feringhee[78] woman is in my Zenana[79]—to you I give a bracelet of gold and a purse of mohurs.[80] Destroy the children." Rajah.

MRS. CAMPBELL. My children.

(Sees Achmet raising a knife over Randal—utters a cry. Achmet drops his knife and leaps over parapet. O'Grady utters a cry. Randal fires his revolver at Achmet. Enter Geordie, Mary, Alice, Jessie, Cassidy and Sweeny).

---

73   Hindus' holy city on the Ganges, an important pilgrimage site (also called Varanasi). It mutinied on 4 June 1857.
74   Reddish-brown.
75   Approximately 100 miles northwest of Lucknow.
76   A sacred month in the Muslim calendar.
77   Mountain pass.
78   Euro-Christian (pejorative).
79   Part of a dwelling occupied by a harem.
80   Gold coins.

ALL. What is it?

O'GRADY (*appearing with a smashed umbrella on hat*). It came plump on my umbrella—

RANDAL. Twas nothing—a jackal in that thicket. I fired to frighten him away.

O'GRADY. A jackal! I beg your pardon—

RANDAL. Hush, say it was so—

O'GRADY. A jackal—oh yes—a jackal six feet high.

RANDAL. Don't be alarmed, return to the house all of you—stay you men.

(*All go off except Mrs. Campbell, O'Grady, Cassidy, and Sweeny*).

RANDAL. Mr. O'Grady, moments tonight may be worth lives—we are in danger.

O'GRADY. Here—

RANDAL. Yonder mountains may be swarming with our foes. I cannot tell. Their design is to take us by surprise. The young prince Mour-ed-deen with five hundred men will attack the fort while the Rajah surrounds this place—and puts its inmates to death except Amy whom he destines for his Zenana—

O'GRADY. The monsters—demons—

CASSIDY. Sweeny aye hear that—the naggers[81] is comin—dasen't your mouth wather ye villin?

MRS. CAMPBELL. Does Geordie know our peril?

RANDAL. No—he is young and rash. I must haste back to the fort, and to you, Mr. O'Grady I confide the defence of this house.

O'GRADY. Me defend—but you—oh dear—you don't expect *us* to be attacked tonight.

RANDAL. No but we must take precautions. You were once an officer in the Dragoons, and the men say you distinguished yourself.

O'GRADY. Distinguished—Sir—I beg you won't recall my youthful errors to my mind.

RANDAL. Yes—you behaved gallantly in the Sikh Campaign.[82]

CASSIDY. Oh by dad you may say that—didn't I ride behind him at Chilliawellah[83] and Ferayisheh.[84] Oh if he seen how he tickled the pandies.[85]

O'GRADY. Hold your tongue, sir. I quitted the Army from conscientious scruples.

RANDAL. But if you saw these women and these little ones in the power of our foes?

O'GRADY. I could pray for them.

CASSIDY. It's sure—I've seen him at his devotions. I recollect the way of it—down 'ud go a pandy—repint ye sinners—right wheel—Heaven forgive us—charge—

RANDAL. I will leave you in command here. Geordie, Cassidy, and Sweeny will aid you—

MRS. CAMPBELL. Do you go alone?

RANDAL. My horse is at the foot of the hill—a few moments will take me across the valley—Farewell! (*Exit*).

O'GRADY. Stop Randal—I cannot undertake it—it is impossible. He is gone—

CASSIDY. Now he's in his native iliment. Smoke?

O'GRADY. How can I, a minister of peace—undertake to—to—what arms have you got in the house?

MRS. CAMPBELL. Two double guns—a rifle—my late husband's swords and a pair of pistols.

---

81 Blacks (pejorative).

82 Two wars (1845-46 and 1848-49) between the British East India Company and the last independent kingdom.

83 An engagement in the Second Sikh War (13 January 1849) which resulted in the subjugation of the Punjab.

84 Ferozeshuhur (or Feroshuhr), a battle of 21-22 December 1845.

85 Usually referential to the sepoy mutineers; as this refers to the 1840s, here it is a more general pejorative applied to South Asians.

O'GRADY. My Mission is to save, not to destroy. If I could only speak with those deluded murderers and plead—have you any powder?

MRS. CAMPBELL. A keg of cartridges.

O'GRADY. I tremble in every limb. Cassidy take the garden front outpost duty—fall back on the kitchen door if pressed. Sweeny that rock yonder commands the valley—I wish this shrubbery was not so near the house—that wash house gives me a flanking fire—such is life my respected friends. Here today—gone tomorrow—let us go in and inspect the ammunition.

(Scene closes in).

Scene 2

The Garden. Enter Cassidy R.H.

CASSIDY. Whist.[86] Sweeny, come here.

SWEENY *(enter L.H.)*. Vats hup?[87]

CASSIDY. Spake low—d'ye see that wood beyond? There's fifty black divils hidin' in it—they're poppin in an out like rabbits in the back of a ditch—here's one of their rapin hooks[88] I found below in the grass.

SWEENY. Rebels in this 'ere vicinity—

O'GRADY *(enters)*. Rebels here—

CASSIDY. As thick as boys[89] they are—if your reverence 'ud like to see them I'll go down and stir up the nest of 'em wid this—

O'GRADY. And Randal?

CASSIDY. I'm afeard he's tuck—

O'GRADY. A prisoner?

CASSIDY. I watched him—he rode into the wood but he never came out on the road beyant.

O'GRADY. He must be rescued—rescued at any risk—what's to be done?

CASSIDY. Axin your honer's pardin—if ye'd rather me and Sweeny to crape down on beknowns[90]—throw me out in front to skirmish—when we get amongst the varmin—Sweeny would give a rawl[91] on his drum—that 'ud make them lep, and before they'd cry—Banagher[92]—I'd jump in and cut the Captain loose.

O'GRADY. What then?

CASSIDY. Then I'd form a square[93] on Sweeny and put the Captain in the middle and retreat in ordher.

O'GRADY. Have you reckoned the odds?

CASSIDY. I'm no hand at countin sir, but Sweeny's a dab.

SWEENY. What's the hodds so long as you're 'appy—

O'GRADY. My poor fellows it is a desperate enterprise. What temerity[94] you must have to propose it?

---

86   Hush.
87   What's up?
88   For pillage.
89   Clustered, "as thick as boys around a circus tent."
90   i.e., unbeknownst.
91   Roll.
92   An English garrison town along the river Shannon, in the Irish midlands.
93   Infantry formation of the hollow square: two or more ranks of musket or riflemen poised to volley fire at charging cavalry.
94   Boldness.

SWEENY. Cassidy—what's that—have you got any?

CASSIDY. No, but I think it's something in a battle.

O'GRADY. Delay however is death. The attempt shall be made. I will secure the doors and bring up your rear with a pair of double guns—

CASSIDY. More power to your reverence—sure wid me and Sweeny and the Captain that'll make four—and the drum five—

O'GRADY. Not a word of this to the ladies—

CASSIDY. Never fear, sir, we'll be a dumb as oysthers.[95]

(Exit O'Grady).

CASSIDY. Now Sweeny, whatever you do kape a whole skin[96]—

SWEENY. I shall expase my body has little as possible.

CASSIDY. 'Tisn't your dirty body, it's your drum I mean—

O'GRADY *(enter with the guns).* All's well—the door's bolted, they have no suspicion yet of our danger. Cassidy you in front—it is a fearful enterprise, their numbers are unknown to us.

CASSIDY. The more the merrier as the ferret said when he enthered the rat hole.

(Exit Cassidy, Sweeny, and O'Grady L.H.).

ACHMET *(enter).* This way Sahibs—

(Enter Achmet, Mour-ed-deen, and the Rajah).

MOUR-ED-DEEN. The Kaffirs[97] are in our hand—why delay their death?

RAJAH. The woman must be spared—she is mine.

MOUR-ED-DEEN. She has turned the heart of the Rajah to her own colour—white—how many more of these giaours[98] must be saved?

RAJAH. None—Jahannam[99] have them all—let fire pass over their dwellings and the edge of the sword be their fate.

ACHMET. May your servant speak, Behala[100]—she shall be told that the Captain Sahib is our prisoner— we shall promise them life and mercy if they yield.

MOUR-ED-DEEN. I will ask nothing of the Kaffirs but their blood.

ACHMET. Our attack will alarm the fort and bring the soldiers down upon us.

RAJAH. This slave[101] is right. Mour-ed-deen, they will surrender—the men and children shall be given to death, the plunder and the woman to our troops.

ACHMET. For my share, I ask only the young McGregor Sahib and the Scotch Ayah[102] Jessie.

MOUR-ED-DEEN. And for mine, nothing. Neither plunder nor love—I ask only to witness the death of each foul unbeliever and see their houses given to the devouring flames.

---

95 Oysters, possibly as in "they are stupid as oysters, and as slow as tortoises." Augustus von Kotzebue, *Virgin of the Sun,* trans. Anne Plumptre (London: R. Phillips, 1799) 45.

96 Keep out of harm's way. (In his next line Cassidy puns on the skin of a drum).

97 Infidels.

98 Whites (pejorative).

99 (Muslim) hell.

100 Possibly Behárá: a low-caste member (palanquin bearer).

101 As a vakeel, Achmet is probably already a slave; the Rajah uses the term to indicate inferiority.

102 Nursemaid.

(Jessie sings inside).

ACHMET. Hark—'tis the Scotch ayah—yonder window is where the children sleep.
RAJAH. Lead us beneath it.

(Exit all).

Scene 3

The interior of the Bungalow.[103] *Mrs. Campbell discovered. Charlie, Effie, Alice, and Mary R.C.*

MRS. CAMPBELL. No. I shall not undress the children. Take Effie with you, Alice—
ALICE. Poor child, she is almost asleep now.
CHARLIE. Mamma, I want to go to bed. Where is Jessie—
JESSIE *(enter)*. Here, my precious one.

(Exit Alice and Mary).

MRS. CAMPBELL. Place him in his cot, do not remove his clothes. *(Aside)* I cannot repress my agitation—dare I impart the news of our peril to this girl?
CHARLIE. Jessie, sing me "Charlie"; you are not tired are you?
JESSIE. Nae—darling, I'm never tired o' teaching ye' the airs o' Scotland. *(Sings a verse of "Charlie is my Darling")*[104]
  'Twas on a Monday morning,
  Right early in the year,
  When Charlie came to our town,
  The young Chevalier.
  (Chorus) O! Charlie is my darling,
  My darling, my darling,
  O! Charlie is my darling,
  The young Chevalier.
MRS. CAMPBELL. Jessie!
JESSIE. Aweel,[105] my lady?
MRS. CAMPBELL. There's danger near. Don't start, don't cry. The rebels are expected in this neighbourhood—our murder is planned, but so is our escape.
JESSIE. It canna be, wha tould[106] ye this?
MRS. CAMPBELL. Randal McGregor.
JESSIE. Then it's true. Mercy on us! Can nothing be done?
MRS. CAMPBELL. Randal has promised to rescue us—
JESSIE. The McGregor has said it dinna ye fash yersel[107]—gin he said it he'll do it—
MRS. CAMPBELL. Go, Jessie—see to the fastenings of all the doors, but show no fear—excite no suspicion—

---

103 One-storey house of light construction, usually with a thatched roof.
104 A traditional song by J. Hogg about Bonnie Prince Charlie, the last of the Stuarts, claimant to the Scottish throne. For variants, see *The Universal Songster; or, Museum of Mirth* (London: Jones and Co., 1825), 224.
105 Well.
106 Who told you?
107 Don't worry.

JESSIE. I hae no fear[108]—Has not the McGregor gi'en[109] his word to coom back? He'll tak it up and under his claymore[110] there cannae[111] be fear—*(exit hastily).*

MRS. CAMPBELL. This girl gives me a lesson in courage. What reliance, what noble confidence she has in Randal. How calm she turned, when she heard he had given his word to secure our escape—

(Music. Mour-ed-deen and Achmet appear on the balcony. Achmet points to Mrs. Campbell—The Rajah of Mour-ed-deen enters the chamber. Achmet disappears).

MRS. CAMPBELL. What is the hour? *(Looks at watch)* It is now past eleven, Randal must have reached the city by this time. It is time to prepare—*(She turns and sees the Rajah beside her.)* Mercy!

RAJAH. Be silent—you know me—

MRS. CAMPBELL. The Rajah—

RAJAH. The officer who intercepted my letter to Achmet is my prisoner—my men are now surrounding your park, escape is hopeless.

MRS. CAMPBELL. Randal taken prisoner! Then we are lost.

RAJAH. Listen! I saw you at Benares—your soul entered through my eyes into my heart, and thrust out my own. I followed you, until like the sun you passed away, where I could follow no more. I went to Bithoor and my wives offended your soul within me. I gave them riches and sent them away. My Zenana is cold. I am there alone! It awaits the form to which the soul here belongs.

MRS. CAMPBELL. You would murder my children and dishonour their mother.

RAJAH. Your children shall be mine, princes of the Maharatta:[112] follow me and no blood shall flow. I will withdraw my men—Lucknow shall be spared and peace restored.

MRS. CAMPBELL. England would spurn the peace—bought thus, with the honour of one of her people.

RAJAH *(approaching the bed).* This is your child?

MRS. CAMPBELL. My child.

MOUR-ED-DEEN *(draws his yataghan).* No cry! Or this steel is in his throat—

CHARLIE. Oh dear mamma, help me—

MRS. CAMPBELL. Oh! Rajah, spare my child!

(A roll of the drum outside).

MOUR-ED-DEEN. The Kaffirs are upon us—away?

MRS. CAMPBELL. My child!

RAJAH. Mine you shall be by force. None under this roof, but you, shall see tomorrow's sun.

(Distant shots. Achmet appears).

GEORDIE *(enter).* What shots were those—ah—

(Mour-ed-deen and the Rajah face him. He stands a moment irresolute. Achmet fires at him from the window. He staggers back and places his hand over his eyes. Mour-ed-deen and the Rajah escape, taking with them the child. Enter Jessie, Alice, Mary and Effie).

JESSIE. What has happened—Geordie are you hurt?

---

108 I have no fear.

109 Given.

110 Scottish broadsword.

111 Cannot.

112 (Or Mahratta) The princely and military classes of the former Hindu kingdom of Maharashtra in central India (now Maharashtra).

GEORDIE. No blinded, and, I—I am faint.

JESSIE. You are pale, you tremble. He is wounded. Where is Charlie—where the bairn?[113]

MRS. CAMPBELL. Gone.

JESSIE. Gone!

MRS. CAMPBELL. Carried off before our eyes, but they will not harm my poor child. Oh they will not harm any helpless little one—

JESSIE. Who has been here?

MRS. CAMPBELL. The Rajah with a horde of the rebels besiege us in this house. Randal is their prisoner. Randal who promised to rescue us.

JESSIE. Prisoner or free, the McGregor will keep his word—

MRS. CAMPBELL. The impassibility[114] of that girl drives me mad.

(Enter Cassidy).

JESSIE. He's comin thunder and turf, he's fightin like a cat wid tin legs and fifteen claws on aich foot—

ALICE. Who?

CASSIDY. The Captain; Sweeny is fightin' beside him.

(Guns)

Hurroo! They're at it. Where's a gun?

JESSIE. Here is one.

(Pistol shot)

CASSIDY. Hoo! There goes a bullet through my leg.

(Geordie staggers back very pale. Jessie runs up with the gun).

The devils see us in the light here, and they're papperin'[115] us handsome—

JESSIE. Look, Cassidy, look there's a big fellow making for Sweeny, quick—

CASSIDY *(fires)*. Hoo! There's a dead nigger—

JESSIE. Here they come—quick by this ladder—

(Enter Sweeny and Randal).

RANDAL. Cassidy stand to your arms—

CASSIDY. Ay! your honour—

MRS. CAMPBELL. Oh, Randal you have escaped!

JESSIE. I told you the McGregor would keep his word.

RANDAL. I was taken prisoner by about fifty men, who be just this side of the bridge—their main force is still beyond the river. They are led by Mour-ed-deen.

MRS. CAMPBELL. No, by the Rajah in person, he was here. They snatched my little one from his cot, and bore him away—

RANDAL. Cowards! They hope to make our hearts quail, and fear for those we love. Do not lose your courage Amy, the child shall be rescued. Let us prepare to repel these wretches. The fort is in danger— our men if not warned will be taken by surprise. Where is Geordie?

---

113 Child.

114 Flawlessness and unsusceptibility.

115 Peppering (targeting).

GEORDIE. Here Randal.

RANDAL. How pale you are—are you wounded?

GEORDIE. No, it is nothing—

RANDAL. A scratch, eh, well—that's right you must start at once for the fort. My horse is picketed[116] just beyond the bridge. You know the spot—

GEORDIE. Y-yes—I know?

RANDAL. Creep down by the mango grove and swim the river—mount and spur for the fort. On your arrival train the guns on the wood below—the main force of the rebels is there.

MRS. CAMPBELL. But can Geordie escape through the lines of the enemy who surround us? Death must be nearly certain.

RANDAL. It is possible—we must provide against that chance—I will write a dispatch to the sergeant in command—if you reach the mare tie the letter in her mane—then should you fall let her go—she'll bear the dispatch to the fort. Come Amy, give me paper and ink. Geordie—while I am gone see to your arms.

(Exeunt all but Jessie and Geordie).

JESSIE. Eh! but the McGregor is grand in the hour of battle, and firm in the face of death.

GEORDIE. Death—he said that death is nearly certain—

JESSIE. How pale you look! Geordie, speak are you hurt?

GEORDIE. Oh, Jessie!

JESSIE. You tremble—what is it Geordie dear? Tell me—

GEORDIE. I can't Jessie. My tongue fails me as my limbs do. Oh! Jessie I feel I cannot face the fire.

JESSIE. What say ye?

GEORDIE. They came, they stood before me, and I could not strike. They took her child and my arm was nerveless to defend. I was paralysed. I was a coward!

JESSIE. No—hush, dearie; there's nae drop of coward bluid in the McGregor. Tak' time, Geordie—

GEORDIE. I cannot help it Jessie; the passion of fear is on me. I cannot stir— *can't move*

JESSIE. Oh, my heart! Oh my Geordie, think of what Randal will say if he sees ye so—his ain brither—his ainly one. Think, dearie there are women here and bairns, puir helpless things—and if ye flinch noo, they will be killed!

GEORDIE. I know it *(hides his face in his hands).*

JESSIE. Think of the auld mither,[117] at home Geordie, the proud one that nursed ye Geordie—the leddy[118] that awaits her twa boys cumin back fra the wars, what! Will ye bring yer mither back a blighted name? Oh, hae courage for her sake! Oh—for mine. Oh, why canna I gang beside ye to show ye how to bleed for the auld braes[119] o' Scotland—

(Enter O'Grady).

Who's there? Gang awa'—oh, 'tis the minister.

O'GRADY. Is he wounded? My poor boy, is he hurt?

JESSIE. Oh! Sir help him; his heart fails him—it is his first fight, and he flinches.

---

116 Tethered.
117 Old mother.
118 Lady.
119 Hills.

O'GRADY. Pooh, you are as brave as a lion. In my first action I felt just the same—first powder smells sick, but after you see a few men fall, that goes off.

JESSIE. Yes, it clears awa'?

O'GRADY. Take your lip between your teeth and choose your man—

JESSIE. Think of the bairns they've slaughtered in cauld bluid—

O'GRADY. Don't trust to pistols, I always preferred steel, it's more reliable and doesn't misfire; use the point, it kills when the blade throws open your guard. Heaven forgive me! I am teaching this boy how to murder—

(Re-enter Randal, with the order, followed by Sweeny and Cassidy, Mrs. Campbell, Alice, etc.).

RANDAL. Here is the dispatch. Where is my brother?

JESSIE. He is here—

O'GRADY. Randal I've been thinking that—ahem! If I were to go in Geordie's place—

RANDAL. You! My dear O'Grady why should I deprive my brother of his opportunity to distinguish himself. This daring act will cover him with honours.

JESSIE. Oh, don't let Maister Geordie leave us—cauld na one of the laddies do as well?

MRS. CAMPBELL. Oh yes, let one of the men go?

RANDAL. Well Jessie there is the dispatch—which of your lovers shall be chosen for this desperate duty?

CASSIDY. Now's the time darling to say which you love best—

JESSIE. Which—

CASSIDY. Cover me wid honour—choose me—

JESSIE. What can I do?

O'GRADY. She is going to put her own lover in the jaws of death. God bless her.

JESSIE *(giving paper)*. Sweeny, Heaven protect you—Heaven be wi ye' laddie—

CASSIDY. She loves him best. I knew it, well good luck to ye' Sweeny—I'll take care of Jessie for ye—

(Jessie weeps).

SWEENY *(offers his hand)*. He'll deserve her—

CASSIDY. Look at the concait[120] of him now—paycocks is nothing' to him—

GEORDIE. Oh, Jessie—Jessie?

SWEENY. Hif you please, sir—I propoge[121] ta go hout on the balcony—as hif to take a hairing—they'll fire hon me—I'll drop hover hinto the garden has hif I was shot, and they won't look harter me—rule[122] him hon any road to the fort—

RANDAL. Well let me see you try it.

JESSIE. Oh 'tis for Geordie's sake—

(Randal and Sweeny go onto balcony).

MRS. CAMPBELL. But why should Randal go?

O'GRADY. To lead his man, habit?[123]

(A pistol shot—Sweeny falls over—a cry from Jessie. Randal, after watching, returns).

---

120 Conceit.
121 Propose.
122 Guide.
123 Custom.

RANDAL. 'Tis all right, he has escaped.

JESSIE. But he may be wounded?

RANDAL. No I think not, unless there were two bullets. I have got one here—*(takes off his cap—his temple is bloody).*

MRS. CAMPBELL. Oh Randal!

RANDAL. Tut! We have other things to do. Now Amy to work, there are but three of us here, Geordie, Cassidy, and I—

O'GRADY. You may say four! I will lay aside my conscientious scruples—and like my namesake, David, I will strike the Philistines.[124]

RANDAL. You have three native servants who I think may be trusted. There are not more than fifty sepoys on this side of the bridge—now if we can destroy that bridge, we shall divide our foes and hold our own for a few hours.

O'GRADY. There's a keg of powder downstairs. I'll take it down under my arm and blow up the bridge. This enterprise is bloodless, it suits me exactly.

RANDAL. You propose with your form to creep down unobserved? You would be cut to pieces—

O'GRADY. But if the piece of me that held the keg got there, I might accomplish the good deed. *(Aside)* I'm afraid he will send Geordie—

RANDAL. Geordie, quick, you must see to this.

GEORDIE. I'm ready *(rises).*

JESSIE. He's ganging,[125] look, look, he goes bravely. The McGregor bluid is in his cheek, the dark fire is lichted.[126]

GEORDIE. The cloud has passed away—you have given me courage. Jessie, my heart thanks you. Now Randal—

O'GRADY. Stop—stop—till you are calm and steady—you are excited now and ready to be foolhardy.

GEORDIE. Oh! Sir, I have a score against myself to wipe out. My sword must wear the blushes that are still upon my cheek.

RANDAL. Come Geordie. O'Grady, secure the door after us.

(Exeunt Randal, Geordie, and O'Grady—Mrs. Campbell watches them from the window).

JESSIE. They are gone, and I ha' sent the puir boy to his death may be, and Sweeny too puir Sweeny.

CASSIDY. Oh! Jessie, darlin'—

JESSIE. Eh! Gang away—I hate ye!

CASSIDY. God bless you jewel all the same—

ALICE. Foolish fellow, can't you see 'tis you she loves—are you so blind?

CASSIDY. Me—but she chase Sweeny.

ALICE. Yes, for your sake, and she's angry with you for making her so selfish and unjust—

CASSIDY. But she says she hates me.

ALICE. You're a fool! *(Turns away).*

CASSIDY. Females is quare things *(goes up).*

MRS. CAMPBELL. Oh, my only one—my child—are you alone left to me?

Jessie loves cassidy and want doesn't want to get him hur.

---

124 1 Chronicles 14:8-17.
125 Proceeding.
126 Lit.

JESSIE. The puir Charlie, the bairn o' my heart. It's no in Jessie's arms ye'll sleep the nicht, it's no Jessie's song will put thee to rest—

O'GRADY *(enter)*. They are gone. I'm afraid Geordie will do some mad thing—he's all out like a young colt.

ALICE. All is quiet.

O'GRADY. That's a bad sign. But let us extinguish the lights, they serve the enemy. *(He puts out the candle)*.

MRS. CAMPBELL. Oh, Heaven protect us in this dark hour of peril, preserve my poor little children.

O'GRADY. Amen! They come! I see white figures in the garden.

JESSIE. My Sweeny, have they killed my poor Sweeny? Oh this suspense is worse than death.

O'GRADY. The house is surrounded, the whole collection is here—

MRS. CAMPBELL. Cassidy fire, why don't you fire on them?

CASSIDY. Please yer honour, ma'am. Them savages is like birds—firin' frightens them away, and if we coax them here awhile, sure they won't be seeing after the Captain Randal?

O'GRADY. Good heart, noble heart, it is a pity such good people should die. Have pity on these weak ones, and upon these little ones.

JESSIE. Oh! Protect my puir Geordie—don't let his blood lie on my hands, don't break puir Jessie's heart.

(A distant explosion. Music).

O'GRADY. They are coming! I hear Randal's voice.

RANDAL. Cassidy! Help! Cassidy!

CASSIDY. That's me! Here I am, your honor. Hoo—*(leaps over balcony)*.

O'GRADY. The door, the door is fast inside—*(runs out R.H.)*.

MRS. CAMPBELL. They come, they are safe.

(Music. Enter Randal bearing Geordie in his arms).

RANDAL. See to the doors—

ALICE. He is dead?

JESSIE. Dead! Who's dead? *(Sees Geordie and screams)* Geordie what have ye done? Ye have killed the bairn. Stand awa' o' ye' Geordie, Geordie look to me. Oh! I did it, I have killed him, only for me he wad nae have gone.

RANDAL. We might have returned undiscovered, but as we returned we heard the child's voice.

MRS. CAMPBELL. My child—Charlie—he lives!

RANDAL. I could not restrain Geordie, he sprang amongst them to rescue the boy. The attempt was madness—and failed.

CASSIDY. They are coming down on us your honour.

RANDAL. Sweeny has fallen then. The fort is silent—we are lost—

(A flash from the distant fort is seen and report).[127]

CASSIDY. No—he's safe. Look at that now—there's a round shot on to them—

(Another flash and report).

---

127 Report: heard.

JESSIE. Garryowen[128]—yer soul—give it 'em Sweeny—

(*Another flash and report*).

Ah! that's a nasty one. They're off sir, we're relieved—

JESSIE. Geordie—speak to me, dear. Oh, I shall go mad, Geordie, if ye' dae not answer me—if ye' do not luk to me.

(*Reports of guns are heard all through this scene*).

GEORDIE. Jessie, Jessie, do you hear those guns? Sweeny has escaped, and after all Geordie is not a coward.

Act II

Scene 1

A ruined city. The Encampment of the Rajah. Hindus and rebel soldiers.
Rajah R. and a group of girls. Jessie and the child Charlie L. Achmet R. Geordie bound.
Music. Enter Mour-ed-deen and Hindus L. The Rajah rises.

RAJAH. What news?

MOUR-ED-DEEN. They have escaped. The troops from the Fort have returned on the road to Lucknow.

RAJAH. The prize I risked so much to gain has been torn from my hands.

ACHMET. But mine is here! Bring forth the prisoners.

(*Geordie and Jessie are brought down*).

These are my share.

MOUR-ED-DEEN. Dog of a giaour, twas by his hand our men were slain.

---

128 Originally a drinking song, referential of Limerick Ireland, widely adopted in the British Army as a marching tune.

> Let Bacchus' [Greek god of wine] sons be not dismayed,
> But join with me each jovial lad
> Come booze and sing and lend your aid,
> To help me with the chorus.
>
> (*Chorus*) Instead of spa [water] we'll drink brown ale
> And pay the reck'ning on the nail,
> No man for debt shall go to jail,
> From Garyowen in glory.
>
> We are the boys that take delight
> In smashing the Limerick lights when lighting.
> Through all the streets like sporters fighting,
> And tearing all before us.
>
> We'll break the windows, we'll break the doors,
> The watch [lookouts] knock down by threes and fours
> Then let the doctors work their cures,
> And tinker up our bruises.

RAJAH. Hold Mour-ed-deen—the cup of vengeance should be quaffed slowly or we lose the flavour of its blood.

GEORDIE. For every drop you spill, there's an account kept at home.

RAJAH. The tiger of Bengal has risen from his jungle and his cry shall be heard all over the world.

JESSIE. Tak heed it doesn't rouse the English Lion eh, Rajah, but ye'll find he's an awfu' beast!

CASSIDY (outside). Aisy now. Aisy ye devils.

JESSIE. 'Tis Cassidy's voice.

(Enter Cassidy on horseback with Hindus).

RAJAH. A prisoner!

CASSIDY. One at a time now, sure there's no hurry—take care of the beast, he's a Christian horse, and worth forty of your mothers' dirty sons (dismounts).

GEORDIE. Cassidy, my poor fellow, I'm sorry to see you a prisoner.

CASSIDY. Divil a prisoner I am. I'm out on lave sir, and the Captain lent me his horse for the day.

MOUR-ED-DEEN. It is true—he rode out from the enemy's ranks and gave himself up to our men.

RAJAH. What brought you here?

CASSIDY. The horse avich[129]—devil a hap'oth[130] else.

MOUR-ED-DEEN. For what have you come?

CASSIDY. I've come for that child if ye plase, and if ye'd send the nurse wid it, I'd be more obliged to you.

JESSIE. Oh Cassidy, are ye daft laddie?

CASSIDY. I couldn't help it, Jessie. I axed the Captain to let me come and save ye or die beside ye darling. Oh, don't be too hard on me darling. Whist darling, whisper, the mistress is breakin' her heart after the child. We must save it.

JESSIE. How?

CASSIDY. Get a hould of the child some way and when ye get a chance and nobody lookin' swing the creature on the mare's back, jump after him and ride like the devil. I know ye can.

JESSIE. How can I get the bairn, it's guarded by a native woman.

CASSIDY. Dhress yourself in one of them night shirts.[131]

RAJAH. You say you have come for the child.

CASSIDY. If ye plase.

RAJAH. It shall be sent to its mother from the mouth of a cannon. Secure those unbelieving dogs. Tonight is our sacred feast, and they shall serve as a life offering to Seeva.[132] The blood of the infidels shall anoint our idol and gratify our goddess.

A Grand Ballet, during which Jessie appears as a Hindu girl; while the Hindu woman is engaged she carries off Charlie and carries him on horseback across stage. All is confusion and amidst cries of rage the scene closes.

---

129 (Var. a mich) son.

130 Ha'penny (halfpenny) worth.

131 He conflates the kurta with European nightwear.

132 Shiva, the supreme Hindu deity. Muslims would not sacrifice to a Hindu God, but that was immaterial to Boucicault.

Scene 2

A rocky wood. Enter Soldiers, Alice, Randal, Mrs. Campbell, and Effie.

RANDAL. The mountain road ends here.

ALICE. I hear the roar of a waterfall to the left.

RANDAL. That is the cataract of the Ghoorka[133]—it falls from this height to the Ghat below.

MRS. CAMPBELL. Are we in safety here?

RANDAL. We are now beyond pursuit. That deep cleft in the mountain is the bed of the torrent, it intercepts between us and the rebel forces. I have halted the men to give them some rest, poor fellows, for they have a tedious march before them.

MRS. CAMPBELL. Where's Charlie? Ah, my brave my gentle boy. I would give half my life to press him once more to my heart.

RANDAL. Courage Amy. Oh, had I only a handful of my own gallant Highlanders—one poor company, my own men alone—I'd bring our people safe from the midst of these black orgies.

ALICE. Hark! what's that! There again.

RANDAL. It seems like confused cries from the river below.

(Enter Sweeny and Soldiers).

SWEENY. If you please Sir, the henemy is comin' up the walley sir, in a few moments they will be in range.

RANDAL. Impossible! They will not expose their lives so madly.

MRS. CAMPBELL. See, look below there—a white figure upon horseback seems to fly, while others are in pursuit.

RANDAL. Where is my fieldglass? What can it mean. Yes, by their speed it must be cavalry.

MRS. CAMPBELL. Do you see them?

RANDAL. By heaven it must be—I cannot be mistaken—'tis my mare, my black Jenny and ridden by a Hindu woman. She rides well.

MRS. CAMPBELL. No—no—look again, 'tis Jessie, my throbbing heart tells me 'tis Jessie.

RANDAL. I can't see her face. She looks back, now she turns, yes—yes—'tis she and in her arms she holds the child, brave girl.

(Distant shots).

She bends over the saddle to cover the boy, ah—the mare's down—they're on her.

ALICE and MRS. CAMPBELL. Ah!

RANDAL. No she's up again. Gallant horse, brave girl.

SWEENY. If you please, sir, the men would like to give an ooray if it ain't again the regulations.

RANDAL. Cheer my lads—cheer with all your hearts.

(Soldiers shout).

Now she's well in sight—wave your caps men she sees us—ah—despair—she's caught—the torrent is before her.

MRS. CAMPBELL. No. She dashes in—she swims it, look see?

---

133 Nepalese.

RANDAL. But the cataract bars her path—the Ghoorka falls are right before her. Away men scatter yourselves along the precipice—pick off the enemy as they approach her.

MRS. CAMPBELL. Oh! heaven preserve my child!

RANDAL. Come.

(*Exeunt*).

Scene 3

The Ghoorka Falls. Enter Mour-ed-deen and Hindus.

MOUR-ED-DEEN. Dismount there, hem her in. She cannot escape.

RAJAH (*enter*). See yonder she turns—she is ours again. A thousand gold mohurs for him who recaptures the Scotch ayah.

(*Randal and Mrs. Campbell appear on the rocks above*).

RANDAL. Steady men—don't fire—you may hit the child.

MRS. CAMPBELL. My child. Charlie! Charlie!

RAJAH. She comes—now—now, men bar her path, cut down the horse.

RANDAL. Jessie, Jessie we are here.

Jessie on horseback with the child in her arms enter R. and, uttering a loud cry to the horse, gallops up the cataract dashing through the water and escapes. Picture.

Act III

The interior of a Hindu Temple in Lucknow; curtains at back, C. Jessie chained, L, to a pillar. Geordie is lying on a pallet, R, chained also. Rebel Sepoys at the back; a divan, L. Stage somber.—Music.

GEORDIE (*awaking*). Where am I? Oh, these chains, those dark walls, those darker faces—I am a prisoner—why did I awake?

JESSIE (*L.*).Geordie, dear, you are better now, the fever has left ye.

GEORDIE. Jessie, are you there? Come near me.

JESSIE. I can't, dearie, the savages have tied me like a dog to the wall.

GEORDIE. What place is this?

JESSIE. It's a church where they worship the devil.

GEORDIE. How long have I been here?

JESSIE. For six lang weeks.

GEORDIE. Does the Residency still hold out against the rebels?

JESSIE. I dinna ken.[134]

GEORDIE. Were you taken prisoner when I fell into their hands?

---

134 I do not know.

JESSIE. Na, but when we heard that you were dying here, for want of Christian help, I came across to nurse you.

GEORDIE. My poor girl! But they will murder you, they show no mercy for age or sex.

JESSIE. I know it, here is the *Calcutta News*. It is full o' the bluidy wark the Rajah made at Cawnpore.

(Drums. Enter the Rajah and attendants).

Eh! talk of the deevil—

RAJAH. Sahib, open your ears, your countrymen are dogs, they still lie howling in the Residency—they dare not come forth—Inshallah![135]

GEORDIE. They look for aid.

RAJAH. Their hearts lie, and hope will not feed them; their food is out, they cannot feed on air.

JESSIE. Ye mistake! they are living on an air noo, and it is ca'd, "The Campbells Are Comin'." And oh, could I but hear one screel of the pibroch,[136] could I see the wavin' o' the bonnie tartan, and the braw hue o' the Shinin' steel, I'd na gie ye twa minits,[137] but ye'd find the deevil before ye could say "Cawnpore."

RAJAH. Woman, be silent, read your printed words, and leave men to speak with men. *(To Geordie)* Your countrymen are in our hands. Beneath this mosque, even below our feet, we have a mine. It passes beneath the fort, commanded by the Sahib, your brother. Behold the powder is laid, the match is ready; we can destroy him utterly, his fort once taken, the Residency is ours, Bismillah![138] Have I defiled my tongue with lies?

GEORDIE. The Redan fort is the key to our position.

RAJAH. Enough blood has been shed—let him yield, his men shall go forth unharmed, we will pour the oil of mercy on their wounds.

JESSIE *(reading)*. "And under these conditions, Cawnpore was surrendered, the garrison marched out, and entered the boats provided for their safe transport."[139]

RAJAH. You say your countrymen still look for aid, but they know not that the Sahib Havelock was defeated by my troops.[140] From Lahore[141] to Allahabad,[142] Hindoostan is ours, you shall write these things that they may know. They will believe your word, and they will yield. Inshallah! they shall go forth safely; we will show mercy—on my head be it.

JESSIE *(reads)*. "No sooner were the boats containing the troops, the women and children, in the midst of the stream than the enemy opened a murderous fire, and a work of slaughter began."

RAJAH. What writing has she in her hand? Tear it away!

(Achmet does so).

What says the pen there?

---

135 If Allah wills it.

136 Piercing cry of the Scottish bagpipe.

137 I'd not give you two minutes.

138 In the name of God.

139 This foreshadowed greater terror: the civilians were promised escape but were instead taken prisoner and later slaughtered.

140 General Henry Havelock advanced on Lucknow three times before he succeeded in lifting the siege on 25 September 1857. He died of dysentery on 24 November, his fame secured.

141 A city in the Punjab.

142 He stresses the breadth of the mutineers' reach: from Lahore in the Punjab (Britain's northwestern-most holdings) to Allahabad in Uttar Pradesh (also called Aggra, 140 miles south-southwest of Lucknow), a total of 695 miles (1120 km).

JESSIE *(rising)*. I'll tell ye in broad Scotch. It says that you have taught baith[143] women and children to fecht,[144] for you have found something that they fear muir[145] than death.

ACHMET. What's that?

JESSIE. The mercy of the Rajah.

RAJAH. Let my ferooshees[146] come here.

(Enter two Hindus).

Take that woman and let her die.

(Music).

GEORDIE. Stay, Rajah, you would not kill that poor child.

(Cords descend from roof).

RAJAH. You would have her life? Give me the letter to your brother; she herself shall bear it to the Redan fort.

(They unbind them).

GEORDIE. That letter will not serve you. You do not know Randal McGregor—he will die, but will never yield.

RAJAH. Be it so. Achmet, hew away the right hands of these prisoners, and let their bodies swing from the heights of this mosque.

ACHMET. On my head be it.

JESSIE. Geordie, Geordie!

GEORDIE. No, Rajah, do not give me the death of a dog. Spare that poor child.

RAJAH. Stifle the howling of that hound.

JESSIE. Geordie, far'weel,[147] Geordie!

GEORDIE. Hold! what would you have me do!

RAJAH. Do you see yonder ropes? They ascend to the minaret of this mosque. *(To Achmet)* Prepare the means in yonder room to write.

(Exit Achmet).

Behold! write as I have said, or give your neck to the cord—choose—I have spoken.

JESSIE. Aye, but you have spoken to a McGregor.

(Re-enter Achmet).

GEORDIE *(aside)*. One day more—aid may come. Havelock, Outram,[148] cannot be far.

JESSIE *(aside)*. He hesitates—if he pens that letter a' is lost again, yet if I speak the deevils will murder me.

GEORDIE *(aside)*. She shall not die.

---

143 Both.
144 Fight.
145 More.
146 Obscure (evidently some kind of retainers).
147 Farewell.
148 Generals Havelock and Outram relieved Lucknow and held it until it could be evacuated.

(Exeunt all but Jessie).

JESSIE. He will do it, to save my life, he will write down his infamy; nae if I bear it to the fort, but then they will kill him after a', and I ainly can be saved. Yonder he sits, he takes the pen, his hand shakes, but still he writes, he writes. Oh, what are the words? Words of infamy, that will gae hame, and fill the faces of a' the Christian world in shame. Oh, could I reach his heart, I could stay his hand, but that black Beelzebub is wi' him. Eh! haud a wee,[149] I'll speak to him. *(Sings)*[150]

Oh! why left I my hame?
Why did I cross the deep?
Oh! why left I the land
Where my forefathers sleep?
I sigh for Scotia's[151] shore,
And I gaze across the sea;
But I canna get a blink
O' my ain[152] countrie.

(After first verse. Speaks.) He stops, his head fa's in his hand—tears, tears—he minds me, he minds me. *(Sings)*

The palm-tree waveth high,
And fair the myrtle springs;
And to the Indian Maid
The ballad sweetly sings.
But I dinna see the broom,
Wi' its tassels on the lea;
Nor hear the lintie's[153] sang
O' my ain countrie.

(Speaks) He knows what I mean!

(The floor L. partially sinks).

Ah! what is that?

(Cassidy puts his head through the orifice L.C.).

CASSIDY. What a dust. *(Sneezes)* That was a big pinch of snuff anyway.
JESSIE. Wha's that? 'Tis Cassidy's voice.
CASSIDY. I'll call Sweeny!

(Sweeny appears).

JESSIE. Sweeny!
CASSIDY. Sweeny!
SWEENY. What's the matter?
CASSIDY. Mather! Bedad there's an echo here that spakes first—a Hindu echo, that takes the words out a yer mouth.

---

149 Hold a while.
150 Robert Gilfillan, "The Exile's Song."
151 Scotland's.
152 Own.
153 Linnet bird.

JESSIE. Hush, 'tis I, Jessie.

SWEENY. Jessie!

CASSIDY. Hoo! Garryowen yer soul! Hurroo!

JESSIE. Hush! gae down quick, they are comin'.

(They disappear. Jessie draws the carpet of divan over the orifice. Sings "My boy Tammie!" unconcerned. Enter the Rajah with light. Examines the place, looks in Jessie's face and exits R. Jessie draws carpet).

JESSIE. Hush, silence, whisper.

(Sweeny and Cassidy reappear).

CASSIDY. Where the divil are we at all.

JESSIE *(sings with affected unconcern)*.

Whar' hae ye been a' day,
My boy, Tammy?
An' whar' hae ye been a' day,
My boy, Tammy?
I've been by burn and flow'ry brae,
Meadow green and mountain grey
Courtin' o' this young thing,
Just come frae her mammy.

(Enter Achmet with light. Examines the place, looks in Jessie's face, and exits. Jessie withdraws the carpet).

JESSIE. Hush, silence, whisper.

(Sweeny and Cassidy reappear).

CASSIDY. Where the devil are we at all?

JESSIE. This is a mosque, they ca' it. It is my prison and Geordie's. How did you get here?

SWEENY. We were working in the countermine,[154] ordered by the Captain, when we struck right into the mine prepared by the rebels to blow us up. We removed their powder, of which we were running short, and then Cassidy and I took a stroll along the mine, to see the country.

CASSIDY. The road was mighty dirty, but the view at the end of it is worth the walk.

JESSIE. Then this passage goes underground to the fort.

CASSIDY. Bedad[155] Sweeny, we never thought o' that. It comes this way, but I don't know if it goes back the same.

JESSIE. D'ye see yon ropes dangling there. They are ready for me and Geordie. Twa hours mair[156] and ye'd been too late, down wi' ye now and don't stir, til I tell you.

CASSIDY. We'll be as dumb as oysthers.

(Music. They disappear, Jessie replaces carpet. Re-enter the Rajah, Achmet, and Sepoys).

ACHMET. A flag of truce from the fort.

(Enter Randal and O'Grady).

---

154 A defensive mine dug to intercept besiegers.

155 A mild oath.

156 Two hours more.

JESSIE. The McGregor!

RANDAL. You are the Rajah?

RAJAH. I am he.

RANDAL. I command the Redan fort. I came to offer you an exchange of prisoners. We have taken sixty of your men.

RAJAH. They are in your hands, Inshallah! Mohammed Allah! Death is their portion. To each man his fate.

(Exit Achmet).

RANDAL. We fight our foes, we do not murder them.

O'GRADY. Stay, Randal, don't be so fiery, let me speak to the Rajah. Salam, Alleikoom![157]

RAJAH. Allah, Resoul Allah![158] speak! There is no God but God, and Mohammed is his prophet.

O'GRADY. There I can't agree with you, and I shall feel pleased to discuss that question. I am a minister of peace and a herald of mercy. Let me touch your heart. This girl came here on a mission of mercy, she is not your prisoner; in every religion, of all time, the weakness of woman protects her life, and makes her safety sacred.

RAJAH. The shepherds from the hills of the Himalaya came to me and they said, "Behold the tigers come out of the jungle and prey upon our flocks, and we fear."[159] Which hearing I arose. I sought the lair of the noble beast. I found there the tigress and her cubs. I slew them, until they died, but lo, the tiger came, but did he whine and weep sayin, you have done evil, my mate and my little ones are sacred—their weakness should protect them?

O'GRADY. Are we tigers?

RAJAH. The tiger was placed here by Allah. He eats for his hunger, and kills that he may eat. Did Allah send the Briton here to make us slaves, to clutch us beneath his lion's paw,[160] and to devour the land?

(Enter Achmet with letter).

Has the English prisoner written as I have said?

ACHMET. 'Tis done!

JESSIE. Na, it canna' be!

RAJAH. The officer, your brother, knowing the folly of further resistance, writes here to you Sahib, and counsels you to yield up the Redan fort.

JESSIE. Oh, I dare not luk[161] at Randal.

GEORDIE *(enters)*. Randal!

RANDAL. Stand back Lieutenant McGregor! the Rajah declares that in this letter to me you have counseled to surrender—you are silent.

GEORDIE. Randal, you will forgive me when you know all, but now here I cannot speak.

RAJAH. The proud brow of the Englishman our tyrant can be bowed down with shame. Achmet read the letter.

GEORDIE. No, no, not here.

---

157 Peace be with you.

158 Usually "Allah il Allah, Mohammed resoul Alah," the translation of which he speaks in full. The Rajah's response to O'Grady should be the customary "aleikum salaam," but instead he offers the creed.

159 Paraphrases Jeremiah 49:19.

160 As in the lion rampant, symbol of England on the United Kingdom's coat of arms.

161 Look.

ACHMET. I cannot, it is in a foreign tongue.

O'GRADY *(looking over it)*. 'Tis in Gaelic, the native tongue of Scotland; I do not understand it.

JESSIE. Oh, I do, let me see. There's nae words in Gaelic that would serve a coward's tongue. Eh, sirs, it is pure Gaelic, and runs so. Open your lugs,[162] ye deevil, for here's porridge for you, hotter than ye can sup it, maybe. *(Reads)* "To Captain Randal McGregor, Her Majesty's 78th Highlanders, My dearest brother, the Rajah has doomed me to the death of a dog. My execution will take place at seven o'clock, you can spare our mother that grief and me that disgrace. Jessie will point out to you the window of my prison, it looks over the Redan fort and is within gunshot of our men. As the clock strikes six I will be at that window. Draw out a firing party, and let them send three honest volleys through my heart. God bless you, give my love to Alice and Mary, remember me to all the fellows of our mess, let them give me a parting cheer when I fall. Your affectionate brother, Geordie McGregor."

RANDAL. Geordie, my brother, my own brother!

GEORDIE. Randal!

O'GRADY. I can't resist any longer. God save the Queen! *(Shouts. Embraces Jessie)*.

(Guns and cannons outside).

RANDAL. What guns are those?

RAJAH. My artillery cover the advance of the faithful on the Redan fort. Bind these men. Your hours are numbered.

RANDAL. Traitor, we are protected by a flag of truce.

RAJAH. Your flag of truce shall be your winding sheet. Swing their bodies to the Minaret.[163] As the hour strikes seven let it be done.

(Hindus seize Randal, Geordie, and Jessie).

Let the old man go, that he may bear witness over all the earth, and strike white with terror the hearts of England, when they hear the vengeance of the Rajah *(exits)*.

O'GRADY. Don't, hang me too—I'll be hung if I die for it.

ACHMET. Slaves, see the Rajah's order done, on your heads be it. On the stroke of seven, draw the ropes. My duty calls me to the mine, the mine below your countrymen. In five minutes the match will be lighted, and from above you will be able to see your soldiers blown to the skies *(exits)*.

(Hindus bind them and exit).

JESSIE. Are they gone?

RANDAL. Yes, and we shall be gone too, unless Heaven perform a miracle to save us.

JESSIE. So it has. *(Calls)* Cassidy! Cassidy!

CASSIDY *(appears)*. Here I am Captain—it's an Irish miracle. Phew! I'm choked wid keeping the fight in me.

RANDAL. Quick, cut us loose.

(He cuts all the ropes).

RANDAL. How came you here?

CASSIDY. By that rat hole you call a mine.

---

162 Ears.

163 The mosque's tall tower from which the muezzin calls at hours of prayer.

JESSIE. Where's Sweeny?

CASSIDY. Bedad, as soon as he heard that nagger-in-chief order them to hang you like onions on a string, he scuttled away like a rabbit.

(*The ropes ascend*).

RANDAL. See the ropes. We were liberated just in time.

(*Drum*)

Hark! The alarum is given, away by the mine, quick ere it be too late.

(*Enter Achmet and Hindus*).

ACHMET. Treachery! Help! The kaffirs escape.

GEORDIE. 'Tis too late!

ACHMET. Take them alive, 'tis the Rajah's orders they should hang.

(*Enter Sweeny and soldiers from the mine. They form a line and fire on the Hindus and Achmet. Picture*).

Act IV

The Redan fort, forming an outpost near the Residency. The scene showing marks of a severe attack. Groups of soldiers, children, women, Cassidy, Jessie, Mrs. Campbell and her children, Mary, Alice, Sweeny, Geordie and sentinel at back.

MRS. CAMPBELL. Geordie, what can you see?

GEORDIE. I can see the road to Alambagh,[164] from whence we expect relief, but there is no sign of troops there.

MRS. CAMPBELL. Day after day we hope, until hope itself dies away. For three long months we have resisted.

CHARLIE. Mamma, I'm hungry.

MRS. CAMPBELL. God help you my poor child.

GEORDIE. Lads, here's a little child starving, is there a crust among ye?

SWEENY. Not a crumb, your honor, except it's in Phil Regan's kit—he died an hour ago. There he lies.

GEORDIE. Search and see.

(*Exit Sweeny*).

RANDAL (*enter L.*). What news of the night?

GEORDIE. Nine men dead of their wounds and six gone into the hospital.

RANDAL. Inglis[165] is hemmed in and can scarcely hold his own. If the columns of General Havelock's force do not appear today, we must make Lucknow our permanent residence, Geordie.

GEORDIE. You mean that you will die at this post?

---

164 The direction from whence Generals Outram and Campbell marched to Lucknow.

165 Colonel John Inglis commanded the garrison at Lucknow after Sir Henry Lawrence was wounded on 2 June; promoted to Major-General upon General Havelock's arrival on 26 September, he continued in command until Sir Colin Campbell broke the siege on 18 November. His wife and three sons were in Lucknow throughout the action.

(Sweeny re-enters with bread and gives it to children L.C.).

MRS. CAMPBELL. How is Jessie?

SWEENY. She sleeps, but the long weeks of suffering has worn her spirits out at last.

RANDAL. Poor Jessie, has she lost her spirits?

CASSIDY. Lost her spirits? Bedad, the strongest keg of spirits will wear out at last, if ye go drainin' at it ev'ry miniute. But, shure, Jessie 'ud have a song about the ould country that'd warm our hearts, or a gay word to throw us in passion that 'ud fetch the tear into our eyes. Oh, Achone![166] them spirits was brewed in Heaven above—they niver touched the head but the heart could get dhrunk upon them.

MRS. CAMPBELL. Poor Jessie! She has been in a state of restless excitement through all the siege, and has fallen away visibly during the last few days. A constant fever consumes her, and her mind wanders occasionally when recollections of home seem powerfully present to her. She has lain there since midnight wrapped in her plaid, poor child! It is strange, Randal, to see those rough men watch over her with the tenderness and grief of a mother over a sick child.

(Enter O'Grady).

O'GRADY. No news of relief?

RANDAL. None yet, but our fort here is cut off from the Residency, and Colonel Inglis may have dispatches.

O'GRADY. Cheer up, lads, there's a good time coming. The old folks at home will long remember the defence of Lucknow, and every man here will be a hero in his own native village.

CASSIDY. Except me, your reverence, devil native village I've got. I was born under a haystack, me father and mother had crossed to England for the harvest.[167] My mother died of me and my father bruk his heart wid drinkin', so when they sent me home to Ireland, my relations wouldn't own me, bekase[168] I was an Englishman.

O'GRADY. My good Cassidy, hearts like yours are never without a home, while there is goodness in earth and room in Heaven!

CASSIDY. I am content, Sir! if Jessie was not sick and I'd an ounce o' baccy,[169] I wouldn't call the Queen my uncle.[170]

(Enter Sergeant and two men).

RANDAL. Now, lads, there's no bugle to call you to breakfast, so fall in and fall to,[171] this is the last of our food, so make it go as far as you can. As soon as the sun is up, we shall have warm work, so buckle your belts tight.

(Gun).

There goes a how d'ye do from the enemy.

SWEENY. Please your honour, the men wants to know very respectfully, Sir, if this here ration is the last of our food? What's the children and ladies a' going to have served out?

---

166 Alas.

167 Prior to the Great Famine that began in 1845, countless Irish labourers made an annual migration to assist with the English harvest.

168 Because.

169 Tobacco.

170 I would be content (colloquial).

171 Fall into line in the ranks.

RANDAL. That is a mutinous question sir, fall in your ranks.

CASSIDY. Ax pardon sir, please the men won't eat their rations till they know. They say they wouldn't fight no how sir, any way comfortable, if they ain't allowed to share all fair with the women and the little 'uns.

SOLDIERS. Share alike! Share alike!

RANDAL. Silence in the ranks! fall in, my good lads. Listen: for eighty days we have held this fort against eighty thousand rebels. A few hours more, and General Havelock may arrive—

(Gun)

but those few hours will be terrible. The rebel Sepoys, grown desperate by repulse, will try to overwhelm us with their whole force.

(Gun)

To preserve the loss of these weak ones, you must have strength to repel this attack. You are starving— the food you eat is their protection.

SWEENY. Please, Captain, the men say they'd feel worse after such a meal.

RANDAL. Do as you will, there is a Captain above who commands your hearts. Break ranks.

(They do so and go up to women and children R. and L.).

GEORDIE *(to O'Grady)*. Will you not eat sir?

O'GRADY. How can I, boy? My heart is in my mouth, I have food enough in that. *(To groups)* Stay, my dear ones! the food is poor, but let us not forget *Him* who gave it.

(All take off their hats).

God bless us, and give us strength in this dark hour of our lives.

JESSIE *(waking)*. I'm cauld—I'm verra cauld.

CASSIDY. Cauld, darlin! Sure it's September and as hot as blazes.

MRS. CAMPBELL. Jessie, are you better?

JESSIE *(looks round)*. I maun get my father's breakfast. The gude man will be bock soon from the field.

CASSIDY. What is she talking about?

SWEENY. Eat, Jessie dear, we have kept your ration till you awoke.

JESSIE. Eat! Na—ah! *(Rejects the bread)* Dinna ye see! there's bluid upon it!

CASSIDY. Blood!

GEORDIE. Jessie!

MRS. CAMPBELL. Jessie! *(To her)* Jessie, you are ill—look at me—speak to me? Do you not know me? *(Kneels beside her).*

JESSIE. Knaw ye! knaw ye! Nae, but I ken[172] a bonnie song of Scotland—it's made o' heather and bluebells, woven in a tartan, it is so gladsome that it makes me weep.

MRS. CAMPBELL. Randal, Randal! her senses have gone—her mind wanders.

CHARLIE. Jessie, my own Jessie—don't look so.

JESSIE. We'll gang hame—come to me—what's yer name?

CHARLIE. Charlie Fergus Campbell.

JESSIE. Then ye'ar Scotch to the core of the heart. Listen. *(Sings)*[173]

---

172 Know.

173 A traditional Scottish air, "Tak Your Auld Cloak about Ye."

In winter when the rain rain'd cauld,
An' frost an' snow on ilk a hill,
An Boreas,[174] wi' his blasts sae bauld,
Was threatnin' a' ou kye[175] to kill,
Then Bell, my wife, wha lo'es nae strife,
She said to me, right hastily
"Get up gude man, save Crummie's[176] life,
An' tak your auld cloak about ye."

SWEENY. Jessie, Jessie dear don't you know me? Sweeny.

JESSIE. Sweeny—where is he? He'll be outside the Byre,[177] doon by the gates after milkin' the coos, I'll coom t'ye, my lad. I'll steal away to the trystan,[178] Sweeny. Fear nought. *(Sings)*[179]

Oh, whistle and I'll come to thee, my lad,
Tho' feyther and mither and aw should goo mad;
Oh, whistle and I'll come to thee, my lad.

RANDAL. Do not weep, Amy. She is happier so—and if we fail in repulsing the rebels today, or if we are not relieved by sundown, her madness will be a blessing—she will be insensible to her fate.

O'GRADY *(enters)*. Randal, Randal, there is a movement among the enemy I do not understand.

(Three guns).

SWEENY. A movement! I understand! He calls that a movement.

(Drums).

RANDAL. To arms! Men.

SWEENEY *(up C.)*. A flag of truce from the enemy.

RANDAL. Fall in. Pass flag of truce!

(Enter Sepoys, one bearing flag, and Rajah).

RAJAH. Englishmen, your last day of defence has arrived, you are beleaguered[180] by fifty thousand men. In a few hours the Residency must fall.

RANDAL. Then it is for us to ask terms, not for you to offer them.

RAJAH. I offer none, you die to the last man, but I would spare the women.

RANDAL. Aye for worse than death—for torture and mutilation—to see them murdered as at Cawnpore.

RAJAH. No, but for the sake of one, of her who is yonder *(pointing to Mrs. Campbell, L.C.)*.

MRS. CAMPBELL. She fears your love more than hate, sooner would seek the tiger in his lair, and trust herself within his fangs, than fly from death to the arms of the Rajah. Go—I am dying.

SWEENY. Hurrah! here's a sentiment after that toast—

(Offers to fire. Randal prevents him).

---

174 God of the north wind.
175 Cattle (kine).
176 Her milk cow.
177 Cow shed.
178 Lovers' meeting place.
179 Words by Robert Burns, tune by John Bruce, "Whistle and I'll Come to Thee, My Lad."
180 Besieged.

RANDAL. Recover arms! Would you fire on a flag of truce? And disgrace our colours?

CASSIDY. Bedad, the nagger beyant wasn't so mighty particular.

RANDAL (to Rajah). Begone! You say that this day is our last, let it be so, go write another page in history and call down the curses of god and man upon the name of the Rajah of Bithoor—rather than see our women yield to such mercy as you would show them, we would ourselves kill them and our little ones.

RAJAH. Dead or alive, yonder woman is my captive and by tonight Lucknow is ours.

(Drums and exit).

RANDAL. We have repulsed the first attack, but the enemy is too strong for us, they will try a second and a third. We have now only thirty men left, their next attack will succeed.

GEORDIE. Alice, Amy, and Jessie—must they fall into the hands of these wretches. Oh, Randal, remember Cawnpore!

O'GRADY. Let them decide. Let them know the worst, that they may prepare to meet their dreadful fate.

RANDAL. I cannot speak it. I can face the enemy but I cannot face the pale features of the women and tell them that my arm is powerless to defend their honour and their lives.

O'GRADY. This is my mission. I will speak to them. Heaven inspires me with courage! Geordie, tell me when the last moment is come—let me know when death is near.

MRS. CAMPBELL. Her temples throb and burn. My poor Jessie, lie down awhile and rest your head in my lap.

ALICE. How she trembles, her hands are icy cold.

MRS. CAMPBELL. Jessie, are you cold?

JESSIE (sings). In winter when the rain rained cauld.

ALICE. Her senses wander again.

MRS. CAMPBELL. Jessie, my dear Jessie, try to rest your wearied brain, try to sleep.

JESSIE. Sleep! Aye, let me sleep awa', but you'll awake me when my father comes from the ploughin'.

MRS. CAMPBELL. Yes Jessie, when the gude man comes home I will awake you. God help her.

JESSIE. I'm his ainly bairn, and he loos me weel. (Sings)[181]

When the sheep are in the fauld, and the cows come hame,
And a' the weary warld to quiet rest are gane;
The waes o' my heart fa' in showers frae my ee
Unken'd by my gudeman, who soundly sleeps by me.

Young Jamie loo'd me weel, and sought me for his bride;
But saving ae crown-piece, he'd naething else beside,
To make that croun a pound my Jamie gaed to sea;
And the croun and the pound, oh! they were baith for me.

Before he had been gane a twelvemonth and a day,
My faiher brak his arm, our cow was stown away;[182]
My mother she fell sick—my Jamie at the sea—
And Auld Robin Gray, oh! he cam a-courting me.

---

181 Lyrics by Lady Anne Lindsay [Barnard], set to various traditional airs. "Auld Robin Gray," based on the Bannatyne Club edition of 1825, ed. J.L. Weir (Brechin: D.H. Edwards 1938) runs to 26 verses.

182 Stolen away.

GEORDIE. The enemy are moving sir, the time has come.

(Drums).

RANDAL. The Enemy! Fall in men!

(They do so).

Thirty men alone are fit for service, thirty men to repulse a thousand *(turns aside).*

O'GRADY. My gentle friends, to you, weak in body but so strong in soul, I speak. It is fitting that you should know that the last hour has arrived.

(Guns)

The last earthly hope is gone. Let us address ourselves to heaven.

ALICE. Will these men desert us?

O'GRADY. In an hour not one of those men will be living.

MRS. CAMPBELL. But we shall be living. Oh, recollect Cawnpore. These children will be hacked to pieces before our eyes, ourselves reserved for worse than death—will you not preserve us from this fate?

RANDAL. Amy my heart is broken, what can we do?

MRS. CAMPBELL. *Kill us,* put us to a merciful death ere you fall. Oh, Randal, do not turn away from me, think of the fate reserved for her you love. Oh! death! a thousand times death! Take us with you Randal, if you leave us here you are accessories to our dishonour and our murder.

O'GRADY. They come. Already they begin to ascend the hill.

ALICE. Geordie! *(Goes up).*

MRS. CAMPBELL. Quick, or it will be too late. Oh, Randal! remember, we are cowards, we are women and may not have the courage to kill ourselves.

RANDAL. I cannot Amy, I cannot.

MRS. CAMPBELL. Lend me your dirk[183] then, rather than see my children mutilated, tortured, they shall die. God will forgive a mother when her children plead for her.

O'GRADY. They are here Randal—

RANDAL. Murderers! They come for their prey. Soldiers one volley, your last, to free your countrywomen from the clutches of these demons, one volley to their noble and true hearts, and then give your steel to the enemy. Shoulder arms. Ready!—

(Bagpipes heard).

JESSIE. Ah! Hark—dinna' ye hear that? I'm no dreaming, it's the Slogan[184] of the Highlanders we're saved. *(Falls on her knees)* Thank God whose mercy never fails the strong in heart and those that trust in him.

RANDAL. Relief! No it is impossible!

(Guns).

JESSIE. To the guns men! Courage! Hark to the Slogan of the McGregor, the grandest of them a'—

RANDAL. Jessie, Jessie, your ears deceive you.

MRS. CAMPBELL. She is mad!

JESSIE. I am not daft, my Scotch ears can hear it far awa'—

---

183 Highlander's dagger.
184 Battle cry; particularly, among Scots and Irish, a surname or gathering-place.

Illustration 23. Agnes Robertson as Jessie Brown, depicted near the close of act 3; song sheet cover for "The Pipes at Lucknow," by E.B.W. Wiebe. Courtesy of the Harvard Theatre Collection, Houghton Library.

(Bagpipes)

There again, will ye believe me, noo? D'ye hear? "The Campbells Are Comin'."

(Guns. Drums and shouts heard).

GEORDIE. See, the flag runs up at the Residency. 'Tis true.

(Cannonade till fall of curtain).

RANDAL. To arms! Men! One charge more, and this time drive your steel down the throats of the murderous foe.

(Charge and Grand Tableau).

Ours (1866)

Interpretive Issues

The comedy *Ours* opens benignly with news of Sergeant Jones's newborn twins. Critics have remarked that this is not exposition; indeed, in marked contrast to the typical well-made play there is no neatly laid-out antecedent action given in the initial scene.[1] Robertson relies on dramaturgy of situation rather than plot, and nothing happens in the entire first act apart from establishing an array of characters. Though never seen on stage, the Jones's newborns are the through-line, as the other characters reveal individuated traits based on their readiness to mark the births and assist the Sergeant's family. This is what Martin Meisel astutely refers to as "expressive attitude": the relationship between members of the group and accessory items, not as profound internal depth but in toned-down effects accruing through serial and multiple situations.[2] Incidentally, Robertson delineates the military class system, with the miserable wages paid to the rank and file such as Jones, minimal accommodation for their families, and no provision at all when noncommissioned husbands and fathers are sent abroad; the compromised social status of commissioned officers such as Captain Angus MacAlister, whose prospects radically differ from his own cousin's, the heiress Blanche Haye; and the regimental officer, Colonel Alexander Shendryn, whose familial wealth is evident in the park and townhouse settings of acts 1 and 2. In this conjunction between the social elite and the Joneses—the least privileged of the military caste system, who nevertheless plan careers for their sons in "ours"—the regimental cohesion of precisely who is "ours" is enacted in multiple deeds of concern, largesse, charity, consideration, and lineage.

Although *Ours* does not overtly cite the historical events that frame it and that transport the characters from the English countryside to the Crimean battlefield, it prompted the audiences of 1866 to remember the political circumstances of that disastrous conflict of 1854-56. Britain had not engaged in a European war since defeating Napoleon, but the balance of power that had held since 1815 was increasingly precarious. This time the agitator was Russia, not France. Tsar Nicholas I expanded Russia's eastern frontier, bellicosely confronted Russia's southern neighbour the Ottoman Empire, and warily watched the 400-mile border with Austria. In July 1853, Russia moved preemptively to occupy the principalities of Moldavia and Wallachia,[3] and thus constricted Austrian shipping in the lower reaches of the Danube, threatened Austria's outlet to the sea, and signalled a step toward flanking Turkey from the west. Britain stood by as the allegiances of three major powers remained in question: the waning Ottoman Empire, centred in Turkey, which controlled Russia's access to the Mediterranean through the straits of Marmara; France, which had cooled toward Russia yet not been a friend to England for 400 years; and the Austrian Empire, whose territories buffered Russia from western Europe but which faced unrest in its Slavic and Hungarian possessions. *Ours* commences in autumn 1853 as tensions mount yet their resolution is still thoroughly in doubt.

In January 1854, Britain and France—which shared no border with the Russian, Ottoman, or Austrian empires—allied to claim predominance at Constantinople.[4] They moved warships into the Black Sea. In

---

1   Anthony Jenkins, *The Making of Victorian Drama* (Cambridge: Cambridge UP, 1991), 74.
2   Martin Meisel, *Realizations: Narrative, Pictorial, and Theatrical Arts in Nineteenth-Century England* (Princeton, NJ: Princeton UP, 1983), 354-56.
3   Currently part of Romania, in 1853 it was part of the Ottoman Empire.
4   Now known as Istanbul.

March, the Sultan invited them to help repel Russia and thus stabilize Europe by establishing an eastern front; war was declared on 28 March. Robertson sets act 2 in the spring or summer of that year as regiments were mobilized. British and French troops amassed at Malta, then Varna[5] (south of Wallachia along the Black Sea), to await further orders during this period preceding active hostilities. Russia withdrew from the principalities in August, signalling the anticlimactic and even ridiculous nature of the stand-off, yet the allies had already resolved not to go home. They selected the Crimea[6]—a peninsula protruding into the Black Sea along Russia's southern boundary, where the Russian navy harboured—as the locus for war.[7] The allies reckoned that though Sebastopol was heavily fortified from sea attack, it was vulnerable from the land. They strategically erred by disembarking too far north, a nine-day march from Sebastopol, which needlessly exhausted troops and expended lives. By November, after hard-won progress across three rivers, they discovered that Sebastopol was better fortified than they had expected. A siege set in. The allies were undersupplied and ill-equipped to survive the winter; their regiments were unaccustomed to acting in concert; and the generals were so inexperienced that the war was, in effect, commanded by staff officers (liaising with line officers such as Colonel Shendryn). Disease and frostbite, rather than battle wounds, caused massive casualties. Reports in the British press emphasized the appalling hospital conditions, shocking disparities in quartering for officers and the rank and file, and growing desperation during this war of attrition, endured in the trenches rather than fought in combat. Skirmishes rather than campaigns characterized this phase. Robertson sets act 3 during this bitter winter, as the British public became alternately irate and exasperated at the ruptured image of the gallant armed forces that had set out less than a year earlier.

At the start of hostilities, British and French forces outnumbered the enemy two to one; by the next spring 225,000 allied troops[8] faced 300,000 Russians. The fortress of Sebastopol was captured on 3 September 1855, but as the allies advanced, the Russians blew up the battlements and made an orderly retreat to fortified positions across the bay. The allies found themselves occupying not a stronghold but a pile of rubble, and opposing not a weakening force but an undaunted enemy. The stalemate extended for six more months. Russia held its own in not just the Crimea but also the Caucasus, where they fought the Turks. Only by threatening to escalate to a naval assault in the Baltic and a land war along the border with Austria did the allies persuade Russia to sign an armistice (the Treaty of Paris) in March 1856.[9]

The Crimean War commenced with fervent patriotism: British colours flew, bands played, and pride overspilled at the prospect of the first major engagement since the Napoleonic Era. Optimism was short-lived. The lavishly dressed officers leading the charges became such easy targets that their mortality significantly exceeded that of soldiers in the field.[10] During the calm of the siege, however, the rank and file died at five to ten times the rate of officers, not from battle wounds but from disease and exposure. Britons' attitude toward the campaign changed markedly once reports turned gloomy. In contrast to the play's brilliantly crafted dialogue in act 1 and the rousing departure of the troops in act 2, the battlefront situation of act 3 has been criticized as preposterous. It would be more correct to characterize it as depicting fully warranted anxieties, on the part of the women characters, as a backdrop to a particularly upbeat

5   Currently part of Bulgaria, in 1853 it was under Ottoman rule.

6   Currently part of Ukraine, in 1853 it was controlled by Russia.

7   Trevor Royle, *Crimea: The Great Crimean War* (London: Little Brown, 1999), 183-200.

8   By this time, Sardinia had joined the alliance. Turkish troops fulfilled support functions but were never taken seriously as co-combatants by the British or French.

9   Mortality figures are dire: approximately 19,500 British, 80,250 French, and up to 450,000 Russians. J.A.S. Greville, *Europe Reshaped, 1848-1878*, 2nd ed. (Oxford: Blackwell, 2000), 166-202.

10   Ulrich Keller, *The Ultimate Spectacle: A Visual History of the Crimean War* (Amsterdam: Gordon and Breach, 2001), 19.

vision of the front, on the part of the regiment. Most troops were quartered in conical canvas tents, not the kind of wooden hut depicted at the Prince of Wales's Theatre. Lieutenant-Colonel Dallas of the 46th Foot wrote to his mother: "Conceive a tent with 2 foot of snow on the ground & of course in drifts many feet of it. This morning we literally had to dig our way out of ours." He reported that officers who could acquire charcoal for cooking and heating were afraid to use it, as three had asphyxiated in their tent trying to warm themselves.[11] The scene designer captured the sense of cold and snow, but Robertson has Hugh Chalcot improbably well provisioned: despite the ice on his washing bowl, he has both a stove and a fireplace where he finds hot coffee upon waking and later cooks his dinner. There are precedents: Chalcot and MacAlister's hut closely resembles structures in a few contemporary illustrations.[12] Nevertheless, Simpson's depiction of joints of lamb and bottles of champagne in an illustration of officers' *Christmas Dinner on the Heights Before Sebastopol*, which substantiates Robertson's choices in act 3, must be understood to be an exceptional feast resulting from an extraordinarily resourceful caterer.[13]

Camp conditions varied by rank and regiment—Henry Clifford (third son of Lord Chudleigh) described the interior of his "comfortable little tent" as having "a brisk warm fire, with plenty of clothing, and a good bed of straw, a camp stool and table, with a Bolognia [*sic*] sausage and some good ration biscuits"—but overall the reports were bleak. Sergeant William Jowett, for example, stressed the combined privations of cold and hunger:

> Well, you have some raw coffee, some pork, and a little biscuit…. [but] you have no wood; none to be got, only the roots of brushwood. You manage to steal a pickaxe, for you cannot get one without, and then you commence grubbing for these roots…. But the next thing is, how are you to light a fire?… You manage to get your fire lighted after a great deal of trouble, and perhaps burning half of the only shirt you have (that on your back); you then have your coffee to roast or burn…. All this time, perhaps, you are almost frozen to death.[14]

Soldiers faced an endless physical slog. Cholera was endemic, and the hospitals offered no effective relief. *Ours* dramatizes the consequences of such reports inflaming anxiety in every military family and kindling indignation in the public at large, even as it foregoes the political dimensions in favour of interpersonal concerns. By depicting both the commissioned officer (Chalcot) and the sergeant (Jones) wounded in battle, Robertson reminds audiences of the hazards of war (reinforced by the distant booming cannon). That memorable winter's suffering is theatricalized by the roaring wind and swirling snowfall

---

11   Michael Hargreave Mawson, ed., *Eyewitness in the Crimea: The Crimean War Letters (1854-1856) of Lt. Col. George Frederick Dallas* (London: Greenhill, 2001), 71.

12   See the illustrations in George Brackenbury, *The Campaign in the Crimea: An Historical Sketch*, 2 vols., illustrated by William Simpson (London: Longman, Brown, Green, and Longmans, 1855), especially vol. 1, plates 2, 8, and 15-17, and vol. 2, plate 10; *History of the Russian War, 1854-5-6* (Edinburgh: W. & R. Chambers, 1866), 321, 391, reproduced in Mawson, *Eyewitness in the Crimea*, plate 19; and Matthew Paul Lalumia, *Realism and Politics in Victorian Art of the Crimean War* (Ann Arbor: UMI Research Press, 1984), plate 28.

13   Brackenbury, *Campaign in the Crimea*, 99-100.

14   Keller, *Ultimate Spectacle*, 20. Compare Jowett's discursive description with John D'Albiac Luard's painting *A Welcome Arrival* (1857), depicting the painter and two other Crimean officers gathered around a newly arrived crate of provisions from London. A reproduction of *A Welcome Arrival* is included in Stephanie Markovits, *The Crimean War in the British Imagination* (Cambridge: Cambridge UP, 2009), 170. Also compare George Cadigan's sketch *My Room*, showing him seated in repose on a folding chair, his sturdy-walled room with a view furnished with bookshelves, table, chairs, cot, and hearth (Keller, *Ultimate Spectacle*, plate 3), and William Simpson's sketch *The Heights Before Sebastopol*, depicting a dozen officers dining on several joints and drinking heartily in a tent draped with patriotic flags (Keller, *Ultimate Spectacle*, fig. 66), to documentary photographs of amputees or drudgery in the trenches (John Hannavy, *The Camera Goes to War: Photographs from the Crimean War, 1854-56* [Edinburgh: Scottish Arts Council, 1974]).

just outside the thin door.[15] The occupants of this hut are comparatively well provisioned—they have food as well as fuel—but this, like so much in the British Army, involved a little luck and lot of subsidy from officers' pockets. Sergeant Jones, who shuttles cooking implements between officers' huts, does not—significantly—sleep or dine with them.

Ours is not so much evidence of the Crimean War—even a romantic or commodious version of it—as an impression of characters engaging with each other in the midst of historical forces. Littering the set of act 3 with realia—straw and commonplace gewgaws evoking sensibility and place—helped audiences recall how the Crimean conflict was the very first war to be covered by picture journalists. This referent to authenticity and documentation—rather than the commercially mounted panoramas and theatrical spectacles that the public also eagerly consumed during wartime,[16] or battle paintings[17]—is the long-term memory evoked by *Ours*. Patriotic sentiments aside, the aesthetic approach is as different as possible from a performance that Henry Morley saw at the Adelphi in December 1854:

> It has little story, being chiefly a vehicle for the introduction of effective scenery, views in the Baltic and Black Seas, in Wallachia, Constantinople, St. Petersburg, etc., and of such effective business as belongs to a dramatic enforcement of the popular opinions about the Russians, and a putting of them down, so far as it lies in the power of an enterprising playhouse manager to do it. The piece is received with full applause, and a French dance, *La Flotte*, now extremely popular in Paris, has been introduced with success. I cannot say that I find much wit, and certainly I see no grace, in the representation of a naval combat by the dancing of ladies and gentlemen with ships on their heads.[18]

Early theatrical representations of the Crimea, such as this one, tended toward the capricious; but once the ground war was underway, news of the campaign was relayed to the London public on a very short turnaround, as journalists and photographers reported developments by telegraph and quick trans-Europe rail service to London presses. As one popular chronicle reflects, "The Russian War of 1853-56 differed from all preceding wars" in that "it admitted, to a very remarkable degree, of historical narration during the progress of the events themselves."[19] When the military developments became infrequent, the press was never short of reportage of a sociological nature.[20]

Robertson looked back upon this, a decade later, in a more contemplative mood. Portraits of the period—the gallant lieutenant, distinguished foreign prince, and good-natured sergeant—cast the milieu romantically but not necessarily naïvely. Robertson and the Prince of Wales's manager and leading actress Marie Wilton capitalized on the middle class's fascination for unsentimentalized popular illustrations of the war to move the action of the play from the pastoral first act to the fashionable London residence of act 2 and, finally, to the inelegant realism of act 3 where the men—now bearded, battered, and bedraggled[21]—prosecute the war.

---

15   William Archer, *The Old Drama and the New* (Boston: Small, Maynard, 1923), 262.

16   For discussion of entertainments, see J.S. Bratton, "Theatre of War; the Crimea on the London Stage, 1854-55," in *Performance and Politics in Popular Drama: Aspects of Popular Entertainment in Theatre, Film and Television, 1800-1976*, edited by David Bradby, Louis James, and Bernard Sharratt (Cambridge: Cambridge UP, 1980), 119-38; for panoramas see Keller 60-65; and for circus see Erroll Sherson, *London's Lost Theatres of the Nineteenth Century: with Notes on Plays and Players Seen There* (London: John Lane, 1925), 61.

17   Lalumia, *Realism and Politics*.

18   The piece was *The Zig Zag Travels of Messrs. Danube and Pruth*. Henry Morley, *Diary of a London Playgoer* (1866; reprinted by Leicester: Leicester UP, 1974), 88.

19   *History of the Russian War*, v.

20   Andrew Lambert and Stephen Badsey, *War Correspondents: The Crimean War* (Stroud: Alan Sutton, 1994).

21   See illustrations of Squire Bancroft, Johnny Clarke, and C. Young in the Victoria and Albert's collection of Guy Little's cabinet photographs (S.142:64-2007 and S.142:67-2007).

The Shendryns' bitterness, Mary and Chalcot's disillusionment, and Blanche's overt status as a commodity ensure that marriage—the theme established in the antebellum period and which runs parallel to the war—is the comedic heart of the play.[22] Even so, the cause of the Shendryns' rift—the embezzling brother—is not just a convenient plot point but also information regarding the regiment's condition: colonels' fortunes equipped and clothed the men, so the perfidy of Lady Shendryn's brother not only deprived her of a new carriage but literally took good cloth from soldiers' backs and better rifles from their hands. Prince Perovsky, suitor to the Shendryns' niece, implicitly establishes the Shendryns' social standing. His civility also, incidentally, represents the entrenched practices of gentlemen diplomats and officers whose intermarriages made England's prosecution of war with German or Russian speakers so fraught, and even more so when they campaigned on behalf of a waning empire of Muslim Turks. Victoria and Albert's children had intermarried with Prussian and German nobility,[23] but the queen was also keenly interested in Anglo-Russian amity: her own godfather was Tsar Alexander I, and she was christened Alexandrine Victoria in his honour. She was briefly courted by Alexander I's grandson before (like Blanche) marrying her own first cousin. When Prince Perovsky pays compliments to the Shendryns' niece, this insinuates that Blanche Haye is not merely a desirable heiress but is also as eligible as the daughters of the royal family and the queen herself. While this is posited as a love plot it also shadows international relations.

Editing Issues

The 1889 edition of Robertson's *Principal Dramatic Works* briefly quotes from a manuscript draft of act 1.[24] Daniel Barrett's study of 1995 declares this source lost. Not so: it is in the Victoria and Albert Museum's Theatre collection. Four versions of the play warrant comparison. In order of composition, they are the V&A manuscript; the licensing manuscript submitted to the Lord Chamberlain; a printed edition made for Robertson's private use *c.* 1870, based on an unspecified prompt copy; and the 1889 published edition endorsed by Robertson's son.[25] Because it makes explicit many details of staging closest to the original production date (rather than the 1889 version, which likely reflects a later revival), the third version is the one transcribed here.

The play's structure is consistent across all four versions. Act 1 shows many instances of lines expanded or turned to better effect, most likely in a combined effort of playwright and actors in rehearsal, followed

---

22 Fredric Jameson lists eight narrative variants for war. *Ours* evinces three of them: the collective experience of war; the leaders, officers, and institution of the army; and foreign occupation. The predominance of the marriage plots pulls against these explicit war motifs; provided that the men were in danger, many other pretexts could be substituted for the women venturing into the masculine realm. See Fredric Jameson, "War and Representation," *PMLA* 124:5 (2009): 1533.

23 Several matches were with Germans: Princess Victoria to Prince Friedrich Wilhelm (1857), Princess Alice to Prince Louis of Hesse (1861), and Princess Helena to Prince Christian of Schleswig-Holstein (1866). The Prince of Wales married Alexandria of Denmark in 1863, but in 1874 his brother Prince Alfred Ernest Albert married Grande Duchess Marie, daughter of Tsar Alexander II. One of Princess Alice's daughters eventually married Tsar Nicholas II, and as Alexandra Fedorovna was the last tsarina.

24 T.W. Robertson, *The Principal Dramatic Works of Thomas William Robertson* (London: Sampson Low, Marston, Searle & Rivington, 1889), lii-liii (hereafter *PDW*).

25 *Ours*, Theatre Museum PR 5232.R5; *Ours*, British Library Add MS 53053 (A), licensed on 12 September 1866; *Ours: An Original Comedy*, in the British Library's Department of Printed Books, date stamped October 1870, shelfmark 11780.b.43; and *PDW*, vol. 1. The British Library includes another printed version, bound with alternate blank pages, date stamped 30 October 1874, shelfmark 1568.153; it bears the bookplate of William Hillier (4th Earl of Onslow) and was evidently used for an amateur production at his country home, Clandon Park, in Surrey. Its text and printed didaskalia are closest to Robertson's private edition, which lends credence to the idea that the *PDW* edition reflects changes made for later revivals at the Prince of Wales's Theatre.

by 150 nights of the initial run. Act 2 becomes fleshed out in a few key details, for example Lady Shendryn's report of the letter advising her on how to handle the Prince's suit now that war has broken out. After the Prince presses his suit to Blanche, Chalcot and Mary remark on the troops that pass below their balcony window, upstage of this fashionable drawing-room. Comparison of the earliest manuscript and the 1889 edition documents how Robertson's ideas developed into an elaborate polyrhythmic scene of voice and music: emotions are more fully contrasted between Chalcot and Mary's exuberance, Blanche's pensive politesse, Lady Shendryn's rising alarm when she hears the colonel's voice outside and realizes her husband is off to war, and the Prince's *sang-froid*.

V&A Manuscript (pre-production)	1889 Published Edition
(Enter Lady Lysart L.D.).	*(As Blanche rises, Lady Shendryn enters, L.D. Blanche sits again on sofa. CHALCOT and Mary at window).*
LADY LYSART. My dear Prince. I did not know you were here.	LADY SHENDRYN. My dear Prince, I did not know you were here!
PRINCE *(rising)*. I took the opportunity of your ladyship's absence to urge the suit of which you have been kind enough to approve.	PRINCE. I profited by your ladyship's absence to urge the suit of which you have been kind enough to approve.
LADY LYSART. And have you received an answer?	LADY SHENDRYN. And have you received an answer?
PRINCE. Not precisely.	PRINCE. Not precisely.
DRAYCOTE *(at window)*. ~~They're marching past.~~	*(Music stops).*
(Lady starts).	CHALCOT *(at balcony)*. There's Sir Alick!
There's Sir Alick!	*(Cheers).*
(Lady stands near armchair C.).	
LADY LYSART. I trust to prevail upon my niece to—	
SIR ALEXANDER *(without)*. Right wheel. March!	SIR ALEXANDER *(outside)*. Battalion! Attention! Form fours, right! March off by companies in succession from the front! Number one, by your left, quick march.
(Lady nearly faints. "God Save the Queen" played)	*(Music. Repeat, "The Girl I Left Behind Me."—Lady Shendryn, C., starts. Tramp loud).*
DRAYCOTE. They're marching ~~past~~ off.	CHALCOT. They're marching right past the window. Come here and see. There's the sergeant.
	(Command outside, "Number two, by your left, quick march").
PRINCE. May I be permitted to hope that I may know my fate now?	PRINCE. Miss Haye, may I be permitted to know if I may hope?
MARY. There's Angus.	MARY *(at window)*. There's Angus!

("God Save the Queen" louder. Cheers. Tramp of troops. Lady S. [Lysart]~~faints~~ sinks in arm chair as Blanche rises from sofa—goes to window, returns ~~from~~ and staggers near arm-chair C. giving the idea that she has seen Angus. Prince standing in front. Mary & Draycote cheering and waving pocket hand[kerchiefs]. Machine to imitate horse's hoofs on stone & gravel. Gravel for men to march on. Entr'acte Music Dead March & Lively Airs blended).

(Blanche rushes u.)
ANGUS *(without)*. Number three, by your left! Quick march!
(Music forte. Band plays "God save the Queen." Cheers. Tramp of soldiers. Excitement. Picture. Chalcot and Mary waving handkerchiefs, and cheering at window. Prince, L., taking snuff. Lady Shendryn, C. Blanche totters down and falls fainting at her feet).

Stage directions at the top of the act indicate that the window is within sight of Birdcage Walk (along the southern edge of St. James's Park in front of Wellington Barracks). The Shendryns live within a stone's throw of Buckingham Palace; therefore, when the band strikes up "God Save the Queen," the audience might envision them rounding the corner at Buckingham Gate to salute the monarch.[26] Sir Alick and Angus commend themselves to the state, and the women who love them collapse according to their onset of sentiment. Mary, the onlooker to history, waves and cheers with the throng below. Chalcot has resolved to buy a commission and join up, so though he is still physically with the women his allegiance is with the marching regiment. The Prince, over to one side, takes snuff, indifferent to the spectacle suggested by the emotional range and offstage soundscape of regimental tunes, national airs, mustering cavalry, and drill commands. According to William Archer, "this effect" of the patriotic departure, offstage rather than as a spectacle, "since so familiar, was then novel and intensely moving."[27]

The first two versions bear out Marie Wilton's claim that Robertson was at a loss over how to bring Mary Netley to the fore in act 3: "he begged me to do all I could in the scene which concerned me in the last act ... so at the rehearsals I set to work, and invented business and dialogue, which, happily, met with his approval.... The audience laughed at the fun, and forgave the rest."[28] The scene was developed through improvisation instigated by Wilton and retained with Robertson's blessing. The earliest manuscript and the licensed version contain only perfunctory mention of the lamb roasting for dinner. When Lady Shendryn and Blanche step out to watch the regiment, Mary is left alone with Chalcot. Sparring at first, though not as acerbically as their Beatrice and Benedick personae of act 1,[29] Mary dons an apron, ascertains what ingredients are at hand, and concocts the homey luxury of a roley-poley pudding (a dough of suet and flour spread with jam, rolled into a ball, tied with a cloth, and steamed for several hours) to cap off the dinner of roast lamb and potatoes. This provides the opportunity for Mary to soften to Chalcot, lamed by a bayonet and thus temporarily in charge of the culinary arrangements, and for him to marvel at her domestic aptitude. They emerge from the scene affianced, but the transformation in attitude that enables this is more fully laid out in each successive version of the play. In the earliest version, by contrast, Chalcot

---

26   Queen Victoria often personally inspected the troops at embarkation. Lalumia, *Realism and Politics*, 77.

27   Archer, *Old Drama and the New*, 262.

28   Marie Bancroft and Squire Bancroft, *Mr. & Mrs. Bancroft On and Off the Stage* (London: Richard Bentley, 1889), 415. The *Morning Herald* insisted that there was much to forgive: "The episodes in the park are the most interesting portion of the work, and they held out promises of a really bright and original comedy, which the subsequent scenes did not wholly realize. The figures in the drawing-room were less finely drawn and coloured, and the third act was a still inferior representation of life and character, and afforded little more than a mere farcical and extravagant view of the discomforts of Crimean campaignings." *Morning Herald*, 17 September 1866: 6.

29   The resemblance was noted by both the *Times* (19 September 1866: 10) and the *Observer* (16 September 1866: 7).

experiences an almost miraculous sensation of love after knocking heads with Mary as they search for a dropped hair pin:

> DRAYCOTE. ... I wouldn't lose that for the world.
>
> *(Draycote and Mary go on their knees to search for it).*
>
> > Where is it!—I want to wear [it] there *(hitting his breast)* like a medal. *(Knocking his head against Mary's)* I beg your pardon.[30]
> > MARY. O never mind.
> > DRAYCOTE *(seizing her hand).* Forgive my sudden familiarity but if I should ever leave the Crimea may I hope that you will permit me to, to, to pay my addresses to you.

In the later versions, it is Mary's resourcefulness in the camp kitchen that removes the last of Chalcot's resistance toward her charms. What *she* sees in *him* is never made explicit in the text.

Genre Issues

Robertson came from a family of actors but resolved to be a dramatist. He wrote in a variety of genres—eighteen comedies, nineteen dramas, eleven farces, and three novels[31]—finding his first fame and true home with Marie Wilton at the Prince of Wales's Theatre. The earliest of his successes with Wilton was *Society* (1865), followed by *Ours* (1866) and *Caste* (1867), his best-remembered play. Marie Wilton had made her name playing burlesque; Robertsonian comedy represented her way out of travesty roles into the line of quick-witted, sometimes sharp-tongued maidens that she played the rest of her life. At this point, she was tenant of the Prince of Wales's Theatre, a relatively small and off-the-beaten-track house elegantly refitted to appeal to the growing middle class. She managed the theatre for C.J. James, who leased the property and contributed to the manageress's success with his skilfully painted scenery.

Though act 3 includes numerous inversions of conventional social roles—the millionaire cooks, commissioned officers squabble over frying pans, and society women go to the battlefront—it relies upon none of older comedy's formula of disguised ingénues and their clever ladies' maids. Instead, Blanche has a female companion whose social inferiority is solely financial, and except for some high-spirited mock sword-play in the Crimean hut[32] and imitation of drawling clubmen, there is no hint of older comedy's recourse to breeches roles. Instead, it is a war play whose staged battles are wholly matrimonial. And while it is assuredly a comedy—the marriage plots guarantee that—the characterizations and style aim for a newly anglicized claim upon comedy featuring an indigenous yet modernized morality and a small ensemble of characters equal in importance within the story.[33]

Ours was recognizable in 1866 for offering characters plausibly drawn from London society.[34] Only Sergeant Jones resembles the stock comic man (though even he is stolidly droll and not merely

---

30   Another inked line in the upper margin: "*Engagement. Dray [Chalcot] derails his first action making love at same time on his knees.*"

31   Robertson, *PDW*, vol. 1, lxxix.

32   This is the iconic moment portrayed in the *Illustrated London News*, 20 October 1866.

33   Robertson, *PDW*, vol. 1, xiv. The Prince of Wales's company sought to play down the idea of stars, even though Marie Wilton was a clear favourite. The Bancrofts' revivals included Ellen Terry (not yet a star) and Lillie Langtry (a society novelty) as Blanche. A later production, not with the Bancrofts, included no fewer than five of London's actor-managers.

34   Robertson struggled repeatedly to adapt Thackeray's *Vanity Fair* for the stage, but its scope always eluded him. In fact, he evidently took the title *Ours* from the novel: "Run Simple (Ensign Simple, of Ours, my dear Amelia. I forgot to introjuice him to ye)" and "a stout jolly lady, in a riding-habit, followed by a couple of officers of Ours, entered the room" (chapter 26). See Clement Scott, *The Drama of Yesterday*, vol. 2 (London: Macmillan, 1899), 510, 515.

convenient). Notably, the play has neither hero nor villain and makes an explicit point of neither having nor needing fortune-hunters to make the marriage plots thrive. Unlike figures in melodrama, the principals require nuanced playing: Sir Alick is determined to shield his wife from her brother's misdeeds yet must silently endure her misplaced jealous scorn; Chalcot overcomes his dread of being publicized as a philanthropist and gives Sergeant Jones a large sum, yet must seamlessly accept the donation's exchange for a smaller one when Jones assumes a mistake; and Blanche is onstage with her sanctioned suitor (the much older Russian prince) and Angus (her cousin and childhood companion), yet must give Prince Perovsky a thorough chance while not comprehending what she feels towards Angus. Lady Shendryn is also a challenging part. Her original proponent's characterization is described as that of "a self-willed and discontented great lady," "a bit of a shrew," and a "jealous and affected lady" played "in a truthful and telling style": she must modulate the character's unbecoming attitudes with elegance as well as genuine surprise and compassion upon discovering the truth of her husband's mysterious expenditures.[35]

Polished dialogue and smart repartee propel *Ours* forward.[36] The comedic tone of act 1 is underscored by a concurrent stagecraft of falling leaves, midday gloominess succumbing to a patter of rain, then thunder presented in parallel with the scornful interchange between the Shendryns and the shy banter between Angus and Blanche, each pair caught unaware of the other taking shelter from the cloudburst under three-dimensional trees. Their contrapuntal dialogue is further enhanced by a verse of "Le Chanson de Fortunio" (from Offenbach's *Maître Fortunio*) which is used as a kind of leitmotiv throughout the play: heard as an overture as the curtain rises, invoked while the couples shelter from the storm, dolefully picked out on the piano in act 2, and reprised in act 3 as "Captain MacAlister's March."[37] While Robertson's plays became a lodestar for the emergence of stage realism—dubbed "cup and saucer realism" in reference to his next play, *Caste*—it would be a mistake to confine this development to tea parties or the textured set dressing of the Crimean hut's snow-laden rafters, door chinked with insulating straw, or the infamous roley-poley pudding. His handling of atmosphere and dialogue is at least as deft and as much of its time as photo journalism, the novels of George Eliot, and the paintings of John Everett Millais.

Performative Issues

Comparing his own plays *The Colleen Bawn* and *Arragh-na-Pogue* to Robertson's *Ours* and *Caste* in 1868, Dion Boucicault stated: "Robertson differs from me, not fundamentally, but scenically; his action takes place in lodgings or drawing-rooms—mine has a more romantic scope."[38] Debates about "truth" versus "staginess" notwithstanding, Boucicault had a point, for even though only one act of *Ours* transpires in a drawing-room, drawing-room manners and concerns pervade the whole.

The drawing-room of act 2 is the play's pivot point, where the imminence of both marital and martial engagements are depicted. Blanche and Angus's tableau, one of the most recognizable moments in the performance, forms Millais's iconic 1860 picture of a woman barring her lover's path to war.

---

35 *Morning Herald*, 17 September 1866: 6; *Liverpool Mercury*, 24 August 1866: 7; and *Observer*, 16 September 1866: 7.

36 "'Ours' at the Prince of Wales's Theatre," *Reynold's Newspaper*, 22 September 1866: 4.

37 Squire Bancroft describes hearing the tune as the curtain rose on act 1 so many times that he thought it would become his requiem (Bancroft and Bancroft, *Mr. and Mrs. Bancroft*, 405). A contemporary of Bancroft also remembered the tune as extremely catchy: "It soon became the rage, and the simple love song ... was sung in every drawing room in London." "A Veteran Actor and a Play. Mr. Hall's Interesting Recollection of the Early Days of *Ours*," clipping file, Harvard Theatre Collection. The tune was published for Wallack's New York production as "Secret Love," arranged by Edward Mollenhauer (New York: J. Schuberth, n.d.).

38 Archer, *Old Drama and the New*, 88; from Bancroft and Bancroft, *Mr. and Mrs. Bancroft*, 118.

BLANCHE. No—yes! You confuse me so—I hardly know what I'm doing!

(Bugle without, at distance. Roll on side drum, four beats on big drum, then military band play "Annie Laurie"—the whole to be as if in the distance. Angus starts up, and goes to window. Blanche springs up and stands before door, L. Angus goes to door, embracing Blanche. They form Millais's picture of the "Black Brunswicker").

BLANCHE. Oh, Angus—dear cousin Angus!

Briefly, the couple forms Millais's composition of Prussian lovers (a young woman poignantly standing between her soldier-beau and a partly open door) caught up in the conflict with Napoleon.[39] In *Ours*, the door opens and Prince Perovsky is announced. His entrance literally rends the pair apart. Subtly, the audience is reminded that Tsar Nicholas I is now the foe, not Napoleon as in Millais's setting, yet instead of the cannonade of battle and warring forces of empire, "Annie Laurie" wafts in from the street below and a rival suitor steps through a doorway. Perovsky, a perfectly charming enemy, is not exoticized like *The Relief of Lucknow*'s Rajah or *Elphi Bey*'s Osmyn. John Hare made himself up to resemble Nicholas I's son Tsar Alexander II—aged forty-eight in 1866—and so Hare's Prince Perovsky contrasted with Angus by virtue of age and wealth rather than ethnic alienism. If anything, Angus the Scot is the home-grown exotic, splendidly clad in his dress uniform.[40] As Meisel observes, the historical indirection of Millais's picture (from Napoleon to Tsar Nicholas I, and from epic struggle to a young woman's heartbreak) required an audience attuned to subtleties: "Robertson appeared as a dramatic realist to an audience prepared to see realism in texture and detail." Robertson relied upon his audience's familiarity with realist painting, in particular, to decode the stage action. This enabled, in turn, new stage conventions. "In the negation of strong contrast, broad effect, and violent gesture and rhetoric, he remained in dramaturgy a pale scion of Romantic theater,"[41] scaling emotion to sentiment rather than transcendent experience. Subsequently, in act 3, where the "private" realm of the field hut is full of utensils and the paraphernalia of domesticity, affairs of the heart preoccupy the warriors' business. As it draws to an end, Prince Perovsky strolls in, a genial prisoner to his former hosts, and in giving up his sword (and his suit for Blanche) effects a gentleman's capitulation as a gentleman—neither villain nor hero—would do.

While "completeness"[42] characterized the Bancrofts' stage management,[43] their deployment favoured surface effects. The hut occupies the centre of the stage space in act 3, and though the space beyond is filled with atmospheric detail, it is not the panoramic sweep of romantic drama that postulates the human condition *per se*. Robertson accomplishes something similar in the act 2 drawing-room, as lovers spark against a background of sound. Robertson's textural engagement with props, polished dialogue, composition among figures, and background soundscape demonstrates technical finesse that became accentuated as the play entered rehearsals and settled into a pattern in performance and revivals. William Archer aptly called him a "Pre-Raphaelite of the theatre" for his "illusion of reality by minute but characteristic touches."[44] Pre-Raphaelite illustrators utilized masterful technique to render

---

39   A photograph depicting Mabel Terry Lewis and Frank Seymour in the 1897 Globe Theatre production demonstrates the pose. See Victoria and Albert Museum, Guy Little's cabinet photographs S.133:691-2007.

40   In act 1, Bancroft as Angus wore a velvet jacket, striped trousers, and derby hat, so his second act military regalia must have constituted an impressive contrast to his civvies. See Victoria and Albert Museum, Guy Little's cabinet photographs S.142:62-2007 and S.142:65-2007.

41   Meisel, *Realizations*, 358. See also Markovits, *Crimean War*, 168-69.

42   *Morning Herald*, 17 September 1866: 6.

43   Marie Wilton and Squire Bancroft married in December 1867.

44   Archer, *Old Drama and the New*, 260.

surface details yet their vivid colours mitigated against the immanence of experience. Like Robertson, they stressed the importance of narrative, not arrested in monumentality like the grandeur of history painting but breaking through tableaux into action on a human scale. Fidelity to nature, in any aesthetic, always lacks an absolute standard.

Music in *Ours* is wholly diegetic: always motivated by the action whether sung on stage (as in acts 1 and 3) or justified by an offstage band (as in acts 2 and 3) yet also underscoring the narrative and emotionally illustrative. During the "Black Brunswicker" tableau, a passing regimental band strikes up "Annie Laurie." A parlour favourite, the song "Annie Laurie" is narrated by a Scottish lad who remembers the "brae" (hill) where his true love gave her promise. The refrain, "I'd lay me doon and dee" (I would lie down and die), though unsung in *Ours*, would nevertheless resound in audiences' minds. While Blanche has not made a promise, Angus asks her for it, and after the line "May I hope?" must break from her. Once Blanche tears off her locket and gives it to him, the music stops. She sits on the ottoman (no coincidence, that), and Prince Perovsky begins his one-way colloquy. When he mentions the disparity between their ages, the fifes and drums outside strike up "The British Grenadiers." This rousing song, a favourite of the Redcoats since the Napoleonic Era, makes Chalcot and Mary struggle to be heard in the first part of their conversation. The music ceases, Mary throws open the window, and a bugle calls. Horses tramp, then fade away. Chalcot, replacing Blanche on the ottoman, declares his intention to buy a commission. Mary commends him, and a band strikes up the sprightly song "The Girl I Left behind Me."

The final act begins with the girls—presumably—left very far behind. The curtain rises—again—with "Chanson de Fortunio," and at the conclusion of Angus's monologue, he exits singing "Le Sire de Framboissey" though he breaks off before reaching the song's moral: "A jeune femme, il faut jeune mari!" (A young woman must have a young husband). Chalcot wakes, singing another jaunty song about a daughter who refuses to marry and so her father withholds his fortune. "Willikins and His Dinah" was sung by troops in the Crimea, and its "rattling chorus" broke what was "otherwise all gloom and despondency."[45] Later, conversing with Blanche, he reprises "Willikins" as a contrast to the band's "Chanson de Fortunio," marching the regiment into a skirmish. "Captain MacAlister's March" is heard once more as the men march back to their tents: the principals are all gathered safely in the hut, the three couples are happily matched, and everyone makes preparations to lay the dinner table.

The regimental band, which somewhat implausibly performs in the offstage milieu of winter, takes the soldiers into battle during a lull in the blizzard. In reality, bandsmen served not only as musicians but also as riflemen and stretcher-bearers during the Crimean conflict.[46] While they gave panache to military spectacles and regulated the cadence of soldierly movement,[47] the final tableau holds on the revelation of the enemy's captured colours: Sir Alexander whispers to Lady Shendryn, "Ours;" Chalcot identifies the returning troops as "Ours"; and Angus takes Blanche's hand saying, "Ours." The "Chanson" continues, quietly. For once, the band did not need to lay down their instruments and carry bodies home on stretchers.

---

45   L. Winstock, *Songs and Lyrics of the Redcoats: A History of the War Music of the British Army, 1642-1902* (London: Leo Cooper, 1970), 158.

46   Ibid., 169.

47   Scott Hughes Myerly, *British Military Spectacle: From the Napoleonic Wars Through the Crimea* (Cambridge, MA: Harvard UP, 1996), 8.

Ours[48]

BY T.W. ROBERTSON

First performed at the Prince of Wales's Theatre, Liverpool, 23 August 1866; premiered at the Prince of Wales's Theatre, London, 18 September 1866.

	Liverpool	*London*
Prince Perovsky	Mr. Hare	Mr. Hare
Sir Alexander Shendryn, Bt.	J.W. Ray	J.W. Ray
Captain Samprey		Mr. Trafford
Angus MacAlister	Squire Bancroft	Squire Bancroft
Hugh Chalcot	Johnny Clarke	Johnny Clarke
Sergeant Jones	F. Dewar	Frederick Younge
Houghton	Mr. Tindale	Mr. Tindale
Lady Shendryn	Sophie Larkin	Sophie Larkin
Blanche Haye	Louisa Moore	Louisa Moore[49]
Mary Netley	Marie Wilton	Marie Wilton
Jennings, Lady Shendryn's maid		
Soldier		

Scenic design C.J. James

Act I

An avenue of trees in Shendryn Park; the avenue leading off to R.U.E. Seat round tree in foreground, R. Stumps of trees, L.C. and L. The termination of the avenue out of sight. Throughout the Act the autumn leaves fall from the trees. Chalcot discovered asleep on ground under tree, L.2 E., a handkerchief over his face. Enter Sergeant Jones (L.1 E.), meeting Houghton, R.U.E.

SERGEANT *(L.).* Good morning.
HOUGHTON *(L.).* Good morning.

(Sergeant shakes Houghton's hand warmly. Houghton surprised).

SERGEANT. How are you?
HOUGHTON. Quite well; how are you?
SERGEANT. I'm—I'm as well as can be expected.
HOUGHTON. What d'ye mean? *(With dialect).*
SERGEANT *(with importance).* I mean that last night my missus—*(whispers to Houghton).*

---

48   Based on a prompt copy printed recto only and bound for T.W. Robertson. Dedicated to Joseph M. Levy, London, October, 1870. After Robertson's death, this copy passed to his sister, Madge Kendal, who gave it to the British Library (shelfmark 11780.B.43).

49   Later replaced by Lydia Foote.

HOUGHTON (*surprised*). Nay!

SERGEANT. Fact.

HOUGHTON. Two!

(*Sergeant nods*).

Twins?

(*Sergeant nods*).

Well, mate, it does you credit! (*Shakes hands condolingly*) And I hope you'll soon get over it.

SERGEANT. Eh?

HOUGHTON. I mean I hope your missus 'ull soon get over it. Come and ha' some beer.

SERGEANT. I must go to the hall first. I wish they'd been born at Malta.

HOUGHTON. Where?

SERGEANT. At Malta.

HOUGHTON. Malta! Be that where they make the best beer?

SERGEANT. No; it's foreign. When a child's born in barracks there, it gets half a pound o' meat additional rations a-day.

HOUGHTON. Child does?

SERGEANT. Its parents. Twins would ha' been a pound a-day—pound o' meat, you know. It's worthwhile being a father at Malta.

HOUGHTON (*looking at Sergeant admiringly and shouldering his gun*). Come and ha' some beer to drink this here joyful double-barreled event.

(*Exeunt Sergeant and Houghton, R.U.E. Chalcot wakes up, lights his pipe, and looks round moodily; then rearranges the handkerchief over his face, and lies down again. Enter Blanche and Mary, both with baskets, through trees, R.U.E.*).

BLANCHE (*R.*). Don't walk so fast, Mary. Lady Shendryn said she'd overtake us. Let us rest here.

(*They sit on seat R.*).

It's charming under the trees. I mean to look after the little boy. That's for him. (*Puts portemonnaie*[50] *into basket*).

MARY (*L. Taking out portemonnaie*). And I mean to look after the little girl. This is for her. (*Puts portemonnaie into basket*).

BLANCHE (*R.*). But, Mary, dear, can you afford it?

MARY. Yes; though I am poor, I must have some enjoyments. You rich people mustn't monopolize all the pleasures in the world.

BLANCHE (*hurt*). My dear Mary, you know I didn't mean—

MARY. And I didn't mean; but I can't help being sensible. I know my place; and if I didn't, Lady Shendryn and the world would make me. I haven't a penny, so I'm a companion, though I don't receive wages, which the cook does. But then she's respected—she's not in a false position. I wish I hadn't been born a lady.

BLANCHE. No you don't.

---

50 Wallet or folder holding money.

MARY. Yes *I* do. I should have kept a Berlin-wool[51] shop, and been independent and happy. And you, Blanche—you could have rolled down in your carriage, and given your orders—Miss Netley, please send me home this—or that—and so on *(with imitation)*.

BLANCHE. Mary, do talk about something else.

MARY. Well, I will, dear, to please you; but it is annoying to be a companion. Not your companion, Blanche—that's charming—to know that you're kept in the room to save another woman from rising to ring a bell, or to hand her the scissors, or to play the piano when you're ordered. *(Imitating)* Miss Netley—oh!—yes, a very nice person; so useful about the house. Useful—oh!—There, I beg your pardon, Blanche; but really Lady Shendryn's temper does upset me—one minute she's so tender and sentimental, and the next—Poor Sir Alick. Then there's that Mr. Chalcot—I detest him.

BLANCHE. Why?

MARY. Oh, for his gloomy air, and his misanthropic eyeglass. *(Imitating)* Liking nothing, and dissatisfied with everything.

BLANCHE. Despite all that, he has a very good heart.

MARY. My gentleman is rich, and thinks that every girl he speaks to is dying for his ugly face, his stupid bank notes, and his nasty brewhouse. When I look at him I feel that I could smack his face.

BLANCHE. For being rich!

MARY. Yes—perhaps. No, for being disagreeable.

BLANCHE. I'm rich; at least, they tell me so.

MARY. But you're not disagreeable.

BLANCHE. Talk about something else.

MARY. Who—what?

BLANCHE. Anything—anybody.

MARY. Of the people staying at the Hall?

BLANCHE. Yes.

MARY. Prince Perovsky?

BLANCHE. If you like.

MARY. He means you;[52] I can see it in his eye. I know Sir Alick would say yes, and so would my lady. Blanche, what would you say?

BLANCHE *(pensively)*. I don't know.

MARY. That means yes! A Russian prince—wealthy, urbane—the grand air, but dried up as a Normandy pippin.[53] Will my Blanche be a princess?

BLANCHE. Prince Perovsky is a little old.

MARR. Not for a prince. Princes are never old.

BLANCHE. And I'm a little young.

MARY. Not too young for a princess. Princesses are never too young.

BLANCHE. Why, Mary, you're quite worldly.

MARY. On your account I'd like to see you a princess. You'd be charming as a princess.

BLANCHE *(smilingly)*. And if I were and had a court, what would you be?

MARY. Mistress of the Robes, and First High Gold Parasol in Waiting! Oh, my charming, darling Royal Highness. *(Rises)* My Highest, Mightiest, Most Serene Transparentissima![54]

---

51   Wool embroidery on tapestry canvas; produces a three-dimensional effect.
52   He intends you for his wife.
53   A variety of apple: sweet, late-ripening, and long-keeping.
54   Radiance.

(Chalcot wakes up, and looks about him).

BLANCHE *(laughs)*. How silly!

MARY. Who—me?

BLANCHE. Yes.

MARY. Then I renounce my allegiance. I turn Radical,[55] and dethrone you. I wish the prince would ask me.

BLANCHE. Ask you what?

MARY. To be his wife.

CHALCOT *(aside)*. Devil doubt you!

BLANCHE. How would you answer?

MARY. I'd answer—No!

CHALCOT *(aside)*. Dreadful falsehood!

MARY. Though I'd like to be a princess—a Russian princess—and have slaves.

BLANCHE. Oh! I shouldn't like to have slaves.

MARY. I should, particularly if they were men.

CHALCOT *(aside)*. Nice girl that!

BLANCHE. Let's leave off talking Russian.

MARY. What shall we talk then? Scotch? *(Sits again)*.

BLANCHE. What a time Lady Shendryn is!

MARY. About Angus MacAlister? *(Maliciously)*.

BLANCHE *(seeing Chalcot)*. Hush! *(Rising and crossing, L.)*.

MARY *(R.)*. What?

BLANCHE. There's a man.

CHALCOT *(rising)*. Don't be alarmed; I've heard nothing that I oughtn't to.

MARY *(primly)*. Impossible you should.

CHALCOT *(C.)*. I fell asleep under that tree *(down C.)*.

MARY *(R.)*. Why did you wake up?

BLANCHE *(L.)*. Asleep, just after breakfast!

CHALCOT. Humph! There was nothing else to do.

MARY. You mean nothing else that *you* could do.

CHALCOT. I thought of climbing the tree; good notion, wasn't it?

MARY. Excellent—if you'd stayed up there!

CHALCOT. Eh?

MARY. I mean, if you hadn't come down.

(Guns fired without. Mary rises).

CHALCOT. Sir Alick might have brought me down.

BLANCHE. Mistaken you for a rook!

MARY *(aside)*. Or a scarecrow!

CHALCOT *(pointing to basket)*. What have you got there?

BLANCHE. Guess.

CHALCOT. Can't. Never could make out conundrums—or ladies.

MARY. Beyond your comprehension?

---

55   Anti-monarchist.

CHALCOT. Quite *(annoyed)*. Confound the girl! *(Aloud)* But what's in the baskets?

BLANCHE *(L.)*. Fowls, jelly, sago,[56] tapioca,[57] wine!

MARY. Wine, tapioca, sago, jelly, fowls!

CHALCOT. That's variety! Somebody ill?

(Mary sits, R. Enter Lady Shendryn, a languishing, sentimental, frisky person, who heard the last few words, U.E.R.).

LADY SHENDRYN. No—no! Nobody. They're all doing well *(down, L.C.)*.

CHALCOT. All! Who?

LADY SHENDRYN *(L.C.)*. The Twins!

CHALCOT *(R.C.)*. Twins! What twins?

LADY SHENDRYN. Ours.

CHALCOT. Yours? Yours and Sir Al—

LADY SHENDRYN. Mine and—no, no. What a man you are! When I say Ours, I mean Sergeant Jones's.

CHALCOT. Sergeant Jones's!

LADY SHENDRYN. Of Ours—of Sir Alexander's regiment. Alexander is very fond of him; and I quite dote on Mrs. Jones. You know the barracks are not eight miles off, and the railway drops you close to—Miss Netley, I'll sit down—

(Mary rises, and crosses, L.C. Lady Shendryn sits, R.).

So I gave Mrs. Jones the use of the Cottage—and it's—a most agreeable circumstance; isn't it?

CHALCOT. Very—for poor Jones!

MARY *(aside to Blanche, L.)*. Make him give you something—subscription—you know.

CHALCOT *(R.C. Overhearing)*. Make me! I should like to see anyone make me!

BLANCHE *(rising, and crossing to Chalcot)*. By the way *(to Chalcot)* I'm collecting for them. *(Taking out pocketbook)* How much shall I put you down for?

CHALCOT *(R.C. Seeing Mary's eyes on him)*. Nothing.

MARY *(L.)*. Nothing!

LADY SHENDRYN *(R.)*. Oh, Hugh!

BLANCHE. Oh, Mr. Chalcot!

MARY. Oh, these men!

BLANCHE. Consider poor Mrs. Jones!

LADY SHENDRYN. And the twins!

CHALCOT. Twins! I don't think those sort of women ought to be encouraged.

MARY *(aside)*. And that's a man worth thousands!

BLANCHE *(coaxingly)*. Let me put you down for something!

MARY. A shilling!

CHALCOT *(to Mary)*. I'm not to be put down.

LADY SHENDRYN. Miss Netley, pray don't interfere.

(Girls go up, L.).

How charming it is here, under the trees!—so poetical and leafy!

---

56   A pure carbohydrate produced from the trunk of a sago-palm; boiled with milk or water into a pap.

57   A starch produced from the cassava (manioc) root; small pearls are soaked or boiled until chewy.

CHALCOT (*throwing insect off her mantle*). And insecty!

(*Lady Shendryn starts up. Enter Prince, R.U.E., smoking a cigarette. Chalcot crosses to L.*).

LADY SHENDRYN. Ah! here's the Prince. How charming!
MARY. He'll give something.
BLANCHE (*L.C.*). Prince, I'm begging—make a subscription.
PRINCE (*R.C.*). Let me trust I may be permitted to become a subscriber.
BLANCHE. For any amount you please. How much? (*With pocket-book*).
PRINCE. I leave that to you.
LADY SHENDRYN (*R*). Oh, Prince, you are so kind!
MARY (*L.C.*). What a difference! (*To Chalcot*) A noble nation the Russians! (*Goes up, R.*).
BLANCHE. Will that do? (*Writing, and showing him*).
PRINCE. If you think it sufficient.

(*Blanche joins Mary*).

LADY SHENDRYN. Charmingly chivalric!
PRINCE. Shall I be indiscreet in asking the object of—
LADY SHENDRYN. *Objects!* There are two!
PRINCE. Two objects!
CHALCOT. Yes—babies.
LADY SHENDRYN. Twins.
CHALCOT (*L.*). The Jones's gemini!
PRINCE (*to Chalcot*). Twins! Extraordinary people you English.
LADY SHENDRYN. We're going to take these things to the Cottage for them. (*Crossing L.*) Prince! will you come as far?

(*Chalcot crosses, and sits under tree, R.*).

PRINCE. If I may be allowed to take part in so delicate a mission (*following Lady Shendryn*).
LADY SHENDRYN. Blanche! The Prince will escort you.

(*Blanche crosses, L.*).

PRINCE. May I carry the basket?
BLANCHE. Can I trust you?
PRINCE. With what?
BLANCHE. The sago.

(*Exeunt Prince and Blanche, L.1 E.*).

LADY SHENDRYN. Miss Netley will be my cavalier.[58]
MARY. What a treat! (*Coming from back, R. to L.C.*).
LADY SHENDRYN. Unless you, Mr. Chalcot—
CHALCOT (*eye to eye with Mary*). Thanks, no. I'll stay where I am.
LADY SHENDRYN. We shall leave you all alone.
CHALCOT. I don't mind that.

---

58 Gentleman escort (or a lady's dance partner).

MARY. That's just the sort of man who would pinch his wife on his wedding-day.

(*Exeunt Lady Shendryn and Mary, L.1 E.*).

CHALCOT. That's a detestable girl! Whenever I meet her, she makes me thrill with dislike.

(*Sergeant and Keeper enter at end of avenue, R.U.E., carrying a large hamper. They go off, L.U.E.*).

SIR ALEXANDER. Hugh—that you?

CHALCOT. Yes (*seated, R.*).

SIR ALEXANDER. What have you been doing here?

CHALCOT. Sleeping. Shot anything?

SIR ALEXANDER. A brace.[59] I'm nervous. I've been annoyed this morning.

CHALCOT. I'm annoyed every morning—and evening, regularly.

SIR ALEXANDER. I'd bad news by post—and then my lady—(*sitting down*) and I'm so horribly hard up.

CHALCOT. A little management—

SIR ALEXANDER. I know; but I've other troubles, Hugh. You're an old friend, and so was your father before you. If you only knew what was on my mind. There's my lady wrangling perpetually.

CHALCOT. People always quarrel when they're married—or single; and you must make allowances—her ladyship is much younger than you.

SIR ALEXANDER. She might remember how long we have—But it isn't that—it isn't that.

CHALCOT. What then?

SIR ALEXANDER. I mustn't tell—I wish I could.

CHALCOT. I'm open to receive a confession of early murder, or justifiable matricide.

SIR ALEXANDER. It isn't my secret, or I'd tell it you. Oh! my lady is very wrong. The idea of her being jealous!

CHALCOT. I've heard that years ago you were a great killer.

SIR ALEXANDER (*not understanding*). Killer! Of what—birds?

CHALCOT. No. Ladies.

SIR ALEXANDER. Oh!—like other men.

CHALCOT. That's bad—that's very bad. But surely my lady knew that before marriage you were not a Joseph?[60]

SIR ALEXANDER. Not she.

CHALCOT. But she must have guessed—

SIR ALEXANDER. Pooh! pooh! You're talking like a bachelor.

CHALCOT. A bachelor may know—

SIR ALEXANDER. A bachelor can know nothing. It is only after they're married that men begin to understand the purity of women—(*aside*)—or their tempers.

CHALCOT. But do you mean to tell me—between men, you know—that Lady Shendryn has no cause for—

SIR ALEXANDER. Has no cause? Certainly not—

CHALCOT. *Had* no cause, then?

SIR ALEXANDER. *Had!* Um—well—the slightest possible—

CHALCOT. Did she find it out?

---

59   A pair of birds.

60   A man who is impervious to temptation, as in the enslaved Joseph who resists Potiphar's wife (Genesis 39:1-20).

SIR ALEXANDER. Unfortunately she did.

CHALCOT. Ah! Nuisance that—being found out. Is the cause removed now?

SIR ALEXANDER. The what?

CHALCOT. The cause—the slightest possible—

SIR ALEXANDER. Oh yes—long ago. Gone entirely.

CHALCOT. Dead?

SIR ALEXANDER. No—married.

CHALCOT. Better still. Further removed than ever.

SIR ALEXANDER. But my lady has never forgotten it. It was an absurd scrape; for I cared nothing about her.

CHALCOT. About my lady?

SIR ALEXANDER (irritably). No—the—

CHALCOT. Slightest possible—no, no.

SIR ALEXANDER. Where is my lady?

CHALCOT. She has gone to the cottage to see the interesting little Joneses. The Prince went with her—and Blanche—and—that other girl.

SIR ALEXANDER. Mary Netley! Charming girl that!

CHALCOT. Very.

SIR ALEXANDER. She's the daughter of very dear old friends, who died without leaving her a penny.

CHALCOT. Very dear old friends always do.

SIR ALEXANDER. What?

CHALCOT. Die without leaving pennies.

SIR ALEXANDER. Poor little thing! I wish I could find her a husband!

CHALCOT. What a misanthropic sentiment!

SIR ALEXANDER. Now, there's Blanche; she's a fortune. She, like Mary, has no guardians but us—neither father nor mother.

CHALCOT. Splendid qualification that; but Blanche is much too nice a girl to have a mother.

SIR ALEXANDER. She's another anxiety.

CHALCOT. All girls are anxieties.

SIR ALEXANDER. You were wrong to let Blanche slip through your fingers.

CHALCOT. Me marry an heiress! Ugh! (Shudders) That Prince Perovsky is very particular in his attentions.

SIR ALEXANDER. Yes; it would be a good match. He owns two-thirds of a Russian province.

CHALCOT. Poor devil! Isn't it rather awkward, his staying here? If war is to be declared—

SIR ALEXANDER. He's off in a couple of days; besides, after all, Russia may not mean fighting.

CHALCOT (rising). There's Angus, coming down the avenue!

SIR ALEXANDER (rising). Between you and me, Hugh, I wish he wouldn't come so often. He's too fond of teaching Blanche billiards. I'm always finding them with their heads closer together than is warranted by the rules of the game. When children, they saw a good deal of each other. Blanche is my ward, and an heiress; Angus, a distant cousin, poor as a rat—the Scotch branch of the family. I shouldn't like it to be thought that I threw them together.

CHALCOT. No, no.

SIR ALEXANDER. I'll go and meet the people at the Cottage. I promised to join them. (Taking letters from his pocket, selecting one) I daren't take this into the house with me; eh—yes I may—this from Lady Llandudno. She's in a terrible fright about the prospect of war. You know her boy's in Ours. Asks me if

I think the regiment will be ordered out. I may show my lady that. (*Replaces letter in pocket, then tears another into very small pieces. Sighs deeply*) Heigho! It's not much use. It is sure to be found out at last.

(*Exit Sir Alexander, L.1 E. As he goes off, Angus MacAlister comes down the avenue, U.E.R. Chalcot smokes incessantly; as soon as one cigar or pipe is out, he lights another*).

CHALCOT. Well, Gus. Just got in? (*Sit, L.*).

ANGUS (*R.*). Yes. Slept last night in barracks. Got leave again for today. (*Angus is grave and composed in manner; as he speaks, he looks about him, as if his thoughts were away*).

CHALCOT. Bring down a paper with you?

ANGUS. Yes.

(*Gives him newspaper, which Chalcot looks over*).

Where are all the people gone? There's nobody in the Hall[61] (*sits down, R.*).

CHALCOT. Gone to the Cottage to try on a pair of new twins—born on the estate. My lady, Sir Alick, Miss Netley, the Prince, and Blanche.

ANGUS (*rising, and crossing to him*). Have they been gone long?

CHALCOT. No. I haven't quite made up my mind whether I like that Prince Perovsky or not. Do you like him?

ANGUS. I never think about him.

CHALCOT (*aside*). That's not true, Angus, my man. (*Aloud*) I wonder if we shall have war with Russia? (*Eyeing Angus*).

ANGUS. I don't know—I don't care—I wish we had!

CHALCOT. Out of sorts?

ANGUS. Yes.

CHALCOT. Have a weed.

(*Handing cigar-case. Angus smokes*).

Why want war? For the sake of change?

ANGUS. Yes.

CHALCOT. Change of scene?

ANGUS. Change of anything—change for anything—silver, copper—anything out of this! (*Putting his foot on trunk of tree*).

CHALCOT. Out of what? (*Puffing smoke*).

ANGUS. Out at elbows! If there's no war I shall go to India. What use in staying here—without a shilling or a friend? (*Plucking leaf*) What chance is there?

CHALCOT. What chance! You mean what chances? Plenty. You're young—good family—marry a fortune.

ANGUS. Marry for money! That's not the way with the MacAlisters.

CHALCOT. Umph! Marriage is a mistake, but ready money's real enjoyment; at least, so people think who haven't got it. I suppose you've made your choice?

ANGUS. I have. Perhaps you're aware of that?

CHALCOT. Yes.

ANGUS. And who it is?

CHALCOT. Yes.

---

61   The Shendryns' home.

ANGUS. I'm a bad hand at concealment. I'm too proud of loving her. I have to hide it. That's why I mean to go to India. (*Crosses to tree, R.*).

CHALCOT. Better stop here and smoke. I feel in a confidential humour.

(*Angus sits again, or leans against tree, R.*).

So you're in love with Blanche?

ANGUS. Yes.

CHALCOT. I saw that long ago. You know that I proposed to her? (*Sitting on ground*).

ANGUS. Yes.

CHALCOT. But I'm proud to say she wouldn't have me. Ah! she's a sensible girl; and her spirited conduct in saying "No!" on that occasion, laid me under an obligation to her for life.

ANGUS. She declined?

CHALCOT. She declined very much. I only did it to please Sir Alick, who thought the two properties would go well together—never mind the two humans. Marriage means to sit opposite at table, and be civil to each other before company. Blanche Haye and Hugh Chalcot. Pooh! the service should have run: "I, brewhouses, malt-kilns,[62] public-houses, and premises, take thee, landed property, grass and arable, farm-houses, tenements, and salmon fisheries, to be my wedded wife, to have and to hold for dinners and evening parties, for carriage and horse-back, for balls and presentations, to bore and to tolerate, till mutual aversion do us part;" but land, grass and arable, farm-houses, tenements, and salmon fisheries said "No"; and brewhouses is free (*strikes match*).

ANGUS. At all events, you could offer her a fortune.

CHALCOT. And you're too proud to make her an offer because you're poor!

(*Angus sighs*).

You're wrong. I have more cause for complaint than you. I'm a great match. My father was senior partner in the brewery. When he died, he left me heaps. His brother, my uncle, died—left me more. My cousin went mad—bank-notes on the brain. His share fell to me; and, to crown my embarrassments, a grand-aunt, who lived in retirement in Cornwall on four hundred a year, with a faithful poodle and a treacherous companion, died too, leaving me the accumulated metallic refuse of misspent years. Mammas languished at me for their daughters, and daughters languished at me as their mammas told them. At last my time came. I fell in love—fell down, down, down, into an abyss where there was neither sense, nor patience, nor reason—nothing but love and hope. My heart flared with happiness as if it were lighted up with oxygen. She was eighteen—blue eyes—hair yellow as wheat, with a ripple on it like the corn as it bends to the breeze—fair as milk. She looked like china with a soul in it. Pa made much of me—ma made much of me; so did her brothers and sisters, and uncles and aunts, and cousins and cousinettes, and cousiniculings.[63] How I hated 'em! One day I heard her speaking of me to a sister; she said—her voice said—that voice that, as I listened to it, ran up and down my arms, and gave me palpitation—she said, "I don't care much about him; but then he's so very rich!" (*His face falls.*) That cured me of marriage, and mutual affection, and the rest of the poetical lies. (*Knocking ashes out of pipe*) You've youth, health, strength, and not a shilling—everything to hope for. Women can love *you* for *yourself*. Money doesn't poison your existence. You're not a prize pig, tethered in a golden sty. What is left for me? Purchasable charms; every wish gratified; every aspiration anticipated, and the

---

62   A kiln in which barley, etc., is dried after steeping and germinating.

63   Robertson invents a diminutive form for cousin.

sight of the drays[64] belonging to the firm rolling about London with my name on them, and a fat and happy drayman sitting on the shafts, whom I envy with all my heart. Pity the poor! Pity the rich; for they are bankrupts in friendship, and beggars in love.

ANGUS *(standing over him)*. So, because one woman was selfish, you fall in love with poverty, and the humiliations and insults—insults you cannot resent—heaped on you daily by inferiors. Prudent mothers point you out as dangerous, and daughters regard you as an epidemic. You are a waiter upon fortune—a man on the look-out for a wife with money—a creature whose highest aim and noblest ambition is to sell himself and his name for good rations and luxurious quarters—a footman out of livery, known as the husband of Miss So-and-so, the heiress. You talk like a spoiled child! The rich man is to be envied. He can load her he loves with proofs of his affection—he can face her father and ask him for her hand—he can roll her in his carriage to a palace, and say, "This is your home, and I am your servant!"

CHALCOT. You talk like a—man in love. Couldn't you face Sir Alick?

ANGUS. No.

CHALCOT. His marriage hasn't made him happy. Poor Sir Alick! He never could have been happy with his weakness.

ANGUS. You mean Lady Shendryn?

CHALCOT. No; she's not a weakness—she's a power. No; Sir Alick's great regret in life is that he isn't tall. There's a skeleton everywhere; and his skeleton lacks a foot. He can't reach happiness by 10 inches. He's a fine soldier, and an accomplished gentleman; his misery is that he is short. An odd sort of unhappiness, isn't it, from the point of view of men of our height?

ANGUS. What's that to do with the subject of money versus none?

CHALCOT. Nothing whatever—that's why I mentioned it.

ANGUS. Talking of money—you lent me £50. Here it is. *(Giving him note from pocket-book)* I got a note for fifty, because it was portable.

CHALCOT *(taking it reluctantly)*. If it shouldn't be quite convenient—

ANGUS. Oh, quite *(goes up, R.C., cutting at leaves of tree with cane)*.

CHALCOT *(aside)*. Now this would be of use to him; it's of none to me. I know he wants it—I don't; I didn't even remember that I'd lent it him. Confound it. *(Putting it in his pocket)* It's enough to make a man hate his kind, and build a hospital.

ANGUS *(at top of avenue)*. Coming in?

CHALCOT. No; I shall stay here. *(Turning, and lying on ground)* The comfort of the country is, one can enjoy peace and quiet *(turns to L.)*.

(A large wooden ball is thrown from L.1 E. It falls near Chalcot's head. He starts up).

Eh!

(Four more balls are thrown, each nearly hitting him).

By Jove!

ANGUS. Here they are!

(Enter Prince, Blanche, Lady Shendryn, Mary, Sir Alexander, and Captain Samprey, L.1 E.).

PRINCE *(looking at bowls. To Blanche)*. Yours—that's ten. It's your first throw. Permit me *(picks up the ball)*.

---

64   Low carts built for hauling heavy loads.

ANGUS (*comes down between them*). Good morning.
BLANCHE. Oh, Cousin Angus, how you made me start!

(*As the Prince hands her the ball, she drops it with a start*).

LADY SHENDRYN. My dear child, my nerves! (*Leans against Sir Alexander*).
SIR ALEXANDER. Don't be so affected (*aside to her*).

(*Lady Shendryn sits L.*).

ANGUS. Good morning, Lady Shendryn; good morning, Miss Netley. (*Crossing to each, and shaking hands*) How are you, Samprey?
SAMPREY. How d'ye do, Mac?

(*The Prince and Blanche are a little up, R.C. Angus joins them*).

CHALCOT (*R.C.*). Who threw that ball? (*Pointing to the first one thrown*).
MARY (*L.C.*). I did.
CHALCOT. It only just missed falling on my head.
MARY. I'm very sorry.
CHALCOT. That it missed me?
MARY. No; that it fell so far off.
CHALCOT. My head?
MARY. No; that other wooden thing (*pointing to ball*).

(*Chalcot goes up*).

ANGUS. May I join in the game?
SAMPREY. Take my hand, Mac (*giving him ball*).
LADY SHENDRYN (*getting between Blanche and Angus*). It's going to rain. We'd better get indoors.
BLANCHE. Oh no, it won't. It never rains when I wish it to be fine. Now, where shall I throw it?
PRINCE (*R.C.*). I would suggest this side of the hillock.
ANGUS (*L.C.*). I would advise the other. We couldn't see what became of it then.
BLANCHE. The other side. There! (*Throws ball off, R.1 E.*).
ANGUS (*about to throw*). Now then!
LADY SHENDRYN (*interposing*). It's for the Prince to throw first.
ANGUS. I beg your pardon.
PRINCE. No; after you.

(*Angus refuses. Prince throws*).

   There!

(*Angus throws*).

CHALCOT (*R., to Mary*). Are you going to throw now?
MARY. Yes; why do you ask?
CHALCOT. That I may get out of the way. (*Crosses, L.*).

(*Mary throws, then goes up, and sits on stump, L., looking at paper*).

PRINCE (*R.*). Now, Lady Shendryn.

LADY SHENDRYN (*L.C.*). Oh, I am so fatigued! My dear Prince, pray throw for me.

(*Prince throws. Lady Shendryn goes up*).

SAMPREY. All thrown. Who's won?

(*Prince and Angus start together, then stop*).

ANGUS. I beg your pardon.
PRINCE. After you.

(*They hesitate, each unwilling to precede the other*).

BLANCHE (*crossing R.*). Oh, do go! You can't stop to behave prettily across country.

(*Blanche exits, R.1 E., followed by Angus and the Prince, then Samprey*).

LADY SHENDRYN (*coming down, L.C., trying to take Sir Alexander's arm*). I'm so tired, Alexander.
SIR ALEXANDER (*avoiding her*). Do leave me alone (*exit, R.1 E.*).
LADY SHENDRYN. Miss Netley, I must trouble you.

(*Mary is seated on stump, L.2 E. Lady Shendryn takes her arm*).

CHALCOT (*aside*). Serves her right.

(*Lady Shendryn and Mary cross, and exeunt, R.1 E. Mary and Chalcot exchanging looks*).

Poor Angus Mac-Moth. He'll flutter round that beautiful flame till he singes his philabeg.[65]

(*The patter of rain heard upon the leaves*).

Lady Shendryn was right. It's coming down. That'll break up the skittle party.

(*The Sergeant enters, L.1 E., puts out his hand, feels the rain, and takes shelter under tree, L.2 E.*).

There's the Sergeant. I must tip him something in consideration of his recent domestic—affliction. (*Takes out pocket-book*) I'll give him a fiver[66]—eh? Here's Angus's fifty, I'll give him that. (*Pausing*) No; he'll go mentioning it, and it will get into the papers, and there'll be a paragraph about the singular munificence of Hugh Chalcot, Esq., the eminent brewer!—eminent!—as if a brewer could be eminent! No; I daren't give him the fifty.

(*Stands under tree, next to Sergeant, L.1 E. Sergeant touches his cap*).

Wet day, Sergeant (*turning up coat collar*).
SERGEANT. Yes, sir.
CHALCOT. Glad to hear that Mrs. Jones is getting over her little difficulty—I should say difficulties—so well.
SERGEANT. Thank you, sir; she is as a person might say, sir, as well as can be expected (*with solemnity*).

(*During this scene the rain comes down more heavily, and the stage darkens*).

CHALCOT. Have a pipe, Sergeant?

---

65 Kilt.
66 Five-pound note.

SERGEANT. Thank you, sir.

(Chalcot gives him tobacco and fuse.[67] They fill and light pipes).

   Thank you, sir.

CHALCOT. Sergeant, how many are you in family now?

SERGEANT. Eight, sir *(lighting pipe)*.

CHALCOT. Eight! Good gracious! *(Aside, and looking at note.)* If I were only sure he wouldn't mention it—

SERGEANT. Yes, sir. Six before, and two this morning—six and two are eight.

CHALCOT. Rather a large family. May I ask what your pay is?

SERGEANT. One-and-tenpence a day, sir.[68]

CHALCOT. One-and-tenp—*(Aside)* P'raps he wouldn't mention it! *(Aloud)* A small income for so large a family!

SERGEANT. Yes, sir; the family is larger than the income; but then there are other things, and Sir Alick is very kind, and so is my lady, and I hope for promotion—I may be colour-sergeant[69] some day, and my eldest boy will soon be in the band; and so you see, sir, it's not a bad look-out, take one thing with another.

CHALCOT *(astonished. Aside).* Happiness and hope, with a wife and eight children on one-and-tenpence a day! Oh, Contentment! in what strange, out-of-the-way holes do you hide yourself? If he wouldn't mention it! *(Looking at note. Aloud)* Twins!—both of the same sex?

SERGEANT. No, sir—one boy, one girl.

CHALCOT. Which is the elder?

SERGEANT. Don't know, sir. Don't think Mrs. Jones knows. Don't think they know themselves. We never had a baby-girl before, sir. It's quite a new invention on Mrs. Jones's part. We always have boys, 'cos they make the best soldiers. There's one thing as strikes me with regard to these twins as being odd.

CHALCOT. Odd!—you mean even. What's odd?

SERGEANT. I'm their father, and so the credit of them must be half mine; and yet everybody asks after Mrs. Jones, and nobody asks after me.

CHALCOT. Oh, vanity! vanity! poor human vanity!

(Rain hard).

   By Jove, it is coming down. The skittle party must be broken up. *(Crossing up, C.)* Well, Sergeant, I wish the twins all sorts of good luck, and their mamma and papa likewise. Please buy 'em something for me. *(Giving note)* Good morning *(hurries up avenue, and goes off, R.U.E.)*.

SERGEANT. Here's luck! *(Looking at note)* Hey! Hullo! Here's some mistake! *(Calling after Chalcot)* Hi! Sir! Sir!

(Chalcot re-enters, R.U.E.).

   I beg your pardon, sir, for calling you back; but you've made a mistake; you meant to give me a five-pun' note—and many thanks, sir; but this here's for fifty.

---

67 Match with large head of combustible material tipped with blue-burning brimstone.

68 One shilling and ten pence equals half a guinea (just under £1).

69 Sergeant who guards and attends to the officers (ensigns) who carry colours in the field. A reward for courageous and long service.

CHALCOT (*After a pause, with suppressed rage*). Thank you,—yes—my mistake (*takes bank-note, and gives Sergeant the other, and goes off, R.U.E. biting his lips with fury*).

SERGEANT. Five pounds. He's a trump![70] Who'd a thought it?—and him only a civilian. My twins is as good as promotion. I'll go and show Mrs. Jones.

(*Exit Sergeant, L.1 E. Rain and wind. Enter Blanche and Angus, R.1 E. Blanche carries the skirt of her dress over her head*).

BLANCHE. How unfortunate, the rain coming on! (*Under tree, R.*).

ANGUS. Very.

BLANCHE. Where are all the other people gone?

ANGUS. I don't know. (*Aside*) And I don't care. Your feet will get wet through on the grass. Better stand upon the seat. Allow me (*helps her to get on seat*).

BLANCHE. You're very careful of me.

ANGUS. As careful of you as if you were old—

BLANCHE. As if I were old?

ANGUS (*R.*). Old china. (*Gets up on seat, and stands by her side*) This is more comfortable, isn't it?

BLANCHE (*L.*). Infinitely.

(*Enter Lady Shendryn and Sir Alexander, at end of avenue, R.U.E.*).

LADY SHENDRYN (*her skirt over her head*). I said it would rain.

SIR ALEXANDER. I didn't contradict you.

LADY SHENDRYN. No, but I understood your silence (*sitting on stump of tree, L.C.*).

SIR ALEXANDER. Now you're under shelter, I'll leave you.

LADY SHENDRYN. Leave me by myself in the Park?

SIR ALEXANDER. Do you suppose you'll be attacked by freebooters?[71] What are you afraid of?

LADY SHENDRYN. Of—of the deer!

SIR ALEXANDER (*sitting down, back to back with Lady Shendryn. Aside*). The deer! They're more likely to be afraid of you.

LADY SHENDRYN (*sentimentally*). Ah! You would have been glad to have sat with me beneath the shelter of this verdant canopy years ago!

SIR ALEXANDER. Years ago, I was a fool!

(*Rain and wind*).

ANGUS. Quite a storm! Your hair will be wet!

BLANCHE. It is already.

ANGUS. Take my hat (*takes off Blanche's hat and puts his own on wide-a-wake[72] on her head. Then hangs Blanche's hat by ribbon on branch of tree above his head*).

BLANCHE. How do I look in a man's hat?

ANGUS. Beautiful! Take this, too (*takes off his coat, and wraps it round her shoulders; puts his arm round her waist, and ties coat over her bosom by its sleeves*) That's much better, isn't it?

BLANCHE. But you'll catch cold.

---

70   First-rate fellow.

71   Pirates.

72   In production photos, Angus, in civilian clothes, sports a rounded-crown, narrow-brimmed hat. Wide-a-wakes are broad-brimmed.

ANGUS. No; we're used to cold in Cantyre;[73] besides, we're trained not to care for it. There's a special sort of drill that makes us almost mackintosh![74] You've seen troops marching in the wet?

BLANCHE. Often.

ANGUS. That was rain drill!

LADY SHENDRYN. If you walked to the Hall, you could send me an umbrella.

SIR ALEXANDER. I'd rather you got wet. Just now you wished me to stay for fear of highwaymen.

LADY SHENDRYN. I might catch cold.

SIR ALEXANDER. I should be sorry for the cold that caught you.

LADY SHENDRYN. It might be my death.

SIR ALEXANDER. Lady Shendryn, the rain fertilizes the earth, nourishes the crops, and makes the fish lively; but still it does not bring with it every blessing. You have no right to hold out agreeable expectations which you know you do not intend to realize.

(These conversations to be taken up as if they were continuous).

ANGUS. What was that song you sang at the Sylvesters'?

BLANCHE. Oh!

ANGUS. I wish you'd hum it to me now.

BLANCHE. Without music?

ANGUS. It won't be without music.

BLANCHE. You know the story: it is supposed to be sung by a very young man who is in love with a very haughty beauty, but dare not tell her of his love.

ANGUS. Of course he was poor.

BLANCHE. N—o.

ANGUS. What else could keep him silent?

BLANCHE. Want of—courage.

ANGUS. How does it go?

BLANCHE (*Sings. Air, "Le Chanson de Fortunio," in Offenbach's* Maître Fortunio).[75]

If my glances have betrayed me, Ask me no more,
　For I dare not tell thee, lady, Whom I adore.
　　She is young, and tall, and slender.
Eyes of deep blue,
　She is sweet, and fair, and tender,
Like unto you.
　　Unless my lady will me,
I'll not reveal,
　Though the treasured secret kill me,
The love I feel.

LADY SHENDRYN. Advertising our poverty to the whole county; a filthy, old rumbling thing, not fit for a washerwoman to ride in. I won't go out in it again!

SIR ALEXANDER. Then stay at home.

LADY SHENDRYN. Why not order a new carriage?

SIR ALEXANDER. Can't afford it.

---

73   Now spelled Kintyre, a peninsula in western Scotland.

74   Rainproof, as in a rubberized fabric used for raincoats.

75   Words by Alfred de Musset. Published as sheet music, *Love's Secret* (London: Metzler, [1866]). The New York production substituted a composition by Edward Mollenhauer, words by T.W. Robertson, *Secret Love* (New York: J. Schuberth, [1866]).

ANGUS. The air has haunted me ever since I heard you sing it. I've written some words to it myself.

BLANCHE. Oh, give them to me, I'll sing them.

ANGUS. Will you? *(Gives her verses, which he takes from pocket-book in coat pocket).*

BLANCHE *(reading verses which Angus has given her).* They're very charming *(sighs).*

ANGUS. You're faint. They'll lunch without us.

BLANCHE. Never mind.

ANGUS. You're not hungry?

BLANCHE. No; are you?

ANGUS. Not in the least.

BLANCHE. Cousin, do you know I rather like to see you getting wet. May I keep these?

ANGUS. If you wish it.

BLANCHE. But tell me, cousin, have you ever been in love?

ANGUS. Yes.

BLANCHE. How many times?

ANGUS. Once.

BLANCHE. Only once?

ANGUS. Only once.

BLANCHE. I shouldn't like a husband who was too good, he'd become monotonous.

ANGUS. No husband would be too good for you; at least, I think not!

LADY SHENDRYN. Oh! I feel so faint I think it must be time for lunch.

SIR ALEXANDER. I'm sure it is. *(Looking at watch)* And I'm awfully hungry. Confound it!

LADY SHENDRYN. Where does all your money go to then? And what is that Mr. Kelsey, the lawyer, always coming down for?

SIR ALEXANDER. You'd better not ask. You'd better not know.

LADY SHENDRYN. I know where the money goes to.

SIR ALEXANDER. Do you? I wish I did. Where?

LADY SHENDRYN. I know.

SIR ALEXANDER. Where?

LADY SHENDRYN. I know.

LADY SHENDRYN. Isolating me from my family! Never letting me see my brother!

SIR ALEXANDER. Your brother—

LADY SHENDRYN. Poor Percy! only twenty-two, and—

SIR ALEXANDER *(in a fury).* Don't mention his name to me! I won't hear of him! Infernal young villain! always in scrapes himself and dragging others into them! Don't mention his name!

LADY SHENDRYN. I should not have been so treated if I'd married a man of decent height. What could I expect from a little fellow of five feet two?

SIR ALEXANDER. Lady Shendryn! *(Rising, out of temper).*

LADY SHENDRYN. Such violence! 'Tis the same as when years ago I discovered your falsehood. I know why we live so near.[76] You have too many establishments to provide for!

---

76 Frugally.

SIR ALEXANDER. Madam!

LADY SHENDRYN. I suppose that when that woman—

SIR ALEXANDER. Lady Shendryn!

LADY SHENDRYN. That Mrs.—

SIR ALEXANDER. Silence!

(Distant thunder).

LADY SHENDRYN *(rising and clinging to Sir Alexander).* Alexander!

SIR ALEXANDER. Don't touch me!

(Exits quickly).

ANGUS *(nearing her).* Blanche!

BLANCHE. Angus!

The Prince enters, R.U.E., with umbrella up, followed by Servant with another, which he takes to Lady Shendryn, holding it over her as she exits, R.U.E. The umbrellas to be wet. The Prince goes down to Blanche, and takes her off under umbrella, R.U.E, leaving coat in Angus's hands; at same time, Chalcot and Mary enter, R.1 E., wrangling, she saying, "I never saw such a man! you want all the umbrella," etc., snatches it away from him, and runs off, R.U.E. Angus, who is reaching Blanche's hat from tree, drops coat over Chalcot's head, as drop descends.

ACT II

Drawing-room at Lady Shendryn's, in the neighbourhood of Birdcage Walk.[77] C. folding-doors, closed. Door L.2 E. Chandelier and lamps, lighted. Cup of tea and gong-bell on small table, L. Mary discovered, presiding at tea-table, R. Blanche looking over book of engravings on ottoman,[78] C. Lady Shendryn on sofa, reading letter, L.

LADY SHENDRYN. My dear Blanche, I must request your attention to the subject of this letter again.

BLANCHE. I'm listening.

LADY SHENDRYN. Although I am all excitement at Sir Alexander's departure tonight, still, this affair must be settled, and at once; for not only Sir Alexander, but the Prince leaves town tonight. I'll read Lady Maria's letter again.

(Mary and Blanche exchange looks).

The last side is all that I shall trouble you with. *(Reads)* "It could easily be arranged, and though a formal contract could not be entered into, a mutual agreement might be ratified, and when the war is concluded—and I hear from the very best authority"—"Best" underlined, my dear—"that it cannot last long"—"Cannot" underlined, my dear—"the Prince could return to this country and renew his suit. This is my opinion"—"My" underlined, Blanche—"and it is also the opinion of the Duchess, with whom I

---

77   Birdcage Walk runs along the south side of St. James's Park, in front of Wellington Barracks. At its west end it splits into the two Spur roads leading in front of Buckingham Palace.

78   Low upholstered seat without back or arms.

have held counsel"—"Duchess" underlined.—"It is most desirable"—"Most desirable" underlined—"that the match should be made."—"Made" underlined.—"Ever your own Adelaide." There, Blanche! now you know what Lady Maria thinks! and when the Prince comes here tonight to make his adieux, you can act in accordance with the views she has so feelingly, so very feelingly, expressed.

BLANCHE *(rising, and putting down book)*. But why should I be engaged to Prince Perovsky?

LADY SHENDRYN. Because he's a great match.

BLANCHE. But to engage oneself to a Russian at the very time we're going to war with them!

LADY SHENDRYN. But when the fighting is over, you can be married.

MARY *(aside)*. And then the fighting can begin again!

BLANCHE. And Sir Alick going away this very night!

LADY SHENDRYN *(with suppressed emotion)*. It is my husband's duty to go.

MARY *(aside)*. And his pleasure.

LADY SHENDRYN. And go he must.

MARY *(aside)*. And will!

BLANCHE. Poor Sir Alick! I am so sorry.

LADY SHENDRYN. Duty, my child! duty!

BLANCHE *(to Mary)*. But I don't want to get married at all!

MARY *(to her)*. Duty, my pet! duty! And in this case duty ought to be a pleasure.

BLANCHE. Duty! The same as it is Sir Alick's duty to go and fight?

LADY SHENDRYN. Precisely.

BLANCHE. And a girl must put on her wedding-dress for the same reason a soldier puts on his regimentals?

MARY. Just so. And seek the mutual conflict at the altar.

BLANCHE. Oh, Mary—conflict!

MARY. I repeat it—conflict. And let the best man win.

LADY SHENDRYN. Miss Netley, I think you talk too much.

BLANCHE. Why do girls get married?

MARY *(aside)*. That's a poser![79]

LADY SHENDRYN. O—h. For the sake of society.

BLANCHE. That means for the sake of other people?

LADY SHENDRYN. Naturally. If people didn't marry there would be no—evening parties.

MARY *(aside)*. And what a dreadful thing that would be!

BLANCHE. But I don't want to get married.

LADY SHENDRYN. Then you ought to do.

BLANCHE. Ought I, Mary?

MARY. I don't know—I never was married.

LADY SHENDRYN *(severely)*. And never will be. With your views, Miss Netley, you don't deserve to be. Marriage is one of those—a—dear me—I want a word. Marriage is one of those—

MARY. Evils?

LADY SHENDRYN. No *(angrily)*.

BLANCHE. Blessings?

LADY SHENDRYN. Blessings—yes—blessings, which cannot be avoided.

BLANCHE. What do you think, Mary?

---

79 Difficult question.

MARY. It is woman's mission to marry.

BLANCHE. Why?

MARY. That she may subdue man.

LADY SHENDRYN. Quite so.

MARY. The first step to man's subjugation is courtship. The second matrimony. Any more tea?

(They signify No).

BLANCHE *(in a pet).*[80] Don't talk about it any more. Think of poor Sir Alick!

MARY *(rising. To Blanche).* And Angus MacAlister.

LADY SHENDRYN. What's that? *(Sharply).*

BLANCHE. Nothing! What's what?

(Rising with Mary quickly).

LADY SHENDRYN. Didn't I hear the name of Angus MacAlister?

BLANCHE and MARY *(together).* Oh, no.

BLANCHE. She doesn't believe us.

MARY. She knows better.

(Enter Sir Alexander, L.D., in regimentals).

SIR ALEXANDER *(L.C.).* Well, girls, my time is up, and I've come to bid you good-bye.

BLANCHE *(R.C.)* and MARY *(R.).* Oh, Sir Alexander!

SIR ALEXANDER. You won't see me again till I come back—if ever I do come back. One word with my lady.

(The girls go up, and sit at tea-table. Sir Alexander sits beside Lady Shendryn on sofa, L.).

Diana, you know the dispositions I have made, and how I have left you—in case any—in case anything should befall me. For ready money, there is £2,000 at Coutts's[81] in your name.

LADY SHENDRYN *(dignified).* You are very kind—indeed, you are very liberal.

SIR ALEXANDER. With every possible allowance for your temper, and customary misapprehension of my conduct, I cannot understand why you should meet me in this way.

LADY SHENDRYN. £2,000! Where does the rest of the money go? I know your income. What have you done with it?

SIR ALEXANDER. Is this the moment—when I am about to leave you—perhaps never to return—to quarrel about money?

LADY SHENDRYN. Money! You know that I despise it. I only speak of the disappearance of these large sums as a proof—

SIR ALEXANDER. Proof!—proof of what?

LADY SHENDRYN *(with tears).* Of your faithlessness—your infidelity!

SIR ALEXANDER. Consider the girls.

LADY SHENDRYN. They cannot hear me.

BLANCHE *(to Mary).* That's all very dreadful. I don't think I'll ever marry.

MARY. Yes, you will.

---

80   Sulking.

81   A London bank.

BLANCHE. To quarrel with my husband?

MARY. Think how pleasant it is to own a husband to quarrel with!

LADY SHENDRYN. Such large sums unaccounted for!

SIR ALEXANDER. I know it.

LADY SHENDRYN. Where do they go?

SIR ALEXANDER. I cannot tell you. You are the last person in the world I would have know.

LADY SHENDRYN. Doubtless!

SIR ALEXANDER. Diana, you are wrong—very wrong!

LADY SHENDRYN. Alexander Shendryn, you know how you have treated me. You know—

SIR ALEXANDER. I know that at one time you had just cause of complaint. I confessed my fault, and entreated your forgiveness. Instead of pardoning, you have never forgotten my indiscretion; but have dinned—dinned—dinned it into my ears unceasingly.

LADY SHENDRYN. And, pray, sir what divine creature is a man, that he may be faithless to his wife with impunity? What are we women, that our lot should be, that we must be deceived that we may forgive; that we may be deceived again that we may forgive again, to be deceived again? Sir Alexander, these expenses from home demand my scrutiny, and I insist on knowing why they are, and wherefore? But perhaps I am detaining you, and you have adieux to make elsewhere!

SIR ALEXANDER (rising). Diana, I lose all patience!

(Enter a Servant, L.D.).

SERVANT. The orderly is below, Sir Alexander, and wishes to speak to you.

SIR ALEXANDER. May he come up here?

LADY SHENDRYN. If you wish it.

SIR ALEXANDER (after motioning to Servant, who goes off, L.D.). Consider, £2,000 is a large sum—more than enough for your immediate requirements!

LADY SHENDRYN (with exultation). My requirements! All I ask is a cottage, and a loaf of bread—and all your secrets told to me!

(Enter Sergeant, L.D.).

SIR ALEXANDER. Now, Sergeant!

SERGEANT (saluting). This letter, Colonel. Mr. Kelsey, the lawyer, brought it himself.

LADY SHENDRYN. Mr. Kelsey?

SIR ALEXANDER. To the barracks?

SERGEANT. Yes, Colonel; he said it was of the utmost consequence, and that you was to have it directly, and that he would be back in half-an-hour at your quarters to receive your instructions.

(Sir Alexander goes up, and reads).

LADY SHENDRYN. Mrs. Jones quite well, Sergeant?

SERGEANT. Middling, my lady, thank you.

BLANCHE. And the children?

SERGEANT. Quite well, thank you, miss; all but the twins. The twins has got the twinsey!

BLANCHE and MARY. The what?

SERGEANT. The twinsey, inside their throats—just here—under the stock.

MARY. You mean quinsy?[82]

---

82   Throat inflammation such as tonsillitis.

SERGEANT. Very like, miss. It's a regulation infant complaint!

BLANCHE. And what does Mrs. Jones think of your going away to Varna?

SERGEANT. Well, mum, she don't like it much. She is a little cut up about it, and has made me an outfit—six new shirts complete. *(Piqued)* The twins don't seem to care much—but children never seem to know when you've done enough for 'em!

MARY. And how do you like it?

SERGEANT. Well, miss, I'm sorry to leave the missus and the children—'specially them twins, who wants more looking after than the others, being two; but I shouldn't like to stay behind. I don't think the company could get along without me.

SIR ALEXANDER *(coming down, violently agitated)*. Good heavens!

LADY SHENDRYN. What's the matter?

(All rise).

SIR ALEXANDER. Nothing! *(Pacing stage).*

LADY SHENDRYN. Can I—*(offering to take letter).*

SIR ALEXANDER *(crushing letter in his hand. Aside)*. What's to be done? What's to be done? What's to be done? *(Looks at time-piece)* Sergeant, take a cab, drive to the Garrick—the Garrick Club—as hard as you can go. Ask for Mr. Chalcot; bring him here directly. He's dining there, I know. Lose no time, for I haven't a moment to spare.

(Exit Sergeant, L.D.).

LADY SHENDRYN. More mystery! *(Sits, L.).*

BLANCHE *(together)*. You quite frighten me.

MARY *(together)*. Can I be of any—

SIR ALEXANDER. No, my dears—no. I must speak to your aunt again, but alone. Step into this room for a few minutes *(opening folding-doors, C.).*

(Mary and Blanche go in, exchanging glances. Sir Alexander closes door after them).

LADY SHENDRYN. What's coming now?

SIR ALEXANDER *(looking at letter then advancing)*. Diana, I grieve to tell you that I cannot leave you the £2,000 I spoke of.

LADY SHENDRYN. What?

SIR ALEXANDER *(looking at letter)*. I can only leave you £500.

LADY SHENDRYN. This is that letter?

SIR ALEXANDER. Yes.

LADY SHENDRYN. From Mr. Kelsey! Whenever that fellow shows his face, there is always trouble.

SIR ALEXANDER. Don't wrong poor Kelsey. He is an excellent man.

LADY SHENDRYN. £2,000!—£500! Why this sudden call for £1,500?

SIR ALEXANDER. I dare not tell you.

LADY SHENDRYN. Show me that letter.

SIR ALEXANDER. Impossible!

LADY SHENDRYN. Why not?

SIR ALEXANDER. I cannot tell you. I must ask you to have confidence.

LADY SHENDRYN. Confidence!—in you?

SIR ALEXANDER. I have sent for Chalcot to—to—

LADY SHENDRYN. To borrow money of him?

SIR ALEXANDER. Yes.

LADY SHENDRYN. For me?

SIR ALEXANDER. No.

LADY SHENDRYN. And I am not to know the reason of this sudden call upon your purse?

SIR ALEXANDER. You must not.

LADY SHENDRYN (rising). I will! (Advancing).

SIR ALEXANDER (about to tell her). Diana—no! no! You must not know!

LADY SHENDRYN (trying to snatch letter). That letter!

SIR ALEXANDER (struggling). Diana!

LADY SHENDRYN. I am your wife. I will have it. I will know this woman's name. (As she gets hold of the letter, it tears in half. She has the blank side).

(Enter Sergeant and Chalcot in evening dress, D.L. Blanche and Mary, hearing the noise, enter from inner room, and go down R.).

LADY SHENDRYN (showing blank). The blank side!

SIR ALEXANDER (showing written side). Thank heaven! (Crosses, R.).

CHALCOT (L. Aside). There's been a row.

SERGEANT. Colonel, I met Mr. Chalcot as I was going to the cab-rank.

SIR ALEXANDER (crossing, L.). Chalcot, a word!—Sergeant.

(Speaks to Sergeant, who salutes).

In this room, Chalcot.

CHALCOT. An awful row! (Aside).

(Sir Alexander and Chalcot go off through folding-doors).

LADY SHENDRYN (after a pause, crossing and sitting, R.). Sergeant, I shall take care of your wife while you are away.

SERGEANT (L.). Thank you, my lady (dolefully).

BLANCHE. And the children.

SERGEANT. Thank you, miss.

MARY. And the twins.

LADY SHENDRYN and BLANCHE (together). Oh, the twins! certainly.

SERGEANT (affected). Thank you, ladies. Mrs. Jones expects one or two more in the course of a few weeks; and I've never known her to break her word, or forfeit her engagements upon that subject—never!

MARY. You may rely that we—

SERGEANT. Thank you, ladies. It'll make me more comfortable to know that they'll be cared for, if anything should—if anything—'cos accidents will happen with—the best regulated enemy. She's waiting below to march with me to parade,[83] so as to see the last of me. (A pause) Thank you, ladies. Good evening. (Salutes. Exit, L.D.).

(The Women look sorrowfully and go up, R. Enter Sir Alexander and Chalcot, C. door).

---

83   Assembly of the troops for public procession.

SIR ALEXANDER. You understand?

CHALCOT. Perfectly!

SIR ALEXANDER. And you'll see that it's explained as I—

CHALCOT. Certainly.

SIR ALEXANDER. Thanks. *(Shaking hands)* You are a friend indeed.

(Sits on sofa, L., Lady Shendryn and Blanche up, R, Mary in chair at table).

CHALCOT *(C.)*. This is a charming wind-up to a jolly evening. Parting with all my pals. I didn't know I cared at all about them; and now they're going, I find out I like them very much. Saw Sergeant Jones's wife crying in the hall. Why don't she stop at home and cry? Why does she come and cry where I am?

MARY *(half crying, coming down, R.)*. What a world this is!

Illustration 24. Sophie Larkin as Lady Shendryn, Marie Wilton as Mary Netley, and Frederick Young as Sergeant, in *Ours*, act 2, carte-de-visite, 1866. Bequeathed by Guy Little, courtesy of the Victoria and Albert Museum.

CHALCOT (*L.C.*). Sad hole, I confess.

MARY (*R.C.*). And what villains men are!

CHALCOT. They are!—they are!

MARY. To quarrel and fight, and bring grief upon poor women—and what fools women are—

CHALCOT. They are!—they are!

MARY (*impatiently*). I mean, to cry about the men! How stupid you are!

CHALCOT. I am!—I am! You're quite right. I agree with you entirely.

BLANCHE. You two don't often agree.

(*Coming down, R. Lady Shendryn sits at table, R.*).

CHALCOT. No; but then we very seldom meet.

MARY (*C.*). Thank goodness!

CHALCOT. Thank goodness!

MARY. At all events, Mr. Chalcot does not deny that women are far superior to men.

CHALCOT. Pardon me. He does deny it—he denies it very much.

BLANCHE (*R*). Which, then, are the better?

CHALCOT. Neither!—both are worst.

BLANCHE and MARY. Oh!

CHALCOT. And, as a general axiom, this truth is manifest. Whatever is—is wrong!

(*Goes up L. Blanche and Mary go up R. Lady Shendryn comes down a little to C.*).

SIR ALEXANDER (*advancing to Lady Shendryn*). And now there is no more to say, but good-bye, and God bless you!

(*Holds out his hand. Lady Shendryn remains motionless. A pause. Chalcot on sofa, L.*).

Won't you bid me good-bye?

LADY SHENDRYN (*R.C.*). The letter!

SIR ALEXANDER (*L.C.*). Impossible! It would make you more miserable.

LADY SHENDRYN. Doubtless.

SIR ALEXANDER. Diana! (*Holding out his hand*).

LADY SHENDRYN. You are waited for elsewhere. Kiss and bid good-bye to those you love.

SIR ALEXANDER. It may be for the last time.

LADY SHENDRYN. The letter!

(*Sir Alexander dissents, and again holds out his hand*).

Your lady-love is waiting. Waste no more time with me.

SIR ALEXANDER (*aside*). Ah! I may find peace in the campaign—I cannot find it here. I can control a regiment, but not a wife. Better battle than a discontented woman. (*Aloud*) Good-bye, Chalcot—(*shaking hands*)—and remember! Good-bye, Blanche—Good-bye, Mary (*kissing them*).

BLANCHE and MARY (*hanging about him*). Oh, Sir Alick!

(*They look appealingly at him, and then towards Lady Shendryn. Sir Alexander again goes to her, and offers his hand. She takes no notice of him. He bows and goes off hurriedly, L.D., followed by Blanche, crying. Mary, who turns at door to look at Lady Shendryn, and meeting Chalcot's eye, bounces out of the room. Chalcot looks with contempt at Lady Shendryn, and is about to follow. A carriage is heard to drive off. Lady Shendryn starts, and nearly falls. Chalcot stops her fall*).

LADY SHENDRYN *(R.C.)*. Mr. Chalcot—don't leave me! Ring for Jennings, my maid. Give me some air—the heat overpowers me. Open those doors.

(Servant enters, L.D.).

LADY SHENDRYN. Send Jennings.

(Servant goes off, L.D.).

Thank you Mr. Chalcot.

(Enter Jennings, L.D. Lady Shendryn takes her arm).

To my room—and—thank you, Mr. Chalcot. I'm better—much better.

(Is led off, L. door, nearly fainting).

CHALCOT. No better than you should be.

(Piano played in inner room).

Temper—temper! *(Opening folding-doors)* How people, with these before their eyes, can fall in love!

(By this time he has opened folding-door, R. As he takes hold of handle of L. door, he pauses, his back to the audience. At the same moment, the "Chanson" is played on the piano. Blanche is discovered at piano, playing; Angus, in regimentals, leaning over her, his cap and gloves on piano. Chalcot opens L. door noiselessly, shakes his head, and steals off, L. door, on tiptoe. The inner drawing-room discovered, the lamps lighted. Piano, R.; flowers on it. A large bay-window at back, opening on to a balcony. Blanche sings the song of Act 1. She breaks down at the last words with a sob, and lets her face and arms fall on piano. Pause).

ANGUS. Won't you sing the words I wrote?
BLANCHE. I can't sing tonight. I can't play *(rising, and coming forward. Sits on ottoman, C.)*.
ANGUS. I shall often think of that air, when I am far away *(sitting by her side)*.

(This scene to be broken by frequent pauses).

BLANCHE *(L.C.)*. I—I am very sorry you are going.
ANGUS *(R.C.)*. I have few reasons for wishing to remain—hardly any—only one.
BLANCHE. And that one is—
ANGUS *(nearing her)*. To be near you!
BLANCHE *(averting her eyes)*. Oh, cousin!
ANGUS. In the old days a soldier wore a badge, bestowed on him by the lady he—he vowed was the fairest in the world! They were his own individual personal colours! Some people say the days of chivalry are over! Never mind that! Give me a token, Blanche—Cousin Blanche—a ribbon—anything that you have worn!
BLANCHE *(trembling. Rises, and goes to couch, L.)*. But, cousin, these exchanges are only made by those who are—engaged!
ANGUS *(sitting on couch, by her side)*. And if this war had not been declared, should you have been engaged to Prince Perovsky? Should you have exchanged tokens with him?
BLANCHE *(troubled)*. Oh! How can I tell?
ANGUS. I should like to know before I go.

BLANCHE. And when must that be?

ANGUS *(looking at time-piece)*. In five minutes!

BLANCHE *(approaching him)*. So soon! *(Pauses)*.

ANGUS. Have you nothing to say to me?

BLANCHE. I—I hardly know—what would you have me say?

ANGUS. Only one word—that you care what becomes of me!

BLANCHE. You know I do.

ANGUS. Care for me?

BLANCHE. Yes—no—Oh, cousin! you make me say things—

ANGUS. That you don't mean?

BLANCHE. No—yes! You confuse me so—I hardly know what I'm doing!

(Bugle without, at distance. At drum Angus starts up, and goes into inner room for his hat. Blanche springs up, and stands before door, L. They form Millais's picture of the "Black Brunswicker." A passing military band outside, plays, distant, "Annie Laurie").

BLANCHE. Oh, Angus!—dear cousin Angus!

ANGUS *(faltering)*. Blanche! you are rich—an heiress. I am but a poor Scotch cadet; but Scotch cadets ere now have cut their way to fame and fortune; and I have my chance. Say, Blanche, do you love me? Say, if at some future day I prove myself not unworthy of you, will you be mine?

BLANCHE. Oh, Angus!

ANGUS. Answer, love; for every moment is precious as a look from you. May I hope?

(Handle of the door moves; they separate, Blanche, L., Angus, R. of door. Enter Servant, L. door).

SERVANT. Prince Perovsky!

(Enter Prince, L.D. Exit Servant. A pause).

PRINCE *(crossing R.C.)*. I fear that I arrive inopportunely?

BLANCHE *(advancing, L.C.)*. No, Prince; my cousin is just bidding us good-bye. He is about to sail for—he is about to leave England.

(Angus comes down L.).

PRINCE *(smiling)*. On service?

ANGUS. Yes, on service. I have the honour, Prince, to take my leave.

(They bow).

  Cousin!

(Blanche presents her forehead, which Angus kisses. Prince looks at pictures, R. Blanche tears the locket from her neck, and gives it to Angus, unperceived by Prince. Angus holds her in his arms, kisses her, and exits hurriedly, L.D. The music of band ceases as Blanche sits, L. Pause).

PRINCE *(R.D.)*. Miss Haye, I am charmed to find you alone; for what I have to say could only be said tête-à-tête.

(Blanche rises).

  Pray don't rise. Both Sir Alexander and Lady Shendryn are aware of the object of my visit, and do me the honour of approving it. Have I the happiness of engaging your attention?

(Blanche assents. Prince sits by her side, R.).

I leave London for Paris tonight *en route* to Vienna. I mention that fact that it may excuse the apparent *brusquerie* of what is to follow. Have I your permission to go on?

(Blanche assents. He bows).

My mission here was not, as many supposed, diplomatic, but matrimonial. I may say, as the man said when he was asked who he was, "When I am at home, I am somebody." I came to England in search of a wife—one who would be an ornament to her station and mine. I wished to take back with me, to present to my province and to my Imperial master,[84] a princess.

BLANCHE. A princess?

PRINCE. Unhappily, this Ottoman difficulty has arisen. I thought that diplomacy would have smoothed it away. I was wrong—and so my mission, which was so eminently peaceful, must be postponed until the war is over.

BLANCHE. Until the war is over?

PRINCE. That will be in very few months.

BLANCHE *(eagerly)*. Why so?

PRINCE. Wars with Russia never last long.

BLANCHE. Why not?

PRINCE. Pardon me, if for a moment I am national and patriotic. Against Russian power, prowess and resources are useless. The elements have declared on our side, and in them we have two irresistible allies.

BLANCHE. And they are—

PRINCE. Frost and fire! If cold fails, we try heat—that is, to warm the snow, we burn our Moscows.[85]

(Blanche shivers).

But, pardon me, you are thinking of those among your relatives who hold rank in the English army? *(Significantly)*.

BLANCHE *(hesitating)*. Yes; Sir Alexander.

PRINCE. Of course—Sir Alexander. As I alighted, I saw troops mustering outside—a pretty sight. Fine fellows! fine fellows! But I fear I am fatiguing you; for I am—*hélas!*[86] too many, many years your senior to hope to interest you personally. *(Rising with courtliness and dignity)* Miss Haye, with the permission of your guardians, I lay my name and fortune at your feet. Should you deign to accept me, at the end of the war I shall return to England for my bride.

BLANCHE *(rising, confused)*. Prince, I am sensible—

PRINCE. Should you honour me by favourable consideration of my demand, in return for the honour of your hand, I offer you rank and power. On our own lands we hold *levées*[87]—indeed, you will be queen of the province—of 400,000 serfs—of your devoted slave—my queen!

BLANCHE *(Sits on sofa, L.).* Queen! If I should prove a tyrant?

PRINCE *(standing)*. I am a true Russian, and love despotism!

---

84   The tsar.
85   As Napoleon's troops entered Moscow in 1812, departing saboteurs set fire or blew up anything that might be of use to the French. The wooden buildings burned for four days, destroying three-quarters of the city.
86   Exclamation of grief or sorrow (alas!).
87   Receptions.

BLANCHE *(smiling)*. And could you submit to slavery?

PRINCE. At your hands—willingly. *(Sits on her R.H.)* I assure you, slavery is not a bad thing!

BLANCHE. But freedom is a better! And you came to England, Prince, to seek a wife?

PRINCE. Not only to seek a wife—to find a princess!

BLANCHE. You can make a princess of anybody!

PRINCE. But I cannot make anybody a princess! Let me hope my offer is not entirely objectionable, despite the disparity of our years.

(Music—"British Grenadiers"[88]*—drum and fife heard outside).*

CHALCOT *(without)*. I beg your pardon.

MARY *(without)*. Beg my pardon? Couldn't you see?

CHALCOT *(without)*. I didn't.

MARY *(without)*. I was right before your eyes *(enters, L.D.)*.

CHALCOT *(entering, L.D.)*. Perhaps that was the reason.

MARY. Tearing one's dress to pieces![89] *(Coming down, R.)*.

CHALCOT. Really, what with the troops, and the bands and the bother, I feel I must tear something! *(Down, R.H.)*.

MARY. Poor fellows—leaving their wives! *(Going up)*.

CHALCOT. They consider that one of the privileges of the profession, like the non-payment of turnpikes![90]

(Music grows distant).

MARY *(up, C. Excitedly)*. Oh, when I hear the clatter of their horses' hoofs, and see the gleam of the helmets, I—I wish I were a man! *(Walking about in inner room)*.

CHALCOT. I wish you were! *(Standing, C., his glass in his eye)*.

MARY *(opening window at back)*. We can see them from the balcony.

(Bugle. Music ceases. When she opens window, the moonlight, trees, gas,[91] etc., are seen at back. Distant bugle).

MARY. There's Sir Alick on horseback.

(Distant cheers. Music).

    (On balcony) Do you hear the shouts?

CHALCOT. Yes *(up at window)*.

MARY. And the bands?

CHALCOT *(on balcony)*. Yes; there they go, and the chargers prancing.

MARY. And the bayonets gleaming.

CHALCOT. And the troops forming.

MARY. And the colours flying. Oh, if I were not a woman, I'd be a soldier! *(Going down a little)*.

(Music ceases).

---

88   Dense crowds sang this to departing soldiers at Waterloo Station; many troops heard it again as they disembarked at Varna. Winstock, *Songs and Lyrics*, 152, 156. See also above, Introduction: Repertoire, p. 22.

89   Evidently Chalcot has bumped into Mary offstage.

90   Toll-gates.

91   Gas-lit street lamps.

CHALCOT. So would I.

MARY. Why are you not?

CHALCOT. What?—a woman!

MARY. No—a soldier. Better be anything than nothing. Better be a soldier than anything!

(Goes up again. Tramp of troops marching heard in the distance).

CHALCOT *(catching Mary's enthusiasm).* She's right! She's right! Why should a great hulking fellow like me skulk behind, lapped in comfort, ungrateful, uncomfortable, and inglorious? Fighting would be something to live for. I've served in the militia—I know—I'll buy a commission—I'll go! *(Going up).*

MARY *(meeting him, as he goes up).* That's right. I like you for that.

(Music—"The Girl I Left behind Me").

CHALCOT. Do you?

(Distant cheers).

Come and shout.

(To Mary, then to Prince, who is seated on sofa, with Blanche)

Come and shout. Oh, I beg pardon!

PRINCE. Not at all—not at all! *(Rises, and goes up to window, and looks out)* In splendid condition. Fine fellows! Fine fellows! Poor fellows! *(Taking snuff, and coming down, L.)* Won't you come and look at them, Miss Haye?

(As Blanche rises, Lady Shendryn enters, L.D. Blanche sits again on sofa).

LADY SHENDRYN. My dear Prince, I did not know you were here!

PRINCE. I profited by your ladyship's absence to urge the suit of which you have been kind enough to approve.

LADY SHENDRYN. And have you received an answer?

PRINCE. Not precisely.

(Music stops).

CHALCOT *(at balcony).* There's Sir Alick!

SIR ALEXANDER *(outside).* Battalion! Attention! Form fours, right! March off by companies in succession from the front!

(Lady Shendryn, C., starts. Tramp loud).

CHALCOT. They're marching right past the window. Come here and see.

PRINCE. Miss Haye, may I be permitted to know if I may hope?

MARY *(at window).* There's Angus!

(Blanche rushes up).

ANGUS *(without).* Number three, by your left! Quick march!

Band plays "God save the Queen." Cheers. Tramp of soldiers. Excitement. Picture. Chalcot and Mary waving handkerchiefs, and cheering at window. Prince, L., taking snuff. Lady Shendryn fainting, C.

ACT III

Interior of a hut, built of boulders and mud, the roof built out, showing the snow and sky outside. The walls bare and rude, pistols, swords, guns, maps, newspapers, etc., suspended on them. Door, R.2 E. Window in flat, R.C., showing snow-covered country beyond; rude fireplace, L.; wood fire burning; over-hanging chimney and shelf; small stove, R., very rude, with chimney going through roof, which is covered with snow and icicles; straw and rags stuffed in crevices and littered about floor; a rope stretched across back of hut, with fur rugs and horse-cloths hanging up to divide the beds off; camp and rough makeshift furniture; camp cooking utensils, etc.; armchair, made of tub, etc. Cupboards round L., containing properties; hanging lamp, a rude piece of planking before fireplace, stool, tubs, pail, etc. Portmanteau, L. table, L.C., rough chair, broken gun-barrel near fireplace, for poker, and stack of wood. Stage half dark, music, "Chanson," distant bugle and answer, as curtain rises. Angus discovered, very shabby, high muddy boots, beard, etc., seated at head of table, reading by light of small lamp letters which are lying on an open travelling-desk.

ANGUS *(reading old note).* "Dear Cousin Angus,—Lady Shendryn desires me to ask you to come and dine on Thursday. The usual hour. Do come.—Yours, BLANCHE. P.S.—Which my lady does not see. Mary says that men ought not to be believed, for all they say is fable." *(Smooths note, and folds it, puts it away, reads another)* "Dear Cousin Angus,—I shall not be at dinner, but I shall be in the drawing-room, for inspection, as you call it. I don't believe a word that you said the night before last. You know.—BLANCHE." *(Folds it, and places it in a large envelope, with other letters, an old glove, a flower, which he kisses, and a ribbon, seals them up, leaving packet on top of desk. Rises)* If the attack is ordered for the morning, Hops will find this on the table as I told him. *(Crossing to R., and back to table. Taking letter from his pocket, sits on stool, R. of table)* How much oftener shall I read this? It contains the last news of her. *(Reads)* "Dear Mac,—London is terribly slow, no parties no nothing"—um—um—um—"All the news comes to the Rag;[92] but of course you know that before we do." *(Turns over)* Here it is! "I saw the fascinating party, the thought of whom occupies your leisure hours, yesterday; she was in a carriage with Lady Shendryn, and Dick Fanshawe sat opposite. Dick has been often seen at Lady Shendryn's lately. I keep you posted up on this subject, because you told me to. Dick's uncle, the old mining-man, died two months ago, and left him a pot of money. Such is luck! My uncles never die, and when they do, they leave me dressing-cases![93] Damn dressing-cases! Dick's name, and that of the divine party, have been coupled, *apropos d'amour.*[94] I am awfully hard up. Little Lucy has left me. She bolted with a Frenchman in the cigar-trade, taking all she could with her." *(Rising)* Um—that's four months ago. What a fool I am! Fanshawe's very rich, and not a bad fellow—as well he as another. *(Sighs)* The next six hours may lay me on the snow, as has been the fate of many a better fellow. Oh! when I think of her, I feel that I could charge into a troop of cavalry, sabreproof with love. *(Pause)* This won't do!—I'm getting maudlin! *(Looks at watch, and takes fur great-coat and cap from barrel, R., buttons up his coat, etc.)* Mustn't be maudlin here. There's work! *(Smiling sadly, and taking up packet)* If I can't live to marry Blanche, and make her Lady MacAlister, wife of General Sir Angus MacAlister, I can, at least, die a decent soldier. So there, Master Hops! *(Placing packet on table, and lighting pipe by fire, L. Exit, R. door, singing—*

---

92 The Army and Navy Club.
93 Cases of toilet utensils.
94 In the matter of love.

Parti-t-en guerre, pour tuer l'ennemi,
Parti-t-en guerre, pour tuer l'ennemi;
Revint de guerre, apres six ans et demi,
Revint de guerre, apres six ans et demi;
Que va-t-il faire? Le Sire de Framboissey—
Que va-t-il faire? Le Sire de Framboissey."[95]

(All exits and entrances are made from door, R.2 E. Wind is heard as door opens, and snow is driven in. Chalcot sneezes, then sings behind curtain, L.C.; then draws it, and is discovered on a rude bed of straw, rough wrapping, etc., his appearance entirely altered, hair rough, long beard, face red and jolly, his whole manner alert and changed. He wears an old uniform coat; one leg is bandaged at the calf, the trouser being cut to the knee, and tied with strings and tape; he sits up in bed and yawns).

CHALCOT.—A—choo! *(Sings)*
In Liquorpond Street, London, a merchant did dwell,
Who had one only darter—an uncommon nice young gal;
Her name it was Dinah, just sixteen years old,
And she'd a very large fortin' in silvier and gold.
Ri-tiddle-um, etc."[96]

(Rubbing his eyes, and hitting his arms out with enjoyment. Speaks) What a jolly good sleep I have had, to be sure! *(Takes flask from under pillow, and drinks)* Ah! What a comfort it is that in the Crimea you can drink as much as you like without it hurting you! The doctor says it's the rarefaction of the atmosphere. Bravo, the rarefaction of the atmosphere!—whatever it may be. I must turn out. *(Takes pillow, and addresses it in song).*

Kathleen Mavourneen, arouse from thy slumbers.[97]

(Hits pillow, and gets out of bed. Speaks) Gardez vous the poor dumb leg. It's jolly cold! I must make my toilette. *(Goes to bucket, R.U.E.)* Ice, as usual. Where's the hammer? *(Takes gun-barrel from fireplace. Takes straw, and cleans gun-barrel. Breaks ice in bucket, and puts it in kettle, which he places on fire, L. Stirs fire, etc.)* Now for the towel. *(Takes straw)* What lots of luxuries those fellows in London do enjoy: Coffee for ringing the bell; soap for asking; and towels everywhere! Here, my towel varies between a bit of stunsail[98] and a hard snowball. *(Pours water from kettle into pitcher; goes behind curtain; Comes out, wiping hands and face with straw)* If the water's cold, the straw's warm. *(Puts on coat from off line,*

---

95   A popular song in the "medieval" style, by E. Bourget and L. de Rille (1855).
        Away to war, to kill the enemy,
        Returned from war, after six years and a half;
        What will he do? The Sire of Framboisssey [Raspberry].
96   During the first months of the war, regimental music was heard less often; basic supplies were wanting so perhaps this change passed with less notice than it otherwise might. But on 20 November 1854, when the guard arrived, they played "Cheer, Boys, Cheer" and this song, "Villikins [or Willikins] and His Dinah," composed by Sam Correll (Winstock, *Songs and Lyrics*, 158). It chronicles a wealthy London merchant (Villikins) whose daughter refused the husband he chose for her. Dinah is disinherited, kills herself by poison, and discovering this Villikins kills himself too.
97   An Irish ballad, which begins:
        Kathleen Mavourneen! The grey dawn is breaking,
        The horn of the Hunter is heard on the hill,
        The lark from her light wing the bright dew is shaking
        Kathleen Mavourneen! What slumb'ring still.
98   Studding sail: canvas sails set during a fair wind.

and gets jug from cupboard, L.) The sergeant left the coffee—good. *(Takes coffee pot from stove, and pours out coffee. Sees packet on table)* Gus is gone, and left his love-traps to my care, in case he should be potted. *(Drinking coffee, and shaking his head. Sings)*

Oh! father, says Dinah, I am but a child,

And for to get married just yet I don't feel at all inclined;

If you'll let me live single for a year or two more,

My werry large fortin' I freely will give o'er.

(Puts packet in portmanteau, L., and hurts his leg) Oh! this poor dumb leg of mine! Just my luck! I obtain my commission all right—get into the same company as Angus—went into action—and was wounded in my first engagement. If it hadn't been for the sergeant, I should have been killed. He received cut No. 5, which the Russian meant for me. Down went the Russian and up I got. *(During this he has got biscuit and canister of sugar, etc., from locker, L.)* And while on the ground, the brute ran his bayonet into my calf. A mean advantage to take—to stick me while he was down. However, I split his skull *(cracks biscuit)*, so he didn't get the best of it; and here I am—lame for another month. Where's the spoon? Oh, this'll do. *(Takes quill, and stirs coffee. Fetches marmalade)* The first fortnight's dressing did my leg no good, for that fool of a sergeant made a mistake, and instead of putting on the ointment given him by the doctor, went and spread the bandages all over orange marmalade; and I should never have found it out if he hadn't served up the salve for breakfast along with the anchovies. *(Eating and drinking)* Now, I superintend the cookery department—when there's anything to cook.

(Knock at door, R.).

Who's there? If you're French, *Entrez*; if you're Sardinian, *Entre*; if you're Turkish, *Itcherree*; if you're Russian, *Vnutri*; and if you're English, Come in!

(Enter Sergeant—ragged great-coat, long beard, his left arm in a sling, bundle slung over his R. shoulder, straw bands on legs, snow on coat, boots, beard, etc. Wind heard as door opens, and snow driven in).

CHALCOT. Shut the door; shut the door—it's awfully cold.

SERGEANT *(shutting the door by placing his back against it. Saluting)*. Good morning, sir. How's your leg this morning sir?

CHALCOT. It feels the cold, sergeant. How's your arm?

SERGEANT. Thank you, sir, it feels frosty too; but I can move it a little *(moves arm, and winces)*.

CHALCOT. Gently, Sergeant, gently. About dinner?

SERGEANT. Here you are, sir. *(Placing bundle on table)* Mutton, sir—for roasting.

CHALCOT. And vegetables!

SERGEANT. Under the meat, sir.

CHALCOT *(lifting up meat)*. Capital! The muddy, but flowery potato; the dirty, milky, turnip; and the humble, blushing, but digestive carrot. Can you cook 'em? *(Putting them near cupboard)*.

SERGEANT. Not today, sir. I'm on hospital duty.

CHALCOT. Then I suppose I must.

SERGEANT. But I shall be able to look in, sir, now and then.

CHALCOT. Do; for your legs are indispensable. Any news outside?

SERGEANT. They say, sir, there's to be an attack shortly.

CHALCOT. Um!

SERGEANT. And the enemy was heard moving in the night.

CHALCOT. Oh!

SERGEANT. And that they're very strong in artillery.

CHALCOT. Oh! *(Drinking)*.

SERGEANT. Talking of artillery, sir, Captain Rawbold sent his compliments to you, sir, and would you oblige him with the loan of your frying pan, a pot of anchovies, and a few rashers of bacon.

CHALCOT *(annoyed)*. Anything else?

SERGEANT. No sir.

CHALCOT. Confound Captain Rawbold!—he's always borrowing something. Last week I lent him our own private and particular gridiron, and he sent it back with one of the bars broken. *(Aside)* Those damned gunners!—borrowing one's *batterie-de-cuisine*[99] *(rising)*.

(Knock, D.L.).

SERGEANT. I dare say that is Captain Rawbold come himself to—

CHALCOT. Open the door.

(Sergeant opens).

I'll tell him my mind about his conduct respecting that gridiron. Well *(taking frying pan)*, you don't deserve it; but here's your frying pan, and—

(Sir Alexander enters. Chalcot sees him).

Eh!—Colonel!

(Sergeant salutes, shutting door with his back. Chalcot puts frying pan behind him. Wind heard as door opens. Snow).

SIR ALEXANDER. Good morning, Chalcot. I want to speak to you *(goes to fire, L.)*.

CHALCOT. Sergeant, my compliments—and frying pan to the captain—and—and—*(aside to Sergeant)* he mustn't do it again.

(Opening door for Sergeant. Sergeant. Sergeant salutes with frying pan, and exits, holding it before his face. Wind heard as door opens).

Did you meet MacAlister?

SIR ALEXANDER *(at fire, L.)*. Yes; and that's what I came to speak to you about. He reminded me of the documents that I intended to entrust to your care—should anything befall me. *(Gives him packet, which Chalcot places in portmanteau)*.

CHALCOT. Is there any news, then?

SIR ALEXANDER. I think we shall be ordered to the front—and I believe there is to be a combined attack, which is likely to be decisive. Angus told me that he had made his last will and testament, and confided it to you. I have done the same.

CHALCOT *(who is arranging a rude spit and string for suspending mutton before fire, L.)*. And while you're fighting, I shall have to stop in here, cooking—like a squaw in a wigwam.[100]

SIR ALEXANDER. I'm sorry you can't go with us.

CHALCOT. Just my luck! Where's the cookery book? *(Gets book from mantelpiece, and goes to table)*.

SIR ALEXANDER. Hugh—you've been a good friend—a real friend! At that time, when Kelsey came with that terrible news just before we sailed—

CHALCOT *(at table. Reading, and feigning not to hear)*. "Roast"—"boil"—"bake"—"fry"— "stew"—

---

99   Cooking utensils.

100 Indigenous North American's lodge or teepee.

SIR ALEXANDER (*taking book from him*). Put that down and listen to me. You know the original cause of my quarrel—with my lady.

CHALCOT. The slightest possible—Oh, yes.

SIR ALEXANDER. You know, too, how she has wronged me since by her suspicions. I wrote a long letter to her last night—here it is. (*Showing it*) If this general engagement should give promotion to our senior major, send it home at once. My lady will find—when it is too late—how far she has been mistaken (*gives him letter*).

CHALCOT (*endeavouring to hide his feelings, goes to fire and hangs mutton*). You don't know how mutton is usually roasted, do you—I mean, which side up?

SIR ALEXANDER. I had more to say to you—but I must go (*rises*).

CHALCOT. I'd hobble with you as far as the hill, if it wasn't for the mutton.

SIR ALEXANDER (*crossing, R.*). And I could speak to you as we walked.

CHALCOT (*putting on cloak, etc.*). The sergeant will be back directly. I can leave it for a few minutes. I have it! (*Writes on a piece of paper, folds it, and sticks it on the point of sword, then fixes sword in drawer of table, so that the point is upwards*) He can't help seeing that. (*Putting on cap and cloak*) I believe I've hung it wrong side up. Now, Sir Alick; since my wound, this will be my first walk (*taking stick from R.C.*).

SIR ALEXANDER. And perhaps my last.

(*Wind and snow, as door opens. Exeunt Sir Alexander and Chalcot. Music. A pause. Captain Samprey, Lady Shendryn, Blanche and Mary, and Soldier, pass window, from L. Knocking heard at D.L. Knocking repeated*).

SAMPREY (*without*). Chalcot, MacAlister—nobody at home. (*Wind. Looks in, then enters*) This way, we have the field to ourselves.

(*Enter Blanche, Lady Shendryn and Mary, and Soldier, with whip, L.D.*).

These are their quarters.

LADY SHENDRYN. Oh, thank you, major—so kind of you to have escorted us from Balaklava.

SAMPREY (*R.*). So kind of you to have accepted my escort. They are out, but I should think they're sure to be back directly. In the meantime—

LADY SHENDRYN. We'll stay here. I suppose we need be under no apprehension.

SAMPREY. My dear Lady Shendryn, let me reassure you. Sir Alexander is quite well—so is Chalcot—and so is MacAlister. I'll now go and seek Sir Alexander—(*all this lively*)—and tell him who is here (*crossing, R.*).

BLANCHE (*R.C.*). Where are they? (*Crossing to door, L.*).

SAMPREY. I don't know. Pray be under no alarm—nobody will come here. There's no fighting going on—nor is there likely to be. We've no employment here but to keep ourselves warm—and to go without our dinners.

(*Exit Samprey and Soldier, D.L. The ladies, who are shivering with cold, run to fire*).

BLANCHE. Mary, your nose is red.

MARY. So's yours.

BLANCHE. So's my lady's.

LADY SHENDRYN. Blanche, how can you take such a liberty?

BLANCHE. It was the frost, not me. Let us warm our noses.

(*They go on their knees, and warm their noses at fire, rub them with handkerchiefs, etc.*).

LADY SHENDRYN. I wonder when Mr. Chalcot will come back.

(They examine furniture, peep behind curtain, see bed, and drop curtain).

BLANCHE *(coming down)*. And this is a hut. And this is the Crimea which we have all heard about and read about so much. And neither Sir Alick, nor Mr. Chalcot—

MARY. Nor Captain MacAlister—

BLANCHE. Expect us, and here we are. *(Seeing sword)* What's that?

LADY SHENDRYN *(R.C.)*. Looks like a sword, with a note at the top of it.

MARY *(L. of table)*. Perhaps that's the Crimean method of delivering letters.

BLANCHE *(R. of table. Taking Mary's hand sentimentally)*. Perhaps, Mary, Chalcot—

MARY. Or MacAlister—

BLANCHE. Or some comrade, has left that letter containing his last request.

MARY. Or a letter to his wife.

LADY SHENDRYN. More probably to his sweetheart.

BLANCHE. A few lines to his mother.

LADY SHENDRYN. Or his children.

MARY. Or his tailor.

BLANCHE. I wonder what *is* in it! *(Crossing round table)* I declare I feel like Bluebeard's wife at the door of the blue chamber.[101]

MARY. So do I.

LADY SHENDRYN. What absurdity! *(Sits at stove, R.)*.

(Blanche, L., Mary, R., on each side of the table).

MARY. There's no address on it.

BLANCHE. Then it's intended for anybody.

MARY. Or nobody.

LADY SHENDRYN. Do you consider yourself nobody, Miss Netley?

MARY. Almost.

BLANCHE. My fingers tingle to know what's inside it.

LADY SHENDRYN. Blanche I'm surprised at you. Open a letter not addressed to you! Most unladylike.

MARY *(whispering to Blanche)*. Tell her you think it's in Sir Alick's handwriting.

BLANCHE. It's open at this end. I can read *T-h-e*, "the." I think it's Sir Alexander's handwriting.

LADY SHENDRYN *(rising)*. Eh?

BLANCHE. But we mustn't open it, Mary; so whether it is Sir Alexander's or anybody else's—

LADY SHENDRYN *(down, R.)*. My dear Blanche, if you insist on gratifying this childish whim—

BLANCHE. You'll let me?

LADY SHENDRYN. To please you, my dear.

BLANCHE. You take it off.

MARY. No, you.

BLANCHE. No, you.

(Pushing each other forward. Mary snatches letter, the sword falls to the ground. All frightened).

ALL. Oh!

BLANCHE *(L.C.)*. It's like the taking of Sebastopol.

---

101 Allusion to Charles Perrault's famous folk tale published in France in 1697 and frequently adapted for the English stage. Bluebeard forbids his new wife to enter one room in his castle; overpowered by curiosity she enters and discovers the butchered bodies of Bluebeard's previous wives.

MARY. Yes; only that we've got it.[102]

MARY *(opens letter, and reads)*. "Please to look after the mutton!"

ALL. Oh! *(They go back to fire)*.

LADY SHENDRYN *(down, R.C.)*. Sir Alexander never wrote that; it's not his style. *(Takes off mantle and wrapper. Goes to fire, R.)*.

MARY. Such a stupid thing to say! Now put the sword and letter back.

BLANCHE. No; that would be mean. We'll look after the mutton ourselves. I feel so excited; I think it must be the air. *(Twirling mutton)* Isn't it fun seeing it go round? *(Standing with her back to fire)* Upon my word, Mary, I think I should make as good an officer as any of the men. I could stand with my back to the fire, as they do *(imitating)*.

MARY *(C.)*. But you couldn't face the fire, as they do.

BLANCHE. I don't know that. I could talk just as they do. *(Imitating slow swell smoking, and taking cigars from case on mantelpiece)* Yaas, it's a very fine cigaw—but I know a man—Bedfordshire man—who imports—for his own smoking, very finest cigaws evaw smoked. Now, Mary, you go on.

MARY *(sitting, L.C., back. Imitating a different sort of swell, with eye-glass, and hands in pockets)*. Look here, old fella, if you talk of cigars—I know some cigars that are cigars—and such cigars as no other fella's got the like cigars.

BLANCHE *(slow)*. You don't say so *(smoking)*.

MARY *(quick)*. Assure you—never saw such cigars before in all my life. *(Rising)* Oh! ain't they nasty?

(They put them down).

BLANCHE. Mary, let's play at soldiers *(snatching up sword, C.)*.

LADY SHENDRYN. Oh! you stupid girls *(rises, and goes to fire, L.)*.

MARY. Oh! It's such a silly game.

BLANCHE. No, it isn't. To please me! There, take one of those guns.

MARY *(takes gun hesitatingly, from R.)*. D'ye think it'll go off?

BLANCHE. No; it is not loaded. Now, you be the soldier, and I'll be the officer.

MARY. No; I'll be the officer.

BLANCHE. No; I'll be the officer.

MARY. No; then I shan't play.

BLANCHE. We can't both be officers.

MARY. Yes we can.

BLANCHE. Then who's to give the word of command?

MARY. Both.

BLANCHE. And who's to obey it?

MARY. Neither.

BLANCHE. Nonsense.

MARY. It's going off, Blanche.

BLANCHE *(in tone of command)*. Hi! Ho! Ha! Attention! Form hollow square![103] Prepare to receive *(prancing over to R.)* cavalry!

(Blanche charges upon Mary. Mary, somewhat frightened, retreats to the corner, R. Door opens; Angus and Chalcot enter. Mary gets R. corner, Blanche L. corner).

---

102 Sebastopol was the Russian stronghold that constituted the object of the British and French operations from November 1854 to September 1855.

103 Close combat formation assumed when infantry battalion is threatened by a cavalry attack.

CHALCOT (R. corner). Lady Shendryn!

ANGUS (R.). Blanche!

CHALCOT. Miss Netley!

LADY SHENDRYN (R.C.). How do you do, Hugh.

(General shaking of hands).

How are you, Angus?

BLANCHE (L.C.). We're so glad to see you, Mr. Chalcot. (Embarrassed) And you too, Captain MacAlister.

MARY. How do you do, Captain? How do you do, Mr. Chalcot? (Places stock of gun in his hand. Goes up and disrobes).

(Blanche, L. Chalcot and Angus take off overcoats, etc.).

CHALCOT (R. aside). She's looking very well. (Aloud) But you must have dropped from the clouds.

LADY SHENDRYN. It was all done in a moment. Lady Llandudno felt that she must come over here to see her boy—you know he's her only one. She sent Lord Llandudno to Southampton, where his yacht was lying, to ask the captain if the Curlew was big enough to make the voyage to the Crimea.[104] The captain answered that it was, and that it could be ready in two days. During that time, Lady Llandudno called on me to bid me good-bye. I was seized with the desire to come out too. Lady Llandudno acceded to my wish. Blanche asked to accompany me: I acceded to her wish. I brought Miss Netley as a companion for Blanche; and here we are. Major Samprey brought us from Balaklava in a cart.

CHALCOT. I saw female figures entering our hut from the top of the hill, and hobbled on as fast as I could. I took you for vivandières.[105]

(Angus and Blanche never take their eyes off each other).

LADY SHENDRYN (L.C.), BLANCHE (L.), and MARY (L.C.). Vivandières!

BLANCHE. Do vivandières ever come here?

CHALCOT (exchanging glances with Angus, R.). No; but seeing petticoats—it seems a dream. By Jove! If this were put in a play, people would say it was improbable (knocks his wounded leg against gun, and winces).

LADY SHENDRYN (seeing his leg). What's the matter with your leg?

CHALCOT. I'm wounded.

BLANCHE and MARY. Wounded?

CHALCOT (R. corner). Yes.

MARY. But how?

CHALCOT. A Russian infantry man ran his bayonet in the calf of my leg.

MARY. Oh! how horrid! (Hiding her face).

CHALCOT (crossing, C.). I brought it away as a trophy.

BLANCHE. The leg?

CHALCOT. No—the bayonet. (Pointing to bayonet on wall) That's the bayonet—this is the leg.

(Lady Shendryn and Angus go up).

BLANCHE (L.). What's the matter, Mary?

MARY (L.C.). Nothing; but to find oneself close to the realities—to the horrors of war!

---

104 Many aristocrats visited the Crimean War, usually sailing there by yacht. The German term for them is Kriegsbummler (war idlers).

105 A woman who supplies food to the field troops.

CHALCOT. Eh?

BLANCHE (*L.C. Laughing*). She says you're one of the horrors of war.

MARY. Oh! Blanche! How can you!

(*Blanche, Mary, and Angus go up*).

CHALCOT (*aside*). She looks deuced handsome.

MARY. If I had to fight, I'm sure I should run away.

CHALCOT. Run away! In action, running away is the first thing you think of, and the last thing you do.

LADY SHENDRYN (*coming down, L.C. Aside to Chalcot*). Are Sir Alexander's quarters near here?

CHALCOT. No. (*Aside*) If he only knew who was here! At some distance.

LADY SHENDRYN. Is he likely to come here?

CHALCOT. I think so—shortly—yes. (*Aside*) This is awkward. (*With fashionable air. Going up*) Well, ladies, happy to see you in the heart of luxury and civilisation; welcome to this baronial hall, which, by the way, we built ourselves. Chalcot *fundavit*—Chalcot *pinxit*—Chalcot *carpetavit*.[106] This is the boudoir. Won't you come upon the Turkey carpet?[107] (*Standing upon the piece of planking, which rocks to and fro*).

ANGUS (*bringing down rude arm-chair, R.C.*). Allow me to offer your ladyship a chair.

(*Mary sits at head of table, and Blanche at end, L.*).

CHALCOT (*R.C.*). Put your feet on the hearthrug—I made it myself; it's beautifully stuffed. Dinner will be ready, when it's done. The *menu* is substantial, but not various. A *grand gigot de mouton rôti au naturel, pas de sauce*.[108] In the meantime, can we offer you any light refreshment—any lunch? We have an admirable tap of rum, and as for fruit, I can strongly recommend our raw onions. After dinner we can go to the opera.

(*Cannonade, distant*).

LADY SHENDRYN. What's that?

CHALCOT (*looking at Angus*). The overture! May I offer you some coffee?

(*Lady Shendryn seated at stove, R., Mary at head of table, and Blanche at foot, L. Angus, L.C.*).

LADIES. Oh, yes.

(*Chalcot hands coffee to Lady Shendryn and Mary; Angus to Blanche, fetching cups, etc., from cupboard, R., then a cup for himself; crossing to Blanche, stirring coffee, with his eyes fixed on her; sees she has no spoon, gives her the fork he is using, squeezing her hand*).

ANGUS (*conscious that Lady Shendryn's eyes are upon him. To Blanche*). I hope I have the pleasure of seeing you quite well!

BLANCHE. Quite well; and you?

ANGUS. Quite well.

MARY. I want a spoon.

(*Chalcot gives her the wooden one*).

CHALCOT. Our family plate.

(*A pause. They sigh*).

---

106 Literally, Chalcot founded, painted, and seized it.

107 Chalcot calls attention to their lack of comforts by calling to mind one of Turkey's luxury exports to western Europe.

108 Roasted leg of mutton without sauce.

ANGUS. Any news in London, when you left it?
BLANCHE. No; none.

(Pause)

ANGUS. No news?
BLANCHE. None; none whatever.
MARY. It's so hot!
CHALCOT. Have some ice in it?
BLANCHE *(pauses)*. You remember Miss Featherstonhaugh?
ANGUS. No—yes. Oh—yes.
BLANCHE. The Admiral's second daughter, the one with the nice eyes; used to wear her hair in bands.[109]
   Her favourite colour was pink?

(Angus puts cup to his lips, but does not drink).

ANGUS. Yes.
BLANCHE. She always wears green now.
ANGUS. Good gracious!
CHALCOT. Can I offer your ladyship the spoon?
ANGUS *(not knowing what to say)*. I heard that London had been very dull.
BLANCHE. Oh! very dull.
ANGUS. Seen anything of our friends, the Fanshawes?
BLANCHE. No.
ANGUS. Not of *Mr.* Fanshawe?
BLANCHE. Oh—Dick! He's married!
ANGUS. Married?
BLANCHE. Yes; one of Sir George Trawley's girls.
ANGUS *(with a sigh of relief)*. Poor old Fanshawe! *(He empties cup at a draught; sees that Lady Shendryn is not looking, opens his coat, and taking out the locket shows it to Blanche, and whispers)* Do you remember the night we parted?
BLANCHE. Yes.
LADY SHENDRYN *(looking round)*. Blanche, dear, are you not cold out there?
BLANCHE. No; quite warm, I assure you.
ANGUS. You remember it?
BLANCHE. Yes.

(Enter Sergeant with paper, which he gives to Angus. He expresses surprise at seeing ladies. Chalcot comes R. of Angus. Sergeant takes sword and belt from cask, R., and gives them to Angus. Wind heard).

ANGUS *(aside to Chalcot)*. To the front! *(To Blanche, seeing she has observed paper)* So Miss Featherstonhaugh wears green, does she? *(Buckling on sword)* I'm afraid that I must leave you.
BLANCHE. Must you?
ANGUS. Yes.
BLANCHE. On duty?
ANGUS. Yes.
BLANCHE. Shall you be back soon?

---

109 Loops.

ANGUS. I hope so. Good day, Miss Netley. Good day, Lady Shendryn, for the present. *(Pause. To Blanche, after shaking hands with Chalcot)* I hope to have the pleasure of seeing you again.

(Sergeant opens door. Exit Angus, D.L. Wind. The "Chanson" is played as a march by band outside; it grows more and more distant).

BLANCHE. What band is that playing? *(Rising).*
SERGEANT. The band of "Ours."
BLANCHE. I think I've heard that march before.
SERGEANT *(R. corner).* We call it Captain MacAlister's march. He had it arranged by the bandmaster. They often play it.

(Lady Shendryn speaks aside to Sergeant).

CHALCOT *(at back, observing Blanche, sings).*
    And a cup of cold pisen[110] lay close by her side,

(Blanche crosses, and sits at end of table).

    And a billy-dux, which said as how for Villikins she died.[111]
SERGEANT. Thank you, my lady—I'm glad to hear the missus is well, and the children—and the twins—and the new one which I haven't seen.
MARY. There's a letter I promised Mrs. Jones to give you if I met you. *(Giving it)* I saw them all the day before we left. The twins have grown wonderfully.
SERGEANT. Have they now? Clever little things! Grown!—So like 'em—just the sort of thing they would do!
BLANCHE *(rising, crosses R., sighing).* Has Captain Mac—Has the regiment to go far?
SERGEANT. "Ours," mum?
BLANCHE. Yes.
SERGEANT. We're going to the front, into—
CHALCOT *(R.C., coming down, and crossing behind, R. Interrupting quickly).* To parade.
SERGEANT *(catching his eye).* Yes; to parade.
LADY SHENDRYN *(C. advancing, C.).* Will Sir Alexander be there?
SERGEANT *(R.).* Yes, my lady. He wouldn't let the regiment go into—
CHALCOT *(interrupting).* On parade.
SERGEANT. On parade—without him.
LADY SHENDRYN. Can we see them?

(A pause. Chalcot and Sergeant look at each other embarrassed).

    I mean, can we not see the regiment parading? You can't escort us on account of your wound; but the Sergeant could conduct us to some place where we could see them, could he not?
BLANCHE. Oh!—I should so like that!
CHALCOT. Well—if you insist—Sergeant, take the three ladies to the—
LADY SHENDRYN. No. Miss Netley can remain here—she is such a bad walker.
MARY. No, I'm not *(pouting).*
LADY SHENDRYN. We shall not be gone long.

(Lady Shendryn and Blanche put on wraps).

---

110 Poison.
111 A reprise of "Villikins and His Dinah," also all the rage in London. "The Ratcatcher's Daughter," letter to editor, *Musical World*, 3 November 1853: 709-10. See p. 403.

CHALCOT. You'll come back to dinner?

LADY SHENDRYN. Yes. Miss Netley will perhaps be kind enough to assist in its preparation. We shall most likely be back before Sir Alexander or the Captain.

CHALCOT. Most likely.

(Opens door. Wind).

It's not snowing, but you'd better stay here.

LADY SHENDRYN. No, no.

BLANCHE. We've made up our minds.

CHALCOT. I understand feminine discipline too well to make another observation.

Sergeant, take the ladies to Flagstaff Hill. Good-bye, for the present; and *(aside to Sergeant)*, not a word about the action!

(Exeunt Lady Shendryn, Blanche, and Sergeant, D.L.).

CHALCOT. This is a singular *tête-à-tête*—shut up alone with this girl. I always hated her in England! Somehow, the air of the Crimea seems to improve everything. Everything has improved since I've had something to do—and a bayonet in the calf of my leg.

MARY *(sitting at back, L.)*. Now, Mr. Chalcot, what are we to do for dinner?

CHALCOT *(R.)*. Dinner?

MARY *(L. attending to fire, L.)*. Yes; of course I must obey Lady Shendryn's orders.

CHALCOT. Orders! *(Aside)* Lady Shendryn behaves like a perfect brute to this girl. Such a charming girl, too—*(Aloud)* About dinner—shall we have a set dinner?[112]

MARY. If you like; I'm a capital cook.

CHALCOT. Are you?

MARY. Yes.

CHALCOT. What an accomplished creature it is!

MARY. In my poor father's time, I was housekeeper. He wasn't very rich; but he always said his dinners were excellent; and he ought to know, for he was a clergyman *(goes up, L.)*.

CHALCOT *(aside)*. A housekeeper, too—ah! *(Aloud)* Well, then, for this dinner—this grand dinner; to begin at the beginning.

MARY *(coming down)*. Soup?[113]

CHALCOT. We've got no soup.

MARY. Fish?

CHALCOT. We're out of fish.

MARY *(L.)*. Entrées?[114]

CHALCOT *(R.)*. I don't think we'll have any entrées today.

MARY. The joint?[115]

CHALCOT. There we're strong. *(Crossing to fire, L., singing "Barcarolle" from Masaniello)*[116]

Beyond the mutton brightly—brightly burning!

MARY. And the vegetables?

---

112 Fixed menu.

113 Mary runs through the customary order of courses for a formal dinner: soup, fish, entrée, joint (roasted meat) and vegetables, game (such as pheasant), desserts.

114 A savoury served between the fish course and the joint.

115 Roast.

116 From act 2 of *Masaniello, ou la Muette de Portici* (debut Paris Opera 1828). The leader of the revolutionary movement begins "Amis la matinée est belle," obscuring his intentions before the Viceroy.

CHALCOT. *Pommes-de-terre au naturel, dans leur jackets*[117] (*pointing to potatoes*).
MARY. Game?
CHALCOT. No game.
MARY. Sweets—ices?
CHALCOT. Lots of ice outside.
MARY. Puddings?[118]

Illustration 25. Marie Wilton as Mary Netley and Johnny Clarke as Chalcot, making roley-poley pudding, in *Ours*, act 3, carte-de-visite, 1866. Window and Bridge (photographers). Bequeathed by Guy Little, courtesy of the Victoria and Albert Museum.

---

117 Potatoes baked in their skins.
118 A boiled, steamed, or baked dish, in this case sweet rather than savoury.

CHALCOT. Unheard-of luxuries.

MARY. Have you no flour?

CHALCOT. A barrelful *(pointing, R.)*.

MARY. Any preserves?

CHALCOT. Lots—pots!

MARY. I can make a pudding.

CHALCOT *(lost in astonishment)*. No!

MARY. I can—a roley-poley.[119]

CHALCOT. A roley-poley pudding in the Crimea! It's a fairy-tale!

(They clear table. Chalcot rubbing it down with newspaper).

MARY *(taking basin)*. Now the flour.

(Chalcot, waiting on her with wonder and admiration, gets flour from barrel).

I declare! here's some paste ready-made; I shall want a paste-board.[120]

CHALCOT. There's a map *(taking it from wall, R.)*.

MARY. That'll do. *(Seeing lid of flour-barrel in Chalcot's hand)* And an apron.

CHALCOT. This will do. It belonged to a pioneer[121] of ours; he was shot at the Alma.[122]

(Mary shrinks).

But he didn't wear it that day.

(Helps her on with pioneer's apron. She mixes pudding).

MARY *(mixing pudding)*. Oh! I forgot.

CHALCOT. What?

MARY. I shall want a rolling-pin.

CHALCOT *(tries to pull leg out of stool. Producing it)*. Here's a field-marshal's baton, popularly supposed to be carried in every French soldier's knapsack.

(Mary rolls pudding, etc.).

Beauty, accomplishments, amiability, no mother, and roley-poley pudding! *(Approaching her, round backwards, L. to R. of table)*.

MARY. Don't I look funny in this leather apron?

CHALCOT. You look charming!—it beats a ball-dress into fits! *(Approaching her)*.

MARY. Don't come near me—my hands are all over flour!

CHALCOT. What matter? Flour on those hands is more becoming than white kids,[123] be they ever so Houbigant.[124] I never saw hands look so sweet!

MARY. You mustn't talk to the cook. Now, the preserves!

CHALCOT *(crossing, R.)*. Here.

(Giving them. Mary puts preserves in pudding).

---

119 Pudding made of suet pastry spread with jam, rolled together, then baked, boiled, or steamed.

120 A board for rolling out pastry.

121 Infantryman who goes ahead of the army to dig trenches, repair roads, or clear terrain in advance of the regiment.

122 The first battle of the Crimean conflict, September 1854.

123 Kid gloves.

124 A French perfume.

MARY. Now the spoon—*the* wonderful spoon.

CHALCOT. Our piece of family plate.

MARY. Why this is treacle![125]

(Chalcot takes it back and gets jam).

CHALCOT. With such a woman as that to sweeten one's path through life—to put—to put the preserve into one's pudding—metaphorically speaking—that's woman's mission!

MARY. Oh—I forgot!

CHALCOT. What?

MARY. A pudding-cloth.[126] What shall we do for a pudding-cloth?

CHALCOT. Won't the leather apron do?

(Mary shakes her head).

I'm afraid our resources have broken down in the moment of victory! To think that a pudding—and such a pudding—should break down for the sake of a paltry pudding-cloth. *(After a pause)* I have it! *(Crossing, L.).*

MARY. What?

CHALCOT. I received a packet of linen a month ago from England. I've never opened it. *(Opens portmanteau, and takes out towel)* Eureka! I have found it! A towel!—and here have I been wiping my face with straw for the last three weeks!

(Offers it to Mary, who puts pudding in it, pins up the ends, and places it in saucepan, Chalcot burning his hands with lid).

MARY. The mutton's getting on beautifully.

(Pokes fire with leg of stool, and as she turns, hits Chalcot's leg. Chalcot falls into a chair, hurt).

MARY. I have hurt your wound!—pray, forgive me!

CHALCOT. It's nothing—not at all hurt. I like it!

MARY. I'm very, very sorry.

CHALCOT. Don't mention it—hurt me again! But speak in that tone—and look in that way again!

MARY. Shall I loosen the bandages? *(Kneels).*

CHALCOT. If you like; but you can't fasten them up again.

MARY. I can.

CHALCOT. With what?

MARY. A hair-pin *(takes one from her hair, and fastens bandages).*

CHALCOT. Miss Netley—Mary—*(taking her hand).*

MARY. My hands are all over flour!

CHALCOT. Never mind—I like them all the better. You don't dislike me—do you, Mary?

MARY. Oh, Mr. Chalcot!

CHALCOT *(sits, R.C.).* Not very much, I hope? I've always loved you—even when we used to quarrel. May I trust that some day I may not be indifferent to you; and, if so, that I may make you my own—my wife!

(She turns away).

---

125 Molasses.

126 A woven wrapper upon which the pudding pastry is placed; engulfs the pudding and is tied with string.

Don't let me frighten you. I won't tell the Colonel—I mean Lady Shendryn! I know you can't love me now—but I'll try to deserve your love: and perhaps if I try hard—and I will—I may succeed. Sebastopol isn't taken in a day; and you'll let me try—won't you, Sebastopol?—I mean Mary? *(With great agitation)*.

MARY. Mr. Chalcot, you know I am a poor dependent.

CHALCOT. That's the very reason! I couldn't love a girl with money.

MARY. A man of your position—your property—

CHALCOT. For Heaven's sake don't raise up the dismal spectre of my money to forbid a happiness within my reach! Don't let cash forbid the banns![127] If I am rich, don't reproach me with it. I don't deserve it—it isn't my fault! I never made a penny in my life—I never had the talent. Only say you will be mine!

(Bugle call without).

LADY SHENDRYN *(enter quickly)*. Mr. Chalcot!

CHALCOT *(cooking assiduously. To Lady Shendryn)*. The mutton's doing beautifully.

LADY SHENDRYN *(crosses, L.)*. They're fighting!—And my husband is in the action! I—I—I—Oh! I don't know what I'm doing! Give me your hand!

(Enter Blanche, hurriedly).

BLANCHE *(to Mary)*. Mary—he's fighting! He's gone to battle—with two or three thousand others! I heard the officers who galloped by say there was an engagement! He's fighting!

(Chalcot shuts door at each entrance).

LADY SHENDRYN *(L.C.)*. Who?—Sir Alexander?

BLANCHE. No; Angus.

LADY SHENDRYN. Angus! What, then—do you love him?

BLANCHE *(crossing, R.C.)*. Yes, I do; and I don't care who knows it.

LADY SHENDRYN. Well, my child, I don't blame you. We can't help these things *(kisses her)*.

BLANCHE. Perhaps, at this very moment—even now, as I speak—a bullet may have reached his heart.

LADY SHENDRYN. Oh!

(Both women horrified at the picture. Lady Shendryn R.; Blanche L.; Chalcot C.; Mary, L.C.).

LADY SHENDRYN. Do you think he will come back?

BLANCHE. Will he return?

CHALCOT. Of course he will! no doubt of it! *(To Mary)* How the devil should I know?

LADY SHENDRYN and BLANCHE *(together)*. If he should not!

CHALCOT. But he will—they will—they never do get killed in "Ours!"

BLANCHE *(L.C.)*. Oh, Lady Shendryn! I'm so sorry for you *(crossing to her, and kissing her)*.

LADY SHENDRYN *(L.)*. And I for you *(kissing her)*.

(Chalcot makes an offer to kiss Mary).

MARY *(L., repulsing him)*. I'm so glad you are not fighting!

CHALCOT *(L.)*. Are you! *(Pointing to Lady Shendryn and Blanche)* It's wrong of me to be so happy, isn't it?

(Chalcot and Mary go up. She takes off apron).

LADY SHENDRYN. Think dear; it's my husband!

BLANCHE. And the man I love!

---

127 Proclamation in church of an intended marriage, creating an opportunity for anyone to declare an objection to the match.

LADY SHENDRYN. And we parted in anger!

(Distant cannon and bugle calls heard throughout following scene).

BLANCHE. And he never knew how much I loved him! Oh! if I could see him again!

(Knock heard at D.L. All start).

BLANCHE *(together)*. Perhaps Angus.
LADY SHENDRYN *(together)*. If it is he!

(They rush to door, and are met by Prince Perovsky, who wears full Russian uniform, orders, etc.).

BLANCHE and LADY SHENDRYN. Prince Perovsky!
PRINCE *(entering)*. Miss Haye, Lady Shendryn.
LADY SHENDRYN. You here, prince?
PRINCE. Yes—a prisoner—fortune of war.

(Samprey enters, D.L.).

SAMPREY *(R.)*. Pardon me, Lady Shendryn, I have the honour to be the prince's escort. Knowing that you were acquainted, I took the liberty—
LADY SHENDRYN. Sir Alexander—
BLANCHE *(C.)*. Captain MacAlister—
SAMPREY *(very gravely)*. Are in the engagement. I did not see their regiment—I could not for the smoke. Excuse me, I must go. Prince, you have given me your parole.[128]

(Prince bows).

I have the honour—

(Presenting Prince with his sword, who sheaths it. Exit Samprey, L.D. Blanche, sits, L., with her face on table. Chalcot, up L., with Lady Shendryn. Mary goes down, R.).

PRINCE. Pray, ladies, don't be alarmed; it is not a battle—a mere affair of outposts.
LADY SHENDRYN *(seated, at head of table)*. Oh, Prince, I am beyond comfort!
PRINCE *(L.C. to Blanche)*. These are strange circumstances under which to meet. You see I am always a captive in your presence.

(Mary, at door).

BLANCHE. Oh, Prince, to think that battle is raging so near us!
PRINCE. Be under no alarm; my presence—
BLANCHE. It is not that, but—
PRINCE. You fear for those dear to you?
BLANCHE. Yes.
PRINCE. Sir Alexander?
BLANCHE. Yes.
PRINCE. And perhaps for some other?
BLANCHE. Yes—my cousin Angus.
PRINCE. The young gentleman I met in London?

(Blanche assents).

---

128 Oath of honour, e.g., conditional freedom based on an officer's pledge not to escape and to refrain from combat for the duration of the war.

BLANCHE. If he should be killed?

PRINCE. *Hélas!* Fortune of war!

BLANCHE. Or taken prisoner?

PRINCE. As I am. He would be treated with the respect and honour due to the sacred name of enemy. Reassure yourself, my dear Miss Haye; your young soldier is sheltered by your love.

(Blanche goes up, and sinks in arm-chair, R.C.).

Oh, Youth! Inestimable, priceless treasure! Lost forever! To be a *sous-lieutenant*,[129] and beloved as he is—psha! Am I a child, to cry for the moon? *Pas si bête!*[130] *(Goes up, R.C., to Blanche).*

CHALCOT *(coming down, with Lady Shendryn, L.).* If you see Sir Alexander again, of which I have but little doubt, I think what I am going to tell you will make you happy with him ever after. I am aware that you were jealous of him—

LADY SHENDRYN *(seated, L.).* Not without cause. Even years ago I had cause.

CHALCOT. The slightest possible. Since then he has been true and faithful. I know, for I was in his confidence. It was hard on him to be suspected, and have nothing to show for it; for when one is found out, nothing is so sustaining as the sweet consciousness of—guilt.

LADY SHENDRYN. Why all this now? What—

CHALCOT. Hear me out. Sir Alexander's money used to go mysteriously. Do you know where it went?

LADY SHENDRYN. Yes; to some woman.

CHALCOT. No.

(Blanche seated up stage, R.C.; Prince near her; Mary down, R.).

LADY SHENDRYN. To whom then?

CHALCOT. To your brother Percy.

LADY SHENDRYN. Percy!

CHALCOT. To save him—to save you, and his family from dishonour. Five years ago Sir Alick discovered, by his banking account, that Percy had forged his name!

LADY SHENDRYN. What!

CHALCOT. You remember the night that Sir Alick left England, when Kelsey, the lawyer, sent him a letter, and he sent for me?

LADY SHENDRYN. And he withdrew £1,500 from my account.

CHALCOT. Yes; for fresh bills forged by Percy.

LADY SHENDRYN *(hiding her face).* And he concealed this from me.

CHALCOT. Because he preferred to bear the brunt of your suspicions, rather than let you know the extent of your brother's—conduct. There is a letter, which in case of accidents, he gave to me for you; in it is contained the half of the letter you did not see, that Kelsey sent him.

(Mary goes up to back).

You need not read it now. All that I tell you is true. Sir Alick is a gallant officer, and a noble gentleman *(with emotion, then resuming his ordinary manner)*, and let come what come, he's sure to bring the regiment out of it creditably. So when you meet, learn to know him better.

LADY SHENDRYN. When we meet—oh! this suspense is terrible. Any certainty—even of the worst!

(Enter Sergeant).

---

129 Sub-lieutenant: the lowest rank of commissioned officer.
130 Not so stupid.

SERGEANT *(R.)*. If you please, sir—the Colonel—
MARY *(running between them)*. Hush!

(Blanche rises).

LADY SHENDRYN *(L.)*. You need not speak—I know all!—He is dead!

(Sinks in chair. A pause. Sergeant astonished).

BLANCHE *(C.)*. And Captain MacAlister?
SERGEANT *(confounded)*. Captain—

(Blanche covers her face with one hand).

BLANCHE. You may tell me—I can bear it.

(Enter Angus).

ANGUS. Didn't I hear my name?
BLANCHE *(rushing to him)*. Oh! *(Restraining herself)* I'm so glad to see you back!
CHALCOT. All right?
ANGUS. Quite.
BLANCHE. Unhurt?
ANGUS. Yes.

(A pause. They look sympathetically at Lady Shendryn).

BLANCHE. And poor Sir Alexander?
ANGUS. Came with me. He'll be here directly.
LADY SHENDRYN *(rising)*. Here! Is he not killed?
ANGUS. No.
LADY SHENDRYN. Alive?
ANGUS. Yes.

(All look at Sergeant).

SERGEANT. That's just what I was going to say, only this young lady stopped me.

(All go up but Lady Shendryn).

LADY SHENDRYN. Oh—my husband!

(Sergeant opens door. Sir Alexander appears at door, and hears her).

   If I could only see you, to kneel at your feet, and ask pardon for having so wronged your noble nature!
   At the very time I reproached you for ruining your fortune for another, to have borne with me for the ·
   sake of the honour of my family!
SIR ALEXANDER *(advancing)*. Diana! These expressions of affection—
LADY SHENDRYN *(C.)*. Alexander.

(Embracing; about to kneel, he prevents her).

   I know all.
SIR ALEXANDER *(R.)*. All what?

(Lady Shendryn shows him letter).

   Chalcot gave you this?

(Lady Shendryn assents).

Hugh? What right had you to—

CHALCOT (*coming down, L.*). None, whatever. That is why I did it (*goes up*).

LADY SHENDRYN. Forgive me!

SIR ALEXANDER (*R.C.*). Forget it, Diana, and—(*staggers, and nearly falls*).

LADY SHENDRYN. What's the matter?

(*Sergeant and Lady Shendryn assist him into chair*).

SIR ALEXANDER. Nothing. I—

ANGUS (*L.*). A slight fall. Don't alarm yourselves.

(*All down stage but Prince. Lady Shendryn attends to Sir Alexander*).

MARY (*R., to Sergeant*). Why didn't you say that he was wounded?

SERGEANT (*R.*). Just what I was going to do, miss, only you stopped me.

SIR ALEXANDER. It is but a scratch—the affair was but a skirmish. The great event is postponed again. I came here to congratulate Angus.

CHALCOT. On what?

SIR ALEXANDER (*whispering, so that Prince may not hear*). He has taken a Russian colour.

CHALCOT (*L.*). Bravo, Angus! My luck; I am out of all these good things (*goes up to Prince*).

MARY (*to Sergeant*). Why didn't he mention his capturing the colours?

(*All whispering*).

SERGEANT. We never do mention those sort of things in "Ours" (*goes up, and takes off overcoat*).

(*Mary goes up, R.*).

PRINCE (*coming down, C.*). Sir Alexander, I trust that your hurt is but slight; wounded yourself, you will have more compassion upon others.

SIR ALEXANDER (*R.C., surprised*). Prince!

PRINCE (*C.*). Permit me, in the hour of my adversity, to point out to you that those two young people love each other. Don't be surprised. Battle elevates as well as brutalizes us. I withdraw my pretensions; I am too old.

BLANCHE (*L.C., overhearing*). Prince!

SIR ALEXANDER. But Angus is so poor!

PRINCE. No man is poor while he is young. Youth is wealth—inestimable and irretrievable.

SIR ALEXANDER (*together*). Well, but—

LADY SHENDRYN (*together*). My dear Blanche—

BLANCHE. It's no use arguing, because I won't have any body else; and if you don't consent, I'll wait till I'm twenty one. You'll wait till I'm twenty-one, won't you, Angus?

SIR ALEXANDER. Well—well—we'll see about it.

BLANCHE. When?

SIR ALEXANDER. When? When the war is over.

(*Sir Alexander and Lady Shendryn go up stage. He sits*).

BLANCHE. What a horrid thing is war!

ANGUS (*L.C.*). Prince, how can I express my deep sense of obligation?

PRINCE. By silence.

(*All go up. Sergeant at fire, reading his letter. Tramp of Soldiers heard without*).

ANGUS. You engaged to Mary! By what means?

CHALCOT. Roley-poley pudding—in the saucepan—boiling at this moment—tell you all about it!

LADY SHENDRYN. Mary caught Chalcot. What an artful girl!

BLANCHE *(coming down, R. aside to Mary)*. But he's so small!

MARY. You know I've no money—and I couldn't expect so big a husband as you.

(They go up).

CHALCOT. I feel awfully jolly! It must be the prospect of marriage—or the pudding! Sergeant, what can I do for you?

SERGEANT *(coming down, L. corner)*. Nothing sir, thank you.

CHALCOT *(L.)*. But I must—you saved my life!

SERGEANT. You gave me a five-pound note!

CHALCOT. But you've only one life!—I've many five-pound notes. I have it! Your boy—the twin boy! How old is he?

SERGEANT. Nearly two, sir—both those twins is nearly two, sir.

(Mary, Blanche, and Angus begin to lay cloth).

CHALCOT. I'll educate him—and—when he's old enough, I'll buy him a commission *(goes up to Mary)*.

SERGEANT *(affected)*. My boy an officer! I'll have him taught to read and write directly. If Mrs. Jones and the twins could only come in at that door just now!

MARY. What a pleasant day!—capturing flags and princes!—and being engaged! It's delightful!

CHALCOT. I hope you find it so. You don't hate me now as you used to do?

MARY. I suppose you have been very wicked.

CHALCOT *(L.C.)*. Awful! But you don't dislike that, do you?

MARY. Um, I don't know. The Crimea has improved you wonderfully.

(Chalcot helps her off with apron. They go up).

ANGUS *(coming down, R., in corner)*. The place is not the same now you are in it, and that you are to be mine. You illuminate it—you're a chandelier!

BLANCHE. Chandelier, indeed! A pretty compliment—all cut glass and wire!

ANGUS. Lit up by love!

CHALCOT *(at fire)*. The mutton's done!

(General movement. They place seats, etc. All on the alert, as at a picnic. Each person, except Lady Shendryn, Sir Alexander, and Prince, has hold of either plates, or a chair, or a saucepan, etc. Chalcot places mutton on table, which has been laid by Sergeant and Mary and others).

CHALCOT. *Les reines sont servies.*[131]

(Sergeant waits at table. The "Chanson" march played, piano,[132] without. Men heard marching. Cheers. Angus opens door).

LADY SHENDRYN. What's that?

SIR ALEXANDER. The Russian colours.[133] *(Whispering, and pointing to Angus)* "Ours!"

MARY. What troops are those?

CHALCOT *(sitting on the same chair)*. "Ours!"

BLANCHE. And what are we? *(To Angus).*

ANGUS *(her hands in his, leaning over her)*. "Ours!"

---

131 The queens are served.
132 Quietly.
133 Regimental flag.

Dorothy (1886)

Around 1875, Alfred Cellier teamed up with H.B. Farnie to write music and lyrics for a piece they titled *Old London*. They reworked it as *Nell Gwynn*, an homage to the seventeenth-century comic actress, and it was produced in Manchester on 16 October 1876. Cellier and Farnie then decided to recycle their work again but with other collaborators. Farnie's libretto was reset to music by Robert Planquette for a piece also titled *Nell Gwynn*, produced in London at the Comedy Theatre in 1884. In the meantime, Cellier sought B. Charlie Stephenson—whose career spanned diplomacy, management of a railway and a bank, and real estate speculation, in addition to writing nearly a hundred plays—to supply new words to his music. The result was *Dorothy*,[1] a clear instance of the modern musical comedy. Stephenson's comic plot dropped the biographical pretext and moved the action to the eighteenth century. The lovers are tested in three disguise scenarios: Dorothy and Lydia take a lower-class status among the picturesque peasantry of act 1, the entire cast dons antique costuming in the *bal masqué* (costume ball) of act 2, and the women undertake cross-gender impersonations for the duel of act 3.[2] In this, Stephenson reflects elements of Colley Cibber's play *She Wou'd and She Wou'd Not* (1702), in which a woman assumes the guise of the maid of an inn, and Oliver Goldsmith's *She Stoops to Conquer* (1773), in which a country gentleman's daughter is mistaken for a barmaid. The devices of the young woman who scorns marriage, yet becomes fascinated by exactly the man she is intended to wed, and of exchanged rings that unravel the web of assumed identities are so common in English comedy as to defy attribution. The plot was old-fashioned, to put it mildly, but the music was tuneful, and the dresses and scenery offered the novelty of rural England, set nearly a century and a half in the past, with a lavish ballroom scene that afforded opportunities for transformation by "gleaming armour ... heavy silver candelabras, and ... throngs of superbly costumed guests of the wig and powder period."[3]

Cellier conducted W.S. Gilbert and Arthur Sullivan's operettas at the Opera Comique from 1877 to 1879 and then emigrated to Australia. He left the manuscript of *Dorothy* in Stephenson's hands, wishing him well in finding a producer when for so long they had failed to do so. Stephenson took it to George Edwardes, John Hollingshead's recent successor at the Gaiety Theatre which was noted for a celebrated string of burlesques. In order to woo the public to the second production of his lesseeship, Edwardes promoted *Dorothy* as a "new burlesque," but as the *Times* critic wrote, "burlesque of scanty wit and scantier costume, burlesque of the 'cheeky' and slangy order is now a thing of the past," for "*Dorothy* is not a burlesque or anything like it, but an extremely genteel comic opera mounted and dressed with an exceptional affectation of propriety."[4] Though the show was favourably reviewed (everywhere but in the *Times*), it was not immediately a blockbuster. Despite early changes—expanding the comic man's business, trimming the third act, and adding and deleting songs[5]—after three months Edwardes transferred

---

1 This is distinct from Julian Edwards's music for another play titled *Dorothy*, licensed on 29 December 1876, British Library Add MS 53179, which has no relationship to the Cellier and Stephenson collaboration.

2 Flotow's *Martha* also involves a masquerade in humble clothes. Kurt Gänzl notes E.L. Blanchard's accusation that the text was taken from Charles Johnson's *Country Lasses* (1715), with other precedents in William Kenrick's *The Lady of the Manor* (1778), Aphra Behn's *The City Heiress* (1682), John Fletcher's *The Custom of the Country* (c. 1619), and Thomas Middleton's *A Mad World, My Masters* (1605). See Kurt Gänzl, *The Encyclopedia of the Musical Theatre*, vol. 1, 2nd ed. (New York: Schirmer Books, 2001), 528.

3 "Gaiety Theatre," *Reynold's*, 26 September 1886.

4 "Gaiety Theatre," *Times* (London), 27 September 1886: 10.

5 *Dorothy's* "Snuff Song" was deleted. See p. 468 below.

it to the Prince of Wales's Theatre (under Horace Sedger's lease)[6] and shortly afterward sold the scenery, costumes, and all rights to his accountant, H.J. Leslie, for £500.[7] It gained traction at the Prince of Wales's, eventually grossing enough that Leslie could build a new theatre, the Lyric, to which *Dorothy* was again transferred for the remainder of its run.

Edwardes went on to establish his reputation producing musical comedies, with an almost unerring string of long-running successes in the 1890s, including *A Gaiety Girl* (413 performances), *The Shop Girl* (546), *The Geisha* (760), and *San Toy* (778). He moulded the form of musical comedy to distinctively English tastes and, in so doing, established standards that were emulated worldwide, with shows such as *A Country Girl* (729), *The Orchid* (559), and *The Merry Widow* (778).[8] Edwardes had produced *Dorothy* as a stopgap, replacing it with the burlesque *Monte Cristo Jr.* (utilizing the cast that had been on tour with his first burlesque, *Little Jack Sheppard*) for the profitable Christmas season. He must have reckoned he had the better of the bargain with Leslie and that the long-lived genre of burlesque would prove more bankable. It was the worst business decision Edwardes ever made.

Leslie kept *Dorothy* running long after *Monte Cristo Jr.* had closed, reputedly making more than £100,000 with it. This newfound public favour was due to Marie Tempest who replaced Marion Hood as Dorothy on 19 February 1887, bringing a "joyous and arch" interpretation to the title role in contrast to Hood's ladylike gentility.[9] Whereas *Monte Cristo Jr.* lasted 166 performances, a typical run for a Gaiety burlesque, *Dorothy* continued on the boards until spring 1889.[10] Though Edwardes went on to a distinguished and successful career, *Dorothy's* longevity outstripped all of his London productions with a consecutive run of 931 performances. Indeed, it was the longest-running lyric piece of the nineteenth-century London stage.[11] From inauspicious beginnings and a patchwork of sources, *Dorothy* became a phenomenal hit.

Genre Issues

As soon as the show opened, the producers realized that there was no solo for C. Hayden Coffin, the popular baritone playing Sherwood. The composer was in Australia, and his brother and legal representative, Frank Cellier, refused to let any other composer's work be introduced. The song "Old Dreams," written by Alfred Cellier for a Mohawk Minstrels entertainment,[12] was unearthed, and Stephenson hastily substituted lyrics. The resulting song, "Queen of My Heart," sung on a darkened stage after the *bal masqué* guests retired for the night, was a decided hit.[13] Coffin was typically required to reprise it several times before a performance could proceed, and the sheet music became the largest selling drawing-room ballad up to that time.[14] The relationship to blackface minstrelsy was organic, as minstrelsy served—along with ballad

---

6   This is not the theatre on Charlotte Street, Fitzrovia, where Marie Wilton and Squire Bancroft staged *Ours*, but a new theatre opened in 1884 in Coventry Street, Piccadilly.

7   Kurt Gänzl, *British Musical Theatre*, vol. 1 (New York: Oxford UP, 1986), 295. H.G. Hibbert stipulates that Leslie paid £1,000 in H.G. Hibbert, *A Playgoer's Memories* (London: Grant Richards, 1920). Neither gives a source.

8   Gänzl, *Encyclopedia of the Musical Theatre*, vol. 1, 398; and Thomas Postlewait, "George Edwardes and Musical Comedy: The Transformation of London Theatre and Society, 1878-1914," in *The Performing Century: Nineteenth-Century Theatre's History*, edited by Tracy C. Davis and Peter Holland (Basingstoke: Palgrave Macmillan, 2007), 87.

9   Gänzl, *British Musical Theatre*, vol. 1, 296.

10   "The History of 'Dorothy,'" *Dorothy* clippings file, Harvard Theatre Collection.

11   Gänzl, *British Musical Theatre*, vol. 1, 296.

12   Sarah Doudney (lyrics), *The Mohawk Minstrels' Magazine of Favorite Songs and Ballads*, 10:28 (1883). The Mohawks were a popular blackface troupe that performed at the Agricultural Hall. Several of their tunes were borrowed for *Alice in Wonderland* in 1888.

13   "'Dorothy' Comes Back," *Radio Times*, 23 July 1937.

14   Hibbert, *Playgoer's Memories*, 62-63.

opera, burlesque, *opéra comique*, and operetta—as a direct precursor to musical comedy. Compared to the "hotchpotch" assemblies "of song, dance, and sketches" of antecedent lyrical genres, *Dorothy* successfully integrated song and story even if the story was trite and the score was repurposed.[15]

Set in the bucolic countryside of mid-eighteenth-century Kent, *Dorothy*'s debt to traditions of pastoral literature and song are evident even if they are differently deployed. Important to the history of opera, pastoral was satirized by John Gay's *Beggar's Opera*, the first ballad opera (1728), with shepherds and shepherdesses transformed to beggars and whores in Newgate Prison. In *Dorothy* it is the chorus, rather than the principals, who labour in the fields, but all join in song and dance to celebrate the harvest. Laminated onto this pastoral is a standard motif of a profligate gentleman evading his creditors—essentially an urban plot—and the crossed lovers who are fated, by dramatic structure, to be together when the final curtain falls.

Dorothy was billed as a comic opera and has been classed as a musical comedy only in retrospect. (It is also correctly called a light opera, along with Gilbert and Sullivan's collaborations. As the conductor of what later became known as the Savoy Operas—*The Sorcerer* and *H.M.S. Pinafore* were popular in the late 1870s—Cellier knew this repertoire intimately.) Nineteenth-century theatre of all genres was musical, but there is a world of difference between a play with music and a musical play: instead of underscoring emotions or themes, as in melodrama, or interspersing thematic, scene-setting, or character-revealing songs, as in much drama and comedy, lyric theatre takes music as its reason for being. Several lyric genres were popular at the time. Opera utilized more concerted music (duets, trios, quartets, etc.) and choruses, required voices trained specifically to its demands, and had its own venues and a market niche separate from the lighter varieties of lyric performance. Burlesque repurposed music from other sources and was rivalled through the 1860s by *opéra bouffe* (exemplified by Hervé's and Jacques Offenbach's compositions), which utilized original, melodious, and memorable music attached to "beautifully bizarre ideas, with crazy characters, dippy, incoherent dialogue, and plots that ranged from the surreal to the stupefying."[16] Operetta, known chiefly through Johann Strauss's compositions, renounced this "vigorous comedy in favour of sentiment and romance" during the 1870s.[17] In the mid-1880s, lyric comic forms tended toward the sexually suggestive, and much of the fare produced in London (originating in Paris or Vienna) consisted of "leg shows" trading on the appeal of revealing female costumes. Even the burlesques at Hollingshead's Gaiety Theatre retained this flavour though commissioning modern music and dropping rhymed couplets in favour of prose.[18] *Dorothy*, in common with Gilbert and Sullivan's works, reversed the trend by offering something in verse as "perfectly pure" as it was thoroughly English.[19] Significantly, however, even *The Mikado* and *H.M.S. Pinafore* were burlesques (in the parodic, not musical sense) of the comic opera form.[20]

Both in format and tone, *Dorothy* represents a departure from its competition, yet it could also seem insipid. Noting that *Dorothy* was stripped of *opéra bouffe*'s satirical bite and burlesque's sexualized display "with interpolated ballet,"[21] the *Pall Mall Gazette* pronounced the piece "curiously devoid of any

---

15   Len Platt, *Musical Comedy on the West End Stage, 1890-1939* (Basingstoke: Palgrave Macmillan, 2004), 1.

16   Kurt Gänzl, *The Musical: A Concise History* (Boston: Northeastern UP, 1997), 30. Emerging in 1858 and popular from the mid-1860s, *opéra bouffe* was farcical, upbeat, and sentimental. It flourished in the 1870s, with prominent examples including *Le Roi Carotte*, *The Black Crook*, *Les Cloches de Corneville*, and *Falka*.

17   Ibid., 66. Strauss's most notable production of the period was *Die Fledermaus*.

18   Ibid., 93.

19   "Last Night's Theatricals: Gaiety," *Lloyd's Weekly*, 26 September 1886.

20   Gänzl, *Musical*, 86.

21   Hibbert, *Playgoer's Memories*, 28, 31.

interest, the dialogue is of the weakest, and lyrics have no point."[22] *Dorothy* represented a way to staunch continental imports, the "vulgarity of so-called comic opera, senseless puns and word-twistings" through tasteful staging, "decently clad" actresses, and an inoffensive premise; its strongest feature, however, was the music.[23] Cellier secured unanimous praise for songs that were "almost always pleasing—never coarse or vulgar" and ballet music that was "vivacious without being flippant." Altogether the music "leaves a pleasant impression, and contrasts favourably with much of that of the present day, in which exaggerated effort is more apparent than even moderate attainment."[24] The music is not as technically demanding as opera, nor do the dances require extensive balletic training. Buoyant tunefulness and rhythmic promenades (with traditional country and historic dances) better describe the demands placed by Cellier and the choreographer Katti Lanner. Action may seem to be suspended, or elongated, through lyric episodes, yet the musical element is integral rather than incidental, most notably in act 2's succession of the gavotte, leave-taking, presentation of rings, alarm, and preparation for the hunt.

Pantomime also uses music throughout, whether original or borrowed (in the tradition of ballad opera), paired with new lyrics. *Dorothy* borrows only from its own composer's earlier work and avoids pantomime's miscellaneous musicality in favour of a consistent style. Musical comedy came to rival pantomime in popularity while operating on almost opposite principles. Millie Taylor explains that in pantomime, "the stable structure of the form allows the exceptional hero to move forward, but the form, like society, does not change." In its structure, "the journey [is] away from, and back to, equilibrium ... mirrored to reflect the stability and fixity of society."[25] Musical comedy, in contrast, is about society in flux, navigated by characters that need not be exceptional. Defying the traditional view of modernism, Peter Bailey argues that the new genre of musical comedy is as significant a development as the so-called New Drama of socially engaged realism and naturalism. Both musical comedy and New Drama offer different kinds of responses to a changing world, including—in their distinct ways—greater self-determination for women, with New Drama focusing on how sexism limits women's potential (as in Netta Syrett's play *The Finding of Nancy*) and musical comedy giving scope for women's self-determination through romance.[26] Yet, as the final stage direction in one of *Dorothy*'s prompt books specifies, "*the prospective brides and bridegrooms embrace ... ladies* [of the chorus] *look on sympathetically, the gentlemen approvingly, while the old women shake their heads wisely and knowingly.*"[27] This mode of commentary on how gender constrains women is gentler than what is employed in New Drama, but the silent scepticism of older women still serves to question the comic exuberance of young lovers' gravitational pull toward matrimony.

Interpretive Issues

Musical comedy developed as a form well adapted to the new century, and its longevity was secured by adaptability to perennial anxieties. *Dorothy* looks forward to this history while also reaching backward, not only to earlier comedies but also to the social practice of the *bal masqué* (a thematic costume ball). On 6 June 1845, Queen Victoria and Prince Albert hosted a *bal masqué* at Buckingham Palace, the "1745 Fancy Ball," which harked back to fashions of a hundred years before. The Queen and the Prince sported

---

22   "'*Dorothy*' at the Gaiety," *Pall Mall Gazette*, 27 September 1886.

23   "Music," *Graphic*, 2 October 1886.

24   "Gaiety Theatre," *Daily News*, 27 September 1886.

25   Millie Taylor, *British Pantomime Performance* (Bristol: Intellect, 2007), 83.

26   Peter Bailey, *Popular Culture and Performance in the Victorian City* (Cambridge: Cambridge UP, 1998), 192-93; and Peter Bailey, "Theatres of Entertainment/Spaces of Modernity: Rethinking the British Popular Stage, 1890-1914," *Nineteenth Century Theatre* 26:1 (1998): 5.

27   White-Smith Stage Manager's Guide, Mills Music Library, University of Wisconsin at Madison, Tams-Witmark Collection UW Box 229A.

white wigs and specially made antiquated costumes, as did their assembled guests. The royal couple was depicted in souvenir lithographs dancing a minuet with their guests of honour, the Duc and Duchess de Nemours (son and daughter-in-law of King Louis-Philippe of France). The lithographs suggested a time before revolutions tore at the social fabric of France and when courtly activity still dominated the social hierarchy of England.[28] Louis-Philippe, the last king of France, was ousted from the monarchy in 1848; by 1886, the hereditary peers of England were noticeably being bought out of their country houses by newly monied industrialists and entrepreneurial Americans.[29] Setting *Dorothy* in 1740, among commoners, allowed audiences to enjoy the spectacle of antique clothes and manners purely as dress-up, an homage to noble authority that had long since faded in potency. Squire Bantam's eagerness to accommodate the Duke of Berkshire (a fictitious title taken by someone bent on felonious action) passes without commentary, but in terms of 1886, the Squire's self-deception was naïve and quaintly old-fashioned. One might be neighbourly to a distressed traveller of any station in life, but to then give them the benefit of the doubt on money matters was an action worthy only of the stage. Both the pastoral and courtly settings of *Dorothy* registered as long, long ago, yet they provided attractive backdrops to the parallel romantic and comic plots. When critics commented on the deficiencies of Stephenson's plot, they implicitly noted its failure to challenge late-Victorian sensibilities; however, they also registered its triumph in pleasing playgoers who did not go to the theatre to be challenged.

While *Dorothy* draws upon earlier stage repertoire and the courtly entertainment of the *bal masqué*, it also utilizes several other forms of social revelry and ritual. Indeed, these constitute the pretexts for the spectacles of acts 1 and 3, and are crucial to the comic opera's impression of creating integrated music and action. The hop-pole celebration and harvest feast of act 1 might be regarded as mere backdrops to introducing the courting quartet except that these rites of country life establish Dorothy and Lydia's aliases as the country lasses Dorcas and Abigail. Wilder and Sherwood's flirtations gain ground (and greater tension) when city collides with country, and gentlemen think they pursue serving wenches of the lower classes. Without the rituals of country life, the women's pretence for disguise would have neither credibility nor forward momentum. In act 3, the framing rite is the marriage of Phyllis and Tom, true country folk, celebrated by their entire village. Somewhat improbably, this occurs in a wooded coppice in order to double locations with the duel between Percy Dasher (seconded by Tilbury Slocomb)—actually Dorothy and Lydia—and Wilder (seconded by Sherwood). The beginning and end of this bit of plot are framed by a country dance by the bridal party and a song urging everyone to be content with their lot. These framing devices make music, song, and dance diegetic—justified within the logic of the plot—rather than merely incidental. They ground the story of the marriage (and the betrothals of the quartet) as the form of musical comedy.

Stephenson's integration of public rituals into *Dorothy* underscores the waning dependence upon theatrical sources (the mode of much burlesque) and highlights the growing importance of other kinds of entertainment in the public's acceptance of the new genre of the musical. As Peter Bailey has stressed, subsequent British musical comedies explored the milieux of modernity: department stores, hotels, and exhibition grounds, the "social spaces of distraction and display."[30] By the 1890s, British musical comedy deployed a "coherent book, characters, and score," but just as importantly, it was modern in setting and sensibility.[31] What, exactly, was novel about it, given that the plots and sub-plots were borrowed and

---

28   Watercolours by Louis Haghe and Queen Victoria are in the Royal Library, Windsor, Royal Library 13348, Victoria; Royal Library 13347; and Royal Library 19907.

29   David Cannadine, *The Decline and Fall of the British Aristocracy* (New Haven, CT: Yale UP, 1990), 725-26.

30   Bailey, "Theatres of Entertainment," 12.

31   Gänzl, *Musical*, 103.

the framing entertainments constituting each spectacle and dance episode were also old? How does repertoire ever reconstitute into something new? *Dorothy* provides an excellent case in point: the music (though recycled) was unfamiliar (though its harmonic structures were standard), the dances (though choreographed for the occasion) were recognizable as social dances, and the story harks back to multiple comic precedents. This leaves three factors that account for *Dorothy*'s novelty: the catchiness of the tunes, the performances by starring principal performers, and the moment-by-moment gorgeousness of the unfolding *mise en scène*. Like so much nineteenth-century fare, *Dorothy* coheres as a recognizable piece of stage work through its masterful recombination of elements rather than as a breakthrough innovation in any part. While it does not warrant the status of "inventing" musical comedy, *Dorothy* helped to establish the popularity of elements that became an enduring performance genre, and its financial success encouraged other creative teams to work in its generic mould. Thus it is recognizable, in retrospect, as near the vanguard of a trend without being so decisive a break with tradition as to constitute a watershed.

Performative Issues

Dorothy was one of the first West End hits to garner multicontinental attention within months of its London success. Productions opened in New York and Budapest and toured circuits in Australia, South Africa, and Asia.[32] It was not a short-lived success but sustained repeated British, American, and Australian revivals. London revivals opened in 1896, 1908, and 1937; provincial and suburban tours occurred between London runs. *Dorothy* proved easily susceptible to updating, accommodating music-hall gags and new fads such as the serpentine dance[33] despite their anachronisms. A pack of foxhounds—probably not used in the first production—is documented in a suburban touring company in 1895. This novelty appeared late in act 2, as the hunters prepared to greet the dawn; at the final moment, the pack encircled Dorothy for an effective curtain tableau.[34] Less constrained by a management bent on a standardized *mise en scène*, *Dorothy*'s popular endurance compares to the best Savoy Opera favourites for half a century.

A critic who had seen the first production and returned in 1908 to witness *Dorothy*'s 2,031st London performance verified that the music stood the test of time, both in solos and concerted numbers. Two of this cast had been in the first production and all interim London revivals: Arthur Williams and C. Hayden Coffin. Williams had made the peripheral role of Lurcher into a significant comic feature by improvising lines and augmenting the by-play between himself and Mrs. Privett, his love interest, at the *bal masqué*. A list of costumes documents how they were marked out for each other: Lurcher in an oversized coat and red wig and Mrs. Privett in an exaggerated court dress, excessively high hair, and a gigantic fan.[35] Just as romantic couples visually harmonized with colour and vestimentary finesse, comic couples could be easily spotted and paired off. It was predictable but satisfyingly so. Williams continued to amplify Lurcher's gags in revivals, and other actors mimicked his inventions.[36] Coffin's career was made by "Queen of My Heart," but he was not the only one who profited. Sarah Dowdney published new lyrics in a "ladies' version"

---

32 Gänzl, *Encyclopedia of the Musical Theatre*, vol. 1, 528; and Gänzl, *British Musical Theatre*, vol. 1, 290, 310.

33 A music-hall turn featuring a voluminous silk skirt manipulated under coloured electric light to create impressive effects, popularized by Loïe Fuller in the early 1890s. It was introduced by Brenda Harper into the suburban touring company in 1895.

34 "The Parkhurst," *Era*, 5 October 1895; see also the White-Smith Stage Manager's Guide, Mills Music Library, University of Wisconsin at Madison, Tams-Witmark Collection UW Box 229A.

35 From Julian Edwards, comp., Costume Plot for *Dorothy*, UW Box 229A. A photograph of Harriet Coveney in the role documents the effect of her embellished costume. Victoria and Albert Museum, Guy Little Theatrical Photograph Collection, Walery (photographer), Museum no. S.148:638-2007.

36 "'*Dorothy*' Revived: Successful Performance at the New Theatre," 22 Dec. 1908, *Dorothy* clippings file, Harvard Theatre Collection; and *Era*, "The Standard," 2 May 1896.

in 1887, and the music-hall comedian Dan Leno capitalized on the song's popularity by performing a misogynist satire (in drag) in 1888.[37]

Frequent professional repetition cemented certain traditions within *Dorothy*, but these were optional in the countless amateur productions that kept *Dorothy* in the repertoire until World War II. In New York, the Tams-Witmark agency supplied these companies with band parts, annotated prompt books, and simple scene plots for versions that retained the best of the music but truncated elements with dispensable technical complexity.[38] The hop poles, banked bridge piece, and Tuppitt's cottage of act 1 could be whittled down to a village backcloth and tables. Act 2 was written for a two-level design, with staircases right and left leading to the balcony and multiple doors leading off the upper corridor and stage-level side flats. The levels and the high window upstage centre, framed by a garden backing, afforded the best ways to show off the court costumes and the reappearance of sleepy-eyed revellers in their nightclothes, as well as to atmospherically light the contrasts between the brilliant *bal masqué*, the pranksters' arrangement of the "theft" sequence in darkness, candlelight for the awoken guests who pour in after the alarm is raised, and the first light of dawn. However, a less elaborate set could carry off the changes in mood if carefully lit. The last act required the simplest of scenery: pairs of forested wings, a three-dimensional tree downstage, and a backdrop depicting the exterior of Chanticleer Hall. Yet again, stock woodlands scenery would suffice perfectly well. Thus, *Dorothy* was a romantic spectacle, enhanced by period design elements but not dependent on them.

Design pointed spectators away from their own historical moment but without the exoticism of the Crimea *(Ours)*, the Indian subcontinent *(The Relief of Lucknow)*, Egypt *(Elphi Bey)*, or Senegambia *(The Africans)*. Len Platt argues that musicals have a reflexive social relationship with their cultures of origin.[39] In *Dorothy*'s case, this is achieved through temporal comparativism—though the past, it turned out, was remarkably like sensibilities of 1886 (or 1937)—in contrast to the timeless Mitteleuropa (Middle Europe) of *opéra comique* and operetta, or turn-of-the-century Edwardes musical comedies such as *The Geisha*, *San Toy*, and *The Cingalee* in which fantasies of Asian cultures, developmentally fixed relative to modernizing Britain, skirted questions of cultural insularity.[40] As such, *Dorothy* claimed kinship with Shakespeare's comedies *As You Like It* and *A Midsummer Night's Dream*, also antique-seeming in the late nineteenth century due to productions' depictions of a faux-historicist Englishness.[41]

Editing Issues

For sixpence, playgoers, fans, or curious prospective audiences could purchase a booklet with *Dorothy*'s lyrics and a synopsis of the plot: one would need both, for the lyrics explain neither Dorothy and Lydia's nor Wilder and Sherwood's subterfuges, and a synopsis would not be much use in putting words to the eminently singable tunes.[42] Sheet music scored for piano, flute, banjo, violin, harmonium, and orchestra addressed home musicians' desire to play, sing, and dance favourite airs; these were produced in abundance throughout the first long London run. The full score sold for five shillings (or seven and a half shillings hardbound), giving amateurs access to the entire piano reduction. Chappell and Company,

---

37   "Our Musical Box," *Theatre*, 1 April 1887: 217; and Dan Leno's parody on the ballad *Queen of My Heart* (London: Francis Bros. and Day, 1888).

38   University of Wisconsin at Madison, Mills Music Library, UW Box 228A.

39   Platt, *Musical Comedy*, 19.

40   Compare with ibid., 59-82.

41   See Alexander Leggatt, *English Stage Comedy, 1490-1990: Five Centuries of a Genre* (London: Routledge, 1998), 75-93; and Gary Jay Williams, *Our Moonlight Revels: "A Midsummer Night's Dream" in the Theatre* (Iowa City: U of Iowa P, 1997), 76-92.

42   B.C. Stephenson and Alfred Cellier, *The Lyrics of Dorothy: A Comic Opera* (London: Chappell and Co., London [1886]).

a major London music publisher, kept the score in print for decades and reissued it in 1924.[43] This attests to *Dorothy*'s popularity but not to the challenges in producing a modern readable edition.

The only comprehensive source for the book (the spoken words constituting a musical's dialogue) is the manuscript submitted to the Lord Chamberlain for licensing.[44] Without this, key contrivances are indecipherable, such as Dorothy and Lydia's plotting to disguise themselves as villagers and Wilder's plan to rob his uncle's house. In act 2, the conversation between Bantam and Lurcher (preparing the way for Wilder to arrive disguised as the Duke) and then Bantam's kowtowing to the Duke upon his arrival are also contained in the licensing copy. And so it goes on, throughout the remainder of the show, until the ring plot is unravelled and the quartet is reconciled in time for the finale. The licensing copy's version of the lyrics is unreliable (many lyrics changed in rehearsal), but their placement relative to the dialogue can be confidently ascribed. The following edition restores all these passages for the first time in print. While it cannot be verified against a "standard" libretto and book, it is corrected against the published piano/vocal score to indicate the lyrics known best by the public, the dialogue crucial to plot development, and the shape of concerted songs.

Neither the published lyrics nor the score includes stage directions. While some details of the action are supplied by the licensing manuscript, more come from a prompt copy in the Tams-Witmark Collection evidently intended for professional remounts. The latter is especially helpful as it provides business indicative of characters' by-play, the chorus's involvement, and choreography. These have been selectively incorporated into the following edition, depending upon their utility to readers. Whereas the published piano/vocal score establishes the order of songs, some uncertainty arises about the placement of "Queen of My Heart," which was unanticipated in the licensed manuscript but was in use by the time the score was published. The prompt copy includes the crucial notation that Sherwood sings his solo toward Lydia's door, on an otherwise deserted stage. There is only one likely opportunity for this though it requires adding stage directions to evacuate the scene before Sherwood commences and to bring his conspirators on again at the song's (and encores') conclusion.

It is not feasible to reprint the music here. Digital sound files, and perhaps audio and video streaming of performed passages, are better ways for non-musicians to grasp the aural experience of *Dorothy*[45] and the importance of harmonic balance between the voices. Basic information about the characters is inherent to the casting of the lead female as a soprano, her companion as a mezzo-soprano, and the country lass Phyllis as a contralto. Sopranos and mezzos have essentially the same range though the latter offer a slightly darker register. Given Dorothy's more adamant stance against marriage, her voice—lighter than her companion Lydia's—may have immediately signalled that this stance would crumble. It is highly unusual to have an ingénue role, such as Phyllis, in the lower female register; Phyllis sings nothing so low that a soprano could not supply it, though Dorothy's part goes higher than a contralto's range. In practice, there must not have been a great deal of difference between what the musical director, W. Meyer Lutz, required of the three principal females' voices, for Lucy Carr Shaw (George Bernard Shaw's sister) began as an understudy to Marion Hood's Dorothy at the Gaiety and sang Phyllis in the 1892 London revival at the Trafalgar Square Theatre,[46] as if casting depended on neither range nor tonal quality in the female leads. Wilder and Tom are tenors, but so is Lurcher (though in his case his higher register sustains his comedy

---

43   B.C. Stephenson and Alfred Cellier, *Dorothy: A Comic Opera* (London: Chappell and Co., [1886]).

44   British Library Add MS 53364.

45   See Doug Reside, "Byte by Byte, Putting It Together: Electronic Editions and the Study of Musical Theatre," *Studies in Musical Theatre* 1:1 (2007): 73-83. A digital multi-media version of *Dorothy* is under preparation by the Maryland Institute for Technology in the Humanities. See http://mith.umd.edu/mto/.

46   Gänzl, *Encyclopedia of the Musical Theatre*, vol. 1, 296, 310.

rather than marks him as a romantic lead). The older men (Squire Bantam and Tuppitt) are basses, and Sherwood takes the baritone part; curiously, there are no singing females to balance them in the heavy contralto range that is typically given (in Gilbert and Sullivan) to an older female character, for in *Dorothy* neither Lady Betty nor Mrs. Privett has lines or lyrics assigned to them. The company is rounded off by a female and male chorus that does service as villagers and guests of the Squire. Just as a reader of drama must try to visualize the array of costumed, mobile characters on stage, a reader of musical plays must try to imagine the vocal contrasts rendered by their voices.

Dorothy[47]

BOOK AND LYRICS BY B.C. STEPHENSON
MUSIC BY ALFRED CELLIER

First performed at the Gaiety Theatre, London, 25 September 1888.[48]

Squire Bantam (bass)	Mr. Furneaux Cook
Geoffrey Wilder (tenor)	Redfern Hollins
Harry Sherwood (baritone)	C. Hayden Coffin
John Tuppitt (1st bass)	Edward Griffin
Lurcher (2nd tenor)	Arthur Williams
Tom Strutt (2nd tenor)	John Le Hay
Dorothy Bantam (soprano)	Marion Hood
Lydia Hawthorne (mezzo)	Florence Dysart
Phyllis Tuppitt (contralto)	Florence Lambeth
Mrs. Privett	Harriet Coveney
Lady Betty	Jenny McNulty

Produced at the Gaiety Theatre by George Edwardes, 25 September 1886.
Transferred to the Prince of Wales's Theatre 20 December 1886; rights sold to Henry J. Leslie who later transferred the show to the Lyric Theatre 17 December 1888-6 April 1889.
Director Charles Harris
Music director W. Meyer Lutz
Choreographer Katti Lanner
Scenic Design Walter Hann, W. Perkins, W.B. Spong, and E.G. Banks
Costume Design A. Chasemore and Alias

The action takes place in the county of Kent, October 1740.

---

47   Based on the licensing copy British Library Add MS 53364, which supplies the book; B.C. Stephenson and Alfred Cellier, *The Lyrics of Dorothy: A Comic Opera* (London: Chappell and Co., London [1886]), which supplies a version of the lyrics; B.C. Stephenson and Alfred Cellier, *Dorothy: A Comic Opera* (London: Chappell and Co., [1886]), which corrects the lyrics somewhat later in the initial run and provides their vocalized settings; and White-Smith Stage Manager's Guide, Mills Music Library, University of Wisconsin at Madison, Tams-Witmark Collection UW Box 229A, from which some stage directions have been extracted.

48   A full list of cast changes is included in Kurt Gänzl, *The Encyclopedia of the Musical Theatre*, vol. 1, 2nd ed. (New York: Schirmer Books, 2001), 309-10.

Act I

As the curtain rises Tuppitt and Chorus are discovered, young men and women
singing and dancing, old men and women sitting and drinking. The Hop[49] Gardens.
Chorus and Ballet of Peasants and Hop Pickers.

CHORUS.
> Lads and lasses gaily trip,
> Age indulges in a sip;
> With an arm about her waist
> Every lass shall have a taste,
> Then each lad shall toast his lass
> To the bottom of the glass. Ha! ha! ha!
> See the maids their locks entwine
> With the blossom and the bine,[50]
> Gaily tripping in and out,
> Up and down and round about,
> Age and youth with mirth combine
> In the merry hopping time.

(Dance. Enter Phyllis and Tom).

CHORUS.
> 'Tis Phyllis and her lover
> Oh what a fool he looks!

TOM.
> Oh! Muster Tuppitt, here I stand,
>   An honest lad you see,
> To ask you for your daughter's hand,
>   That we may married be.

CHORUS.
> Oh! Muster Tuppitt, there they stand,
> Two nice young folks you see
> Now give to him your daughter's hand,
> That they may married be.

TUPPITT.
> Never!

CHORUS.
> He refuses!

PHYLLIS *(to Tuppitt).*
> Would you see your Phyllis weep,
> Who ever was the gayest of the gay?
> Lose her roses? Miss her sleep,
> And sob a disappointed life away?

---

49   A bitter herb used to flavour beer.
50   Climbing stem of the hop.

CHORUS.
>Forbear defying
>The course of true love!
>By quick complying
>Your better sense prove;
>And see her,
>She is crying!

TOM.
>Happy the home that waits your daughter,
>Honest the heart that I have brought her,
>Sturdy the arm that shall support her;
>You will relent,
>You must consent
>Give me your daughter!

CHORUS.
>You will relent,
>You must consent!
>Sure never man required such earnest pressing!

TUPPITT.
>There, take the child, and with her take my blessing.

CHORUS.
>Ha! ha! ha!

TOM.
>Henceforward I devote my life
>To making her a happy wife.

CHORUS.
>Lads and lasses, etc.

(Repeat and Exeunt dancing).

TUPPITT *(speaks)*. Now my lad, I can't have any loitering about here. My lass has got her work to do. You will have more than enough of her by and by, if she takes after her poor mother.

TOM. All right Muster Tuppitt—I'll be off to parson to get him to name the day.

TUPPITT. Day! What day?

TOM. The wedding day, to be sure! I was thinking that tomorrow would be a likely kind of day.

PHYLLIS. Oh! Tomorrow would be much too soon!

TUPPITT. Nay lass, what has to be done should be done quickly.

TOM. Then tomorrow it shall be.

TUPPITT. Settle it as you please. I shall have no peace till you have your own way. Now Phyllis bustle about and get the tables ready. Dorcas has got her pots on, and there will be a mighty lot of hungry mouths to fill. I'll just go and taste that last cask of ours. Come along, Tom *(exit, L.)*.

PHYLLIS. Father is very fond of that ale, and can't keep his lips off it.

TOM. It ain't easy for a man to keep his lips off anything that he is very fond of *(kisses her and exits L.)*.

(Enter Dorothy and Lydia).

PHYLLIS. Lor'[51] Tom, how could you!

---

51   "Oh lord."

DOROTHY. Oh, Phyllis!

LYDIA. Oh, Phyllis!

PHYLLIS. Miss Dorothy! How you did frighten me!

DOROTHY. Serves you right—

LYDIA. Why did you let him do it?

DOROTHY. Why didn't you slap his face?

LYDIA. Why didn't you scream?

DOROTHY. If it were only for the sake of appearances—

LYDIA. Really, I am ashamed of you!

PHYLLIS. But I am going to be married, Miss—

DOROTHY and LYDIA. To be married?

DOROTHY. To whom?

PHYLLIS. To Tom Strutt.

LYDIA. Dear me! I am sorry for you.

DOROTHY. What a pity to spoil such a nice girl!

PHYLLIS. Lor', Miss! How you frighten me. Why, Tom is as handsome as paint, and as good as gold!

DOROTHY. Paint, my dear, is often used to cover a hole in the plank.

LYDIA. And as for virtue in man, it is here today and gone tomorrow.

DOROTHY. You take my advice and draw back, or you will repent when it is too late.

LYDIA. Don't you have anything to do with marriage.

PHYLLIS. But what am I to do?

LYDIA. Do without it.

DOROTHY. As we do. Listen to us.

(Trio sings).

DOROTHY.
   Be wise in time,
   Oh Phyllis mine,
   Have a care maiden fair,
   Pray beware
   Men that combine such traits divine
   Ever dare, never spare, never care!
   Would you your liberty resign
   To gain a golden ring,
   'Twere best in spinsterhood to shine
   Than do so rash a thing.

DOROTHY and LYDIA *(Chorus)*	PHYLLIS *(Chorus)*
Be wise in time	Come there's a time
Oh Phyllis mine,	Oh mistress mine,
Have a care maiden fair	Mistress fair
Pray beware	Pray be ware
Men that combine	When maids unkind
Such traits divine	Are left behind,
Ever dare, never share, never care.	Nor are there men to share.

Illustration 26. Florence Dysart as Lydia and Marion Hood as Dorothy, in *Dorothy*, act 1, cabinet photograph, 1886. W. & D. Downey (photographers). Bequeathed by Guy Little, courtesy of the Victoria and Albert Museum.

DOROTHY.

    All men deny,

    All men defy,

    Warily, charily, airily.

    Renounce the tie,

    And single die.

    Let all three

    Swear to be ever free.

    Take good advice and pray behave,

    As prudent maidens ought,

    Recall the plight you rashly gave,

    No man is worth a thought.

(Repeat trio chorus).

DOROTHY *(speaks)*. Well there, Phyllis, you have my opinion, and if you don't follow it, you will get no pity from me.

LYDIA. Nor from me. What do you think of our dresses?

PHYLLIS. They are beautiful!

DOROTHY. Do you think anyone will notice us?

PHYLLIS. Oh, dear me, Miss! Nobody would possibly guess that you were ladies.

DOROTHY and LYDIA *(disappointed)*. Oh!

DOROTHY. But, Lydia, you don't want anyone to guess who you are.

LYDIA. I am not so sure of that.

DOROTHY. Did we not agree that we would throw off our hoops and our furbelows[52] for one day, and join in the village feast as if we had done nothing all our lives but milk cows and clean our cottage floors?

LYDIA. But they will know us for all our disguise.

DOROTHY. Without our powder? Don't flatter yourself, my dear. Who will ever guess that I, Dorothy Bantam, the Squire's daughter, and Lydia Hawthorne, his niece, are masquerading amongst the yokels of the village? Come, Lydia, pocket your pride, put on your best smile, and I promise you, before the day is an hour older, that some rustic swain shall be at your feet.

LYDIA. A ploughman, perhaps.

DOROTHY. What of that? A ploughman is better than no man.

PHYLLIS *(to Dorothy)*. And what am I to say, Miss, if any questions are asked?

DOROTHY. Say what you please—stay! We must agree in our story. Say that we are your sisters.

PHYLLIS. But what will father say to that?

DOROTHY. Let him be in the secret. He will find some tale to justify the sudden increase to his family.

PHYLLIS. I will make him understand, and now I must run away and help Dorcas with her pots *(exit)*.

DOROTHY. Poor girl! She will know more about it someday.

LYDIA. When it is too late. I pity her!

DOROTHY. This is the fifth marriage that has taken place during the month.

LYDIA. If we don't take care we shall be the only spinsters left in the village.

DOROTHY. But we shall never swerve from our determination to remain single.

LYDIA. Never!

---

52   Stiffened petticoats, pleated, frilled, flounced, or otherwise ornate.

DOROTHY. Let us once more swear to—

LYDIA. Yes, let us swear.

WILDER and SHERWOOD (*without*[53] *R., shouting*). Holloa there! House—landlord! Some of yet—

DOROTHY. Why, who are these?

LYDIA. Men, my dear, human creatures. They are coming this way.

DOROTHY. Gentlemen—and good looking too!

LYDIA (*going*). They will take us for serving maids. We had best be going.

DOROTHY (*stopping her*). What! Would you fly at the first sign of the enemy? Oh, lud![54] Here they come! (*Going back*).

(*Enter Wilder and Sherwood R.*).

WILDER. Pretty maidens—Stay one moment. Turn and give your assistance to two honest fellows in distress. Our horses are lame. We have lost our way.

SHERWOOD. And we would know—(*aside*) what a sweet girl!

WILDER. Where we can stay tonight? (*Aside*) She is surprisingly handsome.

DOROTHY (*going*). Really Gentlemen—if you will inquire in the house they will help you—

WILDER (*detaining them*). Nay—why such haste?

SHERWOOD. What! Do you run away from your customers?

DOROTHY (*aside to Lydia*). We must act up to our parts, cousin. Put your manners in your pocket.

(*Quartet sings*).

WILDER.
    We're sorry to delay you.
SHERWOOD.
    To pardon us we pray you.
WILDER.
    Aching limbs and weary feet,
    Palates parched with dust and heat;
    With fatigue we're fit to sink,
    Bring us anything to drink.
WILDER and SHERWOOD.
    Have you beer, or ale, or porter,
    To make our anguish shorter?
    Such a thirst,
    At the worst,
    We could almost quench with water.
DOROTHY.
    Be seated, Sirs, we pray you.
LYDIA.
    We will not long delay you.
DOROTHY.
    We have drink and food for all,
    Here you have the house of call,

---

53 Offstage.
54 Lord.

   Where the food is of the best,
   Where the drink can stand all test.
DOROTHY and LYDIA.
   We have beer, and ale, and porter,
   To make your anguish shorter.
   Such a thirst,
   At the worst,
   We can cure without cold water.

(Dorothy and Lydia going).

WILDER *(speaks)*. Don't go yet *(arm round Dorothy)*.
SHERWOOD. You must not stir *(arm round Lydia)*.
DOROTHY. But if you do not let us go, how shall you quench your thirst?
WILDER. I had forgotten that I had a thirst.
SHERWOOD. And I that I had anything but a heart.
WILDER. They have the perfect mien of fine ladies at St. James's.[55]
SHERWOOD. I am surprised—such dialect too! Don't let her go, Geoffrey! *(Crosses up with Lydia)*.
WILDER. Not I.
DOROTHY *(trying to get away)*. Pray, Sir! As you are a gentleman.
WILDER. You would not leave us all alone in a strange place?
DOROTHY. Give me my hand, and let me go.
WILDER. Not till you have told me who and what you are *(up following Dorothy)*.
LYDIA *(down, followed by Sherwood)*. Nay, Sir, I beg of you!
SHERWOOD. It is impossible to see you and not to talk in raptures.
LYDIA. And yet you have only just set eyes on me.
SHERWOOD. A good reason for never having loved you before, and a better one for loving you now.
LYDIA. Your speech is involved, Sir.
SHERWOOD. Shall I make my meaning plainer to your lips? *(About to kiss her)*.
LYDIA *(escaping him, and running to Dorothy)*. Oh, Dorothy! What shall I do?
DOROTHY. What is the matter, cousin?
LYDIA. He offered to kiss me!
DOROTHY. Did he? How nice of him!
WILDER. Answer our question, and you shall be free to go where you will, provided you promise to
   return immediately.
DOROTHY. You will forget all about us, even if I tell you who we are.
WILDER and SHERWOOD. Never!
DOROTHY. Well then, I am Dorcas, and this is my cousin Abigail—
WILDER. Now we know—
DOROTHY *(aside to Lydia)*. Come along, or you will mix up the relationship so that there will be no
   disentangling the confusion. And now, gentlemen, having satisfied your curiosity we will bring you
   that which shall appease your thirst. Come, cousin!

(Exit Dorothy and Lydia).

WILDER. Stay!

---

55   An affluent residential district in eighteenth- and nineteenth-century London.

SHERWOOD. What is it?

WILDER. The relationships in this fair hamlet seem somewhat mixed.

SHERWOOD. Simple enough it seems to me.

WILDER. What! When your charmer declared herself to be her own cousin?

SHERWOOD. Do you doubt her word, Sir?

WILDER. Nay; heaven forbid!

SHERWOOD. I never beheld anything so charming.

WILDER. What a shape!

SHERWOOD. What a neck!

WILDER. What an instep!

SHERWOOD. What a foot!

WILDER. You don't mean my girl, I hope, Sir,—

SHERWOOD. Nor you mine, I trust, Sir!

WILDER. Mine is the most beautiful piece of flesh and blood—

SHERWOOD. Mine the sweetest—most angelic little rogue—

WILDER. Hang your St. James's manners and brocades, say I!

SHERWOOD. I am stark mad for dairymaids and dimity.[56] Ten thousand—thousand—

WILDER (interrupting). Pray give me leave, Sir—

(Solo ballad)

WILDER.

> With such a dainty maid none can compare,
> Ten thousand, thousand Cupids play in her hair
> A million little loves within her eyes
> Lie wanton waiting for some sweet surprise;
> Her smile can bid me feel as light as air,
> Her frown can throw me into deep despair,
> Her varied charms to me such joy impart
> That I would gladly yield to her my heart.
>
> But, if my heart has now ceased to be mine,
> However much I may thereto incline,
> I could not; if I would, give what I lack,
> Nor would I, if I could, receive it back.
> Alas! I know not how, or when, or where,
> But love, who never yet was known to spare,
> Has fled victorious from his battle-field,
> And left me weeping with no heart to yield.

WILDER (speaks). What say you, Sir, do you accept my toast?

SHERWOOD. With all my heart—for my girl.

WILDER. Of course!

SHERWOOD. And to think that we should have been wasting our time among the rouged and painted sirens of the ring,[57] while such a pair of beauties were waiting for us.

---

56 Coarse cotton fabric.

57 Women of ill-repute who attend boxing matches.

WILDER. Harry! I renounce the town and all its ways. From henceforth behold me the slave of my country goddess!

SHERWOOD. Until your rural peace be disturbed by our friend Lurcher.

WILDER. Our worthy friend, the sheriff's officer! I had forgotten all about him.

SHERWOOD. He will not have forgotten all about you after the fall you gave him as we came out of the Wells.[58]

WILDER. Ha! Ha! And we took the last of the nags and left him to pursue us on foot.

SHERWOOD. He is sure to track you here.

WILDER. And, if he does, I shall throw myself on my uncle's mercy, as was my purpose when first I started. Cry "*peccavi*,"[59] promise to be a good boy, and try my best to swallow my cousin Dorothy, though the pill will be a bitter one!

SHERWOOD. I wish you well out of your scrapes with all my heart. What is the account of the debt?

WILDER. Nay, Harry, why worry our heads about the figures on a writ when we have other figures to think of—and such figures!

SHERWOOD. There is a touch of gentility beneath those rustic ways.

WILDER. There is some mystery about them.

SHERWOOD. We shall soon know, for here comes the father.

TUPPITT (enter). Gentlemen, your humble servant!

WILDER. The landlord!

TUPPITT. At your service, Sir. Your horses have been attended to. Have you far to ride?

WILDER. As far as Squire Bantam's.

TUPPITT. Then you are close to the end of your journey, for he lives but two miles from here.

SHERWOOD (aside). I would it had been further by some miles—

TUPPITT. I will see that your nags are fed, and ready for you to proceed at once.

WILDER. Nay—there is no great hurry so that we find shelter at the Squire's tonight.

TUPPITT. You will find a goodly company there, and a hospitable welcome. Do you know his worship?

WILDER. I should know him, but it is some years since we met. I am his nephew.

TUPPITT. I am pleased to see you, Sir.

WILDER (aside). Egad![60] It is more than my uncle will be.

TUPPITT. Will you dine, Sir? We have a bean-feast[61] preparing.

SHERWOOD. The bean-feast by all means. What say you, Wilder?

WILDER. It depends on the company—you are bidden?

TUPPITT. All the village.

WILDER. Men—?

TUPPITT. And women.

WILDER. Then the bean-feast by all means!

SHERWOOD. And in the meantime we would ask for a taste of your ale.

TUPPITT. You shall have it, Sir. My daughters have just gone to draw it.

WILDER. Your daughters—!

TUPPITT. Yes Sir.

(Quintet sings).

---

58   Royal Tunbridge Wells, a town in west Kent, 33 miles (53 km) from central London.
59   I have sinned.
60   Interjection ("by god").
61   A country dinner; specifically, the annual dinner given by an employer for his workers.

TUPPITT.

    A father's pride and joy they are—
    Renowned for beauty near and far;
    I'm told they much resemble me,
    The likeness you of course can see.

WILDER and SHERWOOD.

    Of course the likeness we can see,

TUPPITT.

    Their hair exactly mine, you know.

WILDER *(aside)*.

    It must have been some time ago.

WILDER and SHERWOOD *(aside)*.

    It is a most outrageous whim,
    To think that they resemble him!

TUPPITT.

    I think I've got my story pat;
    I wonder what they're laughing at.

WILDER and SHERWOOD.

    Upon my word, it's hardly fair
    The Beast with Beauty to compare.

(Enter Dorothy and Lydia).

WILDER.

    Ah! Here's the liquor come my lass,
    Fill to the brim a foaming glass.

(Dorothy and Lydia fill glasses).

DOROTHY *(aside)*.

    What sense is o'er my spirit stealing,
    Half joy, half pain to me revealing?
    Why was I scorning
    Only this morning
    Maidens who suffered from any such feeling?
    Nay, let me rather steel my heart
    Against the point of Cupid's dart;
    Pride shall assist me,
    None shall resist me,
    I'll arm myself in every part.

WILDER *(at table)*.

    Come fill up your glass to the brim
    With a bumper[62] of foaming October,[63]
    And drink to the honour of him
    Who never was sulky or sober.

---

62   Full glass.

63   Strong ale brewed in October.

SHERWOOD.

> Here's a glass to the lady who bores me,
> And one to the girl whom I bore—

WILDER.

> A bumper to her who adores me,
> And another to her I adore.

TUPPITT *(speaks)*. Come, come, lasses—Bustle about! The tables have to be laid *(exit into house)*.

WILDER *(to Dorothy)*. One word—

DOROTHY. Nay, Sir, not one.

WILDER. Then let it be two or more.

DOROTHY. I must not listen to you.

WILDER. If your duty forbids let your inclination yield.

DOROTHY. And what if my inclination lies in the same direction as my duty?

WILDER. Then you should have said, I will not listen to you.

DOROTHY. It is easy to say that now.

WILDER. Yes; if you have the will. But you have not; I can read it in your face.

DOROTHY. And who are you, Sir, that read so readily in the pages which you first studied half an hour ago?

WILDER. I should have presented myself before. I am Geoffrey Wilder.

DOROTHY. Geoffrey Wilder!

WILDER. Your most obedient servant and slave, nephew to Squire Bantam of Chanticleer Hall, in this very neighbourhood, who lays himself, which is all he has, at your feet, and implores—

DOROTHY *(interrupting)*. Stay, Sir, has not the Squire a daughter called Dorothy?

WILDER. I understand that there is something of that kind about his premises.

DOROTHY. And you are the Mr. Wilder who is destined for the Squire's daughter. At least, so my father tells me.

WILDER. What! I marry Dorothy Bantam? A stuck-up, pert, conceited little minx!

DOROTHY *(aside)*. Oh!

WILDER. Who gives herself the airs of a beauty because, forsooth, she once managed to get up to town and squeeze herself into decent company.

DOROTHY *(aside)*. He shall suffer for this. *(Aloud)* But you have never seen the lady, Sir—at least, so my father says.

WILDER. No, thank Heaven! I was absent from town when she arrived. But I have heard of her—

DOROTHY. Heard what of her?

WILDER. Nay, child, do not let us discuss her further. It is you and you alone I love! *(kisses her hand)*.

DOROTHY. But you are bound to the Squire's house, and tonight you will see your cousin Dorothy, and you will swear that you love *her*, and you will kiss *her* hand.

WILDER *(kissing her hand)*. Never! I swear it! Not if she begs for it on her knees.

DOROTHY. She is not likely to do that.

WILDER *(turning from her)*. One never knows what these little country girls are likely to do.

DOROTHY *(aside)*. Oh! Wait till we meet this evening! *(Exit rapidly into house L.). (Enter Sherwood from house)*.

WILDER *(turning back)*. And so, my darling—you—*(seeing Sherwood)* Hulloa! How did you get there?

SHERWOOD. Tell me, is there a very red mark on my cheek?

WILDER. Yes, rather. Where did you get it?

SHERWOOD. She is as powerful as she is beautiful.

WILDER. Oh fie! Well, Harry, I have made up my mind to marry Dorcas.

SHERWOOD. To marry her? But how about your cousin Dorothy, and your plan to propitiate your uncle by accepting her hand, and having your debts paid?

WILDER. I will have none of my cousin Dorothy and her fine airs!—Give me dimity and sweet simplicity—

SHERWOOD. And the money—

WILDER. Money! What is money, compared to true love?

SHERWOOD. Have you ever tried that sentiment on your creditors?

WILDER. Not yet.

SHERWOOD. Then now's your chance—for, if I mistake not, here is our friend Lurcher close on your heels.

WILDER. What! The Bailiff?[64] I thought we had given him the slip!

SHERWOOD. He must have followed us—

WILDER. What is to be done?

(Song)

LURCHER *(enter).*
I am the Sheriff's faithful man,
The King's own writ I hold,
Sir! I pray you, pay up if you can,
If I may be so bold, Sir.

The debt amounts to twenty pound
The costs to fifty more, Sir—
The sum now owing will he found
To come to eighty-four, Sir!

The bill of costs be pleased to scan;
It surely is not much, Sir,
To levy from a gentleman,
For treating him as such, Sir.

So will you pay the debt you owe
Or else, I am afraid, Sir,
That into prison you must go,
And stop until it's paid, Sir.

WILDER *(interjected).* Costs—fifty pounds. Fifty and twenty make eighty-four!

SHERWOOD *(interjected).* Preposterous!

LURCHER *(sings).*
Attorneys' bills do not decrease
In size by contemplation,
And arguing does not release
A debtor's obligation.
You surely would not let me see

---

64   An officer of justice under a sheriff, who executes writs and arrests.

Illustration 27. Arthur Williams as Lurcher, in *Dorothy*, act 1, cabinet photograph, 1886.
Walery Limited (photographer). Bequeathed by Guy Little, courtesy of the Victoria and Albert Museum.

A man in your position,
Object to pay a little fee
Or cavil at addition;
A six and eightpence less or more,
You really must not grudge, Sir,
And two and two make more than four
When ordered by a judge, Sir!

TRIO (chorus as before).

So will you pay, etc.

LURCHER (speaks). And since the costs in the writ have been incurred, there is a matter of personal damage to settle. Look at my hat, gentlemen! Then there is a charge for delay, discomforture, loss of temper, loss of time—

SHERWOOD. How loss of time?

LURCHER. Not a nag to be had at the last stage—my own worn down to knacker's meat,[65]—I have had to tramp through the mire six weary miles in discharge of my duty to the Court.

WILDER. I have no doubt the Court will requite thee.

LURCHER. Will the Court give me a new hat?

WILDER. Let me but give thee the slip once more, and my eternal gratitude—

LURCHER. Will eternal gratitude mend my breeches? And now, Sir, are you going to pay?

WILDER. It is a most preposterous thing to ask a man to pay when he has not got the money.

SHERWOOD. You will have to give in to your uncle's wishes and marry your cousin after all.

WILDER. What! Give up Dorcas and dimity? Never! Stay—I have an idea. What if I can get the money?

LURCHER. How?

WILDER. From my uncle.

LURCHER. Your uncle? There isn't one in the neighbourhood!

WILDER. I mean Squire Bantam, who inhabits the great house in the neighbourhood. He shall lend me the money, and not know that he lends it to me—I'll extort it from him by stratagem.

LURCHER. But how?

WILDER. You know the Squire. He is excessively fond of quality, and piquet,[66] and prides himself upon being the most hospitable man in the country.

LURCHER. What then, Sir?

WILDER. Why then, I will be a man of quality—I'll clap a blue ribbon across my shoulder,[67] and a patch upon my face[68]—and, if you will both assist me, we will wait upon the Squire tonight, and be received with as much joy and ceremony as if we were really what we appeared.

SHERWOOD. And his Grace will play the Squire at piquet after supper and bite him[69]—

WILDER. No, no—the Squire never plays—I have a more honourable design than that, I assure you.

SHERWOOD. What is it? Out with it, Geoffrey.

WILDER. Why, when the family are fast asleep, we will clap on our masks—

---

65 Suitable only for dog food; a knacker is someone who buys and slaughters worn-out horses.

66 Spelled "piques" in original. Two speeches later, Sherwood refers to "piquet." Probably both should be "piquet" (or piquette), a two-handed card game.

67 Order of Bath.

68 A black leather patch, originally used to fill a pockmark but latterly a fashion accessory used by the wealthy over white make-up.

69 Ask for a loan.

SHERWOOD. And rob the house!

LURCHER. Rob the house! What? Do you think I will be hanged for your projects?

WILDER. There shall be no robbery. We will bind him first, and ourselves afterwards, and yet not rob the house of a shilling.

LURCHER. Nay, Sir—I will not be fooled like this. I have business in the neighbourhood which will take me some five minutes and when I return to town it must be with your money or yourself *(going)*.

WILDER. But my good friend—

SHERWOOD. My worthy Lurcher!

LURCHER. It is impossible, Gentlemen—*(exits)*.

SHERWOOD. What is to be done now?

WILDER. I must carry out my design without him.

SHERWOOD. And what is it, Dick?

WILDER. Don't enquire further. Trust me with the conduct of this affair, and if I can but convince that surly bailiff, I'll venture my life I shall succeed—

SHERWOOD. I'll ask no more questions. I am ready to follow where you lead. Here come our charmers once more.

(Exit Wilder and Sherwood. Enter Dorothy and Lydia with tablecloths, etc.).

DOROTHY *(to Lydia)*. Now, cousin, if you will follow my lead, I will show you what a base and faithless thing is a man.

LYDIA. But how?

DOROTHY. Have you the ring I gave you?

LYDIA. What with the green stone? I never part with it *(showing it)*.

DOROTHY. Nor I with that you gave me with the red stone, but we shall have to part with them today.

LYDIA. What! Give them away?

DOROTHY. Nay! Only loan them for a time. We shall recover them tonight.

LYDIA. What do you mean?

DOROTHY. Follow my lead, I say. Do as I do, and you shall see *(beginning to lay tablecloth)*.

WILDER *(to Dorothy)*. Will you not let me help you? *(Busy with tablecloth)*.

SHERWOOD *(to Lydia)*. Let me show you the way.

DOROTHY *(to Wilder)*. Nay, no more love I entreat you.

LYDIA *(to Sherwood)*. I know by your looks what you mean.

SHERWOOD. Have you no pity?

(Lydia and Sherwood go up).

WILDER. Nay, child, it is you and you alone that I love. In you I see the most perfect charm!

DOROTHY. But can you love me for your life? A poor country girl without a position—

WILDER. I would marry thee though I worked with my own hands.

SHERWOOD *(coming down with Lydia)*. I will not—cannot live without you!

LYDIA *(aside)*. Oh, man!—for flattery and deceit renowned.

WILDER *(to Dorothy)*. Let me speak to your father.

DOROTHY. Not today. But meet me here tomorrow at the same hour. Take this ring *(gives ring)* and shew it to me tomorrow as a token of your promises.

LYDIA *(to Sherwood)*. Meet me here tomorrow at the same hour, and when you shew me this ring you shall have my answer.

WILDER. I swear that it shall never leave my fingers. *(He puts on ring)*.

SHERWOOD. I will never part with it *(putting on ring).*

(Quartet)

DOROTHY and LYDIA.
> Now swear to be good and true—
> To the maid whom you say you adore,
> And promise to love her as few
> Have ever loved woman before.

WILDER and SHERWOOD.
> I swear to be good and true
> To the maid whom I fondly adore—
> We promise to love you as few
> Have ever loved woman before.
> I never was in love before,
> 'Tis only you that I adore.
> We will devote our lives to you
> And swear to be for ever true.

DOROTHY and LYDIA *(aside).*
> We don't believe a word they say,
> They swear the same thing every day.
> Oh! never—never—never—
> Were such gay deceivers!
> We will defy
> The men who try
> To make us weak believers.
> And yet 'tis sweet
> When, at your feet,
> A lover kneels a-sighing,
> And says it's true
> He loves but you,
> Or swears that he is dying.

(Exit Dorothy and Lydia. Enter Lurcher with his hat smashed—his clothes torn, followed by an indignant crowd who menace him. He gets behind Wilder).

CHORUS.
> Under the pump! Under the pump!
> And into the brook with a kick and a jump.
> He's frightened old Margery out of her wits,
> A-sneaking about, and a-serving out writs!

LURCHER.
> They've battered my hat, and they've ruined my clothes,
> They've pulled out my hair, they have pummelled my nose
> Each bone in my body has suffered a wrench,
> And look at the writs of the Court of King's Bench.[70]

---

70   Formerly, the supreme common law court in London.

Look at the writs
Torn into bits *(shows writs torn)*.
CHORUS.
Under the pump etc. *(as before)*.
We'll teach him his betters to grind and oppress
By serving upon them a writ of distress.
He's frightened and bullied a helpless old wench,
And we don't care a rap for the Court of King's Bench.
LURCHER *(speaks to Wilder)*. Save me, Sir, for mercy's sake!
WILDER. One good turn deserves another. If I do will you follow me tonight?
LURCHER. Indeed I will, Sir—anything you please!
WILDER. My lads—this gentleman is a particular friend of mine, and anyone who touches him will have to deal with me.

(Crowd murmurs).

Nay, here comes the dinner. This is no time for quarrelling.

(Enter Dorothy, Lydia and Phyllis with dishes etc., which the women arrange. Song).

DOROTHY and LYDIA.
Now take your seats at tables spread
With best of British beef and bread,
Potatoes—cabbages all hot,
And bacon steaming from the pot.
SHERWOOD.
Who can refuse?
WILDER.
Not I for one,
The rest already have begun.
DOROTHY.
Be pleased, kind Sir, to take a seat,
LYDIA.
And tell us what you wish to eat,
SHERWOOD.
The sight of you is more than quite
Enough to stay my appetite.
WILDER *(seizing Dorothy's hand)*.
There is no lady in the land
With such a dainty little hand.
DOROTHY.
Release my hand, for that at least
Is not included in the feast.

(He tries to kiss her hand, she slaps his face).

CHORUS.
Ha! Ha! Ha! That's right my lass,
And now, my lads, another glass.

(Finale song)

WILDER *(aside to Sherwood).*
　How perfect every feature,
SHERWOOD *(the same).*
　A most delicious creature.
WILDER *(the same).*
　My heart I must resign
　To such a queen divine.
TUPPITT *(to Tom).*
　Tomorrow let it be,
TOM *(to villagers).*
　And all we hope to see
CHORUS.
　That's right! That's right!
　And we will dance all night.
DOROTHY *(to Phyllis).*
　And are you not afraid,
　You most imprudent maid,
　To trust a life's long span
　To any living man?
　You'll find when it's too late
　You've brought about a fate
　You don't anticipate,
　Be wise then while you can.
MEN.
　With indignation great,
　We must repudiate
　The notion that such fate
　Awaits her with a man.
CHORUS.
　Ah! why should you upbraid,
　And why should any maid
　Of wedlock be afraid
　With such a charming man?
　With such a pretty mate,
　We all congratulate
　The bridegroom on his fate,
　He is a happy man.
TOM.
　My love for her is great,
　And she at any rate
　Shall guide my future fate;
　I am a happy man.
PHYLLIS and TOM.
　Ah! why should you upbraid?

And why should any maid
Of wedlock be afraid
With such a charming man?
My love for him is great,
And he at any rate
Shall guide my future fate,
Not any other man.

WILDER.

Tomorrow, Sherwood, then we meet
To make our joy complete.

DOROTHY.

Such infamous deceit

LYDIA.

Due punishment shall meet.

ALL.

Farewell!

Act II

Chanticleer Hall, the interior of Squire Bantam's house; the hall with staircase leading R. and L. to a gallery [second floor] on which the bedrooms are supposed to be situated. In the centre at back is a large door leading into the outer hall. Large old-fashioned mullioned[71] windows. Fireplace. Tables in corners of hall. Some of the guests are seated at tables, some dancing. The Act opens with a country dance, which is danced by the Squire with one of his guests. At end of dance.

BANTAM *(to his guest)*. Madam—I am your most obedient—will you take any refreshment after your exertions?

(Lady declines with a bow).

You will not perhaps object to my putting my lips to the parson's brew[72]—surely—to test it—ha! ha!

(They go up—a servant enters, speaks to Bantam).

What say you? A gentleman to speak with me? Bid him join us—

(Exit servant, and re-enters with Lurcher, who is dressed in the fashion).

Sir—I am proud to know you—

LURCHER. My name, Sir, is Blazes—Secretary to His Grace the Duke of Berkshire.

BANTAM. Sir, I am prouder to know you—

---

71   Divided into smaller panes.

72   A well-hopped and well-aged beer. See *Memoirs of the Society of Grub Street* 2:96 (1737): 162.
     True British doctrine, strong, and proud, and clear,
     Well brew'd, well hopp'd, well ag'd, like Parson's Beer,
     Diffuses health and strength through every part,
     Informs the head and fortifies the heart. (lines 116-20)

LURCHER. His Grace is on his way to the South Coast for the benefit of his health, but on the road his carriage has broken down.

BANTAM. In this neighbourhood?

LURCHER. At your very gates—

BANTAM. Lord—Lord! That any ruts of mine should so behave to his Grace!

LURCHER. And now he craves for us your hospitality for a night, until his carriage be repaired.

BANTAM. Craves it! Why he should command it—And where is he?

LURCHER. He is without—

BANTAM. Without! And here am I standing in my own hall, with a duke knocking at my front door. Nobody of any degree or quality passes by my house. Nobody entertains like me—there is a kind of grace, an art, a manner in these things which naturally slips from me. But I forget myself, and must hasten to greet my noble guest—

(*Goes up to meet Wilder who appears disguised, with Sherwood—they come down together*).

Ah! Here he comes! Sir, I am your Grace's most obedient—humble servant.

WILDER. Mr. Bantam—I am your most faithful and obedient servant, I am glad of the accident which makes me your guest. I could by no means have excused myself if I had passed by and not paid my respects. (*Presenting Sherwood*) My personal friend. (*Presenting Lurcher*) My Secretary—a faithful soul.

BANTAM (*bowing*). Gentlemen! I am proud to welcome you to my house, though 'tis but a doghole,[73] may it please your Grace, a mere doghole. I have a clean bed or so—a bottle or two of good wine (*bowing*). But your Grace's goodness—

LURCHER. His Grace's goodness Ha! ha! ha!

BANTAM. What!

SHERWOOD (*aside to Lurcher*). Silence, fool!

WILDER (*explaining to Bantam*). My secretary is of a somewhat hilarious turn of mind. I love to be surrounded by mirth (*aside*) and beauty (*looking round—aside*). Where can they be?

SHERWOOD (*aside to Wilder*). Do you spy your cousin, Geoffrey?

WILDER. Not I! But patience, she will be here in good time. Remember, I am not to be plagued with her. She is yours.

SHERWOOD. I accept the gift.

BANTAM (*whom Lurcher has lured toward the punch-bowl, and taken a bottle*). Nay, Sir, it is the raw material.

LURCHER. So much the better. It warms the inside. (*To old lady*) Your health, Ma'am—(*about to drink*).

WILDER. No, Mr. Lurcher!

LURCHER. Sir—I mean your Grace—

WILDER. Put it down!

LURCHER. That is what I was about to do.

WILDER. Put the bottle down, I say.

(*Lurcher puts bottle back*).

(*To Bantam*) A good soul, but rough in his ways.

BANTAM. But serves you well, I doubt not, your Grace.

WILDER. Serves me excellently well (*aside*) with writs. (*To Bantam*) You have a charming house, Squire.

BANTAM. Your Grace is pleased to admire my humble abode.

---

73   A vile or modest dwelling.

WILDER (*looking round, sees strong chest*). And a cozy little strong box for the guineas. Eh! Squire?

BANTAM. A paltry few, but, such as they are, entirely at your Grace's commands.

WILDER (*aside*). Egad! My dear uncle I have a good mind to take you at your word.

BANTAM. Your Grace's condescension in observing these trifles quite overwhelms me.

WILDER (*about to sing*). Though—

BANTAM. I am positively overpowered—

WILDER. My good Sir, you do not observe that I am about to make a remark.

BANTAM. I humbly crave your Grace's pardon.

WILDER (*sings*).

Though born a man of high degree,
And greatly your superior,
I trust I know that courtesy
Is due to an inferior.
So, conscious that a ducal bow
Will liquidate the debt I owe,
I bend my back and bow my head,
And thus accept your board and bed.

CHORUS.

He bends his back and bows his head,
And thus accepts your board and bed.

WILDER.

Exalted rank should condescend,
On festival occasion,
And even dukes must learn to bend
Before a host's persuasion;
So, being graciously inclined
To take whatever I can find,
I bend my back, and bow my head,
And thus accept your board and bed.

CHORUS.

He bends his back etc.

BANTAM (*speaks*). If I may be permitted to say so—the grace, the ease, the facility, the excellence, the

(*Lurcher falls against him*).

Good Lud![74] (*Falls into Wilder's arms*) I humbly crave your Grace's pardon!

WILDER. 'Tis granted. (*Aside to Lurcher*) Be careful, knave, or I will have you turned out of the house.

LURCHER. I budge not without your worship.[75]

WILDER (*aside to Sherwood*). Look to him, Harry, or his follies will mar our plot.

BANTAM. Will your Grace be pleased to sup—

WILDER. We have already supped on the road.

BANTAM. A glass of old hock,[76] with a little dash of palm.[77]

---

74   Lord.
75   Term of respect for a person of high degree.
76   German white wine.
77   A palm-toddy (alcoholic drink sweetened with palm sugar).

WILDER. By no means.

BANTAM. Or a Seville orange squeezed into a glass of old Canary?[78]

WILDER. Not one drop.

BANTAM. Well, well, what news? What news in London? I have a nephew there—I have not seen the profligate there these ten years.

(Servant comes up with a glass of punch on a waiter).[79]

Your Grace must taste one glass of our own especial brew—come, come—

(Wilder accepts).

This nephew of mine has been a very wild lad.

WILDER. I am sorry for this.

BANTAM. He disobeys me, and yet he is my kin.

WILDER. And spends your money: eh! Mr. Bantam?

BANTAM. Nay, none of that, your Grace—He shall not have a groat[80] of mine while I live, but when I die he must.

WILDER *(aside)*. I must have a small matter while you live, dear uncle.

BANTAM. What's your Grace's pleasure? My ears did not rightly lay hold of your last words.

WILDER. I say you should allow him a small matter while you live.

BANTAM. No, no—not while he squanders it as he does, and refuses to settle down and marry his cousin Dorothy.

WILDER. Ah! he has a cousin?

BANTAM. My daughter—your Grace!

WILDER. Like her father no doubt, and surpassingly beautiful.

BANTAM *(bowing)*. Your Grace is pleased to flatter.

WILDER *(to Sherwood)*. Now Harry, I will have none of my cousin Dorothy—I resign her to you.

SHERWOOD. Egad! I am content.

(Enter Dorothy and Lydia).

BANTAM. Here comes my daughter and her cousin.

WILDER *(aside to Sherwood. Speaks)*.

Ye powers! What beauty! What enchanting grace.

SHERWOOD *(aside to Wilder)*.

In such a spot as this quite out of place.

LYDIA *(to Wilder)*.

Your Grace is welcome—

WILDER *(to Lydia)*.

Ma'am I kiss your hand.

SHERWOOD *(to Dorothy)*.

I am your most obedient to command.

DOROTHY *(aside to Lydia)*.

That hand, that figure, I have seen before.

---

78 A light sweet wine from the Canary Islands. Wines were often flavoured to make grog.

79 Salver.

80 An obsolete coin of little value.

LYDIA *(aside to Dorothy).*
  It cannot be!
DOROTHY *(aside to Lydia).*
  I have, and I am sure I recognize the ways.
LYDIA *(aside to Dorothy).*
  It must be so.
DOROTHY *(aside to Lydia).*
  They were our faithful swains not long ago,
LYDIA *(aside to Dorothy).*
  How could they think so shallow a disguise,
  Could serve to hide them from a woman's eyes.
WILDER *(to Bantam).*
  My dear Sir John, I trust my presence here,
  Will never be allowed to interfere
  With any entertainment.
BANTAM.
  Please your Grace—
WILDER *(to Sherwood, ignoring Bantam).*
  What teeth!
SHERWOOD *(the same to Wilder).*
  What lips!
WILDER *(to Sherwood).*
  What eyes!
SHERWOOD *(to Wilder).*
  A perfect face!
WILDER *(to Bantam, who has been waiting).*
  Your pardon. What were you about to say?
BANTAM.
  That if your Grace would join us in the dance,
WILDER.
  My limbs have long since lost their power to prance
  But I could hobble through some stately measure
  (to Lydia) If this fair lady lends her hand.
LYDIA.
  With pleasure!

(Bantam gives orders to the musicians—introduces Lurcher to partner. The guests pair off as partners. Sherwood offers Dorothy his hand. Wilder dances with Lydia, and Bantam selects a partner. Song).

DOROTHY.
  What gracious affability! What condescension!
  Of noble birth how great a proof,
  When scions of nobility with kind intentions
  Honour with their presence a provincial roof.

  With faltering felicity we tread the measure,
  Each maiden blushing with surprise,

Deploring her rusticity, accepts with pleasure
Compliments that fall on her from ducal skies.

Oh! how sweet
Eyes to meet
Beaming admiration!
Eyes that fire
Or admire,
Wrapped in contemplation,

With faltering felicity we tread the measure,
Each maiden blushing with surprise
At the simplicity,
The affability,
The true nobility
That meets her eyes.

LURCHER *(dancing with much action).*
Up and down, and round and round,
With dainty feet that scorn the ground,
Weaving figures in and out
See us whirling round about.

CHORUS *(advancing).*
Gaily tread the dainty measure,
Dancing in the path of pleasure,
Hand in hand,
A merry band,
Tripping feet, despising leisure!

WILDER *(speaks).* No more dimity for me, say I—
SHERWOOD. Hang your beauty unadorned—
WILDER. Now like you my cousin Dorothy?
SHERWOOD. Exquisite! Enchanting!
WILDER. I am glad of it. I give her up to you, Harry—Be happy. As for me I am all for Lydia—
BANTAM *(offering glass).* Your Grace must try the parson's brew—Nay, I will not be denied.
WILDER. Well then, just a sip *(takes glass).*
SHERWOOD. Do you leave the toast to your guests, Sir John?
BANTAM. Nay, Sir, by your leave I will give you one.
ALL. Yes, yes—The Squire's toast.

(Bantam. With a glass in his hand. Guests drinking—on one side Dorothy and Sherwood seated. On the other, Lydia and Wilder—flirtation. Song).

BANTAM.
Contentment I give you, and all that it brings
To the man who is fully decided
To take what he has, and be thankful that things
Are such as his lot has provided.
Some strive for high rank, for preferment, for place,

Ever ready to sell or to barter
Traditions of family, fealty, or race,
For a ribbon, a star, or a garter.
BANTAM and CHORUS.
But here's to the man who is pleased with his lot,
Who never sits sighing for what he has not,
Contented and thankful for what he has got,
With a welcome for all
To Chanticleer Hall,
BANTAM.
The old would be young, and the young would be old,
The lean only long to grow fatter;
The wealthy want health, the healthy want gold,
A change to the worse for the latter.
The single would wed, but the husband contrives
To consider his fetters a curse,
And half the world sighs for the other half's wives,
With the risk of a change for the worse.
BANTAM and CHORUS.
But here's to the man who is pleased with his lot,
Who never sits sighing for what he has not,
Contented and thankful for what he has got,
With a welcome for all
To Chanticleer Hall.

(Quartet of horns. Then, spoken).

BANTAM. Now let's to bed.
WILDER. To bed so soon?
DOROTHY. Good night.
WILDER *(to Lydia)*. We leave our hearts behind us.
LYDIA. Most polite.

(Sung)

DOROTHY and LYDIA *(to each other)*.
Alas! how soon can man forget!
Today he swore that he'd be true
To me—yes, me alone,—and yet
Tonight he sighs and dies for you!
WILDER *(to Lydia)*.
If you and I once more could meet—
SHERWOOD *(to Dorothy)*.
Our happiness would be complete!
BANTAM.
Good night, your Grace, and pleasant dreams
ALL.
Good night, your Grace, and pleasant dreams.

WILDER.
  Good night, mine host, and pleasant dreams!
BANTAM *(showing the way)*.
  This way
WILDER *(aside to Lurcher)*.
  Is all prepared?
LURCHER *(aside to Wilder)*.
  All right!
DOROTHY *(curtseys)*.
  Your Grace, good night!
WILDER *(to Sherwood)*.
  We meet again tonight.
CHORUS and PRINCIPALS.
  Pleasant dreams attend your slumber:
  Happy fancies without number,
  Guide you in the land of sleeping,
  While the fairies, vigil keeping,
  Visions bright your sleep adorning,
  Send you, till the light of morning,
  Through the latticed window breaking,
  Tells you that the day is waking
  And through the pane,
  Creeps day again!
  Good night! good night!

(Quartet)

WILDER *(to Lydia)*.
  One moment, pray!
SHERWOOD *(to Dorothy)*.
  Nay—do not run away.
DOROTHY *(to Sherwood)*.
  Meet me tomorrow.
LYDIA *(to Wilder)*.
  Meet me tomorrow.
WILDER and SHERWOOD.
  Tomorrow is today.
WILDER.
  Oh! fly not yet. 'Tis not too late
  To bid me hope or mourn my fate,
  For lovers learn from early morn
  The cruel hand of time to scorn.
  What matters what the hour may be?
  Time was not made for you and me;
  Then hear my whisper ere we part,
  The promptings of a beating heart!

LYDIA.

    And do you think the test, Sir,
    Of love so light a thing,
    That maids will leave their nest, Sir,
    Like fledglings in the spring,
    Because they've wings to fly with,
    And want to soar above?
    The man I live and die with
    Must prove to me his love.

WILDER *(to Lydia).*

    Accept, I pray, this token
    Of vows ne'er to be broken;
    Let me on your finger place this ring.

DOROTHY *(to Sherwood).*

    This ring I take as token
    Of vows made to be broken;
    Till tomorrow I will keep this ring.

(Dorothy and Lydia cross to R. door and exit, Sherwood opening the door for her and bowing her off. Same business L. between Lydia and Wilder. Wilder exits. Sherwood, alone on stage, sings facing Dorothy's door, the forelight from the large open grate shining on him. If necessary raise footlights a little but put them down again after the following song.)

SHERWOOD.

    I stand at your threshold sighing,
    As cruel hours creep by,
    And the time is slowly dying
    That once too quick did fly.
    Your beauty o'er my being,
    Has shed a subtle spell
    And alas there is no fleeing
    From the charms that you wield so well.

    For my heart is wildly beating,
    As it never beat before
    One word! one whispered greeting
    In mercy I implore.

(Comes downstage for remainder of song).

    For from daylight a hint we might borrow
    And prudence might come with the light
    Then why should we wait till tomorrow
    You are queen of my heart tonight.

    Oh! tell me why, if you intended
    Thus to treat my love with scorn
    Such rents as will never be mended,
    In this poor heart you've torn.

Why, why did your beauty enslave me,
And give me such exquisite pain
Oh say but the word that would save me
And bid me hope again.

For my heart is wildly beating *(repeat, as before).*

WILDER *(enter, speaks).* There go the rings.

SHERWOOD. How shall we answer to dimity tomorrow, for the loss of their love tokens?

WILDER. Tomorrow, Harry, is tomorrow, and will have to answer for itself. But now to business. You understand my plan?

SHERWOOD. Perfectly!

WILDER. Has Lurcher the cloaks and vizards?[81]

SHERWOOD. He brought them with him.

WILDER. Where is the lazy scoundrel? Asleep, I'll wager!

SHERWOOD. I bid him wait in the hall until we called. *(Looks out of door at back)* Ah; there he is! Wake up man!

LURCHER *(half asleep, as if arresting Sherwood).* Very sorry Sir. *(Mumbles)* Dooty is sooty, and I must— *(hand on shoulder).*

WILDER. He has not quite recovered from the parson's brew. Where are our disguises?

LURCHER. Oh, Sir! For Heaven's sake—think better of it! We might be all hung for this job!

WILDER. But, I tell you man, there is to be no robbery.

LURCHER. But assault and battery—and misdemeanour and forgery by strangulation—I know the law, Sir.

WILDER. Come, come, a little courage and you shall have your share, robbery or no robbery. Hand over the cloaks and masks.

LURCHER. Here they are *(producing cloaks and masks from bag—and a pistol).*

WILDER. A pistol! Is it loaded?

LURCHER. Heaven forbid, Sir! It hasn't been loaded these ten years.

WILDER. So much the better! It will be the very thing for our affair. Now let me see whether I can drum your instructions into your muddled pate. First, we shall attract the notice of my worthy uncle.

SHERWOOD. His worthy uncle! Do you understand?

LURCHER *(sleepy).* Worthy uncle.

WILDER. He is sure to think that his house is being robbed, and will be in terror for the safety of his guineas in yonder strong box.

SHERWOOD. Strong box! Do you understand?

LURCHER *(sleepy).* Strong box.

WILDER. Then you shall come in terror from my room, and declare that I have been robbed and bound.

LURCHER. And then? What then?

WILDER. Then we shall see what we shall see. Go into my room, and be ready to obey my further instructions to the letter, or to perish in the attempt.

LURCHER. Oh, Lud! To think that a respectable sheriff's officer should have to submit to commit a breach of the peace! *(Exit).*

WILDER. Now, Harry—are you ready?

SHERWOOD *(cloaked and masked).* Ready to do or die!

---

81 Masks.

(Trio song)

WILDER.

Silence pray—be careful how you tread!

SHERWOOD.

Are you sure that they are all in bed?

Let me bind you—*(business of tying).*

WILDER.

Take care; not too tight!

SHERWOOD.

Now's the time to wake our friend, the Knight!

WILDER.

Ha! ha!

SHERWOOD.

Ho! ho!

BANTAM *(appearing on stairs above).*

Who's there?

WILDER.

Hush, here he comes!

BANTAM *(half way).*

Speak! who is there?

SHERWOOD.

We've got him now!

BANTAM *(falling at last step).*

Confound the stair!

(Sherwood seizes him and binds him).

For mercy, Sir, I humbly crave—

Pray take my cash and all I have,

But spare my life!

WILDER and SHERWOOD.

We want your cash and all you have,

But not your life.

CHORUS *(entering).*

What noise was that—waking us from our slumbers

What to goodness, caused such a clatter?

Hand joined to hand—safety there is in numbers—

Let us find out—what is the matter.

BANTAM.

Help! help! I'm almost dead.

CHORUS.

Help! help! raise up his head.

WILDER.

Help! help! I'm almost dead.

CHORUS.

Lift up the Squire's head.

(Enter Dorothy and Lydia).

DOROTHY.
Oh, father! What a dreadful sight,
To see you in so sad a plight.
CHORUS.
Oh, what a sight!
DOROTHY.
And see, most shocking to relate
LYDIA.
His Grace has met the self-same fate.
BANTAM and CHORUS.
Too shocking quite!
Oh, what a sight!
CHORUS.
Daring a duke to plunder
What's coming next, we wonder?
BANTAM.
My money's safe!
CHORUS.
How very strange!
BANTAM.
There's not a penny missing.
WILDER.
Ah!
BANTAM.
Not one!

(Enter Lurcher from Wilder's room, with cash box broken open and empty).

WILDER.
Speak! What is it?
LURCHER.
Your Grace, I fear—
CHORUS.
Ah!
LURCHER.
Has been robbed!
CHORUS.
Oh!
SHERWOOD.
They've got the swag.
LURCHER.
Yes! Taken every mag.[82]

---

82   Obsolete slang, a copper half-penny.

SHERWOOD.

  See; not one shilling left.

WILDER.

  Of everything bereft!

BANTAM.

  The sum must be repaid at any cost.

CHORUS and BANTAM.

  Pray mention what amount your Grace has lost?

LURCHER.

  The sum amounts to eighty pounds

  Perhaps a little more, Sir;

  And as a host, I think you're bound,

  The money to restore, Sir.

CHORUS.

  Pray take the guineas. He feels bound

  The money to restore, Sir.

WILDER *(after hesitation)*.

  Well, then, I take the money as a loan *(hands bag to Lurcher)*.

LURCHER and SHERWOOD.

  I'm much afraid

  It won't be paid.

WILDER, LURCHER, and SHERWOOD.

  Of course your loan will be repaid.

CHORUS.

  His Grace, we own,

  Accepts the loan

  With such a tone

  That one would feel inclined to think the gold was all his own.

SHERWOOD.

  And when his Grace returns this way

  The money he is sure to pay.

(First chime)

CHORUS.

  Hark! I hear the quarter chime.

(Second chime)

  Off to bed, it is now time;

  What on earth can be the time?

(Third chime)

  There it is, the half-hour sure!

  Midnight not long past be sure.

(Fourth chime)

  Yes—why, the clock is striking four!

BANTAM.
  Once more to slumber.
CHORUS.
  We must all to bed again
  Till the sun shines through the pane,
  And the bright
  Morning light,
  Brings us back the day again.

(The lady guests retire to the chambers—groping up the staircase, L.).

BANTAM *(offering candle, speaks).* Will your Grace resume your broken rest? Or will you be pleased to start the early morning with a fresh brew?
WILDER. No more of the brew, Squire. The day is breaking.

(Horn heard without).

  And as I live, your men are on foot with the hounds!

(Door at back opens, and huntsmen appear, horn repeated).

BANTAM. 'Tis but to blood our cups with an early cub.[83] But if your Grace will join us.
WILDER. The very thing.
BANTAM. I have a nag or two very much at your disposal.
WILDER. And a gallop across the fields shall serve to wipe out the memories of the night, eh, Squire?

(Finale song)

ALL.
  Hark forward! Hark forward! Away!
  A-hunting we'll go today,
  And the early dawn of the autumn morn
  Is ready to show the way.

  Hark forward! Hark forward! Away!
  'Tis a beautiful hunting day,
  And horse and hound
  Shall skim the ground
  To the sound of the horn so gay.

  The fox may bide
  By the cover side,
  But today we are certain to find;
  And well we know
  How the best will go,
  And the timid ones scatter behind.
  Hark forward! etc. *(repeat).*

---

83 Young fox; the whole phrase refers to marking novice hunters with the blood of their first kill.

Act III

*A forest glade in the neighbourhood of Squire Bantam's house. Through a break
in the trees the village church is seen in the distance. Far to the right stands
Chanticleer Hall, an old Elizabethan house. On the right of the stage is an ancient
oak with withered and broken branches, and on a bench, which surrounds the tree,
old women from the village are seated chatting to one another and knitting.
Enter groomsmen and bridesmaids. Ballet. When the ballet is over the dancers
retire up the stage and the old women rise and come forward, singing.*

OLD WOMEN'S CHORUS.
    Dancing is not what it used to be
    In the merry days when our tread was light,
    When our feet were nimble, and our hearts were free,
    We danced from dusk till the sun shone bright.
    Eh! eh! eh! Though feeble we be,
    Better than that we can dance you'll see.

*(Old Women dance. Enter Phyllis who is greeted by the old women and the dancers. Congratulations
pass, and signs that they have come to fetch her to church. Sings ballad).*

PHYLLIS.
    The time has come when I must yield.
    The liberty I loved so well
    To one to whom my heart revealed,
    Sighed forth the love I dared not tell.
    My love, my life, I freely give,
    Myself and all that in me is,
    Henceforth in happiness to live
    For him alone as only his.
    Ah liberty to me so dear
    I now resign without a fear.
CHORUS OF OLD WOMEN.
    Eh! eh! eh! Poor little dear!
    Wait till she comes to the end of the year.
PHYLLIS.
    They say, when wooing days are o'er,
    And there is nothing left to gain,
    That turtles coo their love no more,
    And honeymoons get on the wane;
    But I will bind him to my heart,
    With love that shall not fly too soon,
    And life shall be till death us part,
    One everlasting honeymoon.
    And liberty to me so dear
    I now resign without a fear.

CHORUS OF OLD WOMEN.
>   Eh! eh! eh! Poor little dear!
>   Wait till you come to the end of the year!

(Exeunt Phyllis, old women, and ballet down in the glade leading to the church, to the last movement of the ballet. Enter Dorothy and Lydia R., disguised as men, as the ballet and Phyllis go off C.).

DOROTHY *(speaks)*. There goes Phyllis to be married. Heigh ho! I wonder when our turn will come. Now Lydia—a little more confidence, a dash of bravado.

LYDIA. I feel so strange in this dress. I fear that someone will see us.

DOROTHY. What if they do, cousin? They will but take us for two gallants from town. Have you the pistols?

LYDIA *(who has the case under her arm)*. Here they are!

DOROTHY. Set them down.

LYDIA. Do you think that they will come?

DOROTHY. I haven't a doubt of it. I know they received our letter this morning—

LYDIA. And what shall we do then?

DOROTHY. Why then, my dear, we shall give them the choice of a duel or a marriage with the ladies whom they met last night.

LYDIA. And if they consent to marry?

DOROTHY. If they consent to marry, we will never speak to them again.

LYDIA. But, Dorothy, what if they prefer to fight?

DOROTHY. Then we shall know that they love us, for ourselves, and then, Lydia, then—

LYDIA. But the pistols?

DOROTHY. We shall take good care to load them ourselves only with powder. They will go off with a little puff. You will scream. I shall not. All will end happily, and who knows Mr. Wilder may have to marry his cousin Dorothy after all.

LYDIA. Why, Dorothy!

DOROTHY. Why Lydia! And I'll be bound to say that you will be content to pair off with his friend— Here is his letter—I must read it once more.

(Duet song)

LYDIA *(producing letter, reads)*.
>   "Madam"—so his note begins.

DOROTHY *(producing letter)*.
>   And mine begins the same—

LYDIA.
>   The letters are as like as twins.

DOROTHY.
>   Except the writer's name—

LYDIA *(reads)*.
>   "I cannot keep the pledge I gave,
>   What better reason should you have?
>   I love another. But 'tis true,
>   Last night, I really loved but you."

DOROTHY *(reads)*.

"I cannot keep the pledge I gave,
What better reason should you have?
I love another. But 'tis true,
Last night, I really loved but you."

DOROTHY and LYDIA.

Last night, I really loved but you.
If he but keep his faith with me
His conduct thus shall pardoned be.
I'll marry him—
But, if I do, I'll plague his life
And make him feel he's got a wife
To harry[84] him.

DOROTHY *(looking off L. Speaks)*. Oh, lord, here they come! Let us watch them from behind this tree and see what effect our letters have had on them.

(Drags Lydia behind the oak tree—they stand on the bench, and watch the following scene. Enter Wilder and Sherwood L. Sherwood has a case of pistols under his arm).

WILDER. This must be the spot, Harry.

SHERWOOD. And here is the tree, under which these bloodthirsty provincials would call us to account *(producing letter from pocket)*.

WILDER. One might almost treat the affair as a joke if it were not for our honour which must needs stand up to be shot at for an opinion in favour of one woman against another. Let me see. *(Producing letter from pocket—reads)* "Sir, your letter has been handed to me—"

SHERWOOD *(reading letter)*. "Your letter has been handed to me."

WILDER *(reading)*. "By Miss Lydia Hawthorne."

SHERWOOD *(reading)*. "By Miss Dorothy Bantam, and as that young lady's best friend, I insist upon an explanation or immediate satisfaction."

WILDER *(reading)*. "You will find me ready for either at the Hermits' Oak in Mile Coppice[85] at eleven of the clock this morning—your obedient humble servant to command Percy Dasher."

SHERWOOD *(reading)*. "Tilbury Slocomb." The letters are identical in all respects except the name.

WILDER. There's no doubt about it. They are in earnest. *(Looking at watch)* 'Tis close on eleven. Have you the pistols?

SHERWOOD. Here they are *(producing pistols)*.

DOROTHY *(aside)*. Good gracious! There'll be bullets in there.

WILDER. And now, Harry, if anything should happen to me.

SHERWOOD. Pshaw! Man, what are you thinking of?

WILDER. These rustic blades are dangerous fellows.

LYDIA *(aside)*. Do you hear that, Dorothy?

WILDER. They shoot straight. You will not fail to tell my dear Abigail[86] that I remained faithful to her to the last—that I preferred death to giving her up.

---

84   Harass.

85   A wooded area, cut and replanted.

86   In act 1, Wilder was attracted to Dorcas (Dorothy), so by naming Abigail (Lydia) he is further testing the women's story; Sherwood soon colludes with him by naming "my sweet Dorcas."

DOROTHY *(aside to Lydia)*. What do you say to that?

SHERWOOD. And how about the ring which she gave you, and which you so rashly handed over to Miss Lydia, last night.

WILDER. Say that you buried it with me.

LYDIA *(aside to Dorothy)*. Oh! Why I have it on my finger now.

SHERWOOD. You can depend upon me. And you will do the same by me with my sweet Dorcas.

WILDER. I will, Harry—

SHERWOOD. You will say that never for a moment was her sweet image absent from my heart.

WILDER. And the ring you gave to my little cousin, Dorothy?

SHERWOOD. Say, that it was so tightly and lovingly clasped in my death grasp that no effort could tear it away from the finger which it had never left.

DOROTHY *(aside to Lydia)*. Why I have the ring on my finger now!

(Dorothy and Lydia come down).

WILDER. You can depend upon me. If you lie in your grave I will lie for you, Harry. If I lie in my grave you will lie for me.

(Perceiving Dorothy and Lydia. They bow. Dorothy to Sherwood. Lydia to Wilder. The bow is returned by Wilder and Sherwood. Then Dorothy bows to Wilder and Lydia to Sherwood).

SHERWOOD *(aside to Wilder)*. Why surely these cannot be our opponents!

WILDER *(aside to Sherwood)*. Straight from the nursery!

LYDIA *(to Wilder)*. Mr. Wilder, I believe.

WILDER. At your service, young gentleman.

LYDIA. I am Mr. Percy Dasher.

WILDER *(laughing)*. Dasher! Dash me: a fine dasher!

LYDIA. Sir! *(Upstage)*.

DOROTHY *(to Sherwood)*. Captain Sherwood, I presume.

SHERWOOD. You presume rightly, my young friend.

DOROTHY. Gentlemen, we are here to resent an insult put upon Miss Dorothy Bantam.

LYDIA. And Miss Lydia Hawthorne.

DOROTHY. We have come to ask whether you are prepared to atone for your conduct by offering the only reparation possible, or whether you are ready to meet the consequences.

SHERWOOD. By reparation, I presume you mean marriage.

DOROTHY. I do.

WILDER. And the consequences imply a duel.

LYDIA. They do.

SHERWOOD. In point of fact you mean matrimony or murder.

DOROTHY and LYDIA. Precisely.

WILDER. Then we prefer murder.

SHERWOOD. Our words are pledged to two other ladies.

WILDER. And we mean to keep them.

DOROTHY *(aside to Lydia)*. Do you hear that cousin? But we must keep it up until we are able to change our clothes. *(Aloud)* Then gentlemen, you have only to choose your weapons.

(Lydia goes to box).

WILDER. Weapons! Young gentlemen, I should say that a birch rod, or a good bundle of nettles[87] would best befit your age and dignity.

DOROTHY. I would have you to know, Sir, that this is a serious matter and that your jokes are as misplaced as they are usually ill-chosen.

(Sings)[88]

It surely is not quite
Either right or polite
To treat as light
A summons to fight.

A woman's heart
Is no laughing matter
'Tis ill to start
With jest and chatter.

By such a sign
One might divine
A wish to decline
A taste of lead or steel.

But as for me
As you can see
Which e'er it be
About the same I feel.

WILDER *(speaks)*. Well, gentlemen, since you will have it the consequences of your own foolish little hates.

DOROTHY. I am ready to take the consequences. *(Aside to Lydia)* Where are the pistols? Recollect when you load them—powder first, and no ball. *(Aloud)* Here are the pistols.

WILDER. Pardon me. We are the challenged. We have brought our own pistols.

DOROTHY. And must we use them?

SHERWOOD. Certainly.

DOROTHY *(aside)*. Good heavens!

LYDIA *(aside)*. What's to be done?

SHERWOOD. In order that things should be perfectly fair, you will load one *(hands pistol to Dorothy)*.

WILDER *(beginning to load the other pistol)*. Have you the bullets, Harry?

SHERWOOD. Here they are *(hands one to Wilder)*.

LYDIA and DOROTHY *(aside)*. Bullets!

(Sherwood hands a bullet to Dorothy).

DOROTHY. But how are we to know which of the pistols has no bullet?

WILDER *(finishes loading and primes)*. They will both have bullets inside them, and so may one of us presently.

DOROTHY. Ah! Don't you point it at me! *(Avoiding pistol)*.

WILDER. I did but anticipate a pleasure by a few moments.

---

87   A broad-leafed weed (*Urtica dioica*) with hairs that sting on contact.
88   This is the "Snuff Song" deleted early in the run. It does not appear in the published score.

SHERWOOD. Allow me, Sir. You seem unaccustomed in the ways of these little barkers.

LYDIA (*avoiding pistols*). Ah! Don't!

SHERWOOD. It's not loaded.

LYDIA. But it might go off. (*Aside*) What are we to do?

WILDER. Now, gentlemen, as this is to be a duel to the death—

LYDIA and DOROTHY. To the death!

WILDER. I said to the death. It will be necessary for us to carry out the latest fashion of the duello. We can't all shoot at once. We must begin two and two—

DOROTHY. Then perhaps if you two gentlemen would begin first.

SHERWOOD. We have no cause of quarrel.

DOROTHY. Of course, I forgot. (*Aside to Lydia*) Cousin, we must get out of this as quick as we can.

LYDIA (*aside to Dorothy*). One of these pistols is sure to go off in a minute.

WILDER (*to Dorothy*). You and I, Sir, had best lead off.

DOROTHY. Lead off: where?

WILDER. One of us—possibly both of us to the grave (*flourish pistol*).

DOROTHY. The grave! Don't point it at me—(*putting pistol aside*).

WILDER. Each will have his second. Your friend will serve you. We will place ourselves back to back— each will walk five paces—

DOROTHY. Only five paces!

WILDER. Well six, if you like it better. We shall then both turn on our heels (*presenting pistol*).

DOROTHY and LYDIA (*afraid*). Ah!

WILDER. And fire. One of us will fall—possibly both, and then the others will have a turn—

LYDIA and DOROTHY (*aside*). A turn!

WILDER (*to Dorothy*). Now sir—to place yourself!

SHERWOOD (*to Dorothy giving pistols*). Here is your pistol.

DOROTHY (*aside to Lydia*). Oh! If I only knew how to escape from this!

(*Wilder and Dorothy place themselves back to back C. Dorothy facing R., up. Lydia at her side. Wilder facing L. down. Sherwood at his side*).

SHERWOOD. Now, gentlemen, are you ready?

WILDER. Yes.

SHERWOOD. Then—go!

(*Dorothy marches three steps*).

DOROTHY and LYDIA. Ah! (*They run off R.U.E.*).

(*Wilder having marched three steps—Enter Bantam and Lurcher R. Wilder wheels round and presents his pistol at Bantam's head*).

BANTAM. Stop! Murder! Thieves!

WILDER. Why, what's this?

SHERWOOD. Our adversaries have fled—

WILDER. A pretty couple of cowards.

BANTAM. Pretty couple of murderers, Sir!

WILDER. My dear uncle, I can congratulate you on a very narrow escape.

BANTAM. What! My rascal of a nephew—So, sir! It is you who assume the clothes and manners of your betters and impose upon your too confiding relatives!

WILDER. Necessity, my dear uncle—

BANTAM. Necessity, sir, is the mother of thieves.

SHERWOOD (to Wilder). That rascal Lurcher has peached[89]—

LURCHER. The promptings of my conscience, gentlemen—

WILDER. And your pocket, I'll be bound.

BANTAM (angry). "Though born a man of high degree" Eh! You villain—

WILDER. My dear uncle, I did but assume the part for a while.

BANTAM. "And greatly my superior"—is that it?

WILDER. But Squire—

BANTAM. "I trust I know that courtesy is due to an inferior." Who's an inferior? Your uncle, your dog?—Give me my money back—

WILDER (pointing to Lurcher). I must refer you to this gentleman—

LURCHER. Nay, sir, I must refer you to the Court—

BANTAM. Who may possibly restore the money to my grandchildren after I have spent twice the amount in asking for it.

(Enter Tuppitt).

TUPPITT. I humbly crave pardon—

BANTAM. What is it now?

TUPPITT. The young couple are coming to meet your worship at the old oak!

BANTAM. What young couple?

TUPPITT. Tom and my daughter Phyllis, who have just been married.

BANTAM. What do they want with me?

TUPPITT. Your worship's blessing—

BANTAM. Blessing! Do I look like blessing?

WILDER (aside to Sherwood). In faith, Harry, he does not—

BANTAM (aside). I must be calm—(aloud) I'll deal with you, Sir, anon.

(Enter Tom, Phyllis, Chorus, and Ballet to movement of Ballet).

PHYLLIS (to Bantam). Your worship, the old custom bids us ask your blessing—

(Tom and Phyllis head to Bantam).

BANTAM. There—children—if the blessing of an old man who feels more like swearing be any good to you, you have it.

(Septet and chorus)

TOM and PHYLLIS.
   What joy untold to feel at last
   That all delay and doubts are past,
   My future lot with you is cast,
   My own.

---

89   Informed against.

TUPPITT.

> A parent's feelings who can tell?
> His satisfaction who can quell?
> I wished to see her married well,
> I own.

WILDER, SHERWOOD, BANTAM, and CHORUS.

> They are indeed a happy pair,
> What lot on earth can now compare
> With theirs? I only wish it were
> My own.

PRINCIPALS and CHORUS.

> They're happily married by parson and ring,
> So merrily let the bells chime;
> For marriage to start with is not a sad thing,
> It only gets gloomy with time.

> A husband was ready—the maiden said "aye,"
> She makes a most beautiful bride;
> The knot was remarkably easy to tie,
> It won't be so lightly untied.

BANTAM (to Wilder, speaks). Now sir, you may thank your stars that the sight of these young folks' happiness has put me in a better temper.

WILDER (bowing). I am delighted to think that I have obtained, even if I have not merited, your forgiveness.

BANTAM. None of your London manners with me, Sir. I am ready to forgive you, and even to take you back to my heart, where there has long been an empty corner waiting for you, if you will marry your cousin Dorothy!

(Enter Dorothy and Lydia dressed in their peasant clothes of the first Act).

WILDER. That is impossible.

BANTAM. How, impossible? Are you married already?

WILDER. Nay, Sir, but I hope soon to be—

BANTAM. To whom?

WILDER (bringing Dorothy down). To this Lady, if she will so far honour me—

BANTAM. To her? Why that is your cousin Dorothy.

WILDER. My cousin Dorothy!

DOROTHY (with a curtsey). The same.

SHERWOOD (to Lydia). Then you—

LYDIA (with a curtsey). I am Lydia Hawthorne, her cousin—

WILDER. Then last night we—(aside to Sherwood) oh! Harry, here's a pretty kettle of fish—

DOROTHY (to Bantam). Yes, father—I was anxious to find out whether a man could love a woman for herself and not for her money. The ring, which I gave him, and which he now wears on his finger is a proof of his constancy. (To Wilder) Shew it cousin.

WILDER (hesitating). I—(Aside) What in the world is to be done?

LYDIA. And I too entrusted this gentleman with the ring which he now wears on his finger. *(To Sherwood)* Where is it?

SHERWOOD *(aside)*. What shall I say—

WILDER *(recovering his self-possession)*. Ahem! I confess that recognizing my cousin Dorothy last night I returned to her, as a keepsake, and, and *(hesitating)*

SHERWOOD. That is exactly what I wished to say myself—

DOROTHY *(to Wilder)*. Did the stone change its colour in your pocket, cousin? *(Shewing ring)*.

LYDIA *(to Sherwood)*. Had my ring a green or a red stone? *(Shewing ring)*.

WILDER. I have nothing to say—

DOROTHY. Well then if that is all the explanation you have to make—*(giving Wilder her hand)* I accept it.

SHERWOOD *(to Lydia)*. And you?

LYDIA *(giving her hand to Sherwood)*. I suppose I must follow Dorothy's example.

BANTAM. That's right, children—

DOROTHY *(to Wilder)*. After all you were ready to die rather than marry Lydia—

LYDIA *(to Sherwood)*. I cannot forget that you preferred death to Dorothy.

(Finale song)

DOROTHY *(chaffing Wilder)*.
  Who swore to be good and true
  To the maid whom he dared to adore?
LYDIA *(chaffing Sherwood)*.
  Who promised to love her as few
  Have ever loved woman before?
WILDER and SHERWOOD.
  We gladly yield our lives to you
  And swear to be forever true.
DOROTHY.
  Oh, fie! Oh, fie!
  We spurned the tie
  Did not we
  Swear to be
  Ever free?
  To single die,
  And Hymen fly,
  Warily,
  Charily,
  Airily?
  But Cupid, after all, is blind;
  It would indeed be strange
    To meet a woman with a mind
  That wasn't made to change.
PHYLLIS.
  Very strange.
LYDIA.
  Very, very strange.

DOROTHY.
Very, very, very, very strange.

DOROTHY, LYDIA, and PHYLLIS.
Yes; very, very, very strange.

DOROTHY *(to Wilder)*, LYDIA *(to Sherwood)*, and PHYLLIS *(to Tom)*.
But
Be wise in time,
Oh! husband mine
Have a care:
Pray beware!
Hear me swear.
One word unkind,
Change my mind;
Nor are there
Maids to spare
Everywhere.

BANTAM *(advancing and joining hands of Dorothy and Wilder, and Lydia and Sherwood)*.
There, take him. Be happy.
For what you have got
Be thankful, or never allow that you're not.
And on this occasion I ask the whole lot.
There's a welcome to all
At Chanticleer Hall.

PRINCIPALS and CHORUS.
And lucky the man who is pleased with his lot.
Who never sits sighing for what he has not,
Contented and thankful for what he has got.
There's a welcome to all
At Chanticleer Hall.

Alice in Wonderland; or, Harlequin, the Poor Apprentice, the Pretty Belle, and the Fairy Ring (1886)

Genre Issues

Alice's Adventures in Wonderland (1865) and its companion volume *Through the Looking-Glass* (1871) were classics of the Victorian nursery for a generation before they were adapted for the London stage in fully mounted productions.[1] Two portrayals appeared in the Christmas season of 1886-87. The sanctioned version, by H. Savile Clarke (with new music by Walter Slaughter) was billed as a comic opera and produced at the Prince of Wales's Theatre, Piccadilly,[2] performed at matinees while *Dorothy* ran in the evenings. It stuck closely to the novels and was often revived.[3] Joseph Addison's version (which paired new words to popular tunes) was produced at the Royal Artillery Theatre, Woolwich Arsenal, in southeast London. It borrowed a few characters and motifs from *Alice's Adventures*, but the pastiche principally relied upon plotting conventions of pantomime interspersed with minstrel and music-hall tunes. The result was barely recognizable as being from Lewis Carroll yet was thoroughly familiar as pantomime. It was never revived.

Lewis Carroll's novel functions more as an intertext than a source text for Addison's pantomime. Carroll's Alice is a curious child, while Addison's is a "dutiful" young woman of marriageable age. Whereas Carroll's Alice falls through a rabbit hole and experiences her ensuing encounters with righteous indignation and puzzlement, Addison's Alice is caught up in a terrestrial kidnap plot and sent to Wonderland for safekeeping. There are situations recognizable from Wonderland—for example, the Lobster Quadrille and the petulant Queen of Hearts, along with her various courtiers and the White Rabbit—and riddles and puns keep up the spirit, if not the letter, of antic reversals that Carroll masterfully invoked. But a recruiting sergeant's intoxication and the Baron's fixation on Alice are stage contrivances, the domain of droll comedy and pantomimic disorder rather than the incongruous *esprit* of Carroll's Wonderland.

---

1   There are over 400 dramatic adaptations of Lewis Carroll's work. Carroll had successively approached Tom Taylor, Thomas Coe, Percy Fitzgerald, and German Reed about adapting the books, but nothing came of it. Meanwhile, amateur performances were undertaken by the Arnold sisters in 1874, a reading and dumb show at the Royal Polytechnic in 1876, and the Elliston family at Eastbourne in 1878. Charles C. Lovett, *Alice on Stage: A History of the Early Theatrical Productions of "Alice in Wonderland," together with a Checklist of Dramatic Adaptations of Charles Dodgson's Works* (Westport, CT: Meckler, 1990); and Richard Foulkes, *Lewis Carroll and the Victorian Stage: Theatricals in a Quiet Life* (Aldershot: Ashgate, 2005), 60-61.

2   In addition to the original airs, two older tunes were used: the Stephen Foster standard "Beautiful Star" (1859, for "Beautiful Soup") and "Will You Walk into My Parlour?" (for "Will You Walk"). Foulkes, *Lewis Carroll*, 62; see also Anne Varty, *Children and Theatre in Victorian Britain: "All Work, No Play"* (Basingstoke: Palgrave Macmillan, 2008), 101-02. The Slaughter/Clarke *Alice in Wonderland* played at matinees 23 December 1886 to 2 March 1887.

3   H. Savile Clarke, "Alice in Wonderland: A Dream Play for Children," British Library Add MS 53371, printed (London: The Court Circular Office, 1886). It opened on 23 December 1886 with Phoebe Carlo as Alice and was revived on 26 December 1888 at the Globe Theatre with Ida Bowman; 22 December 1898 at the Opera Comique with Rose Hersee; 19 December 1900 at the Vaudeville Theatre with Ellaline Terriss; December 1902 by a touring company with 30 children; 29 May 1905 at the Comedy Theatre with Rosina Filippi (this is possibly a different version); 23 December 1907 at the Apollo Theatre with Maidie Andrews; and 27 December 1909 at the Court Theatre with Ivy Sawyer. Harvard Theatre Collection, *Alice in Wonderland* clippings file; Foulkes, *Lewis Carroll*, 61; and J.P. Wearing, *The London Stage, 1900-1909: A Calendar of Plays and Players*, 2 vols. (Metuchen: Scarecrow, 1981).

Clarke's adaptation ends with the crowning of Alice by the White Knight and then a grand procession and feast. The chessmen and Alice sing "To the Looking-Glass World" (to an old tune), and a roasted joint and pudding are set out. The gauzes that had revealed "the Realms of Bliss" at the commencement of the performance come down, and the stage darkens. When it brightens again, Alice is discovered asleep at the foot of a tree. She awakens proclaiming, "Oh, I've had such a curious dream!" (as in Carroll's story) and the curtain falls.[4] By contrast, Addison's version features a sixteen-year-old Alice who is kidnapped by a lecherous Baron; her suitor, Jack (played by a woman, in the tradition of English pantomime), who has joined the Royal Artillery in an effort to impress Alice's father, is assisted by the Queen of Wonderland to recover his sweetheart. At the conclusion, all sing in praise of Queen Victoria's golden jubilee, after which the Queen of Wonderland—neither a chess piece nor a British sovereign, but a fairy queen—invokes the harlequinade. Before the audience's eyes, she transforms the Baron into the Clown, Alice's father into the Pantaloon, and Jack and Alice into Harlequin and Columbine. The set transforms from Woolwich Common to the Fairy's Wonderland home: this terminates the script, but a wordless ritual of thievery, tumbling, chases, and slapstick ensues in the harlequinade.[5]

The differences between Clarke's and Addison's versions exemplify extravaganza and pantomime, respectively. Extravaganza and pantomime were holiday genres: initially Easter and Christmas entertainments, the winter version predominated in the Victorian period until it became synonymous with the season. Both genres contrast the idyllic realms with everyday life: the power to alternate between them is given to benevolent supernaturals. Both utilize the dances and processionals of ballet to augment spectacular scenery with the massed feminine form.[6] But there are also important distinctions. A leading writer of extravaganza, James Robinson Planché, described his craft as "the whimsical treatment of a poetical subject."[7] Pantomime could have a portion of whimsy too, but as Addison shows, it could change source material almost beyond recognition, insisting on its own conventions in service of a quest plot. Pantomime was also followed by a harlequinade as surely as night follows day.[8] Michael Booth explains:

> Pantomime audiences were offered two things for the price of one, so to speak: the formality, relative refinement and solemnity, romantic illusion, scenic splendor, idealized love, and ordered progression of the opening were complemented by the fast-paced, extravagant low comedy of a world of ideal disorder and chaos. The governing spirits of the ... harlequinade were misrule and anarchy: the freedom to commit amusing capital crimes and set law and authority at nought was bestowed abundantly upon Harlequin and Clown.[9]

---

4   Clarke, *Alice in Wonderland*; also Foulkes, *Lewis Carroll*, 55.
5   As Hargrave Jennings put it, "In at doors—out at windows—darting through walls—pirouetting like twenty opera dancers in one grand whirligig—springing five yards at a bound—inexhaustible in attitudes—astounding in resources of heel and ancle [*sic*]—indefatigable in flourish of toe and wand. Columbine, too, 'princess of pretty movements' ... queen of the boards, goddess of gazers, the very personification of all that is airy, gay, and capricious—presiding genius of the scene—fascination in a *figurante*.... Their very nature is irreconcileably [*sic*] opposed to the idea of standing still." "Some of the Philosophy of Pantomimes," n.d., bound in *Theatrical Tracts* 7:30 (Garrick Club).
6   Alexandra Carter, *Dance and Dancers in the Victorian and Edwardian Music Hall Ballet* (Aldershot: Ashgate, 2005), 54-56.
7   J.R. Planché, *Recollections and Reflections*, rev. ed. (London: S. Low, Marston, 1901), 268, quoted in Michael R. Booth, introduction to *English Plays of the Nineteenth Century*, vol. 5, *Pantomimes, Extravaganzas and Burlesques* (Oxford: Clarendon, 1976), 11.
8   The "decline" of pantomime was noted from the Regency onward (Booth, *English Plays*, vol. 5, 8), but this is principally meant as a comment upon the growing prominence of the transformations in the first part at the expense of the harlequinade. "The Decline of Pantomime," *Musical World*, 13 March 1858: 173.
9   Booth, *English Plays*, vol. 5, 5.

Pantomime was both topical and timeless. Though the precedents were continental, it became a distinctly English phenomenon, "as natural to Englishmen as grumbling, foggy weather, trial by jury, and the liberty of the press" and "as natural to the Christmas holidays as plum pudding and mistletoe."[10] During the early nineteenth century, gender-reversed casting of the lead male by a vivacious young woman became *de rigueur*; at the same time, the "dame," an old woman, was introduced as a cross-gendered role for comedians, though it was not ubiquitous in the pantomimes until the 1880s.[11] When music halls proliferated after 1850, their singing and dancing talent was annually poached for the pantomimes and stars used the format to deliver what they knew best: topical and comic songs, with the occasional variety act (such as Father William's conjuring). Though family entertainment, pantomimes were raucous and even racy, only nominally built on nursery tales of traditional English or continental origin.[12]

Like melodrama, pantomime utilizes "significant props" that enable the hero to fulfil his quest. In melodrama such props enable recognition, whereas in pantomime they unlock magic and link the hero to his fairy benefactress whenever he is blocked by either benign impediments (such as Alice's father) or malevolent ones (such as the Baron). Melodrama idealizes morality, whereas pantomime indulges vice laughably. This, rather than innovation in plotting or technical theatre, is pantomime's secret to longevity.

Written in rhymed couplets, pantomime relentlessly punned, and even the immortals joined in:

SILVER STAR.
> I must make them halt in their mischief brewing,
> I'll be here on the spot, and will not fail
> When treason's near, to give a warning hail (ale).

Forcing the homophones, and dragging them out, was part of the fun.

ALICE.
> I seem estranged.
> I can't explain myself, I am afraid;
> I seem to grow much smaller than I'm made.
> A Caterpillar and a mushroom I see,
> Which dwarfs me into nothing, makes me wee.

CATERPILLAR.
> Yes—in French?

ALICE.
> No, little.

CATERPILLAR.
> O—U—I see.
> You certainly look little here by me.

As Booth states, "the result may seem endearingly naïve, but it is really precisely calculated and achieved with much creative ingenuity on the author's part."[13]

---

10   Morris Barnett, "A Paper on Pantomimes," *Mirror* 3 (1848): 51-64.

11   David Mayer, correspondence with author, 6 July 2010.

12   David Mayer, *Harlequin in His Element: The English Pantomime, 1806-1836* (Cambridge, MA: Harvard UP, 1969); Jim Davis, ed., *Victorian Pantomime: A Critical Reader* (London: Palgrave Macmillan, 2010); and Laurence Senelick, *The Changing Room: Sex, Drag and Theatre* (London: Routledge, 2000), 243-45.

13   Booth, *English Plays*, vol. 5, 22.

Interpretive Issues

The army's Royal Arsenal at Woolwich was founded for ordnance storage in 1671 on a 31-acre site along the River Thames. Expanded with an ammunition laboratory and gun foundry by 1717, the Grand Depot Barracks in 1787, and Royal Military Academy in 1806, it grew to 250 acres. Downstream from London and the Royal Naval College at Greenwich, during World War I the Arsenal comprised 1,300 acres and employed 80,000 people in armament design and manufacture. The facility faced Woolwich Common, a review ground that connected the Arsenal to the settlement of Woolwich. The Academy featured chemical and mechanical engineering courses for officers who were posted there for up to 18 months at a time. In the Victorian period, whole brigades also relocated to Woolwich, prior to foreign service, for training in the School of Gunnery. Woolwich was a community unto itself. Long-term staff and temporary rotas of students organized a variety of clubs: cricket, football, taxidermy, alpine (which involved circumnavigating the academy buildings at roof-top level), and theatre.[14]

The New Theatre at the Royal Arsenal was converted from a disused chapel in 1864. This "handsome, well-ventilated, and singularly commodious Theatre" formed part of the façade along Woolwich Common, the longest unbroken Georgian frontage in England.[15] Seating 1,500, the facility had all the accoutrements of a regular theatre.[16] *Ours* was produced here in 1884, and *Dorothy* in 1914, among a plethora of other light fare from the West End. Theatricals kept the soldiers constructively occupied, and since Woolwich had an especially good band—led from 1881 to 1906 by Cavaliere Ladislao Zavertal, a student of Antonin Dvořák—the efforts of actors and singers were well supported. The theatre hosted regular concerts, annual displays of gymnastics and swordplay, and plays. In the 1860s, leading actresses were hired to perform the same roles they took in the West End, supported by players from Woolwich. Florence and Ellen Terry are among the most notable of a distinguished list of such visitors.[17] In the 1870s, professional companies were hosted, but when this proved unprofitable, the amateurs resolved to rely on less celebrated local resources.

Several groups used the theatre. The Old Stagers, "a number of gentlemen who under fictitious names are in the habit of taking part in Amateur Performances," drew upon retired staff and men of the neighbourhood, including the Honorable Spencer Ponsonby-Fane (Comptroller of the Lord Chamberlain's office, 1857-1901) and his brother Fred. The Officers' Dramatic Club staged its own productions, but Christmas pantomimes were the province of the Non-Commissioned Officers' Dramatic Club and Garrison Dramatic Club. Thanks to the prowess of Gunner Lee (Custodian of the Field Officers' cows) as Clown, other members of the staff and their families, local residents, and minor professional actresses, the pantomimists earned enough to buy two new billiard tables for the recreation rooms.[18]

Joseph Addison, probably a civilian, appeared in Royal Arsenal shows in the 1880s and wrote for the garrison from 1876 until the end of the century. He wrote and directed the 1883 pantomime *Little Jack Frost*, as well as earlier farces and a burlesque on Jason and Medea. *Alice in Wonderland* launched his professional career: the next year he became resident pantomimist for the Britannia Theatre (Hoxton),

---

14   Brigadier Ken Timbers, consultant ed., *The Royal Artillery, Woolwich: A Celebration* (London: Third Millennium, 2008).

15   Clipping dated November 1868, R.A. Officers' Dramatic Club Woolwich, 1862-1912, Royal Artillery Museum RA/110/1.

16   "Royal Artillery Theatre," *Illustrated Sporting and Dramatic News*, 22 February 1890. Some scenery and most costumes were probably rented.

17   Their performance took place on 7 October 1868. R.A. Officers' Dramatic Club Woolwich, 1862-1912, Royal Artillery Museum RA/110/1.

18   "More about the R.A. Theatre," based on diary extracts from James A. Browne, late Bandmaster, Royal Artillery Woolwich Museum.

where he remained until 1898.[19] *Alice in Wonderland* suggests he was well suited to the Britannia's winning formula of a British fairy tale punctuated by twenty to thirty music hall songs laced with topical allusions.[20]

In scene 8, "the Royal Artillerymen have the satisfaction of seeing how their uniform in silk and satin becomes the gentler sex and also of seeing and admiring the manner in which the feminine character is capable of excellence in military exercises."[21] In addition to such sexualized displays, adult spectators could also enjoy allusions to Home Rule or the unemployment crisis while recognizing songs made popular by the likes of Jenny Hill, Harry Randall, Arthur Williams, and Charles Coburn. Of the two dozen songs in *Alice in Wonderland*, over half were set to tunes introduced in the previous year or two, and at least five were from the blackface Mohawk Minstrels or Moore and Burgess Minstrels troupes. Only three were written more than fifteen years earlier, but they were neither traditional nor well known. The pantomime ran for a month, but its audience base was local. Appealing to denizens of the neighbourhood and tying in Jack's storyline to specifically local sensibilities, scene 9 is set on Woolwich Common and Parade. This view of the Royal Artillery Barracks prompted "a hearty cheer and calls for Mr. Rogers," the scene painter, when the audience recognized the familiar vista.

Performative Issues

The novel *Alice's Adventures in Wonderland* already resembles pantomime, and indeed Lewis Carroll thought it particularly well suited to adaptation into this genre (provided that a harlequinade was *not* appended).[22] His characters (such as the Duchess, with her baby and the cook joining as chorus, and Mock Turtle) break into song periodically, and objects and locations metamorphose without recourse to logic. In form and particulars, some of Carroll's episodes have precedents in pantomime. "The Queen of Hearts," part of a set of playing-card poems from 1782,[23] was used in two Surrey Theatre pantomimes that predate Carroll's book. In 1862, *Harlequin and Mother Goose; or, the Queen of Hearts and the Wonderful Tarts* set a scene in the Palace of Cards in which the Queen of Hearts calls for her missing tarts and Jackaxe the Executioner looms over the Knave.[24] In 1865, *Harlequin King Chess; or, Tom the Piper's Son and Seesaw Margery Daw* included a scene in which the evil King Chess has the game played out by living figures.[25] Recognizable but with a difference, Alice could be cited, miscited, mauled, marred, and meddled with in a pantomime, rather like the Duchess's moral: "'Take care of the sense, and the sounds will take care of themselves.'"[26]

Victorian pantomime loosely drew upon familiar stories—more referentially than literally—hitting high points just enough to keep the story in view while melding secondary plots, topical red herrings, and standardized business into an ebulliently cockeyed whole. *Alice in Wonderland* becomes the foil for a story of thwarted young lovers—one abducted by the villain, the other carried off to war by a recruiting officer—eventually returned to each other by a supernatural figure, even though no such character was written by Lewis Carroll, and indeed no one so wholly benevolent appears in his books. His monarch is the Queen of Hearts; and though she does make an appearance in the pantomime (opposite a King of

---

19   Jim Davis, ed., *The Britannia Diaries, 1863-1875: Selections from the Diaries of Frederick C. Wilton* (London: Society for Theatre Research, 1992), 23. See also *King Trickee*, British Library Add MS 53390 (L); and Allardyce Nicoll, *A History of English Drama, 1660-1900*, vol. 5 (Cambridge: Cambridge UP, 1959), 236.

20   Davis, *Britannia Diaries*, 20-21.

21   "The Soldiers' Pantomime at Woolwich," *Kentish Independent*, 1 January 1887.

22   Foulkes, *Lewis Carroll*, 59; and Varty, *Children and Theatre*, 55-56.

23   *European Magazine*, April 1782.

24   British Library Add MS 53018 (J).

25   Foulkes, *Lewis Carroll*, 56.

26   Chapter 8 of *Alice in Wonderland*.

SCENE FROM THE PANTOMIME OF " MOTHER GOOSE ; OR THE QUEEN OF HEARTS AND THE WONDERFUL TARTS," AT THE SURREY THEATRE.—SEE RECREATIONS, PAGE 69.

Illustration 28. Scene from *Harlequin and Mother Goose; or, the Queen of Hearts and the Wonderful Tarts*, Surrey Theatre, 1862. Courtesy of the Theatre Collection, Victoria and Albert Museum.

Hearts, played by the same actor as the villainous Baron) and illiberally pronounces "off with their heads" in a manic trial scene, her function is transient. Other Wonderland characters make brief or repeated appearances—the Gryphon, Dodo, March Hare, Dormouse, White Rabbit, and Caterpillar, known so well through John Tenniel's illustrations—but fulfil few of the functions or interlocutions of Carroll's invention. It is likely that the Wonderland characters' costumes adhered as closely as feasible to John Tenniel's indispensible drawings even if copyright breach was avoided through textual changes.

The comic business derives chiefly from the Irish recruiting sergeant O'Grady, who is a jovial stage drunk, and Father William, who cross-dresses as a woman in scene 4 in order to become the Baron's cook and thus be near his abducted daughter. He is prepared to poison the Baron to keep him from defiling Alice, and though this may sound like a grave measure, it is rendered lightheartedly and no real damage to either daughter or *roué* can be expected. The plucky Alice is prepared to knock the Baron flat if he tries anything. A duet harmonizes their voices only in order to show how they are at odds:

BARON.
> My darling how I love you, you soon shall be my wife,
> And I will never leave you any more.

ALICE.
> You monster I'll not wed, no, not while I have life,
> I'd rather be an old maid, that I'm sure.

Comic reversals are mandatory. When Alice refuses food, the Baron and Father William (as the cook) join forces to urge her to eat. Though Alice already finds something familiar about the cook, when he defends her from the Baron's advances Father William's disguise is uncovered. Dismolo prepares to hang him, but the Queen of Wonderland and fairy Silver Star intervene; rather than taking in the sudden appearance of the immortals, William continues his banter with the Baron over a wager. The Baron will not relinquish Alice, so the Queen entrances her into a sleep and transports her to Wonderland. The Gryphon, on the side of the evildoers, gives the Baron a magic stick, yet, alas, he takes it up too late. The scene change to Wonderland is verified by the appearance of the White Rabbit, yet it is the Baron and Dismolo who are initially found wandering there, not Alice. Jack (now a playing card) and Alice are lovingly united, whereupon Alice's brother and father fall into a quarrel.

Transformations of locale give licence for implausible plot twists. The next transformation, to a regimental encampment on foreign soil,[27] is facilitated by an olio scene in which Father William does conjuring tricks. A pair of sparring lovers (the *viviandière* Annette and the Lieutenant) are interrupted by Jack, now (through inexplicably quick promotions) a colonel. The Queen of Wonderland behaves as if *this* Jack has not recently seen his Alice, for she is still asleep in Wonderland. Another scene change—not so fully an inversion of mood or contrast from earthly to supernatural realms to be a transformation—finds the three villains and Father William on Woolwich Common awaiting Alice's return. Father William now blesses his daughter's union with Jack, and the pantomime can conclude. Instead of an awakening by her elder sister, as in Carroll's story, Alice is delivered by the Queen into a reconciliation and harmonious reconstitution of family. Instead of the novelistic sisters' "dull reality" of a sunny day, banal farmyard sounds, and the lull of the river, there is a year of Golden Jubilee celebrations to announce.

---

27 Woolwich had most recently prepared soldiers for the war in the Sudan (1884-85). Perhaps that setting was reflected in the scenery.

Editing Issues

There is only one source for Addison's *Alice in Wonderland*: the privately printed licensing copy deposited with the Lord Chamberlain. No other copy survives. The licensing copy closely adheres to performance details described in local newspapers, which suggests that few concessions were made in rehearsal for the complexity of the script and scenography. The first performance (Boxing Day, 1886) attracted a crowded house of around 1,700 eager onlookers—the balcony was crammed with some 200 more people than it was designed to accommodate—and the harlequinade was truncated to compensate for the pantomime running overtime. That was not unusual for amateur or professional pantos. As the cast settled into their roles for the month-long run, technical effects were made routine, comic business ran more smoothly, and the harlequinade was restored in full. Regrettably, there is neither a prompt book nor any textual evidence of the harlequinade to flesh out details.

The source text is somewhat short on stage directions and occasionally contradictory or absent-minded about the characters' comings and goings. What appears below is deduced from the dialogue to make the action easier to follow.

Alice in Wonderland; or, Harlequin, the Poor Apprentice, the Pretty Belle, and the Fairy Ring[28]

BY JOSEPH ADDISON

First performed at the Royal Artillery Theatre, Woolwich Arsenal (London), 26 December 1886.[29]

Queen of Wonderland[30]	Edith Garthorne
Fairy Silver Star	Miss Douglas[31]
Father William, innkeeper	Corporal J.C. Francis, R.V.
Alice William, his daughter	Cissie Judge
Jack, apprentice to the hatter	Josephine Henley
Giles, Alice's brother	H. Miller
Gloss, a hatter (Jack's foster father)	
Sergeant O'Grady, Royal Artillery recruiting officer	Gunner H.N. Lee, R.A.
Simon, a recruit	
Baron Hearthardaswood	F. Hayward
Dismolo	W. Sallenger
Gryphon	J. Wylie
Queen of Hearts	
King of Hearts	F. Hayward

---

28   Based on the licensing copy, British Library Add MS 53370 (O), December 1886.

29   No programme survives; casting is deduced from reviews. Additional roles taken by the adult performers C. Lucas, R. Teeter, and H. Fairbairn and the child actors Master Swinerd (son of the general manager), and the three little Lees (likely the children of Gunner Lee) have not been identified though the performers are named in the press.

30   Called Queen of Reverie in the review in the *Kentish Independent*, 1 January 1887.

31   Both Douglas sisters, Ella and Alice, took part though it is unclear who had which role.

Dodo	O. Morgan
White Rabbit	Miss Douglas
Mock Turtle	
March Hare	
Dormouse	
Caterpillar	
Lieutenant	
Annette (a *viviandière*)	Mrs. Bilton
Sentry, Lobster, Executioner, Recruits, Jury Men, Armed Men, Chorus, Boys, Fairy Elves, and Soldiers	
Clown	F. Hayward
Pantaloon	Corpl. J.C. Francis, R.V.
Harlequin	Josephine Henley
Columbine	Cissie Judge

Director J. Addison
Manager Lieutenant Colonel S.P. Lynes, R.H.A.
Asst. Manager Sergeant H. Swinerd, R.A.
Conductor Sergeant Major Montara
Orchestra Royal Artillery bandsmen
Ballet Mistress Lily Tyrrell
Scene painter Mr. Rogers
Transformation scene design Lieutenants S.G. Horton and F.Y. Young, R.A.
Pantomime arranger Charles Bishop
Stage Manager Quartermaster Sergeant Grieg

Scene 1

A cave in Wonderland.

CHORUS (*singing offstage*).[32]
We float in the air, we glide on the sea,
Our couch is a floweret so wild and so free,
On a sunbeam we ride on the Moon's rays we tread,
As we dance in its light when night's mantle is spread;
O'er hill, and o'er vale we journey at will,
And the woods with our voices in harmony fill;
In a dew drop we bathe at the break of the day,
A life full of joy is the life of a Fay.[33]

---

32 The music for the opening chorus was composed expressly by Cavaliere L. Zavertal, the master of the Royal Artillery
Band.
33 Fairy.

QUEEN OF WONDERLAND *(appears and speaks)*.
    In Wonderland I dwell, and am the Queen.
    Of all the marvels in your childhood seen;
    Of Fairy tales be they on sea or land,
    Of jewelled cavern, and of palace grand.
    In Fancy's world I hold supremest sway,
    I'll take you back to *infancy* today.
    Young ones will go with me and nothing loth;[34]
    But will you go, you of an older growth?
    For once throw off your cares, and seek delight
    In fairy realms of mirth and music bright.
    Forget all ills in pleasures unalloyed,
    And don't by outward troubles be annoyed;
    This time of year is not without its charm,
    E'en snow is greeted with a welcome warm.
    The *yule* log, holly, and the mistletoe,
    How *you'll* greet that, why most of you well know,
    'Tis not for me to say how eyes shine bright
    Beneath the mistletoe with berries white;
    What I suggest, in this, my opening rhyme,
    Is that we start at once our Pantomime,
    So I will summon here a goodly band
    Of subjects mine, who dwell in Wonderland.
    The Dodo first, he shall present his Bill;
    Not one that threatens *unity to kill*.[35]

(Enter Dodo).

    White Rabbit next, a tiller of the earth;
    He is a burrow (boro')[36] member, we all know his worth.

(Enter White Rabbit).

    Mock Turtle third, and of *sou*perior[37] kind;
    He of a restaurant puts one in mind;
    There you will find him on the bill of fare,
    His name takes precedence of dishes rare.

(Enter Mock Turtle).

    The Gryphon next we'll summon; he of late
    Has been most anxious to attend our state;[38]

---

34   Not reluctant; i.e., willingly.
35   She puns on the bird's bill and a parliamentary bill, especially one that can be voted up on a parliamentary majority.
36   The licensing text usually indicates punned homonyms either by italicizing or parenthetically inserting the paired word. The author probably intended that the parenthetical hints guide actors' pronunciation and emphasis. Sometimes this improves the meter, but sometimes not.
37   A pun on turtle soup.
38   Royal or governing council.

He's next myself in power, and knows my charms
You've seen his likeness on the City Arms.[39]

(Enter Gryphon).

The rest I will not call by names apart;
But enter all our council then we'll start.

SONG
Air—"Little Tommy Topweight"[40]

GRYPHON.

I am the monster Gryphon of Wonderland renown,
And many children know me very well;
(Aside) I'm good to make a rumpus, do any person brown,[41]
A friend I would at any moment sell.

MOCK TURTLE.

My name it is Mock Turtle, I am good to one and all,
At nearly every dinner I've a place.[42]

DODO.

I'm the sage old Dodo, and can date back to the fall,
And I am now the last of all my race.[43]

WHITE RABBIT *(alone).*

I'm little Bunny Lightweight quite a little don;[44]
Little Bunny Lightweight, and I've got 'em on.
I'm quite a little masher,[45] and mean to go[46] the pace,
I'm cream of all the fashion, and beau ideal[47] of grace.

CHORUS.

He's little Bunny Lightweight, quite a little don;
He's little Bunny Lightweight and he's got 'em on.
He's quite a little masher, and means to go the pace,
The cream of all the fashion, and beau ideal of grace.

QUEEN. *(speaks).*

We here assemble to suggest a plan
To thwart the evil deeds of mortal man.

---

39 A gryphon statue was erected in 1880 at Temple Bar, the western entrance to the City of London (the Square Mile). Gryphons have the bodies of lions and heads and wings of eagles and may symbolize the guarding of treasure. Two rampant gryphons flank the City's coat of arms.

40 F. Bowyer (music and lyrics), "Little Tommy Topweight" (London: Francis Bros. & Day, 1886). Sung by Herbert Campbell, dressed as a jockey. Campbell was a major music hall star who, from the early 1880s, was featured every winter in Drury Lane pantomimes. See "Herbert Campbell's Start," *Era*, 22 September 1888.

41 Deceive.

42 Mock turtle soup is made from a calf's head.

43 Dodos, native to Mauritius, were first noted by Europeans around 1600 and were hunted to extinction within eighty years.

44 Gift.

45 Fashionable womanizer.

46 Set.

47 Perfection.

Does anyone here know a maiden fair,
Who dwells on Earth, who is of virtue rare,
In need of aid, are any sore oppressed?
We wish to give our help to those distressed;
Though charity 'mongst mortal's not destroyed,
As witness, what they gave the unemployed.[48]
We of the Fairy Realms would use our might
At Christmas time, to set some great wrong right;
So speak at once, you who have been away,
Do'st know where help is needed? If so, say.

WHITE RABBIT.

Most Gracious Queen, here at your feet I bend
To speak of one I hope you will *befriend*;
Be friendly to me: as I plead her cause,
With clasped hands.

GRYPHON.

You mean with outstretched *paws*.
Pause not, proceed.

WHITE RABBIT.

I pray don't interrupt.
She's one the wicked world cannot corrupt,
She's beautiful and fair *if fair* can be;
If e'er you see her you'll agree with me.

GRYPHON.

She did no doubt, and that uncommon well,
Since you so ably can her story tell:
Say who she is, come to the point at once,
Or we'll be *bored*.

WHITE RABBIT.

I am no school board dunce.

QUEEN.

Come, peace I say, let's hear him to the end:
Go on Sir Rabbit, let us know your friend.

WHITE RABBIT.

As I was saying—she is beautiful,
And good—to both her parents dutiful;
She is beloved, and loves an honest lad;
But true love don't run smooth.

DODO.

Dear me, how sad!

---

48 The system of poor relief broke down in the 1860s, and from 1870 to 1913 the overall level of relief steadily declined. The situation came to a head in 1886 when 20,000 labourers rioted in London. The Mansion House fund provided an influx of money, but it was too indiscriminately disbursed, leading to criticism from the middle class. George R. Boyer, "The Evolution of Unemployment Relief in Great Britain," *Journal of Interdisciplinary History* 34:3 (2004): 393-433.

GRYPHON.
  Shut up your bill, *be* quiet, don't you hear?
MOCK TURTLE.
  Your *mouchoir*,[49] pray.
GRYPHON.
  There's too *mouchwa*ter here.
  Too many tears you shed, he a sly fox is;
  With all these tiers we have no private boxes.[50]
QUEEN.
  Come, come, proceed; these interruptions really—
WHITE RABBIT.
  I can't remember where I was now clearly.
MOCK TURTLE.
  Oh, but I can! you said their lives were crossed,
  And on the wave despair, love's barque[51] was tossed.
GRYPHON.
  I'd like to add in manner parenthetical,
  Our friend Mock Turtle's getting quite poetical.
WHITE RABBIT.
  A wicked *Baron*—one Hearthardaswood,
  Who is so *base* though *barren* of all good,
  Would make her his, his *tenor*[52] runs that way;
  He persecutes her daily.
GRYPHON.
  So *you* say.
  I know the damsel and the baron well;
  He only goes to her his love to tell.
  He offers riches for his *spouse* doth he.
WHITE RABBIT.
  He is a villain, and *exposed* (espoused)[53] shall be.
  He slew his brother, so the story goes,
  And stepped into his shoes, likewise his clothes;
  He's persecuted damsels in all climes,
  Committed bigamy, and other crimes;
  He is a monster of the darkest *hue*.
GRYPHON.
  Don't *you* believe it.
QUEEN.
  If it should be true

---

49 Handkerchief (French).
50 The Italian style of theatre building included many tiers of private boxes, whereas the English style (at this time) favoured just a few boxes near the proscenium and rows of seating at the dress circle, upper circle, and gallery levels.
51 Ship.
52 Consistent intent (punning on base/bass in previous line).
53 Married.

We'll soon stop his games of sin and malice,
  Give the maiden's name?
WHITE RABBIT.
  Great Queen, 'tis Alice.
GRYPHON *(aside)*.
  The murder's out! It almost makes me swear.
QUEEN.
  What—Alice William with the flaxen hair?
WHITE RABBIT.
  The same.
GRYPHON *(aside)*.
  'Tis she.
QUEEN.
  The blue-eyed pretty child.
GRYPHON *(aside)*.
  The Baron is my friend; won't he be wild!
QUEEN.
  I know her well, she is a charming maid.
GRYPHON *(aside)*.
  I'll have to choke that Rabbit, I'm afraid.
  My head swims round with rage; I feel a dizziness;
  I'm pledged to aid the Baron in this business:
  I'll *foil* 'em yet; *if oily* words can do it,
  That plan a*grease* with me, and I'll per *suet*[54] (pursue it).
QUEEN.
  What say you Gryphon?
GRYPHON.
  My Queen, I tremble.
  One so vile shan't live. *(Aside)* I must dissemble.
QUEEN.
  Your words are right; we'll *watch* his little game,
  To thwart it be the *mainspring* of our aim;
  We'll *balance wheel* our power, as Scott[55] would say,
  And set our *hands* at work this very day:
  We'll thwart him till he is on ruin's *verge*,
  And every *lever* to this end will urge;
  Each *one* in *Won*derland his *hunter* be,
  And then at last he'll be *wound up* by me.[56]
MOCK TURTLE.
  But how can we upon this Baron wait,
  Who is surrounded by a castle great,

---

54 The solid fat taken from around the kidneys, chopped up, and used in pastries and puddings.
55 Herbert Scott, inventor of the toothed count-wheel that triggered pendulum impulses in timepieces; also punning on Scottish pronunciation of "balance well."
56 All the italicized words in this speech are puns related to clockmaking.

By minions who obey his slightest word?
To storm his castle would be quite absurd.

QUEEN.

You know him then?

MOCK TURTLE.

Indeed my Queen, I do;
He dines off me and puts me in a *stew*;
Each day upon his board I'm duly spread;
His favourite dish Mock Turtle at the head.
I have no cause to love him, that you bet;
If he gets killed I may be happy yet.

QUEEN.

Well ease your mind—our vengeance we will fix,
Upon this Baron, and *suppress* his tricks.

DODO.

Let's find him out at once, without *delay*,
Deal a great punishment this very day
Upon this monster, who in human shape
Combines the serpent with the cunning ape.

QUEEN.

That be my task; I'll seek him in his palace,
And if he has intentions ill to Alice
I'll let you know at once, by telegraph,
And then 'gainst him we're sure to turn the laugh,
The powers of Wonderland we'll bring to bear,
To help the lover and the maiden fair.

GRYPHON *(aside)*.

Oh, oh, she thinks she's got him on the hip;[57]
I'll to the Baron, and give him the tip.
He'll bear her from her home at dead of night.

QUEEN.

What say you all?

ALL.

We say you are quite right.

SONG
Air—"The Kicking Mule"[58]

QUEEN.

Now off we go away at once,
Bad deeds to circumvent.

---

57   At a disadvantage, as when Iago states "I'll have our Michael Cassio on the hip, / Abuse him to the Moor in the rank garb" (*Othello*, 2.1.305-06).

58   Walter Redmond (music) and J.H. Danvers (lyrics), "The Kicking Mule," *Mohawk Minstrels Magazine* 17:49 ([1886]): 37-39. Sung by Johnny Danvers of the Mohawk Minstrels, at the Agricultural Hall, London. A sixteen-bar dance in quadruple time follows the song. Many of the pantomime's tunes were taken from this magazine, which offered the advantage of not requiring any royalties to be paid.

GRYPHON.

    I must be a perfect dunce,

    If I don't that prevent.

DODO.

    We'll catch the Baron on the hop,[59]

MOCK TURTLE.

    And make him cut his stick.[60]

WHITE RABBIT.

    It won't be easy him to cop;[61]

    He's up to every trick.

Chorus

ALL.

    He's sure to cut up rusty,[62]

    His temper is so crusty

    He'll fight and kick just like Old Nick,[63]

    For that we know's his rule.

    If he should raise a riot,

    We'll soon make him quiet,

    We'll stop his little game, quite pat, and make him look a fool.

(Dance)

Scene 2

The Cross[64] *in the High Street in the village of Snow Field.*

JACK.

    Oh dear, oh dear, these mornings are so cold,

    To leap from bed one has to be quite bold;

    'Tis seven o'clock, I know that time is right,

    And yet it seems to me more like midnight.

    There Alice lives, and there my true love sleeps;

    At thought of her, my heart with new warmth leaps.

    Ah! someone comes, Oh! how I hope 'tis she.

    My Alice dear!

GILES *(enter)*.

    It isn't her, it's me.

JACK.

    I see that now.

---

59   By surprise.

60   Go away.

61   Catch.

62   Foul.

63   Satan.

64   Marketplace.

GILES.

Oh do yer? That's all right.

JACK.

Is Alice up?

GILES.

Yes, she's been up all night.

JACK.

What, ill?

GILES.

No stairs *(aside)* my answer makes him frown.

JACK.

I said, "was she up" which meant "was she *down*."

GILES.

Did it though? Well I beg leave to doubt it;

I'm too *downy*[65] to think that about it.

JACK.

But will she soon be out?

GILES.

What, Alice?

JACK.

Yes.

GILES.

I think she will; but your suit[66] do not press.

JACK.

Why not pray?

GILES.

Because Dad does not like it;

Says, that you his fancy do not strike it.

JACK.

If I knew where it lay, I'd like to, straight.

GILES.

You'll have a chance for he'll be down at *eight*.

JACK.

He *hates* me now because I'm poor, I see,

Apprenticed to a hatter I'm not free

To seek my fortune in a foreign *clime*,

And *climb* up to it in a way sublime.

'Twas ever thus, love's pathway can't be smooth,

Heigh ho! I sigh in vain my pain to soothe.

GILES.

Never mind your *sighs*, think of my *sire*;

Drop your love and do not raise *his ire*;

65   Knowing or wide awake.
66   Courtship.

For if you do *as higher* up you raise it,
The more he owes you, and he always pays it.
You'd best look out, I've told you what's the matter
So mind what you are *at*.

JACK.

Yes like a *hatter*.

DUET

Air—"Prince Tiptoe"[67]

Oh when first you fall in love and wish to make your bow,
To a girl whose dad's averse and like[68] to make a row;
You advance beneath her window, and upon tip-toe,
You'd ascend the ladder lightly, so that he shan't know.
"Oh my pretty miss, kiss a kiss,
Pretty miss, kiss a kiss.
Oh darling I am longing for a kiss, kiss, kiss,
And if you will but give me one 'twill be such bliss."
And we have a kiss so silently before we part,
Without a noise I press her gently to my heart.

Chorus

JACK and GILES.

While the old man is sleeping,
Then your tryst be keeping,
Off you'd best be creeping,
Yes, yes, off upon tip-toe.

FATHER WILLIAM (*enters. Speaks*).

You Giles, come here, why don't you open shop?
That useless lot of singing you'd best drop;
To work at once, you lazy rascal you,
And you, Sir Jack, do what you've got to do.

JACK.

I beg your pardon you are not my master.

FATHER WILLIAM.

No, if I were I'd make you move much faster.
The bar's not cleared, Good gracious! I must hurry;
These lounging rascals put one in a flurry (*exit*).

(*Enter Alice*).

JACK.

Oh Alice dear!

ALICE.

Ah Jack!

---

67   Celian Kottaun (music) and Harry Hunter (lyrics), "Prince Tiptoe (Song and Dance)" (London: Francis Bros. and Day, 1886). Sung by Miss Florrie Robina, a music hall singer, dressed as a masher. See "A Chat with Florrie Robina," *Era*, 22 September, 1894.

68   Likely.

JACK.

    Once more we meet,

    To see you yet again, is quite a treat;

    It does my eyes good when I look at you;

    I *see* (eyes see).

ALICE.

    Why yes, dear Jack, of course they do.

JACK.

    Say you'll be mine.

ALICE.

    My father won't allow it.

JACK.

    You love me?

ALICE.

    Yes.

JACK.

    Then to him avow it.

ALICE.

    'Tis useless Jack, he says you are too poor.

JACK.

    Poverty's no crime.

ALICE.

    But it's a bore.

JACK.

    What can I do, cancel my indentures,

    Seek my fortune in some wild adventures,

    Go for a soldier?

ALICE.

    That would better be

    At Woolwich, join the Royal Artillery (artil*erie*).

JACK.

    A good idea, in fact a first class notion!

    I'll go at once and try to win promotion.

    My love be sure it will eternal be,

    I'll crack some *nuts*[69] and gain a *colonel*cy[70] (colonel see).

SONG

Original Air, composed by Miss Amy Carver

JACK.

    I'm going to enlist in the army,

    A soldier I'll be smart and tall:

    The thought of the wars won't alarm me.

    I fear not in honour to fall;

---

69   Heads.

70   Rank of colonel.

The cannon's loud thunder will find me
Facing the foe when in view;
One prayer for the girl left behind me.
Then charge with my comrades so true.

Chorus

Hurrah! for the life of a soldier so brave,
Who fights for his country her honour to save.
Long may the Standard[71] of Old England wave
Over the heads of her army.

(Dance and both exit).

GLOSS *(enters. Speaks).*
　　Now where is Jack? I s'pose he's gone sweethearting;
　　It won't be long before with him I'm parting.
　　He's a real good lad; but I'm sore afraid
　　He don't take kindly to the hatting trade.
　　His *soul's* too large, and he'll the trade not suit;
　　 I'll make him free, and start him well to *boot.*[72]
FATHER WILLIAM *(enter).*
　　Good morning Gloss; you're looking rather seedy,[73]
　　Come, take a dram,[74] I'm sure you're not too needy;
　　'Twill cheer you up.
GLOSS.
　　I feel a cup too low.[75]
　　My business flags, and hats are not a go.
　　I'll take a drop of lotion,[76] something short.[77]
　　What is the liquor, brandy, rum, or port?
FATHER WILLIAM.
　　'Tis whiskey neat, the spirit of *Home Rule.*[78]
GLOSS.
　　Then I'll not drink it, I'm the other school.[79]
FATHER WILLIAM.
　　There I've changed it, it's better now I think,
　　It's Orange gin, for Orange men[80] to drink.
　　The Union's defenders.

71　Flag (the Union Jack).
72　Free him from the obligations of his apprenticeship and help set him up in another trade (as a shoemaker, the puns indicate).
73　Shabby or hung-over.
74　Drink.
75　Hung-over.
76　Alcohol.
77　Undiluted.
78　Irish whiskey is likened to the topical controversy of Ireland's self-governance.
79　Favouring government from Westminster (London) rather than Dublin.
80　Protestant Unionists who favoured British rule over Ireland.

GLOSS.

That suits me well.

FATHER WILLIAM (aside).

It's all the same, a political sell.[81]

(Aloud) Are you aware that your apprentice presses

Upon my daughter his uncalled addresses?

He says he loves her.

GLOSS.

That gives no surprise;

For she is pretty, and has lovely eyes.

FATHER WILLIAM.

Like her father.

GLOSS.

Indeed! I don't know where;

I'd not for your child take her, that I swear.

FATHER WILLIAM.

That's very likely; but some folks are blind.

The question that I asked just call to mind.

GLOSS.

Jack's not my son, he may be nobly born;

I know I found him when a child forlorn

Left right upon my doorstep in dead of night,

Took him in.

FATHER WILLIAM.

As he'll do you[82] and serve you right.

GLOSS.

Pooh! a likely[83] lad, he may do well in life,

Then, let him wed the lass and make her his wife.

FATHER WILLIAM.

Not for the world, shall he my Alice wed,

With my consent.

GLOSS.

He will without instead.

He's made his mind up, in good time you'll see;

I know Jack well.

FATHER WILLIAM.

A *Jack*anapes[84] is he,

A poor apprentice wed my lovely child!

With rage I *bust*, I feel so very wild.

GLOSS.

Your raging *bust* pray calm, keep your spirits up;

---

81   Betrayal or contrivance.
82   Deceive.
83   Handsome, promising.
84   An impertinent, wily, or monkeylike creature.

Take some spirits down, come, in a friendly cup.
If I *cancel* Jack's indentures, how then?

(Enter Jack and Alice).

FATHER WILLIAM.
You *can sell* no such trash to any men.
Who'll buy them?
JACK.
I said *cancel.*
FATHER WILLIAM.
That's a plant;
You say you *can sell*, and I say you *can't.*
GLOSS.
I'll make him free.
JACK.
You will? Then I've a plan
To gain my fortune, that is, if I can.
I mean to try and make myself a hero,
Become a Caesar or a second Nero.[85]

(Enter Giles).

FATHER WILLIAM.
My child the *prize.*[86]
GLOSS.
Then by Great Jove[87] he'll win it!
FATHER WILLIAM *(aside).*
His idle boast I'm sure there's nothing in it.
JACK.
Sur*pris*ed am I; but keep you to your word:
As witness, all who have the statement heard,
Don't fear my love, you soon shall hear from me:
I'll try my luck and will a soldier be.

(Exit Father William).

GILES.
And I'll go too, I fear not war's alarms,[88]
For years these *hands* have been attached to *arms.*
I'll be a soldier, yes, this very day,
For 'mongst the ladies they've a taking way;
They're never vanquished, if in *uniform* they sue;
But steal the darling's hearts, they *uniformly* do.
Love and fighting together long have tarried,
You don't believe it? Wait till you are married.

---

85   Ancient Roman rulers.
86   Reward.
87   A mild oath on the leader of the ancient gods (a.k.a. Jupiter or Zeus).
88   Call to arms.

The 'cruiting[89] sergeant's near at hand, I know;
I saw him here about three years ago.

JACK.

Ha, ha! that sound, it is a *mar*shall strain
To which I'm *par*shall when I hear't again;
It fills my soul with *ardour* and with might:
I long the *harder* for the coming fight.
Back, back, ye knaves, where is your gentle breeding?
This for a *schoolboard* is a vile proceeding;
You have this dame a *deal bored*,[90] that I see:
(To Alice) Fear not dear madam, you rely on me.

QUEEN *(enters)*.

Thanks my gallant lad, I will requite you!
But yon rabble, why—I will indict you!

BOYS of the CHORUS.

The soldiers come!

JACK.

Ah! so they do, this way:
I'll join their ranks, I will *enlist* today.

QUEEN *(aside to Jack)*.

*In list*ing to your words I seem to learn,
You for a soldier's life do greatly yearn.
Is't so?

JACK.

It is.

ALICE.

Yes that ma'am is his aim.
He'd be a soldier, and *aspires* to fame.

JACK.

As spires erect they stand within a town,
My deeds shall be, and chronicle renown.

QUEEN.

Go on young man; in your resolves you're right.

JACK.

This day shall make me, or undo me quite.

(Exit Queen, Jack, and Alice. Enter Sergeant O'Grady, Simon, and Recruits).

SONG
Air—"Later On"[91]

O'GRADY.

When I see a boy sure, I want to enlist
Later on *(whistle)* later on.

---

89   Recruiting.
90   Pun on deal-board (a thin plank).
91   Charles Osborne (music and lyrics), "Later On," (London: Francis Bros & Day, [1885]). Sung and whistled by Harry Randall. The whistled passages in the verse each consists of a triplet arpeggio and whole note.

The tale that I tell bedad,[92] gives him a twist,
Later on, *(whistle)* later on.
To him I promise impossible things;
He goes 'mongst his pals and my praises he sings,
A dozen companions back with him he brings.
Later on, *(whistle)* later on.

(Speaks) Come lads, now gather round; don't be afraid,
I've not come here to carry out *a raid*;
Arrayed in all my glory here you see
A sergeant brave, O'Grady, sure that's me.
Some boys I want to serve the Queen, it's asey,[93]
There's naught to do; the berth is sure to plase[94] ye;
A soldier's life is one great round of pleasure:
A little fighting and a lot of leisure.
The beds on which ye lie, are *down* be sure;
(Aside) Bedad that's true; they're *down* close to the floor.
(To Jack) At morn ye rise and do a little drill,
Then breakfast get, with bacon from the grill;
Of grub there's plenty; faith, there is no stint;
You've but to eat, drink, sleep and be contint.
In fact you are a gent in every sense,
And live entirely at the Queen's expense.
SIMON.
How if you're wounded?
O'GRADY.
That's not worth the mention,
If your head's blown off you can draw a pension:
And there's the pay; ah boys, there's lots of cash
To treat your sweethearts with, and cut a dash.[95]
In a month you'd get a little heap of money,
You can't spend it in a minute; there, my honey!
Won't that tempt ye, an't there any willing,
To 'list[96] at once, come, who'll take the shilling?[97]
SIMON.
I'm not so simple, shillin' moight be bad.
O'GRADY.
You take it then and try it,[98] knowing lad.

---

92   By gosh.
93   Easy (imitating Irish pronunciation).
94   Please.
95   Be impressive.
96   Enlist.
97   Taking the Queen's (or King's) shilling from a recruiting officer was synonymous with enlisting.
98   Bite it to ensure its authenticity.

SIMON.
  It be all right mates, shillin's good enough.
  Here, take it back again.
O'GRADY.
  No, that's all stuff;
  You took it freely, now you are a soldier.
SIMON.
  I only meant to try it, as I told yer;
  And I won't list.
O'GRADY.
  You've done it.
SIMON.
  You're another;
  You'd better let I go, I'll tell my mother.
O'GRADY.
  There, hold him lads, he'll like it by and by.
SIMON.
  I won't I tell 'ee.
O'GRADY.
  Then you'll have to try.
  Come lads, let me persuade you, take the bob,[99]
  You'd best be quick now while I'm on the job;
  So speak at once, where is the lad so brave,
  Who'll serve the Queen, his country help to save

(Enter Jack and Alice).

  From foreign foes?
JACK.
  Here sergeant, I'm your boy;
  I'll serve the Queen, and volunteer with joy—
  I want no bribe—no shilling sir of you.
GILES.
  If I enlist sir may I have the two?
O'GRADY.
  You must accept twelve deno.[100]
JACK.
  Well then here,
  Come, take it lads, and spend it all in beer.
GILES.
  Come, give me one, I'll follow where he's led,
  Here, take it lads—no, I'll keep it instead.
O'GRADY.
  Well come, you are the smartest[101] lad I've seen.

---

99 Shilling.
100 Twelve pence (equivalent to one shilling).
101 Most prompt or quick.

JACK.

Then, I'll perhaps be *welcome* to the Queen.

O'GRADY.

You will, my boy; and I can prophesy

You'll be a *general* soon, there, that's no lie,

For when lads join the army such as you

They rise at once, they *general*ly do.

GILES.

And won't I rise 'cos if I don't I'm danged.[102]

O'GRADY.

You're sure to rise; you'll probably be hanged.

GILES.

Well that's a corker![103]

FATHER WILLIAM *(enter)*.

What is this I hear?

My boy a soldier? Pray excuse this tear.

GILES.

There shut up Dad, you know I gave you warning.

FATHER WILLIAM.

'Tain't shutting up, but opening in the morning

That bothers me—who'll take the shutters down?

CHORUS LAD.

I measter,[104] all the week for half a crown.[105]

GILES.

Come, take him Dad, or else you're pretty green;

I serve for a whole crown so I serve the Queen.

(Enter Gryphon).

JACK.

Come friends we'll drain a glass before we go;

You'll drink with me with*in*?

O'GRADY.

With*out* a no.

With*in* an *inn*, an *in*teresting station:

To drain a glass to mut'al admiration.

Here's to yer my boy; and here's the same to you.

Long life to you; long life to you, Horoo!

So come along.

JACK.

Yes sergeant, lead the way.

O' GRADY.

Come follow lads, remember I've to pay.

---

102 Damned; possibly an elision of damned and hanged.

103 Something that settles a discussion.

104 Muster (attend military roll call).

105 Two shillings and sixpence (2s 6d).

(Enter Baron Hearthardaswood).

GRYPHON.

You saw that lad? 'Twas Jack.

BARON.

He's deuced smart.

GRYPHON.

He's now a soldier and must soon depart;

Then we'll get his sweetheart in our power.

BARON.

Yes, that is good, the pretty little flower.

GRYPHON.

Call in Dismolo, and he will I'm sure

Suggest a plan which we will soon *mature*.[106]

To *meet your* (mate your) approbation there's no doubt.

BARON.

Your jokes do not; such frivolity I scout.

This is serious business we are on,

So cease your trifling, or you'd best be gone.

DISMOLO *(enter)*.

You called me Baron, I am up to time,

What is't you wish me do? Tell me the crime;

Larceny, or murders? I'm on the job;

I'd rather cut a throat, or crack a nob[107]

Than eat my dinner, be it baked or boiled;

For years to gain this excellence I've toiled;

And now I'm perfect in all villainy—

BARON.

Come, cease your chatter, and attend to me:

You'll have to carry off a girl.

DISMOLO.

Ah yes!

BARON.

Of form and beauty rare.

DISMOLO.

Just so, I guess.

SONG
Air—"She's the Only Girl I Love"[108]

BARON.

This girl I love—all things above,

I long for her night and day;

Her pretty feet her ankles neat—

---

106 Fully develop.

107 Head.

108 Gus Williams (music and lyrics), "Pretty Little Dark Blue Eyes (She's the Only Girl I Love)," *Mohawk Minstrels Magazine* 16:47 ([1886]): 22-25. Sung by Johnny Danvers.

DISMOLO.
  Oh be careful what you say.
BARON.
  Her waist and arm have every charm,—
DISMOLO.
  Oh I can't stand much of this.—
BARON.
  Her finger tips—her coral lips,
  It would drive me mad to kiss.

Chorus

ALL.
  She's a scrumptious little tart,
  And the girl that he does/I most prize;
  She's the image in his/my heart
  He looks/I look on her with longing eyes
BARON (*speaks*).
  Have you your band at hand, and is it *trusty*?
DISMOLO.
  As true as steel that never has got *rusty*.
BARON.
  'Tis well,
DISMOLO.
  'Tis so.
BARON.
  Attend to what I say.
  The girl I'd have you seize and bear away
  Is Alice, standing at the *bar*.
DISMOLO.
  What, drinks?
GRYPHON.
  If so 'twill prove her ruin soon methinks;
  For standing liquors to those raw recruits
  Is not a process which one's pockets suits.
BARON.
  Well, it shan't *bar* my progress in the game.
DISMOLO.
  To carry out our *bar*gain be my aim.
BARON.
  You know the great reward?
DISMOLO.
  Yes, half a crown.
  (*Aside*) I'd do it for a tanner,[109] money down.
  (*Aloud*) In villainy I revel deep and dire.

---

109 Sixpence (6d).

Oft have I tried to set the Thames on fire;
But no success attends my aspiration,
Though I'm the deep-dyed[110] villain of the nation.

SONG
Air—"Treading on Dangerous Ground"[111]

I'm the greatest villain that e'er did exist,
And murders I oftentimes plan;
The neck of a victim I give a slight twist:
Do that in a second I can.
It has been forever, my earnest endeavour,
To represent every vile crime;
Sheep stealing or arson; garroting, or larcen;[112]
I'll commit everyone in good time.

Chorus
Air—"Jonathan Joseph Jeremiah"[113]

The object to which I aspire
Is one I'm sure we all admire,
In it I mean to excel,
The worst of crimes, they suit me well.
For sacrilege now I'm your man
And murders do, on a merry plan,
I "polish 'em off" in manner odd
In fact, I'm worse than Sweeney Todd.[114]

BARON (speaks).

Now stand aside, and when the chance you see
To seize the maid, and bear her off for me,
Within my castle, which remote doth stand
Beyond a moat, the broadest in the land.
There to my love I safe can make allusion.

DISMOLO.

My Lord, they come!

GRYPHON.

Ah so they do!

BARON.

Confusion!

(Enter Jack and Sergeant O'Grady).

---

110 Dark.

111 Alfred Lee (music) and Harry Hunter (lyrics), "Treading on Dangerous Ground" (London: J.A. Turner, 1877). Harry Hunter (interlocutor for the Mohawk Minstrels) performed the song.

112 Larceny (theft).

113 W.G. Eaton (music) and Harry Hunter (lyrics), "Jonathan Joseph Jeremiah, or Named after Everybody," The Mohawk Minstrels' Magazine 5:2 ([1881]): 21-23.

114 The Demon Barber of Fleet Street, probably fictional, whose victims were made into meat pies.

O'GRADY.

Good luck to you my boy, you are a trump,[115]
And she's yer sweetheart, and she's nice and plump;
You'll make a pretty pair when e'er you wed;
I wish she'd marry me, my boy, instead.

JACK.

You're too late, I'm the lad, sir, of her choosing.

O'GRADY.

She told me that herself when I was boozing;
She doesn't care a rap I know for me,
You're her 'appy one, I'm a reparee;[116]
But let us march, obey your sergeant's will.
And say fare *well* at once, or you'll fare *ill*.
Recruits, fall in. Now mind what you're about.
Fall *in* I said, bedad, you all fall *out*!
Heads up, be smart, or else beware my frown.
Fall in like this.

JACK.

That looks more like fall *down*.

O'GRADY.

Silence, at once! or else I'll make you feel
You Spalpeens[117] you! Oh curse the Orange peel![118]

(Enter Father William, Gloss, and Alice).

GLOSS.

Jack my boy, although we're going to part,
You have the best of wishes from my heart:
That you may rise, whatever be your station,
And be an ornament to this great nation
Is my sincere desire.

O'GRADY.

A good remark to make;
I am an ornament myself.

GLOSS.

For a twelfth cake.[119]

O'GRADY.

What's that you say?

GLOSS.

I merely was suggesting,
Your uniform's the one men must look best in.

---

115 First-rate fellow.
116 *Réparé*, the past participle of *réparer* (to repair), has a moral connotation of sobriety.
117 Rascals.
118 Orange rind, slippery underfoot.
119 An iced and decorated cake served at Twelfth Night (5 January), at the conclusion of the Twelve Days of Christmas.

JACK.

> And now, dear Alice, let my last words tell
> To you, my love, likewise a fond farewell:
> My love for you is boundless as the ocean,
> My life shall be one scene of true devotion.

ALICE.

> I doubt it not; for I would rather die
> Than wed another, yet I say good bye.
> And if between u*s miles* there may be many
> The*se smiles* will be to me, the best of any.

JACK.

> No fairy face though charming it might be,
> Could e'er ef*face* the one so dear to me.

O'GRADY.

> Cut it will yer? Make yer parting shorter.
> It seems, bedad, he'll never leave your daughter.
> Here take her bonny face.

FATHER WILLIAM.

> Thank you.

(Enter Dismolo and Baron).

DISMOLO.

> Not so fast:
> The chance is mine, I triumph here at last.

BARON.

> Stand back I say, or all my anger dread!
> I've got the maid, and mean with her to wed.

ALICE.

> Let go your *hold*! you monster *old* and frightful.

BARON.

> You little duck, more beautiful when spiteful!

JACK.

> Come, I say that's mine!

BARON.

> I hear you do, what then?
> You'd better take it coolly; what oh! my men!

(Enter Body of Armed Men).

> You see my power is great, at you I scoff.
> I've got your love, and mean to bear her off.

JACK.

> Where would you take her?

BARON.

> Wouldn't you like to know?

JACK.

> I'll follow you myself where'er you go.

O'GRADY.

    I don't think so, that remains to be seen,

    Your time belongs, my boy, now to the Queen;

    And we must march at once.

JACK.

    And leave him here

    With Alice in his power?

O'GRADY.

    Och! don't fear,

    You'll have to leave her, that without a doubt,

    And in his power, unless she can get out!

    But when you are enrolled safe—in due form,

    Ask for leave of absence—his castle storm.

JACK.

    She may be killed meantime.

BARON.

    No not by me;

    I mean to treat her, ah, so tenderly.

JACK.

    What can I do? I stand without a friend,

    Saving poor Gloss; he can't assistance lend.

QUEEN OF WONDERLAND *(enter. Aside to Jack)*.

    I can.

JACK.

    What, you?

QUEEN.

    You need not doubt my power

    I'll follow your sweetheart within his tower,

    And *shield* her from all harm if *she yield* not

    To his entreaty.

JACK.

    Thanks, one friend I've got.

QUEEN.

    This packet take, and when you are away,

    Then break the seal, at night of the third day.

JACK.

    But who are you?

QUEEN.

    You shall know all ere long

    Till then, be sure your love shan't come to wrong.

SONG
Air—"I Can't Get at It"[120]

JACK.

You'd better now give up that girl, or this day's work you'll rue.

BARON.

You must think I am generous, that sort of thing to do.

DISMOLO.

You unsophisticated youth! You think yourself a man.

BARON.

You'd better come up here my boy and take her if you can.

Chorus

JACK.

   I can't get at her, I can't get at her;
   That Baron I should like to kill;
   He's taken her, and has her still,
   I can't get at her, I can't get at her.
   He glories in the wrong he's done; he's stolen her.

Chorus
Air—"I did It"[121]

BARON.

   I did it, I did it,
   It didn't take me long!
   I did it, I did it,
   And you think I've done wrong!
   You may kick up a rumpus,
   I don't care I'm sure;
   I'd like to steal all pretty girls;
   A fellow can't do more.

Chorus
Air—"Charlie Dilke Upset the Milk"[122]

ALL.

   The Baron he's a shameless man,
   As naughty as can well be,
   And we all say he's far too gay,
   And ought to be put in a bag.
   Villainy's representative,

---

120 Harry Randall (music) and Herbert Cole (lyrics), "I Can't Get at It" (London: Francis Bros. & Day, [1886]).

121 A.E. Durandeau (music) and George Horncastle (lyrics), "I Did It!" (London: Hopwood & Crew, [1887]). Sung by James Fawn.

122 Little Fred Gilbert (music and lyrics), "Charlie Dilke Upset the Milk" (London: Charles Sheard, [1886]). This topical song, sung at the Alhambra by Master MacDermott, refers to the scandal in which a prominent Liberal MP was named in a divorce proceeding. The bizarre verdict—that Virginia Crawford had committed adultery with Charles Dilke, but not he with her—capped a thoroughly rivetting trial. W.T. Stead then promoted a muckraking campaign in early 1886, resulting in Dilke bringing a legal action against Mrs. Crawford. Although she probably lied, he came off very badly in the witness box. For the song's British and foreign notoriety, see J.B. Booth, *Old Pink 'un Days* (New York: Dodd, Mead, 1925), 361-63.

A regular wicked old sell, he
Winks his eye, at girls so sly,
He's such a giddy old wag.

Scene 3

Country Lane, Roadside Inn. Enter Jack and Sergeant O'Grady.

O'GRADY.
    Cheer up, my jewel, it is no use graving[123]
    For those at home, whom you've had to be laving.[124]
    Belave in what I say when I remark:
    Your *flame* will be all right, my noble *spark*.
JACK.
    At every halt you make that observation.
O'GRADY.
    Well, as it's true it needs no *alter*cation.
JACK.
    We h*alt occasion*ally thrice a day;
    And yet I can't rely on what you say.
O'GRADY.
    And sure ye might belave it, if ye try.
JACK.
    You say 'twill be so.
O'GRADY.
    And the reason why,
    Is becase—becase—now 'twixt me and you,
    The reason is becase—becase—I do.
JACK.
    Why, that's a woman's reason.
O'GRADY.
    Well, what then?
    A woman's reason satisfies the men,
    They'd have in parliament a female school.
JACK.
    Then we should all be subject to *Home Rule*.
O'GRADY.
    Bedad! I'd rather not, 'tis my opinion
    We'd be worse off with petticoat dominion;
    But see, our *billet*[125] wears a cheery tone,
    Come join us.

---

123 Grieving.
124 Leaving.
125 Lodgings.

JACK.

Thanks, I would *be let* alone.

O'GRADY.

Well, as you will, but I am after thinking,

If you want cheering up, best take to drinking *(exit)*.

JACK.

Alone at last, the prospect now before me

Is not the one to greatly reassure me,

In spite of all the sergeant says to cheer me,

My love I feel would safer be if near me.

That wicked Baron has her in his power,

I cannot see her even for an hour.

Unhappy fate! thus at the call of duty

That I should have to leave her there, my beauty!

And strike no blow to save her, I feel mad!

Was ever lover in a plight so sad?

SONG

Air—"Balradour"[126]

I love a little charmer, and Alice is her name;

But now I am compelled by fate to leave her,

Although she's miles away from me she'll love me all the same,

And I am not the one e'er to deceive her.

The parting makes me sad,

It really seems too bad.

Hope again that quickly I may meet her;

I ne'er shall happy be,

While she is far from me,

And in this way, my love, I long to greet her:

Chorus

U—li—ai—li—e—li—o.

I have come from far away.

U—li—ai—li—e—li—o.

My darling now I pray.

U—li—ai—li—e—li—o.

You name the happy day;

And then while life shall last we'll ne'er be parted.

(Speaks) I had forgotten, that packet might reveal

Some small ray of hope, if I but break the seal;

This is the day! the third from when I started,

Come Jack, cheer up, and don't be so down-hearted.

---

126 Harry Starr (music and lyrics), "Balradour" (London: Hopwood & Crew, 1887). A "Tyrolean song" (with yodelling) sung by the male impersonator Jenny Hill, in the pantomime *Aladdin* (Alexandra Theatre, Liverpool).

Here is the packet safe and sound, I vow,
The day's the right one so I'll break it now.
What's this, a ring? A beauty I declare!
Oh shan't I look *a swell*[127] when this I wear!
Perhaps 'twill be *as well*, if I look more:
Oh! here's a paper, written on I'm sure,
But I can't read it, as I have no light:
I wish the moon would shine for me tonight.

(The moon appears).

Good gracious me! it shines this very minute;
Now for the paper see what there is in it.
(Reads) "Your course is clear, be brave and true,
And all that's good shall come to you;
Fear not for her you leave behind;
But always keep her in your mind.
Wherever honour calls you go,
Ne'er leave a friend, nor fear a foe.
On glory's record carve your name,
A just ambition leads to fame;
If more you wish to ascertain,
There's one you will not ask in vain;
But raise the ring in your left hand,
And call the 'Queen of Wonderland.'"
Can this be true? Well, that is soon found out,
I need no longer here remain in doubt.
I've but to raise the ring—yet stop a minute!
Might this not be a plot with treason in it?
And she who gave the ring a *witch* may be,
Who has an object in *bewitch*ing me.
Who is this Queen, a good or evil fay?
I'll see her soon let her *be which* she may.
Away! all doubts, at once I'll let her know.
I fear her not—in fact "I fear no foe."
"The ring I raise in my left hand,
Approach, the Queen of Wonderland!"

(Enter Queen of Wonderland).

There no one comes—a swindle, what a shame!
Good gracious me! Oh lor'! Is that you dame?
I expected another party quite.
QUEEN.
Well if they come I can wish you good night.

---

127 Stylish gentleman.

JACK.

But how came you so far from where we met?
You could not walk or a conveyance get.

QUEEN.

You called just now the Queen of Wonderland;
Then marvel not that here with you I stand.
Behold in me the one you want to see.

JACK.

Great Queen, to you I now must bend the knee.
Here at your feet a suppliant I stay,
And ask for news of those left far away;
Is my love well? and when was't last you saw her?
Take back my message, tell her I adore her.
Is she quite safe, and free from villain power?
Tell her my love grows stronger every hour;
Make her to know I think of her alway;[128]
And that from her my heart can never stray.
That she's my own, my darling, and my life,
That none but she shall ever be my wife.
Shield her from *harm*, that both our loves may be
United soon in *harm*ony through thee.
Cheer up her spirits, do not let her grieve.

QUEEN.

Come, come, I say, I pray you give me leave:
Your love is well, although she's not yet free;
But for that end I think you can trust me,
The Baron I will find means to outwit,
I have the power you may rely on it.

JACK.

How can I thank you?

QUEEN.

Wait until the end.
Then you'll be sure I really am your friend,
That ring you wear unites you now to Alice,
And though she is imprisoned in a palace,
And far from you, she cannot come to harm;
That ring will hold her by a special charm;
So guard it well, preserve it with your life!
And it shall aid you when you claim your wife.
Apart from this 'twill keep your image near
The one you love; she'll see you just as clear,
As though you stood beside her from the hour,
When I reclaim her from the Baron's power.

---

128 Perpetually.

JACK.

Can this be done?

QUEEN.

It shall be with my aid.

JACK.

Then nought is left of which I am afraid.

QUEEN.

Your future course you know remains with you;
You've but to seek your fortune and be true,
To those few precepts which ere now you read,
The victor's laurels soon shall crown your head;
And though you'll find no easy road to fame,
You must succeed if glory is your aim.
The mystery which now surrounds your birth
Shall be removed if you but prove your worth.

JACK.

I'll do my best, the best can do no more;
This good advice within my heart I'll store,
And every nerve and faculty I'll strain,
Until the goal of fortune I attain.
This is the task which I'll pursue with pride,
Returning then to claim my own fair bride.

DUET

Air—"O May'st Thou Dream of Me"[129]

I feel my heart beat lightly,
And that I owe to you:
You shone in my path so brightly,
And proved a friend so true;
Yet though we now must part,
And journey far away;
You'll live within my heart,
I'll think of you each day.

QUEEN.

You may know that when away,
I'll guard thy interests well;
And will cheer thy true love,
With what you wished me tell;
You need then fear no more,
Thy path with joy pursue;
To guard her you adore,
I bid farewell to you.

---

129 Virginia Gabriel (music), "Oh! May'st Thou Dream of Me: Serenade for Two Voices" (London: Boosey & Sons, 1861).

QUEEN and JACK.
Then fare thee well adieu
I go thy love to see/you go my love to see.
Whilst locked in fairy sleep
She'll think herself with thee/she'll think herself with me.

(Exit Queen. Enter Sergeant O'Grady and Giles).

O'GRADY *(speaks).*
Jack my boy, what the divil are ye after?
I heard some sounds of singing, and of laughter;
What's your little game, are you gone off your head?
It's time that you came in and went to bed.
GILES.
Oh sergeant! ain't it precious cold out here? We'd better go.
O'GRADY.
A soldier knows no fear.
GILES.
Of course he don't, and I am not afraid
Of any mortal, fighting is my trade;
But you know out here in this dismal spot
There may be spirits.
O'GRADY.
Then I'll take them hot.
GILES.
I mean bad spirits; you will own they're risky.
O'GRADY.
I never drink 'em, as I stick to whiskey;
And in that *case* no spirits can be bad,
I've lived on whiskey since I was a lad.
GILES.
I mean ghosts!
O'GRADY.
What?
GILES.
Look there! Oh! Gracious me!
There's something moves! a Ghost! no, it's a tree.
O'GRADY.
Look here! ye spalpeen you want me to frighten,
When danger's near, you'll find my pluck will heighten.
An Irish soldier's far above the livel[130]
Of any fear. Och! murther! here's the devil!
Acushla![131] Now St. Patrick, if yer please

---

130 Level.
131 Darling.

You must not touch a man when on his knees;
Not that I fear ye, no, the deuce a bit!
To take a sultry[132] journey I'm not fit,
If ye want a victim to take down to—
Ye'll find this young man here will do quite well;
He's rough, but ready.

GILES.

Nothing of the kind.
You take the sergeant, and leave me behind.

JACK.

I'll have your blood!

O'GRADY.

Bedad! that's turned to water

JACK.

I'll give you something.

O'GRADY.

Well, then give me quarter.[133]

JACK.

Your abject fear, it really makes me smile.

O'GRADY.

Och! Jack it's you, I knew ye all the while.

GILES.

Oh, that's a whopper![134]

O'GRADY.

So is that you see.
I'm not a *liar* you re*ly on* me.

JACK.

Well, never mind, for bed we will be starting—

O'GRADY.

We'll have a song and dance before we're parting.

SONG

Air—"The Christening"

If you want to go in for promotion,
'Tis the best notion, show your devotion,
By giving up drinking all lotion,
And be the teetotalers'[135] joy.
On guard if you're ever caught soaking,
With girls joking, your pipes smoking,
And about your hard life if you're croaking,
You'll all chance of favour destroy.

---

132 Hot, as in Hades.
133 Clemency, especially from a death sentence.
134 Lie.
135 Abstainers from alcohol.

GILES.

In that, no doubt you are right, you are the man that should be advising 'em.

There's nought like example you see to make folks know what you mean.

JACK.

If you'd stuck to that rule for yourself 'stead of their faults others apprising them.

You'd be more than a sergeant, I'm sure, p'raps commander in chief might have been.

O'GRADY.

By my soul, I have long left off drinking,

And I am thinking, I would like "winking,"[136]

From a quarten[137] of whiskey be shrinking,

If 'twas offered now to this boy.

JACK.

Now O'Grady, your statements astounding,

Most confounding, fibs abounding,

With such virtues yourself you're surrounding.

O'GRADY.

It's all true, and I swear it's no *loi*.[138]

(Dance)

Scene 4

Baron Hearthardaswood's kitchen. Enter Father William disguised as a woman.

FATHER WILLIAM.

Now leave me while I make the favourite dish;

If it got spoilt 'twould be a kettle of fish;

So take your *leaf*, and I'll at once pro*ceed*,

As your assistance I don't further need.

I am head cook, I was brought up at *Cook*ham;[139]

The other scullions[140] here, I overlook 'em.

The way to cook I learned from Mrs. Beeton,[141]

A book that treats of all that should be eaten.

SONG

Air—"True-Born Irishman"[142]

Since last we met, I've changed my trade, I've now become a cook,

And all the recipes I know have borrowed from a book;

---

136 Drink.

137 Quarter of a pint (quartern).

138 Lie (with O'Grady's Irish accent making the rhyme with "boy").

139 A village in Berkshire.

140 Kitchen servants.

141 Isabella Mary Beeton (née Mayson) (1836-65), prolific journalist and editor of *Beeton's Book of Household Management* (London: Beeton, 1859-61), an indispensible and ubiquitous guide for the Victorian housewife.

142 Frank Egerton (music and lyrics), "True-Born Irishman" (London: Francis Bros. & Day, 1886). Sung by Walter Munroe.

To make pea soup, and apple tart, Welsh rabbit,[143] or pancake,
Pie crust, so light, and bread go white, I'm up to every fake;
To make an omelette with jam you squeeze it up quite tight.
A currant roll you make with flies, they look the same at night.
And if you have to get stewed tripe, a dish that somewhat rich is,
Should you find tripe to be too dear, stew up some leather breeches.

Chorus

That's cooking with economy, but I must here repeat,
That what we cooks dish up ourselves we don't intend to eat,
We know a trick worth two of that, and always make a point
To help ourselves to what we like, the best cut off the joint.

(Speaks) As I'm alone, and feel somewhat reflective,
I'll give an explanation retrospective:
When the Baron seized my fair daughter Alice,
A cook was advertised for at the palace;
So I applied, obtained the situation,
Which gave to me a post of observation;
Where I could see my child at dinner hour,
And hold the Baron in an unknown power.
My child resists his suit and will not wed,
He swears he'll make her his without,[144] instead;
And this he hopes to do, but I've a plan
Which holds in check this amatory man.
Sometimes his food with jallap[145] I well[146] ply,
That puts off love making till by and by;
A *dose* of laudanum[147] in the soup he takes,
Will keep him *dos*ing till at length he wakes.
Thus soon I hope to find the *means* to fly
For self and daughter, and I *means* to try.
If I'm not soon successful I've a notion,
That I shall have to try a stronger potion.
His favourite dish tonight is rhubarb tart,
To get it made in time I must be smart.
In making up this tart I feel funky,
But it must be done, Oh! Damn the monkey![148]

(Enter Baron and Dismolo).

---

143 A mixture of toasted cheese and ale on bread.
144 With no cooperation or consent.
145 A purgative drug.
146 Easily.
147 Opium.
148 Rascal.

SONG

Air—"I'm the Captain"[149]

BARON.

I'm a Baron a dasher; and what is much worse:
I am quite a masher, my looks are my curse.
The ladies give way at a glance of my eye;
They fall at my feet if I heave a soft sigh.

Chorus

I'm a Baron bold as brass;
So handsome none can me surpass.
I love the ladies, love them all;
At beauty's feet I often fall—bold as brass.

(Speaks). Here's our new cook, a massive sort of dame,
Come here fair damsel, what might be your name?

FATHER WILLIAM.

It might be Daisy but I fear it ain't.

BARON.

What is it beauty?

FATHER WILLIAM.

That's it without paint.

BARON.

Then Beauty darling, you come here to me;
Come take a seat, no take it on my knee.
Confound it! woman, here's a pretty state,
You for a female, are a heavy weight;
You've squeezed my breath out quite I do declare;
But never mind, let's hear the bill of fare.

FATHER WILLIAM.

From Woolwich town to Greenwich, one penny,
From Greenwich to Blackfriars that's two D.[150]

BARON.

That is the fare of tramways in the street,
I mean the fare for dinner, what's to eat?

FATHER WILLIAM.

I see! of course! you don't want the *tramway*
You want the *carte*[151] for dinner, sir, today.

BARON.

Want the *cart* for dinner! hang me! if I do,
I'd rather try the horse.

---

149 The song "I Am the Captain Boleslas" is from a comic opera produced at the Comedy Theatre (London) on 29 October 1883. Francis Chassaigne (music) and Eugène Leterrier and Albert Vanloo (lyrics), *Falka; or, The Heir-at-Law (Le Droit d'Ainesse)* (London: A. Hays, 1883).

150 Tuppence (2d).

151 Menu.

FATHER WILLIAM.

All right, sir, there's stew.

BARON.

Two horses?

FATHER WILLIAM.

Stew, soup, Mock Turtle very fine.

BARON.

I always take Mock Turtle when I dine.

FATHER WILLIAM.

The fish we have is *ache* (hake).

BARON.

Don't get that again.

If I have so much *ache* (hake) t'will cause you *pain*.

FATHER WILLIAM.

I've veal and ham, what more, I do not know.

BARON.

If you don't think, you'll find I*'ve heal* and *toe*,

So say the lot.

FATHER WILLIAM.

There's parsnips, carrots boiled,

Jugged[152] hare, roast pork, and salads fresh—well oiled,

Roast fowl, and shrimps served with anchovy sauce,

Boiled goose, and pickles, end the second course.

BARON.

A decent snack to start on, that I see.

Dismolo, summon Alice here to me.

Tell her in the kitchen we today would dine;

If she asks the reason, 'tis a whim of mine.

(Exit Dismolo).

You heard me, cook, don't you know what I mean?

It saves you time.

FATHER WILLIAM.

You mean it saves a scene.[153]

(Enter Alice).

BARON.

My dearest love, my dainty future bride,

I with a kiss salute you and with pride.

Is that the way you serve your own adorer?

I ask a kiss and then I get—

FATHER WILLIAM.

A floorer![154]

---

152 Stewed or boiled in a jar.
153 Literally, it spares the necessity of changing scenery (an extra-theatrical joke).
154 Knock-down blow.

ALICE.

That serves you right, you'd better keep your place;
You think that I'd be kissed by such a face?
You're much mistaken!

BARON.

With rage I smother!
How dare you act like that?

ALICE.

Ask me another.

BARON.

Be kind and say you love me.

ALICE.

But I don't.

BARON.

Do say you will a little.

ALICE.

No I won't.

DUET
Air—"Any More"[155]

BARON.

My darling how I love you, you soon shall be my wife,
And I will never leave you any more,

ALICE.

You monster I'll not wed, no, not while I have life,
I'd rather be an old maid, that I'm sure.

BARON.

In that you are mistaken, you'd love me by and by,

ALICE.

I would not if I could do so, and don't intend to try;
You are a dreadful ugly man, you know you are.

BARON.

Oh fie!
I hope you will not say that any more, any more.

Chorus

I hope you will not say that any more, any more,
I hope you will not say that any more,
My tender heart will break,
If my hand you do not take,
For you're the only girl that I adore.

BARON (*speaks*).

Now come to dinner, that you won't refuse?

---

155 By C.J. Taylor.

ALICE.

I only come to dinner when I *chews,*
And of all meals I now have had my last.
My spirits sink *so low,* I mean to fast.

BARON.

But you'll get thin and won't be half so nice;
So take a something.

FATHER WILLIAM.

Yes, take his advice;
A biscuit dry and then a drop of fizz.[156]

ALICE *(aside).*

How like my father that old woman is!

FATHER WILLIAM.

Perhaps my dear, you'd like a drop of short;[157]
A little satin[158] (white) to give *support?*

ALICE.

No wine for me, I'll not *sup port* or sherry,
Nor champagne either, that is all gooseberry.
I'm in the know, my father keeps an inn.
He makes his own champagne, his rum, and gin,
And breaks his spirits down by pails of water.

FATHER WILLIAM *(aside).*

My *spirits* now are *broken* by my daughter.
Who here reveals the secret of my *trade:*
Round on her father in this wild t'rade (tirade).

ALICE.

I'll not eat nor drink, I'll starve myself to death.

BARON.

Have this one *blow out.*[159]

ALICE.

Not while I hold my breath!

BARON.

You are an *insister* upon self-slaughter.

ALICE.

An inn sister no—an inn keeper's daughter.

BARON.

Well, as you will—and have your way this time,
The banquet waits, the viands[160] are sublime;
And you must join us a thing of *course;*
You keep the *courses* waiting—I'll use force.

---

156 Effervescent drink, such as champagne or sparkling water.
157 Distilled liquor.
158 Gin.
159 Exhalation.
160 Provisions.

ALICE.

You would not dare!

BARON.

Dismolo do your duty!

Drag her to me, it's my turn now my beauty;

I'll have you on my knee,

FATHER WILLIAM.

I can't stand this!

I'll smack him on the filbert,[161] hit or miss.

DISMOLO.

Resistance is in vain you must confess.

FATHER WILLIAM.

Stand back! you've roused a British lioness.

Such practices are vile to a young child,

And scarcely yet sixteen, it makes me wild!

Beware the Act—of Parliament—I mean,

You'll be sent to quod,[162] "Baron *versus* Queen."

BARON.

You're not her *mother*.

FATHER WILLIAM.

I regret I'm not.

Or else I'd *smother* you infernal lot.

The wish I find, is *father* to the thought;[163]

I'll do my duty as a mother ought.

BARON.

Go on Dismolo, on to the attack.

FATHER WILLIAM.

Come on Dismolo, I'll give you your whack.

DISMOLO.

You'd better yield!

FATHER WILLIAM.

Who told you so, you looney?[164]

DISMOLO.

If I go there again I'll get more spooney.[165]

At her my men!

You'd best give in or you'll lose every rag.

---

161 Head.

162 Prison. He alludes to the Criminal Law Amendment Act of 1885 (48 & 49 Vict. c. 69) which, in response to W.T. Stead's sensation-provoking article "Maiden Tribute of Modern Babylon," raised the age of consent for girls from thirteen to sixteen years of age (*Pall Mall Gazette*, 6 July 1885). Judith R. Walkowitz, *City of Dreadful Delight: Narratives of Sexual Danger in Victorian London* (Chicago: U of Chicago P, 1992), 81-120.

163 Proverbial, from Shakespeare: "Thy wish was father, Harry, to that thought. / I stay too long by thee, I weary thee." *2 Henry IV*, 4.5.100-1.

164 Lunatic.

165 Sentimentally foolish.

FATHER WILLIAM.

You come and take them, don't stand there and brag.

DISMOLO.

This style of thing to me is somewhat recent,

And 'fore a single man is not quite decent.

Let me persuade you—

FATHER WILLIAM.

Take that for your pains! *(Hits him on the head).*

DISMOLO.

It has not hurt me, as I have no brains.

BARON.

Come seize that girl!

(Father William's disguise is revealed).

DISMOLO.

This woman is a mister! Confound him!

BARON.

Hang her! Bless my soul! I've kissed her!

For this wild business you shall suffer death.

FATHER WILLIAM.

Just you wait a bit until I get my breath.

ALICE.

My father dear!

BARON.

Tie him to the dresser.[166]

As for your daughter, I'll console her, bless her.

Now sound the gong and let us start our dinner,

At the Mock Turtle I'll be a beginner.

This trick is yours, you'll suffer by and by;

The soup's all gone, let's try the rabbit pie.

DISMOLO.

This is witchcraft sire, of that I'm sure;

You'd best not let them practice any more.

Let me deal them death at once, and speedy—

For the joys of hanging I feel greedy,

I like to see the victim struggle hard,

The pain I cause them is its own reward.

Let me but lift him just a foot or two.

FATHER WILLIAM.

I'll lift you my beauty, one foot will do.

BARON.

You'll soon be hung, bring me the *noose*, attendant.

What's this?

---

166 Kitchen cabinet.

DISMOLO.

The news—the Kentish Independent.[167]

BARON.

That *news*paper accords not with my views.

DISMOLO.

And yet you'll find it is the best of *news*.

BARON.

It's useless at a hanging—most absurd.

DISMOLO.

My lord, the Wool[168] with folk hang on each word.

BARON.

Swing him, Dismolo, hang him by the neck.

I'll give no *quarter*[169] as he spoilt my *peck*[170]

On two occasions.

FATHER WILLIAM.

That half-a-bushel makes.

I'll bet you ten to one that this cord breaks.

DISMOLO.

I'll take the bet in quids.[171]

FATHER WILLIAM.

All right, agreed.

(They rig the noose in preparation for hanging).

ALICE.

Hold! You old villain! This shall not proceed.

Hang my dear father 'fore my very eyes?

DISMOLO.

You'd better shut them, as it's now he dies.

Come my pet lambs, pull, do as you are told;

We'll make him dance on air.[172]

(Queen of Wonderland and Silver Star appear).

QUEEN.

You will not! Hold!!

DISMOLO.

Oh! won't we though, we all mean to hold on.

To carry out this job we're bent upon.

QUEEN.

My power despised; that cord now snap asunder.

---

167 A Greenwich newspaper, thus local reading for the audience.

168 A reference to the woolsack, colloquial for the Lord Chancellor, the seat of Speaker in the British House of Lords.

169 One quarter of a hundredweight (28 pounds or 12.7 kilograms); also clemency.

170 He refers to his meals while punning on peck as a measurement (two imperial gallons, or 9.09 litres).

171 Pounds sterling.

172 Hang from a rope.

(The rope breaks, freeing Father William).

SILVER STAR.
Annihilate them all with bolts of thunder,
Destroy this palace, leave no stone upstanding,
They'll fear your power when elements commanding.
BARON.
This is my palace, I am master here,
Who is it dares to thus inspire fear?
FATHER WILLIAM.
I say, my ancient; one thing don't forget,
The cord is broken, so I've won my bet.
BARON.
Stand back, I say! Your answer I command!
QUEEN.
Behold in me the Queen of Wonderland!
These are my subjects faithful to my will.
BARON.
I fear you not, and do defy you still.
This *maid* is mine, *made* so by lawful capture;
She's going to love me with ecstatic *rapture*.
ALICE.
Such mad ideas have *wrap't yer* up of late,
There is no truth in anything you state;
Were I a man, I'd *rap't yer* noddle[173] well,
Ere you so false a *rhapsody* should tell.
I am a captive and I hate you so—
BARON.
You've *captivated* me some time ago.
Since then a *captive loved* have you become.
QUEEN.
I'll pay her ransom if you name the sum.
BARON.
Not untold gold can purchase her I say.
QUEEN.
Then I will have her in another way,
Stand back I say; keep back that motley[174] crew.
You have defied me, and this day you'll rue.
Know 'tis my will that Alice now shall sleep,
And safe within a charméd circle keep!
None shall approach her unless I give power,
And thus she'll stay entrancéd from this hour.
And in her dreams shall rise before her view,

---

173 Back of the head.
174 Miscellaneous.

The land of wonder, peopled there by you;
You'll then appear in very different guise,
And act your parts before her dreaming eyes.
In fairy sleep she'll play her pleasant part,
And be united to her own sweetheart;
The time will then be passed so quick away,
Until her Jack returns; and on that day
She shall awake, her own true love to greet,
And then on Woolwich Common[175] they shall meet.
His birth[176] shall be revealed, each wrong be righted,
And Alice and her Jack shall be united.

GRYPHON *(to Baron).*

To break the magic circle, take this stick,
And seize your lovely Alice, come be quick;
And I will join you when you're far away,
And break the spell that holds her in its *sway.*

BARON.

In its *way* that advice is good no doubt,
And I will carry it, and Alice out.
Your power I do defy, I'll make you quake;
I have the charm your magic ring to break.
Alice I want—I'll have her never fear!
I thus defy you!

(Alice vanishes).[177]

Swindled! She's not here.

GRYPHON *(aside).*

Confound it! Sold![178]

BARON.

I'm duped!

DISMOLO.

Indeed that's true.

QUEEN *(to Baron).*

You need not fear, I am quite up to you,
(To Silver Star) There's treachery at work beyond a doubt,
And when I've time I mean to find it out.
But now away to Wonderland we'll start;
But first a chorus, in it each take a part.

---

175 Military land where the Royal Artillery trained.
176 His real identity and heritage.
177 The *Kentish Independent* of 1 January 1887 specifies that this was *à la* the Vanishing Lady: probably a pivoting trap door.
178 Deceived.

SONG

Air—"The Sun Shines Bright at Last"[179]

You cannot well deceive me, as I told you long ago,
If you persist you're sure to come to grief.
Discovery is certain though its coming may be slow;
You'll find my warning worthy of belief.

FATHER WILLIAM.

They are a set of bad 'uns, and all the villainy they'd dare,
They'd cut a throat and think it quite a spree.
They'd tear a man to pieces, or a woman I declare;
If you doubt it just see what they've made of me.

Chorus

FATHER WILLIAM and QUEEN.

They'll punished be at last, no fear,
They'll punished be at last;
Make no mistake, we're wide awake,
They'll punished be at last.

DISMOLO, BARON, and GRYPHON.

We'll do them brown at last, no fear,
We'll do them brown at last;
Make no mistake, we'll win the cake,[180]
And do them brown at last.

Scene 5

Road to Wonderland by the Rabbit Hole. Enter White Rabbit.

WHITE RABBIT.

Dear, dear, I'm late, I shan't get there in time,
The Duchess won't greet me with smile sublime;
She'll stamp her feet, and pout, and look quite vexed,
And rate me till I feel myself perplexed,
What could I do? I could not go before,
I had to guide Miss Alice to the door
Of Wonderland, where she is safe and sound,
Led through this Rabbit Hole right underground.
It leads us to and from our charmed retreat,
And ne'er till now been trod by mortal feet;
But I must haste, or make the Duchess wait.
No use to hurry now, I'm far too late.

---

179 J.W. Dunn (music and lyrics), "The Sun Shines Bright at Last" (London: Francis Bros. & Day, 1886). Sung by Ben Fielding at Dunn's Promenade Concerts, Britannia Pier, Great Yarmouth.
180 Take the prize.

SONG
Air—"The Pilots of England"[181]

Oh dear, oh dear, oh my dear paws!
Whatever shall I do now?
I've lost my gloves, 'twill give me cause
My carelessness to rue now.
The Duchess, she will not allow
Me to appear before her;
No matter how low I may bow,
Or tell her I adore her.

Chorus

She'll say I'm so careless, so careless, so careless,
And shake her head crossly, and frown so at me.
She is so knowing; it's no use my going
Without fan or gloves; offended she'll be.

(Exit White Rabbit. Enter Baron and Dismolo).

BARON (speaks).
Before the Gryphon comes, let's tell the news
On topics of the times, exchange our views.

TOPICAL SONG
(By permission of Arthur Williams)[182]

(Baron and Dismolo vamp a song on current events).

GRYPHON (enters. Speaks).
Here we must part, your destination's near,
Remember what I've said, and without fear
Approach the portals of this mystic land;
You'll find a deep disguise there to your hand:
Assume it quick, then enter through the *gate*,
With *gait* quite firm you must not hesitate.
Should you be challenged while you're on the march,
Reply as when you're passing the North Arch.[183]
(To Baron) You'll represent a king in your disguise,
And thus you'll pass by scrutinizing eyes.
(To Dismolo) You'll *personate* a headsman.[184]
DISMOLO.
Dismal fate!
Doomed to inspire in each *person hate*.

---

181 David Day (music) and Fenton Gray (lyrics), "The Pilots of England," *Mohawk Minstrels Magazine* 17:49 ([1886]): 30-31.
182 A comedian.
183 A feature on the grounds of the Woolwich regiment, near the guard room of the Royal Horse Artillery and the stables. *The Visitor's Guide to the Sights of London* (London: W. Strange, 1844), 27-28. The "reply" referred to is a definitive affirmation of permission to pass the guard post.
184 Executioner.

BARON.

Let's on at once!—disguise I feel's the thing
Wherein I'll ape the conduct of a king.[185]

SONG
Air—"The Young Man Who Used to Live over the Way"[186]

Well, let us be off, as we've no time to waste,
To don our disguise we had better make haste.

DISMOLO.

I fear that a gentle young stripling like me,
And the part of a headsman will not quite agree;
For though I'm a villain as none can deny,
There certainly is a mild look in my eye.
The innocent chat of a child makes me laugh.

BARON.

You'd better shut up; we have no time for chaff.

Chorus

BARON and DISMOLO.

It's useless for me/you all that rubbish to sing
And say I'm/you're a dear little innocent thing.
I'm/you're as bad as they make 'em at least so they say/I should say
I/you do the worst deeds for the smallest pay.

(Exit Baron & Dismolo. Gryphon is met by Silver Star, entering).

SILVER STAR.

How now, Sir Gryphon, whither go so fast?
You must have knocked me down had you gone past.

GRYPHON.

I wish I had!

SILVER STAR.

That's civil.

GRYPHON.

Not a bit.
I am not civil, don't pretend to it;
So stand aside, and let me take my way.

SILVER STAR.

To your request I simply answer nay.

GRYPHON.

Beware!

SILVER STAR.

Pooh, pooh, your threats are out of place;

---

185 A pun on "the play's the thing / Wherein I'll catch the conscience of the King" (*Hamlet*, 2.2.604-05).
186 Joseph Tabrar (music and lyrics), "The Young Man Who Used to Live over the Way" (London: Francis Bros. & Day, 1886). Sung by the music hall star Charles Coborn, a Cockney comedian. *Era*, "A Chat With Charles Coborn," 3 December 1892.

You'd better mind, or you'll be in disgrace.
The Queen, I think, suspects you.
GRYPHON.
In what way?
SILVER STAR.
In giving aid, Alice to bear away.
GRYPHON.
'Tis false! it can't be proved.
SILVER STAR.
Well, that may be.
If what you say is right 'tis well for thee;
But I've my doubts.
GRYPHON.
You'd better cease your chatter,
Or you'll find out that something is the matter.
My power is great, so don't you go too far;
But stand aside.
SILVER STAR.
Why certainly, ta-ta,[187]
Yet stay, what's this? Come tell me if you can.
Is't not a foot *print* and a *type* of man?
GRYPHON.
It is my foot mark.
SILVER STAR.
Nay, I pray you pause.
This foot I see bore nails,[188] but yours bear claws.
'Tis fresh as paint, that plainly can be seen;
I'll off at once and tell this to the Queen.
If, as I think, it should be mortal's tread,
The one who brought him here has cause for dread.
GRYPHON.
But Alice now in Wonderland is lodging;
It may be some kind friend of hers here dodging.[189]
SILVER STAR.
Should one in substance but approach the land,
He undergoes a change by fairy hand.
And punished then according to desert.
He can't escape be he so e'er alert.
GRYPHON.
How long has this been so?

---

187 Good-bye.
188 Shoe nails, i.e., a boot.
189 Hiding.

SILVER STAR.

   This very day,

   This law was made before I came away.

GRYPHON *(aside).*

   Confusion! hang it, here's a pretty fix.

   An ass was I, in mortals' plots to mix.

SILVER STAR.

   You'd best return at once, and take your place,

   In case the Queen your absence soon should trace.

GRYPHON.

   It shall be so *(aside),* this tip I mean to take:

   I to escape must keep quite wide awake.

   Let's on at once.

SILVER STAR.

   You're getting anxious.

GRYPHON.

   Very.

   We'll have a song and dance to make things merry.

SONG

Air—"Down by the Garden Gate"[190]

SILVER STAR.

   You'd best be off; take my advice; make peace with the Queen,

   She'll punish you if she should find that absent you have been

   Without her leave, as you know well, you have been much of late.

GRYPHON.

To get this weight from off my mind I'd best not make her wait.

CHORUS.

   I'll go or she may make a shine,[191] and punishment be mine.

   I must not make her wait, or stop till it's too late,

   And this double game I'd best resign.

(Dance and exit).

Scene 6

Wonderland.[192] *Enter Queen of Wonderland, Silver Star, and Fairy Elves.*

QUEEN.

   'Tis well, you've done my mission as you should,

   And watched the Gryphon as you said you would;

---

190 G.W. Hunter (music and lyrics), "Down by the Garden Gate" (London: Francis Bros. & Day, 1886). This is a courting song with dance sections.

191 Disturbance.

192 The events in scenes 6 and 7 are those seen by Alice during her fairy entrancement.

The footprint[193] which you saw him try to hide,
Was made by one to whom he'd served as guide.
We'll let him have his way for some time yet;
His falsehood you be sure we'll not forget.
And Jack? Did you see him?

SILVER STAR.

Yes, far away;
We saw him fighting foremost in the fray;
He gains promotion fast, he's brave and true;
He'll not abuse the care vouchsafed by you.

QUEEN.

Well, that is right, his love is in our care;
In fancy she can roam now anywhere.
Wrapped in a fairy sleep she lingers still;
Yet peoples with her friends this land at will,
And mingle with the sports[194] she finds at hand,
And acts her part in dreams in Wonderland.

SONG

Air—"Pretty Pond Lilies"[195]

Alice, we in fairy sleep have bound her,
Quickly shall the time pass by;
She's rescued from the ills in which we found her;
Her happiness will not admit a sigh.
Her lover at her side shall stand,
Companion in her fair dream land;
And thus she'll pass her happy hours
Loading her love among sweet flowers.

Chorus

QUEEN and SILVER STAR.

Fairy-like lilies, pretty to view,
Fairy-like lilies sparkling with dew;
The bee from the cup its honey may take,
Bloom on fair lilies, for fair beauty's sake.
Fresh, pure, lilies so fair,
Flowerets so rare perfume the air;
Sweet flowers simple and fair,
Fairest of all to the view.

QUEEN (speaks).

And now, give way to sport ye fairy elves;
The day is yours, in dance enjoy yourselves.

---

193 Gryphon has large clawed feet.
194 Diversions.
195 Lillie Hall (music and lyrics), "Pretty Pond Lilies" (London: Hopwood & Crew, 1887). Sung by the Moore and Burgess Minstrels and the Mohawk Minstrels. Also published in *Mohawk Minstrels Magazine* 17:49 ([1886]): 34-36.

(Ballet)[196]

ALICE *(enters. Speaks)*.

Oh what a lovely place! how bright 'tis seeming!
Am I awake or can I now be dreaming?
My sense seems in a *daze*, it can't be right
That *days* should seem to me the same as night
And yet 'tis so, for since this land I roam
I haven't once felt sleepy as at home.

SONG
Air—"Close to the Threshold"[197]

Here as I stand, and look around me,
Earth's clad in beauty fair to see;
Scenes like a dream they now surround me;
Where is the land, more bright can be?
What are the visions coming o'er me?
Faces I loved left far away,
Friends of my childhood stand before me,
And in my fancy I hear them say:—

Refrain

Joys of our childhood, though they're fleeting,
Mem'ry renews them o'er and o'er;
Joys of our childhood when departed,
Valued will be in our hearts still more.

(Speaks). I'll look for Jack, he may be near at hand.
Ah, let me think, his favorite spot's the *Strand*;[198]
Close to the sea—that is the *strand*[199] I mean:
If he is *handy*, that's where he'll be seen.
CATERPILLAR *(enter)*.
Who are you?
ALICE.
I at present hardly know,
Although I knew quite well some time ago.
Since I got up one morning I seem changed.
CATERPILLAR.
What do you mean by that?
ALICE.
I seem estranged.

---

196 Performed by "a number of little girls, all soldiers' children, who have been carefully trained for the work by the ballet mistress, Miss Lily Tyrrell." *Kentish Independent*, 1 January 1887.
197 Henry Parker (music) and Nella (lyrics), "Close to the Threshold" (London: J.B. Cramer, 1879). Scored for voice, piano, and violin.
198 A thoroughfare in the West End of London, extending from Temple Bar to Charing Cross.
199 Beach.

I can't explain myself, I am afraid;
I seem to grow much smaller than I'm made.[200]
A Caterpillar and a mushroom I see,
Which dwarfs me into nothing, makes me wee.
CATERPILLAR.
  Yes—in French?
ALICE.
  No, little.
CATERPILLAR.
  O—U—I see.
You certainly look little here by me.
ALICE.
  It's like a show.
CATERPILLAR.
  Oh no, we make no charge,
Most things in Wonderland "are fine and large."

SONG
Air—"They're All Very Fine and Large"[201]

All things you know in Wonderland
Are very fine and large;
And you can see them if you like,
Without an extra charge.
The shrimps the size of lobsters are,
And lobsters like a horse;
And pancakes we have once a year,
As large as Charing Cross.

Chorus

They're all very fine and large,
And wonderfully prime;
If you think you could eat one,
'Twould take you all your time.
One would feed a nation,
The half would swamp a barge;
Would you like to take home a dozen or two?
They're all very fine and large.

(Enter Jack, dressed as a playing card).

ALICE (speaks).
  Good gracious me! this is strange I confess.
  Oh lor'! there's Jack, and what a funny dress.

---

200 Altered from the licensed text: "It seems to grow much smaller I am made."
201 F. Bowyer (music and lyrics), "They're All Very Fine and Large" (London: Francis Bros. & Day, [1886]). Sung by Herbert Campbell.

You are my Jack! the one whom I admire?
But in how strange *a dress*, a new attire!
JACK.
By your *address* I see that me you know,
'Twould be *a tire*some thing if 'twere not so.
ALICE.
But how came you out here in these strange parts?
JACK.
Attendant on the King and Queen of Hearts.
I live a life of ease, do nothing hard;
I'm called by some a "knave"[202]—a knowing card;
At taking tricks they say I have a knack;
Of all court cards[203] I'm smallest in the pack;
An honour in a game of *Whist*[204] you see;
And those who lose for me long *wist*fully
A game of "Cribbage"[205] too my worth reveals,
One for my nob they count, or two my heels.[206]
ALICE.
Well, that is queer, it all to me seems *Greek*.
JACK.
It won't when you've been *Latin* (let in) here a week.
ALICE.
Oh, shades of all my forefathers combined,
It's well for my digestion I've not dined;
That pun I'm sure would give me indigestion.
JACK.
Forgive me then if I ask you one question,
If you've not dined, say, could you eat a tart?
ALICE.
Ah! forty in a minute, so be smart.
JACK.
I'll go and get some, for the Queen of Hearts
Has been all day engaged in making tarts *(exit)*.
ALICE.
The sights I've seen while here are like romances:
A Caterpillar sings, and smokes, and dances;
Who would believe it, though I took a vow—
Good gracious me! what is this coming now?
A Gryphon, or I make a great mistake.
I can't be dreaming! no, I'm wide awake.

---

202 Also known as "jack" in playing cards.
203 King, Queen, and Jack.
204 A card game for four players, forerunner of bridge.
205 A game for two, three, or four players using a deck of cards and peg board.
206 This refers to a counting rule when knaves are played in cribbage: two points for turning up a knave as the start card ("his heels"), and one point for having a knave in your hand matching the suit of the start card ("his nob").

(Enter Gryphon).

Here's another figure, well, this is queer!
And falling from its eye a crystal tear!

(Enter Mock Turtle).

GRYPHON.
A melancholy object, sure enough;
That is Mock Turtle when it's in the rough.[207]
ALICE *(to Gryphon).*
What is its cause of sorrow can you tell?
GRYPHON.
It's all fancy that, he is very well,
Here Mock Turtle! this here young lady, she
Would like to hear your doleful history.
MOCK TURTLE.
I was a real Turtle when we little were,
Went to school within the sea I do declare.
The master was Old Turtle, but you see
We called him Tortoise.
ALICE.
Was that for a spree?[208]
MOCK TURTLE *(angrily).*
We called him Tortoise, and the reason why,
Because he *taught* us. You're so dull. Oh fie!
GRYPHON.
You ought to be of yourself quite ashamed.
Such simple question, how could you have framed?
MOCK TURTLE.
Our school was in the *sea*—you *seem* to doubt it.
ALICE.
I never said so, I said *nought* about it.
MOCK TURTLE.
You're very *naughty*—you did as I say.
GRYPHON.
Come, hold your tongue.
MOCK TURTLE.
We went to school each day
We'd the best of education 'twas allowed.
ALICE.
I've been myself to day-school[209] so don't be proud.
MOCK TURTLE.
With extras?

---

207 Its everyday condition.
208 Merrymaking.
209 A school without boarded pupils.

ALICE *(nodding)*.
  Yes, with French and music too.
MOCK TURTLE.
  And washing?
ALICE *(indignantly)*.
  No, with that we'd nought to do.
MOCK TURTLE.
  Ah! then yours wasn't really a good school,
  For on the bills of first-class, as a rule
  These words I think you're pretty sure to find—
  French, music, taught, and washing extra—mind.
ALICE.
  You'd not want that much, if what you said were true,
  Living in the sea was wash enough for you.
MOCK TURTLE.
  'Twas beyond my means, the regular course took.
ALICE.
  Well then, what was that?
MOCK TURTLE.
  We'll tell you like a book.

SONG
Air—"Solomon's Proverbs"[210]

MOCK TURTLE.
  In the morning we learned REELING, and afternoon 'twas WRITHING;
  Those were the things we both learned when at school.
GRYPHON.
  That, with arithmetic, to which we had to stick;
  AMBITION was in our books the first rule.
MOCK TURTLE.
  DISTRACTION was a teaser, UGLIFICATION proved a sneezer,
  DERISION, that's the thing to drive one mad.
GRYPHON.
  With all these things compounded, we often got confounded
  When leaving off time came we both were glad.
GRYPHON.
  The MYSTERY came next, ancient and modern, vexed
  Us sadly with their soon forgotten dates.
MOCK TURTLE.
  DRAWLING and STRETCHING learned, until a prize we earned;
  We used to do our DRAWLING on our slates.

---

210 Charles Osborne (music and lyrics), "Solomon's Proverbs" (London: Francis Bros. & Day, 1886). Sung by G.W. Hunter, a music hall artist specializing in patter songs. See *Era*, "A Chat with G.W. Hunter," 24 October 1896.

GRYPHON.

And after all these toils came FAINTING then in COILS.

MOCK TURTLE.

Well, what that is I cannot tell I'm sure;

Although we were so tried, it was our master's pride

To stuff our nobs[211] chock full of classic lore.

JACK (enter. Speaks).

Here are the tarts, they're jammy[212] as can be.

ALICE.

Oh! jamais[213] you for bringing these to me,

They're light and flakey, see the crust it parts.

JACK.

They're just like us my dear, they are *sweet hearts*.

GRYPHON.

No, thank you, no, I do not eat such trash.

MOCK TURTLE.

But I do though.

GRYPHON.

Your conduct is too rash,

They're stolen from the palace, and by Jack,

You best not eat them: give them to her back.

The Queen is rather *nutty* on her tarts,

And from this course of justice never parts:

"Who is caught stealing that which isn't his'n,

When proved at court, at once is sent to prison;"

So Jack, the time has come, come weal[214] or woe,

When I shall triumph, and to quod you'll go.

(Enter Lobster).

ALICE.

Here comes a lobster, see his grave advance.

GRYPHON.

He's come in time to join us in the dance.

Say lobster, will you dance?

LOBSTER.

Of course I will.

If you will dance the lobster's own quadrille.[215]

---

211 Heads.

212 Jam-filled.

213 Colloquial: I never!

214 Happiness, well-being.

215 See chapter 10 of *Alice in Wonderland*, chapter 10:

"'You may not have lived much under the sea—' ('I haven't,' said Alice)—'and perhaps you were never even introduced to a lobster—' (Alice began to say, 'I once tasted—' but checked herself hastily, and said, 'No, never') '—so
you can have no idea what a delightful thing a Lobster-Quadrille is!'   (Continued)

GRYPHON.

Agreed.

MOCK TURTLE.

Agreed; but who will take fourth place?

GRYPHON *(indicating Jack)*.

This gent can dance, I see it by his face.

(They dance the Quadrille).

JACK.

Here comes the court, the King and the Prime Minister.

GRYPHON.

The headsman too, for Jack that look most sinister;

I'd have Jack's life, his blood, yes every ounce,

I'll wait my time this robber to denounce.

(Enter Baron disguised as King of Hearts, Queen of Hearts, Executioner, Soldiers, and Court).

KING OF HEARTS.

This programme which I hold now in my hand

Proclaims the sports unusually grand,

Will no one cheer, you all heard what I said?

QUEEN OF HEARTS.

If no one cheers you'd best cut off his head.[216]

KING OF HEARTS.

Thanks, generous subjects, for that hearty cheer.

Commence the sports at once, we hold them here.

'No, indeed,' said Alice. 'What sort of a dance is it?'

'Why,' said the Gryphon, 'you first form into a line along the sea-shore—'

'Two lines!' cried the Mock Turtle. 'Seals, turtles, salmon, and so on: then, when you've cleared all the jelly-fish out of the way—'

'That generally takes some time,' interrupted the Gryphon.

'—you advance twice—'

'Each with a lobster as a partner!' cried the Gryphon.

'Of course,' the Mock Turtle said: 'advance twice, set to partners—'

'—change lobsters, and retire in same order,' continued the Gryphon.

'Then, you know,' the Mock Turtle went on, 'you throw the—'

'The lobsters!' shouted the Gryphon, with a bound into the air.

'—as far out to sea as you can—'

'Swim after them!' screamed the Gryphon.

'Turn a somersault in the sea!' cried the Mock Turtle, capering wildly about.

'Change lobsters again!' yelled the Gryphon at the top of its voice.

'Back to land again, and—that's all the first figure,' said the Mock Turtle, suddenly dropping his voice; and the two creatures, who had been jumping about like mad things all this time, sat down again very sadly and quietly and looked at Alice.

'It must be a very pretty dance,' said Alice timidly.'

216 See *Alice in Wonderland*, chapter 8: "'I see!' said the Queen, who had meanwhile been examining the roses. 'Off with their heads!' and the procession moved on, three of the soldiers remaining behind to execute the unfortunate gardeners, who ran to Alice for protection."

GRYPHON.
  So please your Majesty I mean the Queen;
  I have the proof the plainest ever seen
  Of a base crime, committed at your court.
  Which I'll expose.
QUEEN OF HEARTS.
  You'd better cut it short,
  Or I will you, and that, sir, by a head.
GRYPHON.
  I'll execute my threat, ma'am, as I said.
QUEEN OF HEARTS.
  None order execution here but me;
  So don't try that game, or I'll let you see.
GRYPHON.
  You've lost your tarts, they're stolen, come, that's flat.[217]
  I know who took them.
QUEEN OF HEARTS.
  Can you swear to that?
GRYPHON.
  I can, 'twas Jack, he took them, that I'm sure.
QUEEN OF HEARTS.
  Off with his head! I wish to hear no more.

(Jack is seized by soldiers).

ALICE.
  But I protest, will give this charge denial;
  You cannot sentence him without a trial.
QUEEN OF HEARTS.
  Oh! can't I though, you'll see, if I so choose it,
  We haven't got a court house, so can't use it.
QUEEN OF WONDERLAND *(appearing).*
  You then shall have at once a law-court grand,
  Built in less time than those were in the Strand,
  Where you can bring to book all artful dodgers.[218]

(Characters remain in place for transformation).

---

217 Undeniable.
218 A pickpocket, as in Charles Dickens's *Oliver Twist*.

Scene 7

Scene changes.

QUEEN OF WONDERLAND.
  Our architect you know is Jammie Rogers.[219]
  Now Silverstar, to you I leave the rest:
  You watch the case, and in my interest.
SILVER STAR.
  Your Majesty, I will, fear not for Jack,
  He shall not suffer from this base attack.

(Trial opens—Baron still disguised as King of Hearts. Appear: Alice, Jack, Gloss, March Hare, Dormouse, White Rabbit, Jurymen, Giles, and Father William).

KING OF HEARTS.
  Herald, now at once without persuasion,
  Read at once this direful accusation.
WHITE RABBIT *(reads).*
  The Queen of Hearts she made some tarts all on a summer's day.
  The Knave of Hearts, he stole those tarts, and took them quite away.
KING OF HEARTS.
  Your verdict's come, consider it at once.
  The one who's last, will prove himself a dunce.
WHITE RABBIT.
  Not yet, not yet, a great deal has to come;
  There's witnesses, you'd best examine some.
KING OF HEARTS.
  Call the first witness!

(Noise in court)

WHITE RABBIT.
  Silence! cease your clatter.
  First witness please—come Mr. Gloss, the hatter.

(Hatter advances with tea cup in one hand and bread and butter in the other hand).[220]

GLOSS *(to King).*
  I beg your pardon for bringing these with me;
  But when I was sent for I was having tea.
KING OF HEARTS.
  You should have finished first, when did you begin?
GLOSS.
  Fourteenth of March.
MARCH HARE.
  Fifteenth.

---

219 This is an in-joke: the scene painter was Mr. Rogers.
220 The ensuing scene is derived from *Alice in Wonderland*, chapter 11.

DORMOUSE.

Sixteenth.

WHITE RABBIT.

Cease this din.

KING OF HEARTS *(to Jury)*.

Come, write that down. Now Sir, take off your hat.

GLOSS.

It isn't mine.

KING OF HEARTS.

What do you mean by that?

Stolen? *(To Jury)* Put that down.

GLOSS.

I keep them to sell.

QUEEN OF HEARTS.

Don't contradict, we know that very well.

KING OF HEARTS.

Give your evidence quickly if you can.

GLOSS.

Please your Majesty, I'm a nervous man:

I hadn't had my tea above a week,

When the tea began to twinkle so to speak.

KING OF HEARTS.

What's that you say? Twinkle?

GLOSS.

It began with tea.

KING OF HEARTS.

That's what twinkles should do, it appears to me.

Speak up at once, your voice is getting weaker.

GLOSS.

I'm a poor man.

KING OF HEARTS.

You mean you're a poor speaker.

QUEEN OF HEARTS.

Stick to the case, what do you know about it?

GLOSS.

I know he's innocent, you need not doubt it.

KING OF HEARTS.

Is that all? Stand down at once, you know no more?

GLOSS.

I can't stand any lower I'm on the floor *(retires)*.

KING OF HEARTS.

Call the next witness.

GRYPHON.

Your Majesty, a word;

To call more witnesses would be quite absurd;

I know the case, and state without delay
That Jack's the thief, who took the tarts away;
His guilt is sure.

ALICE.

Because you say't forsooth.

GRYPHON.

You know yourself that I speak nought but truth.

ALICE.

The tarts Jack had, so please you, learned judge,
Were not the Queen's, that statement is all fudge.
(To Gryphon) In vain you try the guilt on him to fix;
Behold the tarts are here, the whole six.

QUEEN OF HEARTS.

The trial's ended; the verdict is quite clear.

JURYMEN.

Not Guilty.—

QUEEN OF HEARTS.

Why of course *(to King)* Come, do you not hear?

KING OF HEARTS.

Oh! yes of course, six months hard labour, right!
(To Jack) And you be glad, I make your sentence light.

WHITE RABBIT.

But he's not guilty.

KING OF HEARTS.

Ah!

WHITE RABBIT.

A trumped up charge,

KING OF HEARTS.

In that case let him go, I you discharge.

QUEEN OF HEARTS.

As all is well and you have not done wrong:
I call upon you, Jack, to sing a song.

JACK.

Extend your mercy further, you'll not rue it,
Let Alice and myself now sing a duet.

QUEEN OF HEARTS.

It shall be so, for that's a happy thought,
And after that we'll give our minds to sport.

DUET

Air—"Slumber oh Sentinel," from *Falka*[221]

JACK.

Dearest, 'tis you I love; my heart now rests securely;
True as the stars above I hope thou'lt be surely.

---

221 See above, p. 507, n. 122.

ALICE.
> Yes, loved one, here behold me never more to part,
> Once more my arms enfold thee, king of my heart;
> Life now is all before us, and skies are bright above,
> One hope is still before us, the hope of true love.

JACK.
> With thee I ever wander, 'tis but truth I tell,
> On thee I love to ponder, I love thee well;
> In thee my love confiding, I am all thine own,
> Faith in this heart abiding, doubt has long flown.

ALICE.
> Cupid speaks in a whisper to all, love,
> He's whisp'ring, we answer, the call, love;
> He's whisp'ring, yes, he's whisp'ring.

GILES *(speaks).*
> You're old, Father William, I've often times said,
> And your hair has become very white;
> I think, if you tried, you could stand on your head.[222]

FATHER WILLIAM.
> You do? Then I dare say you're right.
> In my youth, I can tell you, my worthy young son,
> Such things might have injured my brain;
> To stand on my head in the way I have done,
> So don't ask me to do it again.

GILES.
> That's true, for I've heard you say so before;
> But now you're uncommonly fat,
> You can't turn a somersault in at the door.

FATHER WILLIAM.
> I'll bet you a shilling on that!

GILES.
> You're old, let me say, your jaws should be weak,
> For anything tougher than suet;
> Yet you eat up a goose all the bones and the beak;
> Pray how do you manage to do it?

FATHER WILLIAM.
> In my youth my dear boy, I took to the law,
> And argued each case with my wife;
> And the muscular strength which it gave to my jaw
> Has lasted the rest of my life.

---

222 See chapter 5 of *Alice in Wonderland*, the poem recited by Alice to the Caterpillar, which begins:
> "'You are old, Father William,' the young man said,
> 'And your hair has become very white;
> And yet you incessantly stand on your head—
> Do you think, at your age, it is right?'"

GILES.
　At your time of life one would hardly suppose,
　That your eye was as steady as ever!
　Yet you balance an eel on the end of your nose,
　How come you so awfully clever.
FATHER WILLIAM.
　I've answered three questions, and answered with truth,
　So don't ask me more for a week,
　I learned to conjure when I was a youth;
　So look, and I pray you don't speak.

(Conjuring act by Father William).

Scene 8

　　Field of the Camps. Sergeant O'Grady, reduced to Private, enters along with Annette.

O'GRADY.
　Well here I am, as any one may see,
　Private O'Grady; by my soul that's me!
　I've been reduced:[223] and what for do you think?
　Because I got a drop too much to drink.
　I wasn't drunk, but just a little queer;
　It's true I'd had some whiskey and some beer.
　What's a quart of whiskey to a boy like me
　I could drink it daily in a cup of tea.
　The fault was with my liver, 'twasn't right.
ANNETTE.
　So you fell in a ditch and slept all night!
O'GRADY.
　An eccentricity, a way I'd got.
ANNETTE.
　You know that you were bosky.[224]
O'GRADY.
　I was not.
　I know that you a girl of spirit are;
　Bedad, I love you!
ANNETTE.
　Come, don't go too far.
O'GRADY.
　Well, give me one good drink, and then I'm sure
　I won't come near you for an *hour* or more.

—————————
223 Demoted.
224 Tipsy.

ANNETTE.

You'd best be off at once, here comes *our* guard.

O'GRADY.

Och, so it does bedad! my fate is hard;

Good bye, I'm off.

ANNETTE.

The best thing you can do.

O'GRADY.

Bedad! bejabers! garre! and harroo![225]

(Enter Lieutenant and Men).

LIEUTENANT.

Halt! Front!

ANNETTE *(aside).*

Just so.[226]

LIEUTENANT.

Quick march—relieving sentry.

All correct?

SENTRY.

All correct.

ANNETTE.

Of that I'll make an entry.

LIEUTENANT.

Pass—quick march—halt.

You will walk up and down—

ANNETTE *(aside to Private Brown).*

—your post.

Now mind, you'll drop that lantern Brown.

LIEUTENANT.

In such a manner soldier-like and smart.

ANNETTE.

Attend to this or you'll be in the cart.[227]

LIEUTENANT.

If you see a man attempt his pipe to light

In front of Colonel's tent, know it is not right:

But give at once—immediately—alarm,

As 'bacca for our Colonel has no charm;

No one his tent must enter without knocking,

And when our Colonel sleeps he don't want rocking;

He will see the Colonel's dog kept muzzled,

That, when the bobby[228] comes, he may be puzzled.

---

225 Various mild oaths and growls.

226 Exactly.

227 Taken away as a criminal.

228 Policeman.

He will, of course, inspect the Colonel's dinner,
And taste his soup to see it don't get thinner;
His wine to sample, take a small per cintage,[229]
To see it's good, and of the proper vintage.
At dog bark, cock crow, cat squall, or noise like that,
Fire off his gun, but mind, don't shoot the cat.
He will keep upright, steady on his legs,
And keep an eye upon our chief's tent pegs.
Right—turn upon your post—quick march.

ANNETTE.
They're proper soldiers, quite as stiff as starch.

SONG
Air—"Sweet Are the Moments"[230]

While life it shall last, I'll the regiment's staunch daughter be,
All my brave comrades respect me I'm sure;
They're true to each other, as all soldiers ought to be,
They're true to me, and I'm true to the corps.
When in the battle though danger be pressing me,
I flit here and there, giving help where I can;
I hear their deep voices in accents soft blessing me,
I'm loved by them all, from the rear to the van.[231]

Chorus

Bugle resounding, sweetly they're sounding,
As they proclaim that the battle is done;
Their notes are ringing, and joyful news bringing,
Telling each soldier the battle is won.

(Speaks). Here comes the swell returning, he's a beau,
As great a toff as one would wish to know.

LIEUTENANT.
The fair Annette. Ah! how do my pretty pet?

ANNETTE.
I'm not Annetta Sir, my name's Annette;
And I'm not fair.

LIEUTENANT.
Excuse me you've such charms,
They are a net to catch us men at arms.

ANNETTE.
You're joking now, you mean that but in fun.

---

229 Percentage (dialect).
230 William Francis (music) and Harry Hunter (lyrics), "Sweet Are the Moments" (London: Francis Bros. & Day, [1886]). Sung by Mr. Charles Garland.
231 Vanguard, the foremost division of an army.

LIEUTENANT.

Why don't you laugh, d'you know I've made a pun?

ANNETTE.

No, did you really?

LIEUTENANT.

Yes I did, by jove;

And not to smile's disheartening to a cove.[232]

ANNETTE.

To waste your time on such things is absurd,

LIEUTENANT.

But I've *to haste*, I have upon my word;

I bear some papers, quite a largish batch;

With these *despatches*, I should use *dispatch*.

My in*tent's* to see our Colonel. Where is he?

He's *in tent* yonder?

ANNETTE.

Gone there *intent*ionally.

LIEUTENANT.

I'm content with your answer, never fear;

As a reward I'll kiss you now, my dear.

ANNETTE.

Indeed, you won't!

LIEUTENANT.

Then you will lose a treat.

ANNETTE.

Well, that is good!

LIEUTENANT.

It would be.

ANNETTE.

What conceit!

DANCE and SONG

Air—"Where the Flowerets Grow"[233]

ANNETTE.

Sir, your conceit's absurd; you'd better go away;

For if you stop here for a kiss, you'll stop till the break of day.

LIEUTENANT.

But really that's absurd, it's quite stupid, don't you know

You find my kisses very sweet.

ANNETTE.

That's as well to know.

You're such a conceited thing.

---

232 Chap.

233 The script specifies that this was published by Francis Bros. & Day, London.

LIEUTENANT.
Say now may I buy the ring?
ANNETTE.
With you I will not wed just yet, I told you so,
LIEUTENANT.
But if you wait a year or so, well then I don't know!
Say, will you with me wed? I love you don't you know!
You'll love me more when "yes" you've said, you will fonder grow.

(Exit Lieutenant and Annette. Enter Jack as Colonel).

JACK *(speaks).*
The welcome news to hand, peace is proclaimed;
At last the time has come for which I aimed.
Ambition's reached its *summit*, as it should,
That is, when its sole aim is *summat*[234] good;
Now I return, my wealth and fame to share
With her I love, my Alice, pure and fair.

BALLAD
Air—"Endless Love"[235]

She leaned her head upon my breast,
I gently whispered words of love;
Close to my throbbing heart I pressed
The one I loved all things above.
She said: "Dear heart, I will be true;
My love can only end with life
Of all the world I wed but you!
Return and claim me as your wife.
Ne'er be downhearted,
Though we be parted
Love well remember, and brighten the pain.
Truth be requited,
When we're united.
Then we shall never in life part again."

QUEEN OF WONDERLAND *(enters. Speaks).*
I greet you Jack, you wish to know the news:
All is as well as even you could choose;
Your lover's sleeping *still*, in *still* repose;
The Baron is the same where e'er he goes.
The day of reckoning will be your return,

---

234 Something (dialect).
235 Theo Bonheur (music) and Lindsay Lennox (lyrics), "Endless Love" (London: F. Amos & Co., [1870]). This was reissued as a vocal novelty in the 1886-87 season.

He'll reap the punishment such acts should earn;
His *scornful* treatment of my magic power.
JACK.
We two can settle him in half an hour:
I'll challenge him at once to mortal strife;
For trying to *kidnap* my promised wife,
Which made it needful poor dear child, that she
Be sent to sleep, and a *kidnap*ping be.
I *owe t'* him a debt, not relent;
Nor one *iota* of my act repent.
QUEEN.
Leave all to me—now call your friends I pray;
For all should witness what I have to say.
JACK.
Lieutenant here, Annette you may come too.

(Enter Lieutenant and Annette).

Private O'Grady I've a friend in you.
O'GRADY *(enter).*
Indade yer have, that statement is not risky;
Bedad! I like yer better than nate[236] whiskey.
JACK.
You shan't return to England in disgrace;
I'll recommend that you resume your place.
O'GRADY.
You will! Hooroo! I'll never drink again,
(Aside) Unless I'm ill, or have a griping pain;
And that's a reason.
JACK.
All friends come this way.

(Enter Soldiers who formed the Guard).

I've welcome news, peace is proclaimed.
ALL.
Hooray!
QUEEN.
And I've some more good news—Your Colonel here,
(To one and all of you, he must be dear);
Returns to England to assert his station,
Which is usurped and by a base relation,
Who is his uncle.
LIEUTENANT.
Awe! you are a joker!
To ask conundrums.

---

236 Neat (i.e., undiluted with water).

O'GRADY.

Uncle's[237] a pawnbroker.

ANNETTE.

Yours is of that, there is but little doubt,
For everything you had is up the spout;[238]
You didn't save your stripes.[239]

O'GRADY.

A nasty snack.[240]
The Colonel's going to get them for me *back*.

ANNETTE.

That's where they should be, you would get more polished.[241]

O'GRADY.

But flogging in the Army's been abolished.

JACK.

Come that will do, you interrupt this lady.

ANNETTE.

And in a gentleman such conduct's shady.

QUEEN.

Well Colonel, it is this I should have stated.
In my *relation*, to whom you're *related*:
It is the Baron whom your station pills,[242]
He turned you out to suffer earthly ills,
Placed you in a basket in the street.
Where Gloss he found you crying at his feet,
Your father was the Baron, I declare,
You are his only son "the rightful heir;"
Your uncle was his *steward*, he deceived.

JACK.

Pray no more *it's too hard* to be believed.

QUEEN.

You'll find it true, each statement I can prove.

JACK.

To gain my case, I will not lose a move.
So let us start at once for England's *shore*;
We're sure to reach it in a month or more,

QUEEN.

Your transit be my care, I'll do it smart,
And there you'll be before you've time to start.

---

237 (Slang) pawnbroker.
238 Pawned.
239 He has pawned everything, including his sergeant's insignia.
240 Jibe or bite.
241 Whipped, as with a cat-o'-nine-tails.
242 Rejects or detaches, as in peeling away Jack's rightful social status.

SONG

Air—"Around the Christmas Tree"[243]

JACK.

Now we are going homeward we'll leave this foreign shore

LIEUTENANT.

And we shall not be very sorry if we return no more.

ANNETTE.

You said you would transport us across the briny main;[244]

O'GRADY.

In case we should be seasick, suppose we take the train.

Chorus

JACK.

Then all of us will be jolly, all of us will be gay,

All of us will be full of fun, whenever we start away.

ANNETTE.

No moping or melancholy, when we get o'er the sea.

LIEUTENANT.

'Twill be a jolly time, when we Old England see.

Scene 9

Woolwich Common and Parade. Enter Father William, Gloss, Villagers, Baron and Dismolo.

FATHER WILLIAM.

They tell me Jack's return will wake my child;

If they deceive me I shall be mighty wild.

SILVER STAR *(enter)*.

No fear of that, our Queen her word has passed.

GLOSS.

I'm glad to know I shall meet Jack at last.

Where is your daughter?

FATHER WILLIAM.

Yonder, fast asleep.

BARON *(aside to Dismolo)*.

Ha! ha! my eye upon that girl I'll keep.

Dismolo, when she wakes we'll try again,

The sole desire of my life to gain.

DISMOLO.

It shall be so.

FATHER WILLIAM.

Hark, sure hear a drum.

---

243 Fred Carlos (music and lyrics), "Around the Christmas Tree" (London: Francis Bros. & Day, [1886]). Sung by Fred Carlos.
244 Ocean.

Illustration 29. Woolwich Parade and Royal Arsenal, late nineteenth century. The New Theatre is the building set back on the right. Courtesy of the Royal Artillery Library, Woolwich.

GLOSS.
  You're right my friend, at length the soldiers come.
GRYPHON *(enter)*.
  This is your last, and only chance, I say,
  To seize the girl, and bear her right away.
  When Jack's voice does ar*ouse* her you begin it,
  Your work to bear her to your *house* that minute;
  But if her eyes should fall upon Jack first
  Your game's all up, do you your best or worst.
BARON.
  I'll gain a *coign* of vantage[245] you may bet;
  And in his own *coin* I will pay Jack yet.
DISMOLO.
  It's some time since I've had a coin from you.
  You might pay me.
BARON.
  I'm not a *coin* to (going to).

(Exit Baron, Dismolo and Gryphon).

SILVER STAR.
  What treason are those three knaves now pursuing?
  I must make th*em halt* in their mischief *brewing,*
  I'll *be here* on the spot, and will not fail
  When treason's near, to give a warning *hail* (ale).
  Our Queen shall know the Gryphon's vile deception
  The court attend to give a fit reception.

(Enter Characters of Wonderland).

QUEEN.
  Bring Alice hither.

(Alice is borne in. Enter Baron hurriedly).

BARON.
  Now is my chance.
JACK.
  Stand back. I say! Not one more step advance!
  Arrest the villain and both his satellites,
  He has conspired and robbed me of my rights.
QUEEN.
  So sir Gryphon, base traitor that you are,
  Shall banished be at once to Temple Bar;
  Upon a pedestal there take your station,
  A subject for each driver's execration.[246]

---

245 Advantageous position.
246 See p. 485, n. 39.

JACK.

The Baron we will hang.

BARON.

I mercy plead:

You'd better spare me.

ANNETTE.

So you had indeed.

JACK.

State your reasons, I don't see your aim.

ANNETTE.

Tomorrow, he must play the same old game.[247]

JACK.

In that you're right, so I will cease this strife;

And now to bring my Alice back to life.

My darling love, your sleeping spell I break.

Her eyes they open.

FATHER WILLIAM.

She'll *arise*, awake.

ALICE.

Ah Jack! you there?

JACK.

Yes, never more to part;

I offer you at once, my hand and heart.

ALICE.

My father gives consent?

FATHER WILLIAM.

Oh, don't I? Rather!

'Tis well I'm near at hand.

ALICE.

I love you *father*.

JACK.

Now all is settled we may happy be—

Ah! happy thought; 't'as[248] just occurred to me:

This is the year when we should all rejoice,

And for a gracious Queen sing with one voice;

'Tis fifty years since first she 'gan to reign,[249]

To show our love we'll try with might and main

Our loyalty we'll let the whole world see,

In song we'll welcome our Queen's Jubilee.

---

247   i.e., he must again perform the villain at the next performance.

248   It has. Jack demonstrates his East London credentials by dropping the initial aspirant "aitch."

249   Queen Victoria ascended to the throne in 1837. The Empire celebrated her golden jubilee in 1887.

SONG
"Jubilee"[250]

All loyal hearts rejoice with me,
That they this year have seen.
Which gives a royal jubilee
To England's gracious Queen.
Full fifty years, with pride she's reigned,
O'er lands both far and near,
Her gentle sway our love as gained;
To one and all she's dear.

Chorus

Hurrah! for the Queen of merry England,
Hurrah! for the happy days we've seen;
May heaven protect the right, preserve old England's might,
For we all love our country and our Queen.

QUEEN (*speaks*).
Now come with me to realms of beauty bright,
Through vast domains o'er which I rule with might;
The land of phoenix—fire's almighty King,
With safety you through that vast realm I'll bring;
And then o'er waters turned by winter's hand,
To fields of glass, and mountains vastly grand.
They in their turn shall yield my power supreme,
And be dissolved again by bright sunbeam;
You'll then behold the faithful fairy band,
Who dwell within my home in Wonderland.

SONG
Air—"They Ought to Have a Muzzle On"[251]

QUEEN.
Now time is going we must end our Christmas Pantomime,
ANNETTE.
And hope the hours you here have passed will not be wasted time;
FATHER WILLIAM.
We've tried our best just to amuse both old and young awhile,
ALICE.
And our reward in your applause—to see your faces smile.
GRYPHON.
For laughter's healthful, so they say, and if we raise a share,

---

250 An original air by C.J. Taylor.
251 Edmund Forman (music) and Harry Hunter (lyrics), "They Ought to Have a Muzzle On" (London: Francis Bros. & Day, [1886]). Sung by James Francis of the Mohawk Minstrels, at the Agricultural Hall, as he accompanied himself on the harmonica. Though performed in blackface, this topical song was devoid of dialect or other characteristics of the minstrel genre.

GLOSS.
  Perhaps you'll come another night if you have time to spare,
BARON.
  And bring your friends, each one bring six; 'twill please us to see all;
JACK.
  If the theatre is not large enough we'll soon knock down the wall.
                              Chorus
  We hope that we have made a friend of every one now here,
  To raise his voice, and clap his hands, and give us one good cheer;
  From you must come the verdict which will stamp us with success,
  If you applaud, we shall be pleased we all confess.

QUEEN (speaks).
  Now comes the time for frolic and for fun,
  The opening of our pantomime is done,
  Clown, pantaloon, harlequin, and columbine,
  Shall in a friendly rivalry entwine:
  Baron as clown, Father William—pantaloon,
  Jack as harlequin, shall make the time come soon
  For columbine to dance a graceful measure,
  Their efforts will, I hope, afford you pleasure.
  Such old familiar friends are never strange,
  So sound the gong, each character to change.

(Grand Transformation to)

Scene 10

The Fairy's Home in Wonderland.[252]

---
252 The text ends here.

Ibsen's Ghost; or, Toole Up-to-Date (1891)

Just before the turn of the century, the comic magazine *Punch* printed a graphic panel depicting how various types of late-Victorian repertoire were experienced. A playgoer laughs and relaxes at the music hall and farcical comedy, is emotionally engrossed at the melodrama and comedic drama, is bored at the opera, and sits up proudly at a patriotic drama. None of this prepares him for the wrenching experience of watching a play by the Norwegian master, Henrik Ibsen. In a sequence of three images, he sits with toes hooked below his chair, arms folded, head tilted down, scowling; he then twists in his chair with his hands clenched by his chin, head turned away but eyes locked on the stage; and finally, he collapses knock-kneed in his chair, arms limp at his sides, his head resting on one shoulder, eyes bulging and tongue lolling. This is a fair summary of the impact Ibsen had when a succession of entrepreneurs brought five of his plays to the London stage in the first half of 1891. Whether spectators reacted with fascinated admiration or loathing disapproval, they had never seen, or experienced, anything quite like this.

Genre Issues

Theatre excels in parodying social, political, and artistic trends. When an artistic work of high repute is invoked—as with the Christy's Minstrels' renderings of opera—burlesque was the genre of choice. The 1891 season included *Hedda Gabler* (Ibsen's newest play), *A Doll's House* (previously seen in 1889), the scandalous *Ghosts* (in an unlicensed, private performance), *The Lady from the Sea*, and *Rosmersholm*. Continental capitals—notably Berlin, Paris, Christiania (Oslo), Copenhagen, and Stockholm—had already begun to grapple with the aesthetic and rhetorical challenges inherent in Ibsen. This was London's first taste. It excited some spectators and discomfited others. The *Saturday Review* appealed to writers to deflate the dramatic *cause célèbre* through a spoof: fighting theatre with theatre, as it were. Just such a metatheatrical satire was presented at Toole's Theatre on 30 May. This comic reworking of memorable moments from some of the season's productions featured witty dialogue by J.M. Barrie (at this point, known as a novelist and journalist, his great stage successes a decade in the future). It was, as Clement Scott (Ibsen's strongest critical detractor) put it, much wiser, cleverer, and better "than all the earnest essays that many of us have been writing!"[1] Scott was seen laughing in the auditorium, for as Barrie later reminisced "nonsense acted gravely was at that time an innovation."[2] Rather than innovating, however, Barrie turned to an old format, utilizing up-to-the-minute material.

As with Netta Syrett's drama *The Finding of Nancy*, London's actor-managers steered away from Ibsen's *Hedda Gabler* because it had no part in it for any self-respecting leading man. They closed ranks and made themselves unapproachable. Most actresses would have regarded this as an insuperable obstacle, but Elizabeth Robins and Marion Lea were deeply committed to Ibsen, genuinely bored with the ingénue roles they customarily played, and idealistic about the theatre's future.[3] Robins, in particular, saw the acting opportunity:

> You may be able to imagine the excitement of coming across anything so *alive* as Hedda. What you won't be able to imagine (unless you are an actress in your twenties) is the joy of having in our hands—free hands—such glorious actable stuff. If we had been thinking politically, concerning ourselves with

---

1   Clement Scott, *Illustrated London News*, 6 June 1861: 762.
2   Barrie's holograph note prefacing his 1932 revised typescript of *Ibsen's Ghost*, Beinecke Library Barrie Ib6/2.
3   See Elizabeth Robins, entry for 3 October 1890, chap. 1 in "Whither and How" (typed manuscript), Fales Library, New York University, 11.

Illustration 30. Three Acts of Henrik Ibsen, from Charles Keene et al., *Mr. Punch at the Play: Humours of Music and the Drama* (London: Educational Book Co. [*c.* 1910]), 41-43.

the emancipation of women, we would not have given the Ibsen plays the particular kind of whole-hearted, enchanted devotion we did give. We were actresses—actresses who wouldn't for a kingdom be anything else.

Lea and Robins pooled resources to produce *Hedda* themselves, casting it as though they were "choosing a Cabinet at a national crisis."[4] Demand was strong during a series of matinees, so they transferred *Hedda Gabler* to the evening bill. It offered none of the feminist appeal of *A Doll's House*, yet the unsympathetic and unredeemed Hedda hit a nerve: her ennui, compromised marriage, and private recklessness were compelling to witness.

Hedda Gabler ends with the discovery of Hedda's suicide. George (her husband) and Thea (her fair-haired schoolfriend) are already collaborating to piece together notes from the manuscript that Hedda burnt (the future-looking book by the profligate Lövborg, who has fatally shot himself at Hedda's urging). *Ibsen's Ghost; or, Toole Up-to-Date* is a sequel, portraying the marriage of George and Thea. It captured the spirit of some spectators' frustration with Ibsen by code-switching from tragedy to farce whenever it cited *Hedda Gabler*, *A Doll's House*, and *Ghosts*. Its jokes were best understood by playgoers who had seen the plays, for it opens with Thea throwing George's letters into the fire (cremating 127 of their "children") and culminates with her transforming into Hedda. She is wracked by the hereditary effects of profligacy: she has an urgent compulsion to kiss every man she meets. (This is a jibe at Ibsen's repeated use of heredity as a plot device: Osvald in *Ghosts* is on the verge of insanity from congenital syphilis, and Nora in *A Doll's House* is accused of emulating her father when it is revealed that she has borrowed money from an unscrupulous lender.) Her grandfather admits that he kissed a bridesmaid the night before his wedding, though the remainder of his life has been scrupulously respectable. His wife, fresh from an afternoon at *A Doll's House*, reproaches him for failing to introduce her to disreputable people, thereby thwarting her chance to live an unorthodox life. This couple has no clear counterpart in Ibsen's *oeuvre* and instead represents the excesses of pro-Ibsen enthusiasm.[5] The parody culminates with a mass suicide, *à la Hedda Gabler*, corks dangling from the ends of pop-guns' muzzles, and a jaunty finale suggesting that the characters (resurrected puppets) retire to Toole's, where the fare is infinitely more appealing.

Interpretive Issues

Another burlesque opened a few days after *Ibsen's Ghost*, on 2 June.[6] Robert Buchanan, an author who had engaged in a dispute with someone every year since he first attacked Rossetti's and Swinburne's "Fleshy School of Poetry" (1871), was said to have been incited to anger and jealousy by Elizabeth Robins's production of *Hedda Gabler* at the Vaudeville, the theatre where his plays were customarily performed. Although he publicly denied it, he was accused of taking the Avenue Theatre to produce a vengeful attack on Ibsen.[7] He had included a scathing attack on Ibsen in his book *The Coming Terror* (published in April),[8] and many of the things he complains about there are satirized in his play.

---

4   Elizabeth Robins, *Ibsen and the Actress* (London: Hogarth Press, 1928), 31-32, 16.

5   Penelope Griffin draws a parallel between Old Ekdal (from *The Wild Duck*) and Peter. However, this play was not pro-duced in London until 4 May 1894. More plausibly, the couple represents Nora and Torvald, still married in advanced age. See Griffin, ed., "Ibsen's Ghost and the Theatrical Burlesque Tradition," app. 2 in J.M. Barrie, *Ibsen's Ghost: A Play in One Act* (London: Cecil Woolf, 1975), 77.

6   See Tracy C. Davis, "Spoofing 'The Master': Parodies and Burlesques of Ibsen on the English Stage and in the Popular Press," *Nineteenth Century Theatre Research* 13.2 (Winter 1985): 87-102.

7   See Robert Buchanan, letter to the editor, *Observer*, 24 May 1891: 6. He wrote unfavourably about Ibsen all season. See, for example, Robert Buchanan, "The French Novelette as Norwegian Drama," *Illustrated London News*, 31 January 1891: 152.

8   Robert Buchanan, *The Coming Terror, and Other Essays and Letters* (London: Heinemann, 1891), 376-80.

Buchanan's burlesque, entitled *The Gifted Lady*, is about two emancipated free-thinkers, Badalia Dangleton (modelled on Hedda Gabler) and Felicia Strangeways (modelled on Thea Elvsted), who independently form alliances with Algernon Wormwood, a poet of the "modern horrible school." Wormwood is encouraged by a critic named Vitus Dance (V.D.), who believes that the work of this "poet of the Morgue" will lead to a new sort of writing, "it will no longer deal with subjects.... It will have no more meaning than a chord, no more personality than an influenza." Badalia leaves her conventional husband Charles (an amalgamation of Torvald Helmer and George Tesman), a commercial dramatist. After Charles attends a performance by the Independent Theatre Society (which presented *Ghosts*), he is convinced that his own emancipation can only be complete if he murders someone or commits suicide. It is rumoured that Charles would only be satisfied if Wormwood and Badalia drowned themselves in the mill-race (an allusion to *Rosmerholm*). To complicate matters, Charles discovers that his great-great-grandfather was a polygamist and his uncle married a cook, so he offers to trade his own wife for Felicia. Felicia instead returns to her husband. Badalia, too, goes home, longing for normality and her husband's affection, but he has only delved further into his emancipation. In the final moment, he whistles a meaningless tune, which magically cures him of his mania and reconciles him with his wife. Vitus Dance, the critic of the future, goes to Gatti's Music Hall to efface his hubris.[9]

Some critics of the old guard responded to *The Gifted Lady* with mild enthusiasm, praising the acting and the jibes at emancipated women, aestheticism, individualism, heredity, and the divided skirt.[10] Others, predisposed to disliking Buchanan's work, lashed out against him with the fury of an anti-Ibsen critic at *Ghosts*.[11] The play inspired an unprecedented unity of opinion in anti-Ibsen and pro-Ibsen camps. Compared to *Ibsen's Ghost*, it "constituted a British remedy considerably worse than the Scandinavian disease itself"[12] and was a major disappointment. Part of the problem was its excessive length:

> [In *Ibsen's Ghost*] Mr. J.M. Barrie showed us conclusively just the extent to which Ibsen bears ridicule. He will bear it for half an hour at the utmost, and when that allotted span is exhausted he becomes wearisome. Three acts of Ibsen proper is as exhausting as the depression that succeeds the baleful influenza; but three acts of Ibsen burlesqued is worse than the horrors of catarrh, bronchitis, nervous malaria, and double pneumonia combined. It is unendurable.[13]

The sum effect of *The Gifted Lady* was, according to the *Era*, that a service had been rendered to Ibsen by offering a tribute to his notoriety and by creating such revulsion toward the imitation that one was inclined to feel kindly toward the original.[14]

Except for *The Gifted Lady*, the Ibsen-based burlesques of 1891 were widely enjoyed. Scott describes *Ibsen's Ghost* as less like "the grim and savage warfare of [Jonathan] Swift" than "the graceful method of [Charles Stuart] Calverley," the parodist of Robert Browning's narrative poem *The Ring and the Book*.[15] Penelope Griffin astutely analyzes the burlesque and mock-heroic antecedents of Barrie's gags, tracing a line of descent from John Gay, Henry Carey, Henry Fielding, and Richard Sheridan.[16] In other

9   From the licensing copy, British Library Add MS 53475, licence no. 133.

10   Full-length culottes, part of the wardrobe of so-called advanced women.

11   For a compendium of their vitriol, see George Bernard Shaw, *The Quintessence of Ibsenism* (London: Walter Scott, 1891). In *The Philanderer* (1893), Shaw's second play, he sends up Ibsen's (female) enthusiasts, though not Ibsen's drama.

12   "At the Play," *Observer*, 7 June 1891: 6.

13   *Daily Telegraph*, 3 June 1891: 3.

14   "The Avenue: *The Gifted Lady*," *Era*, 6 June 1891: 7.

15   Clement Scott, *Illustrated London News*, 6 June 1891: 760.

16   Griffin, ed., *Ibsen's Ghost*, 74-85.

words, while Barrie attacked Ibsen's plots and back-stories, character delineations, seemingly disjointed psychological motivations, and ideology, he did so with the time-honoured devices of parody. Despite the jokes made at the expense of atheism, feminism, free thought, and the uncharacteristic celebrity of Ibsen's translators, such parody is an homage to modernism rather than an attack on it.

Editing Issues

Two nineteenth-century manuscript source texts exist for *Ibsen's Ghost*: the licensing copy at the British Library and a copy of Thea's sides[17] at the Beinecke Library (Yale) which includes the melody and verses for the final song. A typescript of the licensing copy at the John Rylands Library of the University of Manchester was also consulted. Barrie revised the play in 1932, eliminating many of the topical references. A typed copy of this revision is in the Beinecke Library, and a limited edition of just a few copies was produced in 1939.[18] The licensed text and an Edinburgh University manuscript were published side by side by Penelope Griffin in 1975, in a variorum edition.[19]

According to the actress Irene Vanbrugh, when the actor-manager J.L. Toole received the text, he looked wistfully at Barrie; this being the author's first play, Barrie complied by reducing a long speech to five or six words, adding the subtitle (*Toole Up-to-Date*), letting Toole "turn suddenly into Ibsen because Thea turns suddenly into Hedda," and adding the song and dance. Toole further embellished his part with ad libs.[20] While Toole's "wistful" requests are reflected in the licensed copy, the play may have been rearranged (or the first pages cut) by the time it opened, for Vanbrugh claims that Barrie told her that her first line would be "to run away from my second husband just as I ran away from my first—it feels quite like old times." In the dedication to his play *Peter Pan*, Barrie also cites Thea's first line; however, her sides conform to the licensing copy, wherein the line falls well into the first scene. Barrie claims to have typed the parts himself to save the management money, but when Vanbrugh got hers at the first rehearsal, "it was all written on half sheets by the author himself," evidently freshly revised but very definitely in holograph.[21] The following edition is based on a comparison of the licensing copy and Thea's sides, favouring Thea's sides (when appropriate) as more likely to indicate the rehearsed lines. A few additional stage directions and other variants have been interpolated, based on Thea's sides and newspaper reviews, to better document how the cast alluded to Ibsen productions.

The licensing copy leaves a great deal to the imagination of a reader, as the resemblances between Toole's production and those that it parodied came through more powerfully in performance than in the textual traces of the script. Two line drawings in the *Illustrated Sporting and Dramatic News* and one from *Theatre* give hints as to how this was achieved. When Thea transformed into Hedda, Irene Vanbrugh ducked behind a sofa, disappearing as the "soft and fair-haired" Thea (which Marion Lea had played with "delicacy, finish, and control"), "reappearing" a minute later "as dark-haired Hedda in evening dress,"

---

17   Catalogued with the date 1893, Beinecke Barrie Ib6/1. Rather than paying a copyist to transcribe the entire script for each actor, it was customary to make a unique script for each character, which included just the cue lines and then that particular character's lines. These manuscripts are called sides or parts. Thea's sides in the Beinecke Library adhere closely to the licensing copy at the British Library. The 1893 date is misleading, however: because the manuscript is definitively marked for Irene Vanbrugh's use, it was prepared by Barrie no later than May 1891.

18   British Library Add MS 53475 (L) licence no. 134; J.M. Barrie Collection lb6/1, Beinecke Library, Yale University. The revision was published in a limited edition as J.M. Barrie, *Ibsen's Ghost* (London: Corvinus Press, 1939).

19   Griffin, ed., *Ibsen's Ghost*.

20   J.M. Barrie, introductory note (written in Barrie's hand) appended to Barrie's typescript of *Ibsen's Ghost*, Beinecke Library Barrie Ib6/2.

21   Irene Vanbrugh, *To Tell My Story* (London: Hutchinson, 1948), 27; and J.M. Barrie, *The Plays of J.M. Barrie* (London: Hodder and Stoughton, 1928), 5. The holograph they are referring to is likely the Beinecke manuscript Ib6/1.

swathed in an enormous feather boa to amplify how Elizabeth Robins appeared in the role, "hateful, morally insane, serpent-like" and capricious.[22] Robins's face was "a sublime study of deceit and heartless- ness" compelling "the morbid attraction that we have felt at the Central Criminal Court at a great murder trial."[23] Vanbrugh had seen Robins perform it a couple of times, and she attested that Robins permitted her to "come and talk to her to see if I could catch something more of her personality in this way."[24] This role was a stretch for Vanbrugh who, as a young member of Toole's company, had performed in farce and comedy but had never before played in a burlesque. Toole deployed his well-wrought capacity for comic transformation, first appearing as Peter Terence in a degenerate manner, standing dramatically with one foot ahead of the other, back arched, and black-gloved fingers spread like talons. He remade himself from a lanky aesthete dressed in a short pea coat and wide-collared shirt into a squat, officious version of the frock-coated Ibsen, his face ringed by a leonine wig and whiskers.[25] This strongly inclined the performance as a burlesque of Ibsen, specifically, as the centre of the critical maelstrom. The spectacle of the suicides—including Toole's (as Ibsen)—must have been cathartic though, in the fashion of burlesque, the characters reanimated as automata (lacking the life that many critics asserted in the originals) to sing and dance until they melted.

Performative Issues

There were three plays on Toole's bill.[26] The evening began with a full-length piece[27] and ended with *Ibsen's Ghost*. In between, from 13 June, the company performed *Ici on (ne) parle (pas) français*, a wordless farce, which burlesqued a standard comedy of Toole's repertoire, *Ici on parle français* (first produced in 1859).[28] For this play Toole whitened his face like a pierrot and sent up the farcical combination of mistaken identities, coincidences, and circumstantially crossed lovers of the original. Incidents were underscored with incongruous music, including "Bogie Man," "Wink the Other Eye," "The Marseillaise," and "Erin go Bragh." Thus, in *Ibsen's Ghost*, Ibsen is not Toole's only target: he also parodies *L'Enfant prodigue*, a mimed play, and his first costume (as Peter Terence) resembles the father from an 1891 production of this play brought to London by a Parisian company.

In *Ibsen's Ghost*, Thea's grandparents arrive from the theatre, having seen *L'Enfant prodigue*. Both this burlesque and the preceding one, *Ici on (ne) parle (pas) français*, make fun of *L'Enfant prodigue*, a "play without words" performed by Jane May (as Pierrot) for Charles Laurie's visiting company at the Prince of Wales's Theatre. It is founded on a cantata by Claude Debussy in which a beloved son leaves home to

22   *Western Mail* (Cardiff), 22 April 1891; and *Reynolds's Newspaper*, 26 April 1891.
23   This is from the veteran court reporter and theatre critic Clement Scott, *Daily Telegraph*, 25 April 1891: 550.
24   Vanbrugh, *To Tell My Story*, 23.
25   *Illustrated Sporting and Dramatic News*, 27 June 1891; and *Theatre*, July 1891: 29, reproduced in Griffin, ed., "Reviews of *Ibsen's Ghost*," app. 1 to *Ibsen's Ghost*, plate 4. The image of Toole as Ibsen was incorporated into the perruquier C.H. Fox's advertisements; see inside cover, *Players*, 16 December 1891.
26   Playbills, Harvard Theatre Collection; and playbills, British Library.
27   First, H.J. Byron's *A Fool and His Money* (1878), then Morris Barnett's *The Serious Family* (1849). See Allardyce Nicoll, *A History of English Drama, 1660-1900*, vol. 4, (Cambridge: Cambridge UP, 1955), 131.
28   British Library Add MS 52982 (P). Spriggins is learning French on the "French before breakfast" plan so he can let rooms to foreigners, sticking up "Ici on parle Français" in his window. In recompense for this, he promises to take the family to London for a treat. However, his daughter Angelina has been to Paris with her aunt and longs to return there instead. The first lodgers see through Spriggins's ruse but take the rooms anyway; one of them, Victor, fell in love with Angelina when she was in Paris, but does not know her identity. They recognize each other, but it appears to Angelina that Victor has run away with a married woman. Meanwhile Major Rattan arrives claiming that this woman is his wife and demanding that she should be handed over. Victor proposes to Angelina. The proper couples are united, and all ends well.

Illustration 31. J.M. Toole as Ibsen, in *Ibsen's Ghost*, cabinet photograph, 1891. Walter and Shead (photographers). Bequeathed by Guy Little, courtesy of the Victoria and Albert Museum.

indulge in worldly pleasures. He falls for the charms of a light-hearted woman, but once his resources are exhausted, she leaves him for another man. He returns as the prodigal and is welcomed by his forgiving parents.[29] Early in the piece, the man's parents try to deduce what troubles him:

MRS. PIERROT. Well, what may be the matter with him?

MR. PIERROT. He told us, he has a headache.

MRS. PIERROT. His head. No ... it is his heart that aches.

MR. PIERROT (*laughing*). His heart, he, in love, he is not higher than that.

MRS. PIERROT. It is his heart, I assure you, there come and see him. (*She takes her husband by the hand and takes him to the garden door and showing him her son under the trees*) Look at him walking, there ... he is sad ... thin ... pale ... he walks slowly, like this, his chin in his hand, I repeat it to you. I am certain of it, it is his heart that is sick.

MR. PIERROT (*incredulous, taking back his wife to the front*). Now then my wife let us reason! Look at me also and understand me well. I am in love of you and yet I drink well, I eat well. I have strong arms, big cheeks, a fat stomach. I am very healthy.

MRS. PIERROT. It is true but you and I are married, we live near each other, we sleep together, in short we are two and our son, he is quite alone.[30]

None of this is spoken, which is the joke in *Ibsen's Ghost*:

THEA. You have been at *L'Enfant Prodigue*?

(*Peter signs yes elaborately*).

That means Yes! How much easier it is than talking! But why has dear, simple, homely, humdrum, domesticated Grandmama not come with you?

(*Peter gesticulates*).

She is cleaning windows?

(*Peter repeats*).

Influenza?

(*Peter repeats*).

She is standing for the County Council?

(*Peter repeats*).

Kangaroos?

The grandmother "went away from *L'Enfant prodigue* in the middle of the first act because she declared she couldn't hear a word they said" and proceeded to another theatre where she saw *A Doll's House*. Grandmama has become a New Woman through exposure to Ibsen: no generation is safe from his "emancipating" influence. Her respectable life becomes anathema to her. Skewing Nora's complaints, she will leave her marriage. Thea urges her grandfather to shoot himself with one of Hedda's pistols, "with

---

29 "Our Ladies' Column," *Wrexham Advertiser and North Wales News*, 2 May 1891: 2; and *Manchester Times*, 19 June 1891.

30 The play was first performed at the Théâtre des Bouffes Parisiens on 21 June 1890. Prior to its run at the Prince of Wales's Theatre from 31 March through 14 April 1891, a synopsis was submitted for licensing: Michel Carré fils (book) and André Wormser (music), *L'Enfant prodigue*, British Library Add MS 53479 (G), fol. 8. (Ellipses in original.)

scorn upon your countenance and vine leaves in your hair." The three of them then debate the best place to direct the bullet.

Though actor-managers would not take on Ibsen's plays, the most prominent of them all, Henry Irving, urged his friend and veteran manager J.L. Toole to do *Ibsen's Ghost*.[31] This is tacit recognition that a community of spectators had been forged by the Ibsen season, as well as a new reading market for modernist plays that found intriguing the idea of two translators fighting for rights to Ibsen's latest work. Approximately 26,000 people saw the 48 performances of Ibsen plays in London in 1891, and approximately 16,000 saw the 27 performances of *Ibsen's Ghost*.[32] The travesty relies on the audiences' knowing repertoire, as much as on the actors' (particularly Vanbrugh and G. Shelton, who played the foolish George Tesman) familiarity with the performances that they referenced.

William Archer, the director and translator of Robins's production of *Hedda Gabler*, appreciated the spoof as "a piece of genuinely witty fooling, which ought not to be missed."[33] Other parodies amused, but as Scott wrote, *Ibsen's Ghost* "not only hit the mark but scored a bull's eye."[34] One critic avowed that the pleasure Barrie afforded justified the pain of sitting through the original plays: "Ibsen is out-Ibsened, and his doctrines pushed to the verge of absurdity. And yet so nearly does the travesty trench upon the original that at times it is difficult not to believe that we are not sitting at the feet of the great Norwegian master himself."[35] Toole's company went on tour that July, cutting short what might have been an even longer run, and did not repeat *Ibsen's Ghost* in the provinces, presumably because audiences that had not seen the London productions would not appreciate the parody.[36]

The variety of styles in which parodists wrote, the selection of journals in which they published, and the packed houses at Toole's reflect a diverse market for Ibsen-based satire and suggest that knowledge about Ibsen was relatively widespread.[37] From early March 1891 until the end of June, Ibsen was a fashionable and widely recognized though contentious topic. As J.H. McCarthy stated, the burlesques at Toole's and the Vaudeville were "the most decisive tribute of recognition that has yet been paid in London to the influence, to the importance, to the genius of Henrik Ibsen," and neither his enemies nor his friends could call him "a 'man of no account,' at a time when he and his creations were made the objects of satire in two leading London theatres by two well-known English authors."[38] Even so, Toole's burlesque reminds later generations that the critical fault-lines wrought by the Ibsen season of 1891 were deeply divisive. Though conducive to humour in this recasting, Ibsen's plays represented a dramaturgical outlook distinct enough to be recognizable even when transformed by satire, and innovative enough to provide the content—though not the format—for sustained parody.

---

31   Irene Vanbrugh claims that at the time Toole did not know anything about either Barrie or Ibsen, and that he produced the piece on the urging of Henry Irving. Vanbrugh, *To Tell My Story*, 25.

32   *A Doll's House* was given two performances, *Rosmersholm* two, *Ghosts* one, *Hedda Gabler* 38, and *A Lady from the Sea* five. See Tracy C. Davis, "Ibsen in England: 1872-1906" (PhD dissertation, University of Warwick, 1984).

33   William Archer, "The Theatres," *World*, 3 June 1891: 872.

34   "The Playhouses," *Illustrated London News*, 6 June 1891: 760.

35   "Toole's Theatre: More Ibsenism," *St. James's Gazette*, 1 June 1891: 6.

36   The report of the summer tour that is given by Griffin contradicts reports in the *Illustrated Sporting and Dramatic News* of 6 June 1891, and in the *Era* of 11 and 18 July 1891. According to these sources, Toole's gout prevented him from preparing any new plays after *Ibsen's Ghost* and from properly performing in a play in Norwich during the first week of July; he subsequently headed for Aix-les-Bains. Penelope Griffin, "The First Performance of *Ibsen's Ghost*," *Theatre Notebook* 23:1 (1979): 30-37; and Griffin, ed., introduction to *Ibsen's Ghost*, 11.

37   For more examples see "The Ibsen Girl," *St. James's Gazette*, 25 April 1891: 5; "Fin de Siecle," *St. James's Gazette*, 27 January 1891: 4; Max Beerbohm, "Drinking Sons," reprinted in Doris Arthur Jones, *The Life and Letters of Henry Arthur Jones* (London: Victor Gollancz, 1930), 353-54; and "An Independent Criticism," *St. James's Gazette*, 17 March 1891: 6.

38   "Pages on Plays," *Gentleman's Magazine*, July 1891: 103.

Ibsen's Ghost; or, Toole Up-to-Date[39]

BY J.M. BARRIE

First performed at Toole's Theatre, London, 30 May 1891.

George Tesman, an idiot	G. Shelton
Thea,[40] his wife for the present	Irene Vanbrugh
Peter Terence, Thea's Grandpapa	J.L. Toole
Delia Terence, Peter's doll	Eliza Johnstone
George's Secretary	

Scene. The room in George's house where rubbish is shot.[41] Note: Peter uses Gosse's translation and the other characters Archer's.[42] Scene as in Hedda Gabler.[43] George sits writing at desk R. Thea is at fireplace L.1. burning letters. She is very mournful. Kisses letters, etc.

GEORGE. Do you know, dear, I think I shall be able to make something of poor Eylbert Lovborg's[44] notes after all. Then I will publish the book as my own, and it may bring me fame. Just think of that now, Hedda!

---

39   Based on the Licensing Copy, British Library Add MS 53475 (L) licence no. 134; compared to a typed transcript at the John Rylands Library (University of Manchester), Nicoll Collection R171506. Corrected to an autograph manuscript of Thea's sides prepared for Irene Vanbrugh, Beinecke Library (Yale University), Barrie Ib6/1. Where additional stage directions are inserted based on press reports, they are indicated in the footnotes.

40   She is called Tia in the licensing copy but Thea throughout the Beinecke copy.

41   In the playbill, "Hedda's shooting gallery."

42   Edmund Gosse published a dozen articles on Ibsen in English periodicals from 1872 to 1879. William Archer's first writing on Ibsen was published in 1878. Archer published a translation of *The Pillars of Society* in 1888 (part of the Camelot edition published by Walter Scott, also including translations of *Ghosts* by Henrietta Lord and *An Enemy of the People* by Eleanor Marx Aveling). Archer followed with an edition of *A Doll's House* in 1889 and four volumes of *Ibsen's Prose Dramas* in 1890. Ibsen's latest play, *Hedda Gabler*, was published in separate translations by Archer and Gosse in January 1891. Archer's brother, Charles, collaborated with him on later translations, including *Peer Gynt* in 1892. William Archer and Gosse published a joint translation of *The Master Builder* in early 1893 and monopolized translations of Ibsen's remaining output thereafter.

43   In Archer's translation,

    A spacious, handsome, and tastefully furnished drawing-room, decorated in dark colours. In the back, a wide doorway with curtains drawn back, leading into a smaller room decorated in the same style as the drawing-room. In the right-hand wall of the outer room, a folding door leading out to the hall. In the opposite wall, on the left, a glass door, also with curtains drawn back. Through the panes can be seen part of a veranda outside, and trees covered with autumnal foliage. An oval table, covered with a cloth and surrounded by chairs, stands well forward. In front, by the wall on the right, a wide stove of dark porcelain, a high-backed arm-chair, a cushioned foot-rest, and two footstools. In the corner to the right, a corner settle [bench] and a small round table. In front, on the left, a little way from the wall, a sofa. Further back than the glass door, a piano. On either side of the doorway at the back a whatnot with terra-cotta and majolica ornaments.—Against the back wall of the inner room a sofa, a table, and a couple of chairs. Over the sofa hangs the portrait of a handsome elderly man in a General's uniform [Hedda's father]. Over the table a hanging lamp, with an opal glass shade.—A number of bouquets stand about the drawing-room, in vases and glasses. Others lie upon the tables. The floors in both rooms are covered with thick carpets.—Morning light. The sun shines in through the glass door.

(William Archer, trans., *Ibsen's Works* [London: Walter Scott, 1907], 243.)

44   Ibsen's detractors enjoyed mispronouncing characters' foreign names: this should be Ejlert Lövborg.

THEA (*she performs in a timid, shrinking manner, with downcast looks and scarcely audible tones*).[45] I wish you would remember that my name is Thea.

GEORGE. I mean Thea. I married you so soon after Hedda shot herself that I mix you up still Thea. How many T's in tentative.

THEA (*indifferently*). Four.

GEORGE. And how many Z's in influenza?

THEA. What does that matter, you take it all the same.

GEORGE. Does civil begin with S?

THEA. Don't know, write polite.

GEORGE. I will Hedda, I mean Thea, and is there a K in Christianity?

THEA. There is nothing in Christianity.

GEORGE. Thea, I think I had better leave the spelling to my secretary, where is he now?

THEA. He is upstairs packing his bag.

GEORGE. Think of that now, Hedda. (*Rises*) He is leaving me, and he is the sixth secretary I have engaged during the last month. I wonder why they all desert me thus? (*Comes to her*).

THEA. Dear simple George. Can he not guess!

GEORGE. And, oh! I say Thea what are you doing there?

THEA (*wringing her hands*). Burning the letters you wrote me before our marriage George.

GEORGE. There now! and Thea what is inside that parcel you have been making up all the morning?

THEA. The presents you gave me George and my engagement ring and my wedding ring. Now surely he will understand, though he is only a man of letters.

GEORGE. My careful little wife.

THEA. O how dense he is. (*Rises*) George I, I am going away.[46]

GEORGE. Do dear, you had better lie down for a little.

THEA. I mean, I mean not to come back.

GEORGE. You mean to your Grandpapa's Thea! But you know he and Grandmama are coming to us. I say Thea, how glad they will be to see you and me so happy together.

THEA. Happy! George do you love me as much as you loved Hedda Gabler?

GEORGE. Yes, I think so. Neither Hedda nor you have ever given me a moment's uneasiness. Simple souls both.

THEA (*aside*). This kindness kills me. George I think I shall write you a letter.

GEORGE. Do Thea.

THEA. You must think it strange George that I should write you a letter?

GEORGE. Oh, no Thea. But I say may I show it to my aunt Juliannia?

THEA. After I am gone George.

GEORGE. Yes, yes. Will you write it now Hedda. I mean Thea.

THEA (*on couch R.*). Now, aye now. The sooner the better.

GEORGE. Let me bring you your writing case, dear. There I have not spilt the ink. Really I haven't Thea.

(*Thea writes in wild haste*).

---

45 According to *Era*, 6 June 1891.

46 Quoting the line that begins the climactic scene in *A Doll's House*, in which Nora engages her husband in the first serious conversation of their marriage and explains she will leave him and their three children.

GEORGE. How beautiful you are Hedda—Thea. Do you know Judge Brack told me yesterday that he envied me my pretty little wife.[47] Just think of that.[48]

THEA. An envelope.

GEORGE. Thea, listen to this. I have been so lucky in my wives that I think I must be a good fellow after all.

THEA. I wonder whom your next wife will be.

GEORGE. I wonder Thea, and oh I say—

THEA. A stamp.

GEORGE (gives stamp). How pretty you—

THEA (reads). "George Tesman, Esq." There now put on your hat George, and take this to the post at once.

GEORGE. Just think of that now. Thea this new proof of your affection for me goes to my heart, and I must tell your grandpapa and grandmama about it. The moment they arrive. How good of them Thea, to offer to come to us for six months.

THEA (aside). I cannot remain here to face simple innocent grandmama. Had I not best tell George all, here this instant. (To him) George, I have not been a good wife to you.

GEORGE. As good as Hedda Gabler herself, dear. Remember what I told you Judge Brack said.

THEA (wildly). Judge Brack! George, Judge Brack kissed me last night.

GEORGE. Fancy that now Thea (exit L.).

THEA (pacing room). How unsuspicious these young men of letters are. I wonder if they are all like that. Oh, but in an hour that letter will be delivered, and then George will know all, he will know why I am going away from him forever. (Gets black bag)[49] It was just like this, that I left my last husband Elvsted, a black bag in my hand, and on my shoulders his little black jacket, if jacket it can be called. To steal away from my second husband precisely as I stole away from my first, it feels quite, quite like old times. (Is going when bell rings). Grandpapa and Grandmama would that I had gone before they came. They are so old fashioned that they will think it wrong of me to desert my home.

(Enter Peter L. with rugs etc.).

Grandpapa!

(Both down C. Peter makes strange faces, gestures, etc.).

Are you not well grandpapa?

PETER (whispers). Can't you follow me? It is so simple that a child could make it out. I was saying Thea, Grandmama and I are so proud that you have at last got a husband to suit you.

THEA. Husband? Ah you mean George. You have been at L'Enfant Prodigue?[50]

(Peter signs yes elaborately).

That means "Yes"! How much easier it is than talking! But why has dear, simple, homely,[51] humdrum, domesticated Grandmama not come with you?

---

47   Echoing a line in *Hedda Gabler*, in reference to a character who attempts to put Hedda in a compromising position.

48   One of George Tesman's catch-phrases in *Hedda Gabler*.

49   This imitates Nora when she prepares to leave Torvald in *A Doll's House*.

50   A "mimic comedy" or "story without words" by Michel Carré with music by André Wormser. First performed in Paris at the Théâtre des Bouffes Parisiens on 21 June 1890, and in London at the Prince of Wales's Theatre on 31 March 1891 (running until 14 April).

51   Homey.

(Peter gesticulates).

She is cleaning windows?

(Peter repeats).

Influenza?

(Peter repeats).

She is standing for the County Council?[52]

(Peter repeats).

Kangaroos?

PETER *(whispers).* You are sure you follow me?

THEA. Yes, but—

PETER. Then I'll tell you what it means. Your Grandmama went away from *L'Enfant Prodigue* in the middle of the first act, because she declared she couldn't hear a word they said.

THEA. But she has not come here?

PETER. No, she went to another play, called *The Doll's House*. A childish piece I should think from the title. She will be here directly. *(Sees letters at fire)* But Thea, what have you been doing here? Burning George's manuscripts. Ah, a good wife, a good wife.

THEA *(aside).* Why should I not tell Grandpapa all? I will! Grandpapa, these are George's letters to me that I am burning,[53] and oh it breaks my heart, for I look upon each of them as a little child, George's children and mine. There are a hundred and twenty-seven.

PETER. Thea Tesman!

THEA. Soon to be Tesman no longer, Grandpapa. I am leaving George.

PETER. Leaving him, what has he done?

THEA. Nothing. It is I who am unworthy of him, Grandpapa. I was at the Leybournes' dance last night and Judge Brack and I went into the conservatory, and he kissed me.

PETER *(shakes and falls on sofa R.).* Ghosts, ghosts![54] Is my forty years' secret at last to be discovered?[55] I, I cannot see Thea, that you are to be held responsible for Judge Brack's misbehaviour.

THEA. I let him do it. I wanted him to do it; and that is not all, for Parson Greig kissed me on Tuesday, and Henrik Barsam on Wednesday and Baron Kleig on Thursday, and I am going mad, mad! mad!! *(Falls on sofa).*

PETER. Ghosts! So the bolt falls. For nearly forty years, have I kept my crime to myself and now it must out, it must out. Thea, I, ah, men don't do these things.[56]

THEA *(starting up).* They do, they do, and oh grandpapa, I like it.

PETER. Ghosts.

THEA. And so grandpapa I must leave George. Oh grandpapa, you who have lived a blameless life do not, cannot understand how unworthy I am of George. It is idle to tell me to be more careful. It is in my blood—

---

52   London's County Council was a new entity in 1888. Formerly the conurbation had been governed by local parish councils; this amalgamated responsibility for the first time.

53   An allusion to Hedda's actions in *Hedda Gabler*.

54   An echo of Mrs. Alving's cry at the end of act 1 of *Ghosts*.

55   An allusion to Oswald Alving's father, part of the back-story to *Ghosts*.

56   At the end of *Hedda Gabler*, Tesman discovers that his wife has shot herself. Judge Brack collapses in a chair and exclaims: "Good God!—people don't do such things."

(Peter jumps).

> and I know—I feel that as I have been in the past so shall I be in the future. I cannot look upon a man without wanting him to kiss me, and he reads my thoughts, and does it. Oh Grandpapa, how can men read a woman's thoughts so well? *(Aside)* So well, that is your cue.

PETER *(aside).* No, "other women" is my cue. I am using Gosse's version you know.

THEA. I am using Archer's, say something.

PETER. All right. Ghosts.

THEA. Grandpapa, you who are so wise and good, tell me why I experience this overpowering desire to be kissed? It seethes through my being. It is a wild uncontrollable passion that I cannot master. Why, oh why am I so different from other women?

PETER. "Other women." Ghosts.

THEA. George wonders why he cannot keep a secretary for more than one day. It is because my kisses frighten them. Grandpapa they run from me.

(Secretary enters C.).

> Ha! See!
> *(Thea runs after him, he dodges her round table C. she catches him, he kisses her and Exits L.).* Grandpapa, tell me, oh tell me why I did it.

PETER. How—how should I know? *(Sinks in chair L.).*

THEA. You do know. I can see it in your face.

PETER *(in horrified tones).*[57] Ghosts. She sees them in my face, and I thought I had kept them hidden inside—inside. *(Aloud)* So be it. Let the bolt fall. Thea I will tell you all, but first, the brandy, quick the brandy.

(Thea gives glass of brandy, he drinks, mutters "Ghosts").

> Thea what I am about to tell you I have kept to myself for almost, almost forty years. Ah do not say I have not suffered. *(Flinging himself at her)* Do not say it.

THEA. You frighten me, Grandpapa. That's your cue.

PETER. Ah! revile me Thea if you choose, but do not say I have not suffered, even if you think I have not. Don't let on, it makes me jump so. Thea, weep no more or if you must, weep and wring your hands, because that is your idea of the character, let it be for me, for it is I who have done this; it is I who have made you what you are! Quick more brandy.

(She brings it, he drinks).

> Ghosts. *(Whispers)* You don't think I am saying "Ghosts" too often do you?

THEA. No, not at all. *(Aloud)* You have not made me what I am, Grandpapa. It is only a wicked impulse of my own.

PETER. Poor Thea Tesman, and whence comes that impulse? It comes from me. It is hereditary, as all impulses are.

THEA. Speak quickly, grandpapa, speak quickly *(seizes him by shoulders).*

PETER. Thickly? Is it quickly or thickly in Archer's version? Never mind. The brandy. *(Drinks. Relates these dread experiences of the past in a grotesquely tragic fashion)*[58] Thea Tesman, nearly forty years ago

---

57   According to *Era*, 6 June 1891.
58   Ibid.

I married your grandmother, my confiding little baby wife Delia—and I have never had a moment's happiness since—that was not her fault, it was mine—mine. Two evenings before the wedding one of her bridesmaids was staying with her and it so happened that the gas suddenly went out.

(Music)[59]

It was relit in a moment but during that time—Thea can you not help me out!

THEA (coldly). Go—on—

PETER. She was pretty. Tobacco-colored hair, impudent nose, soft chin, pleading eyes, laughing shoulders, rather plump and twenty round the waist[60]—round the waist. I never saw her without a mad longing to take her face in my hands, gather her up, and—in short she was the kind I liked. Until that black night, however, I succeeded in stepping back from her, in order to prevent myself stepping nearer, but when the gas went out—when the gas went out. Remember Thea, it must also have been hereditary in my case, otherwise I could not have done it. Thea, I offer no excuse for the impulse was not then so strong (it came from my great aunt on my mother's side) but that I could have resisted it.

THEA. The gas went out?

PETER. Went out—it must have been hereditary—and then, ha, ha! I kissed her, yes Thea I kissed her— she was the kind I liked. (Crosses) In another second the gas was lit, and she was at the opposite end of the room, looking at some photographs. Ay, glare at me, Thea, glare at me. It is I who have given you this fell[61] disease.

THEA. I see. I see, the scales fall from my eyes. Oh you wicked old man (faints R.).

PETER. She was the kind I liked. Fainted. Dead! Don't say you're dead, Thea. Ha, the brandy (pours out) say when Thea, say when. Water?

THEA (faintly). Potash.[62]

PETER. No, thank you, Thea. I take it neat, neat (drinks it off).

(Thea sinks onto the sofa, Peter on a chair. The stage grows dark, and in an instant there is a transformation. Thea removes her jacket and instead wields a feather boa. She is no longer the timid, soft-spoken, kiss-loving Thea but has become cynical, defiant Hedda Gabler. Peter is changed into the living portrait of Ibsen).[63]

THEA (sitting up). Ghosts.

PETER. Have you got 'em too, Thea? What change is this that has come over you?

THEA. You notice it? Grandpapa, your confession has made a woman of me. It has turned me into a Hedda. Look! look! I am no longer Thea Tesman. I am a Hedda Gabler.

PETER. She is a Hedda now.

(Bell rings).

Ha—Grandmama.

THEA. I must away to think—to think.

PETER. About your future Thea. I mean Hedda.

---

59   Probably an ominous chord, the intended effect of which is immediately debunked by the restoration of light.

60   A twenty-inch waist, cinched by a corset and tightly bound, was a goal for young women.

61   Terrible.

62   Potassium carbonate, used as fertilizer. Barrie evidently parodies exclamations such as balderdash and pshaw.

63   The specifics are detailed in Era, 6 June 1891 and The World, 3 June 1891: 872, and the timing in Theatre, July 1891: 28-29.

THEA. No, about yours. How will you do it Grandpapa? *(She imitates Hedda)*.

PETER. Do it?

THEA. You don't mean that you will go on living. No, put vine leaves in your hair, Grandpapa, and do it.[64] Oh, why should you have been able thus to destroy me? Hereditary! Why should I suffer for your sins? Grandpapa, I shut my eyes and see a new era dawning. I tell you, I warn you, that the day is fast approaching when there will be no heredity, a day when old conditions will be played out, and new conditions will take their place, conditions under which there shall be no such thing as grandfathers *(exit C.)*.

PETER *(in chair L.)*. Thea. Thea Tesman, you would not blame me so much if you understood she was the kind I liked. I don't think I can do it. Thea, it will be a more severe punishment to live on, and Delia would not like me to do it. I am glad Delia is coming. Womanly, homely Delia. I wonder if Delia uses Gosse's version or Archer's.

(Enter Delia L. She coughs).

Ah, my pet, and how did she like *The Doll's House*? Delia my dear wife, I don't quite care for Thea. I want to go home.

DELIA *(glaring at him)*. Wife! Home! Oh, how I hate the words!

PETER *(jumps up and then falls into seat)*. You too Delia! The brandy!

(She snatches the bottle from him).

Gosse—I mean Ghosts.

DELIA. How did I like *The Doll's House*? It has made a woman of me. Peter Terence, I have come here to call you to account. I am your doll no longer *(triumphantly)*.

PETER. Have you not been happy, Delia?

DELIA. Because we knew no better. Go on Peter Terence, cast my innocence in my teeth. I know what you will say, that you have been faithful to me. Yes, you have been faithful and yet you call yourself a man.

PETER. A virtuous woman—

DELIA. Virtuous! Have I ever had a chance of being anything else? I am your wife. We were to be complement and supplement, it was on that understanding you got me, and how have you kept your trust? Peter Terence answer me this. Did you ever take me into low society? Dare you answer yes! You dare not. Of the women who have come to our house during these forty years of ridiculous happiness, was there not one who was not a lady? Peter Terence, there was not. You know the world, you see it in all its colours, and yet did you ever bring home a disreputable man to dinner? Not one, Peter Terence. Did you ever make a remark in my presence that was not fit for a lady's ear? Never. When I should have been living my own life, were you not dandling me on your knee, and taking hairpins from my hair to clean your pipes with? I have borne you six children, Peter Terence, and did you propose that they should be sent out to nurse, because a true woman cannot be bothered with children? Did you relieve me of the trouble of rearing one of them? Not one. I had to bring them all up myself, they called me mother. You stood by and let them call me mother!

PETER. The brandy.

DELIA. No.

PETER. But my duck.

DELIA. No.

---

64   Hedda urges Lövborg to do this in *Hedda Gabler*, invoking a romantic view of suicide.

PETER. I mean my wild duck.[65]

DELIA. You disgracefully, healthy-minded old man, for shame.

PETER. Ghosts then. You have no objections to my saying Ghosts? I must say something.

(Thea enters C. and listens).

DELIA. Not to me. Henceforth Peter Terence our paths lie in different directions. You go one way and I go the other.

PETER. Delia Terence. Deliar Tremens. Delirium Tremens.[66]

DELIA. And if you are half a man, you will set off upon yours directly.

THEA *(rushes down L. and hands him a pistol)*. Do, Grandpapa.[67]

PETER *(shrinking)*. Hedda Gabler's pistol.

THEA. One of them. Grandpapa take it and leave this contemptible world, with scorn upon your countenance and vine leaves in your hair. Oh, it is the one course still open to a brave man. *(Whispers)* Archer's version says that you here take the pistol.

PETER *(sadly)*. So does Gosse's *(takes pistol)*.

DELIA. Look sharp Peter.

PETER. D'you know—I don't like London.

THEA. Grandpapa. Do it gracefully.

DELIA. Oh, do it anyhow.

PETER. Patience, my dears. I—I am not used to this sort of thing. It's, it's got very warm don't you think Delia? The—a—summer has come at last, Thea, eh?

THEA. Don't aim so low down grandpapa.[68]

(He aims above his head).

Nor so high up. Be graceful grandpapa, there are several good places.

DELIA. Any place is good enough so long as he can find a way in.

PETER. No Delia—I beg you pardon, but Thea makes a point of my doing it gracefully, with art.

THEA *(eagerly)*. The heart is a good place, a very good place.

PETER. Hedda's pistol, Hedda's.

THEA. The head(a) is a good place too.

DELIA *(tapping him on the throat)*. This is a good place.

PETER. Here, Delia *(puts pistol to neck)*.

THEA. Lower Grandpapa, here *(taps his heart)*.

DELIA. Or here *(lifts pistol to his forehead)*.

THEA. Or here *(points pistol at stomach)*.

PETER. Hadn't I better lie down first? It would be more graceful, Thea, than to fall afterwards—No! Very well then. I'll do it when I say three. One—two—I say I have an idea, why shouldn't you both come with me?

THEA. Why not?

DELIA. Ay, why not?

---

65   In Ibsen's *The Wild Duck*, a lame bird is kept by the Ekdals in their attic home/studio.

66   Trembling and delusion caused by withdrawal from alcohol.

67   In Ibsen's play, Hedda gives Lövborg one of her father's pistols and urges him to commit suicide "beautifully."

68   Hedda envisioned that Lövborg would shoot himself in the heart or the temple; instead, he aimed lower (at his abdomen or groin).

PETER *(handing pistol to Delia).* Ladies first.

THEA. No, all together, see here are more pistols *(gets pistols from table, keeps one and gives Delia one).*

THEA. Grandpapa, we all fire when you say three

(Thea, Peter, and Delia are in a line down C.).

PETER. One—two—Have you found a good place Delia? Have you vine leaves in your hair? Very well. One—two—the brandy!

DELIA. No.

PETER. One—Two—I say, where is it we are going to?

THEA. Where?

DELIA. Ah where?

PETER. Let us say to, to Hedda's, one—two—one, two, three.

(All fire and fall, Peter in centre).

GEORGE *(enter L.).* Someone's been shooting rubbish here, just fancy that *(sits at table C.).*

(George's Secretary enters and shoots him).[69]

PETER. *(sitting up. Sings).*[70]
  Just fancy that, it is my cue
  Well I don't fancy them, do you?
  I think that all the Ibsen ladies
  Should find a place and go to Hades.[71]

GEORGE *(without looking up).*
  Just fancy that. Just think of that.[72]

THEA *(sitting up).*
  You take a Hedda, you're a toff[73]
  She's like her pistol, she goes off.
  Of Ibsen women, boys beware
  They all have vine leaves in their hair.

GEORGE.
  Just fancy that. Just think of that.

DELIA *(sitting up).*[74]
  Oh I am an Ibsen-minded thing
  I'm going on the stage.
  You'll see me at the Vaudeville
  Where Ibsen's all the rage.

---

69 According to *Theatre*, July 1891: 29.

70 The score appears in manuscript with Beinecke Barrie Ib6/1, annotated with this verse. All four verses appear on a separate sheet, slightly amended from the licensing copy.

71 An alternative is given for the last two lines:
    The Ibsen wheeze I've got quite pat.
    Just fancy that. Just think of that.

72 An unattributed line in the Beinecke manuscript reads, "Well I don't fancy them that's flat."

73 Stylish person.

74 Delia's first two verses are only in the Beinecke manuscript, and the last is only in the licensing copy.

I'll wear an emancipated dress,
My hair with vine leaves curl.
The latest dodge to fetch 'em 'tis
Of an Ibsen-minded Girl.

Wives of the future, then begorra[75]
I'm glad that I don't live tomorrow.
I'm flesh and blood, I'll tell you, bah
They're nothing but automata.[76]

(The three rise singing).

ALL.
We're nothing but automata.

(They dance like wooden figures).

PETER *(speaks).* I say there's another verse in Gosse's version.
GEORGE *(sings).*
Let's go to Toole's, my version says,
For it's a rare—a rare good place.
PETER.
Just fancy that.
Your taste his plays are sure to strike
And there you'll find the kind you like.

(Repeat first three lines,[77] then "So go to Toole's." They dance and die as in waxwork).[78]

Illustration 32. "Ibsen," score for the finale of *Ibsen's Ghost* by J.M. Barrie (lyrics),
based on the score in J.M. Barrie Collection lb6/1, Beinecke Library, Yale University.

---

75   Anglo-Irish expletive for "by God."
76   Objects such as toys that move by mechanical or involuntary means; can also mean human beings acting routinely or monotonously.
77   The reference is unclear; most likely Peter's first verse.
78   Melting.

Trilby (1895)

George Du Maurier's *Trilby* was the best-selling novel of the century. The illustrated text's serialization in *Harper's Magazine* (1894) sparked "Trilby mania" of astounding proportions in the United States.[1] To capitalize on the fad, American manufacturers produced *Trilby*-branded cigars, waltzes, corsets, cocktails, perfumes, sausages, coiffures, and foot-shaped ice-cream confections.[2] In the spring of 1895, Paul Potter's stage adaptation of the novel was taken on a short US tour before opening in New York.[3] The pre-eminent London character actor and theatre manager Herbert Beerbohm Tree saw the show in Buffalo, went backstage, and bought the British rights.[4] Tree returned to London in the summer of 1895 and embarked on rehearsals for what became one of his biggest hits.[5]

Tree recognized a great part for himself. Svengali, a lesser character in the novel, is significantly more prominent in Potter's play. Recent commentators have recognized the pejorative depiction of Svengali as a despised Jew, "out of the mysterious East"[6] (an epithet from the novel), and anti-Semitism was evident to playgoers. More notably, however, Victorian audiences subsumed Svengali's accent, demeanour, and musicianship—markers of his Jewishness—to their perception of his ability to fascinate or, more specifically, to keep Trilby utterly in his thrall, converting her from a tone-deaf artists' model to a singer of world renown. It is in the context of persistent interest in occult possession, spiritualism, ecstatic conversion, and phrenology that *Trilby* found a place in nineteenth-century repertoire. A variant on these weird and compelling practices was mesmerism, as it was called in the nineteenth century, originally given in medical demonstrations but by the mid-century also proliferating in commercial performances ("grotesque entertainments given in music halls for the delectation of the gaping multitude")[7] and by amateur practitioners.[8] While the empirical basis of some of *Trilby*'s plot points was contentious, as a stage entertainment its hypnotic pretext was hugely compelling.[9] *Trilby* marks two important developments

---

1   Published January-August 1894 in *Harper's*. See also "Royal Court Theatre: 'Trilby,'" *Liverpool Post*, 1 October 1895; and Jonathan Freedman, "Mania and the Middlebrow: The Case of *Trilby*," in *Lyrical Symbols and Narrative Transformations: Essays in Honor of Ralph Freedman*, edited by Kathleen L. Komar and Ross Shideler (Columbia, SC: Camden, 1998), 149-71.

2   See J.B. Gilder and J.D. Gilder, *Trilbyana: The Rise and Progress of a Popular Novel* (New York: The Critic Co., 1895), 25-26; and "Monday Gossip," *Bailie*, 18 September 1895. In Britain, an effusion of *Trilby*-themed music appeared in 1895-96: marches, waltzes, polkas, and other dance music, as well as ballads (including "Trilby Will Be True," "I'm Looking for Trilby!," "Oh, Trilby, What Have You Done for Me?," "Tricky Little Trilby," "Trilby on the Brain," and "Trilby, the French-Irish Girl").

3   Paul Meredith Potter (1853-1921, a.k.a. Walter Arthur Maclean) was English-born but resided in the United States from 1878. He worked as a journalist for the *New York Herald* and the *Chicago Tribune* and began writing original plays around 1890. *Trilby* was his greatest success, but most of his subsequent plays were adapted from French originals.

4   Philip S. Stetson, "How Mr. Potter Wrote 'Trilby,'" *Metropolitan Magazine* 1 (May 1895): 238; and Madeleine Bingham, *"The Great Lover": The Life and Art of Herbert Beerbohm Tree* (London: Hamish Hamilton; 1978), 71.

5   Profits from *Trilby* allowed Tree to renovate His Majesty's Theatre, where he became Lessee in 1897. Tracy C. Davis, *The Economics of the British Stage, 1800-1914* (Cambridge: Cambridge UP, 2000), 225.

6   Neil R. Davison, "'The Jew' as Homme/Femme-Fatale: Jewish (Art)ifice, *Trilby*, and Dreyfus," *Jewish Social Studies: History, Culture, and Society* 8:2-3 (2002): 73-111; Daniel Pick, *Svengali's Web: The Alien Encounter in Modern Culture* (New Haven, CT: Yale, 2000); and Denis Denisoff, *Aestheticism and Sexual Parody, 1840-1940* (Cambridge: Cambridge UP, 2001), 83-93.

7   "'Trilby' at the Lyceum Theatre," *Edinburgh Evening News*, 24 September 1895.

8   John Hughes Bennett, *The Mesmeric Mania of 1851, with a Physiological Explanation of the Phenomena Produced* (Edinburgh and London: Sutherland and Knox; and Simpkin, Marshall & Co., 1851), 6; and Alison Winter, *Mesmerized: Powers of Mind in Victorian Britain* (Chicago: U of Chicago P, 1998).

9   Fred Nadis, *Wonder Shows: Performing Science, Magic, and Religion in America* (New Brunswick, NJ: Rutgers UP, 2005), 100; and Ernesto Laclau, *On Populist Reason* (London: Verso, 2005), 40-44.

in the popular and medical understanding of hypnosis: a wider knowledge among lay people about how to induce trance and a concern that a subject placed under hypnotic influence could be inappropriately manipulated.[10] Can a hypnotist exert such powers? The play explores what would happen if a beautiful young woman were to fall so thoroughly under a hypnotist's influence that she abandons her life and becomes the automaton of another's will.[11] Young women were considered particularly susceptible (also soldiers, accustomed to taking orders).[12] Critics asked, "What if such a power were possessed by an Anarchist or by a thief? And if by Svengali, why not by either or by both?"[13]

Genre Issues

Two of *Trilby*'s great strengths as a play are its crossover between theatrical genres and utilization of several of the fine arts. Gothicism, horror, and the macabre waft through the scruffy artists' studio, invade the gay surroundings of the Cirque des Bashibazouks, and recur through the eerie power of Svengali's image, intermixing comedy with melodrama. Painting occupies the bohemians, they dance in anticipation of Trilby's wedding, and act 3 is set in an opulent theatre lobby, yet it is music that conveys both affective mood and narrative developments. Sound is contrasted between artistic arrangements by great composers and the catchy melodies of popular tunesmiths; between the musically inept *grisette* and her transformed self on stage; and between the Paris cityscape of church bells and noëls and the foreground noise of tipsy revellers. All Victorian performance is multisensory, but *Trilby* exemplifies how fully this can operate in order for a clichéd romance plot of claptrap and balderdash to become compelling actable stuff.[14]

It also represents how a popular vehicle crosses over from the legitimate stage to music hall and cinema, fulfilling audience demand for a popular story in multiple ways. Following the 254 performances of the initial London run, the Haymarket company toured *Trilby* to suburban theatres, the provinces, and America. Tree briefly revived it numerous times between 1897 and 1912, made a film version with a happy ending in 1914, and played a severely truncated version in the music halls in 1915.[15] By that time, nine other cinematic treatments had been made in Britain, the United States, Austria, and Denmark.[16] By the end of the twentieth century, the number had doubled.

Trilby begins as a comedy and proceeds as a romance, utilizing the stage techniques of melodrama. Three British painters (Billee, Laird, and Taffy), all in love with Trilby, are immersed in the free-and-easy

---

10   The ethical issue was first raised by J. Liégeois in 1884: anyone could learn the techniques of invoking hypnotic trance, so what if they abused their power to command criminal or sexual behaviour? See *De la suggestion hypnotique dans ses rapports avec le droit civil et le droit criminal* (Paris: Alphonse Picard, 1884), quoted in Jean-Roch Laurence and Campbell Perry, *Hypnosis, Will, and Memory: A Psycho-Legal History* (New York: Guildford Press, 1988), 226-27.

11   Charles Barney Cory, *Hypnotism or Mesmerism* (Boston: Alfred Mudge & Son, 1888), 20-21.

12   Ibid., 13-14; and W.H.J. Shaw, *How to Hypnotise and Mesmerise: A Manual of Instruction in the History, Mysteries, Modes of Procedure and Methods of Mesmerism, or Animal Magnetism, etc.* (Chicago: The Author, 1896), 45.

13   "'Trilby' at the Theatre Royal," *Manchester Courier*, 9 September 1895.

14   For gothicism in the novel, see Ruth Bienstock Anolik, "The Infamous Svengali: George Du Maurier's Satanic Jew," in *The Gothic Other: Racial and Social Constructions in the Literary Imagination*, edited by Ruth Bienstock Anolik and Douglas L. Howard (Jefferson, NC: McFarland, 2004), 163-93.

15   *Trilby* was revived for short runs in 1897, 1898, 1902, 1903, 1905, 1907, 1909, and 1912. The 1914 film was directed by Harold Shaw and distributed by the London Film Company. Tree's acting is analyzed in Jon Burrows, *Legitimate Cinema: Theatre Stars in Silent British Films, 1908-1918* (Exeter: U of Exeter P, 2003), 158-62. For the 1915 text, revised by Stanley Bell, see Bristol Theatre Collection HBT/000238/1.

16   Tree's version was produced by Harold Shaw and included none of the London cast apart from Tree. See also the films *Trilby and Little Billee* (Biography 1896); *Etta Lola, à la Trilby* (Edison 1898); *Trilby* (Nordisk 1908); *Trilby* (Kinemacolor 1910); *Trilby* (Osterreichische-Ungarische Kinoindustri 1912); *Trilby* (Biography 1912); *Trilby* (Standard 1912); *Trilby* (Famous Players 1913); and *Svengali der Hypnotiser* (Weiner 1914).

culture of Paris's Latin Quarter. The happy union of Trilby and Billee is prevented by two forces: his uptight family (the Bagots) who object to Trilby's upbringing in Paris—an Irish orphan fostered by a rag-picker—and her occupation as artists' model; and the nefarious Svengali, who perceives Trilby's potential as a singer and uses his hypnotic power to control her. Their community of friends, lower-class women and young Frenchmen slumming it among the bohemians, support the union; but while they can effect subterfuges to thwart Billee's family, they are insufficiently aware of Svengali's villainy to protect Trilby from his manipulation. A series of sensational moments mark the four-act play—Trilby's hypnoses, Billee's departure then reconciliation with Trilby, Mrs. Bagot's refusal to permit the marriage, the friends' discovery that Trilby has disappeared, reunification of the friends after many years, Svengali's collapse, and Trilby's encounter with her late husband's photograph—to give it a series of strong pictorial moments consonant with Du Maurier's illustrations for the novel.[17]

While aspects of the story have many precursors, the Svengali-Trilby dyad has "slipped free" of the novel and the play to gain allegorical status in its own right.[18] As reviews and later commentaries note, Mephistopheles utilized the "mystery and cunning" of black arts to exert demonic power over Gretchen;[19] Ovid's Pygmalion carved a statue which the gods endowed with life; the doll in *Coppélia* danced as an automaton, subject to alien will;[20] and Sleeping Beauty awoke from an induced torpor to discover the treachery of her enchantress and the fidelity of her lover.[21] While Trilby's bohemian backdrop and reluctant in-laws were likened to the play *La Dame aux camélias*,[22] and her trance-state resembles the heroine of the opera *La sonnambula*,[23] Svengali too had clearly recognizable nineteenth-century precursors. As a contemporaneous article points out, "the pushing, speculating Hebrew appears in Balzac. The pathetic figure of the typical world-wanderer in Eugène Sue. Dickens gave us Fagin ... George Eliot, the profound, presents us with Daniel Deronda and Mordecai."[24] These various influences coalesce in *Trilby* into an indelible image of a male taking control over a female's creativity. Thus, in an 1895 circus act, Marie Meers rode bareback dressed as Trilby, with Svengali as the ringmaster; the American impresarios David Belasco and Augustin Daly were said to control their star actresses Mrs. Leslie Carter and Ada Rehan like Svengali; George Edwardes held sway over the Gaiety Girls; and more recently Tommy Mottola was labelled Mariah Carey's Svengali.[25]

---

17   An exhibition of Du Maurier's illustrations for *Trilby* at the Fine Art Society, New Bond Street, coincided with the Haymarket premiere. "Haymarket Theatre," *Times*, 31 October 1895.

18   Pick, *Svengali's Web*, 6.

19   "'Trilby' at the Theatre Royal," *Manchester Courier*, 9 September 1895; "'Trilby' at the Lyceum Theatre," *Edinburgh Evening News*, 24 September 1895; and "'Trilby,'" *Evening News*, 31 October 1895.

20   Jane Goodall, *Stage Presence* (London: Routledge, 2008), 87-88.

21   Carole Silver, "On the Origin of Fairies: Victorians, Romantics, and Folk Belief," *Browning Institute Studies* 14 (1986): 150.

22   Adapted into the opera *La traviata*, *La Dame aux camélias* chronicles a *demi-mondaine* who succumbs to illness and death after her lover's father persuades her to renounce the relationship. "Theatre Royal: Mr. Beerbohm Tree and the Haymarket Company in 'Trilby,'" *Manchester Guardian*, 9 September 1895; and Phyllis Weliver, "Music, Crowd Control and the Female Performer in *Trilby*," in *The Idea of Music in Victorian Fiction*, edited by Sophie Fuller and Nicky Loseff (Aldershot: Ashgate, 2004), 69.

23   For a summary of *La sonnambula*, see commentary above on its burlesque, pp. 290-301.

24   Alex Neuman, "The Significance of Svengali," *Illustrated American*, 11 May 1895: 586. See Balzac's *Splendeurs et misères des courtisanes* (*A Harlot High and Low*) and *Ursule Mirouët*, Sue's *Le Juif errant* (*The Wandering Jew*), Dickens's *Oliver Twist*, and George Eliot's *Daniel Deronda*.

25   Gilder and Gilder, *Trilbyana*, 20-21; Kim Marra, *Strange Duets: Impresarios and Actresses in the American Theatre, 1865-1914* (Iowa City: U of Iowa P, 2005), 47, 56, 178, 203; Peter Bailey, "'Naughty but Nice': Musical Comedy and the Rhetoric of the Girl," in *The Edwardian Theatre*, edited by M.R. Booth and J.H. Kaplan, (Cambridge: Cambridge UP, 1996), 39; and Lola Ogunnaike, "A Superstar Returns with Another New Self," *New York Times*, 12 April 2005: B3.

Interpretive Issues

In the nineteenth century, wealthy patrons commissioned portraits and sat for the artists; anyone else posing for painters was a "body for rent, if not for sale, within the space of the studio, which is not only a site of artistic creativity, but also of commercial exchange."[26] The relevance of this taint to Trilby is the topic of the play's initial dialogue. Respectable young working-class women in the glove factory across the street are horrified that Trilby poses in the nude; she is also a thing apart from what Billee's middle-class womenfolk hold dearest. Though her three British champions claim there is nothing untoward in her posing for them, Billee balks at the thought that Trilby poses for another artist upstairs. What is a twinge in Billee becomes outright revulsion in his mother. When his uncle, Rev. Bagot—almost reconciled to Trilby's early life in the Latin Quarter and her later fame throughout Europe—expresses his final desperate reservation about Trilby's suitability to join his family, he asks, "Has the lady been confirmed?" He reverts to true form: unable to impeach her occupation, he must insist that Trilby is a Christian (and a Church of England member). Her friend the Laird, a Scotsman, drily answers, "Probably not." If he was raised in the Church of Scotland, the Laird would be a Presbyterian (though lapsed, no doubt), who disdains confirmation as well as English religious intolerance and prejudice disguised as religion. Determined to settle the issue once and for all, the Laird turns the ultimate weapon upon the clergyman's bias: a fistful of calling cards, left by pre-eminent European heads of state, inquiring into Trilby's health. Royalty—but perhaps only royalty—can trump English bigotry and middle-class moralizing.

The Laird's indifference to religion and Rev. Bagot's insistence upon it pass as character-establishing by-play, yet by implication they also complicate the terrain for depicting Svengali. Whereas Trilby's presumed atheism is a threat to the Bagots, Svengali's brush with apostasy highlights the indispensability of Judaism to his existence:[27] many reviewers remark on some business in act 2—added by Tree to Potter's play, with Du Maurier's permission—in which Svengali triumphantly declares, "I am my own God," laughing at religion. He is immediately toppled by a heart spasm. Asking God to let him live a little longer, he mutters a prayer extolling monotheism.[28] Thus, Svengali's *hubris* is answered by a wrathful god, and he reverts to a rote prayer in Hebrew. Marking Svengali as an impoverished musician, a proficient hypnotist, an eastern European (from somewhere in the Austro-Hungarian Empire) or Russian (the postmarks on his portrait point to this), and a Jew makes him the consummate outsider, yet one who moves effortlessly among the bohemians of the Latin Quarter, a place almost the antithesis of England.[29] His Jewishness is

---

26   Kay Dian Kriz, *Slavery, Sugar, and the Culture of Refinement: Picturing the British West Indies, 1700-1840* (New Haven, CT: Yale UP, 2008), 89.

27   Svengali is an exotic on the West End stage, not a Jew reconstituted into Englishness as Heidi Holder has traced in East End productions. Heidi Holder, "Nation and Neighbourhood, Jews and Englishmen: Location and Theatrical Ideology in Victorian London," in *The Performing Century: Nineteenth-Century Theatre's History*, edited by Tracy C. Davis and Peter Holland (Basingstoke: Palgrave, 2007), 105-20.

28   "'Trilby' at the Court Theatre," *Liverpool Courier*, 1 October 1895; and "Music and the Drama: Brighton Theatre Royal," *Daily News* (Brighton), 19 March 1897.

29   Another stage adaptation, licensed for the Theatre Royal Eastbourne in April 1896, emphasizes Svengali's accent (and creepy foreignness) more than Potter's. It exaggerates Svengali's speech while making the Laird's more phonetic. This is Trilby's first mesmeric induction:

   SVENGALI. Nein. She has ye Neuralgia. Perhaps I cure He'em. Sit you there mademoiselle. *(She sits on raised seat.)* Now you fix your eyes on the whites of mine. Look hard, intent so yat is well, keep your eyes fixed so.

   (Makes passes gently up and down, music. Trilby's eyes close gradually, he makes more passes, & pause).

   BILLEE. He's mesmerising her *(aside).*
   SVENGALI. Was you pitter. Not so mosh pain, hein?

made synonymous with his lack of conscience towards god and people; contrasted with Trilby's loving heart, Svengali becomes a greater threat than atheism *per se*.

The characters' vocal diversity maps Europe from east to west: Svengali and Trilby represent Europe's geographic extremes, but the Laird's Scottish burr, Taffy's Welshness (implied by his nickname, though not proclaimed),[30] and Zouzou's comic protestations that "I no spik Angliche" also make much of Gaelic and Gallic difference in charting cultural pluralism. This places the Bagots—English, educated, and Anglican—as the normative centre, yet as a family even they are divided. The moral compass of chauvinism is skewed though there is never any doubt for an audience where virtue rests, for it is the business of melodrama to render right-thinking unmistakably. Svengali peppers his speech with German, speaks French Teutonically, and renders English with a stage-Jew lisp: this cannot be good. Mrs. Bagot acts out of fear for her son, but the audience is given ample cause to pass judgement on her brother, Rev. Bagot, who shows his scholar's knowledge of Egyptian, Greek, and Roman erotica while furtively enjoying the sensualism that goes with this arcane knowledge. Thus, Potter melds nationality onto ethnicity and religion onto regionalism to depict English anti-cosmopolitanism as small-minded and stifling at the same time that he makes Svengali a dangerous foreigner. Adapted in 1895 but set retrospectively in the 1850s, the height of the Hapsburg monarchy's political threat to Britain,[31] *Trilby* allegorizes a more morally rigid time, when an expansionist enemy lurking to the east seemed as threatening as religious schisms at home and when continental instability made the importance of concord among the British peoples—English (the Bagots), Scottish (the Laird), Welsh (Taffy), and Irish (Trilby)—paramount.

As a young physician, Franz Anton Mesmer observed French priests performing exorcisms. He rejected the idea of demonical possession and pioneered the use of magnets to induce trance and then bring about physical and psychological cures. His extraordinary claims were investigated and discounted by the French government in 1784.[32] Mesmer claimed to manipulate electric currents passing between bodies (hence, the instigation of trance as *induction* in the practice of "animal magnetism"), but in 1831 the French Academy declared that *assertion* was the means of producing mesmeric effects rather than

---

TRILBY. None at all now Monsieur. Thank Heaven and you!
SVENGALI. You gust set still, sleep, at my will.

(Trilby's head sinks back her eyes close Svengali makes passes. Taffy and Laird R.C. enter).

TAFFY. What are you doing?
SVENGALI. Curing ye Neuralgia. *(To Trilby)* Wake—ask her now if she sleep or not.
LAIRD. Eh! this is verra strange: do you sleep young lassie?
British Library Add MS 53599, licence no. 501, fols. 25-26.
30   Presumed to derive from the river Taff, which runs through Cardiff. It has pejorative connotations, as in the verse (sung in the borderlands of England and Wales on St. David's Day) that begins:
Taffy was a Welshman,
Taffy was a thief.
Taffy came to my house
And stole a leg of beef.
I went to Taffy's house,
Taffy was in bed.
I picked up the leg of beef
And hit him on the head.
31   See the discussion of the political background to *Ours*, above, p. 361.
32   James Stanley Grimes, *Etherology and the Phreno-Philosophy of Mesmerism and Magic Eloquence: Including a New Philosophy of Sleep and of Consciousness, with a Review of the Pretensions of Phreno-Magnetism, Electro-Biology, &c.* (Boston, Cambridge; London: J. Munroe and Company; Edward T. Whitfield, 1850), 45-49.

magnetism.[33] By the end of the nineteenth century, while Mesmer's electric techniques were dismissed as "faith cures," the scientific basis of suggestion as something legitimately efficacious while a subject is in deep relaxation had taken hold.[34] James Braid, a Manchester practitioner, coined the term *hypnotism* in the 1840s. Braid's hypnotism had the same applications and efficacy as mesmerism, minus the idea of magnetic fluids. Braid also desexualized induction by forgoing the physical "passes" performed by the hypnotist over the patient's body and made no claim to impinge mind or will upon another person: a hypnotic patient must be a willing subject.[35] Several aspects of hypnosis were debated for the remainder of the century: whether the inducer needed to be in proximity to the subject, the extent to which inductees retained volition and awareness while in trance, and the duration of the hypnotic state.[36] *Trilby* opts for the most lenient view of all these issues.

Three hypnotic stages were propounded by J.M. Charcot at the Salpêtrière asylum in the 1880s. In act 1, Svengali uses hypnotism to relieve Trilby's headache, demonstrating to her friends the first two stages of hypnosis: drowsiness (reducing the subject's ability to resist suggestions) and hypotaxy (the subject is obliged to obey all suggestions) as a medically documented therapeutic treatment for neuralgia.[37] In act 2, his technique evolves—or rather, it diverges from accepted practice—as one reviewer noted:

> Mr. Tree performs feats which, we suspect, even the 'Nancy school'[38] would repudiate. He hypnotizes Trilby from behind without her knowledge; in obedience to the wave of his long, spider-like arm he fetches her from a room, 'off,' where, presumably, she can neither see nor hear him. And most assuredly the stage Svengali theorizes incorrectly as to the nature of his powers. He believes, what was effectively disproved a hundred years ago, that a certain virtue, an 'odic [hypothetical] force' of some kind, passes from the hypnotizer to his patient.[39]

Though Svengali's technique was erroneous, his kind of flamboyance characterized the craft of hypnosis. In contrast to Mesmer's powers of "fascination"—dramatized in 1788 by Elizabeth Inchbald (*Animal Magnetism*), illustrating the power of a magnetized wand[40]—Svengali's application of hypnosis had some basis in medical literature. Indeed, Du Maurier's idea for training a great singer may have come from a medical case study in Dr. Braid's treatise *Observations on Trance*.[41] Braid describes a patient, unknowledgeable about music and unilingual, who in a hypnotic trance could mimic the great soprano Jenny Lind note for note, in any language, so precisely that listeners "could not for some times imagine that there were two voices, so perfectly did they accord, both in musical tone and vocal pronunciations of Swiss, German, and Italian songs." Her mirroring of an extemporized chromatic exercise was equally

33   Ernest Hart, *Hypnotism, Mermerism and the New Witchcraft* (London: Smith, Elder & Co., 1896), 137-38, 242-43.

34   Cory, *Hypnotism or Mesmerism*, 8.

35   Winter, *Mesmerized*, 185.

36   Cory, *Hypnotism or Mesmerism*, 11; Lew Alexander Harraden, *How to Give Hypnotic Exhibitions: With History of Hypnotism* (Jackson, MI: Betts, 1900), 11; Laurence and Perry, *Hypnosis, Will, and Memory*, 183, in reference to E. Aza, *Hypnotisme et double conscience* (Paris: F. Alcan, 1893); and B. Brown Williams, MD, *Mental Alchemy: A Treatise on the Mind, Nervous System, Psychology, Magnetism, Mesmerism, and Diseases* (New York: Fowlers and Wells, 1854), 167.

37   Shaw and James, *How to Hypnotise*, 13; Cory, *Hypnotism or Mesmerism*, 20-22; and Alan Gauld, *A History of Hypnotism* (Cambridge: Cambridge UP, 1992), 311-13.

38   A.A. Liébeault's practices at the hospital at Nancy became widely known through Hippolyte Bernheim's 1884 volume *De la suggestion dans l'état hypnotique et dans l'état de veille*. By 1895, Nancy had overtaken Paris's Salpêtrière asylum in medical opinion, validating hypnotherapy. Gauld, *History of Hypnotism*, 319-37.

39   "Haymarket Theatre," *Times*, 31 October 1895.

40   The play remained in the English repertoire through the first half of the nineteenth century and was produced by Charles Dickens in 1857.

41   Paul Potter, who did research for his adaptation at New York's Mercantile Library, made this attribution. See Stetson, "How Mr. Potter Wrote *Trilby*," 239.

impressive.[42] In 1847, John Newman reported another case: a flautist who could improvise beautifully but never recall a single note he played. A sleepwalker, this patient responded to a suggestion when in trance and then transcribed his impromptus perfectly.[43] A third musical case is reported by Dr. Quackenbos, a distinguished American medical scientist, who treated a pianist. He instructed the patient under hypnosis "that the subliminal self is now in the ascendancy" and "that it will utter itself fearlessly, without diffidence, without thought of extraneous criticism, unerringly, feelingly, triumphantly." The patient was then able to "read music, to interpret the contents, and to render the thought of feeling through the medium of piano tones evoked by dexterous fingers."[44]

For one sceptical theatre critic, hypnotism was simply "an easy way of bringing anything you please to pass without troubling yourself to find an adequate reason for it."[45] As Gecko (Svengali's faithful but ambivalent sidekick) explains at the moment that Svengali's plot is undone,

> GECKO (L.C.). There are two Trilbys. There is the Trilby you know, who cannot sing one note in tune....
> And all at once this Svengali, this magician—
>
> *(All turn to Svengali, who is listening with a ghastly look on his face).*
>
> can with one look of his eye, one wave of his hand, turn her into another Trilby, and she becomes a mere singing machine, just the unconscious voice that Svengali sings with, so that when his Trilby is singing our Trilby has ceased to exist. Our Trilby is fast asleep—our Trilby is dead.

While expedient, this also resembles the seeming miracles performed by documented hypnotic subjects. Setting *Trilby* four decades in the past—contemporaneous with Braid and Newman's cases—helped to defray critique about the unscientific basis of the hypnotism. It mattered less that the stage truthfully represented all aspects of the phenomenon than that empathy was generated for Trilby and those who mourned her.

Performative Issues

W.S. Gilbert, who was present at the London premiere, said, "Svengali's make-up is marvelous—we could *smell* him."[46] Tree based his physicalization on Du Maurier's illustrations and the virtuoso violinist Nicolò Paganini (1782-1840).[47] Forming a lean figure, his pallor made more eerie by an oft-stroked beard and long, oily, black, matted hair streaked with red, Tree's Svengali suggested something unearthly, like the Flying Dutchman.[48] Putty lent him a hooked nose, and India ink feathered onto his arms, throat, eyebrows, and the backs of his hands added to his hirsute unwholesomeness.[49] Lit in a "play of grayish light and

42   James Braid, *Observations on Trance; or, Human Hybernation* (London: John Churchill, 1850), 43.

43   John B. Newman, *Fascination; or, the Philosophy of Charming, Illustrating the Principles of Life in Connection with Spirit and Matter* (New York: Fowler & Wells, 1847), 153.

44   John Duncan Quackenbos, *Hypnotism in Mental and Moral Culture* (New York and London: Harper & Brothers, 1901), 245-46. Another possible antecedent for *Trilby* is the seduction by the conductor Charles Boscha of Anna Rivere Bishop, with whom he subsequently travelled the globe. Du Maurier knew of the scandal. Pick, *Svengali's Web*, 98.

45   "Haymarket Theatre: 'Trilby,'" *Star*, 31 October 1895.

46   Hesketh Pearson, *Beerbohm Tree: His Life and Laughter* (London: Methuen, 1956), 90. For lists of attendees, see "'Trilby,'" *Evening News*, 31 October 1895; and "Drama: 'Trilby' at the Haymarket," *Daily News*, 31 October 1895.

47   "Theatres and Amusements: Mr. Tree at the Theatre-Royal," *Evening Citizen* (Glasgow), 17 September 1895. Paganini was lanky and spider-like (possibly the result of a connective tissue disorder), which observers found unnerving.

48   The Flying Dutchman captained a spectral ship generally associated with portents of doom at sea. "'Trilby' at the Gaiety," *Freemans Journal*, 8 October 1895. As a "stage Jew," Svengali was also modelled on Shylock; however, late-Victorian portrayals of Shylock, for example Henry Irving's, were sympathetic. Alan Hughes, "Henry Irving's Tragedy of Shylock," *Educational Theatre Journal* 24:3 (1972): 248-64.

49   "A Famous Actor's Make-up: How Mr. Tree Prepares for Svengali," *Morning Leader* (New York), 4 January 1897.

dark shadow on his features," he was a stage villain like no other. He used "his long, octopus-like limbs," "short mirthless laugh," and "kick-out of the leg behind" himself to maximum effect; through repetition of these tics, he fascinated and repelled.[50] His hands were talon-like: the scene with the elder Bagots, "in which the gesture of the hands by which it was conveyed that Trilby had sat for 'the altogether' was half comic and wholly sinister—a very triumph of expressiveness."[51] The loose beret and shoddy coat worn in the Latin Quarter gave way in act 3 to evening dress. Better groomed, he still utilized his defiant stare, harshly modulated voice "breaking occasionally into a shrill treble," and "horrible little laugh" to convey rascality. Despite a more laboured gait from five years of exertion in mesmerizing Trilby, his face still exuded suppressed rage.[52]

In the novel, Svengali is the least credible character, yet in the stage adaptation, Tree's "emotional" acting was proclaimed "amazingly realistic."[53] He "portrayed the character in its varying moods of tender passion, ghastly humour, and fierce malignity, dominated always by the 'uncanny,' with a vivid and realistic force which held the audience spellbound until the terrible death scene in the third act."[54] Already "a physical wreck, his life fast oozing from him," yet thirsting for more vengeance, at the moment of death, he fell backward over a gilded table, his head inverted, eyes staring, tongue protruding, face bloodless, and arms spread as if crucified, forming "surely among the most creepy [effects] known to our contemporary theatre."[55] This was "no mere ogre of pantomime, but a living entity."[56] Therein lay the power of Tree's creation and the secret of Svengali's longevity in the social imaginary. "His death was a most intensely tragic episode—appalling in its realism."[57] Parodies of *Trilby*, which are abundant, mimic details of the Haymarket production and in so doing highlight features that caught the public's attention.[58] Music is particularly prominent in this regard. In a burlesque at the Prince of Wales's Theatre, Arthur Roberts (as Svengali) played a tiny pump organ.[59] This poked fun at Tree's exhibition of musical passion in performing Schubert's *Rosamunde*, then "with a quick revulsion, when he sees Trilby is dead to such influences, he displays his cynical humour by a sudden lapse into a French popular lilt."[60] Tree's digital gymnastics on the dummy keyboard were admired for their felicity amid "wild grandeur,"[61] but Tree no more played the piano than Dorothea Baird (as Trilby) sang at the Cirque des Bashibazouks. Svengali's pieces were

---

50   "Haymarket Theatre," *Times*, 31 October 1895; and "Amusements: 'Trilby' at the Lyceum Theatre," *Scotsman* (Edinburgh), 24 September 1895.

51   "Theatre Royal: Mr. Beerbohm Tree and the Haymarket Company in 'Trilby,'" *Manchester Guardian*, 9 September 1895.

52   "*Trilby* at the Prince of Wales Theatre," *Birmingham Mail*, 6 October 1896; and "'Trilby' in Leeds," *Yorkshire Post*, 11 September 1895. See also photographs in the Harvard Theatre Collection, Guy Little Photograph Collection at the Victoria and Albert Museum, and Bristol Theatre Collection.

53   "Haymarket Theatre," *Standard*, 31 October 1895.

54   "Glasgow," *Scotsman* (Edinburgh), 17 September 1895.

55   "Theatres and Amusements: Mr. Tree at the Theatre-Royal," *Evening Citizen* (Glasgow), 17 September 1895; "Amusements: 'Trilby' at the Lyceum Theatre," *Scotsman*, 24 September 1895; "'Trilby' at the Gaiety," *Dublin Evening Herald*, 8 October 1895; and Kate Terry Gielgud, *A Victorian Playgoer* (London: Heinemann, 1980), 36.

56   "The English Svengali," *New York Times*, 15 December 1896.

57   "'Trilby' at the Gaiety," *Freemans Journal*, 8 October 1895.

58   Within weeks of the London premiere, Marie Lloyd sang a *Trilby* parody in the music halls, and burlesques were staged at the Opera Comique and Prince of Wales's Theatres. Others were published.

59   *Sketch*, 4 December 1895, 295. This was billed as "A Trilby Triflet," inserted into the second act of the melodrama *Gentleman Joe*, "with full organ, bagpipe, and cornet accompaniment" (*Morning Post*, 18 November 1895: 4).

60   This is in reference to the 1910 revival; however, when the production toured in 1896, the provincial press indicated that most of Tree's business was the same as what was seen in the 1895 try-outs. Unless contradicted in successive sets of prompt books, it can be assumed that most business was stable even as casts changed. "Sir H. Beerbohm Tree at the Royal," *Dublin Daily Express*, 14 May 1910.

61   "'Trilby' at the Theatre Royal," *Glasgow Weekly Herald*, 21 September 1895.

performed offstage by the musical director, Raymond Roze.[62] In depicting Svengali sweating and pedalling at the pump organ, the parody not only made him appear less like a concert artist but downgraded him to an accompanist in a parish church, and thus sent up the whole pretext of musical virtuosity.[63]

Thrillby, a parody published in 1896, takes a jab at the gothic pretext that Trilby remains in Svengali's thrall after his death. Only Svengali can break the hypnotic bond, so the Laird declares that he will bring him back to life.

LAIRD *(producing toy bagpipes)*. Wi' these! *(plays)*.

THRILLBY *(reviving and rising to her feet, à la Jessie Brown in the* Relief of Lucknow*).*[64] Hush! hark! Dinna' ye hear it? It's the pibroch[65] o' the Heelanders—the Slogan o' the Campbells—the bonniest lilt o' ae.[66]

One ethnic stereotype is indulged while another is lampooned.[67] This demonstrates the endurance of Jessie Brown in cultural circulation at the same time that it points to the preposterousness of last-minute reprieves as a frequent recourse of melodrama. It is a form of reprieve that *Trilby* (novel and play) denies.

An evening at a nineteenth-century theatre was invariably a musical evening. Just as at the opera and ballet, dramas were preceded by overtures. Usually these were mood-setting classical or popular tunes selected by the conductor. At a melodrama, there might be specific music composed for the production, and these melodic motifs could be interwoven with other music. Potter has several characters introduce songs diegetically—as part of the action—most notably Trilby's "Ben Bolt" but also the Laird's "Willie Brew'd a Peck o' Maut" and Svengali's "Messieurs les étudiants," "Annie Laurie," and the "Last Rose of Summer," most of which the musical director also wove into the act 1 overture. Act 2 has its noisy gallop for the entrance of the diners and quadrille for the dancers, ostensibly played by Svengali and Gecko on stage, and concludes with the strains of "O Holy Night" wafting in from the church organ across the road. Anticipation for the appearance of "La Svengali" in act 3 is established by "Hungarian National music played by [a] Gipsy band." Trilby's rendition of "Ben Bolt" is the highlight, but the act closes to the strains of "'Au clair de la lune' played by [an] Hungarian Orchestra during riot."[68] According to a music plot listing the orchestra's cues, Tree scrupulously crafted the extradiegetic elements as well—music not called for within the action but supportive of it—throughout the performance. Certain scenes with Svengali were underscored with music by Hector Berlioz and Anton Rubinstein.[69] The *entr'acte* between acts 1

---

62 Pearson, *Beerbohm Tree*, 90-91.

63 In the 1912 revival, Julia Neilson-Terry performed Trilby; she was the first actress cast in the role who could tackle "La Svengali's" singing repertoire, so the staging was altered to display her abilities. In the middle of act 3, the stage darkened, and Svengali led Trilby before the curtain (as if at the Cirque) whereupon she sang the coloratura aria "Charmante oiseau" (from Félicien David's *La Perle du Brésil*) and "Ben Bolt." *Daily News*, "The Real Trilby: Miss Neilson-Terry's Triumph," 20 February 1912. Later in the act, when Trilby sings out of tune, Neilson-Terry was offstage as the 1895 text indicates. *Stage*, "His Majesty's," 22 February 1912.

64 For a discussion of the last moments of Boucicault's *The Relief of Lucknow*, see above, pp. 324-25.

65 Bagpipe.

66 William Muskerry, with songs by F. Osmond Carr, *Thrillby, a Shocker in One Scene and Several Spasms* (London and New York: Samuel French; [1896]), 14-15.

67 This was not the first time the joke succeeded: in the 1865 Strand burlesque *L'Africaine*, anthropophagian natives enter to the strains of "The Cannibals Are Coming." Kurt Gänzl, *British Musical Theatre* vol. 1 (New York: Oxford UP, 1986), 5.

68 Bristol Theatre Collection "Note on Music," HBT/000054/59-62.

69 Rubinstein was a flamboyant and unpredictable virtuoso pianist. The selected musical motifs may have been from his opera *The Demon*. Both Rubinstein and Felix Mendelssohn, a particularly intense conductor, provide Jewish antecedents for Svengali's musicianship. Berlioz's music was famously moody; the work excerpted may have been *The Damnation of Faust*, which was written for orchestra, voices and chorus.

and 2 consisted of a Chopin Impromptu, between acts 2 and 3 a fantasia of "Ben Bolt" was performed, and between acts 3 and 4 a medley of airs was reprised.

All the more significant, then, that act 4 commences in silence. Later, hinting at Trilby's renewed betrothal, an orchestral rendering of Schumann's "Der Nussbaum" ("The Walnut-Tree") underscored the action. This song, given by the composer to his bride on their wedding day, is about a bridegroom's deferred arrival, though love is whispered by the walnut-tree and the bride listens until wafted into slumber. This is an excellent instance of how, whether played or sung onstage or provided by the orchestra, music conveys the major arcs of *Trilby*'s plot as well as the emotional shifts in the play. Schubert's "Adieu" (with words equally familiar to any audience member with a parlour piano: "Adieu! 'tis love's last greeting, / The parting hour is come!") was played during Trilby's final scene, but this reinforced expectations hatched during the act 1 overture rather than informing even the densest spectator of a new plot twist. From the opening strains, it was hinted that someone will die. The lover of Annie Laurie croons that he would "lay me down and die" for her; the schoolmate in "Ben Bolt" explains that Alice lies in the churchyard; and in "The Last Rose of Summer" the companions have parted, and the only remaining rose blooms all alone in the bleak world. Lyrics were unnecessary accompaniments to such well-known favourites. As long as the tunes were played, the words resounded without being sung.

The actors augmented the musical score with their vocalizations; these, in turn, were part of the orchestration of sound and silence. Trilby had a distinct voice when hypnotized, and in act 4, as she convalesced, she could barely raise a sound above a whisper. When Taffy and the Laird take Rev. Bagot offstage, leaving Trilby and Billee together, "the voice of Little Billee approaches her, meets it, and there is a kiss, and these two sit silent a very long while, while the others converse in whispers."[70] Her voice resumes a dreamy quality:

> TRILBY. Billee, it's real, is it not? All is going to be as it used to be? *(Playfully)* I'm afraid that Barbizon cottage is a tumble-down ruin now; but we'll live in it, won't we—ruin or no ruin? Oh, my love, my love, I'm so happy. And I thought at one time I was going to die.

He kisses her, and she is left alone. The dreaminess is broken when Svengali reclaims Trilby from beyond his grave. She screams. "Feet scuffle about, and a soft body drops lightly to the floor; then silence, as if death were near. The silence seems interminable. What is happening? Did I hear the faint echo of Svengali's laugh, or was it imagination? The silence continues, no one stirs, no one breathes."[71] Trilby, alone with the audience, has expired. The audience see Trilby die, yet also know Billee's fate.

Editing Issues

Potter adapted the text from Du Maurier's novel, Tree suggested further changes to Potter, additional adjustments were incorporated during rehearsals, more amendments were enacted during Tree's out-of-town try-outs, and still more changes were made following the London premiere.[72] Kate Terry Gielgud complained that by the time she saw it in London, *Trilby* was "a mere patchwork of the book, scraps taken haphazard and dumped down without any context—taking for granted that everyone has read the book

---

70   "Strange Impressions of 'Trilby,'" *Woman*, 13 November 1895: 8.

71   Ibid.

72   Instead of a photograph, an oil painting was used in the provincial try-outs and perhaps also at the London premiere, for Kate Terry Gielgud complained that Tree "put in an appearance as a portrait in a frame (deluged with limelight, of course), at the sight of which Trilby shrieks and presumably expires." This contradicts the manuscript; however, act 4 is the least amended portion of the text. Gielgud, *Victorian Playgoer*, 36.

and will fill up the gaps from memory," yet the production satisfied critics as well as playgoers.[73] Several typescripts for *Trilby* have passed from Tree's possession to the Bristol Theatre Collection. They show how the patchwork became even more strained as Tree adapted the text for film and music hall after the turn of the century.

The following edition is based on two manuscripts for acts 1 and 2 and one version of acts 3 and 4 made for Tree's company. The typescripts are augmented with holograph stage directions, alterations, additions, and excisions of dialogue, making this the most complete and faithful edition yet compiled of the text used in the first English production. The versions of acts 1 and 2 show evidence of being made one before the other though holograph changes to the earlier version are not always typed into the later text; some of the holograph changes are in both texts (in different handwriting), and some appear only in one or the other. One copy was probably kept by the prompter, the other for Tree, who directed.[74] Additional plots with music and lighting cues (gas, electric, and limelight) not integrated into the prompt books suggest that though the manuscripts were updated in rehearsal, they are not the stage manager's prompt book used during the run of the show.[75] As notations of acting, this edition retains the stage manager's shorthand for doorways (L.2 E. is stage left second entrance) and scenery (D.L.F. is downstage left flat) even when the code is obscure.

Trilby was licensed part-way into the provincial try-outs, and the Lord Chamberlain's copy closely adheres to the Bristol Theatre Collection manuscripts, minus the holograph stage directions.[76] This complicates dating the Bristol manuscripts. Using a prompt book fleshes out movements, and sometimes actors' inflections, but fails to determine the text's moment in time relative to the rehearsals.[77] Further-more, notations made in rehearsal were not necessarily retained for the whole run. Prompt books also call attention to the problem of attributing authorship over the *mise en scène*. In April 1896, this came to a head in the lawsuit *Tree v. Bowkett* which established that a copy-cat production had stolen the Haymarket's stage arrangements; as a differentiation between the playwright's work and the producing company's, this is a landmark decision.[78] Still, the present edition offers a rare opportunity to publish a working version of a script, reflective of rehearsal discoveries.

73 Ibid., 35.

74 Bristol Theatre Collection HBT/000030/3 to 000030/6. There may have been a more complete rehearsal copy for acts 3 and 4, no longer extant. Actor's part books (each containing one character's lines and cues) substantiate that these manu-scripts pertain to the 1895 production. The part books are uncatalogued, in the same collection. Two modern editions also derive from the Bristol Theatre Collection prompt books; however, Kilgariff's is much truncated, and Rowell opted to transcribe the 1915 version (because it is easiest to read), incorporating aspects of earlier manuscripts unsystematic-ally. Michael Kilgarrif, ed., *The Golden Age of Melodrama: Twelve 19th Century Melodramas* (London: Wolfe, 1974); and George Rowell, ed., *Trilby and Other Plays* (Oxford: Oxford UP, 1996).

75 For information about the technical specifications, see the notes to the play in Rowell, *Trilby and Other Plays*, 290-96.

76 British Library Add MS 53582 (C) licence no. 241, licensed on 16 September 1895.

77 See Catriona Mills, "Adapting the Familiar: The Penny-Weekly Serials of Eliza Winstanley on Stage in Suburban Theatres," *Nineteenth Century Theatre and Film* 36:1 (2009): 38.

78 Bristol Theatre Collection HBT/000021/1-4.

Trilby[79]

BY PAUL POTTER

First performed at Boston Museum, 4 March 1895 (and Garden Theatre, New York 15-20 April 1895). Revised for Herbert Beerbohm Tree and performed at Theatre Royal Manchester, 7 September 1895.[80] Opened at Her Majesty's Theatre (London), 30 October 1895.

	New York	London
Svengali	Wilton Lackaye	Herbert Beerbohm Tree
Talbot Wynne, "Taffy"	Burr McIntosh	Edmund Maurice[81]
Alexander McAlister, "The Laird of Cockpen"	John Glendinning	Lionel Brough
William Bagot, "Little Billee"	Alfred Hickman	Patrick Evans[82]
Gecko, second violin at the Gymnase	Robert Faton Gibbs	C.M. Hallard
Duc de la Rochemartel, "Zouzou"	Leo Ditrichstein	Herbert Ross
Theodore de la Farce, "Dodor"	Alex L. Gisiko	Gerald Du Maurier[83]
Antony, art student	W.M. de Silke	Berte Thomas
Lorimer, art student	Edwin Brandt	Gayer Mackay
Rev. Thomas Bagot	Edward L. Walton	Charles Allan
Colonel Kaw, a theatrical manager	Reuben Fax	Holman Clark[84]
Philippe, a footman		
Trilby O'Ferrall, an artist's model	Virginia Harned	Dorothea Baird
Mrs. Bagot	Rosa Rand	Frances Ivor
Madame Vinard, a concierge	Mathilde Cottrelly	Rosina Filippi[85]
Angele, a grisette[86]	Grace Pierrepont	Cicely Turner
Honorine, a grisette	Lucile Nelson	Agnes Russell
Musette, a grisette	Josephine Bennett	Sadie Wigley
Ernestine, a grisette		Sybil Erlyn
Mimi, dancer from the Salle Valentino	Menta Elmo	Olive Owen
La petite Noisette, dancer from the Salle Valentino		Winnie Leon

---

79   Based on prompt books for the 1895 production in the Herbert Beerbohm Tree Collection, HBT/00030/3 to 00030/6, Bristol Theatre Collection, University of Bristol.

80   The two Manchester performances secured British copyright for Potter's adaptation. Tree's company then toured, performing *Trilby* in Leeds (Grand Theatre) 11-14 September; Glasgow (Theatre Royal) 16 and 20 September; Edinburgh (Royal Lyceum) 23-27 September; Liverpool (Court Theatre) 30 September-5 October; Dublin (Gaiety Theatre) 7-12 October; Newcastle (Tyne Theatre) 14-19 October; and Birmingham (Theatre Royal) 21-26 October. The London premiere was the company's first presentation at Her Majesty's since returning from an American tour.

81   Later, Percy Brough and Frank McVicars.

82   Later, H.V. Esmond.

83   Son of *Trilby's* novelist, George Du Maurier.

84   Later, F. Percival Stevens.

85   Later, Adrienne Dairolles.

86   A young working-class woman.

Hortense, dancer from the Salle Valentino	Madge Langton
Desirée, dancer from the Salle Valentino	Helen Graeme

Director Herbert Beerbohm Tree
Musical Director Raymond Roze
Choreographer John d'Auban

Act I

*It is the 1850s. A Studio. Large bay window at back, through which is seen a church,
with old houses on either side, and in the distance a glimpse of the Seine. Walls covered
with plaster-casts, studies in oil, foils, masks, and boxing-gloves. Large fireplace, with
log fire, between L.1 E. and L.3 E. Gridiron, frying-pan, toasting fork and bellows hang
on wall near it. Cupboard up C. with crockery. Model throne C. Three easels in different
parts of room. Small table R.1. Two lay figures painted; one dressed as a Toreador, the
other as a rag-picker. Trilby's foot scratched on wall. There are three entrances. The door
is in flat L. of the bay window. There is an alcove, containing piano R.2 E. and another
alcove at an angle L.U.E. Both these alcoves are filled with bric-à-brac, books and
knick-knacks. They serve as passages to other rooms in the apartment. It is late on a
November afternoon. Snow is falling in the street. Discovered—stage empty.*

MADAME VINARD *(heard outside R. at back)*. Monsieur Billee. Monsieur Billee. Voici une dépêche.[87]
(Enter D.U.L. She is a good-looking, dark-haired garrulous woman. She looks round.) But where is he
then, this Litrebili?

(She is about to exit by L.U.E. when she stumbles against Taffy who enters carrying a large log).

MADAME VINARD. Ah pardon, mille pardons,[88] Monsieur Taffy.
TAFFY *(with a drawl)*.[89] Not at all, Madame Vinard. My fault. You see—ha, ha—I'm—a—I'm rather a
ponderous individual even without the—a—log. *(Crosses to fireplace where he puts log on fire)* What's
up?
MADAME VINARD *(R.C.)*. Here is a dispatch, a telegram, for Monsieur Billee.
TAFFY. Hand over. I'll deliver it. *(Takes telegram, looks at it)* More trouble, I suppose *(pockets telegram,
sighs heavily, then proceeds to stir up the logs).*
MADAME VINARD *(crosses to C.)*. Trouble, Monsieur Taffy. Why, never since I have been concierge in
the Latin Quarter[90] have I seen three happier people than you, Monsieur Sandy and Monsieur Litrebili.
TAFFY *(taking bellows and blowing fire)*. You're a good sort, Madame Vinard, but you don't know
everything.
MADAME VINARD *(crosses to L. by couch. Mysteriously)*. I know that you go every day to the Morgue.
It's horrible.

---

87   Here is a telegram.
88   A thousand pardons.
89   Slow habit of speech.
90   The left (south) bank of the Seine, noted for students and artists.

TAFFY (blowing fiercely). A fellow must find inspiration somewhere. This wood's wet (stay seated on couch L.).

MADAME VINARD (mysteriously). And you paint the most dreadful subjects—drowning, murder, the guillotine (turns up C., shudders).

TAFFY (facing fire, same business with bellows). We can't all paint Toreadors[91] like the Laird.[92] Wish you'd oblige me with a dry log now and then.

MADAME VINARD (same business). And I know why you paint terrible subjects. (Looking around to see that nobody listens) It is because you're in love.

TAFFY (turns in horror, bellows in hand). Eh?

MADAME VINARD (same manner). You're in love with Trilby.

TAFFY (scared). Shut up.

MADAME VINARD. What?

TAFFY. Fermez-vous![93]

MADAME VINARD. And you're afraid to let Monsieur Sandy and Monsieur Litrebili know it.

(He protests).

And you're afraid to ask Trilby to marry you.

(He protests).

And Monsieur Vinard, my husband—who is fond of you all as I—Vinard says you're nothing but a great big baby.

TAFFY (angrily). If Vinard has been spreading this story about—(jumps over sofa).

MADAME VINARD. But no; but no—

TAFFY (with determination). There's not a minute to lose. (Crosses R. Aside) I'll tackle Trilby and know my fate. I—(hesitating again) you see, I'm not very good at proposals. I—I'll ask the Laird to coach me—great diplomat, the Laird, and meanwhile, just shut up about it, like a good woman, and—and—I'll get some dry logs (crosses L. to door very hastily. Exit quickly L.U.E.).

MADAME VINARD. Ah, the dear Monsieur Taffy (crosses to R. at table).

(Laird is heard singing "Comin' thro' the Rye").[94]

And here is Monsieur Sandy.

(Enter from door in flat, the Laird. He is jauntily dressed, and carries a bunch of white violets).

Good afternoon, Monsieur Sandy.

LAIRD (in very bad French, L.C.). Bon jour, Madame Vinard.

MADAME VINARD (R.C. near table R.). But how gaily you are dressed, Monsieur Sandy.

---

91   Spanish bull-fighters.
92   Laird indicates a member of the landed gentry in Scotland.
93   Close your mouth!
94   A Robert Burns poem. The most relevant verse may be:
    Gin a body meet a body
    Comin thro' the glen,
    Gin a body kiss a body,
    Need the warld ken?

LAIRD *(puts hat on easel L. Scotch accent).* Benighted Gaul though you are, you may have heard that when my eponym, the Laird of Cockpen, went wooing, he took special pains with his attire. *(Recites)*[95]

His wig was well pouther'd[96] and as gude[97] as new,

His waistcoat was white; his coat it was blue;

He put on a ring, a sword and cocked hat,

And wha' could refuse the Laird wi' a' that?

(Crosses to R.C.).

MADAME VINARD *(L.).* And are *you* going to woo, Monsieur Sandy?

LAIRD. I come from the Flower Market and am about to lay these white violets at her still whiter feet *(crosses L. puts violets on mantelpiece L.).*

MADAME VINARD *(R.).* At whose feet? *(Suddenly understanding)* Ah, Mon Dieu,[98] not—not—at Trilby's?

LAIRD *(L. at end of couch taking off coat).* And pray, Madame Vinard, do you know any just cause or impediment why I should not pay my homage to that angel ever bright and fair?

MADAME VINARD *(getting jacket from dais chair).* Ma foi, non.[99] Only Monsieur Taffy *(laughing)* might object.

LAIRD. I waive Monsieur Taffy's objections. Oblige me with that jacket *(throws overcoat on dais).*

MADAME VINARD *(putting on his coat).* And Trilby might refuse you.

LAIRD. I should console myself with the sentiment of my illustrious namesake. *(Crosses R. Recites)*

And often he thought as he ga'ed[100] through the glen,

She's daft[101] to refuse the Laird of Cockpen.

MADAME VINARD *(L.).* And she might love another.

LAIRD *(R.).* I should call my trusty claymore[102] to my aid and lay that "other" low *(gestures with mighty claymore).*

MADAME VINARD *(L.C.).* Ah, but you are ferocious, Monsieur Sandy.

LAIRD *(R. Sheathing his imaginary claymore).* Voilà l'espèce d'homme que je suis[103] *(goes up to window, at easel).*

MADAME VINARD *(laughing).* I must go. I have to see Maître Galvin, the lawyer, about that wretch Svengali's rent. Bonjour, Monsieur Sandy *(exit D.L.).*

---

95 From "The Laird o' Cockpen," a poem by Carolina Oliphant (Lady Nairne). The preceding verses are:

The laird o' Cockpen, he's proud an' he's great,

His mind is ta'en up wi' things o' the State;

He wanted a wife, his braw house to keep,

But favour wi' wooin' was fashious to seek.

Down by the dyke-side a lady did dwell,

At his table head he thought she'd look well,

McClish's ae daughter o' Claversha' Lee,

A penniless lass wi' a lang pedigree.

96 White-powdered (in the eighteenth-century style).

97 Good.

98 My God.

99 My goodness, no!

100 Went.

101 Foolish.

102 Double-edged Highland broadsword.

103 That is the type of man that I am.

LAIRD (*bowing low*). Bong jour, Madame Vinard (*at piano filling pipe. Lights pipe which he smokes upside down;*[104] *then begins to arrange the lay-figure Toreador, singing as he works*)

> Here are we met, three merry boys[105]
> Three merry boys, I trow, are we;
> And mony a night we've merry been,
> And mony mae we hope to be.

TAFFY (*enter from L.2 E. carrying logs. Sadly*). Hello Sandy (*crosses to fire, throws on the logs recklessly. Back to L.C.*).

LAIRD. Ha, my bold militaire. (*Sings*)

> We're na fou, we're no that fou,
> But just a drappie in our e'e.[106] (*Crosses to L. and R.S.*)

TAFFY (*kicking logs; his back to the Laird, stands in front of dais*). Notice anything odd about me?

LAIRD (*coming down to him, looking at him*). Nothing; your back's still as broad as some of Zouzou's stories. (*Runs, slaps back, sings, going to easel*)

> The cock may craw, the day may daw,
> But aye we'll taste the barley bree.[107]

(*Goes up to easel near door*).

TAFFY (*in front of dais, suddenly*). Shut up. I want your advice. You'll laugh, but I don't care. Laugh, hang it, I say, laugh (*crosses to the rag-picker lay figure and arranges it*).

LAIRD. All right. (*Coming down R.C. mahlstick*[108] *in hand, laughs*) What did I laugh for?

TAFFY (*woe-begone*).[109] Sandy, I'm in love (*sits at foot of dais*).

LAIRD (*R. of dais, sees violets*). Love! (*Begins to laugh, suddenly checks himself*) There's nothing so absurd in that. Still, for a man of your Titanic proportions—

TAFFY (*seated R. at foot of dais, firing up*). Hang my proportions. I knew you'd say that. Big men are just as liable to fall in love as little men. And, I tell you, it hurts them a deuced deal more—for they've farther to fall. What I want is advice, not chaff. I've made up my mind to marry; and when my mind's made up, I stick at nothing (*crosses to R., picks up dumb-bells and exercises*).

LAIRD (*C.*). Right (*gets more sticks*).

TAFFY. Come. How do you propose to a girl? (*dumb-bells business: R.*).

LAIRD (*L.C.*). Eh? I'll be frank with you, Taffy. I've been pondering that momentous question myself.

TAFFY. You. No. By Jove, that's rich. (*L. of table R., by it. Laughing, suddenly checks himself*) After all, it isn't so preposterous.

LAIRD. Preposterous!

TAFFY. Still, for a man of your peculiarly unromantic physique (*dumb-bell exercises*).

LAIRD (*C. Angry*). Hang my physique, and let me tell you, Taffy (*waving mahlstick*)—

---

104 Indicating nervousness or inattention.

105 From Robert Burns's poem, "Willie Brew'd a Peck o' Maut," about three happy comrades:
> Here are we met, three merry boys
> Three merry boys, I trust, are we;
> And many a night we've merry been,
> And many more we hope to be.

106 We are not full, we're not that drunk / But just a drop in our eye.

107 The cock may crow, the day may dawn / And always we will taste the barley-brew.

108 A yard-long stick, padded at one end, used to steady an artist's arm and hand.

109 Woeful.

MADAME VINARD *(enters quickly from door in flat. Down L.)*. Ah, Messieurs, I had a message to bring you. You know that across the street there is a factory, a glove factory, where many young girls are employed, and, as the windows of the factory overlook yourself, the propriétaire asks you to close the blind when you have models like—models who— *(looks down)* who— *(same business, lifts her skirts a little, then laughs)*. Vous comprenez?[110]

LAIRD *(C.)*. Je comprong. Je comprong parfaitemong.[111] But we won't do it, Madame Vinard. Never. Jamais, au grand jamais[112] *(goes up to easel)*.

MADAME VINARD. But Monsieur Sandy—

TAFFY *(R.)*. In the eyes of art, Madame Vinard, a—nothing is—a—so—a—chaste as the nude *(dumbbells business)*.

MADAME VINARD. But the ladies in the glove factory think—

LAIRD. Tell the ladies in the glove factory that all beauty is sexless to the artist.

TAFFY. We decline to close blinds; glove-factory must move *(goes up opposite by table)*.

MADAME VINARD. C'est dommage,[113] Messieurs. I have done of my best. *(Going R. by piano)* You will not even close one shutter?

(Enter Little Billee, from door in flat. Throws paint box on floor. Billee is much excited).

TAFFY *(R.C. alarmed)*. Why, Billee, what's the matter? *(Down L. and up L.)*.

BILLEE. She's sitting at Durien's—upstairs, that's all.

LAIRD *(C.)*. Who's sitting at Durien's?

BILLEE *(L. opposite L. opening)*. Why she—Trilby.

LAIRD and TAFFY *(rising)*. What?

BILLEE. Before all those ruffians.

TAFFY *(R.C.)*. For—for the figure?

BILLEE. Yes. There she was, just as I opened the door *(L.)*. I saw her, I tell you. The sight of her was like a blow between the eyes, and I bolted *(sits L. couch)*.

TAFFY *(furious)*. It's—it's monstrous.

LAIRD *(furious)*. It's a scandal.

(They walk up and down).

MADAME VINARD *(R. by table, business affecting innocence)*. But, Monsieur Taffy, in the eyes of art, nothing is so chaste as the nude *(crosses to C.)*.

TAFFY *(R. up)*. Oh, shut up.

MADAME VINARD *(same business)*. And, Monsieur Sandy "all beauty is sexless to the artist."

LAIRD *(C.)*. Oh, get out *(crosses to L. window)*.

MADAME VINARD *(same business)*. Then Trilby is different from other models? *(Cross L.)*.

TAFFY and LAIRD *(shouting)*. Of course she is. Certainerarong![114]

(A tinkling ring).

---

110 Do you understand?

111 *Je comprends. Je comprends parfaitement* (I understand perfectly).

112 Never ever.

113 That's too bad.

114 *Certainement* (certainly).

MADAME VINARD. There he rings—I tell him now—soufflé[115]—ha, ha, ha. *(Exit gesticulating)* On y va—on y va![116] *(Exit door in flat, laughing).*

BILLEE *(at his easel, rising; crosses up, gets hat; walks).* Personally it's no business of mine. I'm off to Barbizon[117] to paint the forest.

TAFFY *(C., trying to assume a playful tone, though evidently worried).* In mid-November? *(Cross to Billee)* You'll freeze to death—a babe in the wood. And Sandy and I will have to drop leaves on you, like two confounded robins.[118] *(Crosses to C.)* By the way, there's a telegram Mother Vinard left for you.

(Gives telegram. Billee sitting C. opens it).

LAIRD *(coming R. of Taffy. Low to Taffy).* This won't do about Trilby. We must stop it *(goes back to easel).*

TAFFY *(R. of couch).* Quite right—we will. *(Aloud)* What is it, Billee?

BILLEE. Nothing much. My mother and uncle have gone to Florence. They want me to join them there.

TAFFY *(crosses to Billee L.1. Putting hand kindly on his shoulder).* Why, young un, you wouldn't desert your two old pals?

BILLEE *(L. pressing Taffy's hand).* I ... may have to. And if I go, I've done with this beastly Paris for ever. I shall never come back.

(Trilby's cry "milk below" heard outside R. Billee goes to his easel).

TAFFY *(cross R.).* Here's Trilby.

(General movement).

Not a word about this. Not a word, mind. To your easel, Billee *(going to his easel).*

(All three sit at easels. Trilby's cry repeated, but nearer).

TAFFY. Here she comes. Now, mind, Billee. Don't breathe a syllable about her posing.

(All pretend to be intent on their work. Trilby appears at door in flat. She wears gray military overcoat, short striped petticoat, and list slippers).[119]

TRILBY *(at door L.F. making military salute).* Salut, mes enfants[120] *(comes down L.C.).*

(All look up as though they had not expected her. All smile. Billee's smile is forced; he at once returns to his work).

I guessed you were at work and thought I'd just come in for a bit and pass the time of day *(coming down).*

LAIRD *(coming down, R.C. rising and bowing).* Trilby, recevez l'aveu de mes admirations très distinguées.[121]

---

115 Blown.

116 Here we go.

117 A community southeast of Paris, near the forest of Fontainebleau.

118 In the children's tale "Babes in the Wood," frequently adapted for pantomimes, two children are abandoned in the forest on the order of their villainous uncle. They wander until they die. Robins cover their bodies with leaves.

119 Soft slippers made of selvage (non-ravelling) cloth, used by gunners on ships of war; this avoided the possibility of inadvertently sparking gunpowder.

120 Greetings, my children.

121 Please accept my confession of my sincere admiration for you.

MISS DOROTHEA BAIRD AS "TRILBY"   COPYRIGHT

Turner & Drinkwater.

8. Regents Terrace, Hull.

Illustration 33. Dorothea Baird as Trilby in her costume for act 1
of *Trilby*, 1895. Courtesy of David Mayer.

TRILBY (*L.C. crossing to him quickly, and pulling his whiskers affectionately*). What lovely language you do use, Sandy dear. Et puis—zut alors—tarra-pat-a pouffe![122]

LAIRD (*R.C. flattered*). Ventrebleu Sacr-r-r-r-e nom de dieu.[123]

TRILBY (*sits C. on dais, laughing*). And how terribly you do swear, Sandy dear. You swear ever so much harder than Zouzou and Dodor, and they are soldiers and it's their profession (*sits on model throne and produces sandwich from paper*).

LAIRD (*going up to easel, sits*). How you go on, Trilby.

TRILBY (*on dais, motion of rising*). Would you like me to go off?

LAIRD and TAFFY (*quickly*). No, no.

TRILBY (*sits on dais. Doubtfully*). Little Billee doesn't want me.

(*A pause—no answer*)

Do you, Billee?

(*No answer. Pouts*)

But the Laird and Taffy want me. That's a majority of the house. I shall stay. (*Pause—she munches sandwich, and carries on.*) What's the matter, Billee? You look as sad as though Taffy had tried to tell you a funny story (*laughs*).

(*Laird and Taffy laugh*).

Well, life ain't all beer and skittles, and more's the pity; but what's the odds as long as you're happy?

TAFFY (*at easel*). We—we'd give a good deal to have your light heart, Trilby.

TRILBY (*seated on dais*). You wouldn't give as much for my head, for I've oh such a pain in it.

(*All rise in great concern*).

Neuralgia[124] in the eyes, or something.

(*Billee L. and Laird R. of her. They crowd round her, Svengali's laugh heard outside*).

TAFFY (*R.*). Here's that horrible Svengali. Keep him out, Sandy.

(*Come down R. Laird moves towards door R.*).

TRILBY. No, let him in. He'll play; it will do me good.

(*Enter Svengali and Gecko R. of dais from door in flat. Both are shabby and dirty*).

SVENGALI (*R. of couch, rubbing his hands and chuckling*). Ha, ha, good joke; capital.

(*Gecko makes deprecating gesture to the company, comes R. of Trilby, but Svengali continues*).

Madame Vinard laughed so much in telling it that she forgot to tell me that I was to be sued for my rent. Very good. Capital (*R. of couch L.*).

TAFFY (*down R.*). Svengali, give us a little music. Trilby has a touch of neuralgia.

---

122 Colloq.: And then—oops!—a blunder. The more standard expression is: "Patapouf! C'est tombé par terre!" (Oops! What a blunder!) "Patapouf" is onomatopoeic, imitating the thud of an object as it lands on the ground.

123 A French curse; literally, belly of God, in the name of God.

124 Stabbing pain.

(Gecko R. of dais near Trilby).

SVENGALI *(seeing Trilby—crosses to her and makes a mock obeisance).* Tiens, c'est la grande Trilby.[125] Bonjour, ma belle; I will make music for you and take away your pain, and Gecko will play his violin for you. *(Crosses to R. of Gecko)* Gecko plays like an angel; I play like an angel. We are two angels.

TRILBY *(taking cigarette from pouch at her side).* You carry your wings inside, for convenience.

(Music)

SVENGALI. En v'la une orichinale.[126]

(Makes another burlesque bow and crosses to piano in alcove R.2 E. Gecko after a wistful look at Trilby, follows him. Stage music).

TRILBY *(cross L.1 to Billee).* Are you angry with me?

BILLEE. How can I lie about it? You have hurt me—awfully—

TRILBY *(eagerly).* How? What have I said? What have I done?

(Billee is about to answer when Taffy comes up and offers a match to Trilby. She lights cigarette. Billee with a gesture of annoyance returns to his easel. Taffy sits with Trilby, she watches Billee, pretending to listen to the music. Taffy sits by Trilby on couch).

BILLEE *(cross to C. half angrily).* Why don't you play, Svengali?

(Music "Last Rose of Summer").

SVENGALI *(at piano, playing).* What shall I play? I know what *you* call music. "Annie Laurie." "Last Rose of Summer." Bah!

(Music "Annie Laurie," his fingers run over the keys; the playing being really done in the wings).

LAIRD *(at easel, painting).* Do you sing, Svengali?

(Music. Billee at back of dais, standing).

SVENGALI *(beginning to play "Adieu" of Schubert, violin played by Gecko).* Nein.[127] I cannot sing myself. And I cannot play the violin. But I can teach the violin, hein,[128] Gecko?

(Gecko nods and tunes violin).

And I can teach singing—the "bel canto."[129] Ach, Himmel.[130] The "bel canto" was lost; but I found it in a dream—I, Svengali.

TAFFY *(seated on couch up stage, to Trilby).* Is the music doing you good?

TRILBY *(seated on couch DS).* What are you playing, Svengali? Well it isn't very lively. What's it all about?

SVENGALI. It is called the *Rosamunde* of Schubert, Mademoiselle.

---

125 Well, it is the great Trilby.

126 *En voilà une originale* (she is an original).

127 No.

128 Eh?

129 A full, rich-toned, legato sound characteristic of the operas of Rossini, Bellini, and Donizetti. Bel canto waned in fashion by the mid-nineteenth century, so Svengali's remark is nostalgic.

130 Ah, heaven.

(Billee goes to easel, Taffy crosses to window C.).

TRILBY. And what's that—*Rosamunde*?

SVENGALI. Rosamunde was a Princess of Cyprus, Mademoiselle, and Cyprus is an island.

TRILBY. And Schubert then—where's that?

SVENGALI. Schubert was not an island, mademoiselle, Schubert was a compatriot of mine and made music and played the piano—just like me.[131]

TRILBY. Ah, Schubert was a gentleman.

SVENGALI. Yes, Mademoiselle, a perfect gentleman.

TRILBY. Don't know him—never heard his name.

SVENGALI. That is a pity Mademoiselle, he had more talent.

(Taffy rises, crosses to window to easel. Trilby with great puff of cigarette).

You like this better, perhaps? *(Plays "Messieurs les étudiants").*

TRILBY *(seated on couch).* Much. Was that written by a countryman of yours?

SVENGALI. *Heaven forbid.* Are you fond of music?

TRILBY. Oh, maïe, aïe.[132] Indeed I am. My father sang like a bird. He was a gentleman and a scholar, my father was. His name *(with great pride)* was Patrick Michael O'Ferrall, Fellow of Trinity, Cambridge. He used to sing "Ben Bolt."[133] Do you know "Ben Bolt," Monsieur Gecko?

GECKO *(at head of piano).* Mademoiselle, I have that felicity.

(Billee to easel by fire. Svengali plays "Ben Bolt").

TRILBY *(rise and cross to C.).* I can sing it. Shall I?

GECKO *(at piano).* Oh, certainly, if Mademoiselle will be so kind.

("Ben Bolt" on violin. Trilby rises as if to sing).

LAIRD *(sitting at his easel. Low to Taffy).* Stop it. She can't sing a note in tune.

(Trilby sings "Ben Bolt" out of tune).

TAFFY *(R.C. downstage by Trilby, interposing).* Don't sing, Trilby. I'm damned if I let you sing. They are only making fun of you.

TRILBY *(C. amazed).* Fun! Why, it's a capital song. My father used to sing it when he felt jolly after hot rum and water. He used to make people cry.

---

131 Svengali implies that he is Austrian, like the composer Franz Peter Schubert (1797-1828), but more likely he is from one of the eastern principalities of the Austro-Hungarian Empire.

132 Oh my eye (onomatopoetic).

133 "Ben Bolt" was written by Dr. Thomas Dunn English, in 1842. It is addressed to a sailor, the singer's old schoolmate, reminiscing about their childhood twenty years ago. It begins,

>Oh, don't you remember, Sweet Alice, Ben Bolt?
>Sweet Alice, whose hair was so brown,
>Who wept with delight when you gave her a smile,
>And trembled with fear at your frown!
>In the old churchyard, in the valley, Ben Bolt,
>In a corner obscure and alone,
>They have fitted a slab of the granite so gray.
>And Alice lies under the stone!

SVENGALI. So do you, ma belle[134] Trilby?

(Winking at the rest, who turn from him in contempt. Music stops).

TRILBY. I? Never! But I can sing it. Do you know Litolff?[135] Well, he's a great composer.

SVENGALI *(rising and trying to silence her. R.C.).* Yes, yes. Never mind, my dear.

TRILBY *(C. continuing).* He said that Alboni[136] couldn't go nearly as high or as low as I did, and that her voice wasn't half as strong. He gave me his word of honour.

SVENGALI *(R.C. hastily).* Yes, yes. We all know that.

TRILBY *(R. by couch).* And Litolff can compose anything.

SVENGALI. Except your nerves, ma chère.[137] And the head? Does it still ache?

TRILBY. A little.

SVENGALI *(crosses to couch L.).* I have a better cure than music. Sit down.

(Trilby sits on divan. Billee rises and crosses to Laird and Taffy).

Look me in the white of the eyes.

(She does so. He fixes his eyes on hers, then makes passes on her forehead and temples).

Does it pain now?

(All come forward and watch intently. Svengali turns to them).

See! She sleeps not; but she shall not open her eyes.

(Trilby sits rigid).

Ask her.

BILLEE *(next to Svengali).* Are you asleep, Trilby?

TRILBY *(on couch, Svengali in front).* No.

BILLEE *(R. of Svengali who is at couch).* Then open your eyes and look at me.

TRILBY *(strains her eyes).* I can't.

SVENGALI. She shall not open her mouth. Ask her.

BILLEE *(R. of Svengali).* Speak. Trilby.

(Trilby makes an effort to do so).

SVENGALI. She shall not rise from the sofa. Ask her.

BILLEE. Can you rise from the sofa, Trilby? *(Crosses to R.).*

(Taffy crosses to Svengali).

TRILBY *(with effort).* No.

TAFFY *(angry).* This is that devil's trick—hypnotism.

(Billee crosses to R., round divan).

---

134 My pretty.
135 Henry Charles Litolff (1818-91), a violinist and composer.
136 Marietta Alboni (1826-94), Italian contralto.
137 My sweet.

LAIRD. These villains get people into their power and make them do any blessed thing they please—lie, murder, steal, anything.

(Business of three together).

TAFFY *(gripping Svengali's arm).* Release her, man, release her.

(Throws him to R.C. Svengali catches Billee by arm. Taffy follows him and grasps him from behind; picture).

SVENGALI *(R.).* Ah, if you are so imbecile, I will set her free. *(Growls, aside)* Pig-dog.[138] Awake! *(Goes up and sets her free).*

(Trilby jumps up).

Did I cure her? *(Comes down.)*

TRILBY *(seated, rubs her eyes and looks round).* Oh, maïe, aïe! The pain is gone. *(Rises)* You have taken all my pain away.

SVENGALI *(going up R.).* Yes, I have got it myself in my elbows; but I love it because it comes from you.

(Trilby sits on lounge, Billee back of dais).

TAFFY *(R.C., low to Svengali).* All the same, if I catch you at those games again, I'll accommodate you with a much needed bath in the river.

(Movement of hatred between Taffy and Svengali).

SVENGALI *(R.).* Trilby, that's funny! *(After savage look at Trilby, chuckling).*

TRILBY *(on couch, innocently).* Why?

SVENGALI. While you, la belle[139] Trilby, were sitting for the "altogether" at Durien's upstairs.

TRILBY *(rising L., as before).* Why not. Haven't I always ...

SVENGALI. And our Englanders were furious *(laughs and throws himself in chair on dais).*

TRILBY *(as before).* Furious at what. Furious because I ... *(Suddenly flushing)* Is ... is this true, Taffy?

TAFFY *(cross to opening L.).* Trilby, we were vexed; we thought you understood.

SVENGALI *(chuckling).* And Litrebili—ha, ha—ran down to tell the story, white with anger; poor Litrebili; poor innocent Litrebili.

(Billee crosses to Svengali, but is stopped by Laird. Lower lights down gradually).

TRILBY *(L. excited).* Billee, is that why you would not speak to me?

BILLEE *(L.C. turning around, with firmness).* Yes, that was why.

TRILBY *(L.C. above couch).* And I ... I've been here with you all, every day. I liked this studio best in the whole Latin Quarter; and you wouldn't warn me, wouldn't tell me what you thought of me. I never dreamed there were objections to my sitting. It was as natural for me to sit as for a man. And all the time that I was running your errands *(beginning to break down)* and cooking your meals, and mending your clothes, I shocked and disgusted you, you despised me *(bursts into tears).*

(They make a movement towards her).

---

138 This snarling epithet expresses Svengali's contempt for Gentiles *(Schweinhund).*
139 Beautiful.

Please don't say anything. I understand now. I will never sit again; not even for the face and hands. I will go back and be a blanchisseuse.[140] I, I hope never, never, to see any of you again.

BILLEE *(by dais, with movement of repentance)*. Trilby *(goes up to door)*.

TRILBY *(through her tears)*. No, thank you, Billee. *(Goes up to door)* I ... I'm not angry. Only ... only. I see that I have earned your contempt. And I promise you shall have no occasion to ... to despise me any more *(exit door in flight)*.

BILLEE *(pulls out his telegram, coming down L. and cross to R.)*. Boys, I've made up my mind. I will go to Florence *(exit R.2 E.)*.

(Taffy and the Laird come down to Svengali).

LAIRD. Do not make a fool of yourself, Billee. *(Crosses to R.)* Svengali, you are destined to be hanged.

SVENGALI *(laughing)*. That's more than can be said for your pictures.

(Exit Laird R.2 E., shaking his fist).

TAFFY *(crossing to Svengali)*. And when you're on the gallows, I ... I'll come and make a sketch of you.

SVENGALI *(laughing)*. You add a new terror to death, my friend *(rises, laughs)*.

(Taffy goes out angrily, R.2 E. Svengali leans back in chair and laughs heartily. Gecko comes down and sits opposite Svengali. Evening begins to fall).

GECKO *(D.R. seated)*. Why did you silence Trilby when she spoke of Litolff?

SVENGALI *(R. Stops laughing, looks around steadily, then leans both arms on the table)*. My Gecko, you are my good friend *(cross to L. opening)*.

GECKO *(seated R. by table)*. Such as I am—*(sadly)* Second Violin at the Gymnase;[141] such as I am, I owe it to you. You taught me all I know. How shall I forget it?

SVENGALI. Have I money, my Gecko? *(Opens door F. looks out)*.

GECKO *(seated at table R. clicking his nails against his teeth)*. Pas ça.[142]

SVENGALI *(L. by opening)*. Have I debts, my Gecko?

GECKO *(seated R., by table)*. Madame Vinard does not permit us to forget it.

SVENGALI *(coming down L. and crossing C. showing card, chuckling)*. I have the card of Maître Guerin, her lawyer. Well. Now I—I, who have to borrow five francs from these pig-dog Englanders—am going to make millions. *(C. and cross to Gecko. Imaginary gestures of counting money)* Millions millions. And you shall have a part of them; a small part, but enough for you.

GECKO *(seated)*. How?

SVENGALI *(R. by Gecko. After again looking around stealthily)*. With Trilby.

GECKO *(seated, amazed)*. Trilby?

SVENGALI *(by Gecko)*. I am telling you a secret, my Gecko. Litolff had discovered that secret. Litolff the composer has a cunning eye, and Litolff told Meyerbeer[143] that the most beautiful voice in Europe belonged to an English grisette who sat as model to sculptors in the Latin quarter. And that beautiful voice is Trilby's *(cross to C.)*.

GECKO *(startled)*. She is tone-deaf, quite tone-deaf. She can't distinguish one note from another.

---

140 Laundress (literally, whitener).
141 Théâtre du Gymnase-Dramatique.
142 Not that.
143 Giacomo Meyerbeer (1791-1864), German composer.

SVENGALI *(C.)*. Bah. I have looked into her mouth. The roof is like the dome of the Panthéon.[144] The entrance to her throat is like the middle porch of St. Sulpice.[145] Oh, my Gecko, she will bring so much money that we shall weary of counting it *(cross to L. and back C.)*.

GECKO *(at table R.)*. But she has not learned to sing.

SVENGALI *(C.)*. We will teach her. We will teach her together; morning, noon, night—six, eight hours a day. We will take her voice, note by note, till it rains velvet and gold, beautiful flowers, pearls, diamonds, rubies.

GECKO. Then you can work magic?

(It is now dark. Green lens on Svengali's face L.2 E. Red glow from fire).

SVENGALI *(cross a little L.)*. Yes, I can work magic, at least, what fools call magic. *(Leaning over impressively)* I can make Trilby do my bidding.

GECKO. Bah!

SVENGALI. Just now you saw me cure her pain.

GECKO *(seated at table R.)*. A trick of magnetism.[146]

SVENGALI *(C.)*. It was the beginning. Trained by us she shall sing for the world's delight.

GECKO. She can no more sing than a fiddle can play itself.

SVENGALI. Hers will be the voice, mine the feeling, mine the knowledge. I have not studied Mesmer's[147] art in vain. Trilby shall be the greatest contralto, the greatest soprano—the world has ever known—and I, Svengali, will see that that world prostrate itself in admiration at my feet.

(Lens off Svengali. Gecko rises with gesture of repulsion).

GECKO *(stands at piano)*. I fear you, Svengali. Your scheme is of the devil. I will have no share in it.

SVENGALI *(crosses and takes Gecko L. Cross to R.)*. You are in error, my Gecko. We will all go away from Paris together—you and Trilby and I, we will wander eastward and leave these Englanders to daub their little canvasses, addle their little brains, break their little hearts—and when we come back, we will bring with us a song-bird the like of whom has never been heard before and the like of whom will never be heard again.

(Trilby puts in her head at door in flat. Svengali sees her and puts finger to his lips).

Is it not so, Trilby?

(Music orchestra).

TRILBY *(D.L. still peeping in at door)*. Haven't heard a sound. I—I am looking for—for my friends—the Angliches.

SVENGALI *(C.)*. Viens donc,[148] ma belle Chérie. There is not an Anglich here.

(She enters down front, shamefacedly. She is now dressed becomingly as a grisette; she carries a market basket).

So you changed your mind with your clothes?

---

144 A neoclassical masterpiece in the Latin Quarter, burial place of Voltaire, Rousseau, and other public figures.

145 In the Place Saint-Sulpice, Paris, the second largest church in the city.

146 Animal magnetism (mesmerism).

147 Franz Anton Mesmer (1734-1815) developed the theory of animal magnetism, lending his name to the English word mesmerize.

148 Come then.

TRILBY (*L.C.*). No, I didn't. But I knew they had no one to get their dinner and ... and ... I wish you wouldn't stare at me like that, Svengali.

(She strikes a match and lights candles; footlights partly up. She begins to lay the table).

SVENGALI (*L. by couch*). Ah, Trilby, the day will come when you will stare at me; when I am the famous Svengali, and hundreds of beautiful women will go mad for love of me—Prinzessin, Contessen, Serene English Altessen.[149]

TRILBY (*at mantelpiece*). I dare say. (*Leaning across table*) But just now I wish you would let me alone.

SVENGALI (*L. by couch*). The beautiful Prinzessen will invite Svengali to their palaces, and pay him a thousand francs to play for them, and bring him tea and gin and kuchen[150] and marrons glacés;[151] and he will not look at them. He will look inward at his own dream. And his dream will be about Trilby—to lay his talent, his glory, his thousand francs at her beautiful feet. And you shall hear nothing, see nothing, think of nothing but Svengali, Svengali, Svengali. Remember these things, my Trilby, remember them. I will have millions, millions.

(Throw red lens on Svengali's face. Music stops. Crosses R., aside to Gecko).

Come, my Gecko, let us go upstairs and borrow five francs from Durien.

(Goes up crosses back to Trilby—business—leers at Trilby, who stands as if fascinated, then exits L.2 E. with Gecko. Gas higher).

TRILBY (*L., alone, repeating to herself mechanically*). Svengali! Svengali! Svengali! He seems to have thrown some spell on me. (*Rouses herself*) How silly I am. (*Laughing*) He reminds me of a great, big, hungry spider (*cross to C.*) and makes me feel like a poor little fly. I suppose I was rather cross with them, the dear boys (*setting table*).

(Going towards cupboard R. meets Taffy who enters quickly from R.2 E. carrying a salad bowl. He nearly drops it on seeing Trilby. When Trilby gets plates, shakes pepper—business).

TAFFY. Trilby, you—you have forgiven us—

TRILBY (*C. bashfully*). I ... I ... it was nearly dinner time, and I knew how hungry you would be getting, and—and—you will despise me more than ever for coming back (*crosses to cupboard and opens it*).

TAFFY (*cross L. salad bowl in hand*). Trilby, I feel—a—the moment has come to—

TRILBY (*crossing to table C. and laying cloth, then meekly*). Yes, I know, dear, I deserve them all.

TAFFY (*L. on couch seated, mixing salad*). Deserve all what?

TRILBY (*R. laying table. Goes up to cupboard*). All the harsh things you want to say to me.

TAFFY. Harsh? (*Suddenly*) Trilby, I'm awfully fond of you (*sits on couch L. back to fire, facing Trilby*).

TRILBY. You've been like a brother to me, dear Taffy (*passing from cupboard to table and back*).

TAFFY (*seated on couch L. mixing furiously*). Yes, brother's all right. But brother isn't what I mean. You know, I've no family. Father and mother died before I was born, that is, soon after. So I've no more pedigree to brag about than ha, ha—than you have. (*Correcting himself*) No, no, I didn't mean that.

---

149 Princesses; comtessen are technically the daughters of countesses, but colloquially indicates the daughters of Viennese society; and serene old English women.

150 Cake.

151 Chestnuts candied in syrup and glazed.

TRILBY. I don't mind. We weren't all brought up at the Austrian Embassy.[152] *My* mother was a barmaid *(cross to C.)*.

TAFFY *(seated on couch L.)*. So was mine, I mean, I always liked barmaids. But as I don't go in for ancestry, and haven't any brains, and am just an ordinary sort of duffer,[153] I thought you ... you might think—in short—

(Trilby up to cupboard).

(With great triumph) We were made for one another *(rising)*.

TRILBY *(D.R. wondering)*. Why, Taffy, I hardly ...

TAFFY *(cross to Trilby R. resolutely)*. Oh, it's no use. I love you, Trilby *(shakes pepper etc.)*.

(She is startled, drops knives and forks).

I—ha—adore, you. I'd fall on my knees, if I weren't so—a—so thunderingly big. I want you. *(Peppering furiously)* I'll take you away from Paris—out of these cursed studios. I'll make a little nest for you in the country. I'll work for you; I'll slave for you; I'll worship the ground you tread on. And—a—if I don't take a glass of brandy, I'll choke *(pours all the pepper into the salad bowl; sneezes, then looks around for brandy—up to cupboard)*.

TRILBY *(R. of table R.)*. Taffy, you're going to think me the wickedest girl on earth.

TAFFY *(C.)*. No, I'm not *(sneezes)*.

TRILBY. I'm more grateful to your goodness than I can say, and—and—I love somebody else.

TAFFY *(C. aghast)*. Who is it?

TRILBY *(R.)*. Little Billee.

TAFFY *(dazed)*. Billee! Billee! Oh, by Jove, Trilby; you don't mean ... Oh, by Jove, by Jove. *(Sits R. on chair R.C.)* Have you accepted him?

TRILBY *(near Taffy, R. side of table)*. He's proposed to me nineteen times—and I said "no" for his sake.

TAFFY. But if he asked you again—

TRILBY. Then—then—I shouldn't have the heart to say "no" a twentieth time. And you would help us to get married, wouldn't you Taffy? And I shall always have you—as a brother.

TAFFY. Yes, but—ha, I don't want—ha, to be your brother *(seated R.C. on chair above table)*.

TRILBY *(wheedling, arm round Taffy's neck)*. We'd never marry without your consent, for you've taken a father's place to us both.

TAFFY *(blankly)*. Now I'm her father.

TRILBY *(L. of Taffy)*. And you'll say "yes," Taffy? Do say "yes"; say "yes."

TAFFY. Billee's a smart little chap, and isn't half bad; he's got brains, and lots of cheek, and all that. I suppose I'll have a devil of a fight with his mother about it, but by Jove! It's all right, Trilby. I say "yes."

TRILBY *(kissing him)*. You dear, dear Taffy *(crosses to L.)*.

LAIRD *(enters from R.2E. with a long loaf of bread under one arm and a Dutch cheese[154] under the other. R.)*. Hello!

TAFFY *(C.)*. We—a—were just making overtures of peace.

LAIRD *(growling, puts cheese and bread on table R.)*. Wouldn't mind playing a part in that overture myself.

---

152 Here and in the novel, the Austrian Embassy is Trilby's catch-phrase for social pretentions.
153 Fool.
154 Edam is recognizable from its circular shape and wax sealant.

TRILBY (*plucks at Taffy's sleeve, draws him over R.C.*). We've agreed to forget and forgive, and as dinner's nearly ready I'm going to get another log for the fire (*runs off L.U.E. The table is now laid*).

LAIRD. Taffy!

TAFFY (*C., low*). What is it?

LAIRD (*R.C., low*). He's gone.

TAFFY. Who?

LAIRD. Little Billee.

TAFFY. Where to?

LAIRD. Florence. He packed his things, slipped out at the back, and took a cab for the station ....

TAFFY. When is he coming back?

LAIRD. Never. We are going to send his pictures after him.

TAFFY. What's the row?

LAIRD. Trilby. The wee fool's in love with her.

TAFFY. And she with him.

LAIRD (*aghast*). Eh? Are you daft?

TAFFY. No. She has just told me. It's going to break her heart. We must bring him back.

LAIRD. He caught the six o'clock train. No mortal power can overtake him. Trilby in love with ... sacr-r-r-re mille tonnerres[155] (*crosses down to table R. and sits*).

TAFFY (*crosses to L., low*). We'll tell her tomorrow. "Mum's" the word tonight. (*Aloud*) That's a regular Yule log, Trilby.

TRILBY. Yes, I feel so cold and odd. I don't know what it is; a sort of chill—as though I wanted to cry. And (*trying to laugh*) I've nothing to cry about.

(*Music—the "Adieu" of Schubert— in orchestra*).

TAFFY. This stupid model business upset you?

(*Wind effect. Ready snow*).

TRILBY (*looking up earnestly*). Taffy, do you really believe that Billee has forgiven me?

(*Pause. Taffy pretends not to hear*).

  Where is he now?

TAFFY (*L.C.*). Eh? Now, Sandy, where's Billee?

LAIRD (*by table R.*). Didn't he go to buy some wine? Or was it the salad?

TRILBY. Taffy made the salad. Billee must have gone for the wine. (*Cross to window—looks out through blind*) How the wind whistles! (*Looks out of window*) It will be a bitter night. And Billee's out in the snow in his light shoes.

TAFFY (*C.*). Don't worry. He could always look after himself.

TRILBY (*L.*). I must build up the fire before he gets back (*crosses to fire, arranges logs*).

LAIRD (*R. to Taffy*). How she loves that shrimp!

(*Taffy crosses to piano*).

TRILBY (*rousing herself at fire*). I'm a fool to be downhearted. (*After pause*) Has Taffy told you all, Sandy—all about Billee and me?

---

155 A thousand holy thunderbolts.

LAIRD *(crosses to L., shortly)*. Aye. So I hear you are going to make Billee happy.

TRILBY. He and I are going to be so happy; we are to live at Barbizon, where Billee will paint and grow famous. And I—well I don't know what I shall do but go on keeping house for him, and loving him. *(See the violets on mantelpiece)* Whose violets are these?

LAIRD *(L. by couch, confused)*. They ... they were left for you.

TRILBY. By whom?

LAIRD *(after pause)*. By whom? Oh, by Billee.

(The "Adieu" ceases in the orchestra).

TRILBY *(kissing them)*. Dear white violets! Then he *has* forgiven me!

(Enter Madame Vinard with wine).

See, Madame Vinard—the violets that Billee bought me.

MADAME VINARD *(C.)*. Litrebili? Oh no, it was Sandy bought them.

TRILBY *(L.C.)*. Sandy!

(Laird confused).

Why did you deceive me? *(Sees wine on tray)* Ah, you have been deceiving me all along. *(Crosses to table with wine)* Billee isn't coming back to dinner. He hasn't forgiven me. Taffy, tell me the truth, has Billee gone away?

MADAME VINARD *(R. by table)*. Why, Monsieur Litrebili has gone to his mother in Florence.

TRILBY *(L.)*. Sandy, has he really gone?

LAIRD *(L.C.)*. Aye, my poor lass—he has really gone.

(Taffy R. by table).

TRILBY *(fiercely to Taffy)*. Why did you let him go?

(Taffy helpless).

You envied our happiness. How base. How unworthy! No, Taffy, no! I beg your pardon, dear, I'm out of my mind with grief—bewilderment. But Billee won't be so—he won't leave me like this. I can't live without him. *(Sits on couch, overcome with grief)* Sandy, you have always told me the truth. Will Billee come back?

LAIRD *(sits by her L. on couch)*. He has asked us to send his pictures to Florence.

(Taffy goes to window).

TRILBY *(sobbing)*. Then I shall never see him again, never, never. Billee was all the world to me. His love had made me a new woman—to think of it makes me sick with shame and misery. Ah! Sandy, Sandy, you don't know what I am suffering. I believe I shall go mad and die.

TAFFY *(at window, opens it)*. Hush! Listen!

LAIRD *(rising)*. Who is it?

TAFFY *(looking out)*. There's a cab below—someone got out—it's so dark, and the snow is so blinding that I couldn't see who it was; but I'll swear it was a man.

TRILBY *(crosses to R.)*. Oh, Taffy, don't raise false hopes in me—don't even hint that—

MADAME VINARD *(outside)*. Mais, entrez donc,[156] Monsieur.

---

156 Come on in.

(*Door R. in flat is thrown open. Billee enters hastily, then Madame Vinard, beaming. "Ben Bolt" in the orchestra*).

TRILBY. Billee! They ... they told me you were gone.

(*Svengali and Gecko appear in alcove L.U.E*).

BILLEE. I tried to go, Trilby; but I left my heart behind—and I had to come back to find it. For the twentieth time Trilby, will you marry me—answer me Trilby.
TRILBY. And you have come back for good—for good?
BILLEE. For life (*kisses her hands*).
SVENGALI (*low to Gecko*). We will see, my Gecko, *we will see*.

(*Laird and Taffy shake hands warmly with Trilby and Billee. Music of "Ben Bolt" very lively*).

Act II

The same, a month later. It is well lighted, and decorated with holly and greenery. The church across the way is illuminated. The fire burns brightly: the table is now L. The hour is nine o'clock on Christmas Eve. A dinner party is in progress in dining room off L.U.E. Noise of merry-making heard as curtain rises. Discovered: as a shout in the dining room subsides Angele, a pretty blonde girl, dressed as a grisette, comes running on from L.U.E.

ANGELE. Madame Vinard! More wine! (*Cross to R.C.*).
HONORINE (*enter from door in flat, a pretty dark girl, dressed as a grisette*). Am I late, Angele?
ANGELE. Ah, it is you, Honorine. They are calling for more wine.
HONORINE. Who is in the party?
ANGELE. Zouzou and Dodor, those gay militaires; Antony and Lorimer, from Durien's studio, and the Angliches.
HONORINE. And all to celebrate the wedding of Trilby and Little Billee?
ANGELE. Oui ma chère. They are to marry tomorrow, at the embassy. (*Pointing through window*) Where's Svengali? (*Sits R. on sofa*).
HONORINE. He is angry at being invited after dinner.
ANGELE (*on sofa*). Bah! Svengali is only asked to make music for people to dance to.
HONORINE. He is as great a composer as Boieldieu.[157]
ANGELE. Because he teaches you to sing and calls you his (*imitating Svengali*) "gazelle-eyed liddle Cherusalem[158] Skylark." (*Laughs*) Trilby declares he's a big black spider, and he is (*rises*).
HONORINE (*with angry gesture*). Say that again.

(*They draw off as if to fight, when Madame Vinard enters from door in flat, with bottles of wine in each hand*).

MADAME VINARD (*hand to heart*). Ah, mon Dieu! Mon Dieu! (*Recovers herself and crosses to door in flat, which she opens wide*) Entrez, Madame; entrez, Monsieur. I have sent to Monsieur Durien's studio to see if Monsieur Litrebili is there.

---

157 François-Adrien Boieldieu (1775-1834), a noted composer of *opéras comiques*.
158 Jerusalem.

(Enter Mrs. Bagot and the Rev. Thomas Bagot. Mrs. Bagot is a trim little woman, with grey hair; the clergyman is small, thin, round-shouldered, weak-eyed).

MRS. BAGOT *(looking round. C.).* So this is the studio where my boy works. Picturesque, is it not, Thomas?

REV. BAGOT *(examining a nude statue).* Remarkably picturesque; fine copies of the antique. *(With eye-glass on the statue)* I revel in the antique.

MRS. BAGOT *(refers to wall above piano).* And this foot—this foot scratched in outline on the wall, what is that Madame Vinard?

MADAME VINARD *(embarrassed).* That, madame? Oh, that is a little sketch by Monsieur Litrebili.

REV. BAGOT. Mural decoration. The tombs of Egypt are very rich in this kind of ornament.

MRS. BAGOT *(coming down to chair below table L.).* My poor boy. To think that he is working so late at night.

MADAME VINARD. Monsieur Litrebili, he works morning, noon and night.

(Laughter and noise in dining room).

MADAME VINARD *(hastily crosses to L.U.E. Apologetically).* A little dinner party in the next apartment.

(Reverend takes book of sketches and sits L.C.).

MRS. BAGOT. We supposed he was busy. *(Sits down L.)* He did not answer our telegram of a month ago; he has not even written.

REV. BAGOT *(gloating over the sketches).* Exquisite form! Divine!

MRS. BAGOT. What are you studying, Thomas?

REV. BAGOT *(quickly closing book).* Sketches, *(humming business and washing of hands)* my dear Ellen. After Phidias,[159] Praxiteles.[160] Very fine.

(Mrs. Bagot continues talking to Madame Vinard. The Reverend when unobserved reopens the sketch book).

MRS. BAGOT *(to Madame Vinard).* We finally became so anxious about the dear boy that we determined to plan a little surprise for him and come to Paris unheralded. You take so much interest in my son that you will be glad to hear of his forthcoming engagement.

MADAME VINARD. Engagement, madame?

MRS. BAGOT. To a young English lady.

SVENGALI *(heard outside).* Come, my Gecko, we will play for the pig-dogs. Come.

(Enter Svengali and Gecko from door in flat).

MADAME VINARD *(confused. To Mrs. Bagot).* Pardon madame. *(Leading Svengali quickly to L.U.E.)* This way, Svengali. *(Low)* I am showing the studio to this lady.

(Svengali casts suspicious looks at Mrs. Bagot).

(Continues low) The party is in here.

(Svengali turns half to Mrs. Bagot who is watching him through lorgnette).[161]

---

159 Fifth century BCE Greek sculptor, possibly the greatest of the ancient world.
160 Fourth century BCE Greek sculptor, known for his full-length female nudes.
161 Eyeglasses mounted on a perpendicular handle instead of ear pieces.

SVENGALI. They have insulted me—me, Svengali, but we could not refuse—hein—Gecko! We could not refuse to make music while they drowned the latch-key of Litrebili in the punch-bowl.

(Svengali exits with Gecko L.U.E. Madame Vinard closes curtains quickly).

MRS. BAGOT *(amazed).* Drowning his latch-key?

MADAME VINARD *(moves to Mrs. Bagot).* Ma foi,[162] madame, this Svengali is crazy; he has the oddest words; but they mean nothing.

MRS. BAGOT. Drowning my son's latch-key in a punch bowl? Thomas, do you understand?

REV. BAGOT *(closing sketch book with a snap).* A classical phrase. I remember it is Apuleius.[163] Or was it Petronius Arbiter?[164] It means drinking the bridegroom's health.

(Svengali's head appears between the curtains, he listens).

MRS. BAGOT *(to Madame Vinard).* You must pardon me. But does ... does my son ...

(Business for Svengali).

... talk freely with you about his family?

MADAME VINARD. Freely? Monsieur Litrebili?

(Business for Svengali).

Why I knew you from his description.

MRS. BAGOT. Then has he—has he never told you of a young lady, the daughter of an English clergyman, highly connected, and of his intention to conform to our wishes and marry her?

(Svengali withdraws his head, after signifying that he has heard and understood).

MADAME VINARD. Ma foi Monsieur Litrebili has told me many things; he has told me this and that; and no doubt he has talked of the young English miss; but really, really ...

SVENGALI *(puts head through curtains, enters from alcove L.U.E.).* Madame Vinard, the big bullock of an Englander Taffy demands the punch.

(Looks of surprise between Svengali and Reverend. Funny business).

MADAME VINARD. Punch! Bon Dieu! And I must go out for the lemons. *(To Mrs. Bagot)* Excuse me, madame. Do not go. I will soon be back. *(Aside—going)* I must get them out of the house before they learn about Trilby. *(Close to Svengali)* Latch-keys, indeed! You villain! Where do you expect to end your days?

SVENGALI. Where I end them now—in bed.

(Business between Madame Vinard and Svengali).

MADAME VINARD *(exclamation).* Arrrr! *(exit angrily).*

SVENGALI *(aside).* How I adore that woman!

MRS. BAGOT *(hesitating).* Pardon sir, are you the husband of Madame?

SVENGALI *(grinning).* I have not the honour. I am the musician of a wedding-party.

---

162 By my faith.
163 Lucius Apuleius (c. 125-180), author of *Metamorphosis* (*The Golden Ass*).
164 Gaius Petronius Arbiter (c. 27-66), supposed author of the *Satyricon*.

MRS. BAGOT and REV. BAGOT. Wedding party?

SVENGALI. Given in honour of my friend, Monsieur Litrebili.

MRS. BAGOT. In honour of my son?

SVENGALI. Ah, you are the mother of ... Madame, my felicitations. Your son has taste.

MRS. BAGOT *(coldly)*. Well, sir!

SVENGALI. He has chosen well.

REV. BAGOT. Chosen whom? Chosen what?

SVENGALI. Chosen his bride.

MRS. BAGOT. He has told you?

SVENGALI. Told us? They are holding the réveillon[165] to celebrate his marriage.

REV. BAGOT. Isn't it a little premature?

SVENGALI. It was, as you English say, "now or never." The marriage takes place tomorrow. *(Pointing through window)* At the British embassy *(crosses R.)*.

MRS. BAGOT and REV. BAGOT *(rising)*. Marriage between whom? *(cross L.)*.

SVENGALI. Litrebili and Trilby.

MRS. BAGOT. Trilby?

SVENGALI. Miss Trilby O'Ferrall *(business of passing finger under nose)*—the most beautiful grisette in the Latin Quarter.

MRS. BAGOT *(sitting)*. I ...oh ... I ... Thomas! My salts! Water! I am fainting!

(Svengali and the Reverend bustle around her).

SVENGALI. Ah, how I am maladroit.[166] What have I said? *(Aside chuckling)* And the Vinard comes not yet with the punch.

(Mrs. Bagot begins to recover. Reverend crosses to R. of Svengali).

REV. BAGOT. Strange as it may seem, sir, Mrs. Bagot's son, my nephew has preferred to conceal this matter from his relatives.

SVENGALI *(shocked)*. Ah! Undutiful! *(Lip business)*.

REV. BAGOT. So that, in short, we are compelled to ask a stranger—who is Miss O'Ferrall?

SVENGALI. Her father, Monsieur, was son of a great Dublin doctor—who was friend of George Fourth.

(Mrs. Bagot looks up a little comforted).

He became a—what you call—parson, like you *(sits L.)*.

(Same business).

He had all virtues but one. *(Sits on chair straddlewise across chair C., back of chair towards audience)* He drank like a fish. *(Gesture of drinking)* He came to Paris; tumble down, down, down; and when he was right in gutter, Trilby's mother picked him out.

REV. BAGOT. This is very dreadful.

SVENGALI. Trilby's mother was barmaid; she wore tam-o'-shanter cap[167] at the Montagnards Écossais;[168] she was Scotch, like the pig-dog Sandy *(correcting himself)* I mean—pardon—she was Scotch; and

---

165 Christmas Eve dinner.
166 Clumsy.
167 A soft woolen bonnet with flat wide top, typically worn by men in this period.
168 "The Scottish Mountaineers:" the name of the pub where Trilby's mother was a barmaid.

Trilby's father married her, and died, and the mother died, and Trilby was brought up anyhow—Grâce de Dieu[169]—and made her living by washing clothes.

MRS. BAGOT (*rising in horror*). Washing clothes?

SVENGALI. And boarded with Père Martin, a respectable rag-picker.[170]

MRS. BAGOT (*same business*). Rag-picker!

SVENGALI. And finally settled down in the Latin Quarter as a model.

REV. BAGOT (*crosses to C. —eagerly*). Model of what? Head, hands, feet?

SVENGALI (*indifferently*). Altogether (*gesture*).

REV. BAGOT. This is very, very terrible.

SVENGALI. That is her foot in outline on the wall, the masterwork of Litrebili—there's only one foot like it in France, and that's her other foot.

REV. BAGOT (*crossing to see it eagerly*). Abominable! Indecent!

MRS. BAGOT (*faintly*). And ... her life ... has that been irreproachable?

(*Bagot moves round to chair R.C. and leans on back*).

SVENGALI (*shrugging shoulders*). Madame, I had the honour to tell you—she is a model! Perhaps not of virtue, mais que voulez-vous, le quartier Latin nes't ce pas?[171]

(*Reverend moves slowly toward Mrs. Bagot*).

MRS. BAGOT (*in great distress*). Thomas, advise me; what can we do? How can we stop this hideous marriage? The law will prevent it!

REV. BAGOT. M'm! Let us consider! Let us devise ...

SVENGALI. If the matter could rest till morning ...

MRS. BAGOT. No, no. I only want a word with Mr. Wynne ...

SVENGALI. They go at midnight to hear the music at St. Nicholas. The midnight mass. Could not madame wait?

MRS. BAGOT. Wait? You see my distress—advise me, Thomas.

REV. BAGOT. I—I suggest—that if we could learn how the French law stands ...

SVENGALI. There is a notary at the corner. He occasionally calls on me when—(*producing a dirty card*) here is his card; Maître Guerin, Rue St. Anatole, 19. He stays always home at night. Tell him I recommend you—I, Svengali, the great musician (*crosses L.*).

MRS. BAGOT (*giving hand*). I don't know, sir, how we can thank you. My grief has evidently touched you.

SVENGALI (*bowing*). It has madame (*sniffs*).

REV. BAGOT. I trust you may be rewarded, sir (*pocket book business*). If not now, hereafter.

(*Exit Reverend and Mrs. Bagot in flat*).

SVENGALI (*chuckling*). Hereafter! Bah!

(*Enter Gecko from L.U.E. Opens curtains*).

One bird in hand is better than a pig in the poke.[172]

GECKO (*laughs*). They are coming. They wish us to play a wedding march.

---

169 With God's favour.

170 Recycler of used clothes.

171 What do you expect of someone from this neighbourhood?

172 He combines two adages: having anything is better than a bargain for an unknown commodity.

SVENGALI *(following him slowly)*. There will be no wedding, my Gecko.

(Gecko makes gesture of surprise—crosses to piano—Svengali continues.)

I had another way to stop it, but this way is better. It is the kinder way. *(To himself)* Ah Svengali, you are too good. Your heart is soft. It is your only weakness *(laughs)*.

(Music. Svengali sits at piano. The curtains are drawn aside. Svengali and Gecko play a wedding march.[173] There enters a procession from L.U.E. First Zouzou and Dodor in uniform; then Antony with Honorine; then Lorimer with Angele then Taffy and Laird; and last Billee and Trilby.[174] Antony, Lorimer, Taffy and the Laird wear fool's caps. They march solemnly around the room to the music).

DODOR *(L.C.)*. Halt! Attention!

(Music stops. The procession halts).

I call upon my friend Zouzou for a speech befitting the occasion.

(All scatter and sit in various parts of the room. Trilby and Billee being R. on couch).

ZOUZOU *(very French accent)*. Messieurs, Mesdames, I no spik Angliche. My friend Dodor spik Angliche. I no. But I am Français, and for that, as gallant homme, I say 'Eep, 'eep 'eep, for la jolie Trilby and for Litrebili. I shake them the hand. *(Drinking imaginary glass)* À la mariée.[175]

OMNES *(noisily)*. À la mariée.

SVENGALI *(rises R.C. Aside)*. Shout! Have good fun, my Litrebili! Mama has gone to Maître Guerin *(at piano)*.

ANTONY *(R.C. above couch)*. Trilby, as queen of the feast, you are to say what shall come next on the program.

(Trilby consults Billee. Taffy crosses to R. and invites Billee over to L.).

LORIMER *(L.)*. It's your last appearance in Bohemia[176] remember. No more quadrilles.[177]

TRILBY *(merrily)*. Oh, maïe, aïe. Then you shall dance one tonight—something that would please them at the Austrian Embassy[178]—*(at couch)*.

OMNES. The quadrille. The quadrille.

(Svengali, aside, chuckling).

DODOR *(L.C., raising hand)*. My friend Zouzou is anxious once more to address the company.

(Applause).

---

173 Felix Mendelssohn's "Wedding March" (from incidental music for *A Midsummer Night's Dream*) dates from 1842; by the time *Trilby* premiered it was widely used. In 1850, however, the wedding march might be an earlier tune traditionally used for the bride's procession along the church aisle.

174 As Trilby, Dorothea Baird wore "a delicate grey Cashmere gown with muslin collar, cuffs, and apron, and on the bodice a great pink rose, which pales before the softly-flushed beauty of the bride-elect's lovely young face crowned as it is by a full white cap with finely fluted brim" ("'Trilby,'" *Globe*, 31 October 1895).

175 To the bride (a toast).

176 Not the Czech region but the artists' bohemia (the free and easy life).

177 A social dance with four couples formed into a square.

178 Possibly an allusion to the Strauss family, dance composers in Vienna from the 1830s. Trilby habitually refers to the Austrian Embassy as a social scene above her own.

ZOUZOU (*C. stands on chair*). Messieurs, Mesdames, I no spik Angliche, but I am Français, and for that, I say the dance without the drink, it is nothing. So I call my honourable friend Mr. Taffy, and I say, where deuce is ze punch (*falls in Taffy's arms—business*).

OMNES. Madame Vinard. Madame Vinard!

MADAME VINARD (*enters door in flat, carrying punch bowl. She looks around*). Voila, voila, messieurs. (*Aside*) Ah! They are gone. Bon!

OMNES. The punch! The punch!

(*They crowd around Madame Vinard who places the punch bowl on the table L. Trilby is left alone on lounge R. Svengali, seeing this, comes down to her stealthily and leans over the back of the lounge. Honorine watches jealously from the distance*).

SVENGALI. Ah Trilby how beautiful you are (*behind Trilby R.*).

(*She makes a gesture of impatience*).

   It drives me mad.

(*The others rest, drink, chat, fence, box, and occupy themselves during the following dialogue*).

TRILBY. There! How you have spoiled everything. All my fun is over.

SVENGALI. And you will not look at me. Not even when you have the pain—the pain.

(*Trying to make her turn her face*).

TRILBY (*on sofa*). I shiver and sicken when your eyes meet mine. I would rather suffer torture than let you—(*half turning her head: struggling with herself*) no, no, I will not look at you.

SVENGALI (*low in her ear*). All your looks are for Litrebili. I will tell your fortune—let me see your hand.

(*She wavers—he takes it*).

SVENGALI. There is great fortune for you, Trilby, but there is no marriage with the Billee. Look at this line—it leads away from the altar, it leads to fame, to fortune.

TRILBY. No marriage!

(*She draws her hand away—he snatches and retains it*).

SVENGALI. Poor Litrebili, you will wait for him in vain at the church tomorrow.

(*Business with her hand. Laugh from the crowd upstage to break up scene. Dodor and Laird fence upstage. Lorimer and Zouzou pledge each other[179] down at table L. Svengali goes up to piano. Billee crosses to Trilby. Honorine crosses to Svengali and protests in gestures. Svengali pushes her angrily away*).

BILLEE (*with knee on couch R.*). What was that blackguard[180] saying, Trilby?

TRILBY (*rising, then turning passionately to Billee*). Billee, are you sure, quite sure—nothing can come between us, nothing?

BILLEE. Nothing, my sweetheart, what do you fear?

TRILBY (*takes his arm*). I don't know. I have a presentiment. I—I sometimes think I'm going mad.

BILLEE (*fondly*). All love's a madness, dear.

TRILBY (*very earnestly*). Did you ever hear that people could be put to sleep, and forced to do things at someone else's will?

---

179 Drink a toast.
180 Scoundrel.

BILLEE. That's all rubbish, Trilby.

TRILBY. Are you sure—quite sure?

BILLEE *(hesitating)*. I know there are quacks who impose on women.

TRILBY. Did—did Svengali impose on me when he took away my pain?

BILLEE *(after a pause)*. That's different! Any doctor could do that.

TRILBY. Billee, when we are married, we'll have nothing to say to Svengali, will we? I'm afraid of him *(half laughing)*.

BILLEE *(laughing)*. We'll banish Svengali from our Eden.

TRILBY. We'll take a cottage at Barbizon; a tiny, tiny cottage. And we'll be ever so happy in our poverty. Père Martin, the rag-picker, says the raggedest muffs[181] are always the softest inside.

(He stops her mouth and kisses her forehead).

   (She rises. Fondly) Oh Little Billee, how I love you.

(They pass out R.3 E. Taffy makes signal to the Laird to cover their retreat. Laird draws curtain, R.2, then faces Svengali).

TAFFY. Come boys, the quadrille! Svengali, a tune that would make the rafters of the Chaumière[182] ring. Partners, partners, all.[183]

(Music. After clearing many things from centre, they form quadrille. Taffy, Laird, Zouzou, Dodor, Antony, Lorimer, Honorine, and Angele dance as Svengali and Gecko play a wild cancan.[184] Madame Vinard watches from sofa at back. When the dance is at its wildest, enter Mrs. Bagot and the Reverend. They hold up their hands in horror. Taffy sees them).

TAFFY. Billee's mother.

(Stop music. Dance stops. All but Taffy and the Laird[185] scuttle off comically L.U.E. and R.2 E. Svengali comes forward, sees Taffy and the Laird shaking hands with the visitors, who are very stiff. He chuckles).

SVENGALI *(to himself)*. Yes, yes, this way is the better. Poor Trilby! Poor Trilby! Poor Litrebili! *(Exit R.2 E.)*.

MRS. BAGOT *(very stiffly)*. I'm so sorry, Mr. Wynne, if we interrupted your dance.

TAFFY *(putting on coat)*. Not at all, Mrs. Bagot. Christmas, you know. Bound to observe the season—even here among the Parlyvoos.[186]

REV. BAGOT. You were—ahem—hardly prepared for our coming.

LAIRD. Oh yes, quite; that is—not altogether. Suppose you've come to hear the midnight mass at St. Nicholas. Music's grand.

MRS. BAGOT *(coldly)*. Really? *(Turning to Taffy)* Mr. Wynne, we are in great distress.

TAFFY *(uneasy)*. No? Sorry—won't you sit down?

---

181 Cylindrical hand-warmers usually made of fur.

182 La Grande-Chaumiére, a dance hall in southern Paris (*c.* 1787 to the 1840s), now 120 Boulevard du Montparnasse. In the 1830s, it was popular with students, who went there to dance the polka, quadrilles, and the cancan.

183 Taffy calls dancers to the floor.

184 An exuberant dance introduced in Paris in the 1840s. Originally a partner dance (later a line dance of female choristers), it mimics movements of a military rifle drill using the legs, especially in high kicks.

185 Wearing a false nose and banging a tambourine, according to *Illustrated Sporting and Dramatic News*, 9 November 1895: 344.

186 *Parlez-vous* (i.e., French speakers).

MRS. BAGOT. We have just been informed that my son is engaged to—*(with effort)* to be married.

TAFFY. Yes—quite true—so he is.

(Reverend Bagot wishes to protest; Mrs. Bagot raises her hand and silences him).

MRS. BAGOT. Do you know—the young woman, Mr. Wynne?

TAFFY. Oh yes; most charming person—a—isn't she, Sandy?

LAIRD. Heaven never made her like.

REV. BAGOT. Is she Protestant or Catholic?

LAIRD. Really, I don't know—she has no prejudices that I know of.

REV. BAGOT *(horrified)*. You—a—know her well, and don't know *that*?

LAIRD. No, I never asked her. Mrs. Bagot, I ... I am called away. I hope to see you tomorrow, and beg to wish you, in advance—a—a merry Christmas.

(Taffy has been making frantic gestures to him, he takes no notice, but goes out hurriedly, L.2 E.).

TAFFY *(aside)*. Cad[187] of a sneak of a Laird—to leave all this to me *(brings down stool)*.

MRS. BAGOT *(after a pause)*. Mr. Wynne, we know the whole truth.

TAFFY. I—I—congratulate you.

MRS. BAGOT. We know also that this marriage would ruin my son for life.

TAFFY. I can't say I agree with you, Mrs. Bagot.

MRS. BAGOT. Oh Mr. Wynne, Mr. Wynne, if you only knew what my son is to me. He was never away from my side till he came to this wicked city. He was as innocent and pure-minded as a girl. I could have trusted him anywhere. That was why I let him come here—here, of all places in the world. Fool that I was!

TAFFY *(sympathetically)*. Undoubtedly. Won't you sit down?

MRS. BAGOT. And, oh! cannot you, cannot you do anything to avert this awful disaster?

TAFFY. Really, Mrs. Bagot, I—I don't see it in that light at all. You don't know Trilby. You may think it strange, but on my word of honour, she's about the best girl I ever met, the most unselfish, the most—

REV. BAGOT *(in a dry tone)*. Very pretty, I suppose *(seated L.)*.

TAFFY. Very. But that's nothing. She has a good heart, a beautiful nature, and I wish to heaven she had chosen *me*, instead of Billee.

REV. BAGOT *(same tone)*. The lady, I don't doubt, would have been only too happy.

TAFFY *(fiercely—rising)*. Sir!

TRILBY *(comes in hurriedly from R.2 E.)*. Mrs. Bagot, they—they told me you were here *(holds out hand, hesitating)*.

MRS. BAGOT *(not taking hand)*. You are Miss Trilby O'Ferrall?

TRILBY. Yes.

MRS. BAGOT. You are beautiful, beautiful indeed. And you wish to marry my son.

TRILBY. I refused him many times for his own sake, he will tell you so himself. I am not the right person for him to marry, I know that. But he vowed he would leave Paris if I persisted in refusing him. So—so—I was weak and yielded. Perhaps I was wrong.

MRS. BAGOT. Are you very fond of him?

TRILBY. Fond of him? Aren't *you*?

---

187 Ill-mannered person.

MRS. BAGOT. I'm his mother, my good girl. (*Sits*) You have just said you are not a fit wife for him. If you are so fond of him, will you ruin him by marrying him? Will you drag him down, separate him from his sister, his family, his friends? Possibly ruin his career?

TRILBY. Mrs. Bagot, I love him so.

REV. BAGOT (*back to audience*). Love him! Love him! Do you know, Miss O'Ferrall, that if he marries you, that his home may be closed to him. His name will be a by-word to his friends; and in after years, when you witness his poverty, his despair, and know that you, and you alone, are to blame, you will perhaps feel some of the pangs which his mother feels today (*goes to door back L.C.*).

TRILBY. Will it really be all that, Taffy?

TAFFY. I'd rather you didn't appeal to me, Trilby (*R.*).

TRILBY (*R.C.*). You are right. I will ask no advice. You are right, Mrs. Bagot. I had not thought of myself except as Billee's equal—I have not been taught to value those social distinctions which mean so much in the world you live in. Perhaps I thought too much of myself. I will myself tell your son of all you have told me—he shall not marry me till his eyes are opened, I promise you. This time I will be strong. Mrs. Bagot, I give you my promise. I will not marry your son, without your consent.

TAFFY. Don't be a fool, Trilby (*cross C., takes her hand*).

TRILBY. Taffy!

MRS. BAGOT and REV. BAGOT (*together*). Mr. Wynne!

TAFFY (*R.C.*). Mrs. Bagot, I'm not a great genius like Billee, but I love the boy as much as anybody, and if you, his mother, want to break his heart, I, his friend, won't let you.[188] Billee has promised to marry Trilby. He has taken this oath before the world, and if he ventured to break it, he, he's no longer a friend of mine.

TRILBY (*softly*). But Taffy—

TAFFY. Be quiet. Let *me* do the talking (*R.C.*).

REV. BAGOT (*L.C.*). Your attitude in this matter, Mr. Wynne, compels us to resort to extremities. We have just come from the office of a notary. (*Reading card*) Maître Guerin, Rue St. Anatole, 19. (*Continuing*) From him we have learned the French law of marriage. In the case of a youth under twenty-five no union is valid without the consent of the parents or, if one of the parents be dead, without the consent of the surviving parent. Mrs. Bagot refuses her consent to this marriage.

(*Business for Mrs. Bagot making action of refusal*).

If you persist in it, we shall have it stopped by the authorities, and one *more* scandal, I regret to say, will be attached to the name of Miss Trilby O'Ferrall.

TAFFY (*turns to Mrs. Bagot*). I am sorry, Mrs. Bagot, to take a stand which may give you offence (*opens door*).

MRS. BAGOT (*weakly, quite worn out*). Give me your arm, Thomas. Good night, some day you will understand.

TAFFY (*up to door in flat*). Good night Mrs. Bagot.

(*Mrs. Bagot goes out without looking at him. The Reverend throws back a hostile glance, then goes. Trilby breaks down, and goes and sits on lower end of chair lower L.*).

TRILBY (*walking round to L. of Taffy*). Oh, Taffy, what have you done?

---

188 An interesting cut is made (in holograph) at this point: "It's all very well in a play for parents to come between young folks who love each other. Trilby spends half her time in crying over *Camille*, at the Odéon. But in real life people have to keep their words."

(He reassures her with a gesture).

BILLEE *(enter excited from R.2 E.)*. Taffy, they've just told me. *(Runs to D.F. looks out—then to Trilby L.)* It was my mother, wasn't it?

(Taffy answers with a gesture. Enter the Laird, shamefacedly; then, looking round, with burlesque airs of mystery, Zouzou, Dodor, Antony, Lorimer, and last, Svengali. Business of entering in a row).

LAIRD *(enters R.2 E.)*. It's all right, boys, the good folks are gone, you need not try to look respectable.

TAFFY *(L.C.)*. What's to be done? *(Turning to Laird)* Billee's under twenty-five. His mother's consent is necessary.

(Exclamations of surprise).

ANTONY *(R.C. to Laird)*. What's to be done, Sandy? You've the canny head.

LAIRD *(seated on stool C. nonplussed)*. There's the difficulty *(sits in thought)*.

DODOR *(L.C.)*. Zouzou, suggest, suggest.

ZOUZOU *(L. of Dodor)*. Suggest? Ah, oui, messieurs, Mesdames, I no spik Angliche; but I suggest what you call it—évasion—elopement.

(General satisfaction).

TAFFY. What do you say to that, Sandy?

LAIRD *(seated C. hesitating)*. Eh, it might be wise, man. The Belgian law is different from the French.

TAFFY *(rises)*. Then to Belgium, we'll go *(L.)*.

(Enter Svengali R.2 E. to bay window).

We'll have carriages here at midnight; drive post-haste to the Northern Railroad, be over the frontier before noon tomorrow, and get the marriage legally celebrated by nightfall.

OMNES. Hooray!

TAFFY *(L.)*. We'll order the carriages at once. Trilby will wait for us here.

(Cheers. Green lights from Dock).

DODOR. Attention; form battalion; march.

(Zouzou, Dodor, Antony, Lorimer, Laird, and Taffy march and exit door in flat).

TRILBY *(seated at table L.)*. Billee, dear, I—I fear we are doing wrong.

BILLEE *(stands by her L.)*. No, my mother loves me. We'll win her over by and by. Let us do as Taffy tells us. Be strong, love, be strong, and nothing can part us *(kisses her and exits door in flat)*.

(Music in orchestra. Svengali looking through window. Trilby rises smiling, crosses slowly R. Svengali stealthily crosses to door, bolts it, makes hypnotic gesture with R. hand, then with L. hand signals her to chair L. again. Svengali comes down—Trilby attempts to rise, but is overcome by Svengali raising both hands).

SVENGALI *(muttering)*. So, at midnight we say goodbye, my Trilby.

TRILBY *(not looking at him)*. I shall be thankful to leave Paris behind.

SVENGALI *(L.C. above Trilby)*. You will leave it gaily—carriages—shouting, Zouzou blowing the horn— and the organist of St. Nicholas playing "Minuit chrétiens."[189] But you are not listening, my Trilby, you

---

189 A French Christmas carol (same tune as "O Holy Night"); literally "Midnight Christians."

are thinking of Little Billee, you will not look in my face, you are looking at the chimney-pots when Svengali talks! Look a little lower down between the houses at the other side of the river. But see, my Trilby. (*Pointing through window*) There is a light glimmering yonder—the light of ugly little building; and inside are eight slabs of marble, all in a row. It is the Morgue, and oh, be careful, my Trilby, that you who leave Paris so gaily (*gets in front of her so that his eyes are fixed on hers*) do not come back to sleep on one of those marble slabs.

(*She tries to get her eyes away from his, but cannot. She struggles ineffectually, her face wearing an expression of horror*).

So that the people will stare through the plate-glass windows and say, "Ach, what a beautiful woman was Trilby. She ought to be riding in her carriage and pair.[190] But she would not listen to Svengali, and for that she lost him."

(*She attempts to rise—is overcome by Svengali's hypnotism*).

Sleep on, ma mignonne,[191] sleep! (*Gloating sigh*).

(*A pause*).

Trilby, can you hear me?

(*A pause; he repeats*).

Trilby, can you hear me?
TRILBY (*in chair L. below table, in a faint voice*). Yes.
SVENGALI. Rise.

(*She rises, he gives her his hand*).

I wish you to go into the dining room and wait till I call.

(*A pause*).

I wish it! I wish it!

(*She goes out L.U.E., looking straight before her, and smiling. Then Svengali sits and wipes his forehead*).

Ach, Himmel, the other way was better. The other way was better. It is my strength, my genius, my life passing into hers. If I take not care, *it will kill me* (*sits in chair L.*).

(*Music stops. Enter Gecko from R.2 E.*).

GECKO (*R.C.*). Trilby! Where is she?
SVENGALI (*seated in chair L.*). She is going to leave Paris at midnight—she and I, and you, my Gecko.
GECKO (*R.C.*). I? Is this right?
SVENGALI. Right? What is right? Pah! (*snaps fingers*).
GECKO. Svengali, I have served you as a dog, but rather than injure her—
SVENGALI. Fool that you are—(*takes him by the ear*). You owe everything to me—and now when the ball is at my feet you kick it away—you little whippersnapper—whom I picked out of the gutter when

---

190 Pair of horses drawing the carriage.
191 Darling.

you were starving—This Litrebili whom I hate shall not take her—You talk to me of religion—of your God—That for your religion—I laugh at it—I laugh at all the world—I am myself, Svengali—I know my power, nothing can frighten me—I am my own God—*(laughs)* and you dare *(raises his arm—suddenly puts his hand to his heart—staggers—gasps)* I—I—what is this—help—help—Gecko—I faint—I cannot see—brandy—quick—I—I—

(Gecko runs out—Svengali feels his heart—it seems not to beat).

I will not die—*(goes to window—throws it open—gasps—comes down agonized like a rat in a trap).* God! Do not let me die—Death, death, no, no *(gasps)* let me live another year, another month—I will repent—Oh God of Israel—"Shemang Yisrael Adonai Eloheno Adonai Echod"[192] *(continues gibbering).*

(Reenter Gecko with brandy—Svengali drinks).

Ah—ah! *(looks before him, feels himself recovering, puts hand to heart begins a low laugh)* I am not dying, Gecko—feel my heart—unloose my neckcloth—I am not dying.

GECKO. No, no, Svengali, you are better, eh? *(sympathetically).*

SVENGALI. Yes, I—am—better—it was nothing but excitement—a little faint—my father died like that when he was seventy—I shall recover—more brandy—Ah! I am not dying—ha, ha—ha—we will, my Gecko, you and I—

GECKO. What were you doing on your knees when I came in?

SVENGALI. I was offering up a prayer for Little Billee—ha, ha—poor little Billee—we will live—you and I—we will wander Eastward—you and Trilby and I—we will cage the song-bird till it sings velvet and gold and beautiful flowers and pearls and diamonds and rubies—and we will be rich—I will ride in my carriage and smoke the big Havana cigar and I will wear a big fur coat—all the winter and all the summer too. She is going to become the greatest of singers; and emperors and grand-dukes shall kiss her hand, and noblemen shall sing serenades beneath her window.

GECKO *(R.C.).* Your old story Svengali.

SVENGALI *(not heeding).* And you are going to help me—*(rises to C.)* because you love her. *(Pointing finger then taking Gecko's ear)* You see, I know your secret—you love her.

GECKO *(R.C. with sudden fierceness).* Yes, I love her, I would rather die than let a moment of unhappiness come to her.

SVENGALI *(C. softly).* What happiness, my Gecko, awaits her with Litrebili? His mother hates her, his sister would despise her; she would wither under the cold contempt of these prudes Anglaises.

GECKO *(R.C.).* C'est vrai.[193]

SVENGALI *(C.).* She has the artist-nature; the beauty of a queen. Should she hide herself among the swine of an English village?

GECKO *(R.C.).* No. *(Doubtfully)* If I thought she would ever forgive me—

SVENGALI *(C.).* Forgive you? More than that, my Gecko. You shall teach her to sing. She shall love you for your patience—for your kindness—yes, she shall love you, and one day, my Gecko, well, well we shall see.

GECKO *(R.C. weakening).* She would never leave Paris.

SVENGALI *(C.).* We shall see. I have my power still. *(Calls to her)* Trilby. She comes not.

(No answer. He repeats).

---

192 Hear, O Israel: the Lord our God, the Lord is one. (Transliterations vary.)
193 It's true.

Trilby.

(No answer. He repeats).

Trilby, come to me.

(Trilby enters from L.U.E. and goes down by table R. of it. Her eyes are rigid. There is a pleasant smile on her face, and, except her eyes, her movements are all entirely natural. Gecko sinks in amazement on couch R.).

SVENGALI. Trilby! *(C.).*
TRILBY. Yes.

(Trilby's hand touches Svengali—a sigh of relief from Svengali).

SVENGALI. Will you do as I bid you?
TRILBY. Yes.
SVENGALI. Sit.

(She sits at head of table L.).

GECKO *(amazed).* She is asleep *(rising, goes to Svengali).*
SVENGALI. Wake her then.

(Gecko puts hand on Trilby's shoulder—she does not move. Bell strikes twelve immediately following peal of organ).

SVENGALI. Take that pen, Trilby.

(She takes pen).

Write—*(dictating)* My dear Taffy—
TRILBY *(seated writing with smile).* "My dear Taffy—"
SVENGALI *(dictating).* This is to say good-bye.
TRILBY *(writing, her face lights up joyfully as she writes, she speaks the last words).* "To say good-bye."
SVENGALI *(dictating).* Billee's mother is right. I must never see him again.
TRILBY *(writing with the same look of happiness as before, especially at the last four words, which she speaks).* Never see him again.
SVENGALI *(dictating).* I have left Paris forever.

(Noise of footsteps. Gecko goes to D.F.).

TRILBY *(same business).* Paris forever.
SVENGALI *(dictating).* Do not try to find me.
TRILBY *(same business).* To find me.
SVENGALI. I am with friends.

(Noise)

TRILBY *(same business).* Friends.

(Knocking heard at door in flat. Svengali and Gecko disturbed. Gecko goes R. of Svengali. Trilby remains without motion).

GECKO. Too late.

(Knocking repeated).

SVENGALI. No. *(Dictating)* Trilby O'Ferrall.
TRILBY *(writing).* Trilby O'Ferrall.

(Knock repeated. Svengali gives his hand to Trilby—she rises).

SVENGALI *(to Trilby).* You will go with Gecko in a carriage to the station, and you will wait with him
    till I join you. You will start with us for the East.
GECKO *(L.).* And when she wakes?
SVENGALI. She will be far from home.

(Gecko leads her off R. opening).

    You understand it is my wish.
TRILBY. Yes.
SVENGALI *(to Gecko).* Quick take her away.

(Gecko crosses with Trilby to R.2 E.).

    Quick. I will have carriage below.

*(Lights down to ¼ foots and border.[194] The knocking increases; then Svengali sees that Trilby has gone,
blows out the lights on piano, goes to D.L.F. and unbolts it, steps behind curtains in L. opening, after
characters enter and are down steals out D.L.F. The door flies open and Taffy, Laird, and Madame Vinard
rush in. Svengali instantly slips out and disappears).*

LAIRD *(C.).* Why what the devil? Who's been here? Who locked the door? And who let us in?
MADAME VINARD *(R.C.).* Ah who knows! Perhaps it was Monsieur Vinard? He may have come for
    the punch bowl ...
LAIRD. More likely for the punch.
TAFFY *(at R. arch—calling).* Trilby! Trilby! All ready for the departure? *(Crosses to L. arch then to R.C.).*
LAIRD *(calling).* Four carriages at door; drivers prepared to whip like mad, and the word passed for the
    start to be made at midnight. Where's the bride?
LAIRD *(calling).* Trilby! *(Sees letter on table L.C.).*

(Swell for organ).

    What's this? *(Reads).*
TAFFY *(R.C.).* What's up? Injunction—attachment—what?
LAIRD *(giving him letter. L.C.).* Read.
MADAME VINARD *(U.R.C.).* What is it messieurs? Ah Dieu, what a réveillon is this!
TAFFY *(R.C. down—in broken voice).* It's all up. There'll be no elopement.

(Exclamations of surprise)

BILLEE *(enter D.F.).* Well boys—is everything all right? Why what's the matter?
TAFFY. Bear it like a man, Billee. Your mother's won the fight. Trilby has gone.
BILLEE. Gone! *(Reads note)* "Have left Paris for ever—do not try to find me"—oh Taffy my heart is
    broken, my heart is broken.

---

194 Footlights and overhead lights.

(Billee falls slight back, then on Taffy. The organ of the church of St. Nicholas peals forth the "Cantique de Noel."[195] *The characters sympathizing around Billee. Svengali laughs).*

Act III

Five years later. Music at rise on stage. Hungarian Dance.[196] *Foyer of the Cirque des Bashibazouks.*[197] *It is a handsome room, draped and decorated. Busts of famous musicians and singers set round. Pictures of operatic celebrities on the walls. A corridor runs off at back R. and L. Three windows, two with blinds drawn in the corridor. At angle R.3 E. there is a bay window with seat and railing, supposed to look down on the auditorium. The window is curtained and the curtains are half closed. Passage R.1 E. and passage L.2 E. Ornamented furniture. Green baize*[198] *tables, R.C. and L.C. with chairs, sofas and lounges. Stools before all the chairs. Discovered: Madame Vinard in the dress of a theatrical box keeper, watching with opera-glass through curtains of window R.3 E. Enter Colonel Kaw, Manager, hurriedly from L.2 E. He is a vulgar and pompous little man.*

KAW. Ah, bong soir,[199] Madame Vinard *(crossing to R.)*.

MADAME VINARD *(at R.3 E. so startled that she nearly drops opera-glass)*. Bon soir, Monsieur le Colonel *(closes curtains)*.

KAW *(R.)*. Did you ever see such an audience in Paris before?

MADAME VINARD. Never since I left the porter's lodge in the Latin Quarter to become a box keeper at the Cirque des Bashibazouks.

KAW. Gigantic idea! "Col. Kaw's American concerts." Every American goes in Paris. The "Star" is colossal, and the Hungarian gipsy band immense. *(Going R.1 E.)* Now, mind, if you allow anybody to enter when the music is going on, off goes your head, my lady *(exit R.1 E.)*.

MADAME VINARD *(R. by R.3 E. Half opening curtains)*. Bah! They are all in their seats already. *(With exclamation of surprise)* Mon Dieu! I shall not hear a sound.

(Enter Zouzou and Dodor from corridor R. They are in evening dress. Their appearance is entirely changed from that of the previous act. They are as stiff and formal as they were before rollicking. Madame Vinard turns, sees them, and throws up her hands).

Ah! Can it be? Is it possible?

ZOUZOU *(adjusting eyeglass loftily)*. My good woman.

MADAME VINARD *(R.)*. Monsieur Zouzou! Monsieur Dodor! Don't you remember me—Madame Vinard, who was concierge, Place St. Anatole des Arts—five years ago?

---

195 "Minuit chrétiens"; see above, p. 617, n. 189.

196 A review indicates that Hector Berlioz's "Hungarian March" was followed by "a quaint czardas, 'rich in dulcimer effects.'" (Czardas are Hungarian dances: they begin slowly and build to a rambunctious end.) "*Trilby* at the Prince of Wales Theatre," *Birmingham Mail*, 6 October 1896.

197 "Bashibazouks" in the manuscript. Bashi-bazouks were Turkish mercenary soldiers, unpaid, who lived off looting. As a made-up term for a Parisian theatre, Cirque des Bashibazouks connotes a particularly free-spirited and racy atmosphere, possibly decorated in eastern motifs.

198 Coarse woollen cloth.

199 *Bon soir* (good evening); Kaw speaks with an American accent.

DODOR. By Jove, how d'ye do Madame Vinard?

MADAME VINARD. And Monsieur Zouzou talks Angliche now as well as I.

ZOUZOU *(with eyeglass)*. Doosid[200] deal better. I've married an American wife.

MADAME VINARD *(R.)*. Ah, Monsieur Zouzou, if I may felicitate ...

ZOUZOU *(C.)*. Thanks. Wish you'd take our coats to the cloakroom.

(They throw her their coats. She goes off L.2 E. gaily chattering; her voice is lost in the wings).

It's like old times to meet her.

DODOR *(seated L.)*. You're too great a swell to think of old times. You're a duke.

ZOUZOU*(C.)*. Hang it, Theodore! Don't be always reminding a fellow that. You're a haberdasher.[201]

DODOR. Haberdasher as I am, I shudder to think of those Latin Quarter days. Remember the pawnshop, Zouzou?

ZOUZOU. Cut that.

DODOR *(seated L.)*. And the bad dinners; and the racket in the studios; and the "trois Angliches;" and Trilby? *(Rising)*.

ZOUZOU *(sighing)*. Poor Trilby!

(Enter Antony and Lorimer from corridor L.2 E. They are as much changed as the others. They come down).

DODOR. Ever heard what became of her?

ZOUZOU. No; the river keeps its secrets.

(They turn toward R. and meet Antony).

ZOUZOU. Antony!

DODOR. Lorimer!

ANTONY. Why, it's Zouzou and Dodor.

LORIMER *(L. seated)*. The devil.

(They shake hands warmly).

ZOUZOU. This is odd. We just met Madame Vinard. She has turned box keeper here, or something. Heard you'd come into a baronetcy, Lorimer.

LORIMER *(L.)*. Yes; I'm a bloated aristocrat *(sits)*.

DODOR *(R.C.)*. And you into a fortune, Antony?

ANTONY *(R.)*. True! I'm a bloated bond-holder. *(Sits)* Do you remember how ardently we used to hunt the five-franc piece?

LORIMER *(sighing)*. Five years ago.

(They sit).

ZOUZOU *(C.)*. It's just to rub up our memories that we've come here to see Svengali.

ANTONY and LORIMER. Svengali?

ZOUZOU. Don't you know that it's *our* Svengali?

ANTONY and LORIMER. *What's* our Svengali?

---

200 Deuced (devilish).

201 Seller of men's wear.

DODOR. The fellow who leads the orchestra tonight.

ANTONY (R.). What! That fellow in the Latin Quarter—hook nose, black beard? Oh, he was a damned blackguard.

ZOUZOU (C.). All the same, he married la Svengali, the greatest singer on earth.

LORIMER (L.). We're just over from England. We never heard of the Svengali.

ZOUZOU (L.C. dismayed). Never heard of la Svengali?

(Stop band on stage).

DODOR (R.). This is awful! (Takes out programme).

ANTONY (R.C.). Enlighten us.

LORIMER (L.). Who is la Svengali?

ZOUZOU. Svengali, you remember, was always bragging about the "bel canto" and how he found its secret in a dream. Well, somewhere in Poland, he met a woman whom he could teach; and he taught her; and she's going to make her first appearance in Paris tonight.

DODOR (reading programme). Madame Svengali the world-renowned singer. First selection, "Au clair de la lune."

ANTONY (speaking). Why, that's a nursery rhyme!

ZOUZOU. Precisely! (Sings) "Au clair de la lune." Only a nursery rhyme. They say she sings it like an archangel.

DODOR. People declare she's not mortal at all. (Cross R.C.) She's like an enchanted princess in a fairy tale. She makes you cry over the commonest tunes. Fellows tell me at the club that in Petersburg the women were crazy about her, and pulled off their diamonds to give her, and went down on their knees to kiss her hands. At Warsaw, where she had sung in the streets, ay the streets, men gave her their watches, and diamond studs, and gold scarf pins. It's disgusting that a hog like Svengali should have found such a pearl (cross R.).

ANTONY (R.C.). Lucky the "Angliches" are not here to witness his triumph.

DODOR (R.). But they are or will be.

(Surprise of Antony and Lorimer).

I met them this afternoon at the Grand Hotel. You wouldn't know them. Taffy stately and solemn; the Laird an Associate of the Royal Academy[202] if you please; and Little Billee a friend of duchesses and a famous painter. They'd discovered Svengali's name on the posters and were curious to see the ruffian again.

ANTONY. So the old crowd will once more foregather.

LORIMER (L.). By Jove! it's just like a play.

(Enter Kaw very quickly from R.1 E.).

KAW. Gentlemen, I must ask you not to linger in the foyer (cross to L.U.E.).

(All feel for their tickets).

The first two instrumental pieces are over, and we have a rule forbidding entrance while the music is being played.

---

202 The Royal Academy of Arts promotes contemporary British art and design through education and exhibitions. In the mid-nineteenth century, Associate Members were eligible for election to the 42 Members posts. This indicates the Laird's status as an artist: he moves in circles habituated by the preeminent artists of the day, including Edwin Henry Landseer, William Clarkson Stanfield, Daniel Maclise, William Powell Frith, and William Dyce.

(They move towards C.).

DODOR. Well, well! this is queer! That we old Bohemians should meet again to hear a woman Svengali picked up in Warsaw sing *(sings "Au clair de la lune").*

(Omnes singing together in harmony, "Au clair de la lune." They exit R.1 E.).

KAW *(protesting).* Gentlemen! Gentlemen! *(Looks at watch).*

(Re-enter Madame Vinard from L.2 E.).

Madame Vinard, let me know the instant Madame Svengali arrives *(exit R.2 E.).*

MADAME VINARD *(L.).* Svengali? Why, that's the name of, it can't possibly be the same, yet—!

GECKO *(heard in the corridor L.).* In a moment. I will see that the foyer is empty.

MADAME VINARD *(in amazement).* Gecko! It's Gecko's voice. Then Svengali is—is—

GECKO *(enter from corridor L. He is in Hungarian uniform. His hair is almost white. Calling).* Ouvreuse![203] Ouvreuse!

(Crossing to L. meets Madame Vinard. Falls back aghast).

Madame Vinard!

MADAME VINARD *(R. Hands on hips).* Yes, it is I, you little wretch. So you thought to swindle me hein? When you and your master Svengali ran away that Christmas, you thought never to see me again hein? Where is all the money he owes me for his rent?

(Music).

GECKO *(L.C.).* He will pay; he will pay. He is now rich. His pockets are lined with gold. He will pay you as soon as this concert ends.

MADAME VINARD *(R.C. Resolutely).* I won't let him out of my sight.

GECKO *(L.C.).* But no scene, I implore you, no scene! His wife, the great singer is coming, and if you should excite his nerves—

MADAME VINARD *(R.).* I'll excite—*(suddenly)* Bon Dieu! Monsieur le Colonel bade me bring him word. *(Going R.1 E. turns at door)* Ah! mon Gecko, this time your master shall not run away from me *(exit C. off R.).*

GECKO *(follows her up, mopping forehead).* Quelle fâcheuse rencontre![204] If Svengali meets her he will be all unstrung, and our bird will not sing tonight. *(Turns to L.U.E. up stage calling)* Svengali!

SVENGALI *(enter in evening dress. He is not so erect as of old; his face is much whiter. Looking round).* The foyer clear? All gone?

(Gecko makes gesture of assent, crosses to R.2 E. Svengali calls off corridor L. in a soft and caressing voice).

Come, mignonne. We are here *(opposite L.3 E.).*

(Enter from corridor L. Trilby dressed in her robe of cloth of gold. Her eyes are set, but, with that exception her demeanour is normal. She is smiling and waves her hand in the old friendly way, as though acknowledging the applause of the art students. Svengali at C. opposite).

---

203 Usherette.
204 What an unpleasant encounter.

Illustration 34. Herbert Beerbohm Tree as Svengali in his costume for act 4 of *Trilby*, 1895. Courtesy of David Mayer.

TRILBY (*L. by table, to an imaginary gathering*). Oh, I am so sorry. (*Arranging her hair before an imaginary glass; then half aside, smiling*) I must look my best tonight, for the supper's in honour of Little Billee and me (*arranges her hair and the coronet*[205] *that surrounds it*).

SVENGALI (*vindictively, aside*). Always thinking of that miserable little dauber. Gecko! Gecko! (*Cross to R.2 to Gecko*) This number is ended, my Gecko. We are next on the programme (*goes to C. open*).

(*Gecko, after a wistful look at Trilby, goes out L.1 E.*).

TRILBY (*crosses to chair L. of table R.C. and continues as though at the dinner table of the previous act. L. seated at table*). How you shout, Zouzou! What's the toast! "La Mariée." (*Confused*) I'm to reply? No, I won't, I can't, I never made a speech in my life. Little Billee must speak for me.

SVENGALI (*cross to R.2 E. looking round impatiently*). Where's Gecko? What keeps him?

TRILBY (*suddenly rises, crosses to C. and holds out hand timidly*). Mrs. Bagot, is it not? Won't you take my hand? (*In heartbroken voice*) Won't you take my hand?

(*Turning to R. there meets Svengali who has risen. Hypnotic business by Svengali*).

Sandy, Sandy dear, you won't let him give me up. His mother has a gentle voice, but she is unkind to me. Oh, Sandy, you won't let him give me up.

SVENGALI (*L.C.*). If I could awake her.

(*Leads her to chair L. of table L.C.*).

But it is too late. My life has passed into hers. And every note she sings I know that it is killing both her and me.

GECKO (*enter from R.1 E. excited. Crosses to Svengali*). There is yet five minutes. But I have met—the Duke, what you call him? Zouzou, and he tells me the "trois Angliches" will be in the audience.

SVENGALI (*eagerly*). All three?

GECKO (*above Svengali R.3*). All three.

SVENGALI. Hast thou found me, oh mine enemy? (*Cross to R.3 E.*) Then, tonight, she shall sing like a nightingale. I will pour my passion into her heart if it makes my own stand still. (*Hand to heart, pause, as if controlling his emotion*) She shall sing tonight as she never sang before.

GECKO (*behind Svengali, L. of him*). You have been making her work too hard.

(*Trilby rises*).

SVENGALI (*at R.3 E.*). Have I spared myself? Did I not fall down in a fit in the streets of Prague? Would any doctor alive allow that I had a year to live?

TRILBY (*her hands behind her foot raised on stool*). Svengali, do not be cross with me. I am doing my best. (*Weeping softly*) Oh, do not be cross with me. (*Putting up arm as if to ward off blow*) Do not beat me.

GECKO (*L. of Svengali, threatening him*). You have beaten her?

SVENGALI (*by window. Snarling*). Silence, dog.

TRILBY. You call me names, horrid names, but how can I touch that note? Don't be cross with me. (*Shrinking*) Don't call me names. (*Putting up arm as before*) Don't beat ...

SVENGALI (*fixing his eyes on hers, cross to Trilby*). Sleep!

TRILBY (*her voice dying out, she sits L. at table*). Don't beat—beat—

KAW (*enter from R.1 E.*). Ah, Svengali, bong soir, bong soir.

---

205 Decorative metal band.

(Stop music).

Your good lady is ready? *(Sees Trilby)* Ah, bong soir. Let me escort her to the stage.

(Svengali with apparent nonchalance, places Trilby's hand on Kaw's arm).

(Continues volubly) A great house, madame. Magnificent. The Prince of Wales is there, all in your honour, broad blue ribbon on his breast.[206] British ambassador beside him. Great sight, great.

(Exit R.1 E. with Trilby who smiles on him in a friendly way, Svengali is about to follow R.1 E. when Gecko intercepts him).

GECKO *(down to R.2 resolutely).* Svengali, you must listen to me.

SVENGALI *(cross to him).* When Trilby is to sing, bah!

GECKO. If you do not listen to me here, you shall listen to me before all the audience.

SVENGALI. Is this madness?

GECKO. Perhaps! I have for years been your servant, your factotum, your jack of all trades, and so I will be until you die.

SVENGALI. You keep me here to tell me this? *(Cross to C.).*

GECKO *(cross to him R.C. not heeding).* But if you ever raise your hand to strike Trilby, I will forget all. I will defend Trilby against a locomotive going grande vitesse,[207] against my own father, against the Emperor of Austria,[208] against the Pope. For Trilby I will go to the scaffold and to the devil after.

SVENGALI *(raising his hand).* Fool.

GECKO *(falls on knee. His hand drops inert. R.C.).* Ah—*(Rises)* You have just said your life is running out, you can no longer beat any but women. *(Stands aside)* Go. I stand not in your way. *(Sneering)* Litrebili will be there in the audience. Make your song-bird sing as never before.

(Svengali cross to R.2 and exit).

And remember—I will go to the scaffold to defend her.

GECKO *(watches Svengali for an instant after he has gone, then begins to break down. C.).* Beat her! Corpo di Cristo![209] He shall beat her no more. He is killing her. Sweet sister! O Dieu de misèrer! Ich habe geliebt und gelebet! Geliebt und gelebet![210] *(Covers his face with his hands, sits at table L.).*

MADAME VINARD *(enter from L.2 E., comes to Gecko R. of him).* I'll have every sou before Svengali leaves the place. *(Sees Gecko, surprised)* Why, Gecko, Gecko: do you not play tonight?

GECKO *(rousing himself).* Ay yes, I am late. *(Cross to R.2 E.)* And she is to sing as never before! *(Exit R.2 E.).*

MADAME VINARD. I'll make Svengali sing, too *(up to R.3 E., peeps out through curtains).*

(Enter Taffy, the Laird, and Little Billee. They are changed as the other young men were changed).

LAIRD *(looking round).* So this is the Cirque des Bashibazouks? *(pronouncing the name as badly as formerly).* Don't think it existed in our time, eh, Taffy?

---

206 Edward, Prince of Wales, later King Edward VII, eldest son of Queen Victoria. Born in 1841, he would have been a teenager in the mid-1850s. He wears the insignia of the Order of the Garter. (The Prince and Princess of Wales were present at the first London performance of *Trilby*.)

207 At high speed.

208 Franz Josef I, at this time an absolute monarch.

209 Body of Christ.

210 God of mercy, I have loved and lived, loved and lived.

TAFFY (*turning up C.*). All Paris is changed. Doesn't seem like our Paris, does it Billee? (*Going up towards C. opening followed by Laird*).

BILLEE (*sighing*). Ah, we'll never see that Paris again (*cross to L.*).

MADAME VINARD (*turns from window and utters little scream*). Mon Dieu! Les trois Angliches.

BILLEE. It's Madame Vinard! Dear Madame Vinard!

MADAME VINARD (*hugging each of them boisterously in turn*). Yes, it is I. Ah, mes garçons,[211] what happiness to see you again. Ah! how handsome you all are. And Monsieur Litrebili (*shakes his hands*) so tall. Ah, if we were only at home to drink my blackberry brandy together (*turns up to R.*).

TAFFY. Have you given up your lodge?

MADAME VINARD. No, Messieurs, my husband keeps it now, and I earn a few sous as box keeper at the Cirque.

LAIRD (*R.C.*). And our old studio, is that occupied?

MADAME VINARD (*L.C.*). It has been three months to let. But you would not know it. Nothing is as it was but Trilby's foot.

(*Billee starts and turns away, sits at table L. of it*).

LAIRD. Three months to let—je prongs.[212]

MADAME VINARD. That Monsieur Litrebili scratched on the wall. Poor Trilby! So good, so pretty. And how she loved you all. And Monsieur Litrebili—mon Dieu! how she loved him! (*Wipes eyes*) Poor Trilby! (*Goes up*).

TAFFY (*controlling voice. R. corner*). We—we have all three agreed to bury the past, Madame Vinard.

MADAME VINARD (*comes down*). Ah vrai, c'est vrai. She did not treat you well, poor girl (*up*).

LAIRD (*R.C. controlling his voice*). We never speak of Trilby, never think of Trilby, we, in short, we've forgotten her, haven't we, Billee?

BILLEE (*seated L. of table L. In broken voice*). Yes, we've forgotten her.

TAFFY (*R.*). That's a lie. Sandy, the boy is lying (*goes up and crossing to Billee*).

LAIRD (*low to Taffy, cross to R. In choking voice*). Was—was nothing ever heard of her again?

MADAME VINARD (*shaking head sadly, comes down R.C.*). Nothing.

(*Taffy crosses to Billee and puts hand on his shoulder*).

And I have nothing but this plain hair ring which she gave me to remember her.

LAIRD (*bringing Madame Vinard D.R.*). Madame Vinard will you take fifty francs for that ring? (*Showing bank notes*).

MADAME VINARD. Fifty? It's not worth two.

LAIRD (*R.*). I'll give you fifty for auld lang syne.[213]

(*Gives bank notes, she gives ring*).

Merci, je prong. Have you any other souvenirs of Trilby at home?

(*Taffy above Billee at table L.*).

MADAME VINARD. I—I might find one or two.

---

211 My lads.
212 *Je prends* (I take).
213 Old time's sake.

LAIRD. Oh, er, Trilby's foot on the wall.

MADAME VINARD (R.C.). Ah, but Monsieur, I cannot cut the wall.

LAIRD (R.). Then I'll take the wall, too. The whole home, if you like. You understand—je prong! All mine, all. Not a word to Taffy (finger on lips). Je prong; je prong (goes to door R.3 E.).

MADAME VINARD (aside). So the "trois Angliches" have not forgotten poor Trilby (joins Laird at window R.3 E.).

BILLEE (seated table L. of it. Looking up from table). I can't help it, Taffy. The mere mention of her name brings it all back to me. I should have kept away from Paris. What an unmanly duffer you must think me. But I loved her and I do still.

TAFFY (at head of table L. Kindly). Brace up, old man. I've loved her too. And we lost her. Svengali may tell us something of her fate.

LAIRD (turning from window). Come, boys, we've just time to get to our seats.

(Billee rises up to C., looks off R.).

MADAME VINARD. Ah, Monsieur Sandy, I forgot to say. You are too late. They let no one enter when the conductor raises his baton. But you can hear the song from the window. (Drawing curtains) There is Svengali—there.

(Taffy and Billee now join the Laird and Madame Vinard at the window; they form a picturesque group, watching).

LAIRD (with opera glass).[214] How sleek the villain looks—but pale as death. That curly mane makes his face seem ghastly white.

MADAME VINARD. And Gecko, too. Can you pick him out?

TAFFY (with opera glass). How he has aged! Hair white as snow. Poor little Gecko! In his swell hussar uniform.[215] But the woman—the prodigy, where is she?

(Hands glass back to Laird. Applause).

LAIRD (with opera glass). Two pages are pulling the curtain aside.

(Applause)

There she is in some spangled dress: sort of cloth of gold.[216] Arms, shoulders bare. Coronet of stars on head, and ... and ... (In great excitement) Here, Taffy, take these glasses. I always thought something was wrong with my eyes. They make me see the queerest things (cross to chair R. of table L.).

(Taffy meanwhile has adjusted opera glass and is looking at the stage).

---

214 Small binoculars.

215 There are hussars (light cavalry) in western European military; however, Gecko is associated with the original Hungarian connotation. Any uniform consisting of heavy gold or silver braiding across the chest, riding breeches, and possibly a plumed busby and a fur-trimmed pelisse slung over one shoulder would be recognizable as a hussar's.

216 Dorothea Baird, as Trilby, appeared in

the cold stately beauty of ...'Mme. Svengali'—a glorious creature in a clinging robe of cream crépe de chêne, bordered with a band of cloth of gold, like a strip of golden sea, above which radiating suns and stars rise almost to the hips, where, still above them, comes the flash and glitter of a shower of diamonds. There are diamond brooches catching the drapery together on the shoulders, and holding, too, the long flowing drapery of Roman satin which sweeps the ground at the back, and with every movement reveals the glory of a silken linen, covered with gold and jewelled embroidery. A small tiara of diamonds is worn in the hair, and in her right hand 'Mme. Svengali' carries a sheaf of white lilies and one great palm leaf. ("'Trilby,'" Globe, 31 October 1895)

MADAME VINARD (*in unconcerned voice*). Why, what is it, Mr. Taffy?

(*Taffy puts down glasses. He cannot speak*).

BILLEE (*with intuition of the truth, rising*). Taffy, is it, is it, somebody we know?
TAFFY. Yes, old chap, it's ... Trilby.
BILLEE. Come back to life! La Svengali! His wife!

(*Music—Song. Applause*).

LAIRD. But by what miracle?
TAFFY. Hush.

(*Applause*).

BILLEE. Oh, listen, listen!

(*A pause—they listen*).

LAIRD. Trilby, the tone-deaf. Preposterous! (*seated R. of table L.*).

(*Song distant. Billee is behind Taffy*).

TAFFY (*with opera glass*). Svengali's eyes are riveted on hers (*hands glasses to Madame Vinard*).
BILLEE. Don't talk. For God's sake, don't talk.

(*Stop song—at end of applause*).

MADAME VINARD (*looks off R.3 E. with opera glass*). Ah, messieurs, did ever spectators sit like that? Half of them are in tears—tears of joy. (*Comes down C. and cross to L.*) What marvel has this Svengali wrought with our Trilby?

(*Laird snatching glasses. Distant noise—applause*).

LAIRD. Voice, hands, feet, sticks, umbrellas. Now the bouquets. The air's thick with them. She stands in a regular conservatory of flowers. The pages are picking them up. She is bowing. Svengali's hand in hers.

(*Billee makes gesture of anger. Taffy puts arm in Billee's*).

TAFFY. Come away, little Billee. We have seen enough.

(*Brings Billee down stage to L.*).

LAIRD (*looks off R.3 E. through opera glass—sadly*). Well, the age of miracles hasn't passed. And there's an end of it.

(*Stop applause*).

BILLEE (*back of table L. Fiercely*). There'll never be an end of it for me; never, never, oh, never. She would have married me but for my mother's interference. What a wife! Think of all she must have in her head and brain to move a lot of clods[217] like that. If my mother hadn't come to Paris we should have been man and wife for five years, living at Barbizon, painting away like mad. Oh, curse all officious meddling, curse all meddlers. (*Cross to R.*)

---

217 Blockheads.

LAIRD *(comes down to Billee).* Brace up, Billee, there's a good chap.

TAFFY *(L. of Billee).* You swore that you'd forgotten her—as we have.

BILLEE. Oh, Taffy, and Sandy, what trumps you are, and what a selfish beast I am ... I ... I *(Billee between them).*

KAW *(enter from R.1 E.).* Gentlemen, I must ask you to withdraw.

(Billee up to C.D.).

Madame Svengali is coming here to rest between the parts.

TAFFY. Madame Svengali is an old friend of ours. She will be glad to see us.

KAW. Tomorrow, no doubt, or after the concert. For the moment I must ask you ...

(Music on stage)

LAIRD *(goes up to Billee).* But we tell you that Madame Svengali ...

(Enter Trilby from R.1 E. on Svengali's arm, Gecko follows her, laden with bouquets. Taffy advances and holds out his hand to Svengali. Exit Kaw R.2 E.).

TAFFY. Svengali!

SVENGALI *(not taking his hand, affecting surprise).* Monsieur?

TAFFY *(still holding out his hand).* You recall me—Taffy; Talbot Wynne, and my two friends?

SVENGALI *(crossing him, with Trilby on his arm).* Pardon me, sir, I have not the advantage of recollecting ...

LAIRD *(coming down C.).* If I might refresh your memory—

SVENGALI *(coldly).* My memory has no need of refreshment *(crosses with Trilby and seats her).*

BILLEE *(has been gazing open-mouthed at Trilby, advances L.C.).* But, Madame Svengali—Trilby—she remembers us—

SVENGALI *(watching her from L.).* I fear Madame Svengali's memory is no better than mine.

BILLEE. I won't believe it. *(Appealing to her)* Trilby, you know me don't you, Trilby?

(Trilby laughs).

Trilby, don't laugh. Look at me, speak to me, I know that you are this man's wife. But at least you will speak to me.

(Trilby laughs).

Won't you remember old times? Won't you think of the past?

SVENGALI *(from L., where he is watching the scene, sardonically).* My wife, sir.

(Billee starts back).[218]

Never looks backward. To her the past is dead. And so are all who were in it *(over for situation).*[219]

TAFFY. Then she is not Trilby, our Trilby, I'll swear it.

(Trilby, sitting, begins to talk to herself, smiling).

---

218 Reacts with shock.
219 Moves into position for the scene of revelation.

BILLEE *(to Trilby, R. of her)*. Tell me one thing, and I will ask no more. Was it really your regard for my mother's wish that made you give me up? Or was it your desire to be rich and famous with—*(pointing to Svengali)* with Svengali? Won't you answer? Don't you know when you went away it broke my heart.

(Goes to Laird, they go up C.).

TRILBY *(seated R. of table L. Vacantly)*. Yes.

TAFFY *(by Trilby, R. of her. Coming down)*. Trilby, I appeal to you. You know what I always thought of you. I don't mind confessing that I think the same today. I never believed that you did anything on that beastly night, five years ago, but what you thought to be right and proper.

TRILBY *(repeating mechanically)*. This time I will be strong. Mrs. Bagot, I give you my promise. I will not marry your son.

TAFFY *(turns to Laird and Billee)*. Svengali has forbidden her to speak to us. But these were the words she used to your mother. She repeats them to show us why she ran away.

BILLEE *(C.—fiercely)*. Why shouldn't she tell us so herself?

TAFFY. She's afraid. She has made her bed, poor girl, and must lie on it *(crossing down R.)*.

BILLEE *(crosses to Trilby)*. Only tell us, Trilby, that we embarrass you by talking to you.

(Pause—Svengali goes back of table—back to audience—looks towards Trilby intently).

TRILBY *(turning to Billee—pleasantly)*. No.

BILLEE *(surprised)*. You have been forbidden to speak to us.

(Same business from Svengali).

TRILBY *(as before)*. No!

BILLEE. Then you are doing this on your own responsibility.

(She goes on quietly babbling).

You willfully choose to "cut" us,[220] you choose to forget old times—the joy your coming brought to us; the desolation caused by going away?

(She goes on talking to herself).

(Suddenly turns fierce) Why, then let us tell you how heartless we think you.

LAIRD and TAFFY *(R.C. and R., protesting)*. No! No!

BILLEE *(continuing angrily)*. And how we are convinced of what we long suspected, that you left me on our marriage eve, not because you cared for my mother, but because this devil—*(pointing to Svengali)* tempted you with promises of wealth and glory.

(Taffy and Laird try to restrain him).

(Continues fiercely) For that you sold yourself. For that you betrayed me. For that you so crushed my heart, so wrecked my life, that I cannot look upon a woman without hating her.

(She laughs softly).

You laugh, all right. You are famous today. Great! The world is all at your feet, but if your conscience doesn't make you suffer when you think of me, it's because you have no conscience.

---

220 Insult us by refusing to acknowledge us.

(He is in great excitement. Taffy and the Laird try to restrain him—he goes on).

It's because you have bartered your soul for fame—

(Music stops on stage—Laird takes Billee up to C. opening).

KAW *(enter from R.1 E.).* Madame Svengali, we have a few minutes before your next song—"Ben Bolt." If I might again have the honour to escort you to the stage.

(Laird drops down R. of Taffy—Trilby's eyes turn till they meet Svengali's, then she rises quietly, takes Kaw's arm, and they go out together R.1 E. Svengali makes a step to follow her—takes flowers. He is L. Billee is L.C.).

BILLEE *(coming down R.C.).* Svengali, I hold myself responsible for all I said to your wife. We are on French soil, and I await your orders.[221]

SVENGALI *(back to audience—with a grin of hatred).* You are brave, my young friend, but you shall not lack provocation.

(Strikes Billee in face with Trilby's bouquet. Billee attempts to strike Svengali—Laird restrains him and swings Billee up C. Laird goes to D.R.2 as if to bar door—Svengali crosses to C. where Taffy meets him and catches him by the throat).

TAFFY *(R.C.).* Leave him to me.

(Shaking Svengali, who is powerless in his grasp).

I'm glad to get this chance, Svengali.

SVENGALI *(L.C.—struggling and gasping).* Coward! I will send you my seconds.[222]

TAFFY. You are brave, my friend, but ha! you haven't lacked provocation.

(Throws him off, dusting hands. Svengali falls in a heap C. Gecko rushes forward from behind and shakes his fist over the prostrate Svengali).

GECKO *(comes down).* Ah, you who beat women, let us see how you now like to be beaten yourself.

(Svengali makes effort to rise, but falls back).

BILLEE *(coming down).* You mean to say that he struck Trilby?

GECKO. Struck her? Oui, she never complained to me, I never guessed it, but I heard her say it just now—so soft, so gentle. "Do not beat me, Svengali."

(They make angry movement towards Svengali).

SVENGALI *(hand to heart, very feebly totters over to table L.).* My heart, my heart! *(Falls heavily on seat).*

(Taffy turns away in disgust).

GECKO *(L.C.).* He is killing her.

BILLEE *(C.).* Our Trilby?

GECKO *(L.C.—solemnly).* No, it is not!

TAFFY, LAIRD and BILLEE *(R.C. and C.).* What?

---

221 He is taunting Svengali to call for a duel.
222 Svengali takes the bait for the duel: he will send representatives to arrange the place and terms of the fight.

GECKO *(L.C.)*. It is Svengali's Trilby, not your Trilby.

(Svengali rises from table, turns feebly to protest, his face very white. He sinks back again).

LAIRD *(R. corner)*. What do you mean, Gecko?

GECKO *(L.C.)*. There are two Trilbys. There is the Trilby you know, who cannot sing one note in tune. That is the Trilby we love—oui, Messieurs! For even I, Gecko, love her as one loves an only love, an only sister, an only child. And all at once this Svengali, this magician—

(All turn to Svengali, who is listening with a ghastly look on his face).

can with one look of his eye, one wave of his hand, turn her into another Trilby, and she becomes a mere singing machine, just the unconscious voice that Svengali sings with, so that when his Trilby is singing our Trilby has ceased to exist. Our Trilby is fast asleep—our Trilby is dead *(sinks on one knee)*.

(Music on stage—"Ben Bolt"—Laird goes hastily up to the window R.2 E.).

TAFFY. Then, Gecko, Trilby cannot sing unless Svengali is present.

GECKO *(rises)*. Not a note.

BILLEE. But, think—the song she just went to sing.

(Laird flings open the curtains of window).

GECKO *(crosses to R.2 E.—striking forehead)*. Madre di Dio,[223] I forgot.

(Music stops).

LAIRD *(at opening R.3 with opera glass. Pointing down)*. Look! what has happened? The audience has risen to its feet. There's an uproar.

DODOR *(enter from L. opening)*. Ah, my friends, such a scene. Trilby sang "Ben Bolt" just as she sang it in the studios. Hideous! Grotesque!

TAFFY. Gecko was right! That demon had hypnotized her.

ZOUZOU *(enter from C. opening)*. Oh, mes enfants, mes enfants! Pandemonium has broken loose in the Cirque, you never heard such a row as the gallery is making—hoots, hisses, cat-calls, cock-crows.

LAIRD *(at opening)*. We must do something; we can't leave her unprotected.

ANTONY *(enter from R.1 E.)*. Trilby turned on the mob like a lioness. "What's all this about," she cried. "Why have you brought me here? I won't sing another note" *(movement to R.1 E.)*.

TAFFY. Come, everybody, let us bring her from the stage.

LORIMER *(enter from R.1 E.)*. Curtain has been rung down.

(Music stops).

KAW *(enter from R.1 E., furiously, he crosses to Svengali)*. Svengali, Svengali, why didn't you come to my help? Damn you, sir, don't you know that your wife has gone mad—yes, stark, staring mad upon the stage. Come to her at once. Do you hear, man? Are you drunk?

(Svengali rises slowly. He is about to leave table; looks at Taffy with horrible grin of hatred; then throws up his hands and falls forward[224] on the table).

---

223 Mother of God.
224 Reviews specify that Tree fell backwards over the table.

GECKO. His heart, listen!

TAFFY *(his ear on Svengali's heart)*. Dead!

(Music in orchestra. Trilby's voice heard off R., all are startled).

TRILBY *(outside)*. I won't sing—not a note. *(She enters—looks around).*

(The men form a screen before table L.).

Where am I? *(See Billee)* Why, Billee—Taffy—Sandy. *(Hand to forehead)* Why are you here? And Svengali? Where is he?

LAIRD. He has gone to the carriage, Trilby, let me escort you. Come—

(She goes on his arm—the men still forming a screen before Svengali's body, and bowing to Trilby).

Act IV

No Music. Hotel Bristol, Place Vendôme, Paris,[225] *five days later. Four in the afternoon. Philippe (a footman) entering, followed by Dodor, Antony, and Lorimer talking earnestly.*

DODOR *(to Philippe)*. Our cards to Madame Svengali. Ask if she is well enough to see us.

PHILIPPE. Oui, Monsieur *(exit L.)*.

ANTONY *(examining presents)*. Who dreamed we should ever call on Trilby at the Bristol—hostelry of kings?

LORIMER. Poor Trilby! She'd give a cycle[226] of the Bristol for an hour of the Latin Quarter *(sits, turns over pages of illustrated paper)*.

DODOR. Whew! What swells! The Prince of Wales wishes to know—*(Taking card)* the British Ambassador wishes to know—*(Taking card)* the Emperor and Empress of the French[227] wish to know ... Everybody in Paris wishes to know if there is better news of Madame Svengali.

ANTONY. And see these flowers ...

DODOR. Trilby has gone up in the world.

(Antony sits at piano and strums. Re-enter Philippe).

PHILIPPE. Madame Svengali is considerably better today, and will be happy to see Monsieur de Lafarce and his friends in a few minutes. *(Low to Dodor)* Monsieur, the three English gentlemen and Monsieur Gecko, the violinist, are at present with the doctors, who are holding a consultation in another room of the hotel *(bows and exits at door back)*.

(Dodor sits before fire—takes up poker).

ANTONY *(turning on piano stool)*. So Trilby's mending, eh, Dodor?

DODOR *(tapping the logs)*. We shall hear from the doctors soon.

LORIMER. What on earth was the secret of Svengali's control of her?

---

225 Altered in one prompt book to "the old studio."

226 Long indefinite period.

227 Louis-Napoléon Bonaparte was elected President of the Republic in 1848. Following a *coup d'état* in 1851, he was installed as dictator; he was crowned Napoleon III the following year and ruled until 1870.

DODOR (*reflectively*). Heaven only knows! Gecko and the "trois Angliches" have some mystery between them.

(*Re-enter Philippe, door at back*).

PHILIPPE (*announcing*). Monsieur le Duc de la Rochemartel.

(*Enter Zouzou. He is preoccupied; he carries photograph in envelope. Exit Philippe*).

DODOR. Hallo Zouzou!
ZOUZOU (*sitting C.*). Ha, you are there. Bonjour, cher.[228] (*Pause then with air of great anxiety*) Oh, la la!
ANTONY. What's the matter, my bold Zouzou?
ZOUZOU. Nothing.
LORIMER. One would think you had seen a ghost.
ZOUZOU. I have.

(*Antony and Lorimer laugh*).

DODOR. Ho, ho! Whose ghost have you seen, Zouzou?
ZOUZOU. Svengali's.

(*All laugh*).

DODOR. It was that Welsh rarebit[229] last night at Brébaut's.[230]
ZOUZOU (*rising and walking up and down*). It was not the Welsh rarebit; it was Svengali. Don't I know Svengali from a Welsh rarebit? Oh! it's no use, boys. Ever since that fellow died across the table at the Bashibazouks, his eyes have haunted me, his voice has haunted me, his laugh has haunted me. I seem to meet him everywhere. Bootmaker brings a bill; I look at him—Svengali. Club waiter gets a brandy and soda—Svengali. Cabman drives me to theatre—Svengali. And now I'm within an ace of[231] believing that I've received a message from Svengali.

(*All laugh*).

DODOR. That's rich. A message from the dead! Ho, ho!
ZOUZOU (*worried*). Don't laugh, Dodor; you annoy me. I tell you that two hours ago I was dressing for the Bois,[232] when Jean, my man, brought in a strange looking post office agent with a registered letter. The writing was unknown to me. The envelope was covered with strange postmarks; and I was going to ask questions of the agent—a big greasy creature with a worn overcoat and a muffler that half concealed his face—when the fancy came to me—came to me in a flash—that it was Svengali as we knew him in the studios five years ago.
DODOR. Bah!
ZOUZOU. He went without a word, leaving me with the letter staring like a fool; and, as he passed down the stairs, I'll swear that Svengali's horrible laugh came up. What do you say to that?
DODOR. I recur to my theory of the Welsh rarebit.
ZOUZOU. All right. Then look at this envelope (*hands envelope to Dodor*).

---

228 My dear.
229 A dish of melted cheese on toasted bread.
230 A restaurant on the Boulevard Montmartre.
231 On the very point, or within a hair's breadth.
232 The Bois de Boulogne, a newly created park on the outskirts of Paris, popular for horseback riding and promenading.

DODOR (*looking at it*). The postmarks are queer: Skateringsburg, Tashkend.[233] It's an envelope that has travelled. (*Hands it back*) What's in it?

ZOUZOU. A photograph.

(*Antony and Lorimer come behind him*).

Svengali himself.

ANTONY. Hungarian uniform.[234]

LORIMER. Stunning photo.

ZOUZOU. Yes, he looks straight out of the picture—straight at you. But he was a damned blackguard.

DODOR. Why did they send it to you?

ZOUZOU. Who knows? A sheet of coarse paper was wrapped round it, and on this was scrawled: "Monsieur le Duc, you are charged—as you love the living and respect the dead—to deliver this photograph to Madame Svengali." But I doubt if it's safe to let Trilby have it.

DODOR. Safe! Why not?

ZOUZOU. I believe she's still a little shaky (*touching forehead*) here. They say she took the news of Svengali's death with wonderful calmness.

ANTONY. She was his wife only in name.

ZOUZOU. Well, we'll keep the photo out of sight till we know how she is and how she feels about Svengali.

LORIMER. Shhhh. Here she comes.

(*Zouzou hides photo under sofa cushion. Trilby appears at curtained door L.[235] She is dressed simply, but richly. Madame Vinard attends her*).

TRILBY (*faintly*). Zouzou, Dodor, dear friends.

(*They make a movement towards her. She waves them playfully back*).

No, don't touch me. Madame Vinard, I am quite strong enough to walk. (*She walks tottering to sofa C. where she lies*).

MADAME VINARD (*leaning over her*). My lamb, my poor lamb, I will bring your medicines—something nice, with grapes and big glass of cassis;[236] but do not let these magpies chatter. (*Shaking finger playfully at Zouzou and Dodor*) You hear, gredins de militaires?[237] You may talk, but no chatter (*exit L.*).

TRILBY (*smiling faintly*). Dear Madame Vinard. (*To the rest*) Ah! What it is to see you all again!

(*They gather round her*).

---

233 In the novel, the photograph arrives in a crate, having "seemed to have travelled all over Europe to London, out of some remote province in eastern Russia out of the mysterious East! The poisonous East—birthplace and home of an ill wind that blows nobody good" (*Trilby*, Eighth Part). The playwright is more specific by stipulating Tashkend (variant spelling of Tashkent, modern Uzbekistan); Skateringsburg may be a typo for Ekaterinburg, in central Russia, about 982 nautical miles (1820 km) north of Tashkent.

234 Dressed as a hussar.

235 As Trilby, Dorothea Baird's
   dress is again of ivory white c[r]épe de chêne, but this time simply accordion-pleated from the little square yoke of mellow-tinted lace to the hem, and only caught in loosely at the waist by a many-coloured Oriental girdle, with long flowing angel sleeves, leaving the white perfectly-shaped arms quite bare. ("Trilby," *Globe*, 31 October 1895)

236 Crème de cassis, a blackcurrant liqueur.

237 Military rascals.

ZOUZOU *(low to Dodor)*. Now let us see if we ought to give her the photo.

TRILBY. It makes one glad to be alive. Ah, j'aime tant ça, c'est le ciel.[238] I wonder I've a word of English left. Billee and the rest have gone to see the doctors and find out how soon I may be taken to England.

ZOUZOU. Are you anxious to sing in an English theatre?

TRILBY. Sing in an English theatre? I never sang at any theatre—except a few nights ago—if that big place was a theatre. And they didn't seem to like it. I'll take precious good care never to sing in a theatre again. How they howled. It all seems like a bad dream. Was it a dream, I wonder?

DODOR. Don't you remember singing at Vienna, Petersburg, lots of places?

TRILBY. What nonsense, Dodor! You're thinking of someone else. I never sang anywhere. I've been to Petersburg and Vienna; but I never sang there—good heavens!

ANTONY. But these cards, Trilby?

TRILBY. That's only a stupid compliment to poor Svengali; he was very famous.

LORIMER. And the diamonds, trinkets, and beautiful dress you had on.

TRILBY. Svengali gave them to me; he made lots of money.

LORIMER. Did he never try to teach you how to sing?

TRILBY. Oh, maïe, aïe, not he. Why, he always laughed when I tried to sing, and so did Gecko. It made them roar. I used to sing "Ben Bolt." They made me, just for fun. Then they would go into fits. I didn't mind a scrap. I'd no training, you know.

DODOR. And nobody ever told you that you were a famous singer?

TRILBY. You are making fun of me, Dodor. If I weren't so weak, I should be angry.

ZOUZOU *(low to Dodor)*. Decidedly we will *not* give her the photograph.

GECKO *(enter from door at back. Radiant)*. Ah, mes amis,[239] mes amis! Trilby, ma chérie,[240] all is well. The doctors say you will recover when you are taken away from Paris. *(Breaking down)* Merci, seigneur, merci![241]

(Trilby puts hand gently on his arm).

BILLEE *(enter with flowers. Coming joyously to Trilby)*. Has Gecko brought you the good news, dear? I stayed to get you these roses, dear. We are all crazy with delight.

(Trilby takes roses, and holds Billee's hand in hers. Enter Laird and Taffy C. from L.).

TAFFY *(pointing to Trilby and Billee)*. Ha, ha, ha, love among the roses. Paint that, you rogue of a Laird. There's a bit of colour that would make your old Toreadors blush *(down to R.)*.

(Trilby kisses her hand to him.[242] Re-enter Madame Vinard with medicine, cassis, and grapes on tray from L. Antony, Lorimer, and Dodor want to take the tray from Madame Vinard).

MADAME VINARD *(cries)*. Mais non, messieurs, mais non.

(This business brings all but Taffy, Zouzou, and the Laird around Trilby's sofa. Taffy, Zouzou, and Laird talk low R.C. Gecko plays the piano).

ZOUZOU. Well, what news from the doctors?

---

238 Ah, I love this, it is heaven.
239 My friends.
240 Darling.
241 Thank you, my lord, thank you.
242 Blows him a kiss.

TAFFY *(R.—low)*. She has every chance of recovery.

ZOUZOU *(R. corner)*. Ah!

TAFFY *(R.)*. It's only the memory of that cursed Svengali that's haunting her. She will recover if we can get Svengali out of her head.

ZOUZOU. But how to get Svengali out of her head? *(Crosses to Taffy)*.

LAIRD. By marrying her to Little Billee.

ZOUZOU *(amazed)*. Eh? *(Finger to lips)* Ah, I understand. *(Goes to sofa)* Well, as you're in safe hands, we'll be toddling, Trilby.

TRILBY. Don't go. Stay and smoke a cigarette, drink coffee and talk over old times.

ZOUZOU *(makes a signal to the rest)*. No thanks; we've all appointments at ... at ...

TRILBY *(smiling)*. The Austrian Embassy?

ZOUZOU *(confused)*. Not at the Austrian Embassy; but at ... *(low to Taffy)* I leave the photograph to you.

TAFFY. What photograph?

ZOUZOU *(not heeding)*. Good-bye, Trilby. *(Gives hand)* We'll come to see you every day. And don't forget to send us a bit of the wedding cake.

TRILBY *(wondering)*. Wedding cake?

ZOUZOU *(hastily)*. Good-bye.

(Business: Zouzou).

ZOUZOU, DODOR, ANTONY, and LORIMER. À la mariée. *(They drink imaginary toast, kiss their hands to Trilby and exit)*.

TRILBY. Dear fellows! What do they mean?

(Laird and Taffy sit on sofa near her).

TAFFY. Trilby, the doctors give us splendid reports of you *(crosses to L.)*.

TRILBY. Do they?

(Billee presses her hand).

LAIRD *(behind Trilby)*. You've just had a peculiar sort of brain fever,[243] and you've come through it grandly; and we're going to get all this singing and nonsense out of your head and send you away from Paris.

TRILBY *(seated L. of table L. Softly)*. With Madame Vinard?

LAIRD. No, with Little Billee—as his wife.

TRILBY *(with gentle surprise)*. What?

TAFFY. Yes, Trilby, you're getting stronger every minute, and we want to pack you happily off as Little Billee's wife.

TRILBY. Now, I am sure this is a dream.

TAFFY *(L.)*. Little Billee holds you to your promise of five years ago. You and he will begin a new life together, and everything that has gone will be forgotten.

MADAME VINARD *(enters to collect the tray)*. Run away, chatterboxes. Trilby must sleep. Run away.

PHILIPPE *(enter at back)*. The Reverend Thomas Bagot.

(General movement of alarm and annoyance. Enter the Reverend in travelling things. Exit Philippe).

---

243 Victorian designation for meningitis, encephalitis, typhus, or other severe fevers with brain complications.

REV. BAGOT. Ah, I trust I have arrived in time. *(Sees Trilby)* I have. Good, good. Perhaps you don't remember me, Madame Svengali. I am Billee's uncle *(offers hand)*.

TRILBY *(taking it)*. I remember you very well, Mr. Bagot.

REV. BAGOT. My sister-in-law sent to me as soon as she heard of your ... *(checks himself—coughs)* illness. How do you do, Mr. Wynne? And Mr. McAlister? *(Shakes hands)*.

TAFFY. You have arrived in time to give your consent to Trilby's marriage with your nephew.

REV. BAGOT *(startled)*. What?

LAIRD. Trilby might have had her pick of the universe.

REV. BAGOT *(warming his back at fire)*. No doubt, but ... but so shortly after this shocking affair of Svengali.

TAFFY *(low, but threatening)*. Don't talk of Svengali.

REV. BAGOT. Eh, why not?

(Gesture of Taffy, the Reverend subsides).

Has the lady been confirmed?[244]

LAIRD *(drily)*. Probably not.

REV. BAGOT. Oh dear, oh dear—and then think of public opinion, of the days when she lived in the Latin Quarter—sitting to painters and sculptors. So attractive as she is ... *(correcting himself)* was ...

BILLEE. It's no question of Trilby's worthiness, Uncle Thomas, it's a question of mine.

REV. BAGOT. Yours? Good gracious! You can't marry a woman ... less than a week after ... *(coughs)*.

TAFFY *(breaking in)*. I think tea's in the library. We shall have no difficulty in persuading Mr. Bagot, I think *(picking up cards)*.

REV. BAGOT. Really my dear sir ... you must admit it is unprecedented. The papers are still full of Svengali and ...

LAIRD *(reading card)*. "The Emperor and Empress of the French wish to know" ... *(looking up)* Ah, we'll join you, Mr. Bagot.

(Exeunt Taffy, Laird, and the Reverend L. Then Gecko).

TRILBY. Billee, it's real, is it not? All is going to be as it used to be? *(Playfully)* I'm afraid that Barbizon cottage is a tumble-down ruin now; but we'll live in it, won't we—ruin or no ruin? Oh, my love, my love, I'm so happy. And I thought at one time I was going to die.

BILLEE. Trilby, if you had died, I could not have long survived you.

TRILBY. Then I won't die, there—never, never. I'll laugh, I'll sing "Ben Bolt." I'll dance as I danced at the Chaumière. But go, dear. Don't leave your uncle to Sandy and Taffy. We ought to thank him for coming to marry us.

BILLEE *(earnestly)*. Trilby, the shadows have passed from our lives.

TRILBY. Yes, we've had to wait long for our happiness, dear—ever so long. But it's here at last.

(Billee kisses her and exits R. Trilby is left alone).

Billee's wife. I hardly dare say the words over to myself. I haven't been good enough to marry him. But much is forgiven to those who love, and much, I hope will be forgiven to me. *(Rises. Goes toward sofa, raises cushion, finds photo)* What's that? *(Picks up photo—looks at it intently)* Svengali's portrait. In his

---

244 A rite of initiation bestowing full church membership; in Roman Catholicism and the Church of England it occurs in adolescence.

Hungarian uniform. *(Wondering, sits)* Where did it come from? *(Screams)* Ah, don't look at me like that, Svengali. Take your eyes away. Take your eyes away. *(Pause. The photograph fascinates her. Finally the hand which holds it falls beside her, she begins to talk to herself)* Once more? What? The whole song over again. Very well, not too quickly at first. Do mark the time clearly, Svengali. I can hardly see. Everything is so dark. Come, Gecko, give me the note. *(Her head moves side to side as though she were singing.)* There! Is that better, Svengali. I'm glad. I am tired, really tired. I am going to sleep. *(Her head falls back. Then very faintly she whispers)* Svengali! Svengali! Svengali!

(Enter Madame Vinard from R. She sees Trilby and supposing her to be asleep, turns down the lights. Then she crosses fondly to Trilby, looks at her face, is startled, looks again, gives cry of horror and retreats to door L.).

MADAME VINARD. Ah, messieurs, messieurs! *(Exit L.).*

The Finding of Nancy (1902)

Just after the turn of the century, the Dramatists' Club in New York and the Playgoers' Club in London each announced contests for the best new play. George Alexander, the dignified actor-manager who had produced Oscar Wilde's *The Importance of Being Earnest* at the St. James's Theatre in 1895, promised to produce whatever work the London committee should select; Daniel Frohman, who brought many of Alexander's hits to New York, promised to stage the American winner at Daly's.[1] New York came up dry; however, London chose *The Finding of Nancy* by the schoolteacher and novelist Netta Syrett. She was a published author yet one of "the unacted."[2] A litmus test of critical opinion and practical dramaturgy, *The Finding of Nancy* delineates social issues that were debated at the brink of the new century. Though most critics found meritorious the play's situation of a woman trapped by class and propriety into spinsterhood, they quibbled over precisely how Syrett turned away from—or in some cases toward—modernity and feminist self-determination.

The subject matter of Syrett's play, like her work for the literary quarterly *The Yellow Book*,[3] reflects her insight into women's experience of loveless relationships and her ambivalence about marital commitment. In action as well as inaction, her female protagonists portray the social and emotional constraints that box them in. Though unconventional in the degree to which they recognize their desire to act autonomously, they suffer from self-imposed Victorian gender constraints that prevent them from publicly bursting the fetters of feminine modesty. As a young woman, well bred but now entirely dependent on her earnings as a typist, the protagonist of *The Finding of Nancy* is hardly a feminist success story.[4] As Max Beerbohm put it, because such women are

> too fastidious to associate on equal terms with the class with which they are in contact, and too poor and too busy to associate on any terms with their own class (even if their own class encouraged them at all to do so), they are peculiarly stranded, thrown back on themselves and on the contemplation of their wretched present and future. Having little or no chance of marriage, they know that they will probably go down to their graves without ever getting off the miserable path which they are treading. Between them and their graves lies one long, bleak, steep vista of drudgery. There is no apparent escape for them except in a defiance of that moral code to which instinctively they cling. In such a life as theirs, in such bitterness as that life must foster in them, what material for a modern dramatist![5]

Established dramatists, even those—such as Arthur Wing Pinero, Sydney Grundy, and Henry Arthur Jones—who made a mark through representing daring women, focused exclusively on the leisured classes. Working-class women were a staple of musical comedy plots by this time, and at the Gaiety Theatre these women sported great physical beauty and infectious vivacity, and so had class mobility to marry up the social ladder, but that was a theatrical convention rather than real women's lived experience.[6] Syrett's

---

1   "The Stage in Other Lands," *The Sun* (New York), 25 May 1902.

2   "St. James's Theatre," *Times* (London), 9 May 1902: 8; see also Katherine Newey, *Women's Theatre Writing in Victorian Britain* (Basingstoke: Palgrave Macmillan, 2005), 29-34.

3   Netta Syrett, "Thy Heart's Desire," *Yellow Book* 2 (July 1894): 225-55; reprinted in *A New Woman Reader: Fiction, Articles, Drama of the 1890s*, edited by Carolyn Christensen Nelson (Peterborough: Broadview, 2000), 52-56; and http://www.classicreader.com/book/2966/1/ (accessed 23 June 2010).

4   A useful comparison may be made with George Gissing's 1893 novel *The Odd Women* in which typewriting is one of the professions espoused for genteel women fallen upon hard times.

5   [Max Beerbohm,] "Miss Syrett's Play," *Saturday Review*, 17 May 1902: 633.

6   Peter Bailey, *Popular Culture and Performance in the Victorian City* (Cambridge: Cambridge UP, 1998), 175-93.

genteelly raised Nancy Thistleton has only spoken with one man in six months: Will Fielding, a theatre critic whom she met through a family connection. Though tethered to a wife who is an institutionalized alcoholic, Will offers Nancy the companionship and sympathy that she craves, as well as love. At the end of act 1, she agrees to become his mistress. She later recalls their years together—which transpire between acts—as a time of contented domesticity. As they are "too poor, and too obscure to attract comment," and as their acquaintances are unaware of the arrangement, the lovers' reputations suffer no ill effects. When Nancy inherits a small legacy, she moves out of her lodgings and begins to circulate in society. She relocates, alone, to the Riviera where she falls in love with Captain Egerton; Will follows her there and, after being turned down by Nancy, becomes engaged to a young woman whose father's connections will facilitate his political aspirations. At the end of act 3, Nancy, mistaking a message in a telegram, believes that Will has taken his life, and reveals the secret of their past—with socially disastrous results. She hastens back to London, where she breaks off her relationship with Egerton. The gentle conniving of a widowed friend puts Nancy and Will together for the last moments of act 4, and Nancy consents to resume the "old life" of contentment they had formerly enjoyed.

This is Syrett's first play, and though she had a flair for dialogue, she had no theatre experience whatsoever: she had never even been backstage. The rehearsals made her miserable and depressed, and she feared that, in taking minor roles, George Alexander and Herbert Beerbohm Tree—who had both pledged in advance to appear—sought to sabotage the production by making the play farcical. More importantly, however, the "ludicrous and hypocritical invective" wielded by Clement Scott, the critic of the *Daily Telegraph*, made an erroneous conflation of Nancy with Syrett, and the playwright was fired from her teaching job.[7] Dramaturgically also, the play became a minor *cause célèbre*, out of all proportion to its one matinee performance, albeit before celebrities.[8] The terms of critique—written about and for women—reveal how profoundly gendered the theatre was at the start of the new century. As one reviewer put it,

> it is a rather militant pamphlet on the subject of the social disabilities of women, addressed to the rather limited public which occupies itself with these questions. Moreover, it is not only restricted in its appeal but it is not treated with a very thorough knowledge of the theatre or of theatrical effect. On the other hand, the writing of the play is quite delightful. It shows a cultivated intelligence and a grace of style which one had almost begun to feel were banished from the stage.[9]

In other words, a play of limited appeal and inept theatrical prowess was also delightful, intelligent, and graceful. How could this be?

Genre Issues

If early-twentieth-century women playwrights put politics at the centre of their dramas, they warmed up to this by observing how "problem plays" by male playwrights of the 1890s dramatized the sexual

---

7   She subsequently focused full-time on writing. Netta Syrett, *The Sheltering Tree* (London: Geoffrey Bles, 1939), 116-27; Kerry Powell, "Gendering Victorian Theatre," in *The Cambridge History of British Theatre*, vol. 2, *1660 to 1895*, edited by Joseph Donohue (Cambridge: Cambridge UP, 2004), 365-66; and Newey, *Women's Theatre Writing*, 30-33. For background on Clement Scott, see Jacky Bratton, "Clement Scott, the Victorian Tribal Scribe," *Nineteenth Century Theatre and Film* 36, no. 1 (2009): 3-10.

8   Another playwriting contest, in 1843, also resulted in a female winner and this too engendered controversy. Ellen Donkin, "Mrs. Gore Gives Tit for Tat," in *Women and Playwriting in Nineteenth-Century Britain*, edited by Tracy C. Davis and Ellen Donkin (Cambridge: Cambridge UP, 1999), 54-74.

9   "The Theatre," *Speaker*, 17 May 1902: 191.

double standard in plots featuring a "woman with a past" (such as *The Second Mrs. Tanqueray*, *Lady Windermere's Fan*, *The Notorious Mrs. Ebbsmith*, and *The Profligate*). Plays by Edwardian women critically examine marriage (as in Elizabeth Baker's *Chains* and Lucy Clifford's *A Woman Alone*) and complicate women's private dilemmas in relation to work and family (see Cicely Hamilton's *Diana of Dobson's* and Githa Sowerby's *Rutherford and Son*).[10] *The Finding of Nancy* was written at a point when the problem play was turning into the overtly political play of gender that characterized the Edwardian period; as such, it introduces preoccupations characteristic of slightly later drama without making the political stakes so explicit. For example, a dowager comments on the "ideas" that are promulgated by "lady novelists" and hopes they do not infect her own marriageable daughter. She has found a copy of Henrik Ibsen's plays in her daughter's possession, and despite its being a full decade after the Ibsen controversy peaked, she has no idea what this means. Her companion's reaction is ironic:

> MRS. WINGFIELD *(concealing a smile)*. Ibsen! My dear, Mrs. Llewellyn. Burn it! Burn it. Most of it
> is traceable to him after all. It's he who has inoculated woman with the idea-germ, and given her
> the disease of thought. It's not too much to say that he's ruined the marriage market. A girl *thinks*
> nowadays, when it's her plain duty to marry.[11]

In Ibsen's social plays, women's sense of purposefulness and aspiration to self-realization are thwarted by stagnant marriages (*Little Eyolf* and *John Gabriel Borkman*), sexual longing (*The Lady from the Sea* and *Rosmersholm*), and unspecified yet unrealized potential (*Hedda Gabler* and *A Doll's House*). He spurred audiences and readers to reconsider their relationships, especially through modelling the psychological profiles of women and contrasting portraits of the subtle misogyny of self-absorbed men (*The Wild Duck* and *When We Dead Awaken*, as well as all the foregoing titles).

The "New Woman" drama emerged as a classification for British plays that reinterpreted Ibsen in a vernacular setting, taking into account the domestic and public realms more fully than the "problem plays" of the 1890s. *The Finding of Nancy* does not fully conform to this pattern but gives hints of it: the play opens with Nancy striving successfully in one of the newly emergent women's occupations; she proceeds to consciously weigh singlehood versus life with two different men; and other women represent circumstances from Nancy's past as well as her potential futures. But the play's conclusion is the most telling contrast with New Woman plays and fiction. It is also the most contentious aspect of critical reception.

Comedies end with marriage or the pairing of suitable couples for imminent wedlock. *The Game of Speculation*, *Ours*, and *Dorothy* all demonstrate this principle. To the extent that plays mix genres, the comedic element will manifest as a marriage plot, as *The Africans*, *Elphi Bey*, and *Trilby* all bear out. *The Finding of Nancy* is more complicated: one reviewer noted that the couplings of acts 2 and 3 have, despite the gentility of the surroundings, a tinge of farce in act 4, as Nancy treats Will "as Cyprienne in *Divorçons* treats her husband—sends with scant courtesy the gallant captain to the right-about and reunites her fate to that of her former lover."[12] Another critic finds Nancy's revelation that she has had a married lover "the beginnings of tragedy" though Syrett then reverts to "the timid way of sentimentality and melodrama" culminating in "the conventional happy ending" when Will and Nancy (though no one

---

10   Peter Raby, "Theatre of the 1890s: Breaking Down the Barriers," 187-203; and Susan Carlson and Kerry Powell, "Reimagining the Theatre: Women Playwrights of the Victorian and Edwardian Period," 245; both in *The Cambridge Companion to Victorian and Edwardian Theatre*, edited by Kerry Powell (Cambridge: Cambridge UP, 2004).

11   Syrett describes how she read Ibsen's plays aloud to her fellow schoolteachers in Swansea in the late 1880s, which resulted in "fierce arguments." Syrett, *Sheltering Tree*, 58.

12   *Athenaeum*, 17 May 1902: 636.

else) are united.[13] From another perspective, Nancy's ultimate choice may be so idiosyncratic that she has prototypes in neither real life nor drama.[14] A more progressive critic (and Syrett's friend from the *Yellow Book* circle), Max Beerbohm, applauds the "*tranche de la vie*" (slice of life) in act 1 but regrets the "decline into theatricals" thereafter.[15] What had begun as a legitimate and compelling question—"whether a woman should catch at any fair chance of the *joie de vivre* or pine away in waiting"—is cast aside by Syrett's "obvious temptation" to kill off Will's wife so he can remarry.[16] William Archer, the great critical champion of Ibsen in Britain, admired the *tête-à-têtes*—between Nancy and her confidante Isabel (a fellow toiler in drudgery, not yet escaped and still unloved), Nancy's explanation to Will in act 2 that she has changed sentiments, and the meeting of Will and Egerton—yet the "drama of sociology, foreshadowed in the first act" had by the third act "diverged into a drama of sentiment." Instead of scourging a social problem, *à la* Eugène Brieux, Syrett disregards form altogether in the manner of Maurice Donnay's *The Other Danger*. For Archer, the conflicting sentiments are not worked out but denied: in act 3 Nancy reveals her secret and discovers the depth of her feeling, leaving act 4 merely for reconciliation and matrimony. "These concluding acts, though not ill-written, are essentially fortuitous and trivial. They solve neither the sociological problem of the first act nor the sentimental problem of the second."[17]

Susan Carlson observes that reviewers of twentieth-century women's dramatic writing "generally will not attack a play on the basis of its politics alone. Instead, the most common criticisms of contemporary women's comic plays are based on structure and form."[18] Conventionally, in comedy men drive the action, and women exert agency only when in disguise or by means of the virtues that make them marriageable. Men woo; women are wooed. Women do not knowingly enter into illicit sexual relationships and then re-emerge into the social world unscathed or unscatheable. They do not inherit mid-play and proceed to seek a marriage partner without the benefit of a parent, guardian, or other guide.[19] However, these are the traits that make Nancy interesting—dramatically speaking—as well as modern. For her to experience early on the pleasures of quiet domesticity, then blossom forth into society, only to revert again to quiet domesticity with the same partner as before (yet legitimated the second time round), was apt to attract comment in 1902. But instead of critics admitting that they were scandalized, or even charging that the plot was implausible, they condemned the play as a mishmash that finally settled into sentimentality. While Syrett posits Nancy's actions as uniquely hers, borne of her dilemma rather than a model for all women, Max Beerbohm was alone among the London critics in prompting his readers to wonder how "these myriads of creatures, starved and stunted, deprived of all semblance of joy in life, do not feel themselves goaded irresistibly to uprise, and to defy and overturn the injustice of society, to assert and win for themselves ... those rights from which they are now precluded by mere accident of birth?"[20] Only women see the moral codes that bind them *and* seek escape. Syrett uses situation creatively, or perhaps naïvely, but she gives Nancy a *choice* that opts out of comedy's traditions of love-stricken maidens as well as subjugated shrews. According to the *Era*, however, Nancy was guilty of "fickleness ... a quality fatal to heroism," and from the moment she began to "shilly-shally," the play's failure was sealed.[21]

---

13 *Illustrated London News*, 17 May 1902: 708.

14 *Era*, 10 May 1902: 15.

15 *Saturday Review*; see Syrett, *Sheltering Tree*, 76.

16 *Times* (London), 9 May 1902: 8.

17 [William Archer], *World*, 14 May 1902: 30-31.

18 Susan Carlson, *Women and Comedy: Rewriting the British Theatrical Tradition* (Ann Arbor: U of Michigan P, 1991), 177.

19 As Charles James Mathews put it in 1852, little of the Parisian repertoire could be adapted for British audiences. See above, introduction to *A Game of Speculation*, pp. 218-19.

20 [Beerbohm,] "Miss Syrett's Play," 633.

21 *Era*, 10 May 1902: 15.

Interpretive Issues

To a late-nineteenth-century aesthete—such as Aubrey Beardsley, who like Syrett was a contributor to the *Yellow Book,* or his sister Mabel, who played Violet Stuart (Will's fiancée)[22]—a sincere and natural representation did not imply a realist representation. Paul Potter's play *Trilby* is neither aestheticist nor realist, yet in posing the question about how we distinguish between what is and what is not sincere and natural, *Trilby* uses both aestheticist and realist elements. In *Trilby,* song represents the thoroughness of Svengali's mesmeric hold on the unwitting Trilby while measuring the fidelity of one art form (as in the painting of Trilby's foot) against another (music, as a window onto true potential). Painting, like beauty, is merely superficial, whereas music is pure experience. While in Du Maurier's novel *Trilby* the incomparability between truth and appearance is narratively conveyed, it must be conveyed differently on stage. In performance, Trilby's voice is experiential, yet because theatre is inherently *mis*representational (audiences see pretences of reality, not reality *per se*), there are conventions of seeming real, pointing out the ambiguity and slippage of mimetic fidelity and liberties with strict accuracy, and the scaling-up necessary for legibility in a theatre. Whether through literature, illustration, or drama, aestheticism aspires to the condition of music because music transcends mimetic correspondences between art and reality and is not expected to represent reality faithfully. Thus, an aesthetic play aspires to be compelling while being freed from expressing anything specific; realist theatre not only reflects life but dramatizes the politics of living amongst others, setting out a significant problem. In aestheticism, significance is not holistic or cumulative but, as Alison Byerly puts it, "manifests itself in bursts or epiphanies that occur in a single moment" of experience. Nancy has two such epiphanies: calling Will back at the end of act 1, and expressing relief after hearing that Will is not dead at the end of act 3. This may not go as far as Walter Pater's or Oscar Wilde's dicta that reality should be avoided, but the epiphanies defend against any seamlessness between stage art and reality.[23]

The contrasts between female and male characters may, in a similar way, underline distinctions between the lifelike and the expeditious, or depth and surface. According to the *Illustrated London News,* Syrett wrote with "emotional poignancy and an undoubted dramatic instinct" to create young women that "are real flesh and blood, carefully observed types of existing modern womanhood." Her male characters, on the other hand, were barely credible (or, as the reviewer put it, Syrett "can scarcely ... draw men who are alive").[24] As placidly as Will exits after being rejected by Nancy in act 1, she is by contrast deeply agitated.

(Nancy stands passively while he turns away and goes out, shutting the door. She continues to stand a moment as if dazed, then crosses to typewriter, sits down and begins to work it mechanically. All at once she starts up with stifled cry).

NANCY *(incoherently).* Oh! I can't! I can't! Not alone! ... I shall go mad.

(Stands irresolutely for a second, then rushes to door which she flings open. Calls at first wildly, then in a tone which she tries to make natural.) Mr. Fielding! Mr. Fielding! *(She then comes back and stands in the middle of room with her back to the door).*

---

22   Syrett and Mabel Beardsley met when they were both teachers in a London school. Syrett suggested Beardsley for the part when Alexander expressed reservations about actresses in his employ speaking Violet Stuart's catty lines in act 2. Beardsley had left teaching for the stage, and though she appeared in many matinee performances, she never had a London success. Syrett, *Sheltering Tree,* 70-73.

·23   Alison Byerly, *Realism, Representation, and the Arts in Nineteenth-Century Literature* (Cambridge: Cambridge UP, 1997), 11, 189, 194, 12.

24   *Illustrated London News,* 17 May 1902: 708.

(Fielding enters, bewildered. Nancy slowly moves her head. At last she puts out her hand stretching it backward).

When she breaks up with Egerton in act 4, he turns on his heel and leaves. She is demonstrably distraught.

(Nancy stands a moment looking fixedly before her. She throws herself upon the sofa and buries her face in the cushion).

These melodramatic postures and gestures juxtapose emotional extremes within Nancy as well as between Nancy and her suitors. Nancy displays turmoil, but the men are the epitome of *sang-froid*: stoic and unidimensional. Though the play is sometimes stagey, it is conceivable that the strong acting possibilities were rendered effective and convincing by actresses. Isabel, likewise, is emotionally engaged in the action, fearing for Nancy, holding her physically back, marvelling at her choices, and measuring the dullness of her own life against her friend's. Though Nancy's life is dull, her inner life is tumultuous. The women live *intensely*, while the men are prosaic. In the final act, Mrs. Wingfield and Isabel exit, leaving Will alone on stage. He has just been notified by his fiancée that his engagement is broken and has learned from Mrs. Wingfield how Nancy reacted when she mistook the news in the telegram, yet he seems completely blasé.

(A moment and Nancy enters. She looks round for her friends and sees Fielding. Falls back, then makes as though she would rush to him. Finally checks herself).

FIELDING *(calmly)*. Mrs. Wingfield was mistaken about the tea. It doesn't seem to have been made, does it? *(Looking into tea pot)* But it's all ready. Let me!

Will's reversion to pouring tea is closer to T.W. Robertson's plays than Oscar Wilde's, and whereas Nancy uses the gestural vocabulary of melodrama, she signifies choices (or "finding," as in the title) unconventional for the stage. As one of the supporting men in the cast blurted "in no pleasant tone" during rehearsals, "You women have courage.... You say things we men wouldn't dare to say!"[25]

Performative Issues

Halfway through the performance, Max Beerbohm sent flowers to Syrett's box, with the note "Many congratulations. How well it is going!" The actors gave it "a swing and a verve," and all were at their best. Following each act, the audience's ovations compelled the cast to take multiple curtain calls, and at the end, "the audience rose *en masse* and yelled, shrieked, shouted, stamped, and nearly went mad." They demanded to see the author, and Syrett was required to improvise a speech.[26] Alexander's acting and business partner, Mary Moore, acclaimed the play, and though he considered putting on a succession of afternoon performances, he was dissuaded lest this "'sully the purity of the St. James's Theatre,'" reputed, as it was, for problem plays (including *The Second Mrs. Tanqueray*) and the plays of Oscar Wilde.[27]

More than thirty years after she was hired to perform at the Woolwich Royal Arsenal Theatre, Carlotta Addison played Mrs. Stuart in *The Finding of Nancy*. Among the younger players, Kitty Llewellyn was taken by Jean Mackinlay, the daughter of the eminent singer Antoinette Sterling. Her contemporary in the role of Nancy was Lilian Braithwaite, an ethereal beauty but as yet a minor player in George Alexander's company. The play presented the greatest opportunity to Braithwaite, who had made a personal appeal to

25   Syrett, *Sheltering Tree*, 119.

26   Ibid., 123.

27   Ibid., 122, 125-26. See also Kerry Powell, *Women and Victorian Theatre* (Cambridge: Cambridge UP, 1995), 145. Syrett's memory of Tree's and Alexander's input (as well as other details of the production) is dubious: she claims that Tree performed the waiter (a three-line part) and that the production occurred in May 1898.

Syrett to be cast as Nancy: the star-studded matinee was a great chance for her.[28] *The Finding of Nancy* has no part for a leading man: Will and Egerton are too generic to be coveted by any West End actor-manager. The roles taken by George Alexander and Herbert Beerbohm Tree are little more than walk-ons. These characters are highly desirable in the marriage stakes as rival suitors to Kitty Llewellyn, but Tree's has just one line so was far from choice (though he was well suited to play the German nobleman whom young women disparage). Unlike *Trilby, Ibsen's Ghost, The Relief of Lucknow, Ours*, and *The Game of Speculation*, therefore, *The Finding of Nancy* had no chance at a commercial West End run.

There are no sources of information about the staging or acting of the play apart from Syrett's autobiography and comments in newspapers. It would have been mounted with stock scenery and costumes to minimize financial outlay. This was not unusual for experimental matinees or benefits, such as this one, and did not warrant comment in the press. The acting was generally lauded though critics sniped that most of the actors had too little to work with through much of the play.

Formerly called *A Woman's Love Story* and then *A Modern Love Story*, the play was licensed under the title *A Doubtful Case*.[29] Syrett settled on the new title, *The Finding of Nancy*, during rehearsals. As a "doubtful case," it emphasizes the audience's perception of Nancy and Will's actions as something to be dreaded or an exterior judgement connoting the divided or uncertain morality of their relationship. As the "finding" of Nancy, it signals a puzzle in which a spectator is invited to imagine the outcome from Nancy's perspective. What is Nancy's "finding"? Is it something Nancy discovers (as if that something existed separately from her), or is it Nancy's invention (devised by her ingenuity)? Does it pertain to her maintenance or support, as in her findings (at her own cost)? Is this an expense of money, time, reputation, or heart? Alternatively, it may be a finding in the sense of a judicial examination: in which case it can be a judge's decree—as if Nancy assesses herself—or a jury's verdict—in the same manner that neutral peers look upon the facts of her case and pronounce guilt or innocence. Perhaps this is what appealed to the Playgoers' Club in choosing the piece: it posits ways for audience members to regard the central character as their contemporary and to take a position on her life.

Editing Issues

The Finding of Nancy had just one performance and was never published. The following edition is founded on the licensing copy, the only surviving version. As such, it is somewhat sparing with stage directions. Entrances and exits have been clarified, but other markers of delivery, affect, and movement must be inferred. Some of the group business in acts 2 and 3 is standard to the Edwardian stage, and experienced actors would have known how to block themselves in rehearsal. Less conventional moments, such as by-play between Will and Nancy, were rehearsed in Syrett's lodgings until Braithwaite and C. Aubrey Smith achieved just the right note.[30] The licensed typescript contains a few holograph additions and substitutions, but a curious omission of question marks after Isabel's (and in one instance Mrs. Wingfield's) interrogatives is not corrected. These have been retained for this edition in case the intention was to connote a rhetorical tone of delivery.

---

28   Syrett, *Sheltering Tree*, 118.
29   Harvard Theatre Collection, *The Finding of Nancy* clippings file; and British Library Add MS LC Plays 1902/14.
30   Syrett, *Sheltering Tree*, 119.

The Finding of Nancy[31]

BY NETTA SYRETT

First performed at the St. James's Theatre, 8 May 1902, as a benefit for the Actors' Benevolent Fund.

Nancy Thistleton, secretary in a typewriting office	Lilian Braithwaite
Isabel Ferris, her friend; assistant teacher in the Manchester School of Art	Madge McIntosh
Will Fielding	C. Aubrey Smith
Captain Egerton	H.R. Hignett
Reginald Ismay	George Alexander
Count Karl	H. Beerbohm Tree
Mrs. Wingfield	M. Talbot
Mrs. Llewellyn	Ada Ferrar
Kitty Llewellyn, her daughter	Jean Mackinlay
Mrs. Mary Stuart, cousin to Will Fielding	Carlotta Addison
Violet Stuart, her daughter	Mabel Beardsley
Miss Adair	May Saker
Mrs. Moore, the porter's wife at Granby Street Chambers	Bessie Page
Waiter	Carter Bligh
Visitors at the Hotel Beau Séjour	Messrs. B. Hatteras, E. Dennison, Alfred Wareing, and Scott; Misses Mabel DuBois, Muriel Myles, Victoria Millbank, and Mabel Adair

Act I

A room in the Granby Street Chambers for women. The room is furnished very simply, but with evident taste. Mrs. Moore putting tea things, which she fetches from an open cupboard, onto the table. A knock: Isabel Ferris at door.

ISABEL. Miss Thistleton?

MRS. MOORE *(volubly).* No, Miss she ain't in yet. But she told me she was expecting you, Miss, and you was please to wite.[32]

ISABEL *(examining things in room).* She is generally back by this time, isn't she?

MRS. MOORE *(continuing to lay the table).* Well, Miss, it varies as you may sy. Sometimes she's even later. They work 'er cruel 'ard at that there orfice, to *my* thinking.

ISABEL. I was afraid so.

---

31   Based on British Library Add MS LC Plays 1902/14.
32   Mrs. Moore's Cockney accent is rendered phonetically.

MRS. MOORE. Yes, Miss. Reg'ler shime it is. As nice a young lidy as ever stepped, and a pleasure to wite on, slavin' all day long, and of evenings clickin' awy on that there 'orrid thing (*pointing with disgust to typewriter on side table*).

ISABEL (*with concern*). Oh! does she do that at night?

MRS. MOORE. She do, Miss, ruinin' a pair of eyes which God Almight gave 'er ter mike fools of the men with, over a rubbishin' clicking machine that can't mike no response! In my young days, Miss, there weren't no typewriters, but there was plenty of 'usbands. I've 'ad three.

ISABEL (*laughing*). Really?

MRS. MOORE. Yes, Miss. That there typewriter I call a fair insult to Providence; let alone flying in its face.

ISABEL (*amused*). Why, how do you mean?

MRS. MOORE. I don't know as I can rightly expline, Miss, 'cept it seems to me things is all different to what they used to be. There's many a young lidy clickin' on a typewriter that ought ter be at 'ome lookin' after 'er babies with a lovin' 'usband comin' 'ome about tea-time. Sez they to the men "we'll show you we can work sime as you." An' they do. They click away all dy, an' git somethin' less than a 'undred a year to show for it!

ISABEL. It's a mistake, you think?

MRS. MOORE (*with conviction*). It's a mistake that monkeys even are above makin', Miss. They don't talk you know for fear of bein' mide to work. Women ain't satisfied with talkin' (though you'd think they might be), they must needs work too! "To show an independent spirit" sez they. To show 'ow near they can come to starvin' sez I! (*Shaking her head*) I've seen too much of it!

(*The door opens hurriedly. Nancy enters, she has flowers in her hand*).

ISABEL. Nancy!

NANCY. My dear child!

(*They kiss*).

I'm so sorry I'm late. Those wretches at the office as usual. (*To Mrs. Moore*) Is tea ready, Mrs. Moore?

MRS. MOORE. The kettle's on the fire, Miss, and the toast's on the 'ob, and I'll bring up the tea-cakes, when—

NANCY. Thanks so much! Yes, I'll ring.

(*Exit Mrs. Moore*).

ISABEL (*laughing as she puts her arm round Nancy*). Let me at least congratulate you upon your landlady.

NANCY. Isn't she delicious! Has she been discoursing on the marriage question? That's her great subject. Wait! I'll just take off my hat!

(*She goes quickly into bedroom, R. Isabel meanwhile looks at room with interest, taking up books, etc. Nancy reappears. She is in a plain serge[33] gown with tie, collar and cuffs*).

NANCY (*kneeling beside Isabel, and fastening bunch of violets in her dress*). There! Violets for you. It is nice to see you! But why can't you stay longer?

ISABEL. My train leaves at seven o'clock, dear child, I must start at six!

NANCY. Then I'll make tea at once. (*Puts kettle on the fire*) Work begins tomorrow then?

ISABEL (*sighing*). Yes. Tomorrow!

---

33   Durable worsted wool.

NANCY. And you are still boarding at the same place? Do you like it?

ISABEL. At the Art Students' boarding house, yes. Like it? *(She shrugs her shoulders)*. It's dull of course. Very dull. But it's convenient because it's so near the Art School. I'm standing all day you see, and I'm worn out by the time evening comes.

NANCY *(pouring water into teapot)*. I should think so. But isn't it trying to see so much of the students? Girls you are teaching all day long?

ISABEL *(dreary)*. I sometimes forget there are any other human beings in existence. The world is for me a vast Art School with students, students everywhere—

NANCY. And not a drop to drink!

ISABEL *(laughs)*. Well! there's cocoa. *(With a changed tone)* Oh yes! it's deadly dull and monotonous when one has time to think about it. Sometimes, when the girls giggle and chatter more inanely than usual I make up my mind to take furnished rooms. But *(meditatively)* I don't think I could stand the loneliness!

NANCY *(significantly)*. I wouldn't try if I were you!

ISABEL. But you seem very comfortable here. How is this place worked exactly?

NANCY. The whole block is let out into rooms you see, and Mrs. Moore the porter's wife gives attendance. Dear old thing, she gives me far more attendance than I pay for, such is the love she bears me.

ISABEL *(looking at her)*. Yes; you were born to be spoilt ... you've been dreadfully extravagant Nancy. Your pennies go more often upon your room than upon your dinner evidently.

NANCY *(shrugging her shoulders)*. Well! one can't both dine and furnish on eighty pounds a year you know! And I prefer chairs to mutton! There! tea's ready. Come and sit down. This is the fattest of the cushions. *(Puts it at back of Isabel's chair)* Take your hat off. That's right.

(Enter Mrs. Moore with plate of cakes).

MRS. MOORE. 'Ere's the cikes Miss: piping 'ot you'll find them ... And a letter, Miss.

NANCY *(carelessly, as she passes cakes to Isabel)*. Oh! just put it on the table please.

(Exit Mrs. Moore).

NANCY *(to Isabel)*. Sugar?

ISABEL *(taking cup absently, and looking at her friend)*. Thanks—yes. Do you know you're getting awfully pretty, Nancy? What have you been doing to yourself?

NANCY *(delightedly)*. Am I? I'm so glad! Isabel you're an angel. *(She blows her a kiss.)* But I'm afraid I'm only *inclined* to be pretty, and I want to be beautiful—*beautiful*! Give me a pretty face, and an—an opportunity, and I will make ridiculous—the click of a typewriter for instance.

ISABEL. I believe you would.

NANCY *(taking box of cigarettes from mantelpiece and offering them to Isabel)*. Will you try one? I'm afraid it would be wasted on you. I'm morally certain you would eat the end.

ISABEL *(refusing with a smile)*. Surely it's an expensive luxury? You really are abominably extravagant Nancy.

NANCY. These were given to me. *(She lights one. Slight pause)* Mr. Fielding gave them to me.

ISABEL. Who is Mr. Fielding?

NANCY *(in constrained voice, looking at end of cigarette)*. He has the proud distinction of being the only man of my acquaintance.

ISABEL. But that scarcely explains him.

NANCY. Do you want him explained? Well—I don't know what there is to say. I met him at the Stuarts'.

ISABEL. The Stuarts'?

NANCY. Don't you remember old Miss Prendergast who came to Streamford just before Father died, and made such a fuss about him?

ISABEL. Oh yes. That was the year we both left Streamford—to make our fortunes.

NANCY *(with short laugh)*. To make our fortunes—yes ... Well, Mrs. Stuart is old Miss Prendergast's niece. She brought her to call on me when I came to town three years ago and insisted upon her sending me invitations to her parties.

ISABEL. And you meet this Mr. Fielding at Mrs. Stuart's?

NANCY. Not now. Old Miss Prendergast died two years ago you know, so Mrs. Stuart is spared the painful necessity of befriending all her aunt's poor protégés.

ISABEL *(indignantly)*. And they don't ask you now?

NANCY. Oh no! I've seen nothing of them for two years. Miss Prendergast left them the money after all, so there's no need you see.

ISABEL. But this Mr. Fielding?

NANCY. Ah! that's a different matter. A *man's* interest in you doesn't cease because his aunt leaves him money.

ISABEL. But where do you meet him now?

NANCY. Oh!—he sends me theatre tickets occasionally. He's dramatic critic on one of the papers, among other things. Then there are picture galleries, on Saturdays sometimes ... and he's been here once or twice ... And that's all I think. He's abroad now.

(Isabel is silent).

NANCY *(glancing at her)*. You see I can't afford a chaperon on eighty pounds, can I?

ISABEL *(slowly)*. No. It's all right of course, but—

NANCY *(gets up and lights fresh cigarette)*. Besides *(deliberately)* he's his own chaperon. He's married.

ISABEL *(sharply)*. Nancy!—You are not a baby.

NANCY. No. Unfortunately I am not. I am twenty-six. I have two or three remaining years of youth. I don't want to waste them.

ISABEL. But Nancy! What are you thinking about? A married man?—and his wife? Surely you consider—

NANCY *(shortly)*. There's nothing to consider. He hasn't lived with her for ten years. They are separated. It's not a case for divorce. She is engaged in drinking herself to death. But slowly—very slowly. She will probably outlive him.

ISABEL *(timidly)*. Nancy, you don't care for him?

NANCY *(after a pause)*. No.

ISABEL *(in a relieved tone)*. But all the same isn't it rather foolish to see much of him. He may fall in love with you, and then—

NANCY *(half smiling)*. Oh well! of course—

ISABEL *(severely)*. You don't encourage him?

NANCY *(hastily)*. Of course not. I *dis*courage him. But *(flippantly)* you must admit it would be rather slow if there were no occasion.

ISABEL *(glances at her in troubled way, then after pause)*. Nancy ... I'm going in half an hour. It's just possible we may not meet again for years. Father gets weaker, and I must spend every holiday with him at Streamford. I don't want to force confidences ... but we've been practically brought up together, and we've always been friends ...—Won't you be serious?

NANCY (*with a sudden change in manner*). Serious? Heaven knows I am serious enough. Oh Isabel! *you* ought to know, you who also lead a cramped narrow life, like mine. Life? What am I talking about? Do we, and thousands of women like us live at all?

ISABEL. No, you are right. It isn't life.

NANCY. Think! Listen! Let me state the case. My case; your case: the case of most girls nowadays whom (*scornfully*) "it is so nice to see independent and leading their own lives." Oh! we who know what leading our own lives means! Doesn't it make you laugh when you think of it? (*Laughs bitterly*) Take my existence. It will do. It is typical. Take any day—they are all alike. In the morning I walk to the office, I work till one. At one I go to the nearest A.B.C. for lunch.[34] Back again at two. Click, click, till five. Then tea, then more work before the walk home. A meal of sorts, and then the evening is before me.

ISABEL. Yes, the evenings are bad. What do you do with them.

NANCY. What is there to do? I work generally (*pointing to typewriter*) to add to my income. Sometimes I go to the theatre, with one of the girls at the office. But waiting at the pit door after a hard day's work is not exhilarating, is it? Friends? Well! there are the other women at the office, poor and friendless like me. Some of them are pleasant, a few of them are ladies. None of them interests me. One or two of them come occasionally, but most evenings I am alone.

ISABEL. You oughtn't to be alone! I've often thought of it. Why not live at some woman's club—or get a girl to share your rooms.

NANCY. Because I have the misfortune to be fastidious. Theoretically I love humanity. Practically I dislike it babbling on my hearth. Oh yes, there *are* charming people of course. But remember how narrow my groove is. I don't meet them.

ISABEL (*slowly*). That is true.

NANCY. So here I sit alone, and work, or read—or think.

ISABEL. What do you think?

NANCY. I think that I am growing older. That life is short: that the days go on one after another, one after another: that nothing happens, that nothing ever *will* happen. I think of all the glorious places in the world I shall never see. I think of all the people, the dear charming, interesting people I shall never know. I see life with all its colour and glitter sweeping on without me like some great full river, while I am caught in a little stagnant backwater, held fast by the weeds.

ISABEL (*hurriedly*). Oh no! no! Nancy, don't think like that. Something will happen—only wait—

NANCY (*springing to her feet*). Wait? The world is full of women who have waited. One passes them daily in the street. They are grey, faded, withered, yet that terrible "waiting" look is the last to be stamped out of their faces ... And that's how I shall be! grey, and faded and withered! *Now* I'm alive. Frightfully alive! Wait! Yes, there's one thing that always comes to those who wait long enough. Indifference—apathy.

ISABEL (*in low voice*). Not to you.

NANCY. Oh yes! But just because I want things so much I shall be cheated by hope a little longer than some women, that's all. Oh Isabel! I want to *live* so badly. I want all life has to give: all its experiences. Lovers, children, joys, sorrow even, anything but just *nothing*—blankness. (*She breaks off with a laugh, and a change of tone.*) What a fool I am, boring you like this about things you know as well as I do. Only you're so good. You never make a fuss. Tell me all about the Streamford people. What about your father?

---

34 The first A.B.C. (Aerated Bread Company) Tea Shop opened in the mid-1860s. In contrast to restaurants and pubs, the chain provided locations where unchaperoned women could eat inexpensively and without compromising their reputations.

ISABEL *(ignoring the change of subject, and kneeling beside Nancy's chair)*. Nancy dear, it's true I know. It's all as you say. I feel it vaguely all the time. But what can we do? There's no way out of it, is there?

(Nancy is silent).

(Anxiously). Nancy! you are not—

NANCY *(hurriedly)*. No. No. Of course not. As you say there is no way out of it. Why, my dear Isabel, I am a member of the Church of England, and Mrs. Grundy[35] presided at my christening. Whatever are you thinking about?

ISABEL. I hate to leave you like this! No wonder you feel reckless. You are ill ... it's this horrible loneliness. Nancy, do try to alter it. Get some girl to live with you, however you may hate it. You must, you *must*. And promise me you won't see this man! Promise me, or I shall never have a peaceful moment about you.

NANCY *(soothingly)*. My dear child, don't fret! It's all quite right. I'm not going to perdition, I shall have no opportunity. People talk so glibly about going to the devil! It's the one thing that women in our position have little chance to do. If I were a shop girl,[36] I could meet the shop-walker[37] round the corner; if I were a duchess that would account for many little eccentricities. But for the modern young woman who works for a living wage, and has the misfortune to be a lady, there is no chance of any kind. Not even of going to the devil.

ISABEL. You will not see him then?

NANCY *(shrugging her shoulders)*. Don't I tell you he's away? He's been away for six months. In Vienna, I believe, where no doubt he has forgotten my existence in flirtations with Russian countesses clothed in ermine, and powdered with diamonds. How should I look powdered with diamonds, I wonder? I believe I could look quite pretty ... Oh Isabel! if only we had a little money, you and I! Just enough to buy pretty frocks you know, and to take us to places where it's gay, and the sun shines—and there are one or two men about just to tell us we are not absolutely hideous!

ISABEL *(smiling faintly)*. Perhaps your Uncle Joshua will be obliging enough to die before long.

NANCY *(despondently)*. Not till it's difficult to find a becoming hat even back to the light[38] ... Besides he thoroughly disapproves of me you know. I ought to have stayed at home and married the curate ... I wish I had. I might have worked a sewing machine then instead of a typewriter. Let me see, by this time there would have been knickerbockers[39] to make for one—two—three—four—five little red-haired boys!

ISABEL *(half laughing)*. Nancy!

NANCY *(innocently)*. Well my dear, his locks *flamed*.

ISABEL *(putting on her gloves)*. You would never have married the curate.

NANCY. No, I am a complete failure. After all Mary Brown's air of administering tracts[40] was always superior to mine, and her woolwork[41] slippers were my despair. *(Sighing in mock dejection)* No! she deserved the curate. *(Brightening)* I hear she's grown fat, and looks forty!... Oh! you needn't go yet?

ISABEL. I must. It will take half an hour to get to Euston.

---

35   Proverbial priggish arbiter of morality; originally a character in Thomas Morton's play *Speed the Plough* (1798).
36   Store clerk.
37   Superintendent of a shop or department.
38   In silhouette.
39   Knee-length breeches commonly worn by little boys.
40   Delivering "improving" pamphlets to the impoverished.
41   Needlepoint worked in wool on a canvas foundation.

NANCY *(helping her with her coat)*. It was good of you to come.

ISABEL *(in a constrained voice)*. Good-bye.

(She kisses her and turns to door. Nancy hesitates a moment, and then runs after her impulsively).

NANCY. Isabel! Wait! I've been a beast to you. I don't mean it, only *(she breaks down)* oh Isabel! I'm so unhappy, so worried!

ISABEL *(with decision)*. I shall stay with you. Let me go and telegraph! I'll say I'm ill—anything!

NANCY *(half laughing)*. And lose your post as Assistant Teacher at the Manchester Art School, with its splendid emolument of ninety pounds per annum! No, my dear! that's another of the things we women who lead our own lives dare not do. Stop the treadmill one instant, even for the sake of your dearest friend, and the hungry waiting crowd is upon you!

ISABEL. I don't care, I will risk it. I can't leave you like this!

NANCY *(seriously)*. No, no! I won't hear of it. Forget all my ravings. It was nothing but naughty temper … One must grumble sometimes. But, as you say, there's nothing to be done; and I can assure you I don't think of doing it.

ISABEL. And—you won't see him again? Don't think me a prude Nancy, but I too know what it is to be lonely, and how grateful one is to anyone who,—who—

NANCY *(firmly)*. I won't see him again, I promise.

ISABEL *(embracing her)*. Then I shall go away happy about you … What are you going to do this evening?

NANCY. Look! *(Points to table)* Piles of manuscripts to type. I shall be busy till eleven o'clock.

ISABEL *(at door)*. I must really go. Good-bye Nancy.

NANCY. Good-bye.

(They part affectionately. Isabel looking back over her shoulder. As Isabel goes out, Mrs. Moore enters with lighted lamp. Nancy runs to window and waves farewell. Then, as Mrs. Moore comes to pull down blind she turns away and walks slowly and dejectedly towards the fire).

MRS. MOORE *(insinuatingly)*. What time will you 'ave your supper, Miss?

NANCY *(starting as she cowers over the fire)*. Oh! I shan't want any supper, Mrs. Moore. There are some biscuits in the cupboard, and I'll make some coffee presently.

MRS. MOORE *(sniffing the violets in a bowl on the table)*. If you was to have less vi'lets, and more chops Miss, it would be better for you.

NANCY *(penitently)*. Yes, I know. But isn't it a shame one can't have violets *and* chops? Oh! when I'm rich Mrs. Moore we'll go steadily through Francatelli[42] together, and I'll smother the table with violets so that no one shall guess what a pig I am!

MRS. MOORE. Git married Miss, an' then you're sure of your victuals and drink at least, bein' the last thing that a man knocks off, and the first 'is wife profits by, so to speak. *(At door)* There's the 'all bell.

NANCY *(laughing)*. Good evening Mrs. Moore. *(As the door closes her smile fades. She turns wearily to the table and begins to turn over papers. Sees the letter she had forgotten. Her expression changes. She opens it hurriedly, reads it, and glances at clock. Aloud)* Six o'clock! It's more than six already.

MRS. MOORE *(at door)*. Mr. Fielding.

(Nancy comes forward slowly to shake hands).

---

42   A well-known cookbook. Charles Elmé Francatelli (1805-76), an Anglo-Italian cook who trained in France, was chief cook to Queen Victoria and author of *The Modern Cook* (1845), *A Plain Cookery Book for the Working Classes* (1852), and *The Royal English and Foreign Confectionery Book* (1862).

FIELDING. You had my letter?

NANCY. Yes—but it was delayed. I've only just opened it.

FIELDING. But you wouldn't have forbidden me to come?

NANCY (*gravely*). Yes I should have telegraphed, but (*shows open letter in her hand*) you see there wasn't time.

FIELDING. I'm glad there wasn't time ... May I sit down?

NANCY (*motioning him to a chair, while she seats herself slowly*). I thought you were in Vienna?

FIELDING. So I was the night before last. I have come straight through—to see you!

NANCY (*coldly*). I am sorry you had that trouble.

FIELDING. But since I am here I may speak to you?... (*Softly*) It is six months since I saw you, remember.

(*Nancy is silent. After a moment's pause Fielding goes on in quiet controlled voice*).

It's just this; I've been offered an appointment out there.

(*Nancy looks up quickly: recovers herself. A pause*).

NANCY (*faintly*). Well?

FIELDING. I want you to let me refuse it.

NANCY. I? (*Confused*) But I have nothing to do with it. (*Hastily*) Of course you must accept it.

FIELDING (*with quiet insistence*). Let me put the case to you once more for the last time. Six months ago, I left England on your account. I told you I should forget you if it were possible. I can make myself do many things. That isn't one of them. I shall not forget you!

NANCY (*pleadingly*). But why should you? Why can't we be friends?

FIELDING. The usual woman's question. Because *I* can't. No! This must be settled now, once and for all. Listen to me one moment longer. I've thought the question out. (*He laughs shortly.*) In fact I can't remember thinking of anything else for six months. Let us look at *your* side of the question. I'm a selfish devil of course; all men are, but whether you believe me or not, I have considered it. I'm afraid I have no theories: I don't go in for the higher morality, and that kind of thing. Marriage is a clumsy enough institution but I don't know what else to propose for the rank and file of humanity at the moment, and if I thought I was spoiling your chance of a happy marriage—well: I *hope* I should have had the decency to stay in Vienna. But as a matter of fact girls who work as you do, who live in a groove as you must, don't marry. How many men for instance have you spoken to within the last six months?

NANCY (*looking straight in front of her*). Not one.

FIELDING. You have been in town four years and except for our chance meeting at the Stuarts', you have had no opportunity of making any friends besides the other girls at the office. A deplorable state of things. But it exists, doesn't it?

NANCY. Yes.

FIELDING. And it is likely to continue. Years hence it will be the same thing in all probability?

NANCY (*recklessly*). Oh yes! Four, eight, sixteen years hence.

FIELDING. Doesn't that make a difference?

NANCY (*recklessly*). Oh it sounds reasonable enough, but—(*She pauses, and goes on desperately.*) If I loved you overwhelmingly, perhaps—But I don't.

FIELDING. You are not "in love with me" I know. If you were, I should know better than to argue with you. But our friendship has been pleasant, you admit?

NANCY (*impulsively*). It has meant everything in the world to me—(*she stops short*).

FIELDING. You would marry me then, if I were free?

NANCY (*involuntarily*). Yes.

FIELDING (*coming nearer to her*). Then—

NANCY (*hurriedly rising*). No! No! I'm unreasonable of course. We've talked about it before. In theory I agree. In practice—I can't ... I know all you are going to say!

FIELDING (*moving away from her and speaking quietly*). Yet let me say it. I want you to be my wife. The law holds me bound to a woman who has probably forgotten my existence. Because we are powerless to alter the law, are we then to part altogether? Shall we injure anyone by being happy? What possible concern can it be to anyone but ourselves that we are lovers as well as friends? That is a private matter surely about which we do not propose to take the whole world into confidence.

NANCY (*walking to and fro with hands nervously clasped*). I know, I know! It is all very reasonable. I admit it in theory.

(*She sinks into a chair. Fielding comes and leans over the back*).

FIELDING. At least life would not be so lonely, Nancy.

(*Nancy covers her face with her hands. After a pause he goes on*).

It is heartbreaking to think of you spending your youth like this; sitting here alone night after night. You with all your gaiety, your capacity for happiness ...

NANCY (*inarticulately*). I know—don't!

(*She suddenly moves away from him and crosses to corner of mantelpiece, against which she leans. Fielding presently follows her*).

FIELDING. We have been such good friends, haven't we?... nothing would be altered. We are both poor people, too poor, and too obscure to attract comment. I think I could make you love me ... We could meet often, as we have done before. Only if I stay, it must be as your lover as well as your friend!

NANCY (*raising herself*). Go. Please go. It is useless. Don't you see it is useless? No. I'm not angry. I understand. Only I—can't.

FIELDING. Then is this good-bye? My answer must reach the office tomorrow. If you send me away I shall start tonight.

NANCY (*entreatingly*). Oh no! *Not* tonight! *Why* can't you promise—

FIELDING (*shortly*). I can promise nothing. I am going because I dare not stay.

NANCY (*wildly*). But I *can't* lose you altogether! Oh! why are men not different?

FIELDING (*grimly*). You must enquire of the Being who is responsible for this very incomprehensible and—damnable world ... I beg your pardon. Good-bye.

(*Nancy listlessly gives him her hand. He looks at her fixedly a moment, then kisses her hand. Nancy stands passively while he turns away and goes out, shutting the door. She continues to stand a moment as if dazed, then crosses to typewriter, sits down and begins to work it mechanically. All at once she starts up with stifled cry*).

NANCY (*incoherently*). Oh! I can't! I can't! Not alone! ... I shall go mad. (*Stands irresolutely for a second, then rushes to door which she flings open. Calls at first wildly, then in a tone which she tries to make natural*) Mr. Fielding! Mr. Fielding! (*She then comes back and stands in the middle of room with her back to the door*).

(*Fielding enters, bewildered. Nancy slowly moves her head. At last she puts out her hand stretching it backward*).

FIELDING. Nancy! (*Takes her in his arms as curtain falls*).

Act II

Four years later. The hall in the Hotel Beau Séjour on the Riviera. A large comfortably furnished place used by the visitors as a general sitting and smoking room. At the back, glass doors open into the hotel garden. Right and left passageways lead to other parts of the hotel. When curtain rises the hall is fairly well filled. A group of girls with tennis rackets, and men in flannels near the door. Mrs. Llewellyn seated near the fire.

KITTY LLEWELLYN *(looking out of window)*. There! The court's free. They've gone.

ISMAY. Come along then. Where's Miss Adair? Oh! here you are!

KITTY *(to Ismay)*. We mean to give you a tremendous thrashing, don't we? *(Turning to her partner)*.

ISMAY. That depends.

(Mrs. Wingfield comes in from garden, the collar of her fur cape turned up).

Oh! Mrs. Wingfield that's too bad. Aren't you coming?

MRS. WINGFIELD *(shaking her head)*. The balmy air of this place doesn't suit me.

(Mrs. Llewellyn leans forward to nod and smile at Kitty, who goes out with Count Karl).

MRS. LLEWELLYN *(graciously)*. I hope you'll have a good game!

(She sees Mrs. Wingfield who comes shivering to the fire. She is a middle-aged woman of distinguished appearance, well dressed, grey haired with a lorgnette. Mrs. Stuart somewhat younger with an irritable fussy manner).

Why! it's Mrs. Wingfield! I was afraid I should be quite deserted this morning. Everybody seems to be going out.

MRS. WINGFIELD. Well, I watched the tennis till I got frozen to the backbone. But the Riviera exists to freeze you to the backbone in practice and to lure you from your happy English fireplace in print.[43] Sunshine and balmy airs indeed! Why Margate[44] in an east wind is tropical by comparison.

MRS. LLEWELLYN *(taking out her embroidery)*. And yet in half an hour's time it will probably be too hot. A most treacherous climate! I thought so when the doctors ordered my poor husband to Nice. *(With a heavy sigh)* He didn't live through the winter.

MRS. WINGFIELD. Really? Well, doctors generally act for the best ... *(Rather hastily)* I'm sorry to miss Kitty's play this morning. She's in excellent form.

MRS. LLEWELLYN. Dear child! Yes. She and the Count do so well together, don't they?

MRS. WINGFIELD. Er. Yes. Fairly. She's more brilliant I think when young Ismay is her partner.

MRS. LLEWELLYN *(standing up to look out)*. She's with the Count, surely. *(In annoyed voice)* No. He's with Miss Adair I suppose, judging from the size of his partner's feet. I can't see well from here. *(She sits down and works with suppressed irritation.)* I shall have great difficulty with Kitty I'm afraid ... Kitty in fact behaves like a fool!

MRS. WINGFIELD. Ah! She seems to be developing ideas!

MRS. LLEWELLYN. And *how* does she get them I wonder? There are no ideas in our family. We've never had them. Look at her sisters! All of them married well. They never had an idea in their lives, I'm thankful to say. It's in the air, I believe?

---

43 Probably an allusion to travel guides or novels.

44 A resort town on the Kentish coast.

MRS. WINGFIELD. And infectious. It used to be an obscure disease which attacked lady novelists, and lecturers and those sort of women. Now it's spreading to all classes. It's as bad as influenza, and almost as common.

MRS. LLEWELLYN. Terrible! It's really serious, isn't it? How do you account for it? Don't you think it may be due to the pernicious literature our girls read? Now here's a book I found in Kitty's room. *(Takes it up.)* I've been trying to read it, but except that I've come across one or two shocking sentiments, I don't in the least understand it. It's too deep for me.

MRS. WINGFIELD. What is it?

MRS. LLEWELLYN *(turning to title on the cover)*. The plays of Henrik Ibsen. Who *is* Ibsen?

MRS. WINGFIELD *(concealing a smile)*. Ibsen! My dear, Mrs. Llewellyn. Burn it! Burn it. Most of it is traceable to him after all. It's he who has inoculated woman with the idea-germ, and given her the disease of thought. It's not too much to say that he's ruined the marriage market. A girl *thinks* nowadays, when it's her plain duty to marry.

MRS. LLEWELLYN *(in distressed voice)*. Dear me! How shocking, and when *we* were girls, there were such a lot of pretty books. *Only Seventeen*, I remember—a sweet story! And *Her Lord and Master*,[45] and *Buttercups and Daisies* ...[46] We used to rave about them.

MRS. WINGFIELD. Yes. We still rave—though not about buttercups and daisies ... Kitty didn't care to go to the Battle of Flowers[47] by the way?

MRS. LLEWELLYN. No. *(Sighing)* She's seen it three or four times. This is the fourth season[48] I have been out with Kitty you know. It really seems hopeless. Sometimes I despair.

MRS. WINGFIELD. Yes. It appears increasingly difficult. Sometimes when I think of all you mothers endure I am thankful I am childless.

MRS. LLEWELLYN. You may well say so. And what thanks do we receive? Only this morning, for instance, when I was urging Kitty to be a little more gracious in—er—well! a likely quarter, she flew into a violent passion!

MRS. WINGFIELD. How impolitic!

MRS. LLEWELLYN. I really scarcely like to repeat what she said, it was too shocking, but she actually maintained that she would consider it less immoral to live with a man she loved than to marry one she didn't!

MRS. WINGFIELD. Ah! Ibsen and Hardy[49]—plus natural temperament I suppose.

MRS. LLEWELLYN *(without comprehension)*. Er. Yes. I suppose so. The young people of the present day seem to have no reverence whatever for the sanctity of the marriage tie. And really, as to love! When I was a girl, I thought it immodest even to think of such a thing. As I said to Kitty this morning, "look at me! What love had I for your father when I married him? None. Respect of course, the girl who marries without respect is almost as bad as—a—"

MRS. WINGFIELD. The girl who marries without money.

MRS. LLEWELLYN *(with fervour)*. Oh! quite. Respect is so necessary.

---

45 A novel by Florence Marryat, 1871.

46 A novel by Charlotte Grace O'Brien, published 1854 as part of the "Buds and Blossoms" series.

47 These were popular festivals in France and Germany in the late-nineteenth century. Flower-bedecked floats and carriages with dignitaries processed in parades.

48 A mother hopes to find a suitable husband for her daughter in one year, for example, during the London Season which extends from May to July. Kitty Llewellyn has been on the marriage market for as long as four years and so is probably 22 years old.

49 Thomas Hardy, author of *Jude the Obscure* and other realist novels which critique social strictures.

MRS. WINGFIELD. Well! if one has to respect *someone*, let him be the man with a comfortable income.

MRS. LLEWELLYN (*vaguely*). Oh yes! of course ... My husband had *that*. But as I was saying, it all turned out very well. He was trying at times of course, but with proper management he was indulgent enough. I never had any difficulty in getting all I wanted in the way of money, and, as I said to Kitty only this morning, suppose I had married a poor man, what would have been the result?

MRS. WINGFIELD. A decree nisi[50] for Mr. Llewellyn probably.

MRS. LLEWELLYN (*half laughing*). My dear, Mrs. Wingfield, how shocking of you! Well! (*Sighing*) One never knows. I had many admirers of course. And as you say, a good income *is* a safeguard, certainly. But it is hopeless to try and point out sensible considerations like these to Kitty.

MRS. WINGFIELD (*rising to look out of window*). Here come some of the people back from the Battle of Flowers. Did you see Miss Thistleton start on Captain Egerton's drag,[51] by the way? She looked very pretty. I wonder who she is?

MRS. LLEWELLYN (*icily*). I cannot imagine. Everyone is talking about her of course.

MRS. WINGFIELD. Naturally ... But why?

MRS. LLEWELLYN. Well! to come here alone! With such an independent air too. I don't admire her in the least, but she's not plain enough to do a thing like that.

MRS. WINGFIELD. Ah! Well! I suppose it's just that beauty as well as homeliness should have its penalties. How long has she been here?

MRS. LLEWELLYN. Oh! I'm forgetting what a short time it is since you came. Miss Thistleton must have been here three weeks, every moment of which Captain Egerton has been dancing attendance. Quite ridiculous.

MRS. WINGFIELD. It must be. I hear he is a man—er, worthy of any girl's respect.

MRS. LLEWELLYN. A friend of hers arrived this morning. A little late to start a chaperon, don't you think? But perhaps some hint may have reached her.

MRS. WINGFIELD. Of course a hint has reached her. How else should a lot of women at a hotel justify their existence?

(*Enter Mrs. Stuart and Violet Stuart*).

MRS. LLEWELLYN. Why!—not really, Mrs. Stuart! And Violet.

(*They greet with effusion. Mrs. Wingfield also rises to shake hands*).

MRS. WINGFIELD. We met at the Wellingboroughs' last summer, I think.

MRS. STUART. Of course! How pleasant to find friends here.

MRS. LLEWELLYN. You have only just come?

MRS. STUART. Early this morning. We travelled straight through, and went to bed the moment we arrived. What a journey!

VIOLET (*who has been talking to Mrs. Wingfield*). Yes, and since we came downstairs half an hour ago, we've seen three people we know. You, Mrs. Wingfield, and (*turning to her mother*) Miss Thistleton, Mamma.

MRS. LLEWELLYN (*eagerly*). Oh! do *you* know Miss Thistleton!

MRS. STUART. Well, I've met her. Some time ago though, I scarcely recognised her today.

VIOLET. I should think not. She's learnt to dress since then.

---

50   A conditional divorce decree usually issued six months prior to an absolute decree.

51   Cart (probably decked out with flowers).

MRS. STUART. Well, Vi, how *can* she afford it?

VIOLET (*shrugging her shoulders*). There are more ways than one. Perhaps she doesn't pay her dressmaker.

MRS. LLEWELLYN. But who *is* she, dear Mrs. Stuart?

MRS. STUART. Oh she's the daughter of a poor clergyman somewhere up in the north. Aunt Prendergast discovered her! You remember my old Aunt Prendergast? She insisted upon taking me to see this girl, who had come to town after her father's death, to get her own living. Let me see, what did she do. Typewriting wasn't it? Isn't that how girls get their living now-a-days?

MRS. WINGFIELD. Yes, or their death. It's much the same thing I believe.

VIOLET. Oh! Aunt Prendergast was a shocking old bore about that kind of thing. It was only necessary for a girl to be poor and afflicted to win her affection, but the worst of it was she expected us to be affectionate as well.

MRS. LLEWELLYN. But now, how *can* a girl like that afford to come out here? And to dress as she does?

MRS. WINGFIELD. Miss Stuart has already suggested a most interesting solution.

VIOLET (*uneasily*). I? Did I? Oh! well now I come to think of it I believe we heard that she had had money left to her, didn't we mamma? Yes, by that rich old Joshua Thistleton we met at Spa,[52] who turned out to be her uncle. It isn't so very much, I think.

MRS. WINGFIELD. Still, without abandoning the older and more exciting theory the knowledge of Miss Thistleton's private income might be sufficient to account for her pretty frocks, mightn't it? To the credulous, I mean.

VIOLET. Oh of course, certainly. Why not?

MRS. STUART. Dear me! How the mention of Miss Thistleton recalls old times. Let me see. Will Fielding met her once or twice before we shut up the Sloane Street house, didn't he Vi? I remember he thought her pretty.

VIOLET (*indifferently*). Really mamma I don't remember! The only thing I recall about Miss Thistleton is the cut of her skirt. It was appalling.

MRS. STUART (*turning to Mrs. Llewellyn and Mrs. Wingfield*). You remember my cousin, Will Fielding, don't you? Such a sad story ... married at twenty-one ... His wife you know ... a dreadful creature! But he's free at last I'm glad to say. And talking of legacies, you know he's come into money? A moderate fortune to be sure but a most unexpected one—from his godfather!

MRS. LLEWELLYN. Really! His wife is dead you say?

MRS. STUART. Two months ago. Providence is very merciful!

MRS. WINGFIELD. It takes its time about it though, like many another Benevolent Institution![53]

MRS. LLEWELLYN. I'm rejoiced to hear it dear Mrs. Stuart. I remember the case well. Most sad! A young man cut off from all er—natural ties—

MRS. WINGFIELD. Well! as far as that's concerned, a young man may generally be trusted to provide for himself, I think.

MRS. LLEWELLYN. My dear Mrs. Wingfield.

MRS. STUART. How naughty of you.

(*Enter by glass door, Nancy with Captain Egerton. Other people returning from Battle of Flowers come in two or three at a time during the few minutes which follow. They group themselves about the hall, talking. Nancy is talking animatedly as she enters. She recognises Mrs. Stuart and Violet. Hesitates a moment and then comes forward to shake hands*).

---

52   Mineral springs and curative resort in the province of Liège, Belgium.

53   Charity.

MRS. STUART. How do you do? *(Smiling)* We have seen you once before, today.

NANCY. Today?

VIOLET. From the bedroom window. When a lady in a charming gown passed along the terrace, I said to mother at once, that it must be Miss Thistleton.

NANCY *(smiling)*. Not because of my gown I think.

(She remains talking to Mrs. Stuart and Violet. Mrs. Llewellyn goes to glass door and looks out).

MRS. LLEWELLYN. Kitty!

KITTY *(from outside)*. Yes mother.

(Enters followed by Ismay).

MRS. STUART. Now Mrs. Llewellyn, come and give us *your* opinion on this point!

(Mrs. Llewellyn reluctantly turns away a moment).

KITTY *(hastily to Mrs. Wingfield)*. *Do* say you want to see us play or something, or else mother will send me out for the afternoon.

MRS. LLEWELLYN *(disengaging herself)*. Kitty! I want you—

MRS. WINGFIELD *(addressing the company generally)*. Miss Llewellyn, Count Karl, Captain Ismay and Miss Adair will now give the trial match they promised!

(There is a general movement towards the garden).

KITTY *(whispers)*. How clever of you! You didn't forget how to couple us!

ISMAY *(gratefully)*. You *are* a brick[54] Mrs. Wingfield.

MRS. STUART. Aren't you coming Mrs. Llewellyn? Do come!

MRS. LLEWELLYN *(in annoyed voice)*. No thank you. I am a little tired of tennis.

(Exit left. The others go out through glass door into garden. Nancy is left alone with Captain Egerton who has been talking to her for the last few minutes).

EGERTON. Why should "Isabel" come! Don't let Isabel come! I want to talk to you. You never let me talk to you.

NANCY *(laughing a little nervously)*. Indeed? If you do anything else, I have never noticed it.

EGERTON. You will never let me say—

NANCY *(hurriedly)*. Anything but sense. Of course not. Ah! *(Glancing out of window)* Here comes Isabel!

EGERTON *(rising slowly)*. My dismissal, I suppose?

NANCY *(deprecatingly)*. Well you see, except for a glimpse of her this morning, when she arrived tired to death, I haven't seen her for four years. *(Repeats to herself)* Four years!

EGERTON. Ah! the only way for a woman to keep her friends. Half an hour's chat, and a four year's interval.

NANCY. I've often warned you to keep to subjects you understand.

EGERTON. But women's friendships are proverbial.

NANCY. We want a new proverb then.

EGERTON. New women: new proverbs you think. But *you're* not a New Woman![55]

NANCY. Heaven forbid! The same old woman under new conditions, that's all.

---

54   Good fellow (slang).

55   A literary and dramatic figure of the later-1890s who advocates women's independence.

(Enter Isabel R. She is plainly and rather badly dressed. She looks much older than Nancy to whom she is a great contrast. Nancy runs forward to meet her. Egerton strolls off L.).

NANCY *(taking both her hands)*. Here you are at last. I was afraid to come in, in case you might be asleep. Headache better?

ISABEL *(nods assent. Looks Nancy up and down admiringly)*. How sweet you look, Nancy! To think it is four years since I saw you! Wasn't it strange that each holiday when I hoped to come something happened. Father's illness for the first two years. Then you see, I broke down. And after that—well! after that I had no money.

NANCY. You are going to give up all that now! You are to think of nothing but getting well and strong.

ISABEL. Could one do anything else here, in this glorious place? Oh Nancy, do you remember the last time we met how you longed that we might have pretty frocks, and that we might go where it was gay, and sunshiny—

NANCY *(slowly)*. And there were one or two men about—yes.

ISABEL. Well! the dream has come true. It's gay, and the sun shines, and—*you* have pretty frocks.

NANCY. And there *are* one or two men about.

ISABEL *(smiling)*. And do you allow them to tell you *you* are not "absolutely hideous"? You ought not. *(Glancing at her)* One man has been telling you that for a long time, hasn't he?

NANCY. Yes ... it is four years since he began.

ISABEL *(trying to see her friend's averted face)*. I've been longing all this time to hear about it Nancy, ever since I got that first letter.

NANCY *(turning a little)*. What did you think, when you got—that letter?

ISABEL. How can I tell you? At first I was in despair. I waited in fear and trembling expecting to hear that you repented, that you were wretched, desperate. I don't know what.

NANCY. And instead?

ISABEL. Each time you wrote you seemed happier, more content, till at last ... I began to be reconciled. I began to readjust my ideas. One does as one gets older. But after all, letters are poor things. I want to hear from your own lips that you are happy. Now tell me. Where is he?...

NANCY. Coming here ... perhaps today.

ISABEL. *Here*? But how rash, how wrong of him! Why do you allow—

NANCY. He is free. He is coming to ask me to marry him!

ISABEL *(joyfully)*. Nancy! Dear, I'm so glad! It's like a fairy tale. First the princess throws off her disguise and appears gorgeously apparelled. She loads her friends with gifts and honours, and then at last the prince—

NANCY *(bitterly)*. Yes. There is only one flaw in the story. It's the wrong prince.

ISABEL. The wrong—Nancy! Are you mad?

NANCY *(starting up suddenly)*. Oh! I don't know! Yes, I believe I am. I really think I must be ... *(Turning to Isabel)* I'm going to tell you about it, then you will know the worst of me. You will know what a brute I am! ... Oh! I don't know what is the matter with me!

ISABEL *(bewildered)*. But I thought—Surely you *have* been happy?

NANCY *(helplessly)*. Yes, I was, wasn't I? And Will has always been perfect, *perfect* to me. It's just that. The thought of him makes me feel the vilest creature in the world ... I will try to explain. You know how I came to—to—consent in the first place? Isabel I couldn't bear the loneliness. When I saw him going I thought I should go mad with the horror of it ... You know all that.

ISABEL. Did you love him then.

NANCY. No. Now I know I didn't. I tried to think I did. But it wasn't that. I was fond of him. I liked him to love me. He was all I had, remember. He was my dear friend. But now I know I—never loved him.

ISABEL (in low voice). That was the mistake.

NANCY. Yes, yes. But think of the circumstances! You know what my life was! Thousands of women marry for a home, for position, for a title—for *payment* that is to say, with not even affection to give their husbands. And people say "how sensible." I consented for none of these things. For the sake only of a little human love and sympathy. I am disreputable of course. But what would you have done in my place?

ISABEL. I should have done as you did—if I had had the courage.

NANCY. Courage? Yes ... you are right. It takes courage. Life is less dreary, but one pays ... one pays.

ISABEL. You mean—

NANCY. Oh Isabel! Theories are all very well, but there are things women never get used to. Foolish unreasonable things of course, but real to us, all the same. Ridiculous terrors; dreadful misgivings. Words that strike one like a blow. Even now, when I hear someone say "She lived with him for years" or "she's his mistress"—you know the voice! I grow cold with horror. I think, that's what *you* are, you are living with a man like that!

ISABEL. But that is not what you *think*?

NANCY (quickly). No! only what I *feel*. And a man never understands that you can think one way, and feel another, without being fundamentally unreasonable.

ISABEL. Yes. Reason ahead, feeling lagging behind. It's different for men I suppose. For ages they have been free.

NANCY. And so they take such matters easily, naturally. We can't do it, Isabel. There's age-long tradition against us ... training ... the old Puritan instinct. These things cling round us like grave clothes.[56] We may take our freedom, but we can't take it lightly. Take it? We pay for it ... to the uttermost farthing.

ISABEL. But you do not regret?

NANCY (rising and walking restlessly to and fro). If you had asked me that six months ago, I should have said No!—a thousand times No. It has been worth it all—terrors, misgivings—all I have suffered. Life is always a compromise, never a question of black or white, happiness or misery. It's a matter of picking out the brightest skein the Fates offer you and weaving what you can out of it.

ISABEL. And though your garment has been torn—

NANCY. It has been patched with purple;[57] and after all I could never have worn homespun.[58]

ISABEL (meditatively). It must have made all the difference to your life.

NANCY. Difference! I worked just as hard. I had no more money. I was wet and cold and tired just as often, but there was always Will. The books we have read together, the talks we have had, all the beauty he has shown me! All this, and then my devoted lover—always.

ISABEL. And now? What has changed all this?

NANCY. I don't know. A madness—a possession of the devil. A year ago I came into my money. I gave up the Granby Street rooms then, and took the little flat at Kensington. I began to know people, to go out a great deal. Will and I used to meet at other people's houses occasionally. But we had to be more careful. It's only while you are poor and obscure that your concerns are your own, and we were forced to see less of one another. It was then I met Captain Egerton ...

---

56   A shroud.

57   Opulence.

58   Coarse, loosely woven cloth.

ISABEL. Does he care for you.

NANCY. Yes. He is here. He was talking to me just now, when you came.

ISABEL *(breathlessly)*. Nancy!

NANCY. It was not my fault. I will tell you. I did all I could. I said to myself, you are out of your senses. The thing is incredible; go away and forget it! I told Will I wanted to winter abroad, and I left town without telling anyone else where I was going. But he ... Captain Egerton found out, and followed me. Of course he thinks I'm free.

ISABEL. Has he asked you to marry him?

NANCY. No; because I won't let him. I'm always fencing. But I can't do it much longer. I'm nearly beaten. And Will is coming today. *What* am I to say to him? I feel torn in pieces, and I despise myself. *(In low voice)* Just think! What shall I come to be! One lover—yes. But—

ISABEL *(rising suddenly)*. At least you are alive! At least you have lived. Look at *me*. I am one of the women you talked about the last time we met. One of the women who has *waited*. Nothing ever happens to me, nothing ever will happen![59] Do not regret anything. At least you have lived. I wish to Heaven I had had your chance!

(Nancy stands breathlessly looking at Isabel, who suddenly covers her face with her hands, and bursts into tears. There is a sound of voices outside in the garden).

NANCY *(hurriedly)*. Come dearest, quickly! Come up to my room.

(She puts her arm round Isabel and hurries her away as the glass doors open. Enter Mrs. Stuart and Fielding, the former pleased and excited).

MRS. STUART. My *dear* boy! How pleased Vi will be! What a delightful surprise. I could scarcely believe my eyes just now, when I saw you crossing the tennis court.

FIELDING *(drily)*. No. I thought there was something wrong with *mine*. But they're all right. They generally are, I find. *(With an attempt at cordiality)* I had no idea you were here, Cousin Mary.

MRS. STUART. We intended to look you up the moment we returned. I was so *delighted* to hear—

FIELDING. Oh, the legacy. Thanks, yes. It makes a difference.

MRS. STUART. And not only the legacy. *(With change of expression)* That is of course,—most sad, but a happy release.

FIELDING. Er, possibly. May I smoke?

MRS. STUART *(still with appropriate expression)*. The ways of Providence are inscrutable.

FIELDING. Very. How is Violet?

MRS. STUART. I *must* call her. Ah! here she comes.

(Violet Stuart, Mrs. Wingfield, Kitty Llewellyn and Ismay enter at glass doors talking about the result of tennis. Mrs. Llewellyn comes in L.).

MRS. STUART *(archly)*. Vi! Who is this?

VIOLET *(giving him her hand)*. Will, obviously. What are you doing here?

(Mrs. Stuart crosses to speak to Mrs. Llewellyn keeping anxious watch on Kitty talking to Ismay).

FIELDING *(with affected depression)*. My wretched health!

VIOLET *(scornfully)*. Health?

---

59   Excised here in licensing copy: "I have no lovers. I shall have no children."

FIELDING. Ah! the young and charming can afford to scoff. The aged and plain, in the sere[60] and yellow leaf—

(Violet laughs derisively. They move aside and talk).

MRS. STUART *(with a nod towards them)*. So suitable! And now that it has pleased Providence to remove the—er—obstacle—

MRS. LLEWELLYN. Oh! if it were only *Providence*! With a little care and tact Providence can generally be managed, but when it comes to a daughter with modern ideas—

(A gong sounds).

Kitty! *(Sharply)* Kitty.

MRS. LLEWELLYN. There's the dressing gong. You have been late for dinner every day this week.

(Kitty and Ismay part unwillingly).

ISMAY. You'll come out after dinner?

KITTY. If I can manage it.

MRS. STUART *(to Fielding)*. We shall see you at dinner?

FIELDING. Not tonight. I've dined.

MRS. STUART. How tiresome of you! We'll have coffee together then.

(All gradually leave the hall, except Fielding who rings and lights cigarette).

FIELDING *(to Waiter)*. Café noir,[61] and cognac.

WAITER. Yes sare.

FIELDING. Wait! *(Takes out card case)* Send that up to Miss Thistleton, please.

WAITER. Very good Sare.

(Gong sounds. People begin to file across Hall into table d'hôte room.[62] Waiter returns with coffee, and Fielding takes out letter, reads it, and returns it to letter case. When everyone has gone in Nancy enters. She is in evening dress. Fielding rises to meet her. Takes her hands. Nancy draws back confused, and grave).

FIELDING. It's all right. They've all gone in to dinner. We shall have the place to ourselves. But *(looking at her)* you were going too.

NANCY. No. No. Not now. I'll dine with Isabel later, upstairs. This is the only chance we shall have alone, this evening. The whole world is here, you know. I didn't expect you so soon, or I should have telegraphed to stop you from coming.

FIELDING *(in a quiet tone)*. An awful bore, of course. But does it matter much, after all?

NANCY. Matter?

FIELDING *(slowly, and with a certain hesitation, looking at her)*. If in a few days we announce our engagement I mean.

NANCY *(she is at first silent in evident distress. Then she sinks slowly into a chair. In half whisper)*. Will!—

FIELDING *(squaring his shoulders)*. Yes dear? *(Very gently)*.

NANCY. Will—I don't know how to say it.

FIELDING. Shall I say it for you. You don't love me any longer. Is that it?

---

60 Dry.

61 Black coffee.

62 Shared tables where a set menu is served at a fixed price.

NANCY (*starting*). How did you—?

FIELDING (*smiling bitterly*). Oh, in a decadent age like this, intuitions are no longer exclusively feminine.

NANCY (*shrinking*). Ah Will! don't take it like that. Don't sneer, I implore you! If you only knew how wretched I am!

FIELDING (*patting her hand*). Well, I'm not exactly cheerful either. I think we may exercise mutual sympathy.

NANCY. Oh! now, if you are going to be good to me—

FIELDING (*laughing hopelessly*). The same Nancy! I'm not to sneer, and I'm not to be good to you—What am I to do?

NANCY. Nothing but just try to understand. And don't think too badly of me ... Will! I have always been straight with you, haven't I?... I must tell you first—

FIELDING. That there is someone else.

NANCY (*startled*). How ...?

FIELDING. Also that you have never really loved me.

NANCY (*looking at him in frightened way*). I never knew that until—

FIELDING. Until you loved someone else. No, how should you?

(*A pause*).

NANCY (*desperately*). Will! I'll marry you if you wish it. It is what I ought to do.

FIELDING. My dear child, I can stand much; more than I thought in fact—but not a dutiful wife.

NANCY (*miserably*). Oh I deserve you to speak so, I know.

FIELDING (*rising and crossing to her*). No, it's I who deserve to be kicked. I guessed this was coming, but when it actually comes, it's worse than one—but never mind that. I only want to tell you that I haven't been quite blind these four years, and if you've had your bad days—well! so have I!

NANCY (*breathlessly*). Not because you thought our life together wrong?

FIELDING. I? A thousand times no. It was the knowledge that I troubled *you*. I knew your loneliness you see, and I used it as a weapon against you. I won, but you have often made me pay for victory.

NANCY. But I never said one word!

FIELDING. No. It was when you were rather gayer than usual, strange to say, that I felt a blackguard. At such moments, the fact that nine men out of ten would have taken the same advantage scarcely seemed a justification.

NANCY. No! No! You mustn't blame yourself! After all, if you had left me that evening what would my life have been? I should feel now perhaps that I had missed my chance. It is I who am unreasonable. I lost my peace of mind—yes. But oh Will! We have had many happy times!

FIELDING. I may at least remember that?

NANCY (*restlessly*). Oh if only I could get rid of this terrible new feeling, and let things be as they were. It is a madness, and yet—

FIELDING (*looking at her*). Impossible. Nancy you love this man. I see it. For four years I've longed in vain to see you look as you look now. It's like my luck that it shouldn't be for me ... No. Don't be afraid. I shan't whine. Only is he going to make you happy?

NANCY. I feel like the woman killed with kindness!

FIELDING. You—you must marry him Nancy. You will never be happy any other way.

NANCY. But—suppose—(*She looks at him long and searchingly*).

FIELDING. Is there any necessity? You didn't ask for chapter and verse of my past life, I think.

NANCY. No! But my theory and practice will never agree. In theory there is no necessity. In practice, I should certainly tell the man I intended to marry.

FIELDING. Have you reflected that on such a subject the normal man is just the prejudiced animal you would expect him to be?

NANCY *(slowly)*. I can't help it. One must take all the risks if one plays a game of one's own with new rules.

FIELDING *(bitterly)*. So after all, I shall stand between you and your heart's desire—

NANCY. You must never blame yourself for an instant whatever happens. Life is a mixed banquet isn't it, and after all I've had a great many of the coloured sweets. If it hadn't been for you, I should have been put off—with stale buns,[63] perhaps—

FIELDING. I've no right to ask any questions of course.

NANCY *(in hurt voice)*. No right? Who else has the right? He's here.

FIELDING. Here!

(Nancy nods. Fielding looks at her long and earnestly).

NANCY *(timidly putting out her hand)*. Will! I shall not lose my friend?

FIELDING *(without taking it)*. You are in love at last, don't you realize *now* that—I can't be your friend?

(Nancy covers her face with her hands).

FIELDING *(with an effort)*. Don't! Don't cry dear. Good-bye!

(Nancy suddenly takes his hands and clings to him).

NANCY. Oh Will!

(A sound from the garden. Nancy starts and whispers).

Here he is! He's coming.

(She escapes as Captain Egerton enters at garden door. Fielding stares at him incredulously).

EGERTON *(suddenly recognises him)*. What! Fielding? Never! You here?

(The two men shake hands).

Act III

A terrace in the hotel garden, over-hanging a tennis court, which tennis court however, is not visible to audience. Steps L. leading from lower part of garden to terrace. On R. at right angles with terrace, one wing of the hotel is seen with row of French windows on ground floor. These open onto the terrace. When curtain rises, hotel visitors are leaning on the balustrade, eagerly watching tennis tournament below. A moment after curtain rises, applause from spectators indicates the end of a game. Mrs. Wingfield is among the spectators.

ONLOOKERS. Splendid! Well played! Very good game!

MISS ADAIR. The next decides it, doesn't it?

THE COUNT. Yes. I back Miss Llewellyn and young Ismay though.

MISS ADAIR. I don't know. They're pretty evenly matched. Miss Thistleton's style is splendid! and Captain Egerton's very strong. Awfully exciting isn't it!

---

63   Day-old baking.

(Visitors continue to watch the game. From the tennis court occasionally "Serve!" "Fault!" "Fifteen all" etc. Mrs. Llewellyn and Mrs. Stuart come up steps on to terrace).

MRS. LLEWELLYN *(to Mrs. Wingfield who rises)*. We've only just caught sight of you. So glad to see you again!

MRS. STUART *(also shaking hands)*. We can see just as well up here, and talk at the same time.

MRS. WINGFIELD. You've quite deserted the Beau Séjour. Why, you haven't been here once since you left for Beaulieu.

MRS. LLEWELLYN. And that's a month ago.

MRS. STUART. Yes! I've often wanted to come over, if only for the day but Will seems to have taken an unaccountable dislike to the place. It was as much as we could do to drag him with us this afternoon, dear boy!

MRS. WINGFIELD. Hm! His dislikes must grow like mushrooms. He was only here one night.

MRS. STUART. And he began to urge us all to leave and go with him to Beaulieu the very evening of his arrival.

MRS. WINGFIELD. Well he succeeded even beyond the dreams of manly arrogance. It was a clean sweep. You, Violet, Mrs. Llewellyn, Kitty, and the victorious Mr. Fielding. It was a blow under which the Beau Séjour staggered to its foundations, I can assure you.

MRS. LLEWELLYN *(snappishly)*. He was quite right. I *detest* the Beau Séjour. I shouldn't be here today if it were not for this tournament. But Kitty stupidly promised a month ago to play in it.

MRS. WINGFIELD. Kitty is still slow to learn wisdom and understanding then?

MRS. LLEWELLYN. I wash my hands of Kitty!

MRS. WINGFIELD. Wise woman. But you should have called for soap and water and performed the ceremony years ago.

MRS. LLEWELLYN. Years ago!

MRS. WINGFIELD. Yes, the day she put her hair up, and let her skirts down.[64] *(Turning to Mrs. Stuart)* What have you done with Mr. Fielding and Violet?

MRS. STUART *(sentimentally)*. I don't know where they are, but no doubt they are perfectly happy lingering somewhere together, dear things!

MRS. WINGFIELD. Oh! it's reached the lingering stage has it? That's very trying. Can't you quicken the pace.

MRS. STUART *(earnestly)*. Do you think it would be wise? Perhaps ... I don't know *(Sighing)* Will gives me a great deal of anxiety.

MRS. LLEWELLYN *(murmurs)*. You are goodness itself to him, dear Mrs. Stuart.

MRS. WINGFIELD. Poor helpless orphan! How little he looks the part. But what has he been doing to occasion all this solicitude.

MRS. STUART *(mysteriously)*. He almost *lives* at Monte Carlo. Oh! it's a shocking, miserable, *wicked* place!

MRS. WINGFIELD. Doesn't he take Violet with him?

MRS. LLEWELLYN. Very often ... *too* often, as I tell Mrs. Stuart.

MRS. WINGFIELD. Oh no!—not for quickening the pace. Violet has a level head. She may be trusted.

MRS. STUART. But she doesn't know a bit how he stands. Will is so reserved, so secretive. It's the one complaint I make against him.

MRS. WINGFIELD. I really don't think you need worry about Mr. Fielding.

---

64   Victorian rites of passage from adolescence to womanhood.

MRS. STUART (*turning to Mrs. Llewellyn*). But he looks shockingly ill, doesn't he? (*Breaking off*) Ah! here comes Vi! (*Anxiously*) But she's alone ... No! (*With relieved smile*) Will too! (*She moves aside and stands waving and smiling by balustrade*).

MRS. LLEWELLYN (*to Mrs. Wingfield*). Isn't it *ludicrous* to watch Mrs. Stuart's manoeuvres since the legacy! All this for six hundred a year too.[65] But of course Violet's getting on!

MRS. STUART (*returning*). Kitty and Mr. Ismay are fighting well!

(*Mrs. Llewellyn leaves her place to look. Mrs. Stuart turns confidentially to Mrs. Wingfield*).

MRS. STUART. Did you ever see anything so absurd as Mrs. Llewellyn's behaviour about this affair? She has made a desperate struggle for the Count. A German Count too! If I went in for position I *would* ... (*To Mrs. Llewellyn who returns*) Dear, Mrs. Llewellyn, I *do* hope your Kitty will be victorious!

(*Enter Fielding and Violet Stuart. They shake hands with Mrs. Wingfield*).

FIELDING. How goes the game? We've only just arrived so we know nothing about it. (*He arranges cushions for Violet while he speaks, in polite but perfunctory fashion*).

MRS. WINGFIELD (*passing card of events[66] to Violet*). The final. Kitty Llewellyn and Mr. Ismay, versus Miss Thistleton and Captain Egerton.

VIOLET (*looking at card*). That girl still here?

FIELDING (*turning suddenly from watching tennis*). We can't persuade you to join us at Beaulieu, Mrs. Wingfield?

(*The others move aside to watch the game. Mrs. Wingfield and Fielding are left in a corner by themselves*).

MRS. WINGFIELD (*shaking her head*). No. I've been faithful to the Beau Séjour for four or five seasons now. I like it. There's always some amusing little drama going on I find, and for a spectator of the human comedy to move on to another theatre before the third act isn't wise, is it?

FIELDING (*taking out a cigarette*). Have you a good cast just now?

MRS. WINGFIELD. Excellent; but there are only two characters on the stage at the moment, and I don't quite understand the situation. I think I must have missed the first act.

FIELDING. Ah! possibly. And the two characters?

MRS. WINGFIELD. Miss Thistleton and Captain Egerton. By the way, I think you may have been on in the first act.

FIELDING (*pausing in the act of lighting match*). I?

MRS. WINGFIELD. Oh, as a *super*[67] possibly ... You know Captain Egerton don't you?

FIELDING. I was at Oxford with him.

MRS. WINGFIELD. I know friends of his in town ... There's more than one little story, isn't there?

FIELDING (*imperturbably*). Sure to be. There's one about Omdurman and a subsequent V.C.[68] But that's a true story.

MRS. WINGFIELD (*looks at him a moment, and breaks into a laugh*). Not to be drawn? Oh! now, if you were a woman! (*A moment's pause, then Mrs. Wingfield suddenly breaks out*) He may be a good soldier, and he's abominably good looking, but, I hate the man!

---

65   £600 per annum is a more than comfortable middle-class income.

66   A listing of matches, as in racing or other sporting events.

67   Supernumerary (i.e., an extra).

68   A reference to the Battle of Omdurman (2 September 1898) in which Sir Herbert Kitchener was victorious over Sudanese forces. The Victoria Cross (V.C.) is the highest military designation awarded to British or Commonwealth forces at any rank.

FIELDING. Why?

MRS. WINGFIELD. You surely don't expect me to give anything so puerile as a reason for hating anyone? And how a girl like Nancy Thistleton—

FIELDING. My dear lady! A distinguished soldier-man and to use your own words "abominably good-looking"?

MRS. WINGFIELD *(with a sigh).* And the primitive instincts we all so carefully ignore. Yes. I suppose so.

FIELDING *(after waiting a moment).* And—what *dénouement* do you expect?

MRS. WINGFIELD. Oh!—the ordinary one I suppose. They will marry, and live unhappily ever after.

(Applause from spectators on terrace. Cries of "Well played!" "A good fight").

Yes ... Miss Thistleton and Captain Egerton!

(A moment later, the little crowd at the top of the steps parts to let Nancy and Captain Egerton pass. Nancy is laughing and excited).

EGERTON *(coming up steps).* You did splendidly! Splendidly!

NANCY. Ah! but the victory is really yours. *(She sees Fielding, and her face changes. She puts out her hand).*

FIELDING *(looking from Nancy to Egerton).* I congratulate you—both.

EGERTON. Why, Fielding! Glad to see you! Over for the day? What's the attraction at Beaulieu? This is the first time since you left.

MRS. WINGFIELD *(patting Nancy affectionately on the shoulder).* Congratulations, my dear!

(The people on terrace surround Nancy, Kitty, Llewellyn, and Ismay congratulating, commiserating etc.).

KITTY. Well! We'd better all go and look at the prizes. Victors and vanquished together! *(Indicating Nancy and Ismay).*

ISMAY *(turning to Mrs. Llewellyn and Mrs. Stuart).* Won't you come too? They're in the tent down there.

MRS. STUART. The prizes? Oh! I should like to see them. *(To Mrs. Llewellyn)* Come, let us go.

(Everyone goes off the terrace, down steps L. and R. Nancy slips her arm through Kitty Llewellyn's).

VIOLET *(turning at head of steps R.).* Will!

(Fielding at once crosses to her. They stand a moment talking in low tones. Nancy pauses a moment at head of steps L., and watches them before she follows Kitty down the steps. Fielding returns to his seat when Violet has gone).

EGERTON *(leaning over balustrade—enthusiastically).* Pretty figure, hasn't she?

FIELDING *(glancing up from his paper).* Who?

EGERTON. Miss Thistleton—Nancy. *(Turning to Fielding)* Awfully attractive isn't she?

FIELDING. She seems to be.

EGERTON *(glancing sharply at Fielding who returns to his paper).* I thought you knew her very well?

FIELDING *(absently).* What? No. I was introduced to her four or five years ago, at Mrs. Stuart's—my cousin. Quite lately we've met out once or twice. That's all.

EGERTON *(tentatively).* She doesn't strike you as the sort of woman who has been a little—anything of that sort, eh?

FIELDING *(taking up paper).* She doesn't strike me as that sort of woman. No.

EGERTON *(suddenly after a pause).* Chalmers swears she's living with a man.

FIELDING *(calmly).* Who is Chalmers?

EGERTON. I thought you'd met him? In the Black Watch.[69] He was over here from Monaco last week, and saw her.

FIELDING. Don't know him.

EGERTON (uneasily). I told him he's messed it up, of course, as she's a friend of Mrs. Stuart, and all that kind of thing. But he sticks to it. He knew her at once. Swears she used to pass his club every day last spring. He admired her tremendously. Went off his head about her, you know. Used to follow her and all that. And—well! he swears it in fact. (Impatiently kicking up leaves on terrace in front of him) I'm awfully sick about it.

FIELDING. Why?

EGERTON. Well—

FIELDING. You're not going to tell me you're personally interested? If so, there's surely only one answer to a lie that this or any other young blackguard chooses to set about.

EGERTON (apologetically). Well you know my dear chap, I am as a matter of fact, don't mind telling you I'm in a devil of a fix. I'm really hard hit. I'd make up my mind to try my luck. I've been racketty[70] of course, but I meant to wind up various little affairs for good and all. Marry—settle down. The exemplary husband you know—that kind of thing. But, hang it! A man wants to be sure first—

FIELDING. That a woman is worthy of him. Quite so. You seem a good deal in love, Egerton. I congratulate you. (Looks at watch) I must be off; I promised to meet the Stuarts.

EGERTON (hastily following him). But look here, Fielding. I don't believe it, I assure you—(Turns impatiently, as Fielding disappears) Damn!

NANCY (heard calling). Isabel! Isabel!

EGERTON (suddenly). I'll risk it.

NANCY. Oh!... have you seen Isabel? (Laughing and pointing to the garden) I want her to come and look at the prizes. Everyone is down there, valuing silver coffee-pots, and now my back is turned, depreciating our victory. But I don't care! It was a glorious victory, wasn't it?

EGERTON (taking her hand and leading her to a seat). It has so intoxicated me that I'm going to tempt fate once more. Nancy! You must let me say it now. You know I love you.

(Nancy is silent. She passively lets him hold her hand. Then she looks at him in troubled fashion, and finally rises).

EGERTON (tenderly). You will give me a kind answer, Nancy?

NANCY. I—give me a little time please. In a week ... I will give you an answer in a week.

EGERTON. Oh! but why—

(Isabel comes out of one of the bedrooms, opening onto the terrace).

ISABEL. Nancy! Oh! there you are. I thought you were in your room (indicating bedroom from which she has just come).

(Egerton makes a gesture of impatience. Nancy smiles at him in troubled way, as he goes out).

ISABEL (in concerned tone). Oh! I'm so sorry. Did I disturb you?

NANCY (confusedly). No, yes! I'm glad you did. (A pause) Isabel, Captain Egerton has just proposed to me.

---

69   A Highland regiment, so named for its dark tartan.

70   Dissipated or disreputable.

ISABEL *(quietly)*. Why has he been so long about it?

NANCY *(abstractedly)*. I don't know.

ISABEL. When are you going to be married?

NANCY. I don't know. We—I haven't given him an answer yet.

ISABEL. Not? Why not?

NANCY *(restlessly)*. I don't know ... I didn't.

ISABEL *(looking at her)*. Nancy, do you know what you want yourself?

NANCY. Of course not. What woman does?

ISABEL *(desperately)*. But what *will* satisfy you?

NANCY *(shrugging her shoulders)*. Why ask *me*? *(A pause)* Did you see—Will this morning?

ISABEL. Yes.

NANCY *(after another pause)*. Don't you think he looks very ill?

ISABEL. Yes. I heard Mrs. Stuart telling someone that he's always over at Monte Carlo.

NANCY *(anxiously)*. Playing?[71]

ISABEL. I suppose so.

NANCY. I wish he wouldn't.

ISABEL. Mr. Fielding looks too sensible a man to make a fool of himself.

NANCY *(bitterly)*. Oh yes! he's very sensible.

ISABEL. I expect he'll marry Miss Stuart.

NANCY *(turning sharply)*. Who says so?

ISABEL *(shrugging her shoulders)*. Everyone. It's the latest gossip.

NANCY *(incoherently)*. But why? I don't understand. He doesn't care for her! He—

ISABEL. But he's ambitious. You told me so yourself—

NANCY *(slowly)*. Yes. I see. And Mr. Stuart has political influence. Yes ... of course.

ISABEL *(looking over balustrade)*. There they go.

NANCY *(quickly)*. Who?

ISABEL. Mrs. Stuart and Miss Stuart.

NANCY *(breathlessly)*. And—

ISABEL. No. He's not with them.

NANCY. I wonder where he's gone. He scarcely spoke to me this morning?

ISABEL. But you could hardly expect him to, could you?

NANCY *(starting up)*. Oh! for Heaven's sake don't you be reasonable too, Isabel! When a *man* is reasonable it only means that he has ceased to care for a particular woman. When a *woman's* reasonable it means that she has ceased to care for anything! It's the beginning of the end. Let her begin to enjoy her dinner and appreciate the comforts of middle age. It's all she has left.

ISABEL. You won't enjoy your dinner for many years to come, dear child. Why ... Nancy? *(Crosses hurriedly to her)*.

NANCY. Nothing! Nothing! I'm tired. This stupid tennis I suppose ... Oh Isabel! What a hash I've made of life haven't I?

(Ismay's voice heard on terrace steps).

ISMAY. Let's try the terrace.

KITTY *(hypocritically)*. Why here are Miss Thistleton and Miss Ferris. How nice!

---

71 Gambling.

NANCY. Yes, but we're not going to stay. I've just got a new dress home, and I'm longing to try it on. Isabel is going to help me. (*Smiling at Kitty*) I'm sure you will sympathise. You know the awful moment of suspense before trying on a new frock!

KITTY (*nodding and laughing*). I shan't expect to see you again for hours.

(*Isabel and Nancy go towards garden bedrooms, and enter at one of the doors half closing it. Ismay and Kitty sit at the end of the terrace furthest removed from the bedrooms*).

ISMAY (*triumphantly*). I say! Luck at last! the first moment we've had to ourselves all the afternoon.

KITTY (*apprehensively*). Where's mother?

ISMAY. Quite safe. Old Major Sturge is talking to her about Indian curries. She won't escape for half an hour.

KITTY (*sitting on bench*). It is so nice to be back at the dear old Beau Séjour. I hate Beaulieu.

ISMAY (*impressively*). Come back again then!

KITTY. I only wish I could. Mother won't move. She says the people over there are so much nicer. I'm sure I don't see how she can tell, for she won't know anyone but that stupid Count, and we saw enough of him before we left here.

ISMAY. Oh *he's* over at Beaulieu, is he?

KITTY. Yes, and mother drags him everywhere. He came over with us today. Oh he's an awful bore!... But now tell me all the gossip. Why you have a month's news to relate! How is that stupid son of the Major's getting on?

ISMAY. Young Sturge?... oh! as great a fool as ever. He's always over at the tables.[72] Sturge is just the sort of young ass who'll come to grief one of these days.

KITTY. I'm so sorry for his poor old father!... And Miss Thistleton and Captain Egerton?

ISMAY. I say Kitty—never mind the other people. I'm sure we shall have to move on again in a minute. Let's talk about ourselves.

KITTY. Do you think we are more interesting?

ISMAY. You are. You can't think how I've been looking forward to this tournament.

KITTY. And we didn't win after all!

ISMAY. As though I meant that! Kitty you know quite well what has kept me hanging about at this rotten place all the month. I only waited to see you again. Look here! We haven't any time to lose. Someone's sure to come in a minute, so say yes quickly, there's a good girl.

KITTY. Yes Reggie. But Oh! how furious Mother will be!

ISMAY (*rapturously*). Oh bother your mother—I mean we will try to propitiate your dear mother, Kitty (*kisses her*).

KITTY (*hurried*). Here comes Mrs. Stuart and Violet!

ISMAY. Confound! This is the third time we've moved this afternoon. Let's try the Orange Walk. They lay out these hotel gardens most inconveniently.

(*Exeunt R. Mrs. Stuart comes up steps L. She is joined by her daughter a moment later*).

VIOLET (*in annoyed tone*). I can't find Will anywhere. No one has seen him since he was here talking to Captain Egerton.

MRS. STUART. What can have become of him? I've been looking for him everywhere too. He must have gone back to Beaulieu.

---

72   Monte Carlo's casinos.

VIOLET. I expect he's at the tables again—like that young fool Sturge. *(Scornfully)* It looks so well doesn't it, on the first day of our engagement.

MRS. STUART. Your—? My dear child!

VIOLET. Do restrain your transports mother, we don't want to take the whole hotel into our confidence.

MRS. STUART. But why didn't you tell me before? A casual mention of such an event! *(Tearfully)* A mother expects more consideration from her only daughter, Violet.

VIOLET. I've had no opportunity. It has been arranged this morning—since we came over here.

MRS. STUART. My dear girl! I am rejoiced, rejoiced! A mother's feelings ... most suitable ... most providential.

VIOLET *(snappishly)*. I don't see any reason for rejoicing, exactly. It isn't my idea of a brilliant match, but it will do.

MRS. STUART. He has six hundred a year, and with your own allowance—

VIOLET. Mr. Brackenhurst has a thousand.

MRS. STUART *(practically)*. It would probably have never come off. Men of six prefer girls of eighteen, as a rule.[73] Be reasonable, Violet. You are not eighteen. *(Lapsing into sentiment)* Just think how Will will love and cherish his wife!

(Violet suddenly sits down on bench just in front of the garden bedroom. Her mother pauses there).

VIOLET *(in exasperated tone)*. For goodness sake don't humbug, mother. There's no love and cherishing about it. I'm going to marry Will Fielding because I don't see my way to anything better, and he's going to marry me because of papa's influence. It's a mutual accommodation. We shan't fight, but, as to—

A WAITER *(comes up with a telegram which he gives to Mrs. Stuart)*. Madame!

VIOLET. From Will, I suppose. He's had the grace to telegraph then.

MRS. STUART. As you thought. Monte Carlo! *(She glances at it and springs to her feet. Incoherently)* Vi! What does this mean? An accident! Shot! Thought to be dying!... Then he was ruined! Oh, this gambling,—what sin and misery ... We must go. You must be with him.

VIOLET *(seizing the telegram)*. I? Where?

(Bedroom door at back of set is flung open when Mrs. Stuart begins to read the telegram. Nancy stands on threshold followed by Isabel who tries to restrain her. When Violet takes telegram, Nancy springs forward and tries to seize it. Violet draws back).

NANCY *(panting)*. Where is he? Where? Let me see! Let me go!

ISABEL *(frantically)*. Nancy! *Nancy*!

(Mrs. Stuart and Violet stand looking at her. At the moment gong sounds. People begin to come towards the house. Mrs. Llewellyn, Kitty, Ismay, Mrs. Wingfield and others).

VIOLET *(coldly to Nancy)*. I don't understand. What right have you? Unless—*(She steps back and looks her up and down)*.

NANCY *(wildly)*. Yes—yes—yes. It's as you think. I admit it ... anything!... Everything! *(In supplicating tone)* But you will give it to me now? You see I have a right ... I must see him. I have something to say to him ... Oh, you don't understand—you don't understand. Don't you see it may be too late! Too late!

---

73 She compares income (£600) to age (18 years).

(Violet gives her the telegram with disdainful gesture. The rest, who have come near enough to hear, stop in amazement, looking from one another to the group near bedroom door. Mrs. Wingfield crosses over to Isabel who makes a despairing movement. Ismay stoops and mechanically picks envelope of telegram, which is on the ground).

NANCY *(in suffocating voice, passing telegram to Isabel)*. Read it! I can't see ...
ISMAY *(staring at envelope)*. But—look here!... This is Sturge, not Stuart!
EGERTON *(hurriedly running up steps)*. Where's Major Sturge?... Mrs. Stuart I'm so sorry! My stupid mistake to the waiter. The telegram is for Major Sturge, not you. I'm afraid something has happened to his son.

(He breaks off looking in amazement from one to the other. Some of the visitors begin to move away whispering and exclaiming).

NANCY *(breaking down and crying hysterically)*. And I thought he was dead!... As if he would ever have hurt me, even that way.

(The rest of the visitors and Mrs. Stuart and Violet move away. Mrs. Stuart murmuring "disgraceful." Nancy looks from Isabel to Mrs. Wingfield in a dazed fashion. Then begins to realize what she has done. Isabel takes her hand and turns away crying).

NANCY. I don't care. He's not dead. Thank God! thank God!
MRS. WINGFIELD. Oh you poor silly girl!

Act IV

Granby Street Chambers. Nancy's rooms furnished and arranged as before.
Four days have elapsed since the last act.

ISABEL *(followed by Mrs. Moore carrying bundle of rugs etc.)*. We are so glad you can take us in Mrs. Moore! We scarcely expected such good luck.
MRS. MOORE. Bless your heart, yes Miss! And glad to see you again. Where's my young lady?
ISABEL. She's coming. I left her paying the cabman. Here she is.

(Nancy enters: she gives both hands to Mrs. Moore who receives her rapturously).

MRS. MOORE. Well! There! I *am* glad to see you agine, an' no mistake! Let's look at you. Lord love us, what white cheeks. And 'ow thin you've gone! I never *did* 'old with foreign parts abroad. Living on all them French kickshaws[74] *I'll* be bound! Give me an English steak with the gravy in it, an' arf a pint of stout.[75] That's what *you* want my dear!
NANCY *(taking off her hat and smiling wearily)*. It all looks exactly the same Mrs. Moore. I wish we could have come last night, but we got in so late that we thought it better to sleep at the hotel. We were afraid these rooms would be let, weren't we Isabel?
MRS. MOORE. Well no Miss! It was only the post before your letter come that we 'eard Mr. Fielding was going to give them up.

---

74   Fancy cookery.
75   Dark ale.

NANCY. *Mr. Fielding*—!

MRS. MOORE. Yes Miss! Didn't you know 'e 'ad them? To be sure there isn't many gentlemen as tikes rooms 'ere though there's no rule aginst it. Too many females my 'usband says—frightens them like. But Mr. Fielding 'e took them on d'reckly you left. 'E didn't sleep 'ere but 'e was in two or three times a week, reading or writin' an' walkin' up and down sometimes for all the world like a bear at the Zoo. Mide me quite nervous time's agine when I come in to look after the fire. But there: as I sez to my 'usband, 'e's a liter'y gent, an' they're never quite responsible.

NANCY *(moving some books)*. Here's my little old work-basket Isabel.

MRS. MOORE. 'E wouldn't 'ave nothing moved, Miss; that was another of 'is fads. "Leave it all as it is," 'e said one dy quite irritable like, when I was clearing up a bit. And of course I 'umoured 'im. They're nothin' but a set of great babies, the 'ole lot of 'em in my opinion!... But you want yer boxes up, an' 'ere I stand chattering. I'll send my 'usband up with 'em, Miss. 'E *can* 'elp with the boxes, if 'e can't do nothin' else! *(She goes out)*.

NANCY *(looking from room to Isabel)*. I remember he told me he'd found a tenant. Some one who would be careful of the few things I left. I took the Kensington flat furnished for the season, you know, so there was no room for anything but my books.

ISABEL. And he kept them on himself ... Because they were your rooms of course.

NANCY *(who has been examining the books on the shelf)*. Prince Otto![76] We were reading this the last evening we were together.

(She opens it and turns the pages—Something falls from them—Isabel stoops for it).

ISABEL. Violets!

NANCY *(taking them to replace in the book)*. Look! here's a date ... It's the date of that last evening ... I remember he took the violets I was wearing. *(She closes book and turns from the shelf with a hopeless gesture.)* He knew we should never be happy again.

(She sinks down before the table and buries her face in her hands. Isabel crosses the room to her—after a moment she goes on brokenly).

Oh, Isabel, we were so happy—so quietly happy you know ... we were just husband and wife ... It all came back to me at that awful moment when I thought he was dead ... our talks over the fire—our trust in one another—our dependence on one another ... all the little things, you know ... don't you? I remembered it all, as they say you do when you're drowning, and I realised that they were the things that mattered—the things that made us belong to each other as husband and wife should. The other was nothing but a madness—an infatuation which would have passed away anyhow—which *had* passed, even then. *(She breaks down and cries)*.

ISABEL. Nancy dear! We ought not to have come. I *knew* it would be awful for you to see the place again—but you would do it!

NANCY. No, it's all the same. I couldn't rest without seeing it once more ... No, no! Isabel, don't say anything. Nothing will alter it. It's my own fault. I've deliberately thrown my happiness away. *(She rises and crosses slowly to the fire)*.

ISABEL. And yet if it hadn't been for that, you would never have realised what the other meant to you.

NANCY. No. *(Slowly)* That's true. Life's an impossible thing to manage. By the time you understand it a little, its chances are over—your knowledge is useless. It's time to go.

---

76   A novel by Robert Louis Stevenson (1885).

ISABEL. Or else life gives one no chance at all, either to make or mar.

NANCY *(earnestly, taking her hand).* Ah! that's worse! I recognise that it's worse. But, Isabel, for you perhaps, one day—?

ISABEL *(shaking her head).* Never! But don't be sorry, Nancy! A few more years, and that also will cease to trouble me. I shall never have the roses of life ... *(With an attempt at a smile)* Never mind! there are the lilies and the lavender and "all that kind of thing," as you say. *(She moves away, and puts on her hat.)* In the meantime we have a lot to do before Wednesday. I'd better go at once and see about those tickets I think.

NANCY. Shall I come too?

ISABEL. No! you must stay in for Mrs. Wingfield—She's coming to tea, you remember!

NANCY *(listlessly).* So she is. I wish she wasn't. *(Rousing herself)* How horrid of me! She *has* been so good. But I can't see her without thinking of that day—

ISABEL *(soothingly).* Don't think of it!

NANCY. Oh, it isn't that I mind ... I wish I did. It would be better than this awful longing. *(Impatiently)* But what's the use of talking ... of anything ...? Don't be long, Isabel—I hate you to be away!

(Isabel kisses her—exit. Enter Mrs. Moore with travelling bag, etc.).

MRS. MOORE. So you ain't goin' to stay then? Not off to foreign parts agine, surely?

NANCY. Yes, Mrs. Moore, we're thinking of going to foreign parts for a year at least—to Italy. We're only in town for two days just to arrange things before we start. You know I've at last persuaded Miss Ferris to come and live with me? I'm too great a baby to be left alone, even at my age.

MRS. MOORE. At your ige, my dear! *You* ain't got no ige worth mentionin' ... But excuse my boldness, Miss, why not git a 'usband? They're a pore lot, I own, 'aving 'ad three myself and none of them satisfactory. But it's the wy of the world to think more of you if you've got one. Stoopid as a howl, or ugly as Guy Fawkes[77] 'e may be. That don't matter as long as you're married.

NANCY *(laughing).* But I'm afraid I don't want to marry a Guy Fawkes, Mrs. Moore.

MRS. MOORE. Better than a howl, Miss, an' there ain't much choice. Besides, some of them Guy Fawkses ain't got up so badly for stuffed figures ... I've thought sometimes, Miss, pardon my boldness, that Mr. Fielding might 'ave a grine more sense in 'is 'ead than most!

NANCY *(bending over rugs).* Mr. Fielding's engaged to be married, Mrs. Moore.

MRS. MOORE *(bouncing towards the door).* There! I might 'a know'd 'e 'adn't no more gumption than the rest. When would you like a cup of tea, Miss?

NANCY. Presently. But we'll make it ourselves. Don't you trouble.

(Exit Mrs. Moore. Nancy walks restlessly about the room and finally puts her elbows on the mantelpiece and leans her head on her hands. A knock).

NANCY *(wearily).* Come in!

(Enter Captain Egerton. Nancy starts back).

Captain Egerton!

EGERTON. The porter downstairs told me to come up.

NANCY. But how—

---

77 Instigator of the Gunpowder Plot to blow up Parliament in 1605, Guy Fawkes (1570-1606) is burnt in effigy every 5 November.

EGERTON. I saw the address you left at the Beau Séjour ... and here I am. Well, haven't you anything to say to me after all this beastly journey? *(A pause)* Look here Nancy! I ... I hope I'm a gentleman ... and in fact, I've come to repeat my offer ... to ask you again to marry me.

NANCY *(drawing back)*. You forget that I promised to give you an answer in a week. The week has not yet elapsed.

EGERTON. Oh, but come—there have been circumstances ...

NANCY. I need not keep you waiting. My answer is ready. It is no.

EGERTON *(incredulous)*. But come Nancy! Be reasonable. Reflect a moment. If you're thinking of Fielding—

NANCY *(proudly)*. Fielding is engaged to be married to Miss Stuart.

EGERTON. Precisely. Then what is your position?

NANCY *(rising)*. Surely that is my concern.

EGERTON. Not if I choose to make it mine also. I ... 'pon my word. I don't think you understand. Let us look at facts. By your own admission, you have—

NANCY. Lived with a man for four years.

EGERTON. Well, surely you see—*(hesitating)*.

NANCY. That unless some gentleman, like you for instance, take pity on me—

NANCY *(eagerly)*. No! There you misjudge me! It isn't a question of pity, I assure you. *Pity*! I—well—the fact of it is, I just can't give you up Nancy, and that's all about it. I've thought it out, and after all what does it matter? If *I* don't mind, who's to object?

NANCY. I don't know ... unless possibly I!

EGERTON *(puzzled)*. You are afraid this will make a difference to my happiness? *(Meditatively)* I don't think it need. Of course no man cares to risk being made a fool of, you understand. But—

NANCY *(rising)*. You shall run no risk of that ... I need not detain you.

EGERTON. What do you mean? You are surely not—

NANCY. Going to refuse your offer? I have already done so. There doesn't seem any more to say.

EGERTON. Then you have been making a fool of me all along?

NANCY. No ... rather of myself.

EGERTON *(with apprehended fury)*. You encouraged me—

NANCY *(quietly)*. Be just—did I ever encourage you? I went away to avoid you. It was you who followed me, remember.

EGERTON. All the same, you let me think you would accept me. You can't deny that.

NANCY. I do not wish to deny it. At one time I thought I should. But not till after I felt myself free.

EGERTON. So if it had not been for that ... little occurrence at the Beau Séjour I might have remained in ignorance of—

NANCY *(forcing calm)*. On the contrary; if I had decided to marry you, I should have been foolish enough to tell you.

EGERTON. *Foolish* enough?

NANCY. Yes. Would *you* have told me anything about yourself if you thought it likely to impair your cause with me? The particular kind of fool who accepts risks of that sort is always a woman.

EGERTON *(after a pause. Coming close to her)*. Look here Nancy! Let us drop all that. Why are we quarreling? Be sensible and marry me. You shan't regret it. I'm awfully fond of you, and upon my honour I think no worse of you for knowing this—

NANCY *(thinking upon this)*. Captain Egerton, I ask you again to go. I have given you my answer. *(Trying to recover her calmness)* Oh yes! I see your point of view. It is useless to argue. You are quite right of course. Nine men out of ten would call you quixotic[78] ... and perhaps you are ... I haven't kept the rules of the game, and so of course I have no right to—to—complain. But why do we discuss it? You have my answer.

EGERTON *(taking his hat)*. Very well ... I have no choice, of course. *(Hesitantly)* Am I not to see you again? Under no circumstances?

NANCY *(shrinking from him)*. Under no circumstances.

(Egerton goes out. Nancy stands a moment looking fixedly before her. She throws herself upon the sofa and buries her face in the cushion. A moment later there is a knock. The door opens and Mrs. Wingfield comes in. Nancy rises and comes towards her, taking her hand without speaking).

MRS. WINGFIELD *(glancing at her sharply)*. Well, my dear! So here you are. I met that exuberant young man, Captain Egerton, on the doorstep. His remarks were incoherent. He seemed in fact annoyed. What have you been saying to him? Something salutary, no doubt.

NANCY *(trying to speak calmly)*. Oh! don't let us talk about it. *(She turns abruptly away)*.

MRS. WINGFIELD *(kindly)*. Come, come my dear! So few things are worth taking seriously. Why pay tribute to the unintelligent after this fashion.

NANCY *(in shaking voice)*. Oh!... because I'm a fool I suppose. What else could I expect, after all?

MRS. WINGFIELD *(taking off her furs)*. True. We can't disregard the sign-posts and have a comfortable time too. It's a pity, because as most of the sign-posts are erected for the unintelligent, one can't be comfortable without being bored.

(She shakes up the sofa cushions and settles herself against them, glancing at Nancy who is nervously trying to regain composure).

And the sign-posts often lead to such excellent and cosy things, such as tea, muffins and the fireside. But then!... There's generally the man who sits opposite, warming his slippers, and you have to take him with the muffins.

(Nancy comes and sits beside her on the sofa. Mrs. Wingfield pats her hand and continues).

Disregard the warning on the sign-posts and you find yourself in the wilds—with a congenial companion, it may be, but the weather is generally inclement. Ah, well! One can't have everything. Tea and muffins through life for me.

NANCY *(trying to smile)*. And the man opposite?

MRS. WINGFIELD. A merciful Providence removed him early my dear, possibly distrusting my powers of endurance ... *(Putting a hand on her arm)* Theories don't pay, my child. Conformity does. Conform, conform! if you would bask in the fat smile of the unthinking crowd which moves the world, and carries us with it, whether we will or no.

NANCY. But we hadn't any theories! We didn't mind being married, but we weren't allowed to be ... We only wanted to be happy.

MRS. WINGFIELD. Ah! but Mrs. Grundy doesn't want you to be happy. She wants you to be respectable.

NANCY *(gathering up her wraps)*. Do you mind if I go and put these away? I am disgracefully untidy.

MRS. WINGFIELD. Of course, I am unpardonably early I know. Give me a book I shall be quite happy.

(She looks after Nancy with a sigh, as the bedroom door closes. A moment after, Isabel enters).

---

78   Chivalrous.

ISABEL. Why, Mrs. Wingfield, I'm so sorry I was out.

MRS. WINGFIELD. Yes, I'm much too early. But don't take any notice of me till tea is ready and then I'll contrive to attract your attention.

ISABEL *(putting tea-cups on table)*. Where is Nancy?

MRS. WINGFIELD. In her room. Don't go to her for a minute. She's rather upset ... Captain Egerton has been here.

ISABEL. Here! What impertinence! He took good care to keep out of the way till after we left the Beau Séjour!

MRS. WINGFIELD *(shrugs her shoulders and goes to window)*. What a nice little room this is ... What sort of view do you get from the window? *(She stands a moment looking out. Then turns with a sudden exclamation)* Yes! It is!... and coming here!

ISABEL *(surprised)*. Who?

MRS. WINGFIELD *(coming hurriedly towards Isabel)*. Mr. Fielding.

ISABEL *(in consternation. Hurriedly)*. We've just heard he took these rooms. He gave them up only this morning. I expect he's coming back for something.

MRS. WINGFIELD *(suddenly)*. Now listen! Can you overhear what's said in that bedroom?

ISABEL. No. Not a word. The doors are so thick. And the room's at the end of the passage.

MRS. WINGFIELD *(speaking hastily)*. Very well. Go in and keep Nancy there. Tell her I've gone out for a few minutes and am coming back. Say her hair's untidy, and make her do it again—anything! Don't come out till I call you! Leave me here!

ISABEL *(bewildered)*. Very well ...

(Mrs. Wingfield pushes her into the room. As the bedroom door shuts the other one opens. Fielding enters. He stands amazed on the threshold).

FIELDING. *Mrs. Wingfield*! Why what in the world are *you* doing here?

MRS. WINGFIELD *(quietly giving him her hand)*. Young man! Should not the question be, what are *you* doing in the room of my friends—with a latch key?

FIELDING *(half laughing)*. Good Lord! You don't mean to say they're let. Why I only gave them up yesterday, and today I found I hadn't sent back the latch key, and I came to give it up to the porter. He wasn't in the hall; he never is. So I just came upstairs. But I say, how strange to find you here!

MRS. WINGFIELD. Sit down.

FIELDING *(hesitating)*. But—

MRS. WINGFIELD. Sit down. They won't be in yet.

FIELDING *(laughing)*. Well! They'll think it pretty cool[79] when they do come.

MRS. WINGFIELD. They may be delighted to see you, on the contrary.

FIELDING. But this is sudden. I thought you were going to stay at the Beau Séjour till February.

MRS. WINGFIELD. So did I.

FIELDING. What's the news at the Beau Séjour?

MRS. WINGFIELD. You should know better than I. Mrs. Stuart and Violet decided to stay till the end of the week. Haven't you heard from them?

FIELDING *(suddenly)*. Now Mrs. Wingfield, you know all about this! Will you explain two perfectly unintelligible letters I received this morning *(searching in his breast pocket)*.

MRS. WINGFIELD. Yes, with pleasure. I make a speciality of the unintelligible.

---

79 Audacious or impudent.

FIELDING. You—er—know of course that I was going to marry Miss Stuart?

MRS. WINGFIELD. Were? Aren't you?

FIELDING (*shrugging his shoulders*). You never can tell! I thought so till this morning when I got a letter from her, releasing me from my engagement.

MRS. WINGFIELD. Why?

FIELDING. She doesn't explain but encloses her mother's letter. Curious of her, for she must know that in her mother's letters the one thing omitted is explanation. Four sheets, you see, but I remain unenlightened. (*Scans the letter and reads, running the sentences together*) "After the shocking scene of Thursday ... the disgraceful conduct of that young person ... The want of frankness, but men are what women make them, and she hopes we shall meet eventually in a happier world ..." (*Folding letter*) I sincerely hope not. But what does it mean?

MRS. WINGFIELD. You can't guess, of course?

FIELDING. How should I?

MRS. WINGFIELD. Come! You don't act badly for a man. But it's unnecessary ... I came back with Nancy Thistleton.

FIELDING (*looks up sharply. Rises and begins to pace the room. Stops suddenly in front of Mrs. Wingfield*). Mrs. Wingfield I beg you to be frank with me.

MRS. WINGFIELD. You can't expect me to be anything but *giddy* if you continue to walk round me like that.

FIELDING (*sitting down promptly*). I beg your pardon.

MRS. WINGFIELD. You remember the day of the tournament when you disappeared without a moment's warning?

FIELDING. I telegraphed, though.

MRS. WINGFIELD (*significantly*). You did. At the self-same moment probably a doctor, or someone was telegraphing from Monte Carlo.

FIELDING. About that poor chap Sturge? I read of it.

MRS. WINGFIELD (*nodding*). Previously, I must explain, Miss Thistleton had heard of the anxiety you were causing your excellent cousin about Monte Carlo, where you were reputed to be wasting your substance.

FIELDING. On the contrary, I won exactly five francs. Go on.

MRS. WINGFIELD (*shrugging her shoulders*). There doesn't seem much to say. Merely that owing to the waiter's stupidity, the Sturge telegram was brought to Mrs. Stuart. She thought it referred to you—and so did Nancy.

FIELDING. And then?

MRS. WINGFIELD. Well! I can leave you to guess the rest. (*Rising*) Nancy Thistleton has less talent for intrigue than anyone I ever met. A great drawback for a woman.

FIELDING (*under his breath*). Gave it all away...? Poor child!

MRS. WINGFIELD. Well! She was sufficiently explicit.

FIELDING (*puzzled*). But—why? I don't understand. She—is engaged to Egerton, isn't she?

MRS. WINGFIELD. Oh, no! Nobody seems to be engaged to *anybody*. It is most disappointing.

FIELDING. But it's Egerton she cares for.

MRS. WINGFIELD. Who says so?

FIELDING. She told me so herself.

MRS. WINGFIELD. And you believed her!

FIELDING. But (*helplessly*) what can I do?

MRS. WINGFIELD. Ask her of course—and *perhaps* she'll tell you the truth, but she's a woman, you'll have to risk that. Great Heavens! These masterminds! And the simplest things never occur to them! I'd rather keep my puerile feminine intelligence after all.

FIELDING *(starting to his feet)*. Where shall I find her?

MRS. WINGFIELD. Here! *(She opens door L.)* Isabel!

FIELDING. *What?*

(Isabel comes to door. Mrs. Wingfield seizes her arm).

MRS. WINGFIELD. Come my dear! I see there's no cake for tea. I can't do without cake. Come and get some. *(She hurries her to door. At door, Mrs. Wingfield calls)* Nancy! Tea is ready.

(She goes out with Isabel. Closing door immediately. A moment and Nancy enters. She looks round for her friends and sees Fielding. Falls back, then makes as though she would rush to him. Finally checks herself).

FIELDING *(calmly)*. Mrs. Wingfield was mistaken about the tea. It doesn't seem to have been made, does it? *(Looking into teapot)* But it's all ready. Let me!

(He goes to fire and takes kettle from it. Begins to pour water into the teapot while Nancy sinks slowly into a seat by the table. As he closes the teapot lid, she looks up, and their eyes meet).

NANCY *(springing to her feet)*. Will!

FIELDING. One moment. You'll burn yourself.

(He puts down kettle. Nancy half laughing, half crying runs into his arms).

NANCY *(looking up)*. Mrs. Wingfield told you?

FIELDING. Yes. She has been explaining how admirably fitted you are to be trusted alone.

NANCY *(disengaging herself in confusion)*. Oh! don't teaze me!... *(Hurriedly)* Will!—I couldn't help it. When I heard that stupid telegram I knew in a flash all I was losing. It was my friend, my child, my *lover* who was dying. And there she stood! The woman who had just been discussing your income! She wanted to take my place ... I couldn't bear it! It was intolerable! Will! I would have *died* if I hadn't spoken! *(Pleadingly)* You are not angry?

FIELDING. You impossible child!

NANCY *(suddenly)*. But ... Violet Stuart? I forgot ...

FIELDING. So did I. *(With mock dejection) You* must marry me Nancy. She will have none of me. There's nothing else for it. We must just take up life together again, and go on like the old married couple—

NANCY *(earnestly)*. We always have been.